D1180149

The Structure of
LUTHERANISM

WERNER ELERT

The Structure of
LUTHERANISM

VOLUME ONE

The Theology and Philosophy of Life of Lutheranism
Especially in the Sixteenth and Seventeenth
Centuries

By
WERNER ELERT

Translated by
WALTER A. HANSEN

Foreword by Jaroslav Pelikan
"Werner Elert, Professor of Theology" by Robert C. Schultz

CONCORDIA PUBLISHING HOUSE
SAINT LOUIS
1962

Concordia Publishing House, Saint Louis 18, Missouri
Concordia Publishing House Ltd., London, W. C. 1

Library of Congress Catalog Card No. 62-19955

Translated by permission from the original German *Morphologie des Luthertums* published by the *C. H. Beck'sche Verlagsbuchhandlung,* Munich

MANUFACTURED IN THE UNITED STATES OF AMERICA

To Anne, my wife,
whose counsel and comments I have
cherished beyond measure while
translating this important work

Ἀλλήλων τὰ βάρη βαστάζετε, καὶ
οὕτως ἀναπληρώσετε τὸν νόμον
τοῦ Χριστοῦ

Galatians 6:2

Foreword

One of the earliest English names for a "Lutheran" was "Confessionalist." [1] Because the Lutheran Church defined itself in a series of confessions but never adopted an official liturgy or a uniform polity, Lutheran theologians have often supposed that the key to understanding any section of Christendom is its confession or symbol. Thus has arisen the branch of theology called *Symbolik*, or more recently *Konfessionskunde*.[2] In fact, the German word for "denominations" is *Konfessionen;* but at least since the eighteenth century American English has been calling the *Konfessionen* "denominations." [3] For even though academic theologians may wish that the denominations were confessions and expressed their genius in the form of a statement of faith, the mute realities of history make it clear that "in Great Britain and America . . . the chief differences between the religious denominations are not doctrinal but institutional. . . . If therefore any one wishes to make a comparative study of the consensus and dissensus of British and American Christianity, he must pay more attention to religious institutions than to doctrines of Faith and Morals." [4] Therefore American denominationalism as a religious and historical phenomenon [5] has been the despair of scholars in the field of "comparative symbolics," who prefer the neater and more precise interpretations that come from a comparison of confessions and creeds.

Yet it does not take an inordinate amount of historical research to discover that the uniqueness even of the "confessional" denominations

[1] Cf. *The Oxford English Dictionary II* (Oxford, 1933), 802.

[2] See the historical materials in Johann Adam Möhler, *Symbolik*, new ed. by Josef Rupert Geiselmann (Darmstadt, 1958—61), 1, 44—54; also Geiselmann's comments, "Zur Einführung," pp. 73—91.

[3] Cf. *A Dictionary of American English* (Chicago, 1960), II, 747.

[4] Charles Augustus Briggs, *Theological Symbolics* (New York, 1914), pp. 29—30.

[5] See Sidney E. Mead, "From Coercion to Persuasion: Another Look at the Rise of Religious Liberty and the Emergence of Denominationalism," *Church History*, XXIV (1956), 317—337: also the Introduction to F. E. Mayer, *The Religious Bodies of America* (St. Louis, 1956).

is not exhausted by their confessions. Thus a conscientious historian could not interpret Roman Catholicism adequately by expounding the decrees of the councils and the *Catechismus Romanus,* but would have to pay attention to the organization of the church, its speculative theology, its cultic life, its *spiritualité,* its social ethics, its definitions of personal morality, and the myriad of other factors that must be taken together as a *complexio oppositorum* before one can even begin to interpret the Roman Catholic Church.[6] Nor is the *Geist* of Lutheranism intelligible solely on the basis of the *Book of Concord* of 1580. It has been said — and it is probably true — that Luther's Small Catechism has done more to unify Lutheranism than even the Augsburg Confession. Both are part of the confessions. But can one really understand the Lutheran Church without carefully studying (to name only three elements) its treasury of hymns, Luther's translation of the Bible, and the figure of the Reformer himself? To be sure, it would lead to a hopeless relativism if one were to say that Lutheranism is everything that Lutheranism has ever been or that Lutherans have ever said it is. But it is also a hopeless reductionism if one isolates the confessions from Lutheran history and reads them apart from the context within which they arose and through which they have been handed down.

Between (or beyond) this impossible choice of reductionism and relativism is a method that can interpret the Lutheran confessions historically and Lutheran history confessionally. Such was the method of Werner Elert. He was a historian among the systematic theologians and a systematician among the church historians. That combination of gifts was evident in all his works, and most of all in the present one. Elert's career as a historical theologian moved backwards through the history of Christian thought. The first book by him that drew wide attention was a history of Christian apologetics during the nineteenth century set into the framework of general cultural history, particularly, of course, into the framework of the development of German idealism.[7] Then came the present book, which covered the centuries from the sixteenth to the twentieth with astounding comprehension. And in the last years of his life Elert occupied himself principally with the history of the early church, paying special attention to the theology of the Greek fathers.[8] It was a great loss that he did not live to fill one of the great

[6] Friedrich Heiler, *Der Katholizismus. Seine Idee und seine Erscheinung* (Munich, 1923).

[7] Werner Elert, *Der Kampf um das Christentum* (Munich, 1921).

[8] Werner Elert, *Abendmahl und Kirchengemeinschaft in der alten kirche, hauptsächlich des Ostens* (Berlin-Grunewald, 1954); *Der Ausgang der altkirchlichen Christologie,* edited by Wilhelm Maurer and Elisabeth Bergsträsser (Berlin, 1957).

needs of theological scholarship in our time, a new history of dogma, for which he was preparing.

Werner Elert was born on August 19, 1885, in the village of Heldrungen. His university studies, which he began in Breslau in 1906 and which he continued at Erlangen and at Leipzig, were devoted not only to theology but to philosophy, literature, law, history, and psychology as well. His philosophical dissertation at Erlangen, dated May 21, 1910, dealt with the thought of Rudolph Rocholl (1822–1905); his theological dissertation, dated May 18, 1911, was a study of the apologetic problems in the philosophy of history. Elert became a pastor in Seefeld bei Kolberg, Pomerania, in 1912. As his books and articles demonstrate, he never forgot that the final test of any theological system is its value for the proclamation of the Word of God to the man of today. After the First World War, in 1919, Elert became the head of the *altlutherisch* seminary in Breslau. In 1923 his university, Erlangen, made him professor of church history; and after the death of Philip Bachman, Elert became professor of systematic theology in addition. He died in Erlangen on November 21, 1954. Bishop Hans Meiser said of him in his farewell: "If I were to write an inscription on his grave, I would know of none better than the one I read in an Italian cemetery as an epitaph for a man who had given his entire energy to his church: *Dilexit ecclesiam,* he loved the church." [9]

The literary output of Werner Elert covered everything from a psychological study of St. Peter to systematic works on dogmatics and ethics that deserve the overworked label "monumental." [10] But his *Morphologie des Luthertums,* first published in 1931–32 and reissued in 1952, is undoubtedly his most important work. Published just at the time when the author was about to add dogmatics to his *Lehrauftrag,* this book partakes of the nature of both historical and systematic theology. Its foundation is historical research of the highest order. Although Elert was quite diffident about his training as a historian,[11] the historical equipment displayed in this volume amply refutes such diffidence. As was pointed out earlier, one cannot understand Lutheranism unless one sees, for example, that the person and experience of Martin Luther have assumed a paradigmatic role in the history of Lutheran piety.

[9] Cf. *Der Martin Luther-Bund,* XVII (March, 1955), 4.

[10] See the bibliography compiled in Friedrich Hübner, Wilhelm Maurer, and Ernst Kinder (edd.), *Gedenkschrift für D. Werner Elert* (Berlin, 1955), pp. 411 to 424.

[11] In the *Vorwort* to his *Die voluntaristische Mystik Jacob Böhmes* (Berlin, 1913), p. i.

To set this forth, Elert immersed himself in the literature on Luther's development that had been pouring out since the discovery of Luther's early commentaries and since the pioneering work of Karl Holl. The first five chapters of this book show the results. But Elert was an able enough historian to resist the occupational disease of German Luther research, a myopic preoccupation with the young Luther at the expense both of Luther's later life and of the subsequent history of Lutheranism. By contrast with many of his contemporaries, Elert emphasized the continuity between Luther's early thought and later developments, interpreting the Lutheran confessions, including, and especially, the Formula of Concord, as the legitimate outcome of Luther's work; at the same time Elert pointed out the misinterpretations perpetrated by later generations. To document this thesis of continuity and change, Elert drew upon a dazzling knowledge of later Lutheran theology, both before and after the Book of Concord. It seems safe to say that this is the most ambitious and most successful attempt in our time to encompass the whole of Lutheran history.

At the same time, this is certainly not history for history's sake — if indeed there is ever such a thing. Elert wrote as a confessional theologian and a Lutheran churchman. This accounts for the recurrence of the polemical accent throughout the historical expositions. The very structure of the book reminds one of a dogmatics, or of what a dogmatics could be like if more dogmaticians knew more about church history. Despite the abundance of historical and bibliographical detail, there is an organic unity and integrity in these chapters that shows a systematic mind at work. Even when his research ranged beyond the usual boundaries of theology, as it did so often, Elert's theological *habitus* made itself felt. *Der christliche Glaube,* his dogmatics of nine years later,[12] was clearly built upon the systematic schema that was already in evidence here. Elert was a committed and ecumenical Christian, a confessional and loyal Lutheran, and a modern and enlightened man; in the present work he showed that, despite the spirit of the age, one could be all of these at the same time. As a mutual friend has said of him, "he was counted as a Lutheran, and that is what he wanted to be. For many he was the most Lutheran among theologians. Those who were inclined to categorization listed him as a confessionalist. All of this he deliberately sought to be. But only if one reads his writings superficially can

[12] Elert's colleague, Paul Althaus, has pointed out that his major works came at an interval of nine or ten years, *Werner Elerts theologisches Werk* in Hübner et al., op. cit., p. 402.

one fail to notice how involved he was in a continuing dialogue with his time."[13]

Perhaps a personal word of tribute will not be out of order as a conclusion to this Foreword. For a seminarian and graduate student, born in the first year of Elert's professorship at Erlangen and shaped through his family by the confessional tradition of Erlangen, the *Morphologie* came as liberating proof that a historical method and a systematic concern were not as irreconcilable as partisans on both sides were wont to make them. And for a Lutheran theology in America that seeks to be both faithful to its confessional legacy and responsible to its time, few works of European scholarship in the past generation would seem to be more important than this one. One may, of course, raise questions about this or that conclusion in it, as Elert himself did in later years. It seems, for example, that the theological relation between Luther and Melanchthon was not quite what the author of this volume (as well as the author of this Foreword) originally thought, and that the relation of pietism to orthodoxy was perhaps even more complex than these chapters suggest. But these are problems over which debate continues or is about to erupt once more, and it is the measure of Elert's greatness that the debate must still come to terms with his work. So must the theology of this generation.

13 Hanns Lilje, "In memoriam," ibid., p. 7.

JAROSLAV PELIKAN
Titus Street Professor of Ecclesiastical History
The Divinity School of Yale University

Werner Elert, Professor of Theology

Others more closely associated and more intimately acquainted with Werner Elert have described him as a person and as a scholar.[1] I cannot hope to add to or even to summarize what they have written; I merely record some of the impressions which Elert left with one who studied under him with great gain.

Werner Elert studied theology in Breslau, Erlangen, and Leipzig. The names associated with those schools – e. g., Rocholl, Harless, Thomasius, Frank, Zahn, and Ihmels – indicate the broad complex of theological scholarship and emphases which formed Elert's heritage. Elert knew himself not only as a scholar dedicated to the appropriation and transmission of the learning handed down by previous generations of the church but also as a theologian responsible for its creative reinterpretation to meet the needs of the world and of the church in which he lived. On the one hand, Elert stood in organic continuity with the Lutheran Restoration and the Erlangen theology of the nineteenth century; on the other hand, he transcended both of them in the method and in the content of his theology.

In his five major scholarly works [2] Elert was concerned to demonstrate the way in which he met the scholarly responsibility which he bore as a member of the theological faculty, and each of these works is a monument to the dedication and discipline with which he fulfilled each of his assignments. They reveal the unique combination of historical knowledge and systematic insight, of confessional depth and ecumenical breadth, that made Elert one of the most learned and creative theologians of this century.

1 Paul Althaus, *Werner Elerts theologisches Werk*, in *Gedenkschrift für Werner Elert*. Ed. by Friedrich Hübner, et al. (Berlin, *Lutherisches Verlagshaus*, 1955), pp. 400—410. Wilhelm Maurer, *In Memoriam Professor D. Werner Elert, Evangelisch-Lutherische Kirchenzeitung*, VIII (1954), 378 ff.

2 *Der Kampf um das Christentum* (1921), *Morphologie des Luthertums*, 2 vols. (1931 f.), *Der christliche Glaube* (1940), *The Christian Ethos* (1949; Engl. transl. by Carl C. Schindler, Muhlenberg Press, Philadelphia, 1957), *Der Ausgang der altkirchlichen Christologie* (1957).

Elert was a theologian with his whole heart and soul. At the same time he was unusually interested in other disciplines. He devoted 90 percent of some of his university semesters to studies other than theology, e. g., philosophy, psychology, history, and military science. This broad spectrum of knowledge is more apparent in some of his writings than in others, but it underlies all of them. Because he felt that the theologian must constantly remain in conversation with the world in which he lives, Elert was a vocal defender of the theological faculty's place within the structure of the university and had little patience with those who wanted to isolate the study of theology on a seminary campus.

For all the richness of Elert's scholarship, his style as a teacher and as a writer must be described as economical. He justified this stylistic economy with a comparison to the art of painting portraits: everything depends on knowing what to omit. His readers, like many of his students, will find the combination of so much content and so few words forbidding at first glance. Neither in his lectures nor in his books did Elert spread a feast of learning which could be memorized in scholarly indolence and stored for later use. On the contrary, Elert demands that one do the work with him; and for this reason he cannot be scanned or even casually read. Elert limited his scholarly judgments to those areas in which he had worked intensively with the sources, and he requires his students and readers to work through the essential content of the material with him before they can appropriate or even understand his conclusions. A certain type of reader will shy away from this; but those who take the trouble to do the work will learn the truth of the Erlangen proverb that for whatever reason one came to Erlangen to study theology, one stayed longer than planned, because he had come under the influence of Elert.

Elert made no effort to attract students. Indeed, it sometimes seemed that he was unconcerned to the point of turning them away. In time, however, one learned to see that he merely accepted students on the basis on which he himself wished to be accepted as a scholar, and that he required the same intensive study of the sources and the concern to draw relevant conclusions that he demanded of himself. He was a great teacher not only because he constantly maintained this demand at a high level but because he was able to communicate his own scholarly passion and his capacity for intuitively seeking out that chain of development which would be relevant to the problem under discussion. His critiques were honest and frank, sometimes sharp and stinging, always deadly accurate. Yet Elert never short-circuited the painful process of scholarly growth by revealing the way to be traveled or the goal to be achieved. At times it seemed that he wanted only students who did not need him as a teacher. The truth, of course, lay elsewhere. His goal for each student was that he learn to work in absolute independence of any personal authority of and guidance from the teacher. Elert took the idea of the university as a community of scholars, each contributing to the other, with radical seriousness. Membership depended on the capacity to give as well as to receive.

Not all students appropriated Elert's conclusions or even his methods and standards. Yet few students sat in his lectures without being decisively influenced in their theological thinking. His influence reaches far and wide through the Lutheran Church. It will be increasingly felt in the coming years, not only in academic theology but also in the life of the church; for he gave his students the same concern for participation in the practical life of the church that he himself demonstrated throughout his life.

This influence cannot, however, be measured in terms of an "Elertian" school. Elert did not want to establish such a school. He himself was a confessional theologian and was concerned not to make his students over in his own theological image but rather to alert them to the strength and cohesiveness of Lutheran theology. The enthusiasm which he inspired was not enthusiasm for his person; it was enthusiasm for the subject matter and the task of theology. What he communicated was not a set of conclusions; it was a method.

ROBERT C. SCHULTZ

Translator's Preface

Werner Elert (1885–1954) was a giant among the important theologians of recent times. Throughout a long and highly significant career his extraordinarily active, inquisitive, and sensitive mind ranged over a vast expanse of theological lore. It went back to the dim and distant past, it concerned itself with the present, and it never lost sight of the future. Elert investigated with tireless diligence and with unusual circumspection. He sifted and weighed, rejected and accepted. He continued to search and probe until death intervened.

The *Morphologie des Luthertums* shows how zealously and how selflessly Elert sought to answer questions of vital concern to those who busy themselves with the study of theology. The famous scholar strove to be objective, and his very passion for objectivity impelled him at times to lash out with telling incisiveness against conclusions which he held to be incongruous and untenable. Here and there the *Morphologie* contains brief but striking examples of his ability to resort to sharp invective whenever he considered it necessary to do so.

Naturally, many theologians will find fault with some of Elert's conclusions. After reading and rereading his *Morphologie* I myself shake my head now and then in disagreement. Others are bound to have the same experience. But this does not mean that Elert did not strive with self-effacing determination to see and to picture the impressive structure of Lutheranism as it actually exists.

Years ago Anatole France, the famous French critic, pointed out with unassailable logic that no author can fail to be autobiographical in his writings. Elert, too, was autobiographical in what he wrote. The *Morphologie* enables one to envisage the man as he thought and worked; it paints the portrait of a courageous scholar whose richly stored mind invariably revealed honesty of purpose. The disagreements which Elert's epoch-making study of the structure of Lutheranism will undoubtedly call forth in this or that quarter can render a significant service by leading to painstaking examination and reexamination of the points of difference.

Elert did not write for the purpose of seeking publicity; he wrote for the purpose of stating the truth as he saw the truth. His *Morphologie* is an outstanding classic in the field of theological literature. But it is not outstanding as a literary achievement per se. The writing is uneven. Sometimes it is downright cumbersome. In numerous instances, however, it is full of elemental power. Occasionally it is beautiful in its texture. Elert himself was keenly aware of "deficiencies" in the *Morphologie.* He was eager to eliminate them. But death came to him before he had the opportunity to do so.

I have tried in the sweat of my face to reproduce Elert's distinctive way of writing. It has been my purpose to let Elert appear as Elert, not in a garb devised by a translator. Alexander Pope, William Cullen Bryant, and Johann Heinrich Voss translated Homer. But they did not actually reproduce Homer; they mirrored generous portions of their own traits. John Dryden did the same thing when he rendered Vergil's *Aeneid* into English. This was Dryden – even though Dryden told Vergil's story.

Yet it is an axiomatic fact that no translation can ever be a perfect replica of the original. Furthermore, one must always bear in mind that even in this domain there can be differences of opinion with respect to some points. I have tried to hit every nail on the head. Any misses the discriminating reader may discover are altogether unintentional. Elert, like many other lecturers, often crowded numerous thoughts into the confines of a single sentence. This resulted in writing which, in some cases, must be traversed two, three, or more times before one grasps everything that is being said. In addition, Elert frequently switches tenses in the middle of the stream. I have switched in harmony with his switching. I did not consider it my duty to polish Elert's style; it was my business to try to reproduce it. For this reason I have sought to avoid paraphrastic renderings, and I have studiously refrained from any attempts to refine the fine gold that sometimes characterizes his way of expressing his thoughts. Whenever his writing is powerful in its burning eloquence, my translation into English lags far behind the original in forcefulness of expression. Here, in fact, it is bound to be afflicted with an unmistakable limp. Translating is a difficult art, but I have realized again and again that Elert often hurls almost insurmountable difficulties across the path of anyone who undertakes to produce an English version of the *Morphologie.* If I have failed at any point or at numerous points, I shall be grateful for the reprimands that will be showered on me.

Now I must call attention to a particularly perplexing problem – a problem that has been a thorn in my flesh, so to speak, ever since I began to translate the *Morphologie* into English. What is the exact English equivalent of *der evangelische Ansatz?* Is there an exact English equivalent? I have striven long and hard to find one. I have sought help from numerous sources, and I myself have devised and rejected more than one translation. I must add, however, that I have been opposed on principle to the use of any rendering that would require a recasting of the sentence in which the expression occurs; for in such cases one could easily withhold from Peter without being able to reimburse Paul. After long deliberation I have finally decided to translate *der evangelische Ansatz* with "the impact of the Gospel." I realize that this rendering is not completely adequate in every respect. But I have not been able to find anything that is better.[1]

The first edition of the *Morphologie* appeared in 1931, and the late Dr. Theodore Engelder, a member of the faculty of Concordia Theological Seminary in St. Louis, contributed a long and detailed review of the book to the September 1932 issue of the *Concordia Theological Monthly.* Dr. Engelder stated that Elert uses *der evangelische Ansatz* synonymously with "the doctrine of justification."[2] Although there is

[1] Those who understand German will undoubtedly arrive at a clearer understanding of what Elert means when he uses the expression *der evangelische Ansatz* if they give special attention to what Paul Althaus said in the address he delivered at the University of Erlangen on February 19, 1955, at a memorial service in honor of Elert. I quote without translating: *Er unterscheidet bei seinem Erfassen des Luthertums "Dynamis" und "Gestalt," Morphe. Jene ist die Konstante, diese der immer neue geschichtliche Ausdruck, in dem die Konstante aufzusuchen, der zugleich an der Dynamis zu messen ist. Jene Dynamis findet Elert — mit einem seiner seitdem weithin rezipierten Termini — in dem "evangelischen Ansatz." Er versteht darunter das grundlegende lutherische Verständnis der menschlichen Existenz, zuerst als "unter dem Zorne Gottes," sodann unter dem "Evangelium." Wir erhalten hier ein ungemein starkes Bild dessen, was man in Anlehnung an einen Begriff Elerts das evangelische Pathos nennen kann, Luthers "Urerlebnis" unter der Verborgenheit Gottes, seine Erfahrung des Evangeliums und den theologischen Ausdruck von beidem. (Gedenkschrift für D. Werner Elert, Lutherisches Verlagshaus,* Berlin, 1955, p. 403.) I must add that these words of Althaus have strengthened me in the belief that my translation of *der evangelische Ansatz* is by no means an out-and-out blunder or what the Germans would call a *Fehlgriff.*

[2] I quote from Dr. Engelder's review: *In diesem grossartigen Werk wird nachgewiesen, wie die Rechtfertigungslehre, durchweg "der evangelische Ansatz" genannt, dem Luthertum und dem lutherischen Wesen zugrunde liegt. Sie bildet das Herz des Luthertums, hat ihm auch seine äusserlichen Züge aufgeprägt. Wie die Lehre der Schrift das ist, was sie ist, eben weil es eine Rechtfertigung durch den Glauben gibt, so steht auch in der lutherischen Theologie die Rechtfertigungslehre im Zentrum, beherrscht auch den Kultus, die Verfassung und das Leben.*

much merit in what this learned reviewer, for whose theological acumen I have profound respect, said about the meaning of *der evangelische Ansatz,* his explanatory remark does not solve the knotty problem with which Elert's expression confronts the person who undertakes to translate the *Morphologie* into English. Elert frequently uses the word *Rechtfertigungslehre* ("doctrine of justification"). If a translator could substitute *Rechtfertigungslehre* for *der evangelische Ansatz* in every instance, there would be no problem at all. But would this rather simple expedient be completely in keeping with Elert's dialectic? I do not think so. While I recognize the relevance and the pertinence of what Dr. Engelder said about *der evangelische Ansatz,* I do not believe that it would be wise or proper to interchange *Rechtfertigungslehre* and *der evangelische Ansatz* every time these two expressions occur in the book.

In the preface which Elert wrote to the 1952 reprint of the *Morphologie* he states that "for technical reasons improvements are confined, in the main, to the weeding out of typographical errors." But typographical errors are elusive and malevolent creatures. I have discovered a few of these pests in the 1952 reprint of the *Morphologie,* particularly where Latin quotations are adduced. In one instance the punctuation was misplaced. I struggled long and fruitlessly to arrive at a translation before it finally dawned on me that a number of commas were in the wrong places. But I am not finding fault with Elert on this account. In numerous instances the time-honored sources from which he quotes are notoriously inconsistent and seemingly arbitrary with respect to punctuation and uniformity of spelling.

I dare not conclude without expressing my boundless admiration of Elert's penetrating and far-sweeping acquaintance with the writings of Martin Luther. In addition, I must state that this famous scholar, who must be numbered among the most distinguished theologians of recent decades, never fails to stress the difference between Law and Gospel. If he did not do so, his *Morphologie* would fall far short of exhibiting the structure of Lutheranism.

In necessariis unitas, in dubiis libertas, in omnibus autem caritas

WALTER A. HANSEN

St. Louis, Missouri
May 21, 1962

From the Preface to the First Edition

The following presentation strives to accomplish in one respect what I demanded in the inaugural address I delivered here on the necessity of reconstructing the study of the confessions. On that occasion I said that one must give attention to the activity of modern church bodies in its entire extent, even in "nonecclesiastical" areas. Those sections of the first volume that deal with the philosophy of life undertake to comply with this demand so far as Lutheranism is concerned, and the entire second volume seeks to achieve the same end. . . .

Erlangen
January 1931

Preface to the Reprint

Since the first appearance of this work not a few new investigations have been added to the writings mentioned in connection with each part. Since that time Swedish and Finnish research has concerned itself in a particularly intensive manner with Luther's theology. But German research has also done so. Further work has been done with respect to Melanchthon and other Lutheran theologians. Important monographs dealing with problematical historical matters – for example, with the doctrine of Holy Communion in the sixteenth century – have appeared. Furthermore, research that is historical in the stricter sense is overlayed with so many writings that it is well-nigh impossible to examine every one of them. With regard to the questions raised by systematic theology in our time, these writings range through identical subject matter or reflect points of view that are of current significance for the church. In this very respect the theological movement is in a complete state of flux. Therefore it was necessary to ask whether this state of affairs does not confront the *Morphologie* with a new assignment – an assignment that might have to lead to a total recasting of the entire work. Nevertheless, a reprinting of the first edition was preferred, and for technical reasons improvements are confined, in the main, to the weeding out of typographical errors. So far as I myself am concerned, the following considerations have been decisive.

The principal objection to the whole work was directed against combining dogmatical and historical points of view into a homogeneous thought structure. In his *Kirchliche Dogmatik* Karl Barth speaks about the "*Morphologie* that cannot be sufficiently condemned," and Hermann Sasse decrees in his letters to Lutheran pastors that "there is no morphology of the confessions." With respect to this, however, the critics have not convinced me. Even if the work had been revised, the total arrangement would have remained the same. In that case I myself would have had the opportunity to make stylistic improvements, to express myself more precisely in many instances, and to omit a few unnecessary comments. This would have been the only advantage. But attention to works that have appeared in the meanwhile and the discussion of these works would have necessitated making the book almost twice as large as it is. For me it was contrary to the command to love one's neighbor as well as one's enemies to pass this added expense on to the purchaser. Sympathetic reviewers have found the book valuable because it cites sources that are either unknown or have not been considered in the past, and even unsympathetic reviewers have acknowledged this to the extent that they have appropriated not a few of the quotations it contains. In my opinion, a reprint will continue to serve this purpose.

But it is necessary to add that from the very beginning — not subsequently — I myself have regarded the two volumes as a mere torso. At the very outset I intended to expand the presentation in the direction of the present as well as in the direction of the past. The modification of my teaching assignment at the University of Erlangen induced me to establish the relationship to the present in two systematic books — in a Lutheran work on dogmatics, *Der Christliche Glaube,* 1940–41, and in a work on the Lutheran ethic, *Das Christliche Ethos,* 1949. So far as I am able to see now, the presentation of the relationship to the past is still an unsolved problem. Early Lutheranism affirmed its consensus with the early church, and today the whole thinking of the church — the thinking that is expressed in this consensus — has received renewed significance for our time. Consequently, from this point of view it seemed to me to be more urgent to examine the history of dogma of the early church than to revise the two existing volumes of the *Morphologie* and thus to eliminate the deficiencies, which I myself know best. I hope soon to be able to present some of the results of the recent investigations.

Erlangen
June 1952

Contents

Foreword vii

Werner Elert, Professor of Theology xiii

Translator's Preface xvii

From the Preface to the First Edition xxi

Preface to the Reprint xxiii

Abbreviations xxvii

INTRODUCTION 3

PART ONE

The Impact of the Gospel *(Der evangelische Ansatz)*

CHAPTER ONE Under the Wrath of God

1. The Primal Experience *(Das Urerlebnis)* 17
2. Sin 28
3. The Law and the Wrath of God 35
4. Fear 43
5. Natural Theology 49

CHAPTER TWO The Gospel

6. Preliminary Questions 59
7. Luther on Justification 73
8. Justification in the Confessions 90
9. *Propter Christum* 106
10. Reconciliation and Predestination in Luther in Disjunction 117
11. Reconciliation and Predestination in the Confessions in Conjunction 126
12. Faith and the Psyche 140
13. *Unio Mystica* 154

PART TWO

Dogma and the Church

CHAPTER THREE Dogma

14. Holy Scripture 179
15. Canon, Inspiration, Means of Grace, Apologetics 191
16. The Acceptance of the Old Creeds 200
17. The Doctrine of God 211
18. The Doctrine of the Two Natures 222
19. The States and Offices of Christ 236

CHAPTER FOUR The Church

20. The Dogma of the Church 255
21. Catholicity 274
22. The Sacrament of Baptism 291
23. The Sacrament of the Altar 300
24. Worship 321
25. The Office of the Ministry 339
26. The Later Doctrine of the Office of the Ministry and the Nature of This Office 352
27. Church Government 367
28. Missions 385

PART THREE

Philosophy of Life

CHAPTER FIVE The World as Space

29. Justification and Philosophy of Life 405
30. The Relativity of the World Picture 414
31. God and the World 431
32. Close Connection with the Earth 448

CHAPTER SIX Time

33. Cross and Vale of Tears 463
34. History 476
35. The Kingdom of Christ 491
36. End of the World 507

Works by Early Dogmaticians 519

Index 521

ABBREVIATIONS

ADB — *Allgemeine Deutsche Biographie*

AELKZ — *Allgemeine Evang.-luth. Kirchenzeitung*

ARG — *Archiv für Reformationsgeschichte*

BBK — *Beiträge zur Bayerischen Kirchengeschichte*

Bek. d. RK — E. F. K. Müller, *Die Bekenntnisschriften der reformierten Kirche,* 1903

BFchrTh — *Beiträge zur Förderung christlicher Theologie*

CA — *Confessio Augustana* (Augsburg Confession)

ChrW — *Christliche Welt*

Cohrs — Ferdinand Cohrs, *Die Evangelischen Katechismusversuche vor Luthers Enchiridion* (*Monumenta Germaniae Paedagogica,* vols. 20—23)

Conf. Hafn. — *Confessio Hafnica (Copenhagen Articles)*

Conf. Mont. — *Confessio Montana, Bekenntnis der oberungarischen sieben Bergstädte von 1519,* quoted according to Borbis, *Die evang.-luth. Kirche Ungarns,* 1861, pp. 22 ff.

CR — *Corpus Reformatorum*

Denzinger — *Henr. Denzinger et Clem. Bannwart S. J. Enchiridion Symbolorum, Ed. XVI et XVII.*

DG — *Dogmengeschichte*

Diss. — dissertation

Drews — P. Drews, *Disputationen Luthers 1535—45,* 1895

EA — Erlangen edition of Luther's works

EA *ex. lat.* — Luther, *Exegetica opera latina,* Erlangen edition

EA *var. arg.* — Luther, *Opera varii argumenti,* Erlangen edition

Enders — *Luthers Briefwechsel,* edited by Enders, Kawerau, Flemming, and Albrecht

Epit. — *Epitome* of the Formula of Concord

FC — *Formula Concordiae* (Formula of Concord)

Fränk. Bek. — *Die fränkischen Bekenntnisse, herausgegeben vom Landeskirchenrat der ev.-luth. Kirche in Bayern r. d. Rh.*

Gussmann — W. Gussmann, *Quellen und Forschungen zur Geschichte des Augsburgischen Glaubensbekenntnisses,* 1911—30

KG — *Kirchengeschichte*

KO — *Kirchenordnung*

Kopenhagener Art. — *Malmö-Beretningen om Religionsartikler og Forhandlinger paa Herredagen i Kjöbenhavn 1530, udg. af Holger Fr. Rördam,* Copenhagen, 1889

Mirbt — Carl Mirbt, *Quellen zur Geschichte des Papsttums und des römischen Katholizismus,* 4th ed., 1924

Niemeyer — H. A. Niemeyer, *Collectio Confessionum in ecclesiis reformatis publicatarum,* 1840

NKZ — *Neue Kirchliche Zeitschrift*

Plitt-Kolde — *Die Loci Communes Ph. Melanchthons in ihrer Urgestalt nach G. L. Plitt herausgegeben von Th. Kolde,* 4th ed. 1925

PRE — *Realenzyklopädie für protestantische Theologie und Kirche,* 3d ed.

Reu — Johann Michael Reu, *Quellen zur Geschichte des kirchlichen Unterrichts in der evang. Kirche Deutschlands zwischen 1530 und 1600*

RGG — *Die Religion in Geschichte und Gegenwart*

Richter — Aem. Ludw. Richter, *Die evangelischen Kirchenordnungen des 16. Jahrhunderts,* 1846

SA — Smalcald Articles

SchrVRG — *Schriften des Vereins für Reformationsgeschichte*

SD — *Solida Declaratio* of the Formula of Concord

Sehling — Emil Sehling, *Die evangelischen Kirchenordnung des 16. Jahrhunderts,* 5 vols., 1902 ff.

SW — *Sämtliche Werke*

Th. — thesis

ThStKr — *Theologische Studien und Kritiken*

TR — Luther's *Table Talk,* Weimar edition

WA — Weimar edition of Luther's works

ZBK — *Zeitschrift für bayer. Kirchengeschichte*

ZKG — *Zeitschrift für Kirchengeschichte*

ZsTh — *Zeitschrift für systematische Theologie*

ZThK — *Zeitschrift für Theologie und Kirche*

ZW — *Zeitwende*

ZZ — *Zwischen den Zeiten*

The Structure of
LUTHERANISM

Introduction

Ever since the Council of Trent made the Western schism complete, the theology of all churches has been striving for the morphology of the confessions. In the background of the serious controversies in which Martin Chemnitz, Robert Bellarmine, Johann Gerhard, and Daniel Chamier engaged one is already aware of the elemental urge to ascertain and understand one's own position and the position taken by others, in order to present the two correctly in controversy. The picture recurs when Rudolf Hospinian, in his *Discordant Harmony (Concordia discors),* and Leonhard Hutter, in his *Concordant Harmony (Concordia concors),* square accounts between the two main Protestant groups, or when the Wittenbergians cross swords with the Socinians. Of course, these polemical works themselves are still part of the shaping of the modern confessions. But for this very reason their original dynamic is still clearly discernible. To be sure, the "objectivity" sought by the reader of yesterday and the day before in a presentation of information concerning the confessions cannot be found. For these men think existentially, not hypothetically. In their thinking they are obedient to a command to which they feel unconditionally obligated, to a claim which, by turning to them, makes them what they themselves are. In this way their observation of their own position and of that of others is applied to the very last thing that urgently sought to take shape here. Consequently, their writings themselves are not only products of confessional polemics but also reliable witnesses of the confessional morphology.

From a morphology we demand a complete picture of its subject matter. Whether the picture is obtained by fitting separate parts together or by sketching the profile; whether one proceeds from the outside to the inside or vice versa, unfolds the formative dynamic from the final shape, or presents the latter to the reader as resulting from the former – these are only differences in method. It is sufficient if, in the end, a complete picture can be seen. Measured by this demand, the works of those old polemicists appear as fragments. The "comparative study of the confessions" which was pursued during the past generation and, as was natural, made enormous progress accuses the polemicists and, in addition, nineteenth-century "symbolics," which preceded them, of having treated confessional differences with reference only to dogmatics. As if there were in human life a single area – from the state and the formation of capital to divorce and the gypsy plague – which had not been drawn into the discussions by Bellarmine and Johann Gerhard. And even though this accusation actually does apply to many of the nineteenth-century students of symbolics, there is still the question whether they, with their one-sidedness in the matter of dogmatics, were not more closely on the track of the dynamic of the confessions than Troeltsch was when he thought he had discovered the secret of confessional differentiation in the various "social doctrines." Measured by the demand for completeness of the morphology, the one was just as one-sided as the other. The fact that the ethos of the confessions – not only the ethic – proceeds in different directions was known long before Troeltsch appeared. Only the question regarding the relationship to the dynamic of the confessions is worth considering. "Dogmas exercise an influence on man's whole behavior," wrote Johann Albrecht Bengel; [1] and Schneckenburger, in his *Comparative Presentation of Lutheran and Reformed Doctrinal Concepts* (1855), made a very thorough attempt to prove this.

The impression that the early polemicists present only fragments of the confessional morphology is rather to be ascribed to the fact that they themselves wrote when things were beginning to take shape. The shaping itself is a process that goes on for centuries; it never ceases while there is still a spark of life. Even today it continues for Roman Catholicism as well as for Lutheranism. Therefore even today any attempt to present a morphology can result only in a fragmentary picture. Nevertheless, for several centuries the work has been making progress. We know what they already knew or suspected: that it is the aim of the confessional dynamic to take into its service and to shape the entire domain of everything human. Furthermore, we know what they could not yet know: that here there are changes in epochs, an increase in strength and a decrease, a dormant state of the formative will and power as well as an awakening. Finally we know what they indeed could know but did not make clear to themselves: that the confessional dynamic is often thwarted, hidden, and overpowered by other forces of history.

At first glance this threefold knowledge seems to facilitate for us the larger approach to the ideal of an actual morphology. On closer examination, however, it uncovers for us just as many difficulties as we had

[1] O. Wächter, *J. A. Bengel*, p. 370.

before. Every area of the sum total of human interests — something we need take no pride in at all — has become more extensive — so extensive that an individual is no longer able to ascertain at every point the relationship to the confessional dynamic. Furthermore, at the very outset changes in epochs wreck every attempt — easy though it may seem — to gain from a cross section of history at a specific moment an adequate picture of one of the confessions. The forms of expression sought by churches and other groups undergo changes, and the farther they get from their starting point, the greater the changes. There are, to be sure, cases of repristination; but there are no repetitions. In order, therefore, to find the relationship between dynamic and form, one must let the whole succession of epochs pass in review, just as the historian ascertains and describes what took place. But while the historian attempts to trace single events from their immediate causes, a morphology undertakes to find a constant that is effective in all changes, one that is operative beyond individual connections and, as a dominant force, either determines or helps determine the outcome. A morphology proceeds from the assumption that the confessional constant not only controls man, ideas, and patterns of a moment in history and welds them together into a confessional unity but also outlasts the succession of epochs, yes — this is at least possible — even brings about the epochal changes of the whole. Only an examination of history itself can show whether this assumption is correct.

But, as has been said, the task of constructing a morphology is complicated most by the fact that the confessional dynamic is in competition with very many other motives of historical development. It would be conceivable that just as early Christianity was said to be a syncretistic religion, so it would also have to be true of the modern confessional churches that they have no homogeneous blood stream of their own but, on the contrary, are nothing more than a product of heterogeneous components. In Catholicism, Brother Heiler has uncovered seven heterogeneous strata in which, as he says, the whole external world of extra-Christian religions is reflected. To find in them the dominant factor — if this has to do with a form *(Morphe)*, with a homogeneous totality of life, the dominant factor must be postulated — is by no means easy! Here the causal relationship of Lutheranism to the act of the Reformation seems to facilitate the appropriate determining of the morphology. But at the very moment the morphology, as just demanded, seeks to take into consideration the changes in the epochs and focuses its attention on the dynamic that is operative in them, it sees its subject matter exposed to an explanation on the basis of other things — an explanation which, so it seems, arrives at its goal without any employment of the confessional perspective. No one will deny, of course, that the soil in which the Herrnhut Unity of the Brethren *(Herrnhuter Brüdergemeinde)* arose was Protestant. But the motives of its origin and the terminology in which it expressed itself have, when considered from the viewpoint of morphology, such pronounced similarity to contemporaneous phenomena in the history of art, literature, and society that the attempts to treat their peculiarity purely as a question of style seem easily understandable.

What is almost obstrusive in the case of this relatively small group can also occur in the case of large groups. The attempts to establish a connection between the Reformation and the Renaissance, not only with reference to ideas but also so far as the style characteristic of these periods in history is concerned, are not new. The Counter Reformation is baroque, pietism is rococo, the Enlightenment is the style of Potsdam and finally of the Napoleonic Empire, the Restoration of the nineteenth century is neo-Gothic or Biedermeier. It would not be impossible to consider the style changes per se consistent with the assumption of a continuously operative confessional dynamic. Conceivably, this could even bring the style changes into being. In reality, however, this is out of the question; for the changes recur in the terminology of all confessions belonging to the same cultural sphere. In any case, therefore, the historical terminology which churches and groups apply to themselves is also cocontrolled by a dynamic springing from other laws. As a result, a study of the confessions which must confine itself first of all to the historical terminology is confronted by the difficult task of looking for clues to its hypothesis concerning the confessional dynamic. This it must do in spite of the apparent or actual relationship in the matter of style. And it must reckon on principle with the necessity of laying down its arms at one point or another.

The following investigation does not claim to have given a complete solution of these problems for Lutheranism. But it has come to grips with them, and it tries at least to take them into account. So far as method is concerned, the direction in which it proceeded was the reverse of the presentation that follows, i. e., with those phenomena in history in which the dynamic of Lutheranism is still directly to be felt. Individual investigations concerning the relationship of Lutheranism to nations, to the history of marriage, and to the ethos of warfare, as well as investigations concerning the effect its doctrine of the Lord's Supper had on the history of the philosophy of life *(Weltanschauung)*, also concerning the phenomenology of anxiety, were, for this reason, published at an earlier date. Now they have been fitted in part into the larger context. Whenever possible, they sought a confirmation of the confessional hypothesis in matters that had been neglected by previous studies of the confessions. Nevertheless, the hope to arrive at a true morphology of Lutheranism in this way proved delusive.

For it became apparent that even from a purely morphological standpoint it is impossible to evade the media of characterization that had been the one and all for the old "symbolics," namely, the doctrinal features set forth in the "symbols," the official church confessions. To be sure, the problem presented and developed above permitted a deliberate abandonment of the attempt to describe Lutheranism merely as theological subject matter. On the contrary, it also necessitated a treatment of the content of the symbols, not as the dynamic governing the whole but as one of their forms of expression besides which altogether different forms can be seen. What Soederbloem established regarding churches in general — that the knowledge and the forces operative behind the council at Stockholm for "practical Christianity" and behind the council at Lausanne "for faith and church government" would have to be expanded — represents a position reflecting the form *(Morphe)* of Lutheranism either consciously or unconsciously.[2] Troeltsch, with his principle stating that "Christianity is practice" *(das Christentum ist Praktik)* — a principle developed when he occupied the chair of theology at the old university in the Palatinate — could not have arrived at such a judgment. But it is by no means possible simply to coordinate the various categories of expression Lutheranism has created for itself. This is evident from the fact that some are more variable than others and that in individual cases their amalgamation with motives springing from other laws reveals great differences in strength. It is strongest in the domain of sociology, weaker in the domain of the philosophy of life, and still weaker in the terminology of church government and worship. Beyond question, however, theology and, here again, the official church dogma come closest to our objectives — the dominant force.

Moreover, as the source of the morphology the confessions mean something different from the binding norms of doctrine formulated at a given time. For, in the first place, they have characteristics that pertain not only to the date of their origin. Even though the measure of their validity in many areas of later development was emphatically disputed, and even though theology as well as the preaching of the church was often at variance with them, yet they were never completely

[2] Soederbloem, *Randanmärkingar till Lausanne, Svensk Teologisk Kvartalskrift,* 1927, pp. 336 ff.

forgotten. They were known even when they were contradicted. Wherever one either agreed or disagreed when coming to grips with them, they were at least reference points of theological thinking. Yes, whenever in the history of Lutheranism it was necessary to come to grips with opposing groups, they were the point of departure for the necessary renewal of the understanding of Lutheranism's own character. In the second place, therefore, the confessions were never merely of a legal nature. Where there is no strict proof to the contrary, the morphology may rather reckon with the fact that, directly or indirectly, they actually helped shape the total picture of historical Lutheranism. In the third place, the confessions were not only formal norms of doctrine; for the most part, they were synonymous with doctrine itself. This is true in large measure, for example, of Luther's Small Catechism. One can say without exaggeration that the simple appropriation of the doctrinal material contained in this book has been the most important factor even in the social life of Lutheran countries – and for centuries a constantly effective factor. The study of the confessions does not ask whether this is pedagogically right or wrong. On the contrary, it simply establishes this fact; and here it has found one of the dynamic elements to which Lutheranism's more or less peripheral forms of expression in history may be traced with certainty.[3]

But the confessions also point away from themselves to a dynamic of a higher order. Their materials – for example, in the Catechisms and in Melanchthon's treatise on the papacy or in the first and the sixteenth article of the Augsburg Confession – are in part so heterogeneous in character that what determines every single point in a uniform manner has to lie even farther in the past. Here the study of the confessions becomes involved in historical questions it cannot evade, even though, strictly speaking, these questions are not part of the study. For even though it seeks the confessional constant that accompanied Lutheranism for centuries and shaped it as a continuously operative dynamic, still this constant has to have a beginning. And if even the oldest confessions are part of what this constant brought about, the constant must have had its origin in the critical years that lead from the beginnings of the

[3] In his famous essay on the "three main branches of the Lutheran Church" (*AELKZ,* 1927; cf. "The Lutheran Church Quarterly," 1928, pp. 302 ff.) Olaf Moe designates the definiteness contained in the confessions as a special characteristic of American Lutheranism. The correctness of this judgment will be substantiated when the field of sociology is discussed. Yet there, too, the history as well as the present situation is defined by characteristics that are totally different. For the time being I refer only to the collection of essays titled *What Is Lutheranism?* (New York, Macmillan, 1930), with contributions by Weigle, Evjen, Offermann, Wentz, Reu, Hefelbower, Scherer, Haas, Dau, Wendell, Rohne, and Ferm.

Reformation to the Augsburg Confession. But this outer bounding of the time of origin indicates at the same time termini of a series of hypotheses demanding from the morphology a decision that will probably keep it from being praised as "objective."

The one hypothesis proceeds from the character of the Augsburg Confession relating to constitutional law. It stresses the fact that the independence of Lutheranism as a church body was due to action on the part of the central authority of the German Empire. Accordingly – as is still the case of late in the cultural philosophy of Franz Zach – it seeks the origin of the dominant force in the motives and purposes of the German territorial rulers and cities. A second hypothesis prefers to hold to the theological character of the Augsburg Confession. Therefore it seeks a theological origin. It is maintained that Lutheranism, by making this document the starting point of its awareness of being a church body, committed itself to the theology of Melanchthon, which is set forth in the document. Recently this hypothesis has come to the point of stating that the Lutheranism shaped by the Augsburg Confession and therefore directly by Melanchthon signifies a falling away from the "young Luther." This contrasting of Luther with Melanchthon is not really new. It lies at the root of the theological disputes that followed Luther's death and came to an end in the Formula of Concord. At that time, however, the unaltered Augsburg Confession of 1530 was still regarded as giving expression to a theology which Luther himself professed without having to renounce his own theology. And what had to be interpreted as Melanchthon's subsequent apostasy lost its right of domicile in Lutheranism because of the outcome of those disputes. Albrecht Ritschl also put very strong emphasis on that antithesis; but inasmuch as he pointed to the 1530s as the time when the development began to go awry, he remained true to the basic conception of Lutheranism as that conception had existed for centuries. To be sure, he also regarded the movement that led to the Formula of Concord as a faulty development. And when he gave the reason for the manner of expression *(Sprachgebrauch)* which spoke only contemptuously of "Lutheranism" on Lutheran soil, he meant, of course, the Lutheranism which thought it had the right to view the Formula of Concord as the reversion from Melanchthon to Luther.

If since those days – i. e., in this perspective – there were two kinds of Lutheranism – the one, that which is contained in the confessions; the other, that which found its most fitting expression in the theology of the professors of the nineteenth and twentieth centuries – the second has recently made progress insofar as it has again set up an objective norm for what Lutheranism should mean in its original sense. This norm is the "young Luther." His first lectures, discovered in recent decades, have given us very accurate knowledge concerning him. The prospect presented by publicizing the theology contained in them is very bright, because one can reckon with the capital of confidence and authority which the mature Luther acquired. The fact that in those lectures there is still a goodly amount of foreign theology, which Luther took over from tradition but deliberately rejected later on, yes, to some extent fought against with the utmost sharpness, presents no obstacle to this way of looking at the matter. Here the interpreter decides dictatorially what pertains to the Reformation and what does not. This Luther – unlike the later Luther, who, because of his important publications, is under the supervision, as it were, of publicity – may be used more easily as needed. Above all, he does not, like the Luther of 1529, break asunder the "united front of Protestantism," since at that time Zwingli was still an army chaplain and "Protestantism" did not yet exist. Above all, the theology of those lectures still seems to leave room for the claim that Calvin was Luther's "most loyal disciple." Here the reader will discover that even church history is not without humor. For the role of Luther's "most loyal disciple" was once ascribed by Heinrich Heppe, a member of the old Reformed Church, to him, of all persons, who allegedly created the Lutheranism that is said to be routed today by means of the young Luther, namely, to Melanchthon – the Melanchthon, of course, whom his Lutheran opponents linked with crypto-Calvinism.

In this way the other outermost boundary of the aforementioned series of hypotheses is marked. This third hypothesis seeks the origin and the fulfillment of its Lutheranism in the theology of the young Luther. So far as pointing to a person is concerned, this hypothesis is surpassed only by a fourth, advocated by Father Denifle, who undertook to find the key to the whole Reformation, and indirectly to Lutheranism, in Luther's writing *On Monastic Vows (De votis monasticis).*

At the decisive point, therefore, our morphology is confronted with a difficult task. It is unfortunate that in view of the great number of hypotheses – which could easily be increased by a few more – the advice to rely on church history and on the history of dogma does not lead to the goal. If the morphology itself is not to become church history, it cannot enter into an investigation of individual details. At all events, it cannot take these as its point of departure. First of all, it must cling to what is historically incontestable. In this category there are primarily two things. In the first place, there is a Lutheranism oriented toward the confessions, a Lutheranism – sometimes set forth with greater sharpness, sometimes in a manner less strong – which has outlasted the centuries. In the second place, there can be no doubt that this Lutheranism was rightfully derived from Luther, the Reformer. There can be no doubt about this, because Luther's Catechisms and the Smalcald Articles also belong to the confessions.

This means indeed that we seem to be back where we were before. Once again we confront the confessions, and we cannot discover the dynamic that shaped them until we have considered what took place before they came into being. In the following pages we shall designate this unknown as the impact of the Gospel *(evangelischer Ansatz).* To develop this will be the task of the first part. In doing so, however, the mode of procedure is different from what would be done in a purely theological-historical investigation. Naturally, it will be necessary to give ample consideration to the second point mentioned above – the dependence of Lutheranism on Luther. But one cannot take the confessions as the starting point without further ado. Like the Augsburg Confession, let us say, they are only an expression of that deeper-lying dynamic. In addition, it is necessary to consult other theological works of Luther. The morphology, however, does not write Luther's theology. On the contrary, it seeks to discover in Luther's theology only that which is able to carry the whole structure of the historical Lutheranism that followed. This, then, would be the impact of the Gospel *(evangelischer Ansatz).* Whether it has the capacity to hold what is expected of it must then be established in the various categories of historical expression that surround this center in larger and larger circles. To be sure, even this further task cannot do without Luther's theology. For his theology not only contains the impact of the Gospel *(evangelischer Ansatz),* but at the same time it is one of the first manifold embodiments of the effects of this impact.

If it is correct to define the impact of the Gospel *(evangelischer Ansatz)* as the center of the dynamic, there arises the further task of referring to it the demonstrable historical effects in such a way that one can see as complete a "picture" of Lutheranism as possible. This is the real task of a morphology. To be sure, the investigation cannot ignore historical development either as a whole or in detail. But it always traces this development merely for the purpose of discovering everywhere the constant, the permanent, "traits." Here it runs into the aforementioned competition with motives that spring from other laws. At the most widely varying points it will be evident that very often, indeed always, the development has a tendency to drift away from the dominant force inherent in the confessions. But even at its outer fringes one always continues to find a community of interests with its beginnings – even where, in the process, the Gospel dynamic has demonstrably faded from view. Here it is seen that the motives arising from Lutheranism have a supraindividual vitality that is operative and takes individuals into its service even where there is no longer a personal dependence on the impact of the Gospel *(evangelischer Ansatz)*. The same thing could be true of the other great churches and groups. Here we see an indirect confirmation of the confessional hypothesis. The confessions are more than private affairs of individuals. They are supraindividual forces with their own morphology.

At all events, the main difficulty in the way of the task of presenting a morphology of Lutheranism is the change in epochs. In the morphological perspective the epochs appear as segments of the gradual weakening and restrengthening of the confessional dynamic. In the area of Lutheranism the first main phase embraces essentially the sixteenth and the seventeenth centuries. Indeed, within this period of time it could also be possible to establish an undulating motion. Nevertheless, the great constant can be seen clearly and uniformly up to the end of the so-called orthodoxy. Then powerful foreign control ensues, especially from the West. This goes at once to the roots of Lutheranism. The impact of the Gospel *(evangelischer Ansatz)* threatens to be lost. The next result is a deep-going readjustment of the theology as a whole, in part also of worship. Sociologically and in the matter of its philosophy of life *(Weltanschauung)* Lutheranism, so it seems, lives on only in the extreme peripheral categories of its expression. Nominally, to be sure, the churches retain their confessions; but in doing so they are apparently merely dragging along a possession that is dead. Then, in the nineteenth century, the third phase of retrogression follows this one. At first glance it appears to be merely a restoration, because, above all, theology picks up threads dropped at the end of the seventeenth century. But the impact of the Gospel *(evangelischer Ansatz)* itself comes to life again in an unmistakable manner, and now it frequently engenders entirely new forms of expression. This is true of theology as well as of sociology and the philosophy of life *(Weltanschauung)*.

If, in spite of the great episode of retrogression, the constant actually remained operative here, one can hesitate to decide from which strata of sources one should take the colors and the brush strokes for the "picture." It is self-evident that for the impact of the Gospel *(evangelischer Ansatz)* and for theology in general, the sources at the beginning of the development flow at their purest. Here, in the writings of the reformers, in the confessions – even those that were not accepted – in the numerous catechisms and sermons, "classical" material altogether inexhaustible is at our disposal. Certainly here, too, the impact of the Gospel *(evangelischer Ansatz)* must always be employed as the critical standard of measurement. But here everything is being built up from the bottom, not repristinated. This is still true of the generation living at the time of the Formula of Concord. In spite of all statements made by critics to the contrary, the governing motive of this confession is not a theologically lame searching for compromises but the struggle for the purity of the impact of the Gospel *(evangelischer Ansatz)* and its resolute application to the new theological situation. Beyond this the theology of the seventeenth century was drawn upon with greater emphasis – partly to demonstrate the dynamic of the beginning, partly to show the drifting away from the dominant force. The theology of the nineteenth century was touched on only at individual points. This is surely a defect. But it seemed more important to reserve the illustrative material of the past century for sociology.[4]

For this, one cannot confine oneself to Luther's time. It is true that the ethical and the theological impact *(Ansatz)* direct one back to the same starting point. For this reason sociology, too, must, in general as well as in particular, begin again with Luther and, what is especially important here, with Melanchthon. But since experience teaches that in the domain of society – understood in its broadest sense – the ethical dynamic asserts itself much more slowly than new knowledge in the domain of theology, the sociological part of the study must, so far as possible, gather its material from longer periods of time than the theological. Here there will also be opportunity to go into the subject of extra-German Lutheranism with somewhat greater attention to detail than in the theological part. Indeed, for the time being a consideration of the whole political and economic history of the non-German Lutheran peoples goes beyond the ability of one person. For the time being – for it is to be hoped that the sketching of the morphology of Lutheranism might also be undertaken in these nations. Here the German scholar must still rely on more or less productive investigations carried on offhand.

What we lack for the purpose of gaining a "picture" of extra-German Lutheranism threatens – because of its profusion – to overwhelm us when we characterize German Lutheranism. The following presentation

[4] Yet I confess that the wish not to collide, so far as the subject matter is concerned, with my book on *The Struggle for Christianity Since Schleiermacher and Hegel (Kampf um das Christentum seit Schleiermacher und Hegel)* was another consideration that led me to reach this decision.

is concerned to hear from as many different groups of sources as possible: the literature of controversy, books on dogmatics, debates, catechisms, rituals *(Kirchenordnungen)*, and here and there also church hymns and sermons. In the field of sociology inspection reports and decisions of faculties and consistories must be taken into account above all. In the part dealing with economics one must depend in the main on secondary literature. For reasons of space it was impossible to draw more extensively on hymns and sermons. The few funeral sermons that are quoted show that here even the title, though shortened to the barest essentials, takes up a disproportionately large amount of space. In general, titles were named only of such old sources as are quoted or actually made use of in the text. If in this way the impression of arbitrariness arises, one must consider that here an attempt was made to sketch a form. And someone has said that the art of portraying consists in omission.

PART ONE

The Impact of the Gospel
(*Der evangelische Ansatz*)

Chapter One

UNDER THE WRATH OF GOD

1. The Primal Experience [1] *(Das Urerlebnis)*

The first part of the Augsburg Confession begins with an article on God; it ends with an article on the saints. But God is more than the beginning. He is spoken of everywhere, even in the article titled "Of Civil Affairs" *(Von Polizei und weltlichem Regiment)*. And the saints come last only because they are the end of the works of God. The whole confession has to do with these works. Here God is the self-evident presupposition for which one would look in vain in the Augsburg Confession for any "proof." The Augsburg Confession was certainly not written for those who do not share this presupposition – which, of course, is not to be understood as saying that its contents have no validity

[1] With reference to the Introduction it must be emphasized once more that this is not a reconstruction of what took place historically when Luther's person was converted. For accounts of this event I refer once for all — apart from the Luther biographies and the literature dealing with Luther's first lectures — to Heinrich Böhmer, *Luther im Lichte der neueren Forschung,* 5th ed., 1919, and *Der junge Luther,* 1925; Georg Merz, *Der vorreformatorische Luther,* 1926; Otto Scheel, *M. Luther. Vom Katholizismus zur Reformation,* 3d ed., 1921—30, and *Dokumente zu Luthers Entwicklung,* 2d ed., 1929; H. v. Schubert, *Luthers Frühentwicklung,* 1916; Joh. v. Walter, *Der religiöse Entwicklungsgang des jungen Luther,* 1925; A. V. Müller, *Luthers Werdegang bis zum Turmerlebnis,* 1920; Ernst Wolf, *Staupitz und Luther, ein Beitrag z. Theologie des Joh. v. Staupitz und deren Bedeutung für Luthers theologischen Werdegang,* 1927; and *Jahrb. d. Luther-Gesellsch.,* 1929, pp. 43 ff.; Martin Burgdorf, *Der Einfluss der Erfurter Humanisten auf Luthers Entwicklung,* 1926. Concerning literature of Luther in England I refer to W. Vollrath, *Theologie der Gegenwart in Grossbritannien,* 1928, pp. 150—172. Additional literature in *RGG,* 2d ed., III, cols. 1772 ff.

Here, on the contrary, the primal experience of "Lutheranism" is discussed in conformity with the principles put forward in the Introduction. Luther comes into question only insofar as he initiated the Lutheranism that resulted. For this purpose I refer here to Theod. Harnack, *Luthers Theologie,* 2 vols., 2d ed., 1927; C. Stange, *Studien zur Theologie Luthers,* Vol. 1, 1928; Erich Seeberg, *Luthers Theologie* I, 1929, 62 ff. and 140 ff.

for them. On the contrary. What is said about God must have unconditional validity precisely because Law and Gospel, which are appealed to as authoritative, have unconditional validity as the divine Word. But if they have validity even when man knows nothing about them, God is in any case independent of our consciousness. And if one investigates further, one finds as the beginning of everything from there on the knowledge that the consciousness of man as consciousness of himself is in original opposition to God, whether he knows about this or not. No man is without sin. Nor is there any neutral ground between sin and righteousness. And there is no sin that would not be enmity against God.

These statements lie at the bottom of the theses with which Luther attracted widespread public attention for the first time. They are the basis of his bitter fight against every kind of Pelagianism. The vehement struggles that took place in the era of Flacius were brought on by the fear that these statements could be obscured. These statements separate Luther from the idealism that followed. Neither the submersion of oneself in one's own thinking nor the setting-up of one's own idea of the "ethical person" can lead to any other result than opposition to God. For everything man finds in himself and everything he sets up is sin and therefore condemned by God.

At first glance this seems monstrous. It amounts to a condemnation of everything among men that appears to be great and noble. It apparently paralyzes every ethical activity, every step forward. It offends the Catholic, who believes in his saints. It led to Goethe's coldness toward, and Nietzche's hatred of, Lutheranism. It was so hard to bear that again and again Melanchthon was tempted to whittle some of it away and the dogmaticians of the seventeenth century seem at times to have retained it only in form. In all likelihood they would all have become weak in this matter if a break with it had not been felt as an open break with the result of the Reformation itself.

The basic total picture of man's existence is developed by Luther exhaustively but also with unparalleled gloom in the lecture he delivered on Psalm 90 in 1534 (Erlangen edition 18, 264–334). "In the midst of life we are in death" *(Media vita in morte sumus)* is the theme. "Disasters, wretchedness, shortness of life, the pangs of an afflicted conscience, despair, temporal death, eternal death, death" *(Calamitates, miseria, brevitas vitae, angores conscientiae afflictae, desperatio, mors temporalis, mors aeterna, mors)* and again and again "death" *(mors)* – these are the variations. Here the poet who wrote this psalm is "Moses in the superlative degree, that is, the stern servant of death, of the wrath of God, and of sin" *(Mosissimus Moses, hoc est, severus minister mortis, irae Dei et peccati).* One asks oneself whether this black picture painted in black is not a completely personal testimony of Luther, who shows right here that he remained a monk throughout his life. But Luther himself regards this pessimistic view as universally valid. To be sure, he states emphatically that there is also another view of life. He knows very well that there are those who avoid every thought of death (276), who are addicted only to temporal joys and cares (325). He also knows that others do not shun the thought of death but want to have done with death by scorning it (266). On the other hand, he himself knows the value of man and of man's life. The melody of death is so frightful precisely because death strikes "such a noble creature" (286, 292). Here, however, Luther stands for no weighing of what is noble and beautiful against what is bad and base. For such weighing presupposes a dismemberment of life – a dismemberment that ignores the pivotal question. Life must be taken as a whole. But as a whole it is undoubtedly bounded by death.[2]

And death is by no means merely the end of temporal existence. Even if one wanted to evaluate it only chronologically, it would be infinite (284, 310). Life, however, is finite. Why, then, should death not be stronger than life? Life flees like a shadow (321). It is identical with time, which has no dimensions, which never "is." As time, life – even if it lasts a hundred years – is merely a mathematical point *(punctum mathematicum)* (321), merely a point of intersection, without surface, without space. The acknowledgment that our life is a mathematical point is meant when Moses demands "that we transfer ourselves outside time and look at our life with the eyes of God" *(ut transferamus nos extra tempus et Dei oculis inspiciamus nostram vitam)* (291). Here, then, we encounter God. "For man's death is something different from the death of animals, which die according to the law of nature. Furthermore, it does not take place by reason of coincidence or time. It is a threat of God; it has its origin in the wrath and the estrangement of God." (284.) Therefore by taking life as a whole, that is, as a mathematical point, one understands why it is always accompanied by the threat of death.

Yes, why?

That continuous threat which causes life to shrink to a mathematical point whence one can look on all sides into the depths of death must

[2] *Operationes in Psalmos* (1519 and later). WA 5, 207, 32: "Indeed, there is death on all sides, whatever they look at and feel. They are stretched out between life and death; they dread death; they do not have life." *(Est vero mors undique, quicquid aspexerint et senserint. Inter vitam et mortem distenduntur: mortem exhorrent, vitam non habent.)*

really be referred to all life, to the totality of its natural and ethical relationships, yes, even to its relationship to God—to the God whose existence theology, philosophy, and the church had certainly taught Luther to recognize as a great, self-evident truth. After the breakthrough of the knowledge that led to the Reformation he characterized the totality of this relationship as *ratio*.[3] Everything he possessed by reason of thinking and knowing was self-evident, that is, self-evident in itself and from itself: that man as a "moral person" should be subject to God and therefore obey His commandments; that when he does not succeed in doing so or at least does not succeed entirely, he must avail himself of the treasures of relics in the possession of the church; that he must follow the examples of the saved and the saints; that God cannot demand of him anything else than what He demands of them, and also that man will be able to accomplish this if he has the necessary good will. Otherwise God could surely not demand this of him. All this is understandable, yes, self-evident, just like the philosophy of Aristotle, which schools his thinking and feeds his knowledge, and in which everything proceeds in a rational way.

But while absorbed in this rationality of the world and in this clear conception of what should be done man suddenly falls to pieces. Dread takes hold of him. Of what? Perhaps every religion begins with dread. But here it is not a mere feeling of worldly uneasiness—the feeling that the world about him is uncanny, puzzling, and irrational. Neither is it merely a fear of his own insufficiency, of getting old, or of having to die. Nor is it the feeling of being crushed by the infinite. On the contrary, it is the dread one has when in the night suddenly two demonic eyes stare at him—eyes which paralyze him into immobility and fill him with the certainty that these are the eyes of him who will kill you in this very hour. At this moment all the trumpery of the philosophy of religion, which defined God as τὸ ὄν, as "something infinite" *(ens infinitum)*, as "pure act" *(actus purus)*; at this moment all the preventives and relics the church has to offer against punishment for sin, against temporal and eternal destruction—all this is gone and forgotten. From an object of meditation, from a paragraph in a book on dogmatics, God has suddenly become a Person who calls to me personally. And this Person calls to me to tell me that my time has run out. At the sight of this every prayer for delay is frozen. The will to live dies—the will to live the life one has led up to this time. Time stands still.

But why is man filled with such a dread when God calls to him

[3] Luther also used the concept *ratio* in another sense. Cf. Hans Preuss, *ThStKr*, 1908, pp. 70 ff.

directly? To this question Luther sought and found the answer in his book *On the Bondage of the Will (De servo arbitrio)*.[4] Beneath the surface of the exegetical controversies with Erasmus he struggles for an understanding of his dread of God. He has grasped the reason for it. In this situation it is natural to look first at man. One tries to explain this dread to oneself psychologically. But under the eyes of God man comes to an altogether different conclusion. For he is totally in the grip of a power outside and therefore opposed to him. And indeed in a twofold sense. For one thing, God demands of him an accounting. God holds him responsible.[5] The fact that God holds him responsible shows him conclusively that he actually had an obligation to be something, to do something, or to leave something undone. But now the terrible discovery. God holds him responsible for something he can never accomplish.[6] The reason is that for the fulfillment of the great "Thou shalt" which hangs over his whole life he lacks the first and most important thing – free will. His will is in bondage.[7] Only when man can no longer be in doubt as to the mysterious power that binds him unconditionally and therefore keeps him from doing what he should does this knowledge become terrible in full measure. It is God Himself. This is the second sense in which God has power over him. God makes demands of man and, in spite of this, brings about the very opposite in him.[8] As if in mockery, however, He holds him responsible for nonfulfillment. Man *should* do what is good, but he *must* do what is evil. We know why Luther is filled with dread. Now we know the connection between death and God. Furthermore, we know that this death is something different from the outer end. It is the end of the "moral person."

In his anxiety man looks to God, who has inflicted this monstrous thing on him. But what does he learn? He sees burning wrath.[9] The

4 Sebastian Schmidt, *M. Lutheri Liber de Servo Arbitrio cum brevibus annotationibus, ed. 2. cum praefatione apologetica Joh. Joach. Zentgravii contra Petr. Yvonem, Argent.*, 1707; Martin Peisker, *Zum Problem von Luthers De servo arbitrio, ThStKr*, 1926, pp. 212 ff.; Fr. Gogarten, *Nachwort zu seiner Neuausgabe der Übers. v. L.s Vom unfreien Willen*, 1924.

5 WA 18, 686, 10 *(imputat)*; 698, 32; 717, 36; 763, 18 *(reatus)*. Cf. WA 7, 147, 8 *(opera iram merentia)*.

6 WA 18, 707, 33: "that God should require . . . things that are impossible" *(ut Deus exigat . . . impossibilia)*. Cf. WA 1, 224, 13: "man, who has become an evil tree, can will and do only what is evil" *(homo arbor mala factus non potest nisi malum velle et facere)*.

7 WA 18, 636, 4 ff.; 670, 34; 671, 13; 706, 12. Cf. WA 1, 224, 15; WA 7, 445 ff.

8 WA 18, 709, 27: "God works in and through evil men" *(Deus operatur in malis et per malos)*; 709, 32. Cf. WA 7, 145, 33 ff.

9 WA 18, 731, 8; 757, 10 ff.

evil must be blotted out, for it is enmity against God.[10] Indeed, God Himself had put into man's hands the weapons he bore when he did what was evil and thus fought against God (WA 18, 710, 1–30). For everything man has is from God (18, 614, 12). But the outcome of the battle cannot be in doubt. Here man cries for an answer to the why! Why does God put him into this desperate situation?[11] But he gets no answer. He is standing before an inscrutable mystery. He feels the guilt that was bound up with his human nature from the very beginning because of the "Thou shalt." But he does not know why. As he asks these last questions, the darkness becomes impenetrable. There is no answer.[12] This God, who holds us responsible for demands we cannot fulfill, who asks us questions we cannot answer, who created for us that which is good and, in spite of this, leaves us no choice but to do that which is evil – this is the "hidden God" *(Deus absconditus)*. It is the God of absolute predestination.[13] It is the God who hardens the heart of Pharaoh and hates Esau before Esau was born, the potter who forms vessels that fill one with loathing[14] – and, in spite of all this, thunders at these luckless creatures in a brutally despotic manner: "Your fault!" *(Tua culpa!)*

Here morals and *ratio* really come to an end. And one must accompany Luther up to this point in order to estimate what revelation, grace, and faith mean to him. Here at the same time is the turning point. "It is obviously," he writes against Erasmus, "utterly repugnant to common sense, for God to be guided only by His own will when He abandons man, hardens his heart, and damns him. For He seems to take pleasure in the sins and in the eternal torment of the unfortunate ones, even though preachers praise the greatness of His mercy and loving-kindness. It seems that for this reason one must look upon God as unfair and brutal, as unbearable. This repugnant thought has caused many distinguished people of all times to go to pieces. And who would not find it repugnant? More than once it hurled me down into the deepest abyss of despair and made me wish I had never been born – until I learned how salutary this despair is and how close it is to grace." (WA 18, 719.)[15] But without

10 WA 18, 774, 35; 783, 15.

11 WA 18, 631, 34; 684, 32; 688, 8 ff.; 690, 1; 712, 29 ff.

12 WA 18, 631, 34 ff.; 684, 38; 689, 18 ff.; 706, 29; 712, 25; 729, 17.

13 WA 18, 685. More under *Reconciliation and Predestination in Luther in Dtsjunction.*

14 WA 18, 700 ff.; 722 ff.

15 Cf. WA 18, 729, 14 ff. and WA 1, 354, 15.

the Gospel the primal experience *(Urerlebnis)* must end in despair, hatred of God, and blasphemy.[16]

The writing against Erasmus contains the reason for that gloomy outlook on life which Luther develops in his commentary on Psalm 90. It will be seen, of course, that in the light of the Gospel a completely different picture comes into view and that therefore the validity of all this is merely provisional. Accordingly, it would be a mistake to conclude from this that Luther had a closed mind with respect to his pessimistic view of the world. But even this further analysis of what has been developed so far leads to danger of misinterpretation and faulty development — as history teaches. In any case, it is necessary to keep in mind without qualification, in the first place, the bearing the primal experience *(Urerlebnis)* has on God and, in the second place, the indissoluble connection between elements of fate and those of morals.

Luther's denial of free will *(liberum arbitrium)* had already been condemned in the papal bull of June 15, 1520; and Aleander, the papal nuncio, knew what it meant when in the Edict of Worms he let the charge of pagan fatalism be brought up against Luther.[17] Luther's stand against freedom of the will, on which Aleander based his charge, could actually appear as a break with every system of ethics, not only with the official ethic of the church. His burning of the book on church law, referred to further, seemed to confirm that in his case the ethical consciousness was actually out of joint. In this connection the edict pointed out that Luther's doctrine had a line of ancestors, and this was meant to finish him off so far as public opinion in Christendom was concerned. Denial of the freedom of the will amounted, so it seemed, to a denial of responsibility. But then only stoical-fatalistic conclusions or those of libertinism were left. Whether Luther drew the latter or the former, it seemed in any case that he had to put himself in opposition to the Christian belief in God. In the conviction that this belief embraced God's justice as a Judge, which separates man's good works from his evil deeds

[16] WA 18, 631, 14. Cf. WA 5, 622, 33; Erlangen edition *ex. lat.* 18, 298.

[17] Denzinger, p. 260, Art. 36: — *Deutsche Reichsakten unter Karl V.*, II (revised by Ad. Wrede), 1896, p. 647: "He [Luther] also confirms from the poetry of the heathen poets that there is no free will, in the opinion that all things are embraced in a definite law." Thus his statement reads in the official printing, in the version published in Germany. On the other hand, the German original has: "In accordance with the opinion of Manichaeus and Wycliffe, he states and confirms from the poetry of the heathen poets as from an irrevocable argument that there is no free will." In addition, it is stated of Luther: "Then just as he teaches a free, self-willed life that is excluded from all law and is completely beastly, so he is a free, self-willed man who condemns and suppresses all laws, just as he then felt no horror or fear of publicly burning the decretals and the spiritual laws."

and therefore presupposes the free decision and, consequently, the "free will" of man, the representatives of the church had the humanists on their side, that is, in the commonly accepted sense, every normal ethical outlook on life.

Here one can already see a misinterpretation which resulted from the one-sided consideration of one of those two elements which Luther held to be firmly connected. For Luther did not by any means deny man's responsibility. Ever since his theses against indulgences his whole appeal to the church had been one great call to repentance. But it is self-evident that a denial of responsibility would have nullified this call. In numerous sermons on individual questions pertaining to ethics, especially in what he wrote about good works (1520), he had, on top of all this, proclaimed a positive ethos that was in opposition to every form of libertinism as well as to every ethic based on fatalism.

Yes, there was even a point of view on the basis of which Luther was ready to acknowledge that there is a free will *(liberum arbitrium)*. This was the same point of view that Melanchthon stressed. In the *Loci* of 1521, which, by the way, reflect a strictly deterministic way of thinking, Melanchthon himself taught that there is "a certain freedom of external works" *(libertas quaedam externorum operum)* (Plitt-Kolde, p. 71). The counsel given at Ansbach in 1524 expressed itself in an altogether similar manner. As yet, therefore, it was by no means a defection from the original position when Melanchthon again included the subject of ancient morality in his lectures and, as one way of justifying the inclusion, stated that this morality could be achieved through the power of man's will.[18] Accordingly, he asserted in the Augsburg Confession and in the Apology that man has a free will "to some extent" in matters "which reason comprehends." Finally even the Formula of Concord, in spite of its attack on synergism, could adduce similar statements by Luther. For Luther, too, asserted – and precisely in his writing against Erasmus – that man is lord over the things that are under him, that vis-à-vis them he has "right and a free will" *(jus et liberum arbitrium)*.[19] There-

[18] Foreword to *Enarr. aliquot libr. ethic. Aristot.* (*CR* 16, 281): "and the human will does these things itself by its own strength" *(et efficit haec humana voluntas suis ipsa viribus)*. Cf. *Proleg. in off. Ciceronis* (*CR* 16, 534): "And God wants this freedom to be left, in the first place, that we may understand the difference between doing what is free and doing what is not free, and may know that the doing itself is free to the highest degree" *(Ac vult Deus hanc libertatem reliquam esse, primum ut discrimen intelligamus inter agens liberum et non liberum, et sciamus ipsum esse agens liberrimum)*. — *Ansbacher Ratschl.: Fränk. Bek*, p. 305, no. 136.

[19] CA XVIII; Apol. VIII, 70; *FC, SD* II, 20. — WA 18, 781, 9; WA 24, 584, 14 ff. — Friedr. Faber (from Stettin), *Diss. de viribus humanae naturae, praesid.* M. Hafenreffer, Tübingen, 1610.

fore in Luther's writings and throughout early Lutheranism the denial of freedom of the will had its basis neither in libertinism nor in philosophical determinism. When Luther spoke of "the lower things" *(inferiora),* which he wanted to be understood as being subordinate to man's freedom, he meant exactly what Melanchthon had in mind when he said this about the things that are subject to reason *(ratio):* the inner realm of human existence, of the world, of human consciousness insofar as it applies to the world. As long as one maintains the position of immanence, one can bring thoughts and decisions into play at will. Here man is autonomous. Immanence and autonomy belong together.

But the nub of Luther's polemics is not to be found in the question whether man has the ability to do what he *wants* to do; it is to be found in the other question: whether he is able to do what he *should* do. In all circumstances, however, the "should" strikes him from the outside and therefore signifies that a breach has been made in immanence. Moral judgment goes astray when it undertakes to appraise man according to the measure of his agreement with the "moral sense" set up by the "moral sense" itself. What sin is, what a good work is, one should rather "learn from the commandments of God and not from appearance, great or numerous though the works themselves may be, nor from the approval of men or of man's law or custom" (WA 6, 204, 20). Moral autonomy is destroyed as soon as there is a break with immanence, which is subject to the divine commandment. This is what Luther means when he denies that there is freedom of the will. "Freedom of the will is at an end over against God" *(Cessat liberum arbitrium erga deum)* (WA 7, 146, 37). Therefore man's obligation and responsibility over against the "should" ordained by God are not, as the Edict of Worms falsely concludes, weakened or even denied. On the contrary, they are emphasized with the utmost sharpness.

At the same time, however, the realization of responsibility before God carries with it self-accusation *(accusatio sui)* on the part of the sinner. What is more, the admission of guilt extends to every area of life. As long as the moral judgment remains within the framework of what is merely human, one can measure an individual case on the basis of an individual case. According to the first thesis of the Reformation, however, one's whole life should be repentance (WA 1, 233, 10).[20] This word "whole" dare not be taken as the sum total of many individual cases; it must be taken as meaning an overlapping totality. Repentance should lead directly out of the sphere of reflections that are merely

[20] *Lectures on Romans,* ed. E. Hirsch and H. Rückert, 1929, I, 15, 19; II, 105, 30; WA 1, 427, 36; WA 29, 576, 11.

human. It should place the totality of human nature before God. In all circumstances the call to God strikes us from the outside – even when it strikes us in our "own" conscience – because it deals a destructive blow directly to what is purely one's inner nature, that is, one's autonomous self-determination. If the sum total of our moral life is the result of this self-determination, the call to God thus deals a destructive blow also to the whole man, not only to his individual acts. From the inside we are autonomous – therefore also responsible. But when, as Luther demanded, we "look at our life with the eyes of God," life and at the same time autonomy shrink to the "mathematical point." Before God autonomy cannot achieve comprehensive fulfillment. It remains merely as a demand of our ego. But this demand embraces both our responsibility and our guilt before God. Thus what Luther pointed out in his commentary on Psalm 90 becomes entirely clear: the outer side of our life is death.

If, therefore, all libertinistic inferences have been pared away from the primal experience *(Urerlebnis)*, even the fatalistic inferences bring no relaxing whatever of the dreadful tension in which it has placed us. If the former are founded on a false evaluation of the moral element, the latter have their basis in a misinterpretation of the idea of fate contained in them. One could imagine, of course, that all fear of God would be allayed, provided that man were willing to acknowledge the power of fate in an altogether logical way and thus to entrust himself completely to the hand of the Creator. Then this acknowledgment and this entrusting of oneself would surely mean that one "gives the glory to God." In that case the rift would be done away with, and peace would be made between God and His creature. In this belief German mysticism is in agreement with Spinoza and Goethe. And even Nietzsche hit upon this way out: "You can no longer endure your domineering destiny? Love it! You have no other choice!"

This first question is: How does the power of destiny which God has over life really make itself perceptible? Precisely when it rests on absolute authority – only then, of course, would this attempt at relaxing it make sense – must it be thought of as being as extensive as possible. So far as man is concerned, it must, therefore, be found in the totality of his relationship to life. For everything we see and recognize, experience and suffer, is our fate. Obviously, the fact that in the Catechisms and elsewhere Luther describes man's relationship to his environment by emphasizing its divine origin as the reason for giving thanks or as an object of prayer cannot lead us any further along at this point; for there he is speaking from the standpoint of faith. Man, to whom the other creatures are referred there, already stands in another relationship to God than that of the primal experience *(Urerlebnis).*

On the contrary, the question is: How does man experience divine destiny without Christ? Luther's answer is unambiguous. "He who does not have faith," he answers, "is cast down below all creatures, nor is there any creature that could console him. For he who has God as his enemy also has all God's creatures opposed to him; these never stand still." *(Qui fidem non habet, infra omnes creatures deiicitur, nec ulla creatura est, quae consolari ipsum possit. Nam qui deum habet inimicum, is et omnes creaturas dei habet contrarias, hi non consistunt.)* (WA, 24, 23, 1.) According to Luther, it is precisely the identification of God with the creatures round about us, that is, with our environment – the identification which edifies Spinoza and Goethe – which depresses man without Christ, yes, intensifies his fear. "All creatures seem to be nothing but God and the wrath of God, even though it is a rustling leaf, as Moses says in Lev. 16" (WA 19, 226, 14). Here all creatures become "God's whips and weapons" (WA 17 II, 59, 6), whether it is "the sea with its waves and billows" (WA 19, 227, 3) or "sickness, hunger, pestilence, fire, water, war" . . . or "the government" (WA 17 II, 59, 3 ff.). All this terrifies, not because one cannot master it but because, strictly speaking, these are weapons of God directed against us.[21]

Is Luther seeing ghosts? Is it the overwrought fantasy of a monk that is speaking here? Or is he here merely constructing a situation in order later on to be able more effectively to draw from it the freedom and the cheerfulness of the person who has been justified – a situation no man has actually ever experienced? One cannot arrive at a complete answer before one knows what Luther means by sin. If sin were only disobedience, that is, the deviation from a norm, the damage could be repaired forthwith by obedience, and the problem of destiny would be solved by "composure." In reality, however, sin, in the strict sense, is "enmity against God," that is, active opposition to the will of God, which, to an equal degree, is active against sin. God replies to sin with a judgment that can terminate only in our death. But since, as developed previously, in God's eyes the mark of sin clings not only to individual acts but to the sum total of our life, we have become hopelessly subject to this judgment, even if, from a particular moment on, we were to try

[21] WA 5, 213, 1 ff.: "Every creature is against me. . . . At the same time he has the comfort of no creature, but whatever he looks at is against him. For the creature is dealing with its Creator . . ." *(Omnis creatura mihi adversatur. . . . Simul nullius creaturae habet solatium, sed quicquid aspexerit, adversatur sibi. Creatura enim cum Creatore suo agit . . .)* — As God is in accord with the creatures against us (WA 31 I, 147, 10).

to put an end to our opposition to God. It was altogether in conformity with what Luther meant when later on a pupil of Johann Musäus said by way of objection to Spinoza's conception of religion that obedience to God could take neither the relationship of the sinner to God nor the relationship of the justified person to God into full account; for that, too, was determined, among other things, by "fear of divine wrath" *(metus irae divinae)*.[22] This meant that it is not belief in Christ which, in the first instance, runs counter to Spinoza's "love of fate" *(amor fati)*, but that even in the elementary experience of destiny Spinoza overlooked an essential point. Luther, too, says that this is actually the fear of the wrath of God. It is the expectation of divine judgment – not, however, only as mere fear of punishment but as that primal experience *(Urerlebnis)* in which it just is not possible simply to balance sin and punishment against each other. God's power over destiny is seen, not in the fact that He shapes our destiny in general but in the fact that He shapes it in such a way that we cannot escape sin. Logically, "submission to destiny" also means submission to the inevitability of sinning. Accordingly, the "love of destiny" *(amor fati)*, which is thought of as obedience to God, includes corroboration of the opposition to Him. Although it would like to achieve the opposite, it is at the same time a renewed defiance of God.

If, therefore, God's sovereign power over destiny actually embraces all relationships in our life, it is no fantasy of Luther's but an undeniable fact that all creatures, too, must, in their relationship to us, serve to execute His inscrutable judgment on us. To us "all creatures are death, for they all have a connection with God" (WA 24, 578, 5). Even fatalism brings no deliverance from the torment of the primal experience *(Urerlebnis)*.

2. Sin [1]

The primal experience *(Urerlebnis)* must be understood as "natural man's" relationship to God. It is full of existential contradictions. These the Enlightenment aims and seeks to destroy. Readiness for revelation results from realization and recognition of their existence. The contra-

[22] Chr. Fr. Knorn, *Spinosismus, hoc est Tract. Theol.-Polit. . . . ad veritatis lancem examinatus,* Wittenberg, 1708 *(Disput. unter Musäus von 1674),* p. 32.

[1] Fr. H. R. Frank, *Theol. d. Konkordienformel* I, 1858, pp. 50 ff. — Wilh. Braun, *Die Bedeutung der Konkupiszenz in Luthers Leben und Lehre,* Berlin, 1908. — Erdmann Schott, *Fleisch und Geist nach Luthers Lehre unter besonderer Berücksichtigung des Begriffes "totus homo,"* Leipzig, 1928 (here one of the most important sources for this subject, Luther's *Rationis Latomianae Confutatio,* 1521, has not been considered).

diction contained in the whole returns of necessity in connection with all the individual elements embraced by the whole.

This is seen with special clarity in the concept of original sin. This concept is the most elementary synthesis of destiny and guilt, of dependence and responsibility. To be sure, a superficial consideration would seem to indicate that here the real problem should be deferred and that the riddle of our destiny should be "solved" on the basis of some previous history. It is true that original sin has a reference to the past, namely, to the fact that originally all mankind was bound up with the beginning of our race. But for this reason alone it was impossible for Luther to speak of it in the Smalcald Articles as the principal sin. For involvement that lies in the past could, of course, relieve us, at the most, of responsibility. And when the Augsburg Confession says that original sin cleaves to us "from birth" *(von Mutterleibe)*, the point is, not that it is there "from birth" but, as Melanchthon emphasizes untiringly in the Apology, that it has affected everything embraced by the life transmitted to us. The statement that original sin is concupiscence directs attention to this totality. For it is pointed out emphatically that the whole man is under the domination of original sin.[2] But the primal experience *(Urerlebnis)* makes itself heard still more sharply when original sin is characterized by stating that man can have no true fear of God, no true faith in God *(CA* II, *Apol.* I, 8). The error of Flacius stemmed from the fear that something could be subtracted from the totality. And when the Formula of Concord contradicted him, it had no desire whatever to punch holes in this totality – which, on the contrary, it maintained to the full extent (*SD* I, 11) – but it wanted to define the totality only in such a way that man's need for deliverance might not indicate that he could not be delivered. In no case did the Formula of Concord want the possibility of being delivered to be understood as some "religious-moral" predisposition that had been excepted from the guilt-relationship determined by original sin. Luther, too, had maintained the "passive fitness" *(aptitudo passiva)* taught by later dogmaticians. In fact, he had done so even against Erasmus (WA 18, 636, 18 ff.) When the Formula of Concord gives the reason for this fitness by stating

[2] Luther, Erlangen edition *ex. lat.* 18, 301: "For when a man is taken hold of by an emotion, he is taken hold of completely, so that he can see, hear, think nothing else than what the emotion suggests" *(Quando enim homo arripitur ab affectu, totus arripitur, ut nihil aliud videre, audire, cogitare possit quam quod affectus suggerit).* Cf. *Lectures on Romans* II, 143 ff. — Original sin as concupiscence: *Apol.* I, 3, 24, 38. To how small a degree one should think here of limiting concupiscence to "sensuality" *(Sinnlichkeit)* in the Neoplatonic sense is emphatically stressed by Melanchthon.

that in spite of original sin man is God's creature, this is indeed a great comfort for the man of faith, with whose eyes the matter is viewed there. At the stage of primal dread *(Urgrauen)*, however, it is the final push *(Anstoss)* into despair. For the distress *(Not)* of the primal experience *(Urerlebnis)* finds sharpest expression precisely in the fact that God's creature is enmeshed in hopeless opposition to his Creator.

Accordingly, the doctrine of original sin enabled early Lutheranism to keep alive the following factors connected with the primal experience *(Urerlebnis):* first, that our whole life as constituted by nature is far distant from God; secondly, the realization of responsibility before God for the total substance of our life – both lie within the concept of sin; thirdly, however, also the realization that our whole life is dependent on the origin to which we were destined – this lies within the concept of original sin. Thus the doctrine of original sin establishes the contradictory state of affairs in the primal experience *(Urerlebnis)* as comprehensively as possible. Accordingly, one could imagine a doctrinal procedure which derives the concept of sin from that of original sin, since indeed in all circumstances the latter includes the former as a factor and also recognizes the state of affairs in question as comprehensively as possible. Perhaps it was the pattern of scholastic theology – perhaps, too, merely the picture conveyed by the term "original sin" – which induced the dogmatics of a later day to proceed in an entirely different manner. The term "original sin" leads involuntarily into the temptation to interpret its intended content as a special instance of the general concept of sin. But if one were to proceed from the latter assumption instead of from the former, danger of shallowness would arise at once. Then the inevitability of sin easily appears as a mere supplement which could also be lacking. Actually, up to the time of the Enlightenment dogmatics did not yet succumb to this danger, because it adhered earnestly to the doctrine of original sin as upheld by the Reformation and constantly sought to formulate the concept of sin in such a way that original sin could at least be included in this concept. Nevertheless, the contradictory elements inherent in that state of affairs were weakened and, in the end, completely ignored.

For Luther the concept of sin was constantly oriented toward God – not toward an impersonal law that is transgressed. It is oriented toward this law only insofar as this law is felt directly as God's will. Naturally, Luther appropriates the Pauline doctrine of the Law, especially the statements that the Law leads to knowledge of sin and – outwardly – holds the godless in check. But precisely when it reveals its effect completely, it drives – in case the Gospel is not heard – more deeply into enmity against God. Through sin God is hurt. Murmuring against God, yes, hatred of God, is inevitably connected with this.[3] Even in his writing against Erasmus, Luther — in spite of his emphasis on the thesis pertaining to destiny — declared that man is in direct opposition to God. Of Pharaoh he says that, because of the wickedness of his will, he could not do otherwise than hate what was "in opposition to him" *(contrarium sibi)* (WA 18, 711, 35). The hardening brought about by God leads to this *contrarium.* By seeing Pharaoh reply with hatred Luther — in spite of "determinism" — ascribes to him not only independence vis-à-vis God but also an active manifestation of his ego, a manifestation that is more than a mere transgressing of legal bounds. It is stated later (714, 4) that Pharaoh is hardened to such an extent that he resists God. Elsewhere, too, in this book Luther writes about war, fighting, enmity, man's hatred of God.[4] To him all this is an inevitable result of the claim to autonomy, the claim implicit in the delusion that there is a "free will" *(liberum arbitrium).* Here, too, Luther leaves no doubt that in all this hostility toward God sin is not an occasional stumbling but clings without fail to every one of our steps. "The godless man sins against God whether he eats or drinks" *(In Deum peccat impius sive edat, sive bibat)* (768, 23).

"Man's heart is inscrutable" *(Cor hominis inscrutabile est),* says Luther where he appropriates the Pauline expression "enmity against God" (WA 43, 203, 30). Thus the nature of sin itself actually becomes incomprehensible in more than one sense. In his Ascension Day sermon of 1522 Luther reduces the primal relationship *(Urverhältnis)* of man who is still to be born to the unmistakable formula: "Therefore there is always enmity between man and God, and they cannot be friends or be in agreement with each other" (WA 10 III, 136, 7). It is impossible to express with greater sharpness the inadequacy, in Luther's sense, of the conception which defines sin merely as a deviation from the

[3] Smalcald Articles III, 2, at the end; furthermore, WA 5, 50, 8; 16, 320, 1; 39 I, 345, 26; 42, 133, 9; 43, 202, 10; Erlangen edition *ex. lat.* 18, 298; on Ps. 51:6: "If I have sinned, [I have sinned] not against the devil, my conscience, the Law, sin, man, an angel, but against God alone" *(Si peccavi, non diabolo, conscientiae, legi, peccato, homini, angelo, sed soli deo)* (WA 40 II, 378, 13). — "Therefore man is a creature in whom there is real ill will against God. Therefore he shows what all men on earth are. He who flees from Him is hostile to Him. Therefore he blasphemes Him. Therefore these are all hostile to God; they do not want to endure him; they do not want to have the Law." *(Homo ergo est creatura in qua mera invidia contra deum, ostendit, ergo, quid omnes homines in terra sint, qui fugit eum, inimicus est ei, ergo blasphemat eum. Ergo omnes hi sunt inimici dei, non possunt eum pati, legem non habere volunt.)* (WA 16, 417, 8 ff.)

[4] WA 18, 626, 23; 690, 26; 774, 35, etc.

right path. But even in Luther's general conception of sin – not only of original sin – that unresolvable contradiction is kept alive precisely in this way. The Creator creates the creature, watches over it, and guides it. But He creates it in such a way that it is able to fight against Him, yes, to hate Him. As a result, He Himself must reply to this with death and destruction.

Even though one looks in vain in the writings of Melanchthon for the directness of this knowledge which Luther had, still Melanchthon never overlooked the opposition to God that is implicit in sin. Where he defines sin as conflict with God's Law, he does not fail to add "offending God" *(offendens Deum)*. But disobedience to the Law is also "not only actual but universal, which in man's nature is opposed to God" *(non tantum actualis sed universa, quae est in natura hominis adversus Deum)* (*CR* 21, 667). And how seriously he wants the relationship to God to be taken is shown in the statement: "Reason understands that there are offenses against God's Law, but it is indifferent to God's wrath" *(Ratio intelligit vitia contra legem Dei esse, sed iram Dei negligit)*. He, too, is aware of the completely incomprehensible element in the nature of sin. Paul, he declares, made use of that "terrible expression" (Rom. 8:7) to enable the reader to realize that the weakness of human nature is too great to be sufficiently understood and estimated by human reason (*CR* 15, 661). In the Augsburg Confession he says of the godless that they are hostile to God (XX, 25). He is also aware of the possibility of hatred of God (*CR* 16, 286; 21, 98 and 163). In the final edition of the *Loci* it is still stated of those who are not converted to God that they will remain "eternal enemies of God" (21, 876).

As has been stated, it was the primary purpose of later dogmaticians to express the concept of sin in such a way that original sin could be included. On the other hand, man's responsibility was not to be compromised. For a long time a voluntaristic definition, which may have been best suited to prevent one from losing sight of the element of inner contradiction, was avoided, obviously because it seemed to come dangerously close to "free will" *(liberum arbitrium)*.[5] Therefore John's statement that sin is "lawlessness" (ἀνομία) (1 John 3:4) was most wel-

[5] Cf. the debate between Johann Gerhard and Bellarmine, *Loci* V, p. 2; in addition, M. Chemnitz, *Examen Conc. Trid.* I, 161, 32 ff.; 166, 42 ff.; 186, 11 ff.; Joh. Balth. Pleninger, *Disp. de causis peccati, praes. G. Sigwarto*, Tübingen, 1605. — The later dogmaticians, on the other hand, emphasize freedom of the will as an abstract presupposition of sin. E. g., Hollaz, *Examen* II, 73 ff., although he clings to the traditional definition of sin. — Concerning a stronger emphasis on voluntarism (in connection with a psychologizing) in the writings of Buddeus cf. A. F. Stolzenburg, *Die Theol. des Jo. Franc. Buddeus und des Chr. Matth. Pfaff*, 1926, pp. 191 ff.

come. It was so flexible that both the active element of "sins in deed" *(Tatsünden)* and the destiny-controlled *(schicksalhaft)* element of original sin could be included in it; and at the same time it permitted a connection with the Pauline trains of thought concerning Law, sin, guilt, and punishment.[6] Accordingly, from this point on everything the dogmaticians have to say about sin is concentrated increasingly on the statement: "Sin is a deviation from the divine Law" *(Peccatum est aberratio a lege divina).*[7] Naturally, this statement could also be the starting point for the understanding which the Reformation based on Paul. But it did not express the directly personal relationship to God. On the contrary, this definition is founded on the picture of a wanderer who strays from the right path. By doing so he certainly exposes himself to danger, yes, perhaps is already lying in the abyss. Normally, however, rescue comes about by calling him back out of the abyss, pulling him up, or helping him climb out. This definition lacks the element of actual opposition to God which determines Luther's conception of sin. Consequently, it can also delude a person as to that contradictory state of affairs in the primal experience *(Urerlebnis)* and give outright support to the thought that man may make amends for individual transgressions of the bounds of the Law. Then this would be the end not only of Luther's theology but also of Paul's.

The dogmaticians of the Enlightenment succumbed to this danger. From that alleged definition of sin in 1 John 3:4 Johann Gottlieb Töllner developed, among other things, the two statements: "Every actual sin arises from a vague conception" and "Every actual sin arises from failure to make use of freedom."[8] Here the fact that sin is an activity aimed

[6] Johann Gerhard V, 2: ". . . which definition expresses with admirable brevity the true and proper understanding of sin, namely, that it is a deviation from the Law or a nonagreement with the Law, or that this is inherent in nature itself [like original sin] or is found in words, deeds, and the stirrings of concupiscence [like all actual sins]; indeed, in its breadth this definition also embraces the sin of omission, which is lawlessness in the same way" (. . . *quae definitio miranda brevitate veram et propriam peccati rationem exprimit, quod scilicet sit aberratio a lege sive non-congruentia cum lege, sive ea in ipsa natura haereat [ut pecc. orig.] sive in dictis, factis ac concupiscentiae motibus inveniatur [ut omnia actualia peccata], quin et sua latitudine peccatum omissionis haec definitio complectitur, quod itidem est* ἀνομία). — Among earlier dogmaticians cf. Dav. Chyträus, *Catechesis,* 1554, in Reu, *Quellen* III 2, p. 303; Heerbrand, *Comp.,* 1575, p. 117; Selnecker, *Institutio* I, 321; and pointedly against Flacius: *Praemonitio, Bl. iiij.*

[7] Hollaz II, 57. — Buddeus, *Instit.,* p. 545: "that sin consists in violation or transgression of the Law" *(peccatum in violatione seu transgressione legis consistere)* — without adding anything to the definition. Cf. also Baier, *Comp.,* p. 472. — Chr. Matthias, *Syst.,* p. 103. — The corresponding section in Kromayer, *Theol.,* pp. 359 ff., is connected least of all with the statement of John.

[8] Töllner, *System der dogmatischen Theologie* III, Nürnberg, 1775, pp. 16 and 19.

directly against God is completely overlooked. In reality, it is no longer even judged on the basis of the objective Law of God. It is still only that which prevents our realization of the ideal man. Where there is knowledge of sin, man's thinking is no longer directed toward God; it is directed toward himself.

The second of Töllner's statements points beyond itself to Kant's philosophy of religion. Exactly like the early dogmaticians, Kant, too, calls sin a "transgression of the moral law as a divine command." [9] It is true that he does not trace it back to failure to make use of freedom, as Töllner does. On the contrary, he maintains the intelligibility of "what is radically evil in human nature," precisely in order to preserve its character of freedom." [10] Nevertheless, Kant and Töllner are agreed in the conviction that it must "be possible to outweigh" the evil propensity (what is radically evil) "because it is met with in man as something that has freedom of action." Here one sees at once how the humanizing of the concept of sin also carries with it a catastrophic misjudgment of what man can do. It is only logical when in the writings of rationalistic dogmaticians like Semler and Wegscheider the association of sin with the doctrine of freedom leads to a furious attack on the doctrine of original sin as maintained by the Reformation. In it Wegscheider – referring to Reinhard's sermon, "That Every Man Has His Price, for Which He Surrenders" *(Dass jeder Mensch seinen Preis hat, wofür er sich hingibt)* – sees the gravest danger to him who is morally weak.[11] Now there was but one step to Schiller, who considered it the right of a philosopher "to congratulate" human nature on the first sin, this "tremendous progress of mankind." [12] In the first of Töllner's statements, that every actual sin arises from a vague – and, as he says later on, a "confused" – conception, one can find the precursor of Schleiermacher's teaching that every "actual" sin is "a pollution of the consciousness of God" *(Glaubenslehre,* 2d edition §74, 2). Yet one dare not deny that in relating sin to God – even though only in the form of consciousness of God – Schleiermacher is, in a sense, leading back to the doctrine of the Reformation.

To be sure, even in Kant and Schiller one can find suggestions of

[9] Kant, *Relig. innerhalb d. Grenzen d. blossen Vernunft,* 1793, *Ausg. Reclam.,* p. 43.

[10] Op. cit., p. 38: "This inborn guilt, which is called inborn guilt because it can be perceived as soon as the use of freedom manifests itself in man and must nevertheless have sprung from freedom and for this reason can be attributed to it . . ."

[11] Wegscheider, *Institutiones Theol., Ed. 6, Hal.,* 1829, 386.

[12] Schiller, *Etwas über die erste Menschengesellschaft, SW, Ausg. Reclam.,* 10, 238.

the primal experience *(Urerlebnis)* of the Reformation. Schiller the dramatist knows about the tragic synthesis of destiny and guilt – a knowledge which, in view of the facts of our life, no ethically-minded person can escape. In Kant's philosophy of religion, it is true, one seeks for it in vain. On the other hand, his dualism of theoretical and practical reason gives evidence of a related knowledge. The former teaches the unconditional involvement of man in the interdependence of cause and effect in nature; the latter teaches his independence over against nature insofar as he is "a moral being" *(ein sittliches Wesen)*. Yet the second remains but a claim. One can speak of actual moral independence only as long as one measures man merely by his own reason. But this independence appears as an illusion if, as in Luther, it confronts God.

3. The Law and the Wrath of God [1]

Before the "hidden God" the primal experience *(Urerlebnis)* comes to an end. But the fact that God is hidden does not mean that we know nothing at all about Him. Two things we know only too well: that He commands "Thou shalt" and that He lets us be born in a state which makes the fulfillment of this "Thou shalt" impossible for us. The sense and the purpose of this contradiction are hidden from us. God Himself is hidden from us because He has other thoughts about us than these. Logically speaking, however, the mistrust that comes upon us as we realize the inability of our reason to resolve the contradiction must also have a bearing on the whole present attempt to arrive at a knowledge of God. If we are entirely sin – in the totality of our doing and thinking – is this perhaps also the whole primal experience *(Urerlebnis)*? Luther does not hesitate to give an affirmative answer to this question. For the primal experience *(Urerlebnis)* produces unbelief.

But the inevitability of our destiny becomes clear because of the fact that, after all, we can by no means deny the individual facts that have a bearing on one another in the primal experience *(Urerlebnis)*. To preserve us, above all, from self-deception, as though we were able to escape sin by ignoring the "Thou shalt," God "reveals" Himself to us in the Law. Indeed, this revelation has already taken place – according to Paul – in the conscience, which we heard speaking to us in the

[1] Siegfr. Lommatzsch, *Luthers Lehre . . . mit besonderer Berücksichtigung s. Theorie vom Gesetze*, 1879, pp. 43 ff. and 316 ff. — Theod. Harnack, *Luthers Theologie*, 2d ed., 1927, I, 221 ff. and 365 ff. — Karl Holl, *Ges. Aufsätze* I, 4th and 5th ed., 1927, pp. 1 ff. — Hans Mich. Müller, *Erfahrung und Glaube bei Luther*, 1929. Günther Jacob, *Der Gewissensbegriff in der Theologie Luthers*, 1929. — Theod. Siegfried, *Luther und Kant, ein geistes-geschichtl. Vergleich im Anschluss an den Gewissensbegriff*, 1930.

primal experience *(Urerlebnis)*. There, to be sure, we were assailed by doubt, and despair of unbelief overshadowed us. Secondly, however, this revelation takes place in history, when God gives the Law. Scripture tells us about this. These two announcements concerning the divine will have a reciprocal relationship to each other. God's giving of the Law, reported in the Old Testament, must be understood as an announcement to the ancient people of the covenant; it cannot be transferred without further ado to other peoples and ages. Nevertheless, it confirms what the conscience knows: that God makes definite demands on men. Yes, over and above this, the conscience also affirms those demands according to their specific content—insofar as nothing characterizes them as being unrepeatable in history. "Thus I now keep the commandments that Moses gave, not because Moses gave them, but because they have been implanted in me by nature; and here Moses is in agreement with nature" (WA 24, 10, 3). Naturally, the correspondence of the written or proclaimed Law to the implanted Law is not accidental. The former would leave us untouched if the latter did not exist. If it is proclaimed, man's heart replies: "So it is!" But the opposite is also true: Satan's opposition blinds the heart to such an extent that the proclaimed Word must first awaken that voice of the heart (WA 16, 447, 10). By means of that correspondence the voice of the Law in our conscience points beyond itself to something supraindividual and transmundane, to a regulation that has validity whether we affirm it or not.[2] The Law faces the conscience as something else, something that demands without showing the possibility of fulfillment (WA 18, 677, 7 ff.), something that makes an accusation and requires satisfaction (WA 12, 679, 17 ff.). Conscience and the Law are by no means identical. There even comes a moment when conscience frees itself from the Law, when it says to Moses, who wants to frighten it: "You are a heretic!" (WA 40 I, 558, 4.) But this really presupposes the Gospel. Up to this time the conscience must in any case affirm unconditionally the regulation that confronts it. The correspondence of the conscience to the Law points out that both have their origin in the Creator (WA 50, 331, 15).

Recognition of the validity of the Law is not fulfillment. On the contrary, the Law confirms for us the correctness of the primal experience *(Urerlebnis)*. It reveals to us the incompatibility of our ability and our obligation. To be sure, it illumines the darkness in which we were

[2] WA 44, 503, 26: "You cannot shake off the Law, but it itself shakes up your heart" *(Non potes excutere legem, sed ipsa excutit tibi cor)*.—WA 40 I, 569, 9: ". . . because man cannot pass judgment concerning the Law; because it rules in man, therefore it judges man" *(. . . quia homo non potest judicare de lege; quia dominatur in homine, ergo judicat hominem)*.

lost; but it is "a light of such a nature that it shows sickness, sin, evil, death, hell, the wrath of God. But it does not help or deliver from these. It is content to have shown. Then man, after coming to a realization of the sickness of sin, is sad, cast down, yes, in despair." *(talis lux, quae ostendat morbum, peccatum, malum, mortem, infernum, iram Dei. Sed non iuvat nec liberat ab istis. Ostendisse contenta est. Tum homo cognito morbo peccati tristatur, affligitur, imo desperat.)* (WA 18, 766, 25.) The Law shows man "what he *should* do, not what he *can* do" *(quid debeat, non quid possit).* It is a "revelation of the wrath" of God (WA 50, 474, 20). It makes us guilty. It accuses, damns, kills. It makes the heart a hell and confirms for us that the primal experience *(Urerlebnis)* takes place with the cooperation of God.[3]

Yet the Law seems to lead beyond the previously developed situation, in which the sinner is in conflict with God. If in that situation man faced God in absolute loneliness, which "assails" *(angreift)* him altogether personally, plunges him arbitrarily, so it seems, into complete helplessness so far as knowledge and willingness are concerned, yes, drives him to despair, in this way the concept and the content of the Law bring in an element of order, an element which at first appears to serve as a deliverance. After all, God's will vis-à-vis the creature is, therefore, not pure arbitrariness; He has put it into a form that is "eternal and unalterable" and, as a result, also offers some measure of security. In addition, the imperative form of the Law breaks through the compulsion determined by nature and replaces the dull "must" with a shining "shalt." The perception of this "shalt" makes us rational human beings. It is conscience that distinguishes us from the donkey, to which one would proclaim the Law in vain for hundreds of years, because it does not feel the Law in its heart (WA 16, 447, 10).

In connection with these reflections it is certainly correct to say that through the Law something general enters into the seemingly altogether individual character of the divine command, something that in any case forbids the thought of arbitrariness on the part of God. But He is, of course, not only the Lawgiver. He is also the Judge. To have God as Judge, however, forbids one again to refer His judgment solely to individual matters in our life and in what we do, to offer Him deeds or

[3] WA 44, 503, 24: "Because in the heart there is the Law, which terrifies and is the Law of God, therefore every feeling of dismay and trembling of the conscience occurs with the cooperation of God. . . . Because God's judgment is eternal and immutable; you will not easily sustain His attack and accusation." *(Quia lex in corde est, quae terret et est lex Dei, ideo omnis consternatio et pavor conscientiae fit cooperante Deo. . . . Quia est Dei judicium aeternum et immutabile, cuius accusationem et impetum haud facile sustinebis.)*

excuses, works or merits. He is outside the bounds of our life. Therefore He always sees our life as a whole. Accordingly, He must always judge it as a whole. But this immediately causes an element of uncertainty to come over us, because we always see only the individual matter and, as a result, even in the case of fulfillment of individual commandments, we could never be certain that we have satisfied the requirements of the whole (WA 18, 783, 26). Yes, this uncertainty turns very quickly into the terrible certainty that I have been unsuccessful not only in individual matters and, therefore, have committed sins, but that I am a sinner. Man's moral quality cannot be determined from the sum total of his thoughts and actions. The opposite is the case. His thoughts and actions can acquire their moral character only from the total personality (WA 1, 188, 12 ff.; WA 7, 32, 4 ff.). The Law must not only be kept; it must be loved (WA 10 I, 1, 467, 6). But if man can never change himself into another person, neither does the Law by any means lead him out of the distress into which we previously saw him sinking. On the contrary, the Law reinforces with unmistakable clarity the contradiction in which man finds himself by nature: "You have not fulfilled, nor are you able to do so. Nevertheless, you should." *(Non implesti, nec potes, et tamen debes.)* (WA 40 I, 256, 15.)

The heightening which the Law signifies for the tension between God and the sinner does not lie ultimately in the concept of the Law. If it precludes the thought of God's arbitrariness in an evil sense, it likewise precludes the hope for His arbitrariness in a good sense. A judge proceeds according to right and law. Therefore he does not sentence arbitrarily. But neither can he acquit arbitrarily. By facing man as Lawgiver and Judge, God reveals a trait of His nature that is founded, to be sure, on His quality as the Creator but is not exhaustively expressed by this trait. When God imposes legal demands on His creatures, the pure interrelationship of cause and effect between God and man is breached in any case on one side. But in this way a legal relationship is established in which God and man face each other in relative independence. And this legal relationship is already implicit in the concept of the Law – does not, therefore, as may be mentioned here, appear for the first time in the Lutheran doctrine of justification.

In Luther's sense, however, one must keep firmly in mind that the Lawgiver and Judge is and remains the Creator too. If to Him sin is not only the overstepping of a boundary but, as shown, "enmity against God," Luther also learns from Scripture, and especially again from Paul, that God cannot give an answer to this after the manner of a judge who is not personally concerned. "The whole human race was deserving of hatred" (WA 1, 274, 28). God's justice and truthfulness, which compel Him to keep His own Word unconditionally, make Him at the same time a Zealot who cannot tolerate sin (WA 40 II, 332, 3). Over against the sinner this zeal for His justice appears to be wrath, which must consume the sinner precisely because sins are outgrowths of the sinner's whole being (WA 14, 595, 34). As Judge, God *must* punish; as Creator and as Lord over all creatures, He *can* punish and *wants* to do so (WA 28, 582, 3). God in His majesty and the human creatures are enemies (WA 40 II, 329, 10). And because conscience is that place in man where his consciousness of being a creature is aware of opposition to the Law, for Luther it is at the same time the ear with which he hears the voice of divine wrath (WA 42, 429, 6).

Luther points out again and again how reason bristles up at the thought of God's wrath. It would be ready to acknowledge His justice if by this a reasonable relationship between sin and punishment can be meant. But this would amount to an immanent settlement, one which overlooks or denies the very transcendence of the Divine Majesty. It is precisely in His wrath that His majesty finds expression, and His wrath reaches beyond a balancing according to reason. The whole ethic of the medieval church, especially the doctrine of penitence, was concerned with the thought of a settlement according to reason. Therefore the advocates of this doctrine "became disciples of Aristotle, the dead, damned heathen" (WA 10 I, 1, 472, 10). This doctrine presumed "to deal with God as though God and our nature were good friends of each other" (473, 19). Thus it has had the result that "no one acknowledges, bewails, or deplores God's terrible wrath against us." The collision of God's relationship to man as Lawgiver and Judge — which lets Him demand and sentence — with His relationship as Creator — which makes man what he is — this is really the deepest offense to reason. Reason judges: "It is wrong for such a high, merciful Majesty to do this" (WA 36, 556, 12). It demands "that God act according to human law and do what to them seems to be right or what God could permit to be right" *(ut Deus agat jure humano et faciat quod ipsis rectum videtur aut Deus esse sinat)* (WA 18, 729, 15). It tries again and again to find immanent grounds for excusing His attitude. "But faith and the spirit judge otherwise. They believe that God is good, even if He were to destroy all men." *(Sed fides et spiritus aliter judicant, qui Deum bonum credunt, etiam si omnes homines perderet.)* (WA 18, 708, 7 ff.)

Faith and the spirit — naturally, they cannot grow in this soil. If they alone — in spite of this whole state of affairs, which ends with man's damnation — are able to acknowledge the goodness of God, this is final proof of the immanent fact that it is impossible to solve the riddles presented here. At the same time the realization that unbelief is the greatest sin begins to dawn, yes, the realization that unbelief is the real essence of sin (*Lectures on Hebrews*, 188, 7; WA 18, 782, 13). But this realization cannot be complete until man has learned to believe.

In the confessions nothing has as yet been subtracted from Luther's teaching concerning the wrath of God, concerning its close connection with Law, death, and conscience. Like Luther, Melanchthon – in the Apology too – traces the fundamental error of the medieval ethic back to the fact that this ethic no longer knew what God's wrath is. According to him, this is the reason for its belief that one can love God without first receiving forgiveness of sins. One can fear the angered God, but one cannot love Him. It is equally impossible to confront God's wrath with one's own merits.[4] Why? Luther substantiates this with the thought that then God would be dealing with man according to "human law" (*jure humano*). Then one would confuse His wrath with immanent justice. Melanchthon, too, calls the attempt to put God's Law and man's work into a plausible relationship a "doctrine of reason" (*doctrina rationis*) (III, 167). When, in contrast, he points out that God's Law reveals His wrath (II, 79), he also sees in God's wrath an actuality that lies beyond man's concepts of right and justice. Accordingly, he also calls God's wrath "inexplicable" (*inexplicabilis*) (V, 34); and Justus Jonas says in his translation into German that it is "beyond man's understanding and thinking what a terrible wrath of God we have inherited" (43).[5] Exactly like Luther, the Apology sees conscience as the place where God's wrath strikes man (32); and, like him, it teaches that death is not regarded as punishment until this wrath is felt (VI, 56). Accordingly, just as in Luther, we hear that the Law not only has the task to give instruction concerning God's will but also to accuse constantly and to torment consciences (V, 34), because it shows the wrath of God. To be sure, our heart bristles up at this; it seeks to lull itself into security; it "despises God's wrath, judgment, and threats. It is malicious and hostile to His judgment." (II, 35.) But this only aggravates our guilt, for doubt about God's wrath is not an ἀδιάφορον (I, 42). Finally – in contrast with the Calvinistic teaching – one must still point out that according to the Apology all men are deserving of "eternal wrath" (*ira aeterna*) (II, 40).

[4] Apology II, 9, 36 f.; III, 7, 174; VI, 11.

[5] It should be recalled here once for all that the translator conformed exactly to Melanchthon's conception. He worked with the cooperation of Melanchthon. Cf. the letter to W. Reiffenstein (*CR* 2, 541) at the end and the text of the German *Ed. B* (*CR* 28, 87 f.).

In all decisive points the Formula of Concord, too, held on to what Luther taught about the wrath of God.[6] So far as Flacius is concerned, this is self-evident. But then a swift decline ensued. It is true that in connection with the doctrine concerning the Law, punishment, and especially death they regularly use the expression "wrath of God." But this appears as one punishment among others. This becomes noticeable even in the writings of Johann Gerhard. Here sin and the wrath of God stand in a simple interrelationship of cause and effect. Wrath is "the just wrath of a vengeful God" *(justa vindicis Dei ira)* *(Loci* XX, 178); it is in exact proportion to sin (199). Therefore Gerhard must propound the question whether the doctrine concerning the wrath of God is at all compatible with His justice. To this he replies that Scripture uses the expression "only with reference to human feeling" (ἀνθρωποπαθῶς). Without comment he quotes Augustine's opinion that Scripture calls what is done in the case of His servants the wrath of God, because this is done by means of the divine laws. Yes, he appropriates the argumentation of the scholastics, that, strictly speaking, one can ascribe to God no wrath whatever (III, 176). If for Luther and also for Melanchthon's Apology the wrath of God was proof that one dare not or can not understand God's relationship to the sinner according to "human law" *(jure humano)*, in the sense of the "doctrine of reason" *(doctrina rationis)*, security against this error threatens to be lost because of Gerhard's dilutions. This is clearly seen in the fact that with regard to this question he fights against the Arminians and the Socinians with dull weapons (VII, 47 f.). The whole inability of the later dogmaticians to grasp Luther's doctrine concerning the wrath of God in a deeper sense is connected with the headway made by "natural theology," which will be described later.

Gerhard's restrictions made it possible even for the dogmaticians of the Enlightenment to employ the concept of the wrath of God. To them it is merely a Biblical expression for God's disapproval of sin. In accordance with their whole system, sin and God's reaction to sin are, as they see the situation, in arithmetical proportion.[7]

[6] *Epit.* I, 12; V, 9 f.; *SD* I, 6, 62. (A quotation from Luther: "We do not even understand what we suffer!"); II, 54; V, 12, 20; XI, 60.

[7] Töllner, *System d. dogm. Theol.*, Vol. 2, Book 3, p. 71: "God's displeasure or His genuine indignation at sin is called the wrath of God in Holy Scripture. Consequently, God is angry at sin and at every sin." A comment on this: "In a larger sense the wrath of God is God's genuine indignation at sin in general; in a narrower sense, however, it is God's genuine indignation at sins that have actually been committed. Here we take the word in the second sense. Accordingly, this partly designates God's indignation as it is shown even by what He does. When in connection with this everything that is usually physical and unreasonable among men is separated, and

Another attempt was made to take into account, as a matter of dogmatics, the terrible mystery which Luther perceived in the wrath of God. It was the dogmaticians of the nineteenth century who tried to do this. They proceeded from various starting points. Although A. Ritschl wanted to banish this concept entirely from Christian dogmatics, he thought he still had a right to ascribe to it an eschatological meaning in the New Testament. Julius Kaftan had a similar opinion. Philippi's definitions harked back to early dogmatics. He, too, adopted the proportional interpretation — which, incidentally, goes back to Augustine — when he illustrated its force and its magnitude by saying that this wrath "can be satisfied and stilled only by constant and endless wretchedness on our part." At least he comes close to Luther's interpretation when he associates anguish of conscience directly with God's wrath. On the basis of his Biblical assumptions Kähler realized that the concept of wrath stresses God's personality in connection with His reaction to sin. He also says that the outcome points out that he who is excluded from association with God when appraising a thing never gets down to the real value. Frank, too, associates wrath with God's personal reaction to sin. When he traces wrath back "to the absolute, personal God in His relation to the world," one dare not let the recollection of his concept of absoluteness lead to the conclusion that he, too, came very close to Luther's interpretation. At least insofar as here, too, just as in Luther, the supposition that God deals with the sinner according to "human law" *(jure humano)* is out of the question.[8]

only the general aspects of the genuine indignation are retained, God's wrath contains nothing that is improper." — Nor is the conception of an immanent proportion between sin and punishment invalidated by the distinction that Töllner and others make between "natural" and "arbitrary" punishment inflicted because of sin; if anything, it is confirmed. Cf. p. 79: "That God must punish every arbitrary sin arbitrarily."

In *Grundlegung der Theologie*, by the pietist J. A. Freylinghausen, the concept of the wrath of God does not occur at all. — Wegscheider, *Instit.*, p. 254 f., limits himself to the reportorial statement: "Let the Hebrews . . . attribute to God wrath, vengeance, and other human feelings of this nature" *(Hebraei . . . iram atque vindictam aliasque eius generis affectiones humanas Deo tribuant)*, and he adds only this: "In the books of the New Testament the wrath of God is even brought to remembrance, albeit in a sense that is rather mild" *(In N. T. libris etiam commemoratur ira Dei, mitiore tamen sensu)*.

[8] A. Ritschl, *De ira Dei*, 1859; *Recht und Versöhnung*, II, 119 ff. — Jul. Kaftan, *Dogmatik*, 5th ed., 1909, p. 573. — Philippi, *Glaubenslehre*, 2d ed., II, 1867, 99; IV, 2, 29. — M. Kähler, *Wissensch. d. christl. Lehre*, 3d ed., 1905, pars. 327 and 333. — Fr. H. R. Frank, *System d. christl. Wahrheit*, 3d ed., 1894, I, 294, 491 f.

The first volume of Theodor Harnack's book on Luther contains one of the first complete and critical presentations of Luther's doctrine of the wrath of God. I refer to this work for the various problems of Luther interpretation that are involved. These problems could not be presented here.

But this, of course, is Luther's decisive concern in what he teaches about the wrath of God. The Law certainly reveals the "moral law of the world," and conscience can certainly not avoid acknowledging the validity of this law. But the distance which conscience perceives between itself and the Law is something altogether different from the discovery that in place of the moral law man has put confusion, that he has transgressed several sections. The Law can by no means neutralize the personal call of God which man hears in his conscience. Neither can it suggest moral freedom to man. Rather it convinces him of his lack of freedom. Man lacks freedom both because the Law has been given to him and because he is not able to keep it. Mere awareness of transgression could be put at ease if an individual sin could be atoned for by a corresponding individual punishment. This would regulate the matter according to "human law" *(jure humano).* According to divine law, however, an individual transgression makes one guilty of the whole: the whole man is in opposition to the whole Law — as a whole creature he is in opposition to his Creator. Because this is true of man's whole existence as established by the Creator, man concludes: "God hates me" *(Odit me Deus).* This, says Luther, is "the greatest temptation" *(summa tentatio).* But as long as he knows God only as Creator and Lawgiver, man cannot look upon this as a temptation that can be overcome. He is unable to discover any immanent logic in this relationship to God — nor any justice comprehensible according to "human law" *(jure humano).* The law, this "moral law of the world," is the curse that burdens man.

4. Fear [1]

The concepts of fear, of the Law, and of the wrath of God forbid the assumption that the primal experience *(Urerlebnis)* was nothing but an individual occurrence in Luther's life. One should rather say that no one who takes the facts of the "Thou shalt" and the inability to obey, of guilt and destiny, seriously in the same way can escape Luther's realization: "You have not fufilled, nor are you able to do so. Nevertheless, you should." *(Non implesti, non potes, et tamen debes.)* He who recognizes the voice of God in the "Thou shalt," His verdict in guilt, His work in destiny, stands, as Luther does, necessarily before the "hidden God" *(Deus absconditus),* in whose presence one can be filled with nothing but dread. According to what has been set forth concerning the attenuation of the concepts of sin and the wrath of God, it is

[1] With regard to what follows here cf. my essay *Angst und Einsamkeit in der Geschichte des Luthertums* in S. Kadner's *Jahrbuch f. d. evang.-luth. Landeskirche Bayerns,* 1925—26, pp. 6 ff.

not surprising that in early Lutheranism this knowledge very soon was weakened and, in the end, completely lost. In connection with the primal experience *(Urerlebnis)*, which correlates these concepts theologically, the falsification proceeded in two directions. For one thing, Luther's fear, with its existential bases of knowledge, became nothing but a matter of emotion. The task of using the Gospel to overcome the "fear" of those who were troubled was rightfully assigned to the church's proclamation. But this led to the belief – and this was not right – that it was neither imperative nor necessary to pursue further the knowledge on which Luther's fear was founded. What was taught with regard to a pre-evangelical and extra-Christian knowledge of God could, it was supposed, be understood in such a way that consciences need not be terrified because of this. The "natural theology" which resulted was the second path to falsification.

It would be a totally inadequate interpretation of Luther's fear to define it as being merely fear of punishment. Certainly one can also find this fear in it (WA 5, 217, 26). In like manner, it contains a universal pessimism which transfers the gloomy prospect of one's own future to the judgment of the world in general (cf. *Cross and Vale of Tears*). But this pessimism, too, lies on the periphery as an incidental effect. The primal dread *(Urgrauen)* is, of course, not alarm about one's own fate; it is dread of God. It is alarm about one's own fate only insofar as it proceeds from the knowledge that, in spite of the Law and the will to fulfill the Law, one is enmeshed in everlasting guilt and must serve sin (WA 40 II, 8, 7). But this knowledge is terrible because looking at the Creator and the Lord of our destiny does not mitigate it but confirms or rather directly substantiates it. Here indeed man stands before the majesty of God; but "then one's neck is broken, Lucifer falls, and there is everlasting despair" *(da folget hals stortzen, casus Luciferi et desperationes sempiternae)* (ibid., 330, 12).

As has been shown, Melanchthon, following Luther's paths, sought to let not only the active element of sin but also the wrath of God and the doctrine of original sin come into their own theologically. One would think that then he must also have felt the unresolvable contradiction of the primal experience *(Urerlebnis)*. But he immediately adduces qualifications. He timidly side-steps the thought that guilt and destiny are intertwined – the thought that cannot be avoided when the doctrine of original sin is presented logically. He knows only the Stoic thought of destiny, and he warns against it *(CR* 21, 650). Here one is already aware of the first impetus toward rationalization. It would be better not to say anything at all about destiny. Otherwise responsibility, that is, morality, is endangered. The inevitable consequence is that then sin, wrath, and punishment are brought into a simple logical chain which is entirely understandable to reason,[2] whereas Luther speaks about wrath precisely because reason is unable to understand God's attitude toward sin. Accordingly, in Melanchthon the agnostic element of God's "concealment" and the fear of God, which in Luther are inseparably connected, fall apart. It is true that the original, adequate knowledge of God is lost because of sin (21, 669). It will be seen later that in the process "ignorance in the mind" *(ignorantia in mente)* is said to have left behind a variety of good remnants. In addition to these, however, there are, as a further consequence of sin, the fears of the conscience on which Melanchthon also puts strong emphasis, but which no longer have any inner connection with the first result. This is exactly the case in the writings of the later dogmaticians, from Martin Chemnitz on and wholly so since Johann Gerhard. Just as the wrath of God is in arithmetical proportion to sin, so the former is to the fears of conscience. From the primal dread *(Urgrauen)* there has arisen partly fear of punishment, partly an "imperfect" knowledge of God.[3]

If for this reason the profound knowledge which, in Luther's case, is at the bottom of the primal dread *(Urgrauen)* is missing in the dogmaticians, one can scarcely be surprised that in the preaching of the church his fear of God also becomes something completely different. In Luther it is something that must simply be overcome. The Gospel brings a knowledge of God that is the very opposite — a knowledge, of course, that can be gained only from faith, because it is faith that must overcome that primal dread *(Urgrauen)*. But even in the literature of dying *(Sterbeliteratur)* that continues to crop up in Lutheranism in the sixteenth century according to medieval patterns, individual elements of Luther's fear appear plainly as characteristics of a believing Christian. They must not be fought down; they must be cultivated. Naturally, not the fears of conscience — against them Johann Arndt's books on true Christianity (1603) and the *Sacred Meditations (Meditationes sacrae)* (1606) of Johann Gerhard, Arndt's disciple, are directed. What is meant,

[2] Cf. e. g., *CR* 16, 388 f.: "Reason understands that there are three causes for punishments, of which the first is the justice of God, who is truly angry because of sins and wants His wrath to be observed in prompt punishments" *(Intelligit ratio tres esse poenarum causas, quarum prima est justitia Dei, qui vere irascitur peccatis et iram suam conspici vult in poenis praesentibus).*

[3] But cf. the Confession of the Lower Saxons of 1572 and the Formula of Concord, on which Martin Chemnitz collaborated. Here Luther's understanding of the intolerability of "God's bare majesty" *(majestas Dei nuda)* is retained (cf. *The Doctrine of the Two Natures*).

however, are those universally pessimistic elements that are also contained in Luther's fear but, together with this fear, are to be overcome by faith (cf. *Cross and Vale of Tears*). As early as 1593, in the *Manual on Preparation for Death (Manuale de praeparatione ad mortem)* by Martin Moller, pastor in Sprottau, it is stated that a Christian should be brought up to think constantly of death. And Johann Arndt, like Johann Gerhard, undertakes to impress upon his readers the vanity and the transitoriness of the world. In Luther the thought of death and transitoriness is – because he has his understanding of it from God – an element in the fear of God, therefore a way of giving expression to doubt about God, who, with the threat of death, seems to contradict His will as Creator or rather, in view of man's guilt, *must* contradict it. But because of the Word of the Gospel faith comes to the knowledge that the Creator does not deny His creature but acknowledges it. Consequently, the believer, while walking through God's nature, will experience the joys of Paul Gerhardt, not the pains of Johann Gerhard.

In contradiction to its intention of recommending the joys of heaven, the literature of transitoriness clings precisely to the present world by instructing the Christian to make empirical sufferings and the necessity of physical dying the basis of his vital consciousness. Accordingly, Heinrich Müller, of Rostock, in his *Hours of Spiritual Comfort (Geistliche Erquickstunden)* (1664), can give a frank description of "the dangers of a long life" and instruct his readers to fear life in this world more than death. Here another element of Luther's fear is unraveled from the primal dread *(Urgrauen):* the realization of unavoidable entanglement in guilt and the fear of not being able to get rid of sin. But while here, too, Luther gains freedom from this fear through faith, in Müller the bondage must be maintained artificially. Under the influence of pietism, of which Müller is already an adherent, this falsification of the meaning of fear and the thought of death also insinuates itself into orthodoxy. In 1745, therefore, Valentin Ernst Löscher, superintendent in Dresden, founds the "Christian Academy for Preparation for Death" *(Christliche Akademie der Sterbensbereitung),* and in his book with the same title he gives instruction in the art of Christian dying. Sebastian Friedrich Trescho is concerned with the same subject in his *The Science of Dying a Blessed and Happy Death, or Bible of Dying (Wissenschaft selig und fröhlich zu sterben oder Sterbebibel)* (second edition, 1767). How far the thought of death has departed here from the elemental dread of the primal experience *(Urerlebnis)* can be seen from the fact that the same Trescho, on order, could also write a counterpart: *The Art of Living Happily (Die Kunst glücklich zu leben)* (1765). On order –

for the suggestion to do so came to him from Fräulein von Klettenberg, who in Goethe's book, says in the confessions of a beautiful soul: "I realized, of course, where I had been unworthy, and I also knew where I still was unworthy; but the knowledge of my shortcomings was altogether without fear. . . . I did not want to be lacking in seriousness. I let myself be persuaded for the moment, and I would gladly have led a life that was sad and filled with terrors. But how amazed I was that once and for all time this was not possible!" (*Wilhelm Meister*, Book VI.) These sentences show that one still knows the thought of death only as something that must be evoked artificially. The age knows the melancholy of English graveyard poetry as Klopstock feels it, but no longer does it know dread of God.

If through this gradual psychologizing *(Psychologisierung)* fear is deprived of its intrinsic theological meaning, nevertheless others have not entirely forgotten Luther's knowledge. And these others, too, are now historical witnesses that this *is* by no means merely a matter of Luther's individual perspectives. Thus in the writings of Jakob Böhme one can find insights that reveal the same profundity, insights that are all the more important, since Böhme evidently lacked a thorough acquaintance with Luther's works. Besides, he listened for years to the sermons of the aforementioned Martin Moller, whose last pastorate was in Görlitz. It is true that Böhme, too, is acquainted with the purely emotional elements of fear. In addition, he is acquainted with fear of punishment. But he is also acquainted with dread of God's incalculable fury, and he notices how God completely escapes discovery by him who is tortured by anguish of conscience. Like Luther, he sees the devil at work in man's despair; and the devil employs every trick to keep man from believing, to cast his sins into his teeth, and to induce him to commit suicide. Like Luther, he advises to counter Black Hans *(Schwarz-Hans)* with the Word of God, to look to the cross of Christ, and to take refuge in the light of God's love. As in Luther, questions pertaining to predestination *(das prädestinatianische Fragen)* are considered as belonging in the sphere of the thinking of reason *(Vernunftdenken)*, which is to be overcome by faith. In his case, of course, all this is embedded in his magical speculation and expressed in the language of his magical psychology. But the directness of the relation of the primal dread *(Urgrauen)* to God, who demands, compels, and renders guilty in accordance with destiny *(schicksalhaft)*, is clearly discernible in his writings.

In the sermonic literature of the seventeenth century there are also numerous instances of a feeling that man's natural relationship to God amounts to real distress. Of course, it is scarcely ever stated that this is distress so far as knowledge is concerned. Yet at that time renowned preachers of the church reckon all the more earnestly with "terrified consciences." Men like Valerius Herberger, Christian Scriver, and Joachim Lütkemann declare in their sermons that fear should not be evoked but should be overcome by means of the Gospel and faith. Accordingly, they, like Luther, are convinced that man's natural thinking and experience, if actually thought out and experienced to the end, must terminate in disconsolateness at least and that accordingly an optimism that is not based on the Gospel is founded on self-deception. Johann Albrecht Bengel, too, commented pertinently on the artificial way of stirring up thoughts of death. "Many," he says, "put all theology into the art of dying. But this is wrong. For a Christian it is most important to come from sin to grace and then not to await death but to look forward with joy to the appearance of Jesus." [4] Similarly, at the end of the eighteenth century a man like Matthias Claudius also stands in opposition to the "purveyors of graveyard melancholia." In his works, too, there is lyricism pertaining to the grave, but as an element that has been overcome – exactly as fear is contained in Luther's faith as an element that has been overcome. Whether the *Wandsbecker Bote* [5] prefixes *Death the Skeleton (Freund Hein, der Knochenmann)* to Claudius' collected works or puts a large black cross above the *Letters to Asmus (Briefe an Asmus)* [6] – here the bugbears grave, death, and cemetery are conjured up to be scared away. The *Bote* looks them straight in the face. Claudius knows them and their terrors. But his faith in Christ has finished them off.

In his book titled *What Is Fear? (Begriff der Angst)* (1844) Kierkegaard undertook a determined approach to the theological understanding of the primal dread *(Urgrauen)*. He revives Luther's realization that "the individual is fashioned for faith only through fear." Here he no longer means fear in the sentimental sense of pietism and the Enlightenment. He seeks to conceive of it as a transcendental presupposition of freedom and therefore also of sin. For he knows no other freedom than the freedom to sin. Therefore fear is the a priori of guilt. It is true that he also takes it to be the result of sin. He speaks about the fear of evil and the demonic fear of what is good. This is not to say that Kierkegaard's "fear" corresponds perfectly to Luthers' primal dread *(Urgrauen)*. For one thing, it lacks the strictly personal relationship to God. Yet it does contain an insight into the necessity of becoming guilty with-

[4] O. Wächter, *Bengel und Oetinger,* 1886, p. 82.

[5] A newspaper published by Matthias Claudius.

[6] Pseudonym used by Claudius. Asmus is short for Erasmus.

out making the concept of guilt itself fatalistic and thus annulling it. And Kierkegaard, like Luther, also knows that fear of God as doubt about God Himself is the primal sin *(Ursünde).*

Finally one can quote Schopenhauer as a trustworthy witness to the universal validity of the primal experience *(Urerlebnis).* "When I try to imagine," he says, "that I am standing before an individual being to whom I would say: 'My Creator, once I was nothing; but you have brought me forth so that now I am something, and, what is more, that I am I' – and adds: 'I thank you for this kindness' – and finally: 'If I have been good for nothing, it is my own fault' – then I must answer that as a result of my study of philosophy and Hindooism my head has become incapable of bearing such a thought." [7] What Schopenhauer rejects here as something impossible to imagine states the decisive factors that make up the primal experience *(Urerlebnis)* in Luther. Schopenhauer rejects them because he cannot bear them. This inability to bear Luther calls despair. Schopenhauer is in complete agreement with him in this point, that on the basis of these realizations – if they are inescapable – God can be nothing but the "hidden God" *(Deus absconditus).* He takes the way of Buddhism. Luther believes in the revelation of God in Christ. In the last analysis the difference is this, that Luther realizes what cannot be denied, namely, the interlacement of sin, guilt, and destiny, whereas Schopenhauer declares in the end that this, like the world, is make-believe. And Schopenhauer's most profound reason for this is to be found in his unwillingness to realize or to acknowledge that God steps out of His concealment. Nevertheless – or rather for this very reason – Schopenhauer remains a witness against the hope of the Enlightenment, which fancied that it could arrive at knowledge of God without the belief in revelation maintained by the Reformation.

5. Natural Theology [1]

"And if perchance a hawker of indulgences were to appear among us, he would not do a good business; for nobody has a disquieted and alarmed conscience." So spoke August Tholuck in one of his sermons that dates from the middle of the nineteenth century.[2] This was un-

[7] *Sämtliche Werke,* edited by von Frauenstädt, Vol. 6, 404. The quotation has already been used by me in another connection in *Der Kampf um das Christentum,* 1921, p. 178.

[1] Friedrich Gogarten, *Ich glaube an den dreieinigen Gott. Eine Untersuchung über Glauben und Geschichte,* Jena, 1926, e. g., pp. 101 f. and in many other places. — Ernst Troeltsch, *Vernunft und Offenbarung bei Joh. Gerhard und Melanchthon,* 1891.

[2] A. Tholuck, *Gewissens-, Glaubens- und Gelegenheitspredigten,* Berlin, 1860, p. 20.

doubtedly a correct view of the situation. If one asks what led to such a state of affairs, the first cause one encounters is obviously to be found in what the church proclaimed. For a number of years the preaching of the church of the Reformation was directed toward the goal of preventing anguish of conscience through the Gospel. This work was assigned to the church by the Reformation itself. The result was greater than could be expected. Anguish of conscience was overcome in individuals who, as happened to Luther and in his time, felt this anguish "by nature." But later generations had a totally different experience. Here one has a striking example of how a word which originally applies in a wholly personal way to the individual and can be correctly understood only by individuals is capable of bringing about results that go beyond the individual. Just as in Luther's day anguish of conscience was innate, so to speak, in man, so peace of conscience was innate in those who came later. But it was forgotten that there is no sense in speaking about peace unless there has been a battle.

As has been shown, Lutheranism as a whole never went astray. Nevertheless, the fact that it was at all possible to go wrong was not only the fault of the preaching church; it was the fault of theology. Even while the Reformation was coming into being, the church saw itself confronted by a similar situation. At that time the instruction of the visitors for Electoral Saxony in 1528 made an urgent demand not to separate faith from penitence. This was a demonstration of a practical way of forestalling the delusion that faith is possible without a break with human nature. "And they should diligently remind the people that this faith cannot exist without earnest and true repentance and dread of God. . . . The other thing, where there is no repentance, is a fictitious faith; for true faith should bring comfort and joy in God. Such comfort and joy is not felt where there is no repentance and dread." (WA 26, 203, 26 ff.; 34 ff.) Later dogmatics did not do justice to this necessity but drew up its system from the position of faith. In Christian dogmatics this cannot be otherwise. In addition, later dogmatics also spoke of the knowledge attained by "natural man." This it had both a right and an obligation to do – in keeping with the example of Paul. But because it did not want to leave the position of faith, it treated this "natural" knowledge merely as the first step toward the knowledge of faith. It is true that what it taught concerning the relationship of penitence and faith was right in a formal way. But it lost sight of the inner connection between the natural knowledge of God and the necessity for penitence. It forgot that "natural" man's knowledge of God leads to doubt about God, thus to unbelief, and therefore makes penitence necessary, and that in all circumstances faith presupposes a break with the natural knowledge. In the light of this theology it could seem as though the evangelical knowledge of God were really innate in man. Therefore it was possible to understand the church's work of proclamation in such a way that the church need only clarify and bring about the realization of what is more or less self-evident to every man "by nature." It is true that this last conclusion was not drawn until the emergence of the theology and the preaching of rationalism. But orthodox dogmatics had already created the supposition on which it was based.

Because of the importance they attached to the doctrine of original sin, the confessions were forced to deny that natural man can have any saving knowledge of God. In the Apology, Melanchthon numbers "ignorance of God" *(ignorantia Dei)* among the effects of original sin – God can be known in no other way than through the Word. In all circumstances man lacks fear of God – fear to be understood in the sense in which Luther's Catechisms speak about it. Man's heart feels only "that God is horribly angry and oppresses us with temporal and everlasting disasters" *(Deum horribiliter irasci et opprimere nos temporalibus et perpetuis calamitatibus).* The doctrine of the Formula of Concord – that by nature man does not feel even the wrath with which God is filled because of sin – is not strange to Melanchthon either. He even accuses his theological opponents of not knowing what God's wrath and judgment are. Elsewhere he ascribes to sin the fact that man does not acknowledge the wrath of God *(CR* 21, 672). And in any case the Formula of Concord leaves no doubt "that by birth and by nature we all inherit from Adam a heart, a disposition, and thoughts which with all their might and in accordance with the light of reason are minded and constituted directly in opposition to God and His chief commandment, yes, are enmity against God, especially in divine, spiritual matters." [3] This virtually exhausts what the confessions have to say about the "natural knowledge of God." For it is self-evident that what Luther teaches in the First Article of the Creed concerning the relationship of the creatures to the Creator does not belong here, because it is spoken from the position of faith.

Nevertheless, the same Melanchthon already accepted the essential elements of the later "natural theology" so far as the material is concerned. He demonstrates the natural proofs of the existence of God

[3] Apology I, 14, 7 ff.; II 67, 37; III 7. — Formula of Concord, *SD,* II, 21; I, 3. Cf. the third of the *Copenhagen Articles* and the Hungarian *Confessio Montana,* Art. 3.

(*CR* 13, 200 ff.; 21, 641 ff.). To him philosophical morality is — at least in the last period of his life — identical with the divine Law. To teach knowledge of the divine will, it employs grounds based on reason, the causal relationship between failure and punishment; it defines the virtues; it shows man's final moral aim (16, 167 ff.). Proofs of the immortality of the soul are also taken over from the philosophers, from Plato, Xenophon, and Cicero (13, 175). Furthermore, Melanchthon is acquainted with Kant's postulate of an equalization of virtue and happiness — an equalization which is to take place in the hereafter but is missing in the present life (13, 176). Of course, all this knowledge is fragmentary; in part it is also corrupted, concealed — all because of sin. Nor does sin let this knowledge have its full effect in a moral life. Without sin, however, it would present a self-contained system that encompasses the total area of the knowledge of the world and of God as well as the ethical content. It is true that a remnant of the knowledge of God remains — a remnant which in all circumstances should be reserved for the special revelation. It pertains, above all, to the mystery of the Trinity and to God's intention of founding for Himself a church among the human race (13, 199). Moreover, the whole natural knowledge of God is to be made subordinate to the "knowledge of the Law" *(notitia legis).* At no point, therefore, can it ignore completely the element of sin. As "knowledge of the Law" *(notitia legis)* it extends, in the direction of natural laws, to God as Creator, as Preserver, and as Lord of providence; in the direction of moral law it extends to God as Lawgiver, as a Judge who punishes and rewards. Yet among the divine attributes accessible to the natural knowledge the concepts "beneficent" *(beneficus)* and "truthful" *(verax)* appear too, almost furtively.[4] Certainly the knowledge of these attributes is obscured, exactly as natural man lets himself be lulled into security over against God's power to punish. Nevertheless, so far as the idea is concerned, this

[4] The most complete compilation is found in *CR* 13, 198: "There flashes in the mind the knowledge which affirms not only that there is one God, the Maker of the whole world and order, in all nature, but also teaches what kind of God He is, namely, wise, beneficent, just, One who assigns like things to like things, truthful, One who loves moral purity, One who demands that our obedience conform to this His will, and One who punishes with horrible punishments those who harshly violate this order, as the whole history of the human race bears witness" *(Fulget in mente humana notitia, quae adfirmat non solum esse unum Deum, opificem totius mundi et ordinis, in tota natura, sed etiam docet, qualis sit, scilicet sapiens, beneficus, justus, aequalia aequalibus tribuens, verax, amans castitatis, postulans ut ad hanc suam voluntatem nostra obedientia congruat et puniens horribilibus poenis hunc ordinem atrociter violantes, sicut universa historia humani generis testatur).*

knowledge belongs into the rational system actually reached at the peaks of the history of philosophy — for example, in Plato.

How far away from Luther we now are! It is true that Melanchthon would emphasize again and again that by nature no man has the right to refer God's goodwill to himself without forgiveness of sins. Yet here forgiveness of sins, with all its presuppositions, appears from the position of the natural knowledge as merely the restoration of a dilapidated building. Luther would have accepted this as valid if it had been said about the relationship of forgiveness of sins to the "primal state" *(Urstand)*. But the relationship of the primal state — here Melanchthon, too, taught in accord with the Reformation — was said to have been lost, not only corrupted, by the irruption of sin. From this there resulted for Luther a relationship of man to God which — even when reason exerts itself to the utmost, yes, precisely when the matter is thought through — must end in a breakdown of the knowledge of God. Not as though, in Luther's opinion, this were at all lacking to man by nature. But it ends at points that can absolutely not be reconciled in one's thinking. From the thought of the divine Lawgiver and Judge one comes to fear of punishment and to a realization of one's own responsibility. From the thought of the Creator and the Ruler of the world one comes to the experiencing of destiny. Even the breaking of the divine commandment is in itself enmity against God. But here reason, too, revolts against Him. According to Luther, it can reach no other goal. This is God's transcendence in the strictest sense; there are no bridges of knowledge leading to it. All empirical evidences of His goodwill fall to the ground in the face of the knowledge that He has decreed for us an eternal death. And Luther would never have admitted that the knowledge of "God's truthfulness" *(veracitas Dei)* can be developed from the components of rational thought. It is not goodwill that God has in readiness for us; it is wrath, and the question concerning His truthfulness must — without Christ — end in doubt. For Luther the knowledge of God is not ruinous, as it is for Melanchthon; for him it lies beyond all rational possibilities.

Once Melanchthon — like medieval dogmatics — had returned to the path of natural theology, there was no longer any stopping. Only once did the development seem to come to a standstill: in connection with the disputes with Flacius. In order to support his thesis concerning original sin, Flacius himself had to prove the totality of man's corruption. His numerous references to Luther were not merely superficial in nature. It was an out-and-out Lutheran thought when, in opposition to Simon Musäus, he showed that original sin is not "a confused mass of diverse evils" *(chaos diversorum malorum)* but a unified power in man and over man.[5] Above all, he spoke about sinful man's "reason" *(ratio)* in such a way that an impetus to Melanchthon's natural knowledge of God is nowhere imaginable.[6] No one of the theologians of that time preserved as energetically as he did Luther's thought that sinful man is "hostile, militant, and at war" *(inimicus, militans, belligerans)* in relation to God, that reason in particular conducts itself "in a hostile manner" *(hostiliter)* over against Him. And his comments also warned those who were opposed to him in matters pertaining to natural theology to be cautious. Thus indeed in a disputation that took place in 1572 under Tilemann Hesshusius he was confronted with the objection that his doctrine of original sin was untenable because man retained certain knowledge which should be regarded as an outstanding work and gift of the holy God. Yet in spite of all reminiscences of Melanththon the description of this knowledge and these capabilities was phrased in such a way that Flacius' constantly raised charge of Pelagianism even with reference to the ability of reason – should be regarded as groundless.[7] As in other cases, here, too, the final result was that the Formula of Concord returned to the position of Luther.

Later on, however, even in the case of Martin Chemnitz, coauthor of the Formula of Concord, Melanchthon's legacy reasserts itself unre-

[5] Matthias Flacius III, *Refutatio sententiae Doct. Musaei de orig. pecc., Ursellis,* 1572.

[6] Flacius, *De essentia orig. just. et injustitiae, Basil.,* 1568, 47 f. *Compendiaria expos. doctr. de essentia orig. pecc., Urs.,* 1572, 10. Referring to the Apology, he says here: "Therefore there is this corruption in the mind, darkness in divine matters and wickedness that abhors and condemns the divine words and fashions false gods and false cults" — so Luther had spoken about the natural knowledge of God in the Large Catechism in connection with the First Commandment — "and esteems these more highly than it esteems the things that God reveals" *(Est igitur haec corruptio in mente, caligo in rebus divinis et malicia abhorrens et damnans divina dicta et fingens falsa numina falsosque cultus et probans ea magis quam quae Deus revelat).*

[7] *Propositiones de pecc. orig. contra furores Manichaeorum et Pelagianorum, de quibus . . . Preside D. Til. Heshusio . . . disputabitur, Jen. 1572, These 108 f.:* "As in the mind there remains knowledge, a distinction between things that are honorable and things that are shameful, the knowledge of numbers, the principles of the liberal arts, new thoughts, there are also the physical loves in human nature, the love of children . . . in the will there is a certain power to choose things that are honorable and to avoid things that are shameful . . . the desire for life and preservation, the flight from death . . . the work of producing offspring . . . often even heroic impulses are stirred up in men who are not led by the spirit of Christ" *(Ut in mente reliquae sunt noticiae, discrimen honestorum et turpium, noticiae numerorum, principia liberalium artium,* κοιναὶ ἔννοιαι, *sunt et* στοργαὶ φυσικαὶ *in natura humana, amor liberorum . . . in voluntate est quaedam vis eligendi honesta et aversandi turpia . . . appetitus vitae et conservationis, fuga mortis . . . opus generationis . . . saepe et heroici motus accenduntur in hominibus, qui non ducuntur Spiritu Christi).* Cf. the aforementioned catalog of natural knowledge as given by Melanchthon.

servedly. To Chemnitz the natural knowledge of God is "nonexistent or imperfect or faint" *(aut nulla aut imperfecta aut languida).* The first of these three adjectives is correct because philosophy, as the legal adviser of this knowledge, knows nothing about the forgiveness of sins; the second, because without Christ man has but a little part of this knowledge; the third, because man counteracts this knowledge with terrible doubts. Its limits are seen in the fact that although it teaches that there is a God and that it is necessary to revere Him, it is not able to say how this is to be done. It also teaches that knowledge of the Creator cannot be made completely certain and profitable by reason alone; according to Heb. 11:3, faith must be added. Furthermore, it teaches that in case of competition the natural knowledge must, self-evidently, be subordinated to the revelation in the Word.[8] Heerbrand and Hafenreffer give a detailed exposition of the proofs of the existence of God "from the book of nature" *(ex libro naturae).* As the first of these Hafenreffer mentions the evidence from the conscience of those who are good and those who are evil. Here he can say in all innocence: "For those who are good rejoice rightly in the testimonies of their deeds in every aspect of things, trusting in the justice and the goodness of the divine being" *(Boni namque recte factorum testimoniis in omni rerum vultu gaudent, freti divini numinis justitia et bonitate).*[9] What would Luther have said if here in the sphere of natural man there is talk about "good human beings" who, on the basis of the testimony of their deeds, rely on the justice and the goodness of the divine being?

Here one can now see where Melanchthon's method of procedure could lead. It is true that in the writings of the dogmaticians of the seventeenth century one will not find such a break with the basic assumptions of Luther's theology. In the case of some of them – Leonhard Hutter, for example – natural theology plays no role at all worth mentioning. But it is all the more important that in the doctrinal tradition established by Johann Gerhard the clear-cut break between man's natural relationship to God and his faith relationship to Him, as it existed in Luther, is constantly weakened more and more, yes, obliterated. For one thing, the formal usage of reason, the necessity of which Melanchthon had already established in dogmatics, also settled on articles that are materially most important, such as the one concerning the nature and the attributes of God. It is entirely self-evident that the conclusion based on cause and effect is employed in the doctrine concerning God and providence. Gerhard, it is true, considers it impossible to give a real

8 M. Chemnitz, *Loci I.*

9 M. Hafenreffer, *Loci,* p. 30. — J. Heerbrand, *Comp.,* 1585, p. 33.

definition of the concept of God. But his reasons for this are of a logical-dialectical kind. If – as in the first article of the Augsburg Confession – Melanchthon and the earlier dogmaticians – like Heerbrand, Chemnitz, S. Pauli, Selnecker, Hafenreffer, Hutter – have already designated God as "a spiritual essence" *(essentia spiritualis),* Johann Gerhard's metaphysical point of departure is completely neutralized. In his writings, as in the writings of the medieval scholastics and mystics, God is again "the highest being, a pure act" *(summum ens, actus purus).* Calov, König, Scherzer, and Quenstedt adhere more cautiously to Melanchthon. Hollaz and Baier, however, again define "spiritual being" *(ens spirituale).* Here, therefore, God is, in the first instance, a neuter – the characteristics that make up the person are accidental. He who defines God in such a way is no longer conscious of responsibility for what he thinks about Him. These definitions leave out of consideration the unavoidable alternative between unbelief and belief. It is godless to speak about God as if He were a thing or a provable or unprovable hypothesis, whereas in reality every one of our thoughts is a yes or a no to the divine call.

For this reason the last representatives of orthodoxy, like Johann Musäus, fought against adherents of the Enlightenment, such as Herbert von Cherbury, with blunted weapons when they undertook to prove to them the "insufficiency" of the natural knowledge of God. Musäus indeed was not wrong in stating that it depended on whether the natural knowledge of God was sufficient "for salvation" – which must be denied.[10] But he did not draw the necessary conclusion: that for this reason it could lead only to "damnation" *(Unseligkeit).* He was no longer able to draw it, because orthodox dogmatics itself believed it could also speak about God by using the neuter gender, as has been pointed out.

That mixture took place in still another way. Luther heard the Word of Scripture as God's Word, because he heard it as a threat and a promise, as Law and Gospel. And the first edition of Melanchthon's *Loci* is an excellent application of this. But in spite of the doctrine of inspiration, to which it adhered – or by which it perhaps was even misled – orthodox dogmatics considered this work a book of instruction with regard to all its heterogeneous contents. These pertain in part, however, to immanent world conditions, which, as is unavoidable, are also the subject of "natural" knowledge. The fact that this led to conflicts which later on caused the apologetic theology of the eighteenth and nineteenth centuries to bleed to death was not the worst result. The imaginary or real agreements settled on between the "revealed" doctrine, say, concerning the

[10] Joh. Musaeus, *Examen Cherburianismi sive de luminis naturae insufficientia ad salutem,* Wittenberg, 1708, p. 8.

origin of the world and the doctrine concerning the "natural" knowledge — in this case natural sciences or philosophy — were fraught with much graver consequences. One can let it pass when Chyträus finds once again in every chapter of the First Book of Moses the proof for one or more *loci* of dogmatics, or when, a century later, August Pfeiffer, general superintendent of Lübeck, also wanted to find in Genesis all twenty-eight articles of the Augsburg Confession, or when J. Deutschmann gave conclusive evidence that Adam was the first true Lutheran theologian.[11] Luther had led the way with related interpretations of Genesis. It was more important that in the exegesis of those passages the findings of the profane sciences were now employed as proofs of "the truth of divine revelation." Here Kepler, in spite of the warnings of his theological friend Hafenreffer, became the great maker of experiments (cf. *The Relativity of the World Picture*). Actually it was alluring to attest for oneself the harmony of the Word of God with the "science" of the foremost authorities. Not only in the commentaries but also in the works on dogmatics — for example, in Abraham Calov — does one get to feel this. Here natural theology becomes an out-and-out guarantor of revelation. In Otto Zöckler's *Natural Theology* (1862) the air is proved to be "the sphere in which the omnipresence and the spirituality of God are revealed," "the cycle of waters, the place where God's faithfulness or truthfulness (!) is revealed," "the animal kingdom, the place where divine goodness is revealed." "The divine Trinity," is "proved from the real and ideal triads of the creature world." "Healing, convalescence, and the living of one's life" are considered "the sphere in which God's mercy is revealed." Things never went higher! It will have to be shown later that even according to Luther God and the world stand in a positive relationship. But to him this was certain in the strictest manner of speaking by reason of God's promise in Christ, that is, by reason of revelation in an altogether different sense. Belief in this revelation must assert itself in opposition to natural man, even in opposition to his natural knowledge.

The development of "natural theology" is the march of history from Luther's primal experience *(Urerlebnis)* up to the Enlightenment. It ended with the ominous error that Christian faith in God and "natural knowledge of God" are essentially identical. For the naive apologists, for many a dogmatician, even for many a politician who wanted to "preserve religion for the people," this was a comfort and a satisfaction. For

[11] Chytraeus, *In Genesin enarratio*, 1561. — A. Pfeiffer, *Pansophia Mosaica e Genesi delineata*, Leipzig, 1685. — J. Deutschmann, *Theologia primi theologi Adami vere Lutherani*, Wittenberg, 1689.

the church Philistine, as Tholuck addressed him, it was reason for no longer knowing of an anguished conscience. But then came Ludwig Feuerbach. Then came Karl Marx and Nietzsche. They showed that the knowledge of "natural" man arrives at a totally different result. And when it came to the great test of the revelation of God's goodness, faithfulness, and mercy on land, at sea, and in the air – which Zöckler and many others taught – the result was decidedly negative. Was it surprising that the generation of the war and the collapse declared the Christian belief in God to be a delusion because it had been refuted by the terrors and the fate that had been experienced? If that generation had heard Luther instead of the theology of the nineteenth century and the preaching that lives on such theology – it would have understood him and his primal dread *(Urgrauen)*.

Chapter Two

THE GOSPEL

6. Preliminary Questions [1]

Under the impression made by the Gospel, Luther forms contradictory contrasts from the relations hitherto developed. The Pharisee in the Gospel account fulfills the divine Law. "He gives to God what he owes" *(Deo dat, quod debet)*. On the other hand, the tax collector is a sinner in his own eyes and in the eyes of everybody. "Reason" *(ratio)* must conclude that he belongs to the devil. But Christ "concludes the opposite" *(schleusst das widderspil)*. He calls him righteous. Conversely, the Pharisee is cast "into the abyss of hell" by the same verse (WA 12, 654, 12 ff.). The moral man is rejected; the sinner is elected. The sinner is righteous. "The sinner is justified when he is damned; he is alive when he is killed; he ascends into heaven when he sinks down into hell" (WA 5, 164, 23). Hell is heaven for the Christian (WA 16, 405, 4). "The Christian is a sinner and not a sinner; he is in heaven and on earth" *(Christianus est peccator et non, est in celo et in terra)* (WA 15, 728, 19). He is "sinful and holy at the same time, an enemy and a son of God" (WA 40 I, 368, 9).[2] God shows what is good while He is showing what is evil (WA 3, 64, 5). Christ overcomes the powers

[1] Lommatzsch, *Luthers Lehre,* 1879, pp. 361 ff. — K. Heim, *Das Gewissheitsproblem in der systematischen Theologie bis zu Schleiermacher,* 1911. — L. Ihmels, *Das Christentum Luthers in seiner Eigenart,* 1917. — F. Kattenbusch, *Deus absconditus bei Luther, Festgabe f. Jul. Kaftan,* 1920, pp. 170 ff. — Ole Hallesbye, *Den kristelige troslaere,* 2 vols., 1920 and later. — F. Gogarten, *Von Glauben und Offenbarung,* 1923. — E. Brunner, *Erlebnis, Erkenntnis, Glaube,* 2d ed., 1923. — R. Bultmann, *Die Frage der "dialektischen" Theologie,* 1926, pp. 40 ff. — Hans Wilhelm Schmidt, *Zeit und Ewigkeit,* 1927 — Jul. Ebbinghaus, *Luther und Kant, Jahrb. d. Luther-Gesellsch.,* 1927, pp. 119 ff. — Torsten Bohlin, *Glaube und Offenbarung, eine kritische Studie zur dialektischen Theologie,* 1928. — Fritz Blanke, *Der verborgene Gott bei Luther,* 1928. — Walther v. Loewenich, *Luthers Theologia crucis,* 1929. — Rud. Hermann, *Luthers These "Gerecht und Sünder zugleich,"* 1930.

[2] Cf. *Lectures on Romans* II, 105, 16; WA 29, 576, 14.

of the world and of hell by experiencing complete powerlessness on the cross (WA 7, 586, 15). When He should be King, He is crucified; when one despairs of Him, He becomes King over everything (WA 14, 444, 2). "When He wanted to go into eternal life, He went into death" (WA 19, 153, 32).

Does the Gospel mean to induce us to speak differently about everything that makes up the primal experience *(Urerlebnis)* from the way common sense compels us to think? If hell is to be heaven for the Christian – then is heaven merely another name for hell? If the Christian is said to be an enemy and a son of God at the same time, then is he a son by being an enemy or because he is an enemy? "Sinful and holy at the same time" – does one become holy by sinning? Luther's answer to these questions is threefold.

In the first place, the two sides of the pair of contrasts appear as elements of a dialectical procedure based on the will of God. The one element is always the content of the divine plan; the other is the means. "Of him whom He wants to make pious He makes a despairing sinner. Of him whom He wants to make wise He makes a fool. Him whom He wants to make strong He makes weak. Him whom He wants to make alive He puts into the jaws of death. Him whom He wants to lead to heaven He lowers into the abyss of hell, and so on. Him whom He wants to honor, to bring to happiness, to power, to exalt and make great, on him He inflicts every disgrace; He damns him, makes him a servant, base and small. Here the verse applies: 'The first, the last; the last, the first.' He who wants to be great, let him be small. He who wants to walk in front, let him walk in back. Now this is the wonderful and strange King; He is closest when He is farthest away. And He is farthest away when He is closest." (WA 19, 154, 22.) All God's deeds are done in this paradoxical manner. Everything God does is contrary to reason *(alles widdersynnisch, was Gott machet)* (WA 24, 569, 31; Enders 5, 182, 29).

If we think back to the primal experience *(Urerlebnis)* as Luther developed it in opposition to Erasmus, it seems at once that the solution of the problem that was not solved there is beckoning here. Now one could conclude that God brought about that situation in order to arrive at the opposite. He engenders sin and despair to bring piety, foolishness to bring wisdom, weakness to bring strength, death to bring life, hell to bring heaven.[3] In itself, however, this answer is by no means sufficient. It is self-evident that the logic of this procedure, in connection with which the first element always changes to its opposite, would

[3] Cf. also *Lectures on Hebrews,* ed. Joh. Ficker, 1908, 133, 1 ff.

have to be the necessity for an immanent dialectic, that is, the first would always have to be regulated in such a way as to give rise to the opposite. Accordingly, the same necessity that gave rise to sin would change sin to righteousness. For one thing, however, this is impossible because – at least according to Luther's conviction – at the end of the procedure by no means all sinners become saints. For some men sin and death have conclusive significance. Consequently, the dialectical procedure would be only partially complete. Accordingly, its author would have accomplished his purpose only in fragments, therefore not at all as an actual end (τέλος). In addition, there is something else. It is true that in his dialectical antitheses Luther says: "The sinner is righteous." But he never says: "Sin is righteousness." In the matter of a dialectical procedure, therefore, man is concerned only insofar as he has material existence. One element remains stable in connection with this procedure. The dialectical procedure affects man, or it takes place with, in, or through him: man is first a sinner, then he is righteous. In addition to this, however, he always remains a human being with material existence. Therefore the procedure expressed in the aforementioned antitheses cannot exhaust God's relation to man. The I of man – that which experiences the man himself – remains identical with itself.

But even the concept of the procedure itself – which always means a succession of events in time – is not sufficient. "We live, and yet we die" *(Vivimus et tamen morimur)*, it is stated in the *Lectures on Genesis* (WA 43, 216, 36). How? The statement that the one who lives is at the same time the one who dies could give pointed expression to the fact that from his first breath man has in him the germ of death. At times Luther can speak in this way: "death in nature before life" *(mors in natura ante vitam)* (WA 39 I, 347 f.). Then the antithesis – although it speaks of simultaneousness – could express a procedure in time or, strictly speaking, a gradual biological transition from the one state to the other. Apart from the fact that in the passage just quoted he is speaking of the relation to original sin, this would then be a rather trivial truth. Yet the dialectical contrasting of death and life has a deeper meaning. "I live in myself, that is, dead before God" *(Vivo ego in me i. e. mortuus apud Deum)* (WA 40 I, 285, 3). "That which is life in the sight of God is death in our sight. That which is temporal among us is not temporal before God; that which is eternal among us is not eternal before God." *(Quod in conspectu Dei vita est, in nostro conspectu mors est. Quod apud nos temporale est, apud Deum non temporale; quod apud nos aeternum est, apud Deum non est aeternum.)* (Erlangen edition *ex. lat.* 18, 296.)

Here it becomes possible to interpret the dialectical antitheses in another way. The antagonism is based on the difference between the sight *(conspectus)* of God and that of man. The two look at the same facts from opposite sides. Consequently, they also arrive at opposing judgments. This is true not only of the pair of opposites, death and life, but also of the other pair, the sinner and the righteous man. For even when the Pharisee and the tax collector are contrasted, God's judgment and the judgment of men are in contrast. But this judgment, considered separately, cannot satisfy either. For concerning a sinner who is a sinner according to his own judgment and according to the judgment of other men can one say without hesitation and unconditionally: "According to God's judgment, he is a righteous man"? This would have to be possible if the divine and the human judgment were abruptly in contrast in dialectics. Then the one conclusion would always have to be drawn from the other. This is not possible. It is true that the verdict "sinner" applies to all without exception and that it applies to the total extent of their existence. This knowledge is an essential element of the primal experience *(Urerlebnis)*. But the knowledge that God pronounces judgment on sin is equally essential. And this, in turn, includes the acknowledgment that man is a sinner not only according to his own judgment but also according to the judgment of God. Divine and human judging, therefore, are by no means opposed in every respect. In the soil of the primal experience *(Urerlebnis)* it is not at all possible to hope that God makes any other declaration concerning the sinner than the sinner must make concerning himself. God's Law confirms that man is a sinner, and he who acknowledges the Law does not judge differently from God but exactly as He does.

If in spite of this the sight *(conspectus)* of God is said to be different from the sight of man, the possibility that this can be so is an absolute secret so far as the man of the primal experience *(Urerlebnis)* is concerned. Accordingly, the realization of this possibility can only be "revealed." This takes place by means of the Gospel. When it is announced there as a divine declaration that the sinner is a righteous man, man is standing before a twofold divine judgment. If he decides to acknowledge the second, he is again judging no differently from God but once more exactly as He does. Consequently, it is necessary to be precise when substantiating the antitheses by contrasting the divine and the human judgment.

This takes place by means of a third series of thoughts. To faith Luther ascribes the power of mediation. "It [faith] mediates between life and death"; it "reconciles the opposites."[4] One opposite consists, in the first place, in the judgment of God, whose Law declares the sinner to be a sinner, whose Gospel, however, declares him to be righteous. The same opposite is repeated in the judgment of man insofar as he is ready to acknowledge both divine judgments. If faith is to reconcile these opposites, this cannot mean that it paralyzes them by letting the one be done away with by means of the other. For then, of course, faith would really acknowledge neither of the two judgments. On the contrary, it has the key to the secret, just as the acknowledgment of both judgments is mediation. For it puts itself into direct opposition to the position forced on man by the primal experience *(Urerlebnis)*. There man looked for an immanent adjustment between the "Thou shalt" and inability to obey, or, what amounts to the same thing when viewed from the other side, between the justice of God and the gruesome condition into which God has placed man. This attempt on the part of "reason" *(ratio)* miscarried. Faith, on the other hand, does not seek the answer; it hears it – the answer that God Himself gives by means of "revelation." It hears that God calls the sinner righteous in spite of the fact that the sinner is and remains a sinner, that He makes alive in spite of the fact that He kills. The unconditional acknowledgment of this judgment of God's is mediation. It is unconditional because it, or when it, keeps itself completely free from all conditionality of human judgment, therefore also from the knowledge it has gained in the primal experience *(Urerlebnis)*.[5]

The aforementioned second interpretation of the antitheses is also to be understood in accordance with what has just been said. Man's

[4] WA 43, 219, 28 ff.: "Therefore faith reconciles the opposites. . . . But it is its power to slay death, to condemn hell, to be sin to sin, the devil to the devil, to such an extent that death is not death, even if the feeling of all should testify that death is present. . . . This is the power of faith, which mediates in this way between death and life, and transforms death into life and immortality, which, as it knows, has been granted through Christ." *(Fides igitur conciliat contraria. . . . Sed virtus eius est mortem occidere, infernum damnare, esse peccato peccatum, diabolo diabolum, adeo ut mors non sit mors, etiamsi omnium sensus testetur adesse mortem. . . . Haec fidei vis est, quae ita mediat inter mortem et vitam et transmutat mortem in vitam et immortalitatem, quam scit donatam per Christum.)* – WA 44, 718, 1: "So great is the power of faith, which makes us alive when we are dead. . . . Therefore death and life are united with each other more closely than we are able to perceive." *(Tanta vis est fidei, quae nos vivos facit ex mortuis. . . . Propius igitur sibi coniuncta sunt mors et vita, quam nos possumus perspicere.)*

[5] WA 18, 708, 7: "Therefore it [namely, reason] rages and struggles in such a way that it excuses God and defends Him as just and good. But faith and the spirit judge differently; they believe that God is good, even if He were to destroy all men." *(Ideo sic aestuat et contendit [scil. ratio], ut Deum excuset et defendat iustum et bonum. Sed fides et spiritus aliter iudicant, qui Deum bonum credunt, etiamsi omnes homines perderet.)*

sight *(conspectus)*, of which Luther spoke, is the sight of the primal experience *(Urerlebnis)*. God's sight *(conspectus)*, on the other hand, is and remains the sight of God. Man becomes aware of it only when he believes. Here it is by no means the believer himself who judges. On the contrary, he receives the judgment of God. In this way that first impression made by a dialectical procedure becomes understandable. The judgment of God that is perceived by faith puts itself into opposition to the knowledge gained in the primal experience *(Urerlebnis)* and at the same time confirms it by presupposing it. For readiness to believe is conditioned by realization of the "Thou shalt" and inability to obey. In fact, it is identical with this realization. And it can be identical with it because man insofar as he has material existence remains unchanged.

2. Accordingly, the fundamental revision of the relationship between God and man which is indicated by the aforementioned antitheses does not come about as the result of a mere readjustment of our thinking. Luther warns expressly against the error of the pseudo tax collectors *(Pseudopublicani)*, who, like the tax collector in the Gospel, say the words "I am a sinner" and "God is merciful," it is true, but remain Pharisees and scoundrels *(Buben)* in spite of this. They say, of course, that they are sinners, and they even think so; but they immediately cancel the acknowledgment of their sin by eliminating from their minds the thought of God's wrath, which they would have to feel as a necessary consequence of sin, and by substituting for it in their thoughts God's mercy, which, as they allege, applies to them too.[6] In the first place, they do not attain the pardon the tax collector received; for they do not take their penitence seriously. But they are also in error because the source of their faith is not to be found in the Gospel. For "this is the art when one truly feels sin, that he learn from the Gospel *(quando quis vere sentiat peccatum, discat ex Evangelio)*; that he not concern himself much with precepts *(das er nicht viel cum praeceptis umb ghe)* but say that he is a sinner and that God is propitious *(sed dicat se peccatorem et Deum propitium)*. I poor sinner, Thou merciful God." (WA 30 II, 145, 16.)

Faith, therefore, is no autogenous changing of one's thinking. It depends on the hearing of the Gospel. For this it is essential that the Gospel is "God's Word" to the sinner, that it is "revelation." Through the operation of the Law and the wrath of God man came to the knowledge that there is "enmity" between him and God. The Gospel announces the opposite to him. "For by sending His Son He shows that

[6] Cf. the entire sermon for the Eleventh Sunday after Trinity, 1531 (WA 34 II, 138 ff.) and the printing in Cruciger's *Sommerpostille* (22, 203, 24 ff.).

there is no wrath between me and Him *(Nam per hoc, quod mittit filium, indicat, quod non sit ira inter me et se)* and that He cannot be hostile to me" (WA 31 I, 396, 14). "He shows *(indicat)* – this is information. Does it have the sense of instruction? Is it a rectification of false conceptions? An increase of knowledge? Then revelation would be tantamount to enlightenment. The dogmaticians of the seventeenth century – Abraham Calov *(Syst.* I, 270), for example – gave support to this interpretation by equating revelation with the Holy Scriptures and by designating as its purpose the "informing" *(informatio)* of man. But *indicat* can on no account be meant in the purely formal sense of a mere rectification of false conceptions. For better instruction – "God is not hostile to me" – would, if it were nothing more than this, presuppose a mere denial of the previous conception – "God is hostile to me." But this knowledge, too, was a fruit of God's revelation, namely, in the Law and in the conscience. Otherwise God's hostility, that is, His wrath, would have been nothing but a delusion. Then, however, man would be in no need whatever of forgiveness.

On the contrary, the Gospel not only gives information concerning a new relationship between him who hears it and God; but it brings this relationship about – only, however, by calling attention to Christ. The Gospel is "a historical account of Christ, God's and David's Son, who died and arose and was appointed Lord *(unnd tzum herrnn gesetzt)*, which is the sum total *(summa summarum)* of the Gospel" (WA 10 I, 1, 10, 6). This historical account has the noteworthy quality of being at the same time an offer. "In the New Testament the Gospel is proclaimed, which is nothing else than a sermon by means of which are offered the Spirit and the grace obtained for the remission of sins through Christ, who was crucified for us, and all this free, and solely because of God the Father's mercy, which is well disposed toward us though we are unworthy and deserve damnation rather than anything else" *(In novo testamento praedicatur Euangelion, quod est aliud nihil quam sermo, quo offertur spiritus et gratia in remissionem peccatorum per Christum crucifixum pro nobis impetratam, idque totum gratis solaque misericordia Dei patris, nobis indignis et damnationem merentibus potius quam aliquid aliud favente* (WA 18, 692, 17 ff.). The fact that the offer is made to those who deserve damnation *(damnationem merentibus)* is no proof whatever that the knowledge conditioned by the Law is wrong. The very meaning of the word "offer" includes the possibility of rejection. If the offer is rejected, it does not become effective. Then the wrath and the judgment of God remain valid. By making an offer the Gospel becomes a promise. It does not want to instruct; it wants to bestow a gift. It does not want to convict the knowledge of sin of being in error; it wants to convey forgiveness of sin. "Therefore the Gospel is a sermon that forgives sin" (WA 10 III, 394, 21). This is a condensed way of speaking, but one dare not forget that this sermon is delivered in the form of the "historical account" *(Historia)* of Christ.[7]

For whatever may hold true of God's "Word" as having the character of revelation, and whatever may hold true of promise and faith — these concepts are and remain empty categories if, so far as content is concerned, they are not saturated with references to Christ. It is impossible to understand Luther's whole discussion with Erasmus unless the strictly Christocentric character of his theology is recognized. "Whatever is not Christ," he said in that discussion, "that is not a way, but error; not a truth, but a lie; not life, but death" *(Quicquid non est Christus, id neque via, sed error, neque veritas, sed mendacium, neque vita, sed mors est* (WA 18, 779, 12). In the Large Catechism: "We could never come to the point of realizing the Father's kindness and mercy except through the Lord Christ, who is a mirror of His Father's heart, without whom we see nothing but an angry and fearful Judge" (WA 30 I, 192, 4).

[7] Obviously the same thing holds true when Luther says that the Gospel teaches the grace of God. WA 8, 105, 39. — For the complete agreement of earliest Lutheranism with what Luther says about the nature of the Gospel, above all, with his equating of the story of Christ and the promise, as well as with the correlation of promise and faith, cf., e. g., Melanchthon, *Loci* of 1521, *CR* 21, 140, 16 ff. — Andreas Althamer's Catechism, 1528, reprinted in Kolde, *A. Althamer*, p. 98: "What, then, is the Gospel? Answer: It is a power of God that serves those who believe in it. It promises us a merciful God, proclaims to us forgiveness of sins and everlasting life in Christ the Lord. Question: But does the Gospel make pious and save? Answer: Yes, it promises us all the good things of God. That Christ is our own, died for our sins, and rose again for our righteousness. If we have Christ, we have forgiveness of sins, righteousness, and everlasting blessing. Question: How does God's righteousness become ours? Answer: Through the Gospel and the Sacraments of Baptism and the Body and Blood of Christ; for here this is offered and given to us, provided that we believe." — *Gutachten des Georg Amerbacher zu Blaufelden, Fränk. Bek.*, pp. 489 ff.; p. 490, about Christ: ". . . yes, He Himself is the true Gospel for us." — *Ratschlag der Geistlichkeit von Culmbach von 1530,* in Gussmann, *Quellen* I, 2: "Then God's promise and faith are related as follows: Where the promise is, there faith must also be." Cf. Luther, *Lectures on Romans,* I, 40, 24: "Faith and the promise are relative" *(Fides et promissio sunt relativa).* — Urban Rhegius, *Loci Theologici, Francof.*, 1545, 67: "The Gospel is the announcement of grace through Christ, who was promised and has already been shown. It is the good and pleasing Word that announces grace and the forgiveness of sins through Christ, or it is the message that Christ rendered satisfaction for us on the cross and saved the people from sins: He who will give the price, and if we have suffered with Him, we are His kinsmen." *(Evangelium annunciatio gratiae per Christum promissum et iam exhibitum. Est verbum bonum et suave, Dei gratiam et peccatorum remissionem per Christum annuncians, vel est nuncium quod Christus in cruce pro nobis satisfecerit et salvarit populum a peccatis: qui dabit mercedem et si compassi cum eo, cognaturi sumus.)*

In the Smalcald Articles the article with which the church stands and falls is based on this, that "no other name has been given to men" (WA 50, 199, 22). And conversely: "Where there is no faith or no knowledge of Christ, there both doubt and despondency must follow" (WA 46, 27, 39). "For in the Person of Christ there is everything, and without the Son everything is lost. Therefore it is no small matter that without the Son we should seek nothing and will find nothing either in heaven or on earth; for then all is lost" (WA 47, 59, 22). If the aging Luther remained faithful to any point of the theological program of his youth, it was the statement made at the Heidelberg Disputation of 1518: "Therefore in Christ crucified there is the true theology and knowledge of God" *(Ergo in Christo crucifixo est vera theologia et cognitio Dei)* (WA 1, 326, 18).[8] Here, too, one finds the all-decisive connection of the later confessions with Luther. The Augsburg Confession explains the lamentable character of scholastic theology by saying that by it the pious are prevented from coming to the right knowledge of Christ (XXVI, 16, German). Again and again the Apology objects to the doctrine of salvation as taught by the opponents; it points to the words "Nothing without Christ" *(Nihil sine Christo)* (III, 145–149). The Formula of Concord appropriates Luther's statement that "without Christ death and sin are lords over us" *(SD* II, 43). Even though in the writings of the dogmaticians of a later period the Christocentric character of all evangelical knowledge is obscured by their method, the contemporaneous preaching of the church, its prayers and hymns, prove at every turn that in the Lutheran Church it was not lost. It is the last tie that binds pietism with the Reformation. From the "awakening" *(Erweckung)* of the nineteenth century it leads back to the theology of the Reformation.

3. It is only this assumption that enables one to understand what Luther and early Lutheranism mean by faith. The story of Christ would indeed remain mute for us if it were not proclaimed. Where the Gospel "is not proclaimed, there Christ is not present" (WA 10 I, 2, 154, 14). But this does not mean reducing the story of Christ to one Word of Christ *(Christuswort)* or one idea of Christ *(Christusidee)*. It is not necessary to preach Christ merely to prevent information about Him from being lost to men. "The Gospel must not only be written; on the contrary, it must be proclaimed with the physical voice" *(mit leyplicher stym)* (WA 8, 33, 31). And furthermore, the hearer is "accosted" *(gestellt)* in the most direct manner by means of the spoken word, that is, as a hearer he cannot doubt that he, too, is meant. He who reads the Gospel can get the mistaken notion that the story of Christ deals only

[8] Cf. *Lectures on Hebrews,* 127, 7 ff.

with a historical event which he commits to memory just as he memorizes other events, without applying it to himself. On the other hand, the hearer who is really a hearer hears the Gospel as meant for him. "For to preach the Gospel is nothing else than Christ's coming to us or bringing us to Him" (WA 10 I, 1, 14, 22; cf. *Holy Scripture*).

In this way the first constitutive definition of faith is attained. "Let us learn only this word 'Me,' 'for me,' that we may be able in sure faith to comprehend and not to doubt: 'for me' " *(Discamus tantum hoc verbum "Me," "pro me," ut possimus certa fide concipere et non dubitare: "pro me")* (WA 40 I, 299, 9). The offer and the promise mean: The story of Christ applies to *you*. Faith is the certainty that this applies to *me*. The sophists are in error when they make Christ a private person, that is, teach about Him as if He did not concern them (448, 3). The godless and the demons believe that Christ died only for other saints. But the Christian is *certain* that Christ is for *him*.[9] He who does not believe this is not a Christian.[10] This is why Luther always puts such "strong emphasis" *(magna emphasis)* on the words *pro me, pro nobis*.[11] For this reason the Small Catechism points to the "for you" as the purpose of the Sacrament. And the word "our" should be referred to everything proclaimed about Christ.[12]

The "salvation egoism" *(Heilsegoismus)* often cast into the teeth of Lutheranism is, therefore, accounted for in the essence of evangelical faith. Consequently, the reproach must be borne. It depends on how the concept "salvation" *(salus)*, which Luther, in the Western tradition, uses in common with Paul, is to be understood. The thought of the "enjoyment of God" *(fruitio Dei)* — the thought ascribed to Luther in the writings of the dogmaticians of a later period — is just as foreign to him

9 WA 2, 458, 20 ff. L. 30: "Beware of being uncertain at any time, but be certain that in yourself you are lost. It is necessary, however, to work that you be certain and firm in faith in Christ, who was delivered for your sins." *(Cave tu, ne aliquando sis incertus, sed certus, quod in teipso perditus: laborandum autem, ut certus et solidus sis in fide Christi pro peccatis tuis traditi.)*

10 WA 31 II, 432, 17: "These words should be written in letters of gold: Ours, Us, For Us. He who does not believe these words is not a Christian." *(Aureis literis haec verba sunt scribenda Nostrum, Nos, Nobis. Qui haec non credit, non est Christianus.)*

11 WA 40 I, 448, 14; 295 ff.; *Lectures on Hebrews*, 168, 13; WA 16, 428, 8 f.; WA 19, 149, 17 ff.; WA 34 II, 219, 11; 498, 3; 509, 1 ff.; WA 37, 236, 30 ff.; WA 31 II, 434, 21.

12 WA 34 II, 509, 4: "Refer that word 'ours' to all things in faith, not only to Jesus Christ but to the fact that He was conceived, was born, and died *for us*, and sits *for us*, our future Judge" *(Istud vocabulum "nostrum" ziehe ad omnes stuck in fide, non solum auff Jesum Christum, sed nobis conceptus, natus, mortuus, sedens nobis, uns zukunfftig richter)*.

as Zinzendorf's "special covenant with the Savior" *(Spezialbund mit dem Heilande)*.[13] What speaks against this in the writings of Luther, however, is not his emphasis on the "sovereign majesty of God" *(Herrenmajestät Gottes)* or what many understand when they use this term. For this majesty is revealed in the Law, not in the Gospel. In Luther the "salvation egoism" *(Heilsegoismus)* has as its presupposition and its reverse the thought of God's transsubjective legal order (cf. *Luther on Justification*). Without application to the I there can be no evangelical faith. In Luther, to be sure, the I which makes that application to me is used, as is yet to be shown, purely for the sake of making a special point; that is to say, it is transcendental. But it refers to the concrete I of the whole person. How else would it be possible to overcome anxiety and despair that also take possession of the whole man? It is certain that "distress and anxiety . . . preserve us well in Christianity" *(Not und angst . . . behellt uns fein ym Christentum)* (WA 31 I, 95, 14). Yet they cause one "to be all the more eager for joy. He sees to it that His promise makes their joy perfect, that it overcomes and forgets all anxiety, sorrow, and affliction" (WA 46, 91, 8). Joy in Christ, in His incarnation, resurrection, and ascension is the real joy. At any rate, it is the greatest joy "man's heart can experience" (WA 21, 293, 12; 476, 12; WA 36, 396, 5). And this joy, like every other joy, has an egoistical motive. "For how else could we rejoice in Him if we had or could receive as our own nothing of what He has done?" (WA 21, 293, 26.) Yes, Luther does not hesitate to characterize joy as the real motive of ethical behavior.[14] Just as Lutheranism cannot forget the past tense used

[13] Quenstedt, *Theol. did. pol.* I, 250. — J. Fr. Buddeus, *Institutiones*, p. 144. — Baier, *Comp.* I, 6, par. 6. Baier also speaks of the "enjoyment of Christ's satisfaction" *(fruitio satisfactionis Christi)* (ibid. III, 1, par. 7).

[14] WA 36, 394 ff.: "He shall be your Helper, Christ, Savior . . . on account of this joy I shall rejoice from now on and do whatever I should, solely on account of joy, because He does not preach the righteousness of the Commandments but preaches pure joy. He who believes this without doubting, that the Father gave His Son and gave a mother, that she should cherish Him for your good, he, He says, who believes does not need the Law and Moses, but the joy alone will make him pious and will cause him to do and suffer everything with the greatest gladness, because He says: 'Born for us as the Savior.' This should be my comfort. Where there is faith in the heart, such joy and betterment of one's whole life follow." *(Is soll dein Helfer, Christus, Heyland sein . . . propter hoc gaudium wil ich mich fortan freuen et facere quicquid debeo, solum propter gaudium, quia non praedicat justiciam praeceptorum, sed merum gaudium. Qui hoc credit sine dubio, quod pater geschenkt filium et matrem dedit, ut foveret dir zu gut, qui, inquit, credit, Non indiget lege et Mose, sed die einige freud wird yhn from machen, et ut omnia faciat et patiatur libentissime, quia dicit: Nobis natus salvator, des sol ich mich trosten. Ubi est fides in corde, sequitur tale gaudium und besserung totius vitae.)*

by Luther when he said: "Anxiety drove me to despair" *(Die Angst mich zu verzweifeln trieb)*, so it will not let anyone tear out of its heart the jubilant present tense: "Dear Christians one and all, rejoice" *(Nun freut euch lieben Christen gmein)*. "It serves to give me joy" *(Es dient zu meinen Freuden)*, sings Paul Gerhardt even of the Passion. He who is no longer deeply sensible of the joy in Luther's Christmas hymns, of the jubilation in our Easter hymns, of Paul Gerhardt's "God for us" and "Christ for me," should examine himself to see whether his theology is not more closely related to the Koran than to the Gospel.

The I reference *(Ichbeziehung)* of faith, however, is altogether different from man's contemplation of himself. Its content is totally different from man himself; it is Christ. Furthermore, it has already been established that faith is not an autogenous judgment of man but the receiving of the divine judgment, and that it puts itself in opposition to all the "natural" possessions of man. But what brings about opposition to these, that is, to everything man carries about in himself because of intellect and experience? In any case, it would be unnecessary and wrong to find opposition here if faith were founded only on the existence of God. It is true that in a compilation of the year 1523 – a compilation ascribed to Luther – one finds the statement: "The whole foundation of faith is contained in the one little sentence 'There is a God.'" But Luther could not have written this statement.[15] Neither faith, the only important thing, nor the "foundation of faith" is defined in his writings in such a way. This faith "is more a science or an observation than a faith" *(ist mehr ein wissenschaft oder merckung dan ein glaub)* (WA 7, 215, 4). I have the other, genuine faith "when I not only believe that what is said about God is true but place my trust in Him, go to Him with courage to negotiate with Him *(begeb und erwege mich mit yhm zu handeln)*, and believe without any doubt that He will be to me and do to me as is said about Him. . . . Such faith – a faith that stakes everything on God, as is stated about it, whether it be in life or in death – such faith alone makes one a Christian and gets from God everything it wants" (ibid.).

Faith is a venture because it puts itself in opposition to everything else man knows or has. But it would be no less foolish than the statement of the aforementioned compiler if Luther had said that faith is

[15] WA 11, 469, 23. How foreign this statement must have been to Luther becomes especially clear when one adds the preceding statements, which the compiler borrowed from Luther's exposition of the *Magnificat* (WA 7, 574, 18 ff.). The Erlangen edition still regarded the writing as genuine (EA 22, 140 ff.). Concerning the spuriousness cf. WA 11, 462 f.

a venture solely because its content is "invisible" and thus had seen the opposition only in the fact that together with him it enters a domain which, unlike other domains, he cannot test by means of his senses. God's Law and His wrath are also "invisible." To be sure, Luther often defines faith according to Heb. 11:1. But it is significant that he puts the contrast "visible-invisible" on a par with the contrast "hidden-revealed."[16] When considering the primal experience *(Urerlebnis)* we encountered the concept of concealment: the God who has imposed on man the terrible lot of the "Thou shalt" and the inability to obey is the "hidden God" *(Deus absconditus)*. It is the God of wrath and absolute predestination whom causal thinking encounters in connection with our experience or with ethical thinking. But the reverse of this cannot be gained from a purely objective concept of revelation. For, in the first place, to that immanent substantiation on the basis of reason and experience there is added the confirmation or the heightening of the same impression by means of the "revelation" of the divine wrath in the Law. God remains the "hidden God" *(Deus absconditus)* in spite of this "revelation." Secondly, however, one must call attention here also to the dialectical procedure which Luther expresses in the formula: Everything God does is contrary to reason *(alles widdersynnisch, was Gott machet)*. The primal experience *(Urerlebnis)* is not only the opposite of what God wants to achieve. It is at the same time a means of achieving this. It is His purpose to achieve faith and what faith receives: forgiveness of sins, life, and salvation. These possessions are to be received from Him. For this reason there is need of faith, and for this reason man must come into the state in which the primal experience *(Urerlebnis)* finds him. But if this is a necessary means to the accomplishment of the divine purpose, its individual components are in opposition to this purpose only when man is unable to recognize in it God's purpose to save, or as long as man is unable to do so. Faith, on the other hand, is the settling of the differences *(die Mediation der Gegensätze)*. Faith experiences that

[16] WA 18, 633, 7: ". . . faith is concerned with things not seen. In order, therefore, that there may be room for faith, it is necessary that all things that are believed be hidden. But they are not hidden farther away than under the opposite object, perception, experience. Thus when God makes alive, He does so by slaying; when He justifies, He does so by pronouncing guilty; when He takes to heaven, He does so by leading to hell." *(. . . fides est rerum non apparentium. Ut ergo fidei locus sit, opus est, ut omnia quae creduntur, abscondantur. Non autem remotius absconduntur, quam sub contrario objectu, sensu, experientia. Sic Deus dum vivificat, facit illud occidendo; dum justificat, facit illud reos faciendo; dum in coelum vehit, facit id ad infernum ducendo.)* — Statements similar in meaning are to be found in *Lectures on Romans* I, 43, 22 ff.; II, 13, 28; 76, 17; *Lectures on Hebrews*, 234, 14; 235, 2.

God makes alive by putting to death, that He reveals Himself even though He conceals Himself.[17]

Accordingly, faith is indeed always faith contrary to appearance. But what is apparent – contrary to what must be believed – is not the natural experience per se; it is the wrath of God, which is "revealed" in it. The venture of faith consists in this, that one appears before God, yes, throws oneself into His arms with the confidence that under this "revelation" He is concealing Himself as Someone entirely different. "If one thinks that our Lord has cast a person aside, one should believe that our Lord God has him in His arms and embraces him" *(hab jn in den armen und hertze ihn)* (WA 44, 111, 32).

The aforementioned Christocentric definition of the Gospel is most closely connected with this. The Gospel accomplishes its task – so it was established – only by pointing to Christ. Christ is the content of the revelation with which faith, as faith, is concerned. In Christ, God steps out of His concealment – He becomes the "incarnate God, or, as Paul says, Jesus crucified" *(Deus incarnatus, seu, ut Paulus loquitur, Jhesus crucifixus)* (WA 18, 689, 23), or, what amounts to the same thing, the "proclaimed God" *(Deus praedicatus)*, who does not desire the sinner's death. "For the proclaimed God does this in order that after sin and death have been taken away, we may be saved" *(Hoc enim agit Deus praedicatus, ut ablato peccato et morte salvi simus)* (685, 19). The "incarnate God" *(Deus incarnatus)* is the "revealed God" *(Deus revelatus)* (WA 43, 459, 25). Here for the first time it becomes perfectly clear that and why faith in the most profound sense is contrary to appearance. Every appearance contradicts the fact that "in Him God shows and offers you His mercy" (WA 6, 216, 26). For Christ is a human being

[17] WA 18, 633, 14: "Thus He hides His everlasting clemency and mercy under everlasting wrath, His righteousness under unrighteousness. This is the highest stage of faith, to believe that He who saves so few and damns so many is kind; to believe that He who by His own will necessarily makes us damnable is just, so that it seems, as Erasmus alleges, that He is delighted by the torments of wretched persons and is worthy of hatred rather than of love. Therefore if I could in any way understand how this God who shows such great wrath and unrighteousness is merciful and just, there would be no need of faith. Now since this cannot be understood, there is room for the exercise of faith when such things are preached and published, just as faith in life is exercised in death when God slays." *(Sic aeternam suam clementiam et misericordiam abscondit sub aeterna ira, justitiam sub iniquitate. Hic est fidei summus gradus, credere illum esse clementem, qui tam paucos salvat, tam multos damnat, credere justum, qui sua voluntate nos necessario damnabiles facit, ut videatur, referente Erasmo, delectari cruciatibus miserorum et odio potius quam amore dignus. Si igitur possem ulla ratione comprehendere, quomodo is Deus sit misericors et justus, qui tantam iram et iniquitatem ostendit, non esset opus fide. Nunc cum id comprehendi non potest, fit locus exercendae fidei, dum talia praedicantur et invulgantur, non aliter, quam dum Deus occidit, fides vitae in morte exercetur.)*

just as we are. He is under the Law. He experiences God's wrath and dies. That in spite of this He is the "revealed God" *(Deus revelatus)* faith can acknowledge only by adding the "for me" *(pro me)* mentioned before. For only then is the act of God's wrath – the act that takes place on the cross – at the same time a revelation of His mercy. Therefore faith gets its last strength precisely from the act of Christ's deepest humiliation. It must "have its source and flow from the blood, the wounds, and the death of Christ" (ibid., 1. 30).[18] And this is why Luther called his theology a "theology of the cross" *(theologia crucis).* For it lives on the revelation of God, "who is nearest when He is farthest away," who "does everything contrary to reason" *(alles widdersynnisch machet).*

7. Luther on Justification

Luther finds the change brought about by the Gospel definitively expressed in the Pauline concept of justification (Enders 7, 348, 19). It is in this concept that the final opposition to the medieval church is developed. As Martin Chemnitz showed in his critique of the Trent dogma, this concept made it impossible to bridge the opposition. In our earliest confessions it is the nucleus; in the later ones it is the central point; in the most recent ones it is the assumption that can no longer be called in question. To be sure, Troeltsch wanted to count the doctrine of justification as set forth by the Reformation among those elements of Protestantism that give proof of a closer connection with ancient and medieval theology than with modern "culture."[1] This doctrine, he said, is merely a new attempt to solve a problem presented by the theology that is specifically medieval in character. The element of truth contained in this statement is obvious, and it is equally obvious that the statement has its sources in the Enlightenment. Actually there are very close recessive connections with the history of dogma. Even the fact that the questions asked have something in common is not the only evidence of these connections.

All the terminology used in this connection is "medieval." Above all, the doctrine of justification as set forth by the Reformation as well as the same doctrine as set forth from Augustine to Luther makes use of

[18] *Lectures on Hebrews*, p. 102, 30: "The humanity [of Christ] is that sacred ladder of ours by means of which we ascend to the knowledge of God" *(Humanitas [Christi] enim illa sancta scala est nostra, per quam ascendimus ad deum agnoscendum).* Cf. *Lectures on Romans* II, 10, 18, and Enders I, 42, 5 f.: "salvation and peace . . . hidden under the cross" *(salutem et pacem . . . sub cruce absconditam).*

[1] Ernst Troeltsch, *Die Bedeutung des Protestantismus für die Entstehung der modernen Welt,* 3d ed. as the twenty-fourth volume of the *Historische Bibliothek,* 1911. Cf. R. H. Grützmacher, *Alt- und Neuprotestantismus,* 1920. — H. Rückert, *Die Rechtfertigungslehre auf dem Tridentinischen Konzil,* 1925.

a manner of expression which, on the whole, is "juridical." But the attempts made long ago by Troeltsch to replace this way of speaking with a "purely religious" or a "religious-ethical" terminology cannot succeed unless there is a fundamental break – in any case with the theology of Luther. Luther's thinking is by no means less "juridical" than Melanchthon's. If the doctrine of justification as set forth by both men has characteristics that are specifically Western, this is because Western theology grasped Paul's teaching more correctly and more profoundly than its Greek sister did. In the history of theology Paul's Epistle to the Galatians has found no better interpretation than in Luther's commentaries on this book – even in the commentary dating from 1519.

It is self-evident that the concept of the Law – the concept that has decisive significance here, just as it has in Paul – can never be divested of its "juridical" character. This Law has its origin in a giving of the Law. It is an objective norm that obligates unconditionally every individual in its sphere. Its violation engenders guilt and carries with it judicial condemnation and great *(fühlbar)* punishment. It is true that the sphere of the Gospel is in sharp opposition to the validity of the Law. But it is precisely this contrast between the two that Luther makes clear by means of a concept taken from the sphere of the Law – the concept of fulfillment.[2] In nearly every place in which he speaks here about the significance of Christ for salvation he includes, as a necessary element, the fact that Christ fulfilled the Law (WA 2, 466, 14; 497, 28 ff.; 523, 10; 529, 30; 563, 35, etc.). It is certainly true that for him who is justified "all laws cease" *(cessant omnes leges)*, but only because the laws have been fulfilled (490, 32 f.). Self-evidently Luther appropriates Paul's conception that it is not the Law but trust in the works done in accordance with the Law that is rejected by the Gospel (491, 35). Christ is the end of the Law and of its works, in order that faith may seek salvation only in Christ (477, 33). But it is precisely faith in Him who fulfilled the Law that can have validity as fulfillment of the Law (492, 17 ff.; 563, 35). Therefore the concept of the Law can be dispensed with neither in an exhaustive presentation of Christ's saving work nor in a presentation of faith. The situation is no different with regard to other

[2] WA 2, 466, 3 ff.: "The Gospel and the Law differ properly in this respect, that the Law proclaims things that must be done and left undone, yes, that things that have already been done and things that have been left undone and are impossible are done and are left undone — therefore it provides only the knowledge of sin — but the Gospel proclaims that sins have been forgiven and that everything has been fulfilled and done" *(Evangelium et lex proprie in hoc differunt, quod lex praedicat facienda et omittenda, immo iam commissa et omissa ac impossibilia fieri et omitti — ideo solam peccati ministrat cognitionem — Evangelium autem remissa peccata et omnia impleta factaque).*

concepts belonging in the sphere of the Law. "Grace takes away guilt; peace takes away punishment" *(Gratia culpam, pax poenam aufert)* (456, 35). Christ took upon Himself the punishments the Law fixed for sins (534, 36). And since everything that is true of Christ can also be said of those who believe in Him (531, 10), it is likewise true of those who have faith in Christ that "He rendered satisfaction for all" *(Satisfecit omnibus)* (504, 8).[3] Naturally, in Luther, as in Paul, the concept of sin as "transgression of the Law" cannot be treated exhaustively (cf. *Sin*), but neither can this element be dispensed with. Then, however, one is forced to recognize the legal element not only in the concepts "slavery" and "damnation" *(servitus, damnatio)* but also in the other concepts: "just," "justify," "impute" *(justus, justificare, imputare)*. By imparting His righteousness to His body, the church, Christ, the Head, "also renders His body obedient" *(corpus quoque suum reddit obediens)* (497, 32). "He who is free from sin has become the servant of righteousness" *(Qui liber est a peccato, servus factus justiciae)*, and vice versa (560, 5). And, to quote right here the salient statement of Luther's doctrine of justification: "To those who believe in the name of the Lord all sins are forgiven, and righteousness is imputed to them" *(Credentibus in nomine domini donantur omnia peccata et justicia eis imputatur)* (490, 25).

This whole terminology certainly includes altogether different elements that make *this* Law and *this* righteousness basically distinct from all secular parallels. But this cannot mislead one into ignoring the legal element or considering it dispensable. In this terminology there is the acknowledgment of something unconditionally valid. Otherwise the fear of God in the stage of the primal experience *(Urerlebnis)* would become mere fear of demons. But in the sphere of the Gospel the I relationship *(Ichbezogenheit)* of faith (cf. *Preliminary Questions*) would become mere ultilitarianism. Ever since the Enlightenment the legal elements of the Pauline doctrine of salvation were regarded as specifically Jewish conceptions which, as such, were antiquated.[4] But when the connection between the Old and the New Testament was severed — the connection that is essential precisely with reference to this point [5] — the Enlightenment also lost the proper way of looking at the disparity between God and man. It ended exactly in the kind of religion it wanted to get rid of, namely, in purely Jewish moralism. To be sure, the "moral

[3] Cf. *Lectures on Romans* I, 62, 17.

[4] Jos. Fr. Chr. Löffler, *Kleine Schriften*, I, 1817, p. XXVIII.

[5] O. Procksch, *Die hebräische Wurzel der Theologie, Christentum und Wissenschaft*, 1926, pp. 405 ff. and 451 ff.

law" *(Sittengesetz)* of German idealism, from which Troeltsch and his predecessors took sustenance, also demands unconditional validity. But since it was based on the autonomy of practical reason, man appeared here not only as his own lawgiver but also as his own judge. Consequently, here, just as in the Enlightenment, the realization of the "state of guilt and punishment" *(reatus culpae et poenae)*, as early dogmatics enunciated in accordance with Luther, was lost.[6] At the same time, however, the concept of the forgiveness of sins, which, as is logical, presupposes the idea of a breaking of the Law, was also lost.

The connection of the Lutheran doctrine of justification with all pre-Reformation theology extends by no means only to the terminology. Luther's stormy polemic turns against every form of "merit" *(meritum)* that scholastic theology – especially since Duns Scotus – ascribes to man. No "merit" *(meritum)* precedes the receiving of justification. There is no "merit" *(meritum)* that man acquires later. Nevertheless, it is wrong to try to illustrate the contrast by pointing to the extent of the operation of divine grace. Thomistic theology, too, had taught that without divine grace man cannot merit eternal life either in the state of purity or in the state of corruption. In this connection Thomas himself had inculcated the teaching that God alone brings this about *(die Alleinwirksamkeit Gottes)*. Yes, from Lombard on all were agreed in this, that the new man – the ethical, eternal man – owes the inner change to grace alone. When they spoke about "created grace" *(gratia creata)*, "infused grace" *(gratia infusa)*, "grace that makes acceptable" *(gratia gratum faciens)*, and the "infused disposition" *(habitus infusus)* – but also about "grace given for nothing" *(gratia gratis data)* – were they really struggling to arrive at an understanding of the same change that Luther meant by the doctrine of justification?[7] Nor can the belief that the imparting of grace depends on the sacraments be the actual point of divergence, as Troeltsch, in a spirit of friendliness, wanted to concede to Luther. For even Luther did not contest the significance of Baptism and absolution for the pardon of the sinner. Where, then, is the antithesis?

Luther said that his reformatory *(reformatorisch)* knowledge began when the knowledge of the "righteousness of God" *(justitia Dei)* was revealed to him from Rom. 1:17. He believed that together with the sudden change of his understanding of this concept he experienced a new

[6] With regard to the expression cf. WA 25, 329, 18.

[7] Cf. R. Seeberg, *Lehrbuch d. Dogmengesch.* III, 2d and 3d ed., pp. 402 ff., 438 ff., and P. Minges, *Die Gnadenlehre des Duns Scotus auf ihren angeblichen Pelagianismus und Semipelagianismus geprüft,* 1906.

birth and eternal life.[8] Because he had learned to know the "righteousness of God" *(justitia Dei)* merely as an attribute of God "by virtue of which God is righteous and punishes sinners and the unrighteous" *(qua Deus est justus et peccatores iniustosque punit)* (WA 54, 185, 24), he hated God; that the Gospel – which, according to Rom. 1:17, revealed this righteousness just as His wrath is revealed according to Rom. 1:18 – appeared as a worsening of the Law. But then it had become clear to him from the second half of Rom. 1:17 that here Paul is speaking about the righteousness "by which, as a gift of God, the righteous man lives, namely, by faith, and that this means that the righteousness of God is revealed through the Gospel, namely, a passive righteousness, by virtue of which a merciful God justifies us through faith, as is written: 'The righteous man lives by faith' " *(qua justus dono Dei vivit, nempe ex fide, et esse hanc sententiam, revelari per evangelium justitiam Dei, scilicet passivam, qua nos Deus misericors justificat per fidem, sicut scriptum est: Justus ex fide vivit)* (186, 5). Whatever may be true of the gradual development of Luther's doctrine of justification, for him himself, as he looked back at it, the decisive turning point consisted in the knowledge of the "passive righteousness of God" *(justitia Dei passiva);* and when he used this expression, he meant the righteousness given to man "as a gift of God" *(dono Dei).* Otherwise the direct connection of "the righteous man [lives by faith]" *(justus [ex fide vivit])* with the "righteousness of God" *(justitia Dei)* is just as incomprehensible in his writings as

[8] In the well-known passage in the preface to the first volume of the complete edition of his Latin writings (Wittenberg, 1545) Luther says: "Here I realized that I had been truly reborn and had entered Paradise itself through open doors" *(Hic me prorsus renatum esse sensi et apertis portis in ipsum paradisum intrasse)* (WA 54, 186, 8). — Cf. E. Starcke, *Luthers grosses Selbstzeugnis,* 1545, *Schr. VRG,* 140, 1926.

I must call attention once more, by the way, to the fact that this book has refrained on principle from presenting an account of Luther's early development. — From the vast literature dealing with Luther's doctrine of justification I mention Fr. Loofs, *Justitia Dei passiva, ThStKr,* 1911, pp. 461 ff., and *Der articulus stantis et cadentis ecclesiae,* ibid., 1917, pp. 366 ff. — O. Scheel, *Die justitia Dei passiva in L.s reformator. Rechtfertigungslehre, Festschr. f. Th. Brieger,* 1912, pp. 93 ff. — E. Hirsch, *Initium theologiae Lutheri, Festgabe f. Jul. Kaftan,* 1918, pp. 150 ff. — K. Holl, *Die Rechtfertigungslehre in Luthers Vorlesung über d. Römerbr., Ges. Aufs.* I, 4th and 5th ed., 1927, pp. 111 ff. — Cf. the discussion between Holl and Wilhelm Walther, *NKZ,* 1923, pp. 50 ff., 185 ff., 668 ff.; 1924, 47 f., 351 ff. Fr. Gogarten, *Chr. W.,* 1924, No. 3 ff. H. Hermelink, ibid., 1924, No. 7 f. Karl Thieme, *ZThK,* 1925, pp. 351 ff. — Hardeland, *D. Begriff d. justitia Dei passiva bei Luther, Christent. und Wissensch.,* 1926, pp. 61 ff., 110 ff., 146 ff. — H. Mich. Müller, *Theol. Blätter,* 1927, No. 10 — G. Merz, *D. junge Luther u. d. Rechtfertigungsglaube,* ZZ, 1926, pp. 404 ff. — Heinr. Lang, *Die Bedeutung Christi f. d. Rechtfertigung in Luthers Römerbriefvorlesung. NKZ,* 1928, pp. 509 ff. — Hans Joach. Iwand, *Rechtfertigungslehre und Christusglaube, z. Systematik d. Rechtfertigungslehre Luthers in ihren Anfängen,* 1930.

it is in Paul. Thus in any case he also understands the concept in his second commentary on Galatians (1531), where he concerns himself most extensively with this subject.[9]

If it is the receiving of the "righteousness of God" *(justitia Dei)* that constitutes the essence of justification, then the fact that when justification takes place man conducts himself in a purely passive manner must be considered the first characteristic of justification. Yet when Luther explains this by saying that the receiving of justification presupposes or includes that we "let someone else, namely, God, work in us," it seems that there is still a bridge to the scholastic doctrine of "grace that makes acceptable" *(gratia gratum faciens)* – likewise to what the German mystics taught about "imperturbability" *(Gelassenheit)*. For to Luther the new righteousness is identical with "grace" *(gratia)* (WA 3, 47, 11; WA 5, 144, 5; WA 2, 504, 26). It would be conceivable, of course, that the "gift of God" *(donum Dei)* of which he speaks is identical in meaning with what the scholastics call the "gift added to nature" *(donum superadditum naturae)*, "the gift that consists in the conferring of a disposition" *(donum habituale)*: a supernatural influence of the divine Spirit on man's psyche – a gift that gives the psyche a God-pleasing content of strength, of thoughts, and of impulses of the will. Actually, Luther, too, still speaks of an infusing and an inflow of "grace" *(gratia)* after using the new concept of "righteousness" *(justitia)* (e. g., *Lectures on Romans*, II, 59, 18; WA 3, 31, 21; WA 2, 145, 9 ff., etc.). But in his writings this means nothing else than that God works faith in man, who receives grace. For later he rejects sharply the view that "grace" *(gratia)* is a "quality of the psyche" *(qualitas animi)*.[10] Neither is faith "an idle quality in the heart" *(aliqua otiosa qualitas in corde)* (WA 40 I, 228, 3 to 230, 13) that does not bring about "righteousness" *(justitia)* until it is "faith fashioned by love" *(fides charitate formata)*. If one adds that Luther, in order to refute this doctrine, quotes the statement: "Faith

[9] WA 40 I, 41, 3: "The Christian righteousness is the very opposite [namely, in contrast with the righteousness that comes from us]; it is passive, we merely receive it; here we do nothing, but we let Another, namely, God, work in us" *(Christiana judicia est mere contraria, passiva, quam tantum recipimus, ubi nihil operamur sed patimur alium operari in nobis scilicet deum)*. — Cf. WA 1, 703, 34 ff. (WA 9, 195, 30 ff.).

[10] WA 8, 106, 11; cf. WA 5, 33, 7; WA 6, 202, 25; WA 40 II, 353, 3: "You are righteous by reason of mercy and compassion. This is not my disposition or a quality of my heart, but it is something from without, namely, divine mercy, because we know that our sin has been forgiven and because we live in His many great deeds of mercy and compassion." *(Misericordia et miseratione es justus. Das ist nicht meus habitus vel qualitas cordis mei, sed extrinsecum quoddam, scilicet misericordia divina, quod scimus peccatum nostrum remissum et quod vivimus in suis misericordiis et miserationibus multis et magnis.)*

is a certain knowledge that sees nothing" *(Fides est quaedam cognitio, quae nihil videt)* (228, 15) and that he also identifies "faith" *(fides)* with "righteousness" *(justitia)* *(Lectures on Hebrews,* 202, 5), one is confronted by the decisive divergence vis-à-vis medieval theology.

Faith is not a "quality" *(qualitas)* and righteousness is not a "disposition" *(habitus)* of the heart or of the soul. In fact, faith, righteousness, and grace cannot be described in terms of human psychology *(lassen sich vom Bestand des menschlichen Seelentums überhaupt nicht qualifizieren).* Righteousness is the "righteousness of God" *(justitia Dei)* in the strict sense. As will be shown later, it is imparted to man through imputation. When this takes place, God is the one and only subject. But can one say the same thing of faith? Just as God is the only subject of grace, so man is the only subject of faith. If, in spite of this, faith – at least so far as its essence is concerned – cannot be described psychologically *(psychologisch nicht qualifizierbar),* then in Luther's sense only the transcendental I of man can be its subject – the I that remains after the abstraction of the entire content of consciousness and yet only then makes it possible to define this consciousness as consciousness of itself. *Here Luther smashes through the sum total of medieval anthropology and with his doctrine of justification creates the assumption of later critical philosophy.* Therefore his doctrine of justification is not a mere variation of the medieval doctrine; it ushers in a new epoch.

In a way the German mystics were Luther's forerunners in this regard. Their demands that man, in order to find the way to God, must "free himself from the creatures" *(entledigen von den creaturen);* that he must be apart from "all creatures, all comfort from the creatures"; that his will must be "without any attribute" *(on alle Eigenschaft);* that man must become "nothing" – these demands seem to be technical directions for reducing consciousness to the same transcendental I of man.[11] Man should learn to abstract from the images of the external world, from observation and imagination; he should eliminate concrete objectivity from his will, in order to come to the point "where the created nothing sinks into the uncreated nothing" *(do versinket daz geschaffen nit in das ungeschaffen nit)* (Tauler). Furthermore, the German mystics, exactly like Luther, carry on polemics against the saving power of outward virtues and good works.[12] Moreover, in this connection one can

[11] Quoted according to the editions in Lietzmann's *Kleine Texte. Der Franckforter (Ein deutsch Theologia),* p. 8, 5; Meister Eckhart, *Buch d. göttl. Tröstung,* p. 18, 26; *Reden d. Unterscheidung,* p. 16, 10; and *Ausgewählte Predigten Taulers,* p. 40, 24 ff.

[12] *Der Franckforter,* p. 14, 6; 32, 10. — M. Eckhart, *Reden d. Unterscheidung,* p. 24, 35.

totally disregard the analogies in the positive reasons for the ethos. One should not overlook the fact that here Luther and the mystics have something in common so far as the general philosophy of life is concerned, especially since Luther himself admits that, next to the Bible and Augustine, he learned more from "German theology" than he learned from any other book "what God, Christ, man, and all things are" *(was got, Christus, mensch und alle ding seyn)* (WA 1, 378, 23).

Nevertheless, here, too – and precisely here – Luther is in sharp opposition to the mysticism of the Middle Ages. According to the mystics, the reduction to the transcendental innermost part of man comes about by means of a technique of thinking. Here the ethical element is the renunciation of everything external, of the world and sensuousness. Luther, on the other hand, arrives at that point by self-judgment that takes place in acknowledgment of the divine judgment. In his writing *On the Liberty of a Christian Man,* which otherwise is heavily impregnated with the thoughts of mysticism, he demands that the Gospel must be proclaimed in such a way "that you hear your God speaking to you, [that you hear] how all your life and deeds are nothing before God, but that you, together with everything in you, must perish eternally. If you believe this aright – that you are guilty – you must despair of yourself. . . . But in order that you may come out of and away from yourself, that is, out of your doom, He puts before you His dear Son, Jesus Christ, and has Him speak to you His living, comforting Word: You should surrender yourself to Him in firm faith and trust boldly in Him. Then, because of this faith, all your sins shall be forgiven, all your doom shall be overcome, and you shall be righteous, true, pious, reassured, regarded as having fulfilled all the commandments, and free from all things." (WA 7, 22, 26.) The mystic, too, wants to annihilate "what is in you" – to reduce it to nothing. He who seeks God must penetrate to this nothing, because this is the point at which the creatures arose from the Creator, at which, therefore, one must run into Him out of immanent necessity. "The created abyss leads into itself the uncreated abyss, and the two become one, a purely divine essence, and the spirit is lost in the Spirit of God. It is drowned in the bottomless sea." (Tauler.) Here it becomes clear that Luther's own judgment of his inner self is something different from what the mystics mean when they speak of the renunciation of the various contents of consciousness. Luther demands "that you come out of yourself and away from yourself," and he does so in all seriousness. The very opposite – that which makes man "free from all things" – is Christ, the preaching of the Gospel, faith. Tauler lets the empirical I be annihilated – this, too, is freedom. But he lets it be drowned in the sea of uncreated nothing, which man then also finds nowhere else than in himself. The divine abyss appears only as an unimaginable bottom of the human abyss. It is an involution of the transcendental I itself – an involution extended into unreality.

Luther's penetration to this I is not renunciation; it is judgment. It is a canceling of the sum total of the content of consciousness, not for the purpose of forgetting it, of "freeing oneself" of it, but of exchanging it for the "righteousness of God" *(justitia Dei).* Here self-judgment and the "righteousness of God" *(justitia Dei)* are in a relationship that is exactly reciprocal.[13] On the negative side at least the process of justification can be referred only to the transcendental I, since self-judgment is passed on the sum total of the contents of consciousness and still is carried out by the I.

But one arrives at the same result if one starts from the "righteousness of God" *(justitia Dei).* Concerning justification Luther says: "There we shall reach a mathematical point by taking hold of righteousness" *(Illic attingemus punctum mathematicum arripiendo justitiam) (Praelectiones in psalmos,* 45, 1532; WA 40 II, 527, 9). We have already found this concept in his exposition of Psalm 90, where he demands "that we consider what we are and regard even a hundred years of this life as similar to a mathematical point" *(ut cogitemus, quid simus et etiam centum annos huius vitae ducamus similes puncto mathematico)* (Erlangen edition, *ex. lat.* 18, 321). This was a new way of expressing the other demand: "that we transfer ourselves outside time and look at our life with the eyes of God" *(ut transferamus nos extra tempus et Dei oculis inspiciamus nostram vitam)* (291). This assessing of one's own life with the eyes of God as a mathematical point comes about when one is aware of divine wrath (322 f.). It is the very mathematical point at which the aforementioned "taking hold of righteousness" *(arripere justi-*

[13] WA 3, 31, 6 ff.: "Therefore as long as we do not condemn, excommunicate, and detest ourselves before God, we do not rise again. . . . The righteousness of God will not be or arise in us unless righteousness falls utterly and our own righteousness perishes. . . . For the more the grace and the righteousness of God abound in us, the more does sin abound, i. e., the less righteousness we judge that we have, the more we condemn, abominate, and detest ourselves, the more abundantly does the grace of God flow into us." *(Igitur quam diu nosipsos non condemnamus, excommunicamus, detestamur coram deo, tam diu non resurgimus nec iustificamur. . . . Non erit nec oritur in nobis iustitia dei, nisi prius omnino cadat iustitia et pereat iustitia nostra. . . . Nam tanto magis abundat gratia et iustitia Dei in nobis, quanto magis abundat delictum, i. e., quanto minus nos habere iudicamus iustitiae, quanto magis nosipsos iudicamus et execramur et detestamur, tanto abundantior influit in nos gratia dei.)* — The text-critical remarks in which E. Hirsch expresses his belief that he can assign this passage in the *Dictata super Psalterium* of 1513—16 to a later time (op. cit., p. 161, note 2) have no significance in this connection.

tiam) takes place. The righteousness we receive can by no means be extended; it is never something empirical in the sense that it could be pointed out in the contents of our consciousness. Nevertheless, Luther refers it most decisively to "me," and here one should call to mind what has been said before about the "strong emphasis" *(magna emphasis)* on "for me, for us" *(pro me, pro nobis).* But then here, too, the I that receives the "righteousness" *(justitia)* is, as a mathematical point, the transcendental I. The identity of the mathematical point at which our life comes under the wrath of God with the mathematical point at which the "righteousness of God" *(justitia Dei)* reaches us is to be understood according to the canon to which Luther refers in the *Ten Commandments (Decem praecepta)* of 1518: "Righteousness is self-accusation in the beginning, and the righteous man is first his own accuser" *(justitia est accusatio sui in principio et justus primum est accusator sui)* (WA I, 427, 36).

At the aforementioned place in his lecture on Psalm 45 (1532) Luther compares the government and the jurisdiction of worldly rulers with the authority of Christ. Worldly rulers cannot accomplish their government and their jurisdiction "to a mathematical point," that is, "an indivisible point" *(ad punctum mathematicum=punctum indivisibilem)* (40 II, 526, 2 f.).[14] They must adapt the administering of "justice" *(justitia)* to individual cases and chance occurrences. When measured by an absolute standard, their empirical "justice" *(justitia)* is "injustice" *(iniustitia).* Christ's authority, on the other hand, arrives at that [mathematical] point: "because Christ committed no sin; on account of Him we are accounted absolutely righteous in faith. . . . Everything is pure in the most absolute sense, and indivisibly so; there is the greatest security." *(quia Christus peccatum non fecit, propter eum reputamur justi absolute in fide. . . . Omnia absolutissime et indivisibiliter pura, summa securitas.)* (527, 8 ff.) Here one sees new implications in the fact that the new righteousness is a point: it is indivisible and absolute, and it gives the greatest certainty (WA 10 I, 1, p. 343, 25 f.). On the other hand, one could, first of all, question whether it is absolute and secure. But these two qualities are closely related. The concept of absoluteness contains the elements of totality and unquestionable validity. Unquestionable validity, however, is the — transsubjective — correlative of — subjective — certainty. But then one must ask to what extent there can still be certainty with regard to the new righteousness, where the sum total of the contents of consciousness is to be eliminated as its basis — for it is

[14] Cf. *Lectures on Hebrews,* p. 113, 4 ff.

only a mathematical point *(punctum mathematicum).* If there is no certainty, however, then we can say nothing about absoluteness either.

How much importance Luther attached to certainty he expressed in connection with what he taught about predestination. To be sure, this is deliberately overlooked by those who would like to regard him as the forerunner of Calvinism. "For what is more wretched than uncertainty?" *(Quid enim incertitudine miserius?)* he asks Erasmus (WA 18, 604, 30). And to arrive at this conclusion he surely did not – as recent critics of "Lutheranism" contend – need to be misled by Melanchthon. Entirely apart from the breakdown of the scholastic and medieval-ecclesiastical system of giving assurance, with which Luther really began his work, the question concerning certainty had become a burning one precisely when he sharpened his doctrine of justification "to a mathematical point" *(ad punctum mathematicum).* For what was left if all rationality ended in complete helplessness before the "hidden God" *(Deus absconditus)* and still no empirical guarantees were valid? Faith? Certainly, faith! "Faith does all things" *(Fides facit omnia)* (WA 40 I, 368, 8). But by no means the faith Kant meant when he defined it as a cross between knowing and thinking, as a conviction for which there are only subjectively adequate grounds. Then Luther could have asked Erasmus the other question: "What is more wretched than faith?" *(Quid fide miserius?)*

It has already been indicated that for Luther faith is bound to the receiving of forgiveness of sins and that forgiveness of sins is bound to the Person and the work of Christ. Now it is necessary to ask what connection this has with justification and how the statement that all salvation is bound to Christ can be reconciled with the binding of justification to faith alone. The difficulty consists in this, that the righteousness of faith is centered only in the transcendental subject, and faith itself should in no case be assessed or rewarded as an act defined as having a psychological content. The specification of faith and the new righteousness as a point – therefore also their absolute validity – appears to be endangered if faith and the new righteousness are to be bound to definite conceptions of Christ, to "trust" in Him – conceptions that would undoubtedly be psychological as to content. The much-discussed correspondence carried on in the year 1531 by Brenz with Melanchthon and Luther revolves about this question.[15] Here Melanchthon settled the question unmistakably, and Luther agreed. But a long time before this Luther himself, in harsh polemics against Occam, had fought sharply against constructing righteousness from faith and divine imputation

[15] *CR* 2, 501 ff., 504, 510 ff., 516. De Wette 4, 271. Cf. G. Traub, *Ein Beitrag zur Gesch. d. Rechtfertigungsbegriffes, ThStKr,* 1900, pp. 457 ff.

alone. To him a purely categorical definition of faith – a definition that loses sight of dependence on Christ as to content – seemed unthinkable.[16]

In his lecture on Isaiah, Luther explains with reference to 53:11: "Righteousness is knowledge of Christ" *(Justitia est cognitio Christi)* (WA 31 II, 439, 20).[17] This knowledge of Christ has justifying power as "knowledge of Christ, who bears our iniquities" *(cognitio Christi portantis iniquitates nostras).* It is the "formal and substantial righteousness of Christians" *(formalis et substantialis justitia Christianorum)* and means the same thing as "faith in Christ, which I take hold of through the Word. The Word, of course, I take hold of with the intellect; but agreement with that Word is the work of the Holy Spirit, not of reason, which always seeks its own righteousness." *(fides in Christum, quam apprehendo per verbum. Verbum apprehendo quidem intellectu, sed assentiri illo verbo est opus spiritus sancti, non rationis, quae semper justitias proprias quaerit.)* From the statements that follow one sees that here the whole act of justification is meant.[18] Accordingly, the question concerning the relationship of the transcendental subject, in which alone the righteousness of God is centered, to the definition of faith as to content leads to the other question: whether the knowledge of Christ, which is engendered by the "external Word" (WA 25, 336, 34) and

[16] *Church Postil,* 1522 (WA 10 I, 1 p. 468, 16 ff.): "Among the distinguished teachers of today there are some who say that the forgiveness of sins and justification by grace consist entirely in divine imputation, that is, in God's accounting it sufficient that he to whom He reckons or does not reckon sin is justified or not justified from his sins by this. . . . If this were true, the whole New Testament would be nothing and in vain. And Christ would have labored foolishly and uselessly by suffering for sin. Then even God Himself would have practiced mere humbug and trickery unnecessarily. Since without Christ's suffering He could well have forgiven sin and not have reckoned it, in this way another faith than faith in Christ could justify and save, namely, the faith that would rely on such gracious mercy of God that his sins were not reckoned to him. Against this horrible, terrible understanding and error the holy apostle has the custom of always referring faith to Jesus Christ." Cf. *Rationis Latomianae confutatio* (1521): "Behold, faith is not enough, but [there must be] the faith that hides itself under the wings of Christ and glories in the righteousness of His [God's] Son" *(Ecce fides non satis, sed fides, quae se sub alas Christi recondat et in filii illius iustitia glorietur)* (WA 8, 112, 1).

[17] With regard to what follows cf. the more extensive comments in WA 25, 327 ff. and 336 f.; WA 29, 577, 14; Enders 4, 224, 30.

[18] Lines 33 ff.: "But the Word sets forth another righteousness by means of the reckoning and the promises of Scripture that cause this faith to be reckoned for righteousness. This is our glory, that we know for certain that our righteousness is divine, since God does not reckon sins. Persuaded by these words, let the Christian cling to them boldly. . . ." *(Verbum autem aliam justitiam proponit per reputationem et promissiones scripturae, quae faciunt hanc fidem reputari pro justicia. Gloria nostra haec certo scire nos nostram iusticiam esse divinam deo non reputante peccata. Justicia igitur nostra nihil aliud est quam reputatio dei. Istis verbis persuasus Christianus fortiter illis inhereat. . . .)*

the promise contained in it, gives rise to a psychological state of affairs which endangers the specification of faith and righteousness as a point. Then this danger would consist in this, that in the end God still justifies the sinner because of something the sinner possesses – the knowledge of Christ. Later on this danger became acute in the theology of A. Osiander, even though in another form.

Nevertheless, by the fact – established by Luther – that faith is dependent on Christ, Luther's specification as a point and therefore the transcendental character of justification is confirmed exactly in reverse. The righteousness imparted through justification presupposes, of course, the "self-accusation" *(accusatio sui)* of the sinner (WA 1, 427, 36).[19] Accordingly, Luther counts it among the effects of Christ's suffering "that man comes to a knowledge of himself, is terrified of himself, and is crushed" (WA 2, 138, 16). To have Christ as Savior means to need Him (WA 18, 744, 14 ff.). From the fact that He did His work it follows that the *whole* world is subject to sin. If we believe in Him, we must *(cogimur)* confess that the *whole* man was lost (786, 18). "The cross of Christ has condemned everything the world approves of, even wisdom and righteousness" *(Crux Christi omnia damnavit, quae mundus probat, etiam sapientiam et justitiam)* (WA 2, 613, 37). To be sure, Luther is speaking definitively about the fact that Christ is a possession which we have, "a gift, namely, the gift which is given to you by God and belongs to you" (WA 10 I, 2, p. 247, 29). But faith, which is the subject of this possession, also demands that we rely on what Christ did and suffered as if one had done and suffered it oneself (ibid. and WA 2, 531, 10; 140, 7). "Christ is called my death" *(Christus vocatur mea mors)* (WA 40 I, 278, 6). Accordingly, it is precisely in the knowledge of Christ, in "Christ crucified" *(Christus crucifixus)*, that the knowledge of one's own punishability and of one's own death, criticism of one's "free will" *(liberum arbitrium)* and of one's own wisdom and righteousness, is made complete. Therefore it completes the canceling of the sum total of our psychic possessions, with the result that only the entirely depleted I remains as a purely receiving I. Danger to the transcendental character of justification would occur only if this canceling were meant in the sense of mysticism, that is, as a removal of all ideas and conceptions. Then the objection that because of the knowledge of Christ definite conceptions would again fill the psyche would actually be valid. But for Luther the canceling is not an act of the technique of thinking; it is an act of judgment in the real sense. Just as the content of conscious-

[19] WA 1, 427, 36. Cf. the sixth disputation against the antinomians (WA 39 I, 358, thesis 2 and 3).

ness is not annihilated, so an evil deed cannot be rendered undone by means of a judicial decision. Now, however, the content of consciousness is no longer a means of self-assertion. In faith a self of man becomes alive that renounces self-assertion and, under the judgment of God, which takes place on the cross, *must* renounce it. Yet it is still there, but it is there, of course, only to receive and by receiving.

The critical significance Christ has for the sinner points to transcendental relations in which He Himself stands to God (cf. *The Doctrine of God*). In any case, for faith it signifies, in a positive sense, the "glory" *(Ruhm)* with which we "defy God and take away His wrath" *(gegen Gott trotzen und seinen Zorn aufheben)* (WA 36, 450, 9), that is, the transsubjective basis to which God has bound Himself. Without faith – as Luther, at the place cited, sets forth against the Nominalists – the imparting to the sinner of the new righteousness could appear as a purely arbitrary act of God. This would not only deprive faith of the necessary certainty; it would cast doubt on the whole Gospel. For the Gospel stands and falls with God's truthfulness and reliability (WA 16, 53, 20 ff.), with which the statement that He acts in an arbitrary manner would be irreconcilable. But whatever the nature of the aforementioned transsubjective relation, for the individual sinner it becomes effective only by being referred by God to man as sufficient cause for justification. "It is because of Christ that God does not impute sins" *(Deus non imputat peccata propter Christum)* (WA 2, 497, 16). "Righteousness is imputed to them because of Thy name, O Lord" *(Justitia eis imputatur propter nomen tuum, domine)* (490, 26). This means: "What has been said about Christ will, because of Christ, be understood as said about us too" *(Quod de Christo dictum est, etiam de nobis propter Christum dictum intelligetur)* (531, 10). "It is because of Christ that faith is accounted for righteousness" *(Fides reputatur ad justitiam propter Christum)* (WA 40 I, 366, 8).[20] Luther puts the greatest emphasis on the word "to account" *(reputare)*. In his writing against Erasmus he is glad to be able to point out that Paul uses this word ten times in one chapter (WA 18, 772, 18). For him the expressions "to account" *(reputare)* and "to impute" *(imputare)* deny in the strongest way all synergism as well as the scholastic teaching that there is a disposition *(Habituslehre)*. For him they characterize in the sharpest way God's attitude in justification. God speaks the word of forgiveness of sins, and by doing so He declares that He does not debit sins and that He accounts faith in Christ as

[20] Cf. WA 2, 495, 12 f.; WA 25, 337, 33. With regard to *reputare* in *Lectures on Romans* cf. I, 45, 4; II, 2, 32 ff., 104, 16; 104, 25 ff.; 105, 17 ff.; 121, 10.

righteousness. Justification is no psychic change; it is a word of God spoken to the sinner.

This also answers the questions concerning the absoluteness and the certainty of justification. "It is because of Christ that we are accounted absolutely righteous in faith" *(Propter Christum reputamur justi absolute in fide)* (WA 40 II, 527, 9). When the Gospel of Christ is proclaimed, it applies to me too: "Christ for me" *(Christus pro me)*. This application is indisputable – for here the question about God is answered conclusively and exhaustively. The opposition it has to overcome is not ignorance per se; it is the distress felt by the conscience (WA 15, 548, 11; 590, 11; WA 18, 783, 21). Uncertainty would signify that fear of God is victorious. In this sense one must understand that question which Luther asked Erasmus: "What is more wretched than uncertainty?" *(Quid incertitudine miserius?)* Here it is not a matter of the psychological possibility of doubt in the believer – which Luther knew as long as he lived – but of the nature of faith itself. If faith does not have one's own psyche as its basis and content but has Christ, it also has in Him the basis of its certainty.[21] For Luther disbelief in Christ is the main sin

[21] I do not understand the antithesis stated by Paul Althaus the Younger: ". . . I do not know whether I believe. . . . I only know . . . on whom I believe." (*Communio sanctorum* I, *Luther*, 1926, pp. 92 f.) Whether I was justified — which is disputed by Althaus — in quoting Luther in substantiation of the Lutheran certainty of salvation in my sketch, *Lehre des Luthertums* (2d ed., p. 57), may be seen from the additional statements of Luther that are cited above in the text. — Althaus quotes WA 9, 196, 16: "Also that all His people are within and concealed even from themselves." With these words he wants to prove that according to Luther the believers do not know whether they belong to the people of Christ. But at the aforementioned place there is the additional statement: "as stated above." The only place to which these words can refer is p. 191, 3 ff. Here Luther contrasts the external beauty of the world with the internal beauty of the true people of God. Of the latter he says: "But the spiritual honor and holy beauty is so deeply concealed, not only from other people but also from themselves, that they do not know it [how beautiful they are in the sight of God. Nor would it be good for them to know this.] Indeed, they cannot know it; otherwise it would not be a concealed honor. And if they now had all the aforementioned worldly honor, it is as if they had nothing but faith and deformity rather than the deep immersing of their will and desire in the will of God." Thus in Luther's manuscript (WA 9, 191, 17 ff.). In the printed version (WA 1, 700, 1 ff.) the words enclosed in brackets are missing. Since the passage quoted by Althaus refers explicitly to these remarks, it must also be interpreted in accordance with them. Then, however, it proves nothing at all concerning the certainty of belonging to the people of Christ but proves only that the members of the "concealed body of Christ," who are spoken of on p. 196, 12 ff., cannot perceive this body any more than others can.

As the second proof Althaus quotes from *Lectures on Romans* II, 89, 2: "we can never know whether we have been justified, whether we believe" *(nunquam scire possumus, an justificati simus, an credamus)*. A few lines after this Luther says: "For although we are certain that we believe in Christ, yet we are not certain that we believe in all the words that are His" *(Quamquam enim certi simus nos in Chris-*

(WA 52, 291, 24). It is a great insult, namely, to God (WA 37, 564, 13). For it is doubt of the promise given by God; it makes God out a liar (WA 7, 322, 8; Enders 8, 35, 17 ff.). Besides, defection from faith is "the sin unto death – the sin for which there is no help" *(die sunde zum tode,*

tum credere, non tamen certi sumus nos in omnia, que ipsius sunt, verba credere). But what, according to this passage, must still be added to faith in Christ — the faith of which we should be certain? One page ahead of this Luther says what it is: "Therefore the heretics confess and glory that they believe in Christ, according to what the gospels say about Him, that He was born, that He suffered, that He died, etc. But they do not believe in the words that are His. What are these words? The church, of course, and every word that proceeds from the mouth of a prelate of the church or is the word of the good and holy man of Christ, who says: 'He who hears you hears Me.' Accordingly, I ask those who withdraw from the prelates and do not want to hear their word but follow their own understanding how they believe in Christ. Or because they believe that He was born and suffered, is it impossible for them to believe him who teaches the truth? 'Therefore is Christ divided' because there they believe in Him, here they deny Him? By no means. But here, too, they deny the whole Christ, who cannot be denied and confessed at the same time." *(Igitur heretici confitentur et gloriantur, quod in Christum credant, secundum quod evangelia de ipso loquuntur, nato, passo, mortuo etc. Sed non credunt in ea, que sunt ipsius. Que sunt illa? Ecclesia sc. et omne verbum, quod ex ore prelati Ecclesie procedit vel boni et sancti viri Christi verbum est, qui dicit: Qui vos audit, me audit. Qui ergo a prelatis se subtrahunt, verbum eorum nolunt audire, suum autem sensum sequuntur, quero quomodo in Christum credant. An quod natum esse et passum credunt, docentem verum non credunt? Divisus ergo est Christus, quia ibi in eum credunt, hic negant? Absit. Sed totum Christum etiam hic negant, qui non potest simul negari et confiteri.)* (88, 7 ff.) And two paragraphs later: "Since this is the state of affairs, we must humble ourselves without end. Because, since we cannot know whether we live in every word of God or not at all, [since much is said to us by the prelates, much by the brothers, much in the Gospel and in the writings of the apostles, much inwardly by God]" *(Que cum ita sint, in immensum nos oportet humiliari. Quia cum non possimus scire, an in omni verbo Dei vivamus aut nullum [cum multa a prelato, multa a fratribus, multa in evangelio et apostolis, multa interno nobis a Deo dicantur])* — now there follow the words that are quoted out of context by Althaus: "we can never know whether we have been justified, whether we believe" *(nunquam scire possumus an justificati simus, an credamus).* Thus Luther bases the uncertainty of which he speaks here on the necessity of believing not only in Christ but also in the word that is continuously set forth anew by the church, that is, not "to withdraw from the prelates" *(a prelatis subtrahere).* Accordingly, one can burden Luther, the Reformer, with the statements contained in the *Lectures on Romans* only if one regards the "humility" *(humilitas)* toward the word of the prelates as being in keeping with the Reformation. In the face of this I declare herewith that I would rather belong to the heretics who are censured here. They believe *only* in Christ, as he admits on page 89, 5, and can be certain of this faith — as the Reformer himself did after the bitter struggles of 1517—20.

To be sure, this Reformer Luther inveighs sharply against "security" *(securitas)* (thus in the *Lectures on Romans* II, 111, 22; the fifth disputation against the antinomians [WA 39 I, 356, thesis 44 f.; WA 36, 286, 5]). It is clear what "certainty" he means, even though he occasionally also designates the certainty brought about by Christ as "security" *(securitas)* (WA 7, 762, 6; WA 40 II, 527, 11). But even in the *Lectures on Hebrews* (1517—18) he demands that "it is necessary for the Christian to be certain, yes, certain to the highest degree, that Christ appears and

der nicht zu helffen ist) (WA 45, 677, 28). The possibilities of doubt, of unbelief, and of defection accompany faith as the sea accompanies a voyager — just as there is no voyage without a sea, so there is no faith without these possibilities. Nevertheless, only because "Christ wants to arouse in us a desire for Himself, that we may keep crying out. He wants us to cry out that He may hear. He wants to hear that He may save and thus teach us to despair of ourselves and to trust in Him." *(vult excitare sui in nobis desiderium, ut clamemus porro. Clamare nos vult, ut exaudiat. Exaudire vult, ut salvet, ac sic erudiat nos de nobis diffidere et in ipsum confidere.)* (WA 1, 129, 19.) "The sea is calm indeed until Christ comes"; but "if there is a storm *(si tempestas est)*, Christ will certainly come upon the sea" (WA 32, 15, 22). If I believe, Christ is there; for He is there for me. If I am not sure of this, I doubt, and therefore I have no faith. For this reason Luther has Christ say: "I am more certain to you than your own heart and conscience" (WA 33, 88, 27). "Christ came into this world to make us most certain" *(Christus venit in hunc mundum, ut faceret nos certissimos)* (WA 43, 458, 21 ff.). "Christ brings about freedom and security" *(Christus facit libertatem et securitatem)* (WA 7, 762, 6). "But away with the thought that Christ has left us uncertain!" *(Absit autem, ut nos Christus incertos reliquerit!)* (711, 38.)

If, then — because the character of a decision is attached to faith — one wanted to conclude that in Luther's sense man must have a certain freedom of choice, these statements teach that he actually has no choice at all. For the subject of the decision is, of course, the condemned I; this is — in the sense explained above — the transcendental I. It lives only in and from faith in Christ. Without Christ it is condemned to death. Therefore the decision of faith applies, in the strict sense, to the alternative of life or death. But the I that would want to choose death is extinguished by this very choice, or, more accurately, it never comes to life. If, however, it actually hears the sin-forgiving Word of God in

is a priest for him before God" *(oportet Christianum certum esse imo certissimum Christum pro se apparere et pontificem esse apud deum)* (236, 11 f.). In his comments on this passage E. Hirsch, according to the precedent set by Holl, contrasts Luther's "certainty of salvation" with the "certainty of election." What Luther denies is the certainty "concerning perseverance and the future state" *(de perseverantia et futuro statu)* (238, 4). According to Enders 4, 51, 19, Hirsch also wants to read "predestination" *(praedestinatio)* into "perseverance" *(perseverantia)* here. That Luther is actually thinking here, too, of the "security" *(securitas)* that is constantly attacked is certain from the quotation adduced at both places from 1 Cor. 10:12: "He who stands, let him see to it that he does not fall" *(Qui stat videat ne cadat)*. Therefore reliance on "perseverance" *(perseverantia)* is no "certainty of election," because it destroys the basis of faith, namely, exclusive reliance on the promised election in Christ.

Christ, this Word applies to it too. Here there is no doubting question. For doubt would immediately extinguish once more the I that hears. The indisputable validity of the Gospel is identical with the certainty of faith.

8. Justification in the Confessions [1]

Luther's doctrine of justification made great demands on the Christian as well as on the theologian. Strictly speaking, to be sure, it demanded of the Christian only that he let his sins be forgiven. But this implied unconditional and exhaustive "self-accusation" *(accusatio sui)*. And it was precisely to this that the greatest obstacles were presented as a result of the teaching and the training of the medieval church – insofar as one was convinced that it was necessary actually to carry it out "to a mathematical point" *(ad punctum mathematicum)*, as Luther did. Here it was necessary to break with many substitutes, with cherished customs and institutions that were convenient for and plausible to healthy human understanding. Furthermore, here, too, libertinism constantly emerged as an ape of genuine Paulinism. The practical task with which all this confronted the formation of evangelical churches was enormous. It could be carried out only by a systematic and thorough theological education of the clergy. A huge mass of traditional theological work that was Biblical as well as dogmatical in nature had to be digested. It was the great accomplishment of the first two generations of Lutheran dogmaticians and theologians, of Melanchthon above all, that in doing so they understood how to make Luther's doctrine of justification the central point and the reference point of all theology.

The dangers implicit in this development are evident. The most important question was whether Luther's utmost emphasis on the doctrine of justification could be maintained if all individual-personal presuppositions its rediscovery had in his own case were to disappear. It was a great risk to make the doctrine of justification the "main article"

[1] Wilh. Ferd. Schmidt, *Untersuchungen in den "Fränkischen Bekenntnissen,"* 1930, Part 1. — Concerning the *Copenhagen Articles:* A. Th. Jörgensen, *In Augsburg und in Kopenhagen 1530, NKZ,* 1930, pp. 361 ff. — Furthermore, Albr. Ritschl, *Rechtfertigung und Versöhnung,* 4th ed., 1895 ff. — Karl Holl, *Die Rechtfertigungslehre im Licht der Gesch. d. Protestantismus,* 1906. — W. Walther, *Das Erbe der Reformation* II *(Rechtfertigung),* 1904. — L. Ihmels, *NKZ,* 1904, pp. 618 ff. — W. Vollert, *NKZ,* 1906, pp. 623 ff. — O. Ritschl, *Dogmengesch. d. Protestantismus* II, 1912.

Conrad Schlüsselburg, *Catalogus Haereticorum* VII, *Francof.,* 1599. — Fr. H. R. Frank, *Die Theologie d. Konkordienformel,* I and II, 1858, 61. — A. Warko, *Die Erbsünden- u. Rechtfertigungslehre der Apologie in ihrem geschichtl. Gegensats zur mittelalterl. u. gleichzeitigen katholischen Theologie, ThStKr.,* 1906, pp. 86 ff. — Joh. Kunze, *Die Rechtfertigungslehre in der Apologie, BFchrTh,* 1908, No. 5. — Carl Stange, *Studien z. Theologie Luthers* I, 1928, 453 ff.

(Hauptartikel) *(CA* XX, 8) for the Christian church in general – for all those who were immature, frivolous or sad, indifferent or religiously active. But the Lutheran church bodies that arose undertook to do so. Not until they had taken this risk did they have the right to call themselves evangelical. External reforms did not give them this right. And the whole magnitude of their mission for Christendom – as well as all the suffering and all the setbacks they suffered – is closely connected with this risk.

The entire difficulty of the task becomes clear from the documents that pertain to putting theology under the authority of the church. These documents have a close connection with the development of the evangelical state churches. It is understandable that first of all the practical changes in worship, discipline, and jurisdiction demanded substantiation. But the inner right had to be confirmed theologically, not only for apologetic reasons but to make it possible for inner truthfulness to be the basis of the tie that bound individuals to the newly organized church. The *Twenty-three Ansbach Articles in the Form of Questions (Ansbacher Frageartikel)* of 1524, which, by formulating the points in dispute, gave the first impetus to the shaping of the evangelical confessions,[2] read like a row of question marks at the edge of existing ecclesiasticism. One misses the central point and, therefore, the final compulsion to take matters in hand. Not until questions have been asked concerning the number of sacraments, the duty to make confession every year, the papal and episcopal reservations in the matter of absolution, the right to grant indulgences, the withdrawal of the cup, the "pretty tabernacles" *(zierliche sacramentsheuslein)*, the endowment of Masses, the Latin language in the Mass and at Baptism, celibacy, canonical marriage laws, the binding force of monastic vows, and the obligation of priests to preach does the fourteenth article rise to a theological level: "Furthermore, it should also be disputed whether or not only true faith and trust in Christ are sufficient for salvation." After the fifteenth article has asked about freedom of the will, those that follow deal again with the veneration of saints, with images, with ceremonies, and with laws pertaining to fasting. The theological level is not reached again until, in the last three articles, questions are asked concerning the church, councils, and Holy Scripture. The Ansbach Evangelical Counsel of the same year, which is the answer to these questions, placed the question regarding the authority of Scrip-

[2] Text: *Fränk. Bek.*, pp. 180 ff. — Cf. H. v. Schubert, *Bekenntnisbildung u. Religionspolitik 1529—30*, 1910, pp. 67 f., and K. Schornbaum, *Die Stellung des Markgrafen Kasimir zur reformator. Bewegung in den Jahren* 1524—27, 1900, pp. 35 ff.

ture first; but it left the articles concerning faith and free will in their subordinated places. Moreover, in the *Forty Questions of Ansbach* of 1528 no attention is paid to justification until the twenty-eighth article is stated.

In North Germany, it is true, Bugenhagen, by means of his rituals *(Kirchenordnungen)*, had hammered into the individual separate churches the fact that all reformatory work was purposeless if one did not first see to it "that one could preach freely the pure Word and the unadulterated Gospel of Christ." [3] And he took this demand into account by obligating fathers and mothers to instruct their children as well as by coupling school regulations with the reformation of the church. Nevertheless, his regulations, as was unavoidable, are adjusted too much to what is practical to make the central significance of justification felt. – The *Copenhagen Articles* of 1530, on the basis of the Scriptural principle – which they, like the *Ansbach Counsel*, place first – put special stress on the Christocentric character of evangelical doctrine; and they do so even more emphatically than the contemporaneous Augsburg Confession. They also contain many clear allusions to other aspects of the doctrine of justification, but they do not devote a separate article to this subject. Melanchthon's Apology of the Augsburg Confession was the first confessional writing to understand fully how to make the real heartbeat of the Reformation audible and to fit it into, or subordinate it to, all other motives. In this regard the *Instruction to the Visitors* for Electoral Saxony, of the year 1528, is a forerunner of the Apology (WA 26, 195 ff.). But here the doctrine of justification is taken for granted and protected against misunderstandings rather than shown to be the real theological program of the Reformation.

Finally, however, the doctrine of justification asserted itself as the definitive expression for the evangelical relationship between God and man, and it remained lastingly effective as the fundamental impetus for the whole church. But this made sense only if it actually preserved what Luther had come to realize as being decisive. And now, conversely, it is necessary to point out that this is already the case in the *Ansbach Counsel* of 1524. First the seventeenth article wards off with words that leave nothing to be desired in the matter of clarity the misinterpretation of faith as an acceptance as true of Scriptural statements or of the facts of the story of Christ that are enumerated in the Apostles' Creed. This misinterpretation it calls ignorance on the part of the opponents, "an uncertain, unstable thought about the Word of God, a dream and

[3] Thus in the foreword to the Hamburg *Kirchenordnung* of 1529, Sehling, *KO* V, 488 b.

a delusion about faith of which God washes His hands" *(mit welchem Gott nichts zu schaffen hat) (Fränkische Bekenntnisse,* p. 292). The positive definition of faith first quotes Heb. 11:1, but then it interprets the passage by saying: "Faith is living confidence or trust in divine mercy promised to us in Christ. Faith means to cling constantly and firmly to Scripture and to all the words of God, whether they be threats or promise, and to rely wholly and joyfully on them in all trouble." (293.) Therefore faith in something invisible, about which the passage in Hebrews speaks, is immediately defined – exactly as Luther defines it – as faith in divine mercy. This faith is faith contrary to appearances. Accordingly, in what follows – likewise in agreement with Luther – all emphasis is placed on pointing to the salvation of the I *(aller Nachdruck auf die heilsegoistische Zuspitzung).*[4] Concerning this "right, true, Christian, and saving faith" it is then established that it cannot be engendered by the thoughts of men, but that, on the contrary, it is exclusively a gift and a work of God and brings with it "precious company" *(ein köstliche gesellschaft):* (1) true righteousness; (2) proper knowledge of oneself; (3) true love. Later the relationship between faith and righteousness is defined more accurately: "Since we become righteous and pious only through the mercy of God (as has been pointed out above with abundant Scriptural proof), and faith is nothing else than a knowledge of this mercy and grace of God shown to us through Christ, it is not unreasonable to ascribe our righteousness to faith alone" (301). To be sure, the thought of imputation is not expressed here directly. Yet among other passages the one – Rom. 4:3 ff. – from which the whole doctrine of imputation stems is quoted, and it is quoted in Luther's translation (294, 303). Furthermore, justification is defined as "passing muster in God's court" *(Bestehn im Gericht Gottes),* that is, before His judgment (300). Above all, however, the juxtaposition of justification, knowledge of oneself, and love as the "precious company" of faith, that is, as its results, should be noted. The self-knowledge connected with faith is defined –

[4] P. 293: "Therefore it is not enough for a person to believe that there is a God, that Christ suffered, and the like. He, a sinner, must also firmly believe that God is a God for *his* salvation, that Christ suffered, died, was crucified, and rose again for *him;* for it is the manner, nature, and deed of faith to impress the goodness of Christ on the heart of a man in such a way that he expects all grace or good for himself and does not doubt that He will faithfully and certainly fulfill what He has promised him." — From a later period cf., e. g., also the catechism of Heinrich Boethius of 1592 (at Pattensen on the Leine) in Reu, *Quellen* III, 2, p. 909: "To whom, then, are the sins forgiven? Answer: To me and all believers. — Why do you think of your own person? Answer: Because it is not enough to believe in the forgiveness of sins in general when one does not include one's own person. . . ." — Brochmand, *Syst.* II, 160.

exactly as in Luther — as unconditional and exhaustive "self-accusation" *(accusatio sui)*.[5] And love, as an expression of the new attitude, is definitely differentiated from justification. Even those who consistently advocated the doctrine of imputation never denied that the human heart is re-created by the Spirit, who works faith (cf. *Faith and the Psyche*). But this re-creation must be sharply differentiated from the justification of the sinner. If one does not do so, one completely contradicts Luther's sharpening of justification "to a mathematical point" *(ad punctum mathematicum)*. The men of Ansbach did not do so. Yes, it seems that the authors were afraid of already having said too much when they concluded the section on love with the words: "In such a way that men, for the sake of Christ and the Gospel, consider neither father nor mother, neither friend nor foe, neither property nor honor, neither body nor life, and say to God from the heart: 'Father, Thy will, not ours, be done on earth as it is in heaven'" (295). A strange ending for the section on love! What is here defined as the content of love — full trust in God's will — could again be called faith much sooner than it could be called love. One can understand this only from the intention of the authors to avoid at any cost falling back into the scholastic teaching about a "disposition" *(die scholastische Habituslehre)*. To be sure, in this way not much had been gained for the deeper problem of the relationship of faith and love, that is, of the transcendental to the psychological subject. But precisely in this way the purity of the evangelical concept of faith, this most important element of the doctrine of justification, had been emphatically preserved.

In the fifth of the *Schwabach Articles* (1529) the doctrine of justification is developed, in the main, from the following elements.[6] From the universality and inevitability of sin there results man's inability to achieve righteousness and piety by means of what he himself does. On the contrary, faith in Christ is the only way to righteousness and to

[5] P. 294: "In the second place, it [faith] carries with it the proper and true knowledge of oneself, that is, that through the illumination of faith or the Spirit of God man recognizes his faults, weaknesses, and sins with which he has been surrounded and still is. Then he also sees that all his wisdom is foolishness; that his righteousness is unrighteousness; that his thoughts, words, deeds, and his whole life are nothing before God but an unclean cloth, as Isaiah says, because of which he is humbled, accuses himself, confesses that he is guilty of being a sinner, constantly sobs and longs for divine grace, calls and cries, and gives praise and honor to God alone, as we see clearly in the tax collector or manifest sinner . . ."

[6] Text in Kolde, *Die Augsb. Konfession*, 2d ed., 1911, *Beilage* I, pp. 125 ff., and WA 30 III, 86 ff., according to the Strassburg manuscript, WA with the variants that have become known. — Concerning the origin especially H. v. Schubert, op. cit., pp. 21 ff. — Luther is not the only author. Cf. the foreword to his *Auf das Schreien etlicher Papisten* (WA 30 III, 194, 5).

deliverance from sin and death. "Such faith is our righteousness; for God wants to account and consider righteous, pious, and holy, and to have all sins forgiven and the gift of eternal life for all who have such faith in His Son, that for the sake of His Son they shall be received into grace and be children in His kingdom." The sixth article emphasizes that faith is the work and the gift of God alone, given by the Holy Spirit through Christ. It says that faith is "not a mere delusion or fantasy of the heart . . . but a powerful, new, living thing." Faith bears "much fruit, always does what is good before God by praising, giving thanks, praying, proclaiming, and teaching, and to the neighbor by serving, helping, counseling, giving, and by enduring every kind of evil unto death." The seventh article then continues with the statement that God instituted the office of preaching for the purpose of achieving this faith. Later on the Augsburg Confession made use of the same transition from the fourth to the fifth article. In this sketch it is of decisive importance that, in the first place, Christ is named as the object of faith; secondly, that faith is equated with righteousness; thirdly, that this is proved by the fact that God wants to "account and consider righteous, pious, and holy, and have all sins forgiven" as well as by the words "received into grace for the sake of His Son." Here, therefore, the concepts "forgiveness of sins," "imputation" *(imputatio)*, and "acceptance" *(acceptatio)* are sharply formulated as components of justification. On the other hand, by including it in the article that follows, the thought that faith is also "a powerful, new, living thing" which bears much fruit is clearly separated from the proof of the doctrine of justification.

Martin Bucer criticized the fifth of the *Schwabach Articles* in the opinion he wrote. "Of course, this article is Christian. But there is one exception: that it speaks as though God accounted us pious and holy if we believe, and we, on the other hand, did not have to become such people." To be sure, this, as he knows, is not the meaning of the authors. But for the sake of the opponents, he went on, what Paul says in Rom. 8:9-11 would have to be inserted into the article, and this insertion would have to be made at a place which precedes what, as quoted above, the *Schwabach Articles* have to say about justification.[7] Moreover, it had

[7] Bucer's opinion in Gussmann, *Quellen* I, 2, pp. 289 ff. In the copy of the *Schwabach Articles* in Ulm, Gussmann pointed out the sign indicating where Bucer demanded the insertion. Then the context of the fifth article would have been as follows: After the statement "Nor indeed can prepare himself or make himself fit for righteousness; but the more he undertakes to work his way out himself, the worse it becomes for him" Bucer wanted to insert the statements with which he interprets the passage in Romans: "To him He also gives His Spirit, who constantly contends against the flesh and makes them correspond to the image of the First-born, our Lord Jesus,

been stated clearly enough in the sixth article that, according to the authors of the *Schwabach Articles,* the whole man must be renewed, and that here faith proves its living power in the soul. Bucer's insertion, therefore, could be made only for the purpose of giving proof of justification as such or of helping to prove it. Just as this failed to get the meaning of the passage in Romans, so Bucer had not understood the Lutheran doctrine of justification. At the very least his insertion could make it appear that becoming like Christ, the molding of "disposition and life according to the divine Law," belonged, potentially in any event, to the presuppositions of justification instead of — as Luther states — to its results. Luther could have replied that then not faith but unbelief would be the recipient of righteousness. For to him trust in the grace of God in which one's own psychic state of affairs or potentialities play a substantiating role was unbelief. Bucer's demands amounted to a reversion to the doctrine concerning a "disposition" *(Habituslehre)* — the doctrine which really had put very strong emphasis on divine causation. How great the danger was that arose here is clear from a marginal note by pro-Zwingli Conrad Sam in Ulm, who wrote in the margin next to Bucer's opinion: "Here I agree with Buzer and not with Luther. For we must become pious, new men. Otherwise faith is nothing." (Gussmann I, 2, p. 294.) As if Luther has ever disputed this! Bucer, like Sam, had never grasped what Luther considered to be the main point.

On the other hand, the significance of the fourth article of the Augsburg Confession consists, above all, in this, that here what is decisive for the whole Lutheran Reformation is expressed with masterly clarity and brevity. By combining both authentic texts, the German and the Latin, one finds that "to be justified" *(justificari)* should be understood as "attaining forgiveness of sins and righteousness before God" and therefore that forgiveness of sins should be understood as the real content of righteousness. Man's works and merits are harshly rejected as reasons. Faith conducts itself in a purely passive manner — "when they believe that they are received into grace and that sins are remitted" *(cum credunt se in gratiam recipi et peccata remitti).* Neither is faith an objective reason for justification; it is considered and imputed by God as right-

who does not cease until He has made their disposition and life conform wholly to the divine Law — from which no jot or tittle may fall away — just as the same Spirit will then revivify their bodies and make them like the glorified body of Christ." After this the *Schwabach Articles* would have contained the following additional statement: "But this is the only way to righteousness and to redemption from sins and death, if without any merits or works one believes in the Son of God, who suffered for us, etc.; and such faith is our righteousness, etc.," as above in the text.

eousness.[8] And finally by means of the words "on account of Christ, who with His death rendered satisfaction for our sins" *(propter Christum, qui sua morte pro nostris peccatis satisfecit)*, the article also takes into account Luther's aforementioned protest against constructing justification out of faith and imputation (cf. p. 83).

In the Apology, Melanchthon hammered out and underpinned the essential characteristics of the fourth article of the Augsburg Confession even more thoroughly, if this was possible. Especially did he emphasize again and again that justification and forgiveness of sins are identical. As a result, no argument against the purely receptive character of faith is left. The concept of "imputation" *(imputatio)* is made clear: "Faith is that thing which God declares to be righteousness, and He adds [Rom. 4:5] that it is imputed gratis" *(Fides est illa res, quam Deus pronuntiat esse justitiam et addit gratis imputari)* (II, 89). And in the article that follows he also uses the expression "to be pronounced righteous according to the forensic usage" *(usu forensi justum pronuntiari)* (III, 131). Above all, in the third article on justification the correlation of faith and promise is added. Luther set great store by this. Even Christ's historical work, says Melanchthon, would remain dead for us if at the same time it did not contain for us the promise: "Therefore it is not enough to believe that Christ was born, suffered, and was resurrected, unless we also add this article, which is the final reason for the account [of Christ's work]: remission of sins" *(Itaque non satis est credere, quod Christus natus, passus, resuscitatus sit, nisi addimus et hunc articulum, qui est causa finalis historiae: remissionem peccatorum)* (II, 51). Furthermore, everywhere the accents on the salvation of the I *(die heilsegoistischen Akzente)* are added, in Luther's sense as well as with reference to "the terrors of conscience" *(terrores conscientiae)*, "the terrors of sin and eternal death" *(terrores peccati et mortis aeternae)*; to "the wrath and judgment of God" *(ira et judicium Dei)* (II, 20, 34 ff., 79) as well as to "comfort in all afflictions" *(consolatio in omnibus afflictionibus)* (60, 3; 62, 118), "consciences that are tranquil and joyful before God" *(conscientias tranquillas et laetas coram Deo)* (91). The expression "to be made righteous = to be born again" *(justum effici = regenerari)* should mean nothing else than "to be pronounced or accounted righteous" *(justum pronuntiari seu reputari)* (72, 117).[9] Here he states noth-

[8] The idea of accounting is missing in the earliest version of the Augsburg Confession. Cf. Kolde, *Die älteste Redaktion der Augsb. Konfession*, 1906, p. 12.

[9] Thus Carl Stange (*Studien z. Theol. Luthers* I, 1928, pp. 453 ff.) argues correctly against Loofs. Cf. also Wilh. Ferd. Schmidt in *Fränk. Bek.*, p. 147.

ing else than what Lutheranism had always understood this to mean: the transsubjective validity of righteousness through faith.[10]

Both the doubts with reference to this doctrine of justification and the struggles for it that arose after Luther's death have their origin in the effort to find a place in a system of rationally possible or rationally required thinking for the adequate reason for what God does in justification. For Luther justification stood in absolute opposition to all rational correlations between God and man. This was not disputed by Melanchthon, but in the Augsburg Confession and in the Apology it is really expressed only between the lines. Certainly one was still aware of the paradox implicit in the statement that the sinner should be righteous. But the pithy brevity, particularly of the fourth article of the Augsburg Confession, could mislead one into thinking that the prepositions "on account of" *(propter)* and "through" *(per)* – "on account of Christ and through faith" *(propter Christum et per fidem)* – were supposed to make logical what to reasonable thinking is illogical, to make comprehensible what is incomprehensible. Both statements were completely in Luther's sense. But for him the paradoxical character of the act was not only not weakened by the words "on account of Christ" *(propter Christum)* and the words "through faith" *(per fidem);* it was actually confirmed. It clung to faith directly, to Christ indirectly. For him faith, according to its essence, is certainty contrary to appearances, contrary to what rational thinking requires. Consequently, the expression "justification through faith" is the opposite of reasonable substantiation. But neither does the reference to the transsubjective basis of faith – the reference implied in the words "on account of Christ" *(propter Christum)* – bring about any change here. For this Christ likewise breaks through the rational connections at the decisive point: in the place of the logical equivalence of morality, reward, and punishment He puts the forgiveness of sins. This element of the paradoxical which, as Luther states it, lies in the very words "on account of" *(propter)* and "through" *(per)* changes from a determining to an accompanying motif in the writings of Luther's successors, in a certain sense also in the writings of Melanchthon. To be sure, up to the end of the period of orthodoxy it was never wholly forgotten. Not until the emergence of the theology

[10] Cf. e. g., Bugenhagen, *Von dem Christlichen Glauben . . . an die Erenreych Stat Hamburg,* 1527, p. 118: "But the righteousness of God, which avails before God, is when God makes us pious and righteous. This, however, He does not do through our works; He does it through faith in Jesus Christ. If you believe in Jesus Christ, you are righteous through faith and a son of God." On the identification of justification and the forgiveness of sins cf. p. 116: "To be righteous is, as we have often said, to be free and rid of all sins and to be certain of everlasting life."

of the Enlightenment did the paradox flatten entirely into supranaturalism – like medieval scholasticism.

The attempts to gain – in spite of this – a rationally sufficient basis for justification from the paradox implicit in "through" *(per)* and "on account of" *(propter)* took place in three stages. The crude objection of Sam, the Zwinglian, to the *Schwabach Articles* – "We must become pious, new people; otherwise faith is nothing" – recurs in a more polished form in the writings of Georg Major. When Major taught that no one could be saved without good works, one cannot decide against his opponents for being mistrustful of his later defense: that by saying this he did not want to detract from justification through faith alone. For he himself had defined the content of salvation as forgiveness of sins and an incipient renewal for eternal life, and thus had subsumed the good that is identical with forgiveness of sins under the good of salvation, for which works as well as faith were necessary. Furthermore, he had also denied the justifying power of faith in which works were not at least potentially present.[11] Therefore one can understand Mörlin: here he found a reversion from the "faith fashioned by love" *(fides caritate formata)* to the scholastic teaching.[12] But even if one sets aside the thought of a potential presence of works – a thought advocated even by orthodox dogmaticians – there remained in Major's writings an evaluation of justification which could deal a mortal blow to its original meaning. For here there cropped up the possibility of works that were to be evaluated according to a different norm from that of forgiveness of sins, that is, the "righteousness of God" *(justitia Dei)* in Luther's sense. From this there was but one step to the Augsburg Interim, in which forgiveness of sins and moral renewal were classified as equally important elements of justification.

The second danger was even greater – if faith itself was made to be the reason *(= causa efficiens)* for justification. Here not only the grace that is an essential quality of justification had to be lost, but the whole act had to become a deed of man. To be sure, in the realm of early Lutheranism no one fell a victim to such a harsh way of putting the matter. But such a teaching was not very far from becoming a reality.

[11] G. Major. *Sermon von St. Pauli Bekehrung*, 1552, C 1 f.: "Our good works are necessary not only here on earth but also before God in heaven, in order that for them we may receive the glorious reward and recompense of everlasting life and salvation." Furthermore, Y 3 b ff. — *Opera* II, 1569, 332.

[12] Cf. Joachim Mörlin's *Disput. gegen die Majoristen*, in Schlüsselburg VII, pp. 166 ff. Here Statement 30: "He who says that faith without the presence of works is nothing simply says what the papists say, namely, that man is justified by faith that is fashioned by love" *(Qui dicit fidem sine operum praesentia nihil esse, simpliciter dicit quod Pontificii. fide formata charitate justificari hominem).*

In dogmatical terminology that was still undeveloped (1520) Luther had described faith as the "first and highest good work, the noblest of them all" *(erste und hochst, aller edlist gute werck)*,[13] and the teaching he constantly maintained — that faith is the true fulfillment of the First Commandment — could likewise be misinterpreted in such a way. Later on Bellarmine did not fail to reproach his Lutheran opponents by saying that by excluding works from justification they themselves were not consistent, since faith, too, was a work — "and indeed an outstanding one!" *(et quidem insigne!)* (*Disput.* IV, p. 989.) In the disputes pertaining to synergism the first subject dealt with was conversion, not justification. But since Melanchthon included "faith" *(fides)* as well as "contrition" *(contritio)* among the emotions, faith, too, came dangerously close to what he taught about the will. In the final edition of the *Loci* (1559) he prefaces what he taught about the "three reasons" *(tres causae)* — "the Word of God, the Holy Spirit, and the will of man that assents and does not resist the Word of God" *(verbum Dei, Spiritus s. et humana voluntas assentiens, nec repugnans verbo Dei)* — with a twofold reminder: that the promise of the Spirit is received "through faith" *(per fidem)* and that one dare not seek God without His Word (*CR* 21, 658). This means, then, that in the systematic classification of the emotions "faith" *(fides)* and "not resisting" *(non repugnare)* occupy exactly the same place. Yes, somewhat later "believing" *(credere)* is used almost as a synonym of "not resisting" *(non repugnare)*.[14] Even though Melanchthon makes no direct use of this in what he teaches about justification, only a little shifting was necessary to arrive at the position of the Socinians, who divided justifying faith into trust and obedience, and, in accordance with this, characterized it as an accomplishment and based justification on it.[15] In this form Kant later disfigured the face of justification into a grimace, and Wegscheider, proceeding from the same assumptions, summarized the sins of the Lutherans by saying that "our people have sinned too often in this respect, that they kept faith and virtue too far apart" *(Nostros saepius in eo peccasse, quod fidem et virtutem nimium seiunxerunt)* (*Instit.* 1829, 491). What he meant by this one can see from a quotation from the Baumgarten-Crusius *Biblical*

[13] WA 6, 204, 25; *Lectures on Hebrews* 116, 11 ff. Cf. Brenz, *CR* 2, 510 f. — Furthermore, C. W. v. Kügelgen, *Die Rechtfertigungslehre des Johann Brenz*, 1899.

[14] *CR* 21, 659: "The Gospel is the power of God for salvation to him who does not resist, that is, does not despise the promise but assents and believes" *(Evangelium est potentia Dei ad salutem non repugnanti, id est, non contemnenti promissionem, sed assentienti et credenti)*.

[15] *Rakauer Katechismus*, questions 418 f.; Chr. Ostorodt, *Unterricht v. d. vornehmsten Hauptpunkten d. christl. Religion*, Rackaw, 1612, chs. II and XXXVI.

Theology (§ 56) – a quotation which defined justifying faith as "a living, joyfully active practice of virtue springing from piety that must develop and merge in the kingdom of God" *(lebendiges thatenfrohes Halten an der Tugend aus Frömmigkeit, welche sich im Reiche Gottes entwickeln und vereinigen soll)* (Wegscheider, p. 502). "A joyfully active practice of virtue springing from piety that must develop and merge in the kingdom of God" – here one thinks that Albrecht Ritschl is speaking. But this relationship did not prevent Luther scholars of the most recent past from attributing this doctrine of justification or a similar one to the Reformer himself. This was a happy return to medieval "piety."

The third way of rationalizing "through" *(per)* and "on account of" *(propter)* was pursued – on a substantially higher level, it is true – by Andreas Osiander. One must acknowledge that his speculative doctrine of salvation is rich in creative originality [16] and in fruitful and as yet incompletely developed suggestions. But his doctrine of justification ran counter to the basic purpose of Luther's theology. The fact that he bases justification on the essential immanence in the believer of Christ's divine righteousness or on the incorporation of the believer in the incarnate Word stems from the effort to seek sufficient reason in a direct concatenation with immanent facts. Of course, even in Luther the question arose whether the specification of faith as a point *(die Punktualität des Glaubens)* was not lost by binding justifying faith to the knowledge of Christ and thus filling it with a content of knowledge. Only one thing prevented Luther from succumbing to this: faith must constantly be accompanied by "self-accusation" *(accusatio sui)*, which must be applied to all the psychic facts. But in Osiander this is no longer possible. One cannot subject the essential possession of Christ's righteousness to "accusation" *(accusatio)*. No matter how correctly what Osiander taught concerning Christ's indwelling in the believer reflected Luther's views (cf. *Unio Mystica*) – he had given up the decisive point of the "main article."

Against these aberrations the third article of the Formula of Concord presented, as its first argument, the statement that in this way distressed consciences were deprived of the comfort they needed. In doing so it took up a motif which determines Luther's theology in its entirety and also played an important role in what the Apology had to say in the article on justification. One can challenge its telling power

[16] E. Hirsch, *Die Theologie des Andreas Osiander*, 1919. — The investigations of Wilh. Ferd. Schmidt with regard to the *Fränkische Bekenntnisse* have added substantially to Hirsch's book. Cf. especially pp. 71 ff.

only by adducing reasons given by Feuerbach. This motif would be invalid if one could show that a desire for salvation had brought about this doctrine of justification. But neither this desire nor the "pangs of conscience" *(angores conscientiae)* and any immanence at all of consciousness *(überhaupt nichts Bewusstseinsimmanentes)* led to this doctrine; it was simply a special concern of the Lutheran doctrine of justification to preserve the transsubjective Gospel and its transsubjectivity. In justification any psychic or moral cooperation on the part of man would have endangered this and would thus have confirmed the suspicion of illusionism. Therefore the Formula of Concord had to reject Major's teaching as well as Osiander's and also the synergistic approaches of Melanchthon, because if the specification of faith as a point *(die Punktualität des Glaubens)* were lost, not only certainty of salvation as such but any certainty at all of faith would be gone.

As a result, it became necessary to make a conceptually accurate distinction between "regeneration" *(regeneratio)* and "making alive" *(vivificatio)*, which had not yet been done in the Apology (*SD* III, 18 ff.). This is not yet the place to decide whether such a distinction, like the one between the concepts "sanctification" and "renewal" (III, 38 ff.), was made correctly and whether it was exhaustive. On it rests what later dogmaticians taught about the "order of salvation" *(ordo salutis)*, which, as may be admitted for the time being, is open to criticism. Here the important thing was the preservation of Luther's fundamental knowledge concerning the "righteousness of God" *(justitia Dei)*, which is adjudged and acknowledged to be for man and is imputed to him but not implanted. If it were implanted, it would no longer be the "righteousness of God" *(justitia Dei)*; then it would be "man's" *(hominis)* righteousness. Therefore the Formula of Concord could indeed define the concepts of reconciliation and the forgiveness of sins as contents of justification (III, 30), because they do not presuppose any human facts as an objective basis; but it could not do so with regard to those other concepts — regeneration, renewal, sanctification — because then one must think of the very opposite: the nature of man. For the same reason the sharp line of demarcation between contrition and justification was also entirely in order, even though one can ask whether it was good to put such great emphasis on the precedence of contrition in time (23 ff.). But this objection is merely formal in nature, since in the same connection the permanent necessity of penitence is stressed (26). It is Luther's knowledge of the continuous correlation of justifying faith and "self-accusation" *(accusatio sui)* that is expressed in the statement that believers "would be pronounced and considered pious and righteous even though on account of their corrupt nature they are still sinners and remain sinners until death" (22). The whole paradoxical character of Luther's faith is to be found in this "even though." Those who took the three wrong paths mentioned above weakened or denied this paradox.

But opponents like G. Major, Menius, Osiander, and even Pfeffinger, who — each in his own particular way — did not know how to distinguish correctly the acts of regeneration, sanctification, etc., from justification, continued to emphasize that they, too, were preserving the divine initiative, and that therefore all human merit was excluded, just as it was excluded from the purely forensic doctrine of justification. Therefore it was necessary to show further that this was by no means made sure by the medieval teaching concerning "preceding grace" *(gratia praeveniens)* and "grace" *(gratia)* in general. For all Lutheranism it is of constitutive significance that in Calvin's "everything to the glory of God" it did not yet find anything specifically Christian or even specifically evangelical, since this glory is not given to the God revealed in Christ. In this sense Luther repeats tirelessly in his commentaries on Galatians that every form of righteousness by works and every form of synergism, no matter how subtilized, detracts from the merit of Christ — righteousness by works and synergism would, of course, not be incompatible with the "glory of God" provided that one ascribed to God, as all synergists did, the creative or spiritual authorship. In like manner Melanchthon states in the Apology that it is the purpose of the doctrine of justification "to increase the glory of Christ" *(ut amplificetur gloria Christi)*.[17] Likewise the Formula of Concord says that renewal, sanctification, love, virtue, and good works dare not be confused with justification, "in order that Christ, the Redeemer, may not be deprived of His glory" *(auf dass dem Erlöser Christo seine Ehre bleib)* (*Epit.* III, 7; *SD* III, 35). Here again it is a matter of the transsubjectivity of the basis of justification. In Luther this was the formal correlative of the specification of faith as a point *(das formale Korrelat der Punktualität des Glaubens)*, and it is a further concern of the third article of the Formula of Concord to underscore this emphatically.

For this reason the "exclusive items" *(particulae exclusivae)* — according to Melanchthon's procedure — the "apart from works" *(absque operibus)*, "without the Law" *(sine lege)*, "gratis" *(gratis)*, "through faith alone" *(sola fide)*, are declared to be marks of justification that are unavoidably

[17] *CR* 2, 504. Cf. Apology VIII, 83. Furthermore, *CR* 21, 749; 758. Martin Chemnitz, *Examen Conc. Trid.* I, 248; *Loci* II, 271 b.

necessary. Neither penitence nor love dare be assumed on man's part. No virtue is the tool; only faith is (*SD* III, 31). And faith itself dare by no means be taken to be "a good work and a beautiful virtue" (13).[18] Furthermore, it must be sharply differentiated from the new obedience (32). Exactly as in Luther, faith is referred exclusively to the promise (31): as an act of man it is altogether empty. What gives it its significance in the act of justification is exclusively that which is conferred on it from beyond all subjectivity: the "merciful reconciliation or forgiveness of sins, which is presented to us out of pure grace solely because of the merit of Christ, the Mediator, and is received solely through faith in the promise of the Gospel" (30).

The tendency to be precise, which dominated the development of the doctrine of justification up to the time of the Formula of Concord, found a definitive expression when later dogmaticians defined justification as a "judicial" *(judicialis)* or a "forensic" *(forensis)* "act" *(actus).*[19] It has been emphasized previously that just as the "juridical" element cannot be imagined as being absent from what Paul taught about salvation, so it cannot be imagined as being absent from what Luther taught. Melanchthon had used the expression "forensic usage" *(usus forensis)* in the Apology. It was a thought completely in accord with the New Testament when the *Confessio Wirtembergica,* in its article on justification, spoke for the Council of Trent (1551) about "God's judgment seat," before which there is no room for human merit.[20] In connection with the doctrine of justification Luther, too, had spoken about the "tribunal

[18] Cf. the Hungarian *Conf. montana,* Art. 6.

[19] Hafenreffer, *Loci,* p. 664: ". . . the significance being taken from the forensic judgments" *(. . . sumpta significatione ex judiciis forensibus).* — Joh. Gerhard, *Loci* 7, 4 ff. — Baier, *Comp.,* p. 737: "The forensic significance" *(Forensis significatio);* p. 744: "The righteousness that avails at the divine court" *(Justitia, quae in foro divino valet);* p. 746: "the tribunal of God" *(Dei tribunal);* p. 747: "in the judiciary process" *(in processu judiciario).*

[20] Cf. the translation into German in the alleged confession of the city of Reutlingen, in Gussmann, *Quellen* I, 2, p. 232. — Cf. in addition Erh. Weinmann, *Disp. de Justificatione, praes. St. Gerlach,* Tübingen, 1603, where the concept "the tribunal of Christ" *(tribunal Christi)* (Rom. 14:10) is the conclusion. — It is hard to understand why O. Ritschl (*Dogmengesch. d. Prot.* II, 1, p. 250) attaches such great importance to the fact that "the idea of an otherworldly court of God *(forum Dei)* was still completely alien to" Melanchthon and that even in Brenz and Flacius "the idea of an otherworldly court of God" is not yet to be found. The theologians mentioned know nothing as yet of Albr. Ritschl's fear of the otherworldliness of God. On the contrary, for them the judgment seat of God was otherworldly in any case for the very reason that it was God's judgment seat. Otherwise they would have been poor disciples of Luther. Nor, to be sure, did they regard the "beyond" *(Jenseits)* of God as a place above the stars, as the Reformed theology of the time did. (Cf. *The States and Offices of Christ.)*

of God" *(tribunal Dei)*.[21] Accordingly, the expression "forensic act" *(actus forensis)* said nothing that was different. But with this expression two things were sharply underscored. In the first place, the error that the Lutheran doctrine of salvation was tantamount to justification of oneself was warded off. This had to be stressed because Luther's identification of faith with righteousness, when torn out of the context, could be taken as a call to man to justify himself. And many theologians of the nineteenth century fell prey to this temptation. The forensic doctrine of justification, on the other hand, kept alive the realization that even when justification and the forgiveness of sins are equated, the seriousness of the judgment passed on sin dare not be minimized. It is the divine Judge whose verdict faith hears. To be sure, this verdict is altogether different from what reason and morality should expect, and in pronouncing it the divine Judge shows that He is not a punishing but an acquitting Judge. But only when His acquittal actually pronounces a valid verdict has the sinner been relieved of the judgment and the anxiety of his conscience – and this belongs to the essential elements of faith.

In the second place, the forensic interpretation expressed in the sharpest manner the antithesis of the scholastic teaching. It put the emphasis on the declaratory character of justification, and this is the self-evident reverse of faith-righteousness as such. For one can speak of faith only so long as certainty of this righteousness is based not on empirical facts but solely on the "Word of God," namely, on the promise of forgiveness of sins. A righteousness that is put into man's nature like a thing or that qualifies his moral behavior can, as a general principle, be identified empirically at least. Therefore it is not an object of faith. Consequently, it was already the beginning of the end of the Lutheran doctrine of justification when Hollaz, the last of the orthodox dogmaticians, reduced the antithesis of the empirical interpretation to the formula: Imputation in justification is to be understood "in a moral sense" *(in sensu morali)* (*Examen* III, 470). For under the guise of the "moral" sense – although Hollaz himself, by the way, was fortified against this – even the Socinian falsification could slip in – the falsification which paved the way for the destruction inflicted by the Enlightenment

[21] WA 34 II, 140, 6: "But before the tribunal of God, where He Himself is the Judge, where no judge, executioner, or jailer sits, it happens that He is merciful and compassionate to sinners. Before Him no saints carry weight; but only sinners. . . ." *(Sed coram dei tribunal, ubi ipse est Judex, do kein Richter, hencker, stockmeister sitzt, ghets so zu, quod est gnedig und barmhertzig peccatoribus. Vor im gelten kein sancti, sed meri peccatores. . . .)*

on the most precious possession of the Reformation. As long as the forensic character of justification was strictly adhered to, one was protected against this.

9. *Propter Christum*

The later dogmaticians divide justification into two elements: "remission of sins" *(remissio peccatorum)* and "imputation of the righteousness of Christ" *(imputatio justitiae Christi)*. The confessions of the church, including the Formula of Concord, know nothing about this. Even if this differentiation is to serve only to clarify the concept or to suit the variety of the Scriptural statements, it still carried with it serious danger that uniformity in the act of justification might be destroyed because of it. But this differentiation is nothing short of intolerable, because by destroying the consistent nature of faith it must also destroy the specification of faith as a point *(Punktualität)*, and here there is simply nothing more to divide.[1] But if the "on account of Christ" *(propter Christum)* of the Augsburg Confession is an element of justification that is necessary at all, it can by no means undermine the accurate coordination of complete forgiveness of sins, that is, of a complete clearing-up of the relationship between God and man and of faith as the ὄργανον ληπτικόν (the tool for receiving), as Melanchthon called it. On the contrary, it must fill a gap left in the previous development of the doctrine of justification. In fact, this gap is present to a decidedly perceptible degree.

Faith places man before God. Man knows that God is calling to him. The hearing of the divine call is incompatible with the psychologizing "explanation" that man, by the power of his intellect, has lifted himself up from the conception of an angry God to the conception of a merciful, loving Father. For just as he is unable to free himself from the powers of the world and of death that surround and restrain him — because these powers always remain "real" — so he is unable to escape the "Thou shalt" of the Law, the annihilating verdict of his conscience, the baneful conflict between "shall" and "must." But that call cannot be mere information concerning a new "concept of God." For the mere statement that God forgives sin would, in connection with the "primal experience" *(Urerlebnis)*, have to make God appear as an inconsistent Lawgiver and

[1] WA 10 I, 1, p. 343, 24: "Behold, thus you see here how St. Paul teaches everywhere that justification does not come through works but comes solely from faith without any works, not in parts but in one heap; for the testament includes everything: justification, salvation, inheritance, and property *(hewtgutt)*. And all this is possessed at once through faith, not piecemeal." *(Church Postil,* 1522.) Cf. WA 40 II, 527, 11: "Everything most perfectly and indivisibly pure . . ." *(Omnia absolutissime et indivisibiliter pura . . .)*

a softhearted Judge. To believe this would amount to substituting a sure experience of the divine wrath for a wish that is founded on nothing at all.

Actually, however, the concept of forgiveness of sins was a paraphrase of the Lutheran concept of the "righteousness of God" *(justitia Dei)*, insofar as Luther himself understood this to be the righteousness given to man as a gift. Thus the concept moves at once into a greater continuity of ideas. Here, first of all, it is stated in a much more elementary manner than in the concept of forgiveness of sins alone that God, even though He forgives man for transgressing, still does not cease to demand righteousness, in any case does not desist from demanding that man must be righteous. On the one hand, of course, this intensifies the feeling that there is a contradiction. On the other hand, however, it states that the same God pronounces judgment and bestows grace. If it were not the same God, the belief that He bestows grace would, at the very outset, have to give way to the suspicion that this is an illusion. At the very least the fact that it is the same God protects faith from itself against the suspicion that through an intellectual accomplishment of its own it has overcome one concept of God by means of another, "higher" one – one that in reality would be more comforting only to itself. Here faith is primarily not at all opposed to faith, but God is opposed to God. And not even one God to another God; the contradiction lies in the God who is identical with Himself. From the standpoint of faith, therefore, it is of a transcendental nature, in any case of a nature that is transsubjective.

It is still necessary to discuss the fact that there is an approach of Luther's according to which the first impression of God, namely, that He is actually angry with the sinner, is merely an illusion or a product of one's evil conscience – even though a necessary product (cf. *Reconciliation and Predestination in Luther in Disjunction)*. There is no need to prove that this could not be a solution of the difficulty that has arisen. For in any case faith would have to be speechless if it were asked: "From what source do you have the certainty that God's wrath is only an illusion and that His readiness to forgive is in agreement with His real nature? Would it not be true to say that the very opposite is the case?" To be sure, Luther, as previously shown, ascribes to faith the power to mediate antitheses *(mediatio contrariorum)*. But it has been seen that this dare not be understood in the sense of a mere change of approach or point of view *(conspectus)*, and that it is by no means to be understood in such a way that faith could deduce dialectically the central theme of the Gospel from the revelation of the Law. On the contrary, it has been seen that the Person of Christ has integrating significance when the aforementioned mediation takes place. One of the first definitions of this resulted from the connection with the concept of revelation. "In the crucified Christ" *(in Christo crucifixo)* the "hidden God" *(Deus absconditus)* becomes the "revealed God" *(Deus revelatus).* To be sure, this revelation, which was transmitted through Christ, is a "communication" *(Mitteilung);* but it is by no means enlightenment concerning a previous error, at least not in the sense of a later correction of the conception of God as an angry Judge. He is the Merciful One only for faith – for unbelief and therefore also for the unbeliever He remains the Hidden One *(absconditus),* the God of wrath. Even faith receives and retains its certainty of revelation only in the knowledge of "Christ crucified" *(Christus crucifixus).* The relation of faith to Christ was already moved into the actual soteriological connection by means of the formula: "Righteousness is knowledge of Christ" *(Justitia est cognitio Christi)* and its parallels. And the connection with the doctrine of justification became even clearer by means of the statement: "It is because of Christ that faith is accounted for righteousness" *(Fides reputatur ad justitiam propter Christum),* or by means of the other statement: "It is because of Christ that God does not impute sins" *(Deus non imputat peccata propter Christum).*

Therefore in Luther's sense the question that has arisen – what assurance the Christian has that his belief in the forgiveness of sins does not rest on an illusion – must be answered very generally by pointing to Christ. He is the basis of the knowledge of the faith in God's readiness to forgive sins. This is also the sense of Melanchthon's formula: that Christ is the "pledge of all the promises" *(pignus omnium promissionum)* (*Loci,* first edition, *CR* 21, 140). Accordingly, in the definition of faith employed even later, "on account of Christ" *(propter Christum)* is also to be understood as "trust in the mercy promised on account of Christ" *(fiducia misericordiae promissae propter Christum)* – where "on account of Christ" *(propter Christum)* is used to signify the subjectively sufficient basis of "trust" *(fiducia)* (*CR* 15, 98; 21, 422, 743). Yes, in the Apology, Christ Himself is described as the subject of the promise of forgiveness of sins, justification, and eternal life (II, 5). Justice would have been done this significance of Christ for the salvation of mankind with the explanation that Christ has proclaimed the new "concept of God," that is, has announced God's readiness to forgive sins. But this would not solve the real problem, namely, how the inconsistency between God and God is thinkable in spite of God's identity with Himself; it would merely postpone the matter.

To early Lutheranism in its entirety, from Luther up to the most recent orthodox dogmaticians, this problem seemed to be solved by an "objective doctrine of reconciliation." Lutheran pietism held fast, in the main, to this teaching, and confessional Lutherans of the nineteenth century returned to it, even though they expressed it in various shadings. What at first glance appears to be a weakness of this doctrine and was also constantly objected to by its opponents – that the direct moral relationship between God and man is broken down by the assumption that a third person is a substitute to the advantage of others – this, if one still disregards all the details, is precisely what makes the "objective doctrine of reconciliation" indispensable in relation to the doctrine of justification proclaimed by the Reformation.

For the righteousness meant by this doctrine of justification it is essential that vis-à-vis man it be an "alien righteousness" *(aliena justitia)* (Apology III, 184), that it have its foundation "outside us" *(extra nos)* (Melanchthon, *Loci* 21, 743). This was Luther's point when he still used the expression "to infuse" *(infundere).* He calls it an "alien righteousness infused from without" *(aliena justitia ab extra infusa),* and here all the weight rests on the phrase "from without" *(ab extra)* (WA 2, 145, 9). To be sure, the word "to infuse" *(infundere)* could not be brought into agreement with this. Very soon, therefore, it was definitely supplanted by the word "to impute" *(imputare)* (WA 2, 490, 26 etc.). And when later dogmaticians, like Martin Chemnitz, state emphatically that the concepts "alien righteousness" *(aliena justitia)* and "imputative righteousness" *(justitia imputativa) are inseparable,* they do so because for them, exactly as for Luther, the second must bolster the first – not vice versa.[2] This is the source of Chemnitz' vehement criticism of the "inherent righteousness" *(justitia inhaesiva)* advocated by the Council of Trent.[3] And Johann Gerhard's embittered controversy with Bellarmine in the whole seventh volume of his *Loci* reaches its climax in the struggle for the "righteousness placed outside us" *(justitia extra nos posita).*

Chemnitz defends Luther's translation "the righteousness that avails

[2] Chemnitz, *Loci* II, 238—328; cf. especially the statement that "it is necessary that an alien righteousness intervene" *(necesse est intervenire alienam justitiam)* (279a) with the section *De vocabulo imputationis,* 326 ff. — To be sure, Quenstedt, *Theol. did.-pol.* III, 525, it is stated: "This imputation has its very firm foundation, not in man, who is justified, but outside him, namely, in God Himself, who imputes, and in Christ the Mediator, who acquires the imputation by rendering satisfaction" *(Imputatio haec habet fundamentum firmissimum non in homine, que justificatur, sed extra eum, nempe in ipso Deo imputante et Christo Mediatore imputationem praestita satisfactione promerente).* But here, too, the "outside us" *(extra nos)* is expressed with special sharpness, and further substantiation is given by Quenstedt. — In Luther cf. WA 25, 331, 5; WA 39 I, 83, 24.

[3] *Trid. Sess.* VI, *De justif. can.* 11 (Denzinger, p. 278; Mirbt, p. 301). Furthermore, Chemnitz, *Examen* I, 231—314.

before God" *(die Gerechtigkeit, die vor Gott gilt)* against Osiander (*Loci* II, 282b).[4] In this expression the whole crisis of the Lutheran doctrine of justification can actually be felt. If "passive righteousness" *(justitia passiva)* is identical with the forgiveness of sins, then one must ask to what extent it is still "righteousness" *(justitia).* It could be called "mercy" *(misericordia),* "favor" *(favor),* "grace of God" *(gratia Dei);* and even Luther and later theologians gave it this designation. But "righteousness" *(justitia)*? This question demands an answer, even if "righteousness" *(justitia)* is, as Luther says, understood, not as the attribute of God but as His gift to the sinner. Here some "right" *(jus)* has to be in question. But if imputed righteousness is actually an "alien righteousness" *(justitia aliena)* – only when it is this, can it be imputed or, in some other way, be declared, granted, promised, imparted; and without this there would have been no Reformation – the "right" *(jus)* inherent in the new righteousness would have to belong to a transsubjective reality. And this is not something new that would be added to the doctrine of justification or would even destroy it; it belongs to its absolutely necessary presuppositions.

It is self-evident that the "right" *(jus)* inherent in the concept "righteousness" *(justitia)* is in itself identical with the "validity" *(dem Geltenden)* in Luther's "the righteousness that avails before God" *(Gerechtigkeit, die vor Gott gilt).* To this extent one could still say by way of objection that it is a paradoxical expression for the idea that God does not actually make use of the "right" *(jus)* but "shows mercy" *(Gnade für Recht ergehen lasse).* But this changing of the "right" *(jus)* that demands and punishes into a "right" *(jus)* that grants and forgives is itself an arrangement – perhaps of a higher kind – but in any case an arrangement that is likewise valid and the validity of which, when looked at from man's point of view, is plainly transsubjective. There are two ways in which it can be more accurately defined. Since here God stands in opposition to God – the One who demands against the One who forgives – one can try to deduce this tension from the concept of God. The classical example for this is the theory of Anselm, which takes it to be a tension between God's glory and His mercy, and does away with it by means of the satisfaction rendered to the divine glory by Christ in carrying out the divine mercy. In various ways of expression one finds this theory even in Luther, Melanchthon, and later theologians. Concerning this "proper mixing of divine justice and mercy" *(temperamentum justitiae et misericordiae divinae)* Johann Gerhard says: "From this arises

[4] Thus in the *Ansbach Counsel* of 1524, *Fränk Bek.*, p. 293.

our justification" *(Ex hoc oritur nostra justificatio)* (*Loci* VII, 302).[5] But this leads to the abandonment of the previous inductive way of developing the doctrine of justification. Therefore the attempt to deduce the tension in question from the divine "attributes" *(Eigenschaften)* and to remove it in this way must still be postponed.

The other way harks back to the facts and viewpoints established in "Under the Wrath of God" (ch. 1). The relationships developed there of guilt and destiny, of responsibility and curse, of Law and conscience, of enmity against God and God's wrath, are broken asunder at a single point. The Gospel gives us news of *one* Man in whose case the interrelationship of these elements was different. No matter how the significance of the Person of Christ and His work is to be understood, Luther demands that one must "begin from the bottom" *(von unten anheben);* he says that one can know nothing about God's Son except from Him who was born as a man. "And the deeper we can bring Him into the flesh — as you are unable to do to a sufficient extent *(ut non satis potes)* — the better it is."[6] Like every other man, Christ was bound up with the cooperating and the opposing relationships of these powers. By becoming man He, like all flesh, became subject to the Law. He became a "servant of the Law." Thus the Law became exactly as effective in His case as in the case of all flesh: it brought the curse of God upon Him, the wrath of God. By being "wrapped up" *(eingewickelt)* in the flesh He was also implicated *(verwickelt)* in the relationship of sins, death, suffering, crucifixion. He became "a Wanderer, a Guest, and a Pilgrim . . . like another man *(sicut alius homo)*"; and His way was that of "a murderer and a condemned man, so that there is no man who is seen to be condemned to a greater extent than this Man *(ut nemo sit, qui videatur magis damnatus quam iste vir).*" His whole life was one descent "under the Law, under the devil, death, sin, and hell, that is, I believe, into the last and lowest depth."[7] In this way He came into a relationship to us as close as can be imagined among men. "But here there is no comparison *(Ibi vero nulla similitudo).* Christ does not become our brother-in-law *(schwager),* our brother; but He becomes what we are *(quod sumus);* He becomes our nature, part, and a greater nearness than that of husband and wife *(et major propinquitas quam mariti et uxoris).* . . . Who can understand that He is not a companion, a friend,

[5] Cf. N. Selnecker, *Instit.* I, 335.

[6] WA 10 I, 2, p. 297, 9; WA 33, 155, 27; WA 34 I, 147, 10; WA 40 I, 93, 5; Enders 1, 416, 70; 3, 273, 57.

[7] WA 52, 80, 21; WA 2, 517, 27 ff.; WA 40 I, 433 ff.; 434, 8; 442, 10; 451, 4; WA 41, 232, 2 ff.; WA 23, 702, 16.

but that it is He Himself?" Therefore if Christ actually assumed our flesh and thus brought the Law, the wrath and the curse of God, the devil and hell, upon Himself, the curse He bears is our curse, and the death He dies is our death. And because in the end our curse and our death are the unavoidable consequence of our sin, He also bears the cause, our sin, together with the consequence. "His Passion was nothing else than our sin" *(Sua passio nihil aliud erat quam nostrum peccatum)*.[8]

Nevertheless, there is, after all, still another difference in the case of Christ the Man. The curse of His life did not stem from a collision of a striving for autonomy with the divine will – He knew no "vainglory" *(Hoffahrt)*. He was "altogether innocent and without any sin, both inwardly in His heart and outwardly with words and deeds. For where inwardly there is something evil in the heart, this cannot be concealed for long; it must also show itself outwardly, at least in words." He was "pure and righteous . . . without any lies and falsehood . . . there is no weakness or anything reprehensible in such love and obedience." With His perfect love and His perfect obedience He fulfilled the Law in its entirety. He did the outward works that are commanded, obeyed His parents – but willingly – humbled Himself out of love, "served all men with the highest service," and was obedient to God.[9] But just as the first series of thoughts rests on the basic fact that He took upon Himself our "flesh," and this in and with His incarnation, so the second is completed in the fact that His "flesh," from the moment of the incarnation, was without sin, that He was conceived and born of the Virgin without sins. "This they [the Jews] did not know. Nor do I know it. But I hear it, and Holy Writ tells me about it. And I believe it. But if you do not want to believe it, don't. Then the harm will be yours." (WA 33, 126, 8.) This completely positivistic proof of the sinless birth by no means causes Luther to depart from the rest of his train of thought; for to him the other facts, too – Christ under the curse and Christ without a sinful deed – are certain only as the content of the "Word." To be sure, this question about the proof has more than a formal significance. On the contrary, it indicates a point at which the inductive procedure preferred by Luther cannot be carried out further. For if the motive of Christ's free choice extends also to the act of incarnation, in His case a transhuman initiative must be assumed in the will that forms His Person. Consequently, Luther accepts the New Testament doctrine of the Logos and the church's doctrine of the two natures.

[8] WA 29, 644, 3; 645, 2; WA 40 I, 274, 6; WA 10 I, 2, p. 247, 32; WA 31 II, 432, 16.

[9] WA 28, 287, 25; WA 21, 304, 28; WA 46, 641, 12 ff.; WA 10 I, 1, p. 365, 4 ff.; WA 17 II, 240, 24; 244, 17 and 36; WA 31 I, 317, 7; WA 41, 190, 1 ff.

But if we assume for the time being that it can be proved that Christ became man of His own free choice, the following conclusions come about as a result of the juxtaposition of the two series of facts that have been developed. Christ came into the category of those who, inspired, as children of Adam, by a desire for autonomy, wanted to be "sons of God" and therefore are guilty of death. "Therefore it serves Him, Christ, right in this matter, because He took our place. He is, of course, an innocent Person, and the Law does not touch Him *(Est quidem persona innocens et lex non tangit eum);* but because He took it upon Himself to be willing to stand in the place of all men, therefore let Him die honorably *(ideo bene moriatur)* (WA 28, 348 f.). Accordingly, the fact that He "took our place" means, first of all, that Christ wanted to be where all men are who desire to be a "son of God" *(filius Dei)* (348, 6). This also meant that Christ, like man, was under the judgment of God. But in complete reversal of every other human analogy, God's judgment applies to Him who, although He actually was "God's Son" *(filius Dei),* is the only Person to fulfill God's Law perfectly and therefore had given up every claim to autonomy.

This confirms what is certain for other reasons too: that God's relationship to sin is not determined by a justice that repays a particular thing with a particular thing, but that it is a behavior over against "man" in general — a behavior that no child of Adam can escape (WA 21, 513, 11). In addition to this, however, so far as Christ is concerned, there is — always presupposing His freedom of choice — no other sufficient reason why He took the wrath of God upon Himself than His love for mankind, with whom He wanted to throw in His lot. Christ "did not suffer for Himself or out of necessity but for you, and He did so of His own free will *(aus gutem willen).*" The motives of freedom of choice and love subordinate the incomprehensible intertwining of those two series of facts in the life of Christ to the viewpoint of purpose. The news of this is not a mere communication. On the contrary, it makes an appeal to him who hears it and induces him to refer it to himself. Actually this is self-evident on account of the solidarity of all mankind — the solidarity into which Christ entered. At the same time, however, it demands the personal individualization of purpose in faith. When Luther designates this faith expressly as the faith that justifies, he has arrived at the transsubjective reason that was lacking above — the reason at which faith in justification can come to anchor.[10]

[10] WA 40 I, 296, 11; WA 35, 434, 9, and 435, 11; WA 32, 84, 3; WA 21, 304, 27; 37, 236 f.; WA 19, 149, 17; WA 2, 458, 20 ff.; WA 31 II, 20; WA 40 I, 274, 6; 447, 4.

Strictly speaking, to be sure, up to this point nothing more has been said than that the innocent Christ took upon Himself the Law, God's wrath, curse, and death "for us." But one must still ask to what extent this is actually to be efficacious for us, that is, to be for our benefit. Here now the dialectic "mediation of antitheses" *(mediatio contrariorum)* begins through faith – the mediation that has no foundation in actuality apart from the facts of the Person and the life of Christ. Together with the curse that rests on all men, Christ also bore my curse. He did so of His own free will; and since His will was always identical with the will of the Father, He did so according to God's will. In the second place, He bore this curse out of love for me; and here, too, it is true that in Christ's love the love of God reaches us. But the two are inseparable from each other. God lets Christ bear the curse because He loves me, and He loves me by letting Him feel and bear the wrath provoked by me. Therefore Luther can also explain the "for us" *(pro nobis)* by letting the believer say to Christ: "You, Christ, are my sin and curse, or rather: I am Your sin, Your curse, Your death, the wrath of God, Your hell! You, on the other hand, are my Righteousness, Blessing, Life, Grace of God, and Heaven, because the text clearly says: 'Christ was made a curse for us'" *(Tu, Christe, es peccatum et maledictum meum, vel potius: Ego sum peccatum tuum, maledictum tuum, mors tua, ira Dei, infernus tuus! Tu contra es justitia, benedictio, vita, gratia Dei, coelum meum, quia textus clare dicit: Christus factus est pro nobis maledictum).*[11] Here we are at the "commutative (interchanging) imputation" *(imputatio commutativa)* of the later dogmaticians. If the fact that Christ bears the wrath of God that rests on me makes me certain of the love or the grace of God, one must conclude that "on account of Christ" *(propter Christum)* the wrath of God no longer rests on me, but that His grace does. And since, on the other hand, Christ's work consisted in the fact that in what He did and suffered He was perfectly righteous, this is merely a new way of expressing the basic thought of the doctrine of justification: that I am righteous because the righteousness of Christ is "imputed" *(zugerechnet)* to me.

Thus Luther arrives "from below" *(von unten her)* at the concept of substitution, that is, at the thought that Christ bore God's judgment of wrath not only for our benefit but in our stead. But the answer is also given to the question to what extent forgiveness of sins can be designated as an imparting of righteousness. If in faith the Christian and

[11] Here, by way of exception, we are quoting according to the printed version, since the transcript, which is vague at this place, must certainly be straightened out in this sense: WA 40 I, 454, 20 ff. — Cf. *Lectures on Romans* II, 129, 23 ff.; 131, 20 ff.; *Lectures on Hebrews*, 169, 2 ff.; 226, 3 ff.; WA 29, 578, 2 ff.; Enders 1, 29, 33 ff.

Christ become so perfectly interchangeable that my curse is His curse, my death is His death, but His fulfillment of the Law is mine too, I am actually as righteous as Christ was. Naturally, this remains a righteousness of *faith,* but also a *righteousness* of faith. And if finally the former insoluble contradiction was an antagonism of God to God, of the God who demands righteousness to the God who gives it, now it is evident in a paradoxical way that precisely the righteousness granted — to the believer — is identical with the righteousness demanded and — by Christ and "on account of Christ" *(propter Christum),* but also by the believer — fulfilled.

In the older confessions the connection between Christ's Person and work and justification is no different. This was the case even in the *Ansbach Counsel* of 1524, which speaks about the work of Christ only in this context, as well as in the *Copenhagen Articles* of 1530, where, conversely, the doctrine of justification is contained only in what these articles teach about the Person of Christ.[12] To be sure, the third of the *Schwabach Articles* asks about the relationship of Christ's two natures to His work. The third article of the Augsburg Confession discusses it first without reference to the doctrine of justification, and the papal confutation praised it for being in agreement with the "rule of faith" *(regula fidei).*[13] Those who wrote this confutation had obviously overlooked the fact that in the statement of the Augsburg Confession — that Christ's sacrifice is valid not only for original sin but for all sins — a sharp barb had already been aimed at the theology of the opponents. Besides, the Augsburg Confession and the Apology employ a series of modifications that seem to go beyond the train of thought developed by Luther. These are, above all, the concepts "Mediator" *(mediator),* "Propitiation" *(propitiatorium),* "Priest" *(pontifex),* and "Intercessor" *(intercessor)* for Christ (*CA* XXI; Apology IV, 40, 46); furthermore, the concepts "reconciliation" *(reconciliatio),* "redemption" *(redemptio),* "appeasal" *(placatio),* and "satisfaction" *(satisfactio)* for Christ's work (*CA* III, IV, XX; Apology II, 18, 44, 69, 81; III, 185; XII, 23). Christ or His work are designated as a sacrifice and, what is more, as a sacrifice of atonement *(Sühnopfer)* (*CA* III, XXIV). His sacrifice is brought into special connection with His blood, His suffering, His death *(CA* IV, 25; Apology II, 15) — "only the death of Christ is truly a propitiating sacrifice" *(sola mors Christi est vere propitiatorium sacrificium)* (Apology XII, 24).

[12] Cf. the comments of Georg Amerbacher in his opinion of April 1530, *Fränk. Bek.,* pp. 490 ff., especially on "alien righteousness" *(frembde Gerechtigkeit),* pp. 492 f.

[13] The text of the confutation according to Kolde's edition of the Augsburg Confession, p. 149.

Not only a "merit" *(meritum)* of Christ is mentioned (*CA* V, XX, etc.); but the "merits of Christ" *(merita Christi)* are also designated as the "price" *(pretium)*, His "blood and merit" as "the treasure with which settlement has been made for sin" *(der Schatz, durch welchen die Sünde bezahlet ist)* (Apology II, 53, 57).

Luther, too, used every one of these concepts. One need only recall the Second Article of the Second Chief Part or the Fifth Chief Part of the Small Catechism to realize the basic importance all this has for him. He introduces the "main article" *(Häuptartikel)* of the Smalcald Articles with Rom. 4:24, John 1:29, and Is. 53:6! Here – but also in Melanchthon's Apology – the New Testament roots of the doctrine of the Reformation concerning Christ's "objective" work of salvation are evident. One may be in doubt with regard to his concept of "satisfaction" *(satisfactio)*. But here, too, later dogmaticians point out that although the word itself is not a part of Biblical usage, it is supported by a series of New Testament synonyms.[14] One could accept this provided that one avoids the false conception that Christ's work of salvation has to do with something – the value of money, for example – one could consider apart from its motives. Even Luther's expression in the exposition of the Second Article – the expression that is taken from the First Epistle of Peter – could in itself be interpreted in this way. But this would contradict the inseparability of the Person and the office of Christ – the inseparability he always emphasized.[15]

By means of its interpretation of the "righteousness of Christ" *(justitia Christi)* the Formula of Concord built a dam against every misunderstanding of such a nature. This service cannot be valued too highly. It was rendered in the statement, directed against Osiander, that the righteousness imputed to faith was Christ's obedience (*SD* III, 9). Although it is also paraphrased as "obedience, suffering, and resurrection" (15) or as "obedience, suffering, and dying" (32), nevertheless His whole Person, life, and work are included in the concept of obedience.[16] This obedience showed itself in the fact that "He fulfilled the Law for us"

[14] Hollaz, *Examen* II, 239, refers to 1 John 2:2 and 4:10; Rom. 3:24 f. and 5:10; 2 Cor. 5:18; Eph. 1:7; Col. 1:14; Matt. 20:28. – The expression occurs in Luther, e. g., in WA 29, 578, 4; 579, 5, etc.

[15] Here I refer to Theod. Harnack, *Luthers Theologie* II, 2d ed., 1927, pp. 228 ff. – Jul. Köstlin, *Luthers Theologie* II, 2d ed., 1901, pp. 133 ff. – Gottfr. Thomasius, *Christi Person u. Werk* II, 3d ed., 1888, pp. 167 ff.

[16] *SD* III, 58: "And thus faith looks at the Person of Christ, how it was made under the Law for us, bore our sins, and in His going to the Father rendered to His heavenly Father for us poor sinners *His entire, complete obedience from His birth even unto death* and thereby covered all our disobedience."

(30), and this "by doing and suffering, in life and in death" *(agendo et patiendo, in vita et morte)* (15). One can doubt that the sharp conceptual separation of "active obedience" *(obedientia activa)* from "passive" *(passiva)* — the separation which later dogmaticians derived from this and which was again vigorously disputed in the theology of the nineteenth century — was in conformity with Luther's meaning. When Luther speaks about the "fulfillment of the Law" *(impletio legis)* through Christ (WA 2, 466, 14; 523, 15; 561, 39; 563, 35; WA 10 I, 1, p. 471, 2), for him, as for Paul, the Law is always a whole, an objective power — or rather *the* objective power — which, after the appearance of man's sin, makes a determined demand for expiation. Together with the New Testament, Luther sees expiation first of all in Christ's death on the cross. But this should have expiatory significance only because Christ rendered satisfaction to the whole Law, therefore also by means of the active fulfillment of all its commandments. Accordingly, it makes little difference if one regards the active fulfillment of the Law as a prerequisite or as an element within the satisfaction rendered to the Law. Even in Christ's suffering the Formula of Concord emphasizes the active element, namely, freedom of choice (*SD* III, 15), and subsumes the active and the passive fulfillment of the Law under the concept of obedience. Because in this way a purely real *(nur dinglich)* assessment of Christ's "merit" *(meritum)*, of the "price" *(pretium)* paid for the sinners, was withheld, at the same time Luther's urgent concern that justifying faith is always faith in Christ came into its own. Precisely for this reason it is also a matter of importance that the Formula of Concord does not know of the difference later theologians made between "forgiveness of sins" *(remissio peccatorum)* and the "imputation of Christ" *(imputatio Christi)*. Neither can the two be separated conceptually. Otherwise the danger would arise that "on account of Christ" *(propter Christum)* would appear merely as an external supplementation of "through faith" *(per fidem)*, while in reality both statements present nothing more than an unfolding of the single, indivisible act of justification.

10. Reconciliation and Predestination in Luther in Disjunction

In Luther's case the terrors of the primal experience *(Urerlebnis)* reached their climax before the "hidden God" *(Deus absconditus)*. They are by no means exhausted by fear of punishment. On the contrary, they are to be understood as dread of God Himself, of God for His own sake. The God with whom they are concerned is the absolute master of destiny; He keeps us in bondage and holds us responsible as though we were free – responsible for something we simply cannot accomplish. Properly speaking, therefore, this dreadful incomprehensibility of the "hidden God" *(Deus absconditus)* does not spring from His capacity as Lawgiver and Judge but only from the connection His capacity as Lawgiver and Judge has with His power over our destiny. But if for faith the "revealed God" *(Deus revelatus)* abruptly confronts the "hidden God" *(Deus absconditus)* – so abruptly that in his *Lectures on Genesis* Luther, at any rate, reached the conclusion that "one must discuss either the hidden God or the revealed God; with regard to God insofar as He has not been revealed there is no faith" *(aut disputandum est de Deo abscondito aut de Deo revelato; de Deo, quatenus est non revelatus, non est fides)*[1] – one must ask to what extent the cause of that dread of God has been put aside or overcome. The train of thought in the doctrine of justification refers to only one aspect of this cause, namely, to the "righteousness of God" *(justitia Dei)*, that is, to God's capacity as Judge. But what about His power over destiny? It was horrifying to think of this, because "by nature" we find ourselves in the state of sin, that is, of enmity against God, and because when we ask for a reason that is sufficient, we inevitably come up against God Himself as the Cause.

Here a seemingly simple solution presents itself at once. One can take for granted that the only purpose God had in hurling man into the misery of his guilt was to cut him off from every thought of his own merit and to let him see that his salvation is a gift bestowed purely by the grace of God. In this way one can understand what Luther says about "saving despair" *(salutaris desperatio)*,[2] and from this point of view the whole writing against Erasmus would take on a unified meaning. On the other hand, to be sure, Luther's use in that writing of the examples of Esau, Pharaoh, and Judas would immediately cause one to think twice. In their case God's power over destiny does not turn out to be beneficial, and it would be poor comfort for these lost persons if, together with Luther, one wanted to tell them in a reproachful spirit that God rejected Pharaoh in order that *our* faith might be strengthened (714, 6 ff.). But if one pursues the thought of "preparation for grace" *(preparatio ad gratiam)* by means of the divine teleology of our guilt somewhat further, one would have to conclude that our fear of God was only an illusion. In reality the frightful fact that we must stand and fight against God because of a terrible decree was already a bestowal

1 WA 43, 458, 38. But cf. also WA 18, 685, 3 ff.; Enders 7, 6, 73.

2 WA 18, 719, 11. On "confident despair" *(fiducialis desperatio)* see Enders 1, 29, 46. Cf. WA 11, 113, 9.

of grace. For this conclusion one could adduce Luther's belief that God is as we picture Him to ourselves: "If you believe that God is angry – He is" *(Si credis Deum iratum – est)* (WA 40 II, 342, 16). Out of its context this can be understood to mean that God's wrath is nothing but a product of our thinking. And in the nineteenth century even the first paragraph of the explanation of the First Commandment in the Large Catechism was adduced in substantiation of this.

Right here, however, one comes up against the resistance that causes the whole series of thoughts to founder. It is already implicit in the formula "If you believe that God is angry – He is" *(Si credis Deum iratum – est)*. If you are unable to believe that He is merciful, then He is angry, and, what is more, *actually* angry, not only in your imagination (WA 9, 515, 29; 668, 27). For the seemingly purely subjectivistic statement "As you think about God, so He Himself does" *(Sicut de Deo cogitas, sic ipse)* Luther refers to the unfaithful servant who calls his master "hard and crabbed" *(hart und sauer)* and for this reason actually does not find another master (WA 37, 589, 8 ff.). Then one would only have to ask whether unbelief, that is, not being willing to believe that God is merciful, is the first thing to provoke God's wrath. Then one would recall Luther's way of taking it: that unbelief is sin in the outstanding sense of the word. But this would not alter the fact that divine wrath is real in a transsubjective way. Then, however, the same question does not arise here for faith that is asked in connection with the train of thought pursued in the doctrine of justification – the question pertaining to sufficient reason for the believer's certainty that God's wrath does not apply to him. And here Luther leaves no doubt at all as to his conviction that God's wrath had to be appeased and that this was done only through Christ (WA 8, 519, 5 ff.; WA 25, 328, 10; 330, 4; WA 27, 167, 4; WA 40 I, 295, 4). From this it follows that our fear of God, before we believe and if we do not believe, is positively founded on fact. Before God our enmity against Him comes up against real resistance.

This gives Christ's Person and work a new meaning. "Between us and God there are the greatest discord and an eternal separation" *(Inter nos et Deum maxima discordia et aeterna separatio)* (WA 40 I, 504, 2). "We are the ones who offend God; He, together with His Law, is offended in the highest degree, and the offense is such that He cannot forgive it and I cannot cancel it" *(Nos sumus offendentes Dei; offensissimus cum sua lege et talis offensio, ut eam non possit remittere et ego non solvere)* (503, 9). It is the active collision of the sinner with God's wrath or, as a result of this, the impossibility that there can be communion between "sinful man" *(homo peccator)* and the "righteous God"

(Deus justus). In this situation Christ appears as the "Mediator" *(mediator)* who by His death makes peace between God and man, or as the "Propitiator" *(propitiator),* His work as "appeasement" *(placatio),* namely, of the God who has been offended by us, or as "reconciliation" *(reconciliatio),* insofar as that "greatest discord" *(maxima discordia)* had to be overcome. Or to express it in another way: Christ performs the office of the high priest who appeases God and at the same time is the Sacrifice. He makes peace and gives us "access to His grace in faith" *(eynen tzugang tzu seyner gnaden ym glauben).* And to express it in still another way: He is the "Liberator" *(liberator),* the "Redeemer" *(redemptor);* His work is redemption.[3]

If the facts of reconciliation and redemption are bound to Christ's life and suffering, especially to His death, they have their place – in the first instance at least – in a contingency of events on which I, a human being of today, had no influence, not even through my faith. At best I can be a part of this contingency of events insofar as Christ, with the love that determined His course, meant me too, or, to express it in the train of thought of the doctrine of justification, because He imputed His righteousness to me; that is, the effect of His reconciliation and redemption is now applied to me. But since in my state of wretchedness the wrath that could be felt was not imagined but was "real," and faith, on the other hand, certain of reconciliation, has a "merciful God," and this certainty likewise rests on a contingency of events that is transsubjective for me, one must conclude in Luther's sense that through Christ's Person and work the change from wrath to mercy was called forth in God Himself. Here it is not yet necessary to investigate whether and how this is consistent in general with faith in God and whether there is no "concept of God" at all that can be the final norm for this question. On the contrary, now we must establish the fact that at all events the fateful side of our state of wretchedness has also undergone a real change, insofar as the hostile tension between God and us – the tension in which we find ourselves by nature, that is, because of our destiny – has been supplanted by reconciliation and peace with God. For just as the Gospel of Christ really contains the promise that He and His work are valid "for me" *(pro me),* and since the application "to me" is an essential

[3] *Mediator:* WA 18, 778, 9; WA 29, 578, 16; WA 40 I, 503, 1 ff. — *Propitiator, placatio, reconciliatio:* WA 2, 458, 2 ff.; 40 I, 91, 1; 295, 4; 502, 6. High Priest, Sacrifice, Peacemaker: WA 1, 703; *Lectures on Hebrews,* 167, 11; WA 10 I, 1, p. 718, 5; WA 20, 366, 18; WA 23, 615, 13 and 25 ff.; WA 25, 337, 29 and 287, 33; WA 41, 192, 1 ff.; 197, 1. — *Liberator, redemptor, salvator,* redemption; WA 18, 647, 31; 744, 9 ff.; WA 19, 140, 3; WA 25, 326, 22; WA 31 II, 433, 17 ff.; WA 40 II, 3, 7.

function of faith, faith also makes it certain that reconciliation and redemption are "for me" *(pro me),* that I, therefore, as a believer, am reconciled to God. Consequently, faith also sees God as Creator and Master of its destiny in the light of Christ's redemptive work (cf. *The Doctrine of God* and *Close Connection with the Earth*).

If Christ is the "Liberator" *(liberator)* for the believer, "freedom" *(libertas)* is one of the things He brings about. Yet whatever may be understood by "Christian freedom," God's power over man's destiny can by no means be abolished by it. The words "by grace alone" *(sola gratia)* stand above all that was said about justification, reconciliation, and redemption. The whole change the believer experiences in his life rests on God's initiative. Consequently, faith enters into a new relationship to its experience of God's power over destiny – or rather now for the first time into a positive relationship. It is sure that "our salvation depends on the work of God alone" *(in solius opere Dei pendere salutem nostram)* (WA 18, 634, 16). If the word "alone" *(solius)* is emphasized here, this, of course, is not something that leads beyond the concept "by grace alone" *(sola gratia).* But if one emphasizes the word "work" *(opus),* one comes to the concept of the activity of God. This brings one to the problem of predestination.

Not directly, to be sure! The activity of God with which faith is concerned is an activity in the present. Only causal conclusions a posteriori lead to the thought of predestination. One need not yet discuss here whether faith can arrive at or sustain such a causal conclusion, because this is a matter of the relationship of faith to the philosophy of life, while now we are discussing exclusively its relationship to "salvation" *(salus).* In any case such a conclusion would be dangerous for faith, because the mere application of the category of causality to man's relationship to God was, of course, an essential element in the fear of God. Indirectly this is confirmed in the writing *On the Bondage of the Will (De servo arbitrio)* by the fact that here Luther adduces testimonies of non-Christians and of "reason" *(ratio)* to the omnipotence of God that is at the bottom of the doctrine of predestination (WA 18, 618, 8 ff.; 718, 15; 786, 5). Thus if this writing had intended to prove the omnipotence of God – as some "Luther scholars" *(Lutherforscher)* still teach – it could just as well have remained unwritten. Ordinarily at least Luther is not in the habit of occupying himself with things that are certain on the basis of "reason" *(ratio).* In addition, he leaves no doubt here that the trains of thought with reference to predestination come to an end before the "hidden God" *(Deus absconditus),* before "the incomprehensible secrets of the divine majesty" *(incomprehensibilia secreta divinae majestatis)* (631, 34 ff.; 685, 5 ff., 28 ff.; 706, 28; 712, 25); and here again he invokes "reason" *(ratio)* as a witness to the incomprehensibility (784, 27). To be sure, here there is between the attitude of unbelievers and believers toward the incomprehensibility of the God who predestines the very essential difference that the latter are impelled by it to "adoration" *(adoratio)* (631, 40), the former to "despair, hatred of God, and blasphemy" *(desperatio, odium Dei et blasphemia)* (631, 14). From this, however, it follows that the thought of predestination can by no means provide a foundation for faith, but that faith must already be in existence if the thought of predestination is to be at all bearable.

In this writing Luther also set great if not all store by the foundation of faith, namely, by the certainty of salvation (604, 33; 605, 6; 646 2 ff.; 656, 9; 783, 24 ff.). If the mere thought of predestination cannot vouch for this certainty — because, to say the least, it does not exclude the possibility of "despair" *(desperatio)* — the basis of faith has to be something else. And here it is nothing else than it is elsewhere in Luther, namely, "the Gospel, by which the Spirit and grace are offered for the forgiveness of sins through Christ crucified" *(Evangelium, quo offertur spiritus et gratia in remissionem peccatorum per Christum crucifixum)* (692, 21), the "proclaimed mercy" *(misericordia praedicata)* (684, 34), the "proclaimed God" *(Deus praedicatus)* (685, 20), "Christ" as the "Light of the world" *(lux mundi)* (655, 6), as our "Wisdom" *(sapientia)* (638, 21), as the "Lamb of God" *(agnus Dei)* and our "Redeemer" *(redemptor)* (744, 26; 8), "Mediator, and Savior" *(mediator et salvator)* (778, 15). If this were not the case, how could Luther declare against Erasmus, and in this very writing at that: "For we, too, teach nothing but the crucified Jesus" *(Nam et nos nihil nisi Jhesum crucifixum docemus)* (638, 24)? From this it follows that the doctrine of predestination can have only a subsidiary significance. In what sense — this, too, is stated by Luther in a manner that cannot be misunderstood. This doctrine, he says, is necessary for two reasons. "The first is the humbling of our pride and the knowledge of the grace of God, the second is Christian faith itself" *(Prima est humiliatio nostrae superbiae et cognitio gratiae Dei, altera ipsa fides Christiana)* (632, 27). The first touches the general theme of all Scripture: that the doctrine of predestination deals an annihilating blow to "free will" *(liberum arbitrium)* (615, 14; 718, 25 ff.; 783, 29 ff.). God wants to show us "our impotence" *(nostram impotentiam)* (673, 35). But even this would only hurl us into despair if the reverse of it were not the fact that in this way we learn "that Christ is necessary" *(Christum esse necessarium)* (779, 23; 744, 14 ff.;

786, 18). For this reason, and for this reason exclusively, Luther can say that the doctrine of predestination is proclaimed only "for the sake of the elect" *(propter electos)* (633, 2).

The other reason is "Christian faith itself" *(ipsa fides Christiana).* To be sure, this thought – because, strictly speaking, it does not belong to the theme of Scripture – is dealt with only briefly. Nevertheless, it is dealt with in a manner so clear that it cannot be misunderstood. "The second is, that it is faith in things not seen. In order, therefore, that there may be a place for faith, it is necessary that all things that are believed be hidden." *(Altera est, quod fides est rerum non apparentium. Ut ergo fidei locus sit, opus est, ut omnia, quae creduntur, abscondantur.)* (633, 7.) Or a little later: "If by any means I were able to understand how this God who shows such great wrath and unfairness is merciful and just, there would be no need of faith" *(Si igitur possem ulla ratione comprehendere, quomodo is Deus sit misericors et justus, qui tantam iram et iniquitatem ostendit, non opus esset fide)* (line 19). If here the "highest degree of faith" is seen in this, that one believes "that He is forbearing who saves so few, condemns so many . . . is just who by His own will makes us necessarily worthy of condemnation" *(illum esse clementem, qui tam paucos salvat, tam multos damnat . . . justum, qui sua voluntate nos necessario damnabiles facit)* (line 15), it becomes clear that faith, to be faith, must overcome the thought of predestination. For the fact that few are saved and many are condemned, that God "makes answerable" *(reos facit)* (line 10), that "He shows such wrath and unfairness" *(tantam iram et iniquitatem ostendit)* (line 20) – these are precisely the "things seen" *(res apparentes)* behind which God conceals that which must be believed, namely, His "righteousness, making alive, clemency, and mercy" *(justitia, vivificatio, clementia et misericordia)!* These are the obvious things against which one has to believe. Here it is entirely clear that the doctrine of predestination is merely an auxiliary thought. Faith, of course, will never do away with those obvious facts, just as it cannot do away with rational thinking. Yes, it uses those facts constantly in order never to be anything else than a "nevertheless faith" *(Dennoch-Glaube).* Therefore faith will always contain those facts as a necessary element, but as an element that has been overcome and must constantly be fought down. But they can never give positive reasons for faith in the "righteousness of God" *(justitia Dei)* in the sense of the doctrine of justification, in the mercy of God, and in the forgiveness of sins.

To be sure, another series of thoughts seems to stand in opposition to this. Naturally, not the thought that God does everything in everyone, that He hardens, that even sin is not committed without Him – all this is the "hidden God" *(Deus absconditus)*, the "angry God" *(deus iratus)*, *against* whom one must believe. And the same thing is true of God's "twofold will." On the other hand, the doctrine of predestination seems to acquire positive significance for the foundation of faith when Luther says that it is necessary in order that we may be sure of His promises (619, 16 ff.). For to this, he says, belongs the certainty that God does not lie, that His will is irresistible and cannot be hindered. But what are the promises? According to Scripture, they extend to nothing else than they normally do: to the offer of "the Spirit and grace for the remission of sins accomplished for us through Christ Crucified" *(spiritus et gratia in remissionem peccatorum per Christum crucifixum pro nobis impetratam)* (692, 19 ff.). Since, therefore, here, too, as always, faith in the promises is founded on Christ, here, too, the doctrine of predestination can be merely an auxiliary thought. Then, however, the same thing is true of the statements that only the "elect" *(electi)* believe (632, 9) or that "grace comes from a plan or from predestination" *(gratia ex proposito seu praedestinatione venit)* (772, 39). For these statements lead only to the "decree of election" *(decretum electionis)*, not to one of "rejection" *(reprobationis)*. For Luther the certainty of being elected is based only on Christ "for me" *(pro me)*, and the grace he derives here "from predestination" *(ex praedestinatione)* is none other than the "thanks we return for the Word of life and salvation" *(gratia, quam rependimus verbo vitae et salutis)* (628, 12), that is, therefore, the "proclaimed mercy" *(misericordia praedicata)!* If an inconsistency remains here insofar as, on the one hand, Luther looks upon the thought of predestination as something to be overcome and, on the other hand, in spite of this seeks positive threads that lead from it to faith, this second thing can never be meant in such a way that the believer may cling to Christ because, on the basis of predestination, it is certain that grace is promised to him in view of his election. Luther is convinced that the very opposite is true, for – "knowledge of Christ, that is, of the things that belong to salvation" *(notitia Christi, id est, eorum quae sunt salutis)* (779, 6). And if for polemical reasons he did not stay with that subject in this writing, neither did he leave it unsaid here: "It is no concern of ours to what extent God hides Himself and does not want to be known by us" *(Quatenus Deus sese abscondit et ignorari a nobis vult, nihil ad nos)* (685, 6).

Later, therefore, Luther had a right to demand in his great *Lectures on Genesis* that when pointing to his teaching "that all things are absolute and necessary" *(omnia esse absoluta et necessaria)* one should not forget that he added "that one must look at the revealed God" *(quod aspiciendus sit Deus revelatus)* (WA 43, 463, 6; cf. the whole section pp. 457–463). His whole theology is a theology of revelation, and when the doctrine of predestination concerns itself with the "hidden God" *(Deus absconditus)*, it can be a subject of theology only indirectly.[4] Even faith can always concern itself only indirectly with this doctrine. If it actually is faith, it is constantly directed to Christ, sees God only in Christ, and, as a result – if it does not really founder at the thought of predestination – sees the God who predestines only as the Father to whom I am reconciled through Christ. Thus Luther teaches as early as 1519 – dogmatically in his first *Commentary on Galatians* (WA 2, 458, 1–34) and practically in his *Sermon on the Preparation for Death* (WA 2, 690, 10 ff.). If the question of "election" *(vorsehung)*, he says here, arises in you as a doubt, "look at the heavenly picture of Christ. . . . Behold, in this picture your hell is overcome, and your uncertain election *(vorsehung)* is made certain."[5] And in the letter of consolation (*EA* 54, 21 ff.) he wrote in 1528 to an unnamed person he demands that one must "not begin with the Law or with reason when discussing God's electing, but with God's grace and the Gospel that is proclaimed to all men." In like manner he contrasts what Christ says in John 17:6 as the Word of revelation and therefore as a "passage full of consolation" *(consolationis plenum locum)* with the temptation into which predestination leads (WA 28, 114, 5 ff.) – the temptation that ends in despair (122, 1 ff.). For this reason he later (1537) characterizes investigations into predestination as the devil's work pure and simple: "There Satan commands such persons to climb higher than God wants, that they may investigate whether they have been elected, whether they will be saved, and to go from what God has revealed into dreams about other things – things He has not revealed" *(Ibi Satan jubet tales hoher steigen, quam deus wil haben, ut forschen, an sint versehen, obs selig werden, und faren ex revelatione, quam deus revelavit, in alia somnia, quae non revelavit)* (WA 45, 95, 32). And this is no different from what he meant when at an earlier date, in his writing *On the Bondage of the Will (De servo*

[4] Luther to Caspar Aquila, 1528, Enders 7, 5: "It is necessary indeed to teach about the inscrutable will of God in order that we may know that it is such; but to strive that you may comprehend it, this is a most dangerous precipice" *(Docendum est quidem de voluntate Dei imperscrutabili, ut sciamus talem esse, sed niti, ut comprehendas eam, hoc est praecipitium periculosissimum)*.

[5] Cf. also *Lectures on Romans* II, 226, 6 ff.

arbitrio), he characterized the attempt to penetrate the mystery of predestination as a struggle against God *(cum Deo pugnare)* (WA 18, 690, 26).[6]

Luther has to reach this conclusion, not in spite of the basic purpose of this writing but simply in a logical carrying-through of his contrasting of the "hidden God" *(Deus absconditus)* and the "revealed God" *(Deus revelatus).* Even here and, as stated before, as early as 1519 he confronts the Christian with an "either-or" when putting the question why he is saved. Either ask whether you have been "elected" *(versehen),* predestined – then doubt surely leads you into despair. Or ask whether you have been redeemed from God's wrath and are reconciled to Him – then faith in Christ leads you to certainty, and you *are* redeemed and reconciled. In the scope of Luther's doctrine of salvation, therefore, there can be only redemption and reconciliation *or* predestination. Unless, together with later dogmaticians, one equates the concept of "election" *(electio)* with predestination and does so more logically than they themselves do. Then one can teach, as they do, that "predestination" *(praedestinatio)* is "not absolute but ordained" *(non absoluta, sed ordinata),* namely, "founded on Christ the Mediator" *(in Christo mediatore fundata)* – and in this way one would not yet come into conflict with Luther's total view, although he formally rejected a differentiation between the "ordained and the absolute will of God" *(voluntas Dei ordinata et absoluta).*[7] But between Luther and the later dogmaticians there is the Formula of Concord.

11. Reconciliation and Predestination in the Confessions in Conjunction [1]

Brief reference has already been made to what the confessions teach about reconciliation and redemption. Both the Apology and the Formula of Concord understand reconciliation and redemption to mean, now

[6] What Luther teaches about God in this writing without considering the questions of salvation and the certainty of salvation goes beyond the bounds of this chapter, which concerns itself with the "Gospel." Cf. *The Doctrine of God.*

[7] WA 18, 719, 14. Cf. Cundisius-Hutter. *Comp.,* pp. 785 ff. – König, *Theol. posit.,* pp. 110 ff. – Baier, *Comp.,* pp. 931 ff. – Schilter and Harbard, *Capita,* p. 661. – Brochmand. *Syst.* I. 248 ff.

[1] On the debate with Calvinism the best information is to be found in Frank, *Theol. d. Konkordienformel* IV, 1865, and in *Acta Colloquii Montis Belligartensis* (1586), Tübingen, 1587. – In addition, cf. Schlüsselburg, op. cit., Vol. 5, and the collection of quotations made by Joh. Pandocheus, *Consensus orthodoxus eccl. Luth. in doctrina de praedestinatione, Helmst.,* 1596. – Cf. M. Schneckenburger, *Darstellung des luth. u. reform. Lehrbegriffs* II, 1855, pp. 135 ff.

From the time of the Huberian predestination controversy, which cannot be dealt with here, and concerning Huber himself: Samuel Huber, *(1329 Theses!), Chr. Jesum*

something that occurred only once and was bound to Christ's Person and work, now something that happens to believers after this has taken place. Undoubtedly the concepts are understood in the first sense when they are used in connection with "satisfaction" *(satisfactio)* (Apology II, 40; IX, 19) and when it is stated here in the perfect tense that "enough has been done" *(satis est factum)* *(SD* III, 57 f.). Strictly speaking, the concept of imputation, which logically presupposes something that has already taken place, is based on this view. On the other hand, it is not necessarily implied in the formula "on account of Christ" *(propter Christum).* For this formula is applied simultaneously to forgiveness of sins and reconciliation (Apology VIII, 5). Yes, forgiveness of sins as well as justification are actually identified with reconciliation (Apology III, 37, 40, 61; *SD* III, 4, 25, 30). This is what is meant when, together with Augustine, it is stated "that He who justifies is conciliated through faith" *(justificatorem fide conciliari)* (Apology II, 106) or "that we are reconciled through faith" *(nos fide reconciliari)* (VI, 59). In like manner, when reconciliation is designated as what is promised, it appears as something to be carried out.

Accordingly, in the sense of the confessions the concept of reconciliation has to be admissible or necessary in both meanings. Moreover, this can also be pointed out in the private writings of the authors of the confessions. The relationship between Christ's historical work of reconciliation and the reconciliation to God experienced by us at the present time must be understood as being analogous to the relationship between the "righteousness of Christ" *(justitia Christi)* and "justification" *(justificatio).* Just as the "righteousness of Christ" *(justitia Christi)* cannot be handed down, so the historical work of reconciliation cannot be

esse mortuum pro peccatis totius generis humani ("that Christ Jesus died for the sins of the entire human race"), Tübingen, 1589. — *Acta Huberiana,* Tübingen, 1597. — Cf. Walch, *Religionsstreitigkeiten der ev.-luth. Kirchen* I, 2d ed., 1733, pp. 176 ff. — In addition, Aeg. Hunnius, *Art. de providentia Dei et aeterna praedestinatione,* 1596. — Zach. Schilter and Burch. Harbard, *Capita purae et incorrupt. Doctrinae Christ. primaria,* Leipzig, 1598, pp. 654 ff. — Contemporaneously the Dane Nic. Hemming taught as Melanchthon did, *Tractatus de gratia universali, Haffniae,* 1591. Similarly in the next century Joh. Musäus, *Diss. Inaugur. de aeternae praed. decreto,* 1668, and *De aeterno electionis decreto,* 1668, ss., and J. W. Baier, *Disp. de Universalitate Gratiae Divinae,* 1675.

On the controversy of North American Lutheranism concerning the doctrine of the election by grace cf. the periodicals *Lehre und Wehre,* 1880 ff.; *Der Lutheraner,* 1880, No. 2 ff. (here Ferd. Walther above all); and *Altes und Neues,* 1880 f. (here Loy and Stellhorn); Hochstetter, *Gesch. d. ev.-luth. Missourisynode,* 1885, pp. 338 f. — Dieckhoff, *Der missourische Praedestinationismus,* 1885, and *Zur Lehre v. d. Bekehrung u. v. d. Prädestination,* 1886. — J. W. Richard, *Confess. Hist. of the Luth. Church,* 1909, pp. 618 ff. — C. Blecher, *Die L. v. d. Gnadenwahl, mit bes. Rücksicht auf Konk.-Form. Art. XI u. d. Missouri-Synode,* 1902.

handed down. Concerning the latter as well as the former it is said that "we receive reconciliation through faith" *(reconciliationem fide accipimus)* (Apology III, 38) or that "we are reconciled to the Father and receive remission of sins when we are buoyed up by trust in the mercy promised on account of Christ" *(reconciliamur Patri et accipimus remissionem peccatorum, quando erigimur fiducia promissae misericordiae propter Christum)* (II, 81). Concerning the righteousness of Christ, which is identical with His perfect obedience, the Formula of Concord says that it is "the most perfect satisfaction and expiation for the human race" *(perfectissima pro humano genere satisfactio et expiatio).* But at the same time it calls that obedience our "righteousness" *(justitia) (SD* III, 57). In the sense of the confessions, therefore, it is, in the concrete *(in concreto),* the same thing in both instances: Christ's historical work of reconciliation is identical with His perfect righteousness. And likewise: the reconciliation to God received by me is identical with justification. Nevertheless, one must distinguish conceptually in both cases, since the concepts "righteousness" and "justification" consider God as the One who demands; the concepts "reconciliation" *(reconciliatio),* "propitiation" *(propitiatio),* "appeasal" *(placatio),* and "Mediator" *(mediator)* consider God as the One who has been offended; the concepts "redemption" *(redemptio)* and "freedom" *(libertas)* consider the condition that results for us. If one wanted to bring these three groups of concepts into a logical sequence, it is self-evident that logic would cause one to assign the last place to the third group. When the Apology occasionally also lets the first two follow each other – "because we, having been reconciled, are accounted righteous" *(quia reconciliati reputamur justi)* (II, 86) – this has meaning only when at that time it thinks of the historical work of redemption in connection with the term "having been reconciled" *(reconciliati).* If this is assumed, reconciliation and justification stand in relation to each other as the past does to the present. If, on the other hand, the Apology means reconciliation as an act occurring at the present time, it sometimes says "forgiveness of sins and reconciliation" *(remissio peccatorum et reconciliatio),* sometimes the reverse – a proof that between justification and reconciliation in this sense there is no logical sequence either.

Later dogmaticians still treat the concept of "reconciliation" *(reconciliatio)* and the concepts of "expiation" *(expiatio)* and "satisfaction" *(satisfactio)* – designated as synonyms since Johann Gerhard – only under the title *The Works of Christ.* Only "redemption" *(redemptio)* usually appears again in the area of eschatology. Where those concepts are still mentioned within the so-called "order of salvation" *(ordo salutis),* they invariably designate the historical act. The fact that dogmaticians divide Christ's sacerdotal office into the functions of "satisfaction" *(satisfactio)* and "intercession" *(intercessio)*, and with the second also designate Christ's reconciling activity as something that is done at the present time, can be regarded as a kind of equivalent.[2] Self-evidently, Luther and the confessions are also familiar with the Biblical concept of "intercession" *(intercessio)*.[3] But in the case of the dogmaticians — as a result of the place they give to this doctrine in their total arrangement — it can seem as though they did not know how to make proper use of it for the direct relationship of faith to God. To be sure, one can see from the literature of the same period that in the age of orthodoxy the understanding of reconciliation as a simultaneous act was not lost either.[4]

In a letter to Brenz, Melanchthon gives the following reason for omitting the doctrine of predestination from the Apology: "In the whole Apology I have shunned that long and perplexing discussion of predestination. Everywhere I speak as if predestination followed our faith and works. And I do this deliberately, for I do not want to perturb consciences with those intricate labyrinths." *(In tota Apologia fugi illam longam et inexplicabilem disputationem de praedestinatione. Ubique sic loquor, quasi praedestinatio sequatur nostram fidem et opera. Ac facio*

[2] Quenstedt, *Theol. III*, pp. 225 ff. In his *Theologia positiva acroamatica*, which in other respects is rather dry, König quotes the hymn stanza beginning with the words "Be My Intercessor on the Last Day," p. 154.

[3] WA 18, 778, 12; WA 41, 192, 6 f.; 196, 2. *CA* XXI; Apology IX, 31.

[4] M. Dan. Hänichen (court preacher in Electoral Saxony), *Serpens exaltatus, Leichenpredigt f. d. kaiserl. Kammerorganisten Joh. Leo Hassler*, 1612: "During his illness here and after he had realized that the end of his life was at hand, he made his peace with God last Friday after the sermon. He acknowledged his sin in true, heartfelt penitence and sorrow. But in true faith . . . he looked at the exalted serpent Jesus Christ; took comfort in His precious merit, suffering, and death; and, after receiving absolution . . . he partook of the true body and blood of Christ."

Melchior Othonius (pastor at Burgfarrenbach), *Homo Stella . . . Sermon über d. Abschied d. Herrn Thomas Immigers* [a merchant from Regensburg], 1613: "Thus our . . . brother . . . had to go the way of all the world. When he realized this, he sent for me while there was still time and desired to make his peace with God and to strengthen himself with Holy Communion . . ."

Manifestly in the same sense the Apology calls the sacraments "signs of reconciliation" (V, 43; cf. *SD* XI, 38).

In 1667, in answer to the question "What shall one do, or how should one guard against the pestilence?" Christoph Schorer, a physician in Memmingen, replies in his *Kurzer Unterricht vornehmlich von Cur der Pest:* "First make your peace with God the Lord. Then, when you have a merciful God, He will put His blessing on the remedies all the sooner." Cf. Friedr. Braun, *Chr. Schorer*, 1926, p. 138; cf. also pp. 136, 182.

When the physician asked the dying Jacob Andreä how he was feeling, Andreä replied: "Not separated from God." O. Wächter, *J. A. Bengel*, 1865, p. 428.

hoc certo consilio; non enim volo conscientias perturbare illis inexplicabilibus labyrinthis.) (*CR* 2, 547.) The reason given is not unobjectionable, especially when the writer of the letter admits that he has presented the doctrine of salvation as if predestination followed our faith and works. This "as if" *(quasi)* became ominous for the subsequent development of Melanchthon's doctrine, and Luther would hardly have sanctioned it. On the other hand, Melanchthon's reason agrees perfectly with Luther's conception so far as danger to consciences is concerned. It would even have tallied with Luther's conception if Melanchthon had spoken about danger to faith. Even then Melanchthon was not far away from pedagogical opportunism. But the point at which this became dangerous was the doctrine of conversion. To be sure, he also fought his battle against the determinism of the ἀνάγκη (compulsion) of the Stoics by pointing out libertinistic implications *(CR* 7, 331). But the ever-recurring discussion with this opponent reminds one that from the very beginning, even as far back as the *Loci* of 1521, he was in danger of treating predestination first and foremost as a problem of the philosophy of life *(Weltanschauung).* Anyone who finds fault with his philosophical doctrine of freedom and contingency after 1532 should not praise what he taught about predestination before 1527. From the standpoint of evangelical faith the one position was just as untenable as the other. For both had the same point of departure – the same one that makes Zwingli the forerunner of the Enlightenment. The statement of the *Lucubrations* (*Lucubratiuncula)* of 1521 – "that from no other source is there more certain comfort than from predestination" *(non aliunde certius esse solatium ut ex praedestinatione)* *(CR* 21, 15) – was consistent with the other doctrine of salvation of the same year only when, as in Luther, the doctrine of predestination became an auxiliary statement which – substantiated in itself in an altogether different way – could support certainty of salvation against doubt that God is also willing and able to make His promises come true. But certainty of predestination can perform this service only when it is certainty of *election.* Therefore it was in exact conformity with Luther's position when in the later editions of the *Loci* Melanchthon restricted that "comfort" *(solatium)* to certainty of election *(CR* 21, 453; 920). But if one has any right at all to speak of a "comfort" *(solatium)* afforded by this doctrine, it cannot be out of place either to examine the effect of this doctrine on the conscience from the other side too, as Melanchthon did in the aforementioned letter to Brenz. Peace of conscience, which is the important matter here, is not the false security of synergism – just as it should not be the false security of a fatalistic belief in salvation.

On the contrary, the conscience that is reconciled in faith in Christ is meant. This freedom of conscience rests on – or is – certainty of faith, and all its components have the mark of reality. But if the doctrine of predestination is understood in such a way that it confronts the believer with the question whether he is predestined to salvation or to disaster, the most important of those components, namely, God's will over the believer, again takes on the omen of potentiality. But doubt, not faith, is consistent with God's will as a potentiality. Therefore in the Apology, which is not a system of dogmatics but was written for the purpose of establishing the bases of evangelical certainty of salvation, Melanchthon had good reason for declining to include an auxiliary doctrine which could provoke doubt.

Brenz adopted Luther's thought from another angle. His letter of February 1526 to Bernhard Griebler was obviously written because of the strong impression made by Luther's writing against Erasmus.[5] Here Brenz corroborates the statement that "all things in heaven and on earth come to pass because of the compulsion of the constraining almighty or, if I should speak more plainly, all-extensively active will of God and not because of their own choice or freedom" *(alle ding im himel und auff erden auss not des zwingenden almechtigen, Oder so Ich deutlicher reden sol, althetlichen willen gottis und nit auss aigner chur oder freyheit geschehen).* In a supralapsarian vein he emphasizes that God "before the creation of the world sat in secret council and came to a decision regarding all men, ordained some for salvation, the others for damnation; and, as it is there ordained, so it must necessarily continue; no mouse bites off a thread" *(vor erschaffung der Welt ein heimlichen Rat besessen und uber all menschen beschlossen, Ein parthey zur selikait verordnet, die ander zu verdamnus, und wie es darin verordnet ist, also muss es von not wegen furtgeen, da beyst jm kein mauss ein faden ab)* (28). But he proceeds: "We, however, are not capable of understanding this counsel" *(Wir sein aber des Rats unser verstentnus nach nit vehig).* Why not? For one thing, our inability to understand amounts to a lack of knowledge of the final bases of the divine will. "But how all this takes place and what the reason is . . . why . . . it is not possible for any man to think or say; one should rather obediently hold such secret, hidden things in reverence and believe that they are just and wise than indulge in painstaking investigation" *(Wie aber solichs alles zugee und was die ursach . . . warumb . . . ist keinem menschen muglich zugedencken oder zureden, Sonder solche heimliche verborgne ding meher gehorsamlich anzubeten und als gerecht und weys zu glauben, denn sorgfeltiglich zu*

[5] Th. Pressel, *Anecdota Brentiana,* 1868, pp. 26 ff.

forschen) (27). The allusion to Luther's "adoration" *(adoratio)* of the hidden God is clear. But then Brenz continues: "According to my custom, I call this matter the secret, divine chancellery" *(Ich nenne diess stuck meiner gewohnheit nach die heimlich gotlich Cantzlei).* In this chancellery the Father, the Son, and the Spirit take counsel with one another and reach their decision regarding the two divisions of mankind. But we cannot understand the secret language of the chancellery. It must "be transferred and changed into our mother tongue" *(in unser mutersprach transferirt und verendert).* This purpose is served by the sending of the Son, the "Word," whose "work it is to give information concerning His will to those who are waiting before the chancellery for a decision with regard to salvation or damnation" *(vor der Cantzlei eins beschaids warten, der selickait oder verdamnus halben, seines willens zu verstendigen hat)* (28). He speaks the language of mankind. This language states unmistakably: "Believe, and you will be saved. Do good, and you will be rescued *(behalten).* If you do not believe, you will be damned." (29.) Yes, according to God's revealed speech, He can and wants to redeem even a rejected person who repents and, conversely, to forget the righteousness of a righteous person if that person trusts in his own righteousness. Thus the Holy Spirit lets "the language remain in its manner and kind but by it teaches to believe and to revere God's unalterable will, which reason cannot grasp and the speech of man cannot express" *(die sprach pleyben in ir weys und art, lert aber darunter zu glauben und anzubeten den unwandelbarlichen willen gottes, der mit vernunfft nit mag erlangt noch mit menschlicher red gefasst werden).*

Here, in spite of all dependence on Luther, definite modifications are already in evidence. In the first place, Brenz does not have Luther's profound terror of the idea of predestination. The enormity of a possible supralapsarian "rejection" *(reprobatio)* is obviously not felt at all. For Luther, of course, the fear that he himself could be numbered among those who are rejected recedes wholly behind the horrible thought of the demoniacal nature of a God who by virtue of His superior ability forces creatures into a guilt relationship from which He then derives a right to inflict cruel torture on them. If this thought cannot be separated from a general doctrine of predestination, his teaching must be subdued altogether by faith in the God revealed in Christ. In Brenz all this is toned down. Faith clings to revelation because the secret decision in the divine chancellery is unknown to us, not because it is unimaginably horrible. Missing is what Luther calls the close bond between the "hidden God" *(Deus absconditus)* and the angry God *(Deus iratus).* Missing, too, is the knowledge that the whole search for an answer to the why – the search that leads to the docrine of predestination – springs from the hunger "reason" *(ratio)* has for the interrelation between cause and effect *(Kausalitätshunger)* – the hunger which, in this form at least, stands, on principle, in opposition to faith.

In a certain sense the eleventh article of the Formula of Concord is a synthesis of the trains of thought of Melanchthon and Brenz that have been indicated. At first, of course, it could appear strange that the Formula of Concord assigns to the doctrine of predestination any independent position at all in its doctrine of salvation. Here one can totally disregard the question whether this was demanded by the confessional tensions of the moment in history. With Luther, of course, this matter could have called to the predestinarians in the West: "One must treat either of the hidden or of the revealed God" *(Aut disputandum de Deo abscondito aut de revelato)* – we know nothing about the former, and therefore our theology can be concerned only with the latter. Yet the reasons for the adoption of this article were by no means merely external in nature, as if perhaps only Scripture statements had necessitated this action. A confession cannot be a Biblical theology. Neither can mere reverence for the Luther of 1525 have been the decisive factor, even though this article shows the same turning-back to Luther that one sees in the article on free will. For in his disputation against V. Strigel even Flacius, the protagonist of this whole turning-back, wanted to refrain from passing judgment on the writing *On the Bondage of the Will (De servo arbitrio)*.[6] No, the writers of the confession must have felt an inner compulsion to establish their doctrine of predestination. And they leave no doubt as to where they found this doctrine. For them it had conclusive significance. Everything "pertaining to our redemption, calling, justification, and salvation" is, "according to Scripture, contained *(comprehenduntur)* in the doctrine of God's eternal election to filial relationship *(Kindschaft)* and to everlasting salvation" *(SD* XI, 13–24).

On the one hand, of course, there was a restriction here. The foundation of the doctrine of salvation must have a different point of departure. The confession quotes Luther's introduction to the Epistle to the Romans (1522) with its admonition to observe the arrangement of this epistle: first Christ and the Gospel, from which you gain knowledge of your sin and His grace; then your struggle against sin; finally, when, according to Romans 8, one is troubled *(in Anfechtung kommt)*, one must learn from chapters nine to eleven how comforting election is *(SD* XI, 33; cf. Erlangen edition 63, 135). Yet nowhere did Luther speak of embracing

[6] *Disputatio de orig., pecc. et de lib. arbitr. inter Matth. Flacium Illyr. et Victorin. Strigelium a. 1560 habita, ed. Simon Musäus, ed. 2, 1563,* p. 115.

the whole doctrine of salvation in the doctrine of predestination. According to his understanding, it was by no means possible for him to do so. Here there is attached to predestination a significance that seems to go beyond everything Luther, Brenz, Amsdorf, and Flacius — not to mention Melanchthon and his adherents — ever taught about it.

Even from this it follows that the Formula of Concord pursues the whole problem from a viewpoint different from the one Luther has in his writing against Erasmus. And not only this. It understands predestination to be something else. The content of "God's counsel and purpose" *(consilium et propositum Dei)* is His decision that the human race be redeemed and be reconciled to God through faith; that Christ's merit be offered and distributed through Word and sacrament; that through preaching His Spirit convert and preserve in faith; that believers be justified, be received into a filial relationship *(Kindschaft),* and be sanctified in love, strengthened in their weakness, comforted in trouble *(Anfechtung);* that the good work begun in them be preserved to the end; and finally that those who are elected, called, and justified also attain eternal salvation *(SD* XI, 14–22). In other words, the content of predestination is God's whole plan of salvation. Therefore this article *(Lehrstück),* like every other article in theology, is concerned with revelation. No non-Reformed *(nichtreformiert)* reader needs proof that with this interpretation of the idea of predestination the Formula of Concord stands on good Scriptural grounds. Strictly speaking, then, it does not contain a single new element over and above the other constituents *(Faktoren)* of the Gospel. It is rather an analytical judgment which from the sum total of these constituents brings into prominence the one that is common to all: God desires and brings to pass all the work that is done to save mankind.

"Therefore God's eternal predestination is to be considered in Christ and by no means outside Christ the Mediator" *(Aeterna igitur Dei praedestinatio in Christo et nequaquam extra mediatorem Christum consideranda)* (65), the pivotal statement of the whole article, is merely another way of expressing this. The idea of predestination expressed in this way is itself an element of the Gospel. Consequently, it can by no means detract from the universal character of the promise of the Gospel — the character which, according to the New Testament, is incontrovertibly established. On the contrary, it must, conversely, be a part of this character (28). And it lies in the nature of faith itself that we "do not regard as humbug" *(vor kein Spiegelfechten halten)* the call that goes out to all men (29). To be sure, according to the statement of the Gospel, the divine decree of salvation applies also to the individual "persons of the elect who are to be saved through Christ" (23). To this extent it is at the same time particular. But the believer can never refer the designation of individual elected persons for salvation to anyone but himself. By looking to Christ he can be confident of *his* election (43). But since he can do this only because the promise holds true in earnest for all and therefore for him too, the certainty of particular election can by no means do away with the universal character of the divine counsel of salvation.

From the fact that the thought of predestination is firmly anchored in the Gospel there arise two further conclusions. The certainty of being elected can be based on nothing else than the certainty of faith itself, namely, on the Person and the work of Christ. Accordingly, those who are troubled with regard to their election *(die ob ihrer Erwählung Angefochtenen)* are to be referred to the means of grace, to Word and sacrament, in which the promise of the Gospel is offered to them (37 ff.), but not by any chance to "what they find in themselves," namely, to their "piety and virtue," which the Spirit brings about in the elect (73–75). At this point the divergent position of Calvinism with respect to the idea of predestination becomes most clearly apparent from a pracical point of view. If the question whether one is elected diverts one's view for but a moment from Christ to the "fruits of faith," then one has gone back almost precisely to the doctrine of certainty which Luther attacked and which resulted in his book.[7] It is true that the Formula of Concord, in conformity with the Biblical direction, admonishes believers "to make sure," by practicing all virtues "that they have been called and elected, in order that the more they find the Spirit's power and strength in themselves, the less they may be in doubt of this" (73). But the context teaches that it is by no means the purpose of these words to designate one's own moral quality or accomplishments as the reason

[7] Cf. Erasm. Marbach, *Disput. de Gratia unter J. Heerbrand,* Tübingen, 1572, thesis 64: "And what madness this is on the part of the enemies of faith and of the Word of God! They want people to be in doubt concerning the grace of God toward them, even though they rely on His grace and on the merit of Christ. Meanwhile indeed — which is not only strange but horrible to hear — they want people to promise themselves with certainty the favor of God because of their own virtues, if they find these in themselves, and to receive pious confidence from this source. On the one hand, they urge them to be certain because they trust in themselves and in their own virtues; on the other hand, they urge them to be in doubt even though they believe in Christ and rely on His merit." *(Et quis furor hic est hostium fidei et Verbi Dei, quos homines de Gratia erga se volunt dubitare, fretos ipsius Misericordia et Christi merito: Interim vero — quod auditu non mirum tantum sed horrendum est — certo sibi polliceri favorem Dei propter proprias virtutes, si eas in se reperiunt, hincque piam eos volunt concipere fiduciam. Hic in se confidentes et suas virtutes, certos esse jubent, Illinc in Christum credentes, eiusque merito nitentes, dubitare.)*

for the certainty of election. No, shortly before this the person in doubt is unambiguously referred solely to the Word of Christ (70). In addition to this, it is stated: "According to this teaching of His, they should desist from their sins, repent, believe His promise, and rely wholly on Him; and because we are unable to do this of ourselves by our own strength, the Holy Spirit wants to work this, namely, penitence and faith, in us through the Word and through the sacraments" (71). The aforementioned statement with regard to making sure of election is most closely connected with this. It is a matter of making sure of election in an objective sense, that is, the realization in time of God's eternal counsel. By no means does this counsel consider only man's final goal, "everlasting life" *(vita aeterna);* it considers the filial relationship *(Kindschaft)* of the believers – the relationship which includes the definite effects for their concrete humanity. These effects, like all effects of the Spirit, take place only through "Word and Sacrament" – so that the idea of making sure objectively of election cannot be interpreted synergistically. When, therefore, the elect "find the power and strength of the Spirit in themselves," this can contribute toward the overcoming of doubt only when attention is actually directed to the power of the Spirit, who is operative in the Word. This is amply confirmed when it is stated further: "And even though they perhaps come into such deep trouble *(Anfechtung)* that they think they no longer feel any power of the indwelling Spirit of God . . . then, in spite of this, they should say again with David, regardless of what they find in themselves: . . . 'Nevertheless, Thou hearest the voice of my supplications.'" (74.)

Then it follows from the way in which the Gospel presents the idea of predestination that those who are rejected are burdened with their own guilt. If faith is really certain that God's decree of salvation applies to the "world," that is, to the world in the New Testament sense, therefore to the substance of sin and the state of being lost – without this certainty faith might just as well be buried – man's resistance cannot at the same time have God as its instigator. "For this would be falsely ascribing contradictory wills to God" *(Hoc enim esset Deo contradictorias voluntates affingere)* (35). On the contrary, just as "the devil's and mankind's evil, perverse will" is "the beginning and the cause of evil" (7), so contempt for the Word [of calling]" is "not the cause of God's election – either God's foreknowledge or predestination *(vel praescientia vel praedestinatio Dei)* – but man's perverse will" (41). To be sure, there is an impenitence that goes back to a divine decree. But it takes place in the case of those "who are called by means of the Word when they reject the Word and persistently resist the Holy Spirit, who wants to be strong and operative in them through the Word" (40). By distinguishing between "foreknowledge" *(praescientia)* and "predestination" *(praedestinatio)* the Formula of Concord attempted to meet the objection that God's unconditional power over destiny is questioned by tracing damnation back to autonomous resistance on the part of man. "Predestination" *(praedestinatio)*, of course, extends only to the children of God (5); but "foreknowledge" *(praescientia)* extends to all creatures as such (4). One cannot deny that both are necessary assertions of evangelical faith. The constantly repeated charge that the confession is merely a way out of a dilemma is invalid as soon as one grants the premise of the confession that according to the New Testament predestination means God's decree of salvation.

There is another question. When one traces the salvation of believers back solely to God's will, does it not follow logically that in the case of those who are lost this will was simply lacking and that in the final analysis their rejection also goes back solely to divine causation? Then if, in spite of this, rejection is based on sin, one must go to the end of this path and conclude further that God is also the originator of sin. For if sin were based on the human interrelation of cause and effect *(die menschliche Kausalität)*, the divine decree of rejection would still not be absolute; it would be conditional, because it would be dependent on a decision of man. But not even Calvin and Beza dared make God the originator of sin. Therefore at this point, which is most important for them, their system — allegedly so strictly logical — is not a bit more logical than that of the Formula of Concord. But the Formula of Concord by no means claims to be rationally consistent; it claims only that it safeguards what faith knows to be certain. Concerning God this faith knows that He wants to have mercy on all — but concerning itself it knows that it must make a decision when it hears the call "Be reconciled to God" (27). Therefore the only thing it can do is to assume sole responsibility for the possibility of rejecting that call — the possibility implicit in the concept "decision." As actual faith it is constantly concerned with the God who has been revealed in Christ — the God who is not simply the "cause" *(causa)* but the "cause of salvation" *(causa salutis)*. For this reason the decision regarding the doctrine of predestination as set forth in the Formula of Concord has nothing at all to do with the question whether the Formula of Concord is right when it distinguishes between "foreseeing" *(praevisio)* and "predestination" *(praedestinatio)* or when it declares that man alone is to blame for his rejection. No, these are self-evident conclusions which faith must draw from the two facts that (1) salvation comes to it, not as a natural compulsion but as an offer and (2) that Christ's call is expressed in such a way that no one who hears it can doubt that it applies to him too.

Even Brenz could say nothing different about the Word of revelation heard by those who wait outside the "chancellery" *(Kanzleistube)*. But the Formula of Concord was also in agreement with Melanchthon in that it regards certainty of predestination as certainty of election. Luther, too, was on its side. In his writing against Erasmus he had said about the "proclaimed God" *(Deus praedicatus)*: "He wants all men to be saved, since He comes to all with the Word of salvation; and the fault is in the will, which does not grant Him admittaance" *(Vult omnes homines salvos fieri, dum verbo salutis ad omnes venit, vitiumque est voluntatis, quae non admittit eum)* (WA 18, 686, 6).

To be sure, the Formula of Concord is also aware of a secret counsel of God (9, 70). It knows that even of the mystery revealed in Christ God "has held back and concealed much and has reserved it for His wisdom and knowledge" (52). It warns against brooding over this, for such brooding causes either "security and impenitence or despondency and despair" (10). We should not "explore the abyss of God's hidden foreknowledge" (33). The confession designates the content of this foreknowledge when it states "that God foresaw who and how many should be saved and who and how many should be damned, or that He alone held such a review *(eine solche Musterung gehalten)*: this one shall be saved, that one shall be damned; this one shall remain constant, that one shall not remain constant" (9; cf. 54). Furthermore, He alone "sets for everyone the time and the hour when he is to be called and when he is to be converted" (56) – which reminds one of the statement of the Augsburg Confession that the Holy Spirit works faith "when and where He wills" (Art. 5). And God alone knows why He sends out *(freigeben)* His Word for one place or one people but not for the other, for hardening and for a call to turn back (57 f.). Ultimately the danger of brooding over this is traceable to the one-sided causal view of what happens in the world: "What God foresees must take place," "I can neither hinder nor change what God foresees" (10) – this is identical with Melanchthon's warning against the ἀνάγκη (compulsion) of the Stoics. But this brooding is also misleading because it proceeds from the notion that "God's eternal salvation or ordainment for everlasting life . . . contains nothing further or that nothing more belongs to it, or that one has to consider nothing more than that God foresaw who and how many should be saved, etc." – the statement quoted above from Section 9 follows.

Here the weakening of the thought of the "hidden God" *(Deus absconditus)*, which we observed in Brenz, has progressed still further. Whatever part of His secret God does not reveal but reserves formally for His own knowledge can, so far as its content is concerned, not only not contradict His revealed will of salvation, but on principle it cannot detract from what has been revealed when this is applied to the individual person. From the statement quoted last (9) one can see that for the Formula of Concord the questioning aimed at the hidden will appears even as an inadmissible simplification of the thought of predestination. The thought of a simple "review" *(Musterung)* of future generations — "this one will be saved, that one will be damned" — appears to be a theft from the richness of the divine thoughts that planned and carried through the salvation of the world. If at first glance this amounts to a passing look at the horrors felt by Luther at the thought of the "hidden God" *(Deus absconditus)*, still one will have the same right to say that precisely in this way Luther's demand that theology should cling only to the "proclaimed God" *(Deus praedicatus)* was seriously taken into account. To be sure, the important change in usage is this, that here the concept of predestination, which for Luther is closely connected with the "hidden God" *(Deus absconditus)*, is used as a definitive expression for the revealed God's work of salvation. But even here the Formula of Concord adopted a thought of Luther's which found in the idea of predestination a strengthening of the certainty of faith — but could find it only when, as here, predestination is referred to salvation. On the other hand, when in Luther this idea also belonged to faith insofar as faith is faith only when it overcomes what is apparent, it was, of course, not the thought of predestination as such that must be overcome but the necessary connection into which — as Luther expressed it — it entered with the apparent demoniacal injustice of God *against* which one must believe. For Luther, however, this connection was merely a special application of the thought of the wrath of God. And it has already been shown how the Formula of Concord is in agreement not only with what Luther teaches about this wrath but also with what he teaches about reconciliation to God.

If in this way the Formula of Concord attempted to bring the doctrine of predestination more completely into harmony with the doctrine of reconciliation and redemption through Christ than was the case in Luther's writing against Erasmus, still this was done on the basis of the principle Luther had proclaimed in that very writing: "For we, too, teach nothing but Jesus Christ crucified" *(Nam et nos nihil nisi Jhesum*

Christum crucifixum docemus) (WA 18, 638, 24).[8] The statement of the confession that "predestination is by no means to be considered outside Christ" *(praedestinatio nequaquam extra Christum consideranda)* is an accurate application of this. If another confession boasts of having made its doctrine of predestination redound wholly and solely "to the glory of God," Lutheranism may claim that in its confessions everything is said for the glory of Christ.[9] And Lutheranism may confidently look forward to the investigation whether in this way it has decreased or increased the "glory of God." Later it will be pointed out that with regard to God the Formula of Concord has not yet spoken the last word concerning the whole question.

12. Faith and the Psyche

The Lutheran doctrine of justification distinguishes a twofold subjectivity of man. This does not presuppose any critical power of discernment based on special knowledge; it is connected with the elementary fact that man himself becomes the object of reflection. If in his reflections he thinks to a conclusion in the direction of what he is and in the direction of what he could or should be, he stands before that maze of destiny and guilt which was developed as the "primal experience" *(Urerlebnis)*. If finally one takes as the object of reflection the laws of thinking itself that are applied here – for Luther this is "reason" *(ratio)* in the formal sense – the thinking I shrivels to a mathematical point without content and without extent. Nevertheless, the content of my consciousness has not vanished, and all facts and possibilities belonging to it characterize "me." They are my possessions. I myself am all this. I imagine; I know, and I have the will; I feel, and I have the desire. Thus there is a twofold subjectivity: the transcendental I as a "mathematical point" *(punctum mathematicum)* and the psychic I that is saturated with content.

Later we came upon the fundamental difference between Luther and mysticism. Whereas German mysticism, in its technically flawless carrying-through of the reduction of thinking to the transcendental I – or, as German mysticism itself expresses it, to nothing – sees the birth of God in man, for Luther it is a question of a judicial act in the strict sense. That separation of I and I is carried through as "self-accusation" *(accusatio sui)*. I myself am the object of my reflection, because I am

[8] Cf. WA 18, 609, 29; WA 25, 333, 13; Enders 4, 288, 15.

[9] *Epit.* III, 7; *SD* III, 30; 35. — *CA* XXVII, 38. — Apology II, 2; III, 94, 178. 196; VIII, 83; IX, 31. Cf. Luther in *De servo arbitrio* (WA 18, 744, 15, and *Justification in the Confessions*).

compelled to look at the concrete aspects *(das Konkretum)* of my life or, what amounts to the same thing, of my consciousness, with the eyes of God. To be sure, these concrete aspects, too, then shrivel to a mathematical point; yet this does not occur because they should be forgotten or obliterated but because God's judgment, the thoughts of which the transcendental I follows up, lies in another dimension, since it takes all life "from the outside" as a unit. Looked at from within, life keeps its total content as a multitude of separate things – before God it is taken as a whole and condemned as a unit.

Furthermore, this distinguishing of a twofold subjectivity is the formal presupposition of the doctrine of justification. The subject of the faith that receives the "righteousness of God" *(justitia Dei)* is the transcendental I. It is altogether empty, merely a "mathematical point" *(punctum mathematicum).* The righteousness adjudged to it is "alien" *(aliena)* in the strict sense. Here, on principle, the matter could end and, so far as the righteousness "that avails before God" *(die vor Gott gilt)* is concerned, must end. But just as the differentiation between I and I in the form of the judicial act can or should not obliterate the psychic state, so the mere specification of faith as a point *(Punktualität)* cannot do away with the relationship of the transcendental I to the psychic I. Of course, no change can take place when the second is judged by means of the first. The judgment will always be an "accusation" *(accusatio).* But this does not mean that the concrete aspects *(das Konkretum)* of our life undergo no actual change in content because of faith. The very opposite is true. The transcendental I is, of course, merely an abstraction. Although this abstraction is necessary, it is possible and significant only as long as there exist concrete aspects *(Konkretum)* filled with psychic life. Yes, this abstraction is always merely in the process of being carried out, merely an act, never something actually carried out – otherwise it itself would have become a psychic fact. Consequently, it is always in the process of being related to the concrete aspects *(das Konkretum)* of life. Then, however, the transcendental I's turnabout from accusation to faith must become operative or at least noticeable in this relationship too. To express it in another way: what happens or has happened to the transcendental I cannot fail to affect the sum total of the content of consciousness.

By means of a series of Biblical concepts which they group under the title "The Appropriating Grace of the Holy Spirit" *(Gratia Spiritus Sancti Applicatrix)* later dogmaticians attempted to illustrate the change that takes place with regard to all the constituent parts of man.[1] With

[1] Quenstedt, *Theol.* III, 461; König, *Theol.*, p. 184; Hollaz, *Examen* III, 318.

their "order of salvation" *(ordo salutis)* they sought — in accordance with the precedent set by Luther in the explanation of the Third Article of the Apostles' Creed — an answer to the question whether there can also be a contact of the Spirit of God with the concrete consciousness of man, that is, with the consciousness of man when understood with reference to its empirical content, not transcendentally. And in this way they disposed of a task set by Luther's whole theology and by the whole theology of the confessions. This theology had concentrated rightfully on the doctrine of justification — with the result that Hafenreffer, who was the first to enumerate the various parallel acts side by side, could still decide that if one understood the doctrine of justification, everything else was "very easy to grasp" *(sehr leicht einzusehen)* and could therefore, as in his own case, simply be passed over.[2] It is true that from the very beginning Luther and Melanchthon — and the confessions to no smaller extent — had discussed the problem thoroughly from *one* angle when they inquired into the relationship between faith and works. For in doing so they had not only excluded works so far as validity before God is concerned; but at the same time they had demanded them as a necessary result of faith and had thereby maintained nevertheless that faith, when understood transcendentally, affects directly what is empirically concrete in man *(das empirische Konkretum des Menschen).* Here, however, the basic question had been how the experience of justification can turn into moral activity in connection with which, as is self-evident, the accents — decidedly passive in part — of Luther's ethic are also to be rated as moral activity in a broader sense. But for this reason it was also necessary to determine whether the new I of faith did not itself likewise represent a change in the psychic state of affairs in general.

To be sure, the "call" *(vocatio)* and the "enlightenment" *(illuminatio),* the first two of the acts which later dogmaticians put in the foremost place, in no way go beyond what has taken place before, since here one can disregard the "direct call" *(vocatio immediata),* which they found in the case of the apostles and the prophets. The possibility of a "direct

[2] Hafenreffer, *Loci,* p. 662: The benefits *(beneficia)* that are appropriated through faith and the sacraments "are many, namely, justification, regeneration, adoption, renewal, sanctification, salvation, glorification. But all these have been procured in such a way that after the procedure of justification has been set forth . . . it is very easy to understand what one should think about the rest of the benefits and how those benefits, too, accrue to us." *(plura sunt, Utpote, Justificatio, Regeneratio, Adoptio, Renovatio, Sanctificatio, Salvatio, Glorificatio. Sed isthaec omnia ita sunt comparata, ut exposita ratione Iustificationis . . . quid de reliquis beneficiis sentiendum sit et quomodo nobis illa quoque obtingant, facillimum sit intellectu.)*

enlightenment" *(illuminatio immediata)* is contested over against the Enthusiasts. The call never takes place except through the Word, that is, through the Law, to convince us of sin and of the wrath of God, and through the Gospel, to assure us of the grace of God in Christ. The "changes in disposition brought about by the call" *(affectiones vocationis)*, according to which the call is "serious" *(seria)*, "efficacious" *(efficax)*, "resistible" *(resistibilis)*, "inevitable" *(inevitabilis)*, and "universal" *(universalis)*, are taken from the doctrine of predestination as set forth in the Formula of Concord, and only in view of the further development of Calvinism are they intensified. On the other hand, the aforementioned problem is felt directly in connection with the ensuing concepts of "conversion" *(conversio)* and "regeneration" *(regeneratio)*, which, of course, are included in this doctrine by Calov as "concepts related to" *(cognatae)* the "call" *(vocatio)* (*Syst.* X, 1–159).

One can understand Philipp Nicolai's attempt to subordinate the whole process of salvation to the concept of regeneration.[3] No rival concept excludes every Pelagian interpretation as clearly as this one does – if it is taken seriously. It expresses man's passive attitude in an unambiguous manner. In addition, however, it has an advantage in that it binds the "new life" inseparably to the turning to faith. Of course, this did not prevent pietism from using the same concept as a pseudonym for its activistic "striving for sanctification" *(Heiligungsstreben)*. The dogmaticians, on the other hand, follow the narrower interpretation established by the Formula of Concord – the interpretation according to which the word "means only forgiveness of sins and that we are adopted as children of God" *(heisset allein Vergebung der Sünden und dass wir zu Kindern Gottes angenommen werden)* (*SD* III, 19). In support of this it refers to the language used in the Apology. Here, then, the emphasis is on the obvious connection between the new birth and the filial relationship *(Kindschaft)* of those who believe. Then all this is merely a graphic way of paraphrasing the process of justification.[4]

But even if one lets the concept have its full graphic effect, nevertheless an element that was not yet expressed in the previously presented

[3] Then it should embrace the following elements: "(1) The evangelical justification of a penitent sinner; (2) the gracious acceptance into heavenly adoption; (3) our spiritual betrothal to the great Bridegroom Jesus Christ; (4) the indwelling of God in our hearts; (5) the elevation of the children of God to the royal priesthood; (6) the divine renewal of man through the Holy Spirit; and finally (7) the cleansing or testing of the upright Christian." *Theoria vitae aeternae,* 1606 (cf. *Alle Teutschen Schrifften,* ed. by G. Dedekenn, I, Hamburg, 1617, pp. 147 ff. — Cf. the entire third volume.)

[4] Here we are still leaving the relationship of Baptism to regeneration out of account. Cf. *The Sacrament of Baptism.*

concept of justification cannot be separated from it, namely, the fact that through faith the man who believes becomes a different person — from the person he was before. Of course, the Formula of Concord is willing to admit this only when the expression is used in a broader sense, namely, as synonymous with "sanctification and renewal," concerning which it then says that they "follow the righteousness of faith" (*SD* III, 21). But it is precisely at this point that the Formula of Concord insists on strict differentiation, in order to preclude the notion "that after regeneration no unrighteousness clings any longer to the justified and regenerate in their being and life" *(dass den Gerechtfertigten und Wiedergeborenen keine Ungerechtigkeit nach der Wiedergeburt im Wesen und Leben mehr sollte anhangen)* (22). And it must do this to keep from endangering the truth that the justification of a sinner is a whole or something that is completed in faith, that sanctification, on the other hand, is only "piecework" *(Stückwerk)* "all the way to the grave" *(bis in die Gruben).* Luther used the concept of "sanctification" *(sanctificatio)* as a synonym for justification.[5] Accordingly, he looked upon the gift of holiness as a whole. But to declare that faith leads to no change at all in man's psychic make-up never occurred either to him or to the Formula of Concord, not even to Flacius. Luther's whole ethic is based on the knowledge that man has to be good in order to do good works. No matter what a more precise understanding of this may be, it is clear that in this way the assertion was made that faith puts all mankind in a new setting.

Therefore it was not a departure from Luther's view when the dogmaticians maintained that regeneration in the narrower sense also leads to an actual change in the psychic state of affairs. Thus Baier taught that in regeneration God "presents [man] with spiritual strength on the part of the intellect and the will to believe in Christ and to begin a life that is spiritual in the same degree, or brings forth this [strength] in [man] himself" *(ex parte intellectus et voluntatis viribus spiritualibus ad credendum in Christum vitamque adeo spiritualem inchoandam donat aut eas in ipso producit)* (*Comp.*, p. 678). Here the only thing that gives one pause is the fact that Baier lets the psychic change come about for the purpose of faith. But the context shows that for him the thing

[5] E. g., WA 28, pp. 173 ff. and 175, 7: "He who believes that Christ sanctified Himself for us, he has been sanctified" *(Qui credit Christum pro nobis se sanctificasse, hic est sanctificatus).* 178, 2: "Therefore every Christian is holy" *(Omnis Christianus ergo est Sanctus).* L. 8: "that he is sanctified through the Word" *(sanctificari per verbum).* L. 20: "that he is sanctified through an alien sanctity" *(sanctificari aliena sanctitate).* Cf. WA 41, 551, 4 ff. Furthermore, Luther's Catechisms on the Third Article and the quotations, Apology II, 86 and III, 185.

that matters is the fact that this is merely an abstract delimitation, even though it seems to be a delimitation in point of time. It is equally irrelevant that Baier, in accordance with the whole psychology of the dogmaticians, separates intellect and will from each other, and how he does this. Furthermore, the reality of a psychic change is expressed when "regeneration" *(regeneratio)* is designated as "successive" *(successiva)* (König, p. 191) or as "gradual and growing" *(gradualis et crescens)* (Quenstedt, III, 483). Therefore "on the part of God it is perfect, but it is imperfect on the part of the human beings who receive it" *(ex parte Dei perfecta, ex parte vero hominum recipientium imperfecta).*

How the factual change of man is to be understood will become clearer in connection with the discussion of conversion, especially since dogmaticians frequently take up this subject when they deal with the concept of regeneration. The only difference König is able to establish is decidedly external. He states that one can speak of regeneration in the case of children and adults, of conversion only in the case of adults, and that regeneration comes about through Word and sacrament, conversion, however, only through the Word (189). On the other hand, Hollaz wants to limit conversion in the strict sense to the "arousing of contrition" *(excitatio contritionis),* regeneration to the "granting of faith" *(donatio fidei)* (III, 375 ff.). Even though he himself is unable to carry out this distinction strictly, still his definition of conversion causes us to come upon a concept associated with the very beginning of the Reformation, namely, that of penitence.

Luther's public activity had begun with a call to repentance. With this call he comes forward as the termination of a long development of the medieval church, whose earnestness and inmost depth is felt nowhere so clearly as in its preachers of repentance, but also in the pedagogics of its official system of penitence. Here Luther's doctrine of repentance is a termination or a culmination, because it is impossible to go beyond his "self-accusation" *(accusatio sui),* which is actually applied to all constituent parts of the I, and in the face of God's wrath, which is experienced in connection with this "self-accusation" *(accusatio sui),* leaves no room for anything else than hopeless "contrition" *(contritio).* At the same time, however, he led up out of this last abyss of hopelessness by realizing that it is precisely victory over "despair" *(desperatio)* that is the goal of the Gospel. And *only* the Gospel is able to do this. For no matter how much he was in earnest all his life about the statement contained in his instruction to visitors that "without repentance there is no forgiveness of sins" (WA 26, 202, 9), still he knew from experience:

"To repent without a longing for and a love of righteousness, merely out of fear of torment, as they taught, this is to become secretly hostile to God, to blaspheme, to make sin greater; and it is nothing but a Judas repentance." No, only he can "repent with longing and love" who "has for himself sure comfort and the promise of grace, not drawn from his own thoughts (for this is neither lasting nor valid) but offered and presented through a sure Word of God" (WA 30 II, 507, 1 ff.).[6] Luther's brusque rejection of the "false repentance of the papists," as he calls it in the Smalcald Articles, is based on this. True repentance is not active; it is not a work of man which brings about forgiveness of sins. No, it is "passive, the suffering and the sensation of death" (Smalcald Articles III, Art. III, 2). But where it is nothing else than this, there it is "the realm and the power and the might of sin in the heart at which I am terrified, and sin wants to devour me" (WA 34 I, 324, 15). But this is definitely enmity against God (325, 15), because faith is lacking. "In every instance of tribulation and terror that little spark of divine mercy must be put into the hearts, in order that the contrite heart may be buoyed up by this mercy" *(Oportet in omni tribulatione et terrore infixam animis esse parvam illam scintillam misericordiae, qua erigatur animus contritus)* (WA 44, 469, 19). Accordingly, the "call for mercy" *(Anrufen der Barmherzigkeit)* (l. 40) or faith (WA 40 I, 232, 1 ff.) must be part of saving repentance. Therefore Luther expresses his doctrine of repentance conclusively when he says that it consists "both in serious acknowledgment of sin and in laying hold of the promise" *(et seria agnitione peccati et apprehensione promissionis)* (WA 44, 175, 4 ff.). The confessions as well as the later dogmaticians support the same conception of penitence.[7]

According to this, it could seem as if the doctrine of repentance were merely a pleonastic way of expressing the doctrine of justification. And it is certain that the latter is operative in the former as a determining factor. But when the dogmaticians, proceeding from the synonymity of the Bible concepts ἐπιστροφή and μετάνοια, equate repentance with conversion, they see in this at the same time a new modification of the concept of regeneration in the previously established sense; but they

[6] Cf. Luther's letter to Joh. Staupitz of May 30, 1518, Enders 1, 196 ff.; Ernst Wolf, *Staupitz und Luther*, 1927, pp. 223 ff.

[7] *CA* XII; Apol. V, 29, 35; Large Catechism III, on the Fifth Petition. — Joh. Gerhard, *Loci* VI, 228; XVII, 236 f.; L. Hutter, *Comp.*, p. 129; Calov, *Syst.* X, 413 ff.; Baier, *Comp.*, p. 710; Justus Moller (from Bodenbach), *Disp. de poenitentia vel Salutari hominis conversione, praesid. Joh. Winckelmanno . . . , Marp. Catt.*, 1602. — Himmel, *Syntagma Disputationum.* Erfurt, 1630, pp. 203 ff. — A. Galley, *Die Busslehre Luthers und ihre Darstellung in neuester Zeit, BFchrTh*, 1900, No. 2.

see it from a new angle: man is put on a new plane. At the same time, however, this now places the new man in a definite relationship to the old man. As Luther says, "contrition" *(contritio),* which belongs to repentance, consists in "self-accusation" *(accusatio sui),* in "despair of oneself" *(desperatione sui)* (WA 40 I, 232, 3). But this necessarily includes that you "have now become hostile to sin" – self-evidently because this takes place only when one looks to Christ, "out of love, not out of fear of torment" (WA 2, 141, 9; Enders 4, 225, 69 ff.). "[Scripture] calls repentance really a change and reform of one's whole life, when man comes to the realization that he is a sinner and feels that his life is not right, that he must then desist from it and become a new being with his whole life, in words and deeds and also from the heart" (WA 12, 514, 18). This statement about repentance corresponds exactly to the new element which the dogmaticians add to the doctrine of justification when they set forth what they teach about conversion. And this is not contradicted when Luther, in his writing against Erasmus, wants to see the concept "to convert" *(convertere)* used in its evangelical sense – not as "a word of one who demands and commands, which requires, not an attempt but a change of one's whole life" *(vox exactoris et imperantis, quae non conatum, sed totius vitae requirit mutationem),* but as "a word of divine consolation and promise, by which nothing is demanded of us but grace is offered to us" *(vox consolationis et promissionis divinae, qua nihil a nobis exigitur, sed nobis offertur gratia)* (WA 18, 682, 10 ff.). For in this writing, too, he demanded "despair of oneself" *(desperatio sui)* most sharply and designated it as a prerequisite to the receipt of pardon. And conversely, in the sermon quoted above it is said: "'Repentance in His name' takes place as follows: to those who believe in Christ He gives betterment by means of that same faith, not for a moment or an hour but throughout life" (WA 12, 514, 30). Here, too, "to be converted" *(converti)* results as a turning from unbelief to faith, but in faith also as "a change and reform of one's whole life."

But even if we stop for the present at the fact that the believer is "hostile to sins," it becomes apparent that the transcendental birth of faith affects man's psyche. For after faith has been born, it is impossible for him who has been converted by God to God to sanction in himself what he hates as sin in his past life. As a believer he is, of course, also a penitent throughout his life. In the light of God's verdict he will consider good nothing that he himself is or does. Before the eye of God, therefore, he will always subject the whole of his being to the judgment of "contrition" *(contritio).* But this does not *exclude* his own entrance into the battle against sin; it *includes* it. Thus faith – no more need be said at present — becomes an active ferment in the man of sin. If all sin has its foundation in unbelief and unbelief is its real essence, then faith must have the courage to attack its real enemy, unless it wants to capitulate. By showing this courage the believer begins the battle for his psyche, and when fighting this battle it is his goal to come forth again as a unit from the splitting of his I.

In itself, therefore, it was understandable that the dogmaticians from Melanchthon's school associated the "new obedience" with penitence as a third factor in addition to "contrition" *(contritio)* and "faith" *(fides).* Indeed, Melanchthon himself had declared in the Apology that it was possible to add "worthy fruits" *(dignos fructus)* to these (V, 28). One was most likely to do this when, as Nicolaus Selnecker did, one made the concept of penitence or conversion a collective concept for the whole turning from ruin to salvation.[8] To be sure, this was dangerous insofar as the Melanchthonians were the only ones who put strong emphasis on the free activity of the will in the "new obedience" *(nova oboedientia)* of the justified person, and the close proximity of "obedience" *(oboedientia)* to justification under the common cloak of penitence could very easily infect the second with the activistic element of the first. In the case of Selnecker the danger makes itself felt in his description of the new obedience as "retaining faith and a good conscience" *(retinere fidem et bonam conscientiam)* (p. 174). Thus here peace of conscience, which, according to the uninfected doctrine of justification, belongs only to faith, is ascribed to the new obedience! And it is even more dangerous when Simon Pauli does not hesitate at all to designate the "forgiveness of sins" *(remissio peccatorum)* as the purpose of "penitence" *(poenitentia),* to which he also adds the "new obedience" *(nova oboedientia)* as a third element.[9] This one could say only if, as the dogmaticians of the following century did, one limited penitence most strictly to "contrition" *(contritio)* and "faith" *(fides).* But Melanchthon's own doctrine of conversion was, of course, still more deeply entangled in synergism when he traced it back to three reasons: "And when we begin with the Word, here three causes of the good act meet — the Word of God, the Holy Spirit, and man's will, which assents and does not resist the Word of

[8] Selnecker, *Examen Ordinandorum,* 2d ed., 1593, III, 161: "Penitence or conversion to God is contrition, that is, true fear and sorrow of the heart because of our sins, and receiving remission of sins, reconciliation, justification, and quickening through faith in Christ, and beginning a new obedience" *(Poenitentia seu conversio ad Deum est contritio, id est verus pavor et dolor cordis propter peccata nostra, et fide in Christum accipere remissionem peccatorum, reconciliationem, justificationem et vivificationem, et inchoare novam obedientiam).*

[9] Simon Pauli, *Methodi aliquot locorum doctrinae* III, Magdeburg, 1575, 207 a.

God" *(Cumque ordimur a verbo, hic concurrunt tres causae bonae actionis, verbum Dei, Spiritus sanctus et humana voluntas assentiens nec repugnans verbo Dei)* (*CR* 21, 658; 23, 15). The Formula of Concord deals thoroughly with this notorious heterodoxy (*SD* II, 90). It is due to the Formula of Concord that the later dogmaticians actually limit the concept of conversion to repentance and faith again and thus, in principle at least, were fortified against synergism.

Therefore if in conversion one may and must observe the retroactive effect of faith in the constituent parts of the psyche – because the indwelling elements of repentance and faith begin to struggle against sin – it is advisable to bring under another comprehensive concept, as the later dogmaticians do, everything that looks like an active modification. For this they use the expressions "renewal" *(renovatio)* and "sanctification" *(sanctificatio)*, which are usually said to be synonyms – if, together with Scherzer, the concept of "sanctification" *(sanctificatio)* is not avoided entirely. Scherzer recognizes only "justification" *(justificatio)* and "renewal" *(renovatio)*, and by emphasizing strictly the posterior position of the second he most easily escapes the dangers of synergism (*Syst.* 1698, 454 ff.). Theophil Grossgebauer includes both under the concept of rebirth.[10] Quenstedt distinguishes rebirth, justification, and renewal in such a way that the first has the "bringing forth of faith" *(productio fidei)* as its object; the second, the "imputable righteousness" *(justitia imputabilis)*; the third, the "inherent righteousness" *(justitia inhaerens)*; or, with reference to the "effecting causes" *(causae efficientes)*, in such a way that only rebirth and justification are acts of God, while in renewal the person reborn cooperates with God, "not," it is true, "by means of his own strength but by means of strength given by God" *(non per proprias sed divinitus concessas vires)* (*Theol.* III, 632).

Here both the real concern and the danger of this article are to be seen. Here Quenstedt and Hollaz make bold to use the expression "to meet" *(concurrere)* in spite of the synergistic aftertaste, because although they know that in their purely forensic definition of justification they are untouchable, they still, on the other hand, want to give expression somewhere to the activity of the person who has been justified. And one must admit that here this activity is more firmly anchored than, let us say, in Melanchthon's doctrine of good works. But Quenstedt's presentation seems to become even more dangerous when he designates the product resulting from the cooperation of God and the justified person as "righteousness" *(justitia)*, namely, as "inherent righteousness" *(justitia*

[10] Grossgebauer in the appendix to his *Wächterstimme* concerning regeneration. Reprinted in *Drey Geistreiche Schriften*, Rostock, 1667, pp. 419 ff.

inhaerens), or when Hollaz uses the expression "inherent holiness" *(sanctitas inhaerens)* in this connection (III, 506). From this one could conclude that between God and man there is a twofold righteousness — the one, the righteousness that is granted to man; the other, the righteousness in which man himself takes part with what he himself accomplishes. No reference to the fact that the strength employed by man in this connection is "strength given by God" *(vires a Deo concessae)* could do away with the fatal recollection of the medieval doctrine of "cooperating grace" *(gratia cooperans).* For this reason others, like König, have avoided these expressions entirely.

Nevertheless, the confessions were in agreement when they taught that good works resulting from faith please God and are accepted by Him as good works in spite of their imperfection.[11] Luther had taught the same thing (WA 2, 46, 29). Yes, the Apology stated plainly: "Good works in the holy . . . are evidences of righteousness" *(Bona opera in sanctis . . . sunt justitiae)* (III, 131), or that Scripture wants the "righteousness of the heart to be surrounded by fruits" *(complecti justitiam cordis cum fructibus)* (244). Consequently, it was of the utmost importance not to lose the connection between faith and the activity predicated of the person who has been renewed. When this connection was preserved, then, through faith, "contrition" *(contritio)* also hovered above all "good works" and all other changes to be included in renewal — therefore the consciousness that the righteousness that avails before God remains an "alien righteousness" *(aliena justitia)* in spite of all the "inherent holiness that has only begun" *(sanctitas inhaerens inchoata).* And one must admit that even Quenstedt and Hollaz did not lose this consciousness. It was not lost until the emergence of the doctrine of sanctification as set forth by pietism.

Nevertheless, there is still another connection between faith and the concrete state of the "reborn man" *(homo renatus).* It is true that this "reborn man" *(homo renatus)* is and remains a sinner; but for this very reason the believer dare not apply the "for me" *(pro me),* without which there is no faith, only to his past. He must also apply it to his "now" and to his "here," and that in the most concrete sense: God in Christ "for me" *(pro me),* that is, for the whole empirical man. In this way, however, the restoration of oneness in the subject is achieved. At least there is a start. The "righteousness of God" *(justitia Dei)* is received by the transcendental I — but it holds true of the empirical I. And if to

[11] Cf. Bugenhagen, *Von dem christlichen Glauben . . . an die Ehrenreich Stat Hamburg,* 1527, pp. 105 f. — Luther, WA 37, 479, 37 ff.

Luther this "righteousness" *(justitia)* means "Christian freedom" in the original sense, namely, "that we have need of no work in order to achieve piety and salvation" (WA 7, 25, 1 ff.), then this freedom is the opposite of an idealistic freedom.[12] In idealism it is the original deed of the intelligible, that is, the transcendental I; in Luther it is the conceiving of the empirical I – heard by the transcendental I of faith as an acquital but meant as freedom of man in his empirical reality. For faith it is a purely passive receiving; but for the empirical man it is a conceiving – certainly, like every act of conceiving, something that happens to one but at the same time a "making alive" *(vivificatio)* in the most concrete sense. To be sure, it sounds very dull when the later dogmaticians distribute the fruit of "renewal" *(renovatio)* among the individual elements of consciousness, including even man's body (König, p. 216). But even if one resists the temptation to follow them in this and, perhaps as in Luther, to compile the proofs that have been accumulated, yet in no case can one overlook the fact that the same Luther, who emphasized the "purely passively" *(mere passive)* of faith and justification as no other person did, at the same time ascribed to faith the highest vitality, which can no longer be interpreted as being anything but empirical. "Where faith is of the right kind, there the deed also follows; and the greater the faith, the greater the deeds. Faith of the right kind is indeed something powerful, mighty, and active. To it nothing is impossible; nor does it rest and take a holiday" *(er rugett und freyrett auch nit).* (WA 10 I, 1, p. 269, 19.) The fact that faith, as opposed to unbelief, which makes a devil out of God (WA 37, 564, 15; 20), has a merciful God and, in view of this, shows its greatest power does not belong here directly, it is true; but just as fear of God is inseparable from unbelief, so the "joyful disposition" *(affectus hilaris)* (WA 2, 587, 28), of which Luther spoke in his exposition of the *Magnificat* (7, 544 ff.) in inexhaustible variations and in the most inspiring manner, is inseparable from faith. "This same faith," he says here, "is alive and active; it pervades and changes the whole man" (553, 33). And as soon as the believer has become sure of the mercy of God – the God who indeed is also Lord of all things – he sees and experiences the world differently from the way the doubter sees and experiences it. He who is sure of forgiveness of sins is able to cope with every other trouble. "And let everyone also become a falcon, which may soar on high in such trouble" (WA 31 I, 95, 3). "This is then a faith, that is, a heart, which looks to God for all help, grace, and com-

[12] Luther employs the same concept of freedom in his writing against Erasmus, WA 18, 627, 26.

fort in all trouble" (WA 37, 562, 35). Out of works split into many fragments God leads the believer to "oneness of heart" *(unitas cordis)* (WA 14, 614, 25).[13]

Therefore Luther was in earnest when, in his treatise against Latomus, he defended the following statement: "[The Gospel] heals the corrupt state of nature by means of righteousness" *([Evangelium] per justitiam sanat corruptionem naturae)* (WA 8, 106, 1). Through faith the empirical man becomes another person. From a split person he becomes a whole person; from an anguished person, a joyful person; from a person who is not free, a person who is free and "lord of all things." It is not necessary to show again that all this cannot obscure the clarity of the doctrine of justification. Nor need one show that the dogmaticians spoke in Luther's sense when they repeated emphatically and tirelessly that "renewal" *(renovatio)* is and remains "imperfect" *(imperfecta)* "until the Last Day." It could only be questionable whether, after all, the concept of faith is used in a different sense, that is, whether, in the end, faith does not evolve from an act of the transcendental I as a psychological act. But what first led to this question is to be found in the strong emphasis placed on "trust" *(fiducia)* – the emphasis which, since the time of the *Ansbach Counsel,* distinguishes what all the confessions teach about faith. On the part of man, who has been judged by "contrition" *(contritio)* – and, since he has been judged with finality according to his psychical status, is a "nothing" in the eyes of God, which seek righteousness in him – the "trust" *(Vertrauen)* of faith is surrender to the promise. On the other hand, the same trust is precisely the "joyful disposition" *(affectus hilaris)* that is an essential element of renewal and therefore the beginning of the transformation of the empirical man. Even here it is evident that faith cannot exist without this transformation yet must be assessed in the act of justification without any consideration of it. Flacius and Nik. Gallus gave expression to these two aspects of faith in their polemical treatise against Georg Major in such a way that in connection with justification they assessed it as purely a gift of God but after justification let it be considered an activity of man.[14] Thus even

13 Cf. *Lectures on Hebrews,* 116, 22: "faith not idle" *(fides non otiosa).* Enders 4, 224, 42: "Faith is a living thing that changes the whole man" *(Res viva est fides totum immutans hominem).* Similarly WA 1, 364, 31; Smalcald Articles III, 13; WA 20, 367, 6: "faith becomes greater" *(fides major fit);* WA 40 I, 299, 5: "Christ is joy" *(Christus est laetitia).*

14 *Sententia Ministrorum Christi in ecclesia Lubecensi etc.,* Magdeburg, 1553. There in the note of Flacius and Gallus concerning faith and works: "For they are nothing but pure gifts of God toward us and not our works toward God, as is also the very gift of the Holy Spirit. — But if after justification and after we have received salvation we retain those gifts of God, namely, faith and good works, and piously

the master of the "trunk-and-stone doctrine" *(truncus et lapis-Lehre)* could not escape Luther's realization that the faith which receives – and counts before God as that which receives – is at the same time a "mighty, active, busy thing" *(mächtig, tätig, geschäftig Ding)*. And one will let the distinction made by both participants in this controversy hold true if "after justification" *(post justificationem)* is not taken in the sense of a delimitation in time. Strictly speaking, faith, which receives the "righteousness of God" *(justitia Dei)*, is outside space and time – "at a mathematical point" *(in puncto mathematico)*, as Luther says. And conversely, "renewal" *(renovatio)*, like "conversion" *(conversio)*, is not "sudden" *(subita)*; but both take place "successively" *(successive)*. "For," says Martin Chemnitz, "it is impossible to show at a mathematical point where the will that has been set free begins to be active" *(Neque enim in puncto mathematico ostendi potest, ubi voluntas liberata agere incipiat)* (*Loci* I, 214b).

It has already been pointed out that the dogmaticians bore Luther's Small Catechism in mind when they summarized the individual acts under the title "The Appropriating Grace of the Holy Spirit" *(Gratia Spiritus Sancti Applicatrix)*. But in their presentation they avoided drawing the "Holy Spirit" *(Spiritus sanctus)* into the details of their development. This was altogether right. The Spirit of God, who, as they, like Luther, know, works only in the Word and in the sacraments, always stands face to face with man, even with the "reborn man" *(homo renatus)*, as the other. He is the very factor of their doctrine of salvation which can in no circumstances be transferred into the domain of psychology. About Him, therefore, one can speak only in the form of dogma. Besides, the weaknesses of their doctrine of the "order of salvation" *(ordo salutis)* are so notorious that it does not pay to spend any time now to underscore them. In the end they all arrive at the same result: that by the succession of a multiplicity of acts identical in part with one another the clear state of affairs or the inner unity of the Lutheran doctrine of salvation is complicated or obscured. But that the effort of these dogmaticians to find the way to the concrete facts pertaining to the psyche has not been in vain will be seen in their ethic and in what they teach about the philosophy of life *(Weltanschauungslehre)*. It has been pointed out here what led to this teaching.

practice them, then finally our own good works are also done." *(Sunt enim mera et pura dona Dei erga nos et non nostra opera erga Deum, sicut et ipsa S. S. donatio. — Sed si nos post justificationem et adeptam salutem ea Dei dona, fidem scilicet et bona opera retinemus et pie exercemus, tum demum nostra quoque bona opera fiunt.)*

13. *Unio Mystica*[1]

1. The dogmaticians of the seventeenth century divided the "way of salvation" *(Heilsweg)* into a large number of acts or elements. But in the end this does not mean that they considered it necessary to do justice to all the riches of the thoughts contained in the New Testament. Even though they were almost apprehensively at pains not to destroy the fundamental idea of the doctrine of justification, and even though, in reality, this idea was for them a safe guide to keep them from slipping into threatening chasms, nevertheless in the New Testament they also encountered lines of thinking which at first glance could be reconciled with this fundamental idea only by using sheer force. These are, above all, the words of Christ recorded by John. In them Christ speaks about a personal relationship to the disciples which apparently leaps across the Pauline way of reconciliation and justification. Here Melanchthon had called to his aid the concepts of Gospel and faith which he had acquired from Paul. He had done so with amazing skill. Christ wants to be in us, that is – so he remarks with reference to John 15:4 – His words are to remain in us. This follows from verse seven. And from this also follows what it means to remain in Christ, which "signifies nothing else than to believe His Word" (*CR* 14, 1186). Or later: those who truly remain in Him are the ones who keep the Gospel in true faith – they are governed by the Holy Spirit (15, 327). And when Christ states that the disciples are united with one another because He is in them and the Father is in Him (John 17:22 f.), it is His desire "that first they agree with Us, that they be illumined by Our light and truth . . . He wants the minds of all to be linked together with God through the Gospel" *(ut primum consentiant nobiscum, sint illustrati nostra luce et veritate . . . vult copulatas esse omnium mentes cum Deo per Evangelium)* (15, 387; cf. 14, 1207). When one says that Christ is in those who believe, this means that those who believe have faith in Him

[1] I have refrained here from giving a detailed presentation of the development of this doctrine in the seventeenth century. For this I refer to W. Koepp's essay *Wurzel und Ursprung der orthodoxen Lehre v. d. unio mystica (ZThK, NF,* Vol. 2, 1921, pp. 46 ff. and 139 ff.). To be sure, this otherwise very careful investigation missed its real purpose by seeking the root and origin of this doctrine in Joh. Arndt. I confine myself to the proof that, conversely, it is complete even before Arndt's time. In the dogmaticians of the seventeenth century the only thing new is this, that they made this a special article and by doing so got into a predicament when they arranged their "order of salvation" *(ordo salutis).* Koepp either overlooked the Biblical grounds for this doctrine or passed over them in silence. Nor did he give consideration to the connection with the doctrine of the two natures and the doctrine of Holy Communion.

(14, 1209).[2] Although these statements are correct and important per se, still they show that Melanchthon was unaware of the problem which – precisely from the standpoint of the doctrine of justification – it is scarcely possible to overlook here.

But here, too, the problem is to be found in the relationship of faith and the psyche. Faith, as faith in Christ, loses its footing at once if it does not let Christ remain Someone totally different and His righteousness remain "alien" *(aliena)*, if it no longer receives the word of forgiveness as spoken by the other One. But John's statements – "I in them," "God's dwelling place in them," "remain in them" – seem to say the very opposite. Can this mean anything else than that between Christ and those who are His there takes place a union of such a nature that Christ is no longer the other One but belongs to them, is no longer the content of faith but a psychic content? Here, of course, an exegetical way out presents itself. Christ is not speaking about his relationship to the individuals; He is speaking about His relationship to the sum total of the disciples. He is in them, that is, among them, in their midst – through His Word, through the preaching of the Gospel, as Melanchthon aptly points out. In the Pentecost sermon he delivered when the Reformation was introduced in Leipzig (1539) Luther, too, referred the words "make Our abode with him" (John 14:23) to the church (WA 47, 772 ff.). And in accordance with the precedent set by him the dogmaticians of the seventeenth century also apply these and similar words to the evangelical doctrine of the church.

But when at the same time the dogmaticians of the seventeenth century buttressed their doctrine of the "mystical union" *(unio mystica)* with these words, they did so because in this matter, as in others, they sought to bring Paul and John into agreement. Only they had recourse to another sphere of ideas than the one Melanchthon had used. They found that when in Eph. 1:22 ff. and 5:23 Paul pictures Christ as the Head and the church as His body, he has nothing else in mind than what Christ means when in John 15:1 ff. He uses the illustration of the vine and the branches. Furthermore, from the application which Paul makes in 1 Cor. 6:15 ff. of the picture of the body and the members they concluded that the "great mystery" *(mysterium magnum)* of which Eph. 5:32 speaks also holds true of Christ's relationship to the individual believers. They found this confirmed in Gal. 2:20, a passage which they

[2] In the *Annotat.* (14, 1179 f.) Melanchthon completely disregards the expression "make Our home" *(Wohnung machen)* in John 14:23 — the expression that is so important to the later dogmaticians. In the *Enarr. in Ev. Joh.* (15, 317 f.) he refers it to the presence of Christ in the church through the teaching of the Gospel.

separated, to be sure, from Gal. 2:19, where Paul says about himself in a wholly personal way that Christ lives in him. Nor did they consider it necessary to restrict this to unity with Christ, because in John it is also stated that the Father is in the believers (14:23), and Paul is speaking about becoming "one spirit with Him" (1 Cor. 6:17). They adduced 2 Peter 1:4, where it is said that believers should become "partakers of the divine nature" (θείας φύσεως κοινωνοί). And since in 1 Cor. 6:19 the body is designated as "a temple of the Holy Spirit," they thought they had no right to exclude Christ's human nature. In this connection they called attention to the "glorifying" (δοξάζειν) of which Christ speaks in John 17. Finally, when one adds that they distinguished the union with God spoken of here from the general union they found expressed in 1 Cor. 15:28, one has brought together all the essential elements of their doctrine of the "mystical union" *(unio mystica)*.[3]

If there really were important Biblical grounds for this, they must have become evident in the sixteenth century too. It is true that even in the homilies which he based on the Gospel According to St. John, Brenz, like Melanchthon, shows that he is a guardian of the doctrine of justification – even where, and precisely where, God's or Christ's indwelling in the believers is spoken of.[4] "To remain in Christ is to remain in the Word of Christ" *(Manere in Christo est manere in verbo Christi)* (764). And conversely: Christ remains in us if His Word remains in us. If we remain in faith in Christ, we are His friends (773). Christ and the Father want to make Their abode with us. "But we receive Them with hospitality through love or through faith in Christ" *(Accipimus autem eos hospitio per dilectionem seu fidem in Christum)* (742). Obviously Brenz, like the later dogmaticians, calls attention here to the Pauline parallel (1 Cor. 6:19). Even in connection with John 6:56, where Christ ties His remaining in the disciples to the eating of His flesh, he explains emphatically that here only faith is spoken of – this is the exegesis maintained long before this time in opposition to the Swiss (377; 381). Yet he cannot stop with these statements. This statement that Christ and the believers remain in one another – "this is, we are made one flesh, one blood. And he who eats Me also acquires the same nature that My

[3] This, in the main, is the Scriptural proof for the doctrine of the "mystical union" *(unio mystica)* as developed in Calov, *Syst.* X, 505 ff.; Quenstedt, *Theol.* III, 614 ff.; König, *Theol. pos.*, pp. 209 ff.; Brochmand, *Syst.* II, 304. — Concerning Buddeus, who moves the "mystical union" *(unio mystica)* into the center of the "order of salvation" *(ordo salutis)*, cf. Stolzenburg, op. cit., p. 213. Joh. Saubert *(Die neue Creatur*, Nürnberg, 1625, p. 6) declares that the union of the believers with Christ is the sense of all Holy Writ.

[4] J. Brenz, *Evangelium quod inscribitur secundum Joannem . . . , Francof.*, 1554. All the references that follow refer to this.

flesh and My blood have." *(hoc est, una efficimur caro, unus sanguis. Et quam habent naturam mea caro et meus sanguis, eandem etiam consequitur is, qui me vescitur.)* (378.) An actual "sharing" *(communio)* or "participation" *(communitas)* takes place between Christ and those who are His (776). With those who believe in Him Christ has everything in common (774). To be sure, He does not share with them what He knew or was able to do by virtue of His essential connection with the Father; He shares with them only what pertains to the perfect salvation of men. And one cannot include in this the arts of astronomy, geometry, and prophecy (775). Still here, too, Brenz, exactly like the later dogmaticians, adopts from 2 Peter 1:4 the thought that believers become "partakers of the divine nature" (869). To be sure, he includes the church. The disciples are to be one, just as Christ and the Father are One. If it is true of Them that They have "one essence and divinity" *(unam essentiam et divinitatem),* still Their communion with the church holds true only "as the church is able to contain Them" *(pro modo capacitatis ecclesiae).* What the Son has from eternity the church acquires only by adopting it. But all believers who, by reason of their faith in Christ, remain true members of the church also remain indissolubly united with the Trinity (in that very place). Therefore it is possible to draw the final conclusion: "that as many as believe in Christ receive divine majesty and become sons of God, that is, gods themselves" *(ut quotquot in Christum credunt, recipiant divinam majestatem ac fiant filii Dei, hoc est, dii ipsi)* (379). Not even the later dogmaticians went beyond what Brenz sets forth here concerning the acquisition of divine majesty by the believers. But before pursuing his thoughts further it is necessary to look for parallels.

It is clear that these thoughts had to become important in the battle concerning the real presence of Christ. Here they were even intensified, insofar as the real presence according to both natures was the matter at issue. Thus Stephan Gerlach, of Tübingen, adduced 2 Cor. 13:3 ff., Gal. 2:20, and Eph. 3:17 in addition to the passages in John and, like the later dogmaticians, combined the picture of the vine with Paul's picture of the Head and the members.[5] From this he concluded that the whole Christ is present, not only in His church but also, "dwelling in every believer, not cut in half but in His entirety and unchanged, makes them alive by means of the nature assumed, sanctifies, consoles, and saves them" *(singulis fidelibus non dimidiatus sed totus et integer habitans eos per naturam assumptam vivificet, sanctificet, consoletur, salvet)* (383).

[5] Stephan Gerlach, *Assertio piae sanaeque doctrinae de div. maj. Christi hominis,* Tübingen, 1585, p. 383, pp. 388 f.

The indwelling, he says, comes about not only — as the Jesuits and the Calvinists would have it — "through the Spirit, faith, and love . . . but also by means of a real union that takes place after the manner of the sitting at the right hand of God, which is present everywhere and — as Cyrillus says — is a natural sharing of the body and the blood at the sacred meal" *(per spiritum, fidem et charitatem . . . verum etiam coniunctione reali, quae fit per modum sessionis ad dextram Dei ubique praesentem et participationem naturalem — ut Cyrillus loquitur — corporis et sanguinis in sacra coena)* (389). The relationship to the Lord's Supper will be discussed later. But when Gerlach speaks of a "real union" *(coniunctio realis)*, he means, according to the entire context, exactly what the later dogmaticians mean when they speak of a "union in substance" *(unio substantialis)* — whenever this expression is used at all later on.

In connection with the doctrine of the Lord's Supper these or similar thoughts were altogether unavoidable. Even a man like Nikolaus Selnecker, who, in other respects, is as far apart from Brenz as anyone can be and speaks about John 15 almost with the very words of Melanchthon, declares that in the Lord's Supper Christ "dwells in us, not only as this is understood through love but also by a natural participation, corporeally, by the sharing of His flesh, and actually makes us His body and causes us to become one mass with Himself, not only through faith but in reality, nourishes us with His own body and joins and cements us to Himself" *(non habitudine solum, quae per caritatem intelligitur, sed etiam participatione naturali, corporaliter, communicatione carnis in nobis habitare et reipsa nos corpus suum efficere et in unam secum massam reducere, non fide solum sed revera, proprio corpore nos alere et sibi coniungere atque conglutinare)*.[6] In this distinction between two kinds of union with Christ, the one of which comes about "through faith" *(fide)* but the other "in reality" *(revera)*, are contained all the uncertainties with regard to the doctrine of the "mystical union" *(unio mystica)* as well as the final reason for the criticism to which this doctrine has been subjected since the days of Ritschl. And this in the case of a man from the school of Melanchthon! The fact that the Lord's Supper is spoken of here cannot obscure what Selnecker, too, maintains: that there is a union with Christ which goes beyond the faith relationship that is meant in the doctrine of justification. He proves rather that the Lu-

[6] Selnecker, *Ex. Ord.* IV, p. 264. — The expression *conglutinare*, which Selnecker uses here, often returns in the later dogmaticians as *agglutinare.* Koepp (op. cit., p. 69, footnote and p. 143) seems not to have realized that this expression stems from 1 Cor. 6:17, where even the Bible translation of Beza reads: *Qui vero agglutinatur Domino, unus cum eo spiritus est!*

theran Christian of that time had long been familiar with the thoughts of the later doctrine of the "mystical union" *(unio mystica)* — the doctrine developed on the basis of its conceptions of the Lord's Supper.

Nor, as is self-evident, does Martin Chemnitz ignore the New Testament doctrine of Christ's indwelling in the believers as proof of Christ's presence in the church. His interest in this matter is all the stronger because he can have no confidence in Brenz's conception of the omnipresence of Christ — a conception which he rejects. He proceeds from the Pauline statement that Christ dwells in our hearts through faith (Eph. 3:17), and he attacks those who conclude from this that "the Person of Christ dwells in our hearts, not with His essence as this essence consists of two natures and remains in them, but that He dwells in us through faith, as if in this passage faith were a phantasy or an imagination about Christ, who is not actually present with us but is pictured by the imagination as dwelling in us" *(Personam Christi inhabitare in cordibus nostris non essentia sua, sicut duabus naturis constat et in illis subsistit, sed fide inhabitare in nobis, quasi vero fides hoc loco sit phantasia seu imaginatio de Christo, qui revera nobis non adsit, sed per imaginationem fingatur in nobis inhabitare)*.[7] On the contrary, he says, faith is mentioned here only as a means, a tool, an instrument with which we receive and retain Christ. In addition, however, it is mentioned to express that Christ does not dwell in our hearts in an earthly way, under earthly conditions, physically, visibly, spatially, but in a heavenly, divine, incomprehensible manner (p. 506). Here and a little later (p. 508) nearly the entire terminology applied to the "mystical union" *(unio mystica)* by the later dogmaticians is anticipated. In his rejection of the aforementioned interpretation of Eph. 3:17 Chemnitz clearly expresses his own thought that Christ dwells in the believers "with His essence" *(essentia sua)*. Even if in this connection there was no occasion to go into the matter further, still this thought is underscored when Chemnitz adds that Paul teaches not only the participation of the believers in the Spirit (2 Cor. 13:13) but also their participation in the body and the blood (1 Cor. 10:16). This entire chapter of Chemnitz' book undertakes to prove the real presence of Christ also according to His human nature. Concerning Christ's promise that He wants to be united with His members to the highest degree" *(membris suis conjunctissimum esse)* he says, therefore, that this applies to "that nature by which He is our Kinsman and Brother consubstantial with us" *(ea natura, qua nobis consubstantialis cognatus et frater noster est)* (p. 507). And this, Chemnitz goes on, is by no means limited to the Lord's Supper — as has been set forth previ-

[7] Chemnitz, *De duabus naturis in Christo,* reprint in Leipzig, 1580, p. 505.

ously. But concerning the indwelling of the Holy Spirit he quotes Luther's exposition of Ps. 51:12, according to which the Spirit dwells in the believers "not only through His gifts but also as to His substance" *(non tantum per dona sed et quoad substantiam)*.[8]

The final point in this comparison is the fact that the Formula of Concord speaks about the indwelling of the Father, the Son, and the Holy Spirit in the believers and remarks that this indwelling is not our righteousness that avails before God, but that it results from this righteousness.[9] Accordingly, there is proof that even in the age of the Formula of Concord Lutheran theology teaches the indwelling of the Trinity and of Christ in the believers. This is described as a "real union" *(conjunctio realis)* (Gerlach). It signifies that the believers have received divine majesty (Brenz), but also that there is a union in essence *(eine essentielle Einung)* with the human nature of Christ and a union in substance *(eine substantielle Einung)* with the Holy Spirit (Chemnitz). It is specifically distinguished from the act of faith (Selnecker, Formula of Concord).

But one finds the doctrine of the "mystical union" *(unio mystica)* set forth with unsurpassable emphasis and completeness in writings by Philipp Nicolai, and not for the first time in his book on the omnipresence of Christ (1602); it is to be found as early as 1598, in his frequently reprinted *Freudenspiegel des ewigen Lebens*.[10] On the surface, it is

[8] Chemnitz, *Loci* I, 117. The statement occurs in the printed version of Luther's *Enarratio Ps. LI* (1538). The word *substantia* does not occur in Rörer's transcript (WA 40 II, 421). If for this reason we cannot ascribe it to Luther with certainty, still it is significant for Chemitz — and obviously also for Luther's own hearers!

[9] *SD* III, 54. Cf. *Epit.* III, 16; IV, 15, 19; *SD* XI, 73.

[10] Even Koepp cannot refrain from referring to Nicolai, at least in a note (pp. 144 f.), where, to be sure, he mentions only the writing "concerning the omnipresence" *(de omnipraesentia)*. The reference to the *Freudenspiegel*, which appeared four years earlier, would completely overthrow Koepp's construction, which is pointed at Joh. Arndt. The elimination of Nicolai from the genealogical tree of the "orthodox" doctrine of the "mystical union" *(unio mystica)* is accounted for by the statement: "In Nicolai we have the *only* actual restoration in Lutheranism of the *genuinely* Lutheran 'union' *(unio)*" (p. 144, italics by Koepp). This, of course, would be something entirely different from the "union" *(unio)* in Joh. Arndt and his successors, where "an alien piety imposes itself on a sharply orthodox Lutheranism that has become impotent in its religious substance and has been ethicized. Here we recognize again the mysticism of the Middle Ages and the Jesuits in all its shadings." (P. 166.) — Although Koepp, according to his own testimony, "investigated all the traces of the doctrine of 'union' *(unio)* that are still mentioned or to be found before 1620 up to the time of Melanchthon" (p. 70), he overlooked only the trifle that Nicolai, too, brings columns of quotations from Augustine and even from Ludovico Vives! (E. g., *T. Schr.* I, 28; 43 ff., etc.) In the paragraphs that follow we quote the *Freudenspiegel* as well as the writing *Of Eternal Life (Vom ewigem Leben)* according to the edition in Nicolai's *Teutsche Schriften*, ed. by G. Dedekenn, Hamburg, 1617. — In addition, *Sacrosanctum omnipraesentiae Christi mysterium, Francof.*, 1602.

true, the description of eternal life which Nicolai gives in this book has an eschatological character. But from the use of the New Testament statements that are constantly adduced in substantiation of the indwelling and are to characterize the Christian publicly even during the present aeon it can be seen that for Nicolai the boundary between eternal life and life on earth is not chronological in nature. Besides, in the writing *On Eternal Life (Vom ewigen Leben)* he sets forth "that during this time we believing Christians live simultaneously 'from the outside and from the inside' *(ab extra et ab intra)*, that is, outwardly in the world and inwardly in the Holy Spirit," and that I, "according to my spiritual life and my inward, heavenly life, am in heaven and in God's city above together with all the citizens of heaven" *(T. Schr.* I b, 216 f.). Accordingly, there is justification for including Nicolai's observations on the "heavenly, eternal life" in the context of our treatment of the "mystical union" *(unio mystica)*.

In the first main part the *Freudenspiegel* enumerates six "characteristics" *(Eigenschaften)* of eternal life: love and reciprocated love between God and the elect, equality of the elect with God, God's indwelling in them, "God all in all," perfect love for one's neighbor, and "perfect union or harmony *(Einigkeit)* between God and His children." After a description of the fourfold advantage of this knowledge the second main part points out the six blessings with which God prepares for eternal life. Of God's indwelling in the elect it is stated that the means it employs are love and reciprocated love or perfect mutual knowledge. This knowledge must be taken in the Biblical sense — "knowing with feeling" *(nosse cum affectu)*, in the language of the dogmaticians. "Let this now be for me a heavenly joy and a delightful knowledge or a strong, penetrating love in eternal life, since God knows those who love Him in such a way that He resides and dwells in them with His essence" *(Das lasse mir nun eine Himmlische Wollust und eine liebliche Erkändtnuss oder starcke, durchtringende Liebe sein im ewigen Leben, da Gott seine Liebhaber so erkennet, dass er in jhnen wesentlich residiert und wonet)* (I, 24). This mutual, burning love is like the love of bride and bridegroom, who do not rest until they come to a perfect "union" in marriage (26). In inexhaustible turns of expression this picture is also varied with respect to the relationship to Christ. In addition to Biblical references and quotations from medieval literature, Luther, too, is regularly cited (I, 89 ff., 136, 150 ff., 255 ff.; II, 231 ff., etc.). As Father, Son, and Holy Spirit, God Himself is "not three gods, but only one God and a Being in three Persons. And this *unum* or this essential oneness

(Eines) is in Him Himself sheer glory, sheer joy, sheer life, and sheer pure pleasure, because it is sheer pure love and a source of love" (I, 41). This essential oneness, the whole Godhead, enters into the "perfect union" with men and angels (40). According to 1 Cor. 6, Eph. 4, 1 Cor. 12, and John 17, they become a "perfect oneness" "through a heavenly combination" (41). If one adds to this that everywhere "repose," "resting" *(Ausruhen)* in God, is present in the mind as the final goal, that Christians are admonished to concentrate their thoughts constantly on eternal life, and that ascetic conclusions are also drawn from this (I, 62 ff.), no further proof is needed that the doctrine of the "mystical union" *(unio mystica)* is set forth completely in Nicolai's book.

In his book on the omnipresence of Christ, which appeared four years later, Nicolai repeated these thoughts in a manner that is strictly systematized. Here the occasion was the same as it was in the case of Chemnitz and the Württembergians: proof that the human nature is capable of containing God's infinite essence within the frame of the doctrine of the two natures. God is essentially love, he explains. The place of His indwelling in the believers is the divine image, which was lost because of the Fall but has been restored through Christ (pp. 56 f.). Christ won back for man the ability to contain God's essence. Here Nicolai employs the catchword which became a "technical term" *(terminus technicus)* for the later dogmaticians. The fourth chapter is titled "On the Three Mysteries Resulting from the Mystical Union of God and Holy Men" *(De tribus mysteriis ex unione mystica Dei et sanctorum hominum resultantibus).* Here the much-disputed meaning of the word *mysticus* becomes clear. It is nothing more than the adjective for the noun *mysterium.*[11] The "mystical union" *(unio mystica)* takes place in a threefold differentiation *(Staffelung).* By means of idiopoeia (pp. 81 ff.)

[11] A definition of the "mystical union" *(unio mystica),* p. 81: "There God and man grow together so closely, associate so closely, are joined together, bound together, and united so closely that they are not only one spirit, one mass, and one body, so to speak, but that from this union and spiritual interlacing of them three logical consequences, three mystical effects, or three kinds of mutual communication result, the first of which one may call the spiritual idiopoeia of God, who receives; the second, the spiritual metapoeia of man, who has been received; and the third, the spiritual koenopoeia of God and man" *(Ibi Deus et homo tam arcte coalescunt, tam arcte consociantur, tam arcte iunguntur, devinciuntur, uniuntur, ut non tantum sint unus Spiritus, una massa et unum quasi corpus; verum ut ex hac illorum unione et nexu spirituali tria resultent consectaria, tres effectus mystici, sive tria mutui commercii genera, quorum primum libet spiritualem Dei assumentis idiopoeiam, alterum spiritualem hominis assumpti metapoeiam et tertium spiritualem Dei hominisque koenopoeiam dicere).*

König, too, *Theol. pos.,* p. 210, takes the word *mysticus* as an adjective related to *mysterium.*

God — by means of the "bond" *(copula)* of the Spirit — transfers all the suffering of Christians, their pious words, works, and feelings, to Himself, as if they were His own. Here one is reminded of the transference of Christ's righteousness to the sinner — obviously in the sense of "commutative imputation" *(imputatio commutativa)* (Selnecker, *Ex. Ord.* III, 301). By means of metapoeia (pp. 91 ff.) the believer shares in the work and in the powers of almighty God and Christ. By means of koenopoeia God and man unite in such a way in a spiritual *(pneumatisch)* community of action that the one always thinks and acts in common with the other. This is what is meant when it is stated in Scripture that all believers in Christ are priests, judges, and wrestlers (in the struggle against Satan). Here are ascribed to them ability and action which they cannot achieve as mere human beings but only by virtue of their co-operation with God.

The later development of the doctrine of the "mystical union" *(unio mystica)* brought no further progress of any kind. The question whether the union is to be taken as operative, substantial, or both belongs to the uncertainties of exposition which confront dogmatics since Johann Gerhard as genuine scholasticism in all essential points of evangelical doctrine. Even Nicolai teaches an essential union. Here this concept becomes more palatable to the modern reader only because Nicolai describes the divine essence which is united with the believer as "essential love" *(essentialis amor, dilectio, charitas)* (*Omnipr.*, p. 89). But the very fact that he can do this without, as he sees it, scuttling the concept of the "essence" *(essentia)* should be a warning not to reinterpret the same concept, when it occurs in the later dogmaticians, and the analogous concept of the substance, which, as said before, is to be found in a work of Luther's printed in 1538,[12] as something halfway or totally materialistic. Conversely, the later dogmaticians, who stress the "approach" *(appropinquatio)* or the "union of the substances" *(conjunctio substantiarum)*, emphasize that God's indwelling is "not idle" *(non otiosa)*, and, where they do not make this express statement, it can be concluded from their final definitions *(Finalbestimmungen)*. When Nicolai speaks of a "spiritual union" *(unio pneumatica)* or a "spiritual participation" *(spiritualis communicatio)* (*T. Schr.* II, 88; 134), the later dogmaticians attach weight to the conclusion that "this is called a spiritual union according to its real cause, nature, and manner because it is accomplished through the Holy Spirit, who mercifully dwells in us also in a supernatural and spiritual way, not in a fleshly way, by contact, immersion, and placing

12 But concerning the expression cf. also WA 18, 784, 19.

one being into the other."[13] In any case, all the objections raised by Albrecht Ritschl from the standpoint of his own concept of God as well as from the standpoint of ethics to the doctrine of the "mystical union" *(unio mystica)* apply likewise to Philipp Nicolai.[14] These charges — which, in the case of the opponents in the seventeenth century, amount to accusations of Osiandrism and Weigelianism, in Ritschl's case to incompatibility with the doctrine of justification, to pantheism and ascetic-quietistic ethics — are so weighty and, in addition, so obvious that it is now necessary to investigate whether and how this doctrine can be reconciled with the fundamental thoughts of Lutheran theology that have been developed so far.

2. Nicolai bases the possibility of God's essential indwelling in man on the restoration of the divine image through Christ. Brenz goes beyond this thought to the extent that he lets the believer receive "divine majesty," which was designed for man in his primal state *(Urstand)*, was then lost, but was won back for mankind through Christ (op. cit., p. 379). If quotations from Scripture were not adduced here, one would have to establish an almost blasphemous abolition of the distance there is between God and man — the distance that must be preserved even in the faith relationship. According to Brenz, however, it is precisely faith which should be not only the prerequisite but the means by which Christ dwells in the believer and by which the believer shares Christ's nature. This "union" (*communio*, p. 738) with Christ is, as the words of John make clear, a "sharing" *(Gemeinschaft)* of life. "I live, and you shall live" *(Ego vivo et vos vivetis)*, says Christ; "that is, My life is your life" *(hoc est, mea vita est vestra vita)* (737). But this life is nothing else than "righteousness" *(justitia)*. For he who is justified before God through faith has life before God, that is, eternal life. "Preservation in death" *(conservatio in morte)* is of necessity bound up with God's declaration of absolution (*reputamur*, 737) — therefore also "resurrection, eternal life, bliss" *(resurrectio, aeterna vita, foelicitas)* (738).[15] Yet it is by no means a matter only of the judgment pronounced by God, which gives

13 Thus Hülsemann against the misinterpretation by Calixt, *Calixtinischer Gewissenswurm*, Leipzig, 1654, 1102. — Likewise Joh. Gerhard, *Loci* III, 469. In addition, cf. III, 515; XVIII, 233 f. — If Koepp, with his extensive investigations, discovered that "the doctrine of the union is not yet to be found" in Gerhard's *Loci* — the reader can convince himself of the opposite by consulting the passages mentioned.

14 The passages from Ritschl have been assembled by Joh. Wendland, *RGG*, 1st ed., V, col. 1458.

15 Similarly on p. 741, where the "treasure of all good things" *(thesaurus omnium bonorum)* which God's indwelling in us carries with it is described as "forgiveness of sins, adoption, victory in death, eternal life" *(remissio peccatorum, adoptio, victoria in morte, vita aeterna)*.

us righteousness and thus a title to eternal life. On the contrary, here there is an incentive for us to receive with real hospitality the Father, the Son, and the Holy Spirit, who dwell in us, and not to drive Them out but rather to keep Them in us. "But we receive Them with hospitality through love or through faith in Christ . . . we keep Them through the obedience of faith and of an honorable life" *(Accipimus autem eos hospitio per dilectionem seu fidem in Christum . . . retinemus eos oboedientia fidei et honestae vitae)* (742). Referring to Paul (1 Cor. 6), it is then established that man, as the temple of God, must avoid all unholy things. He should devote himself completely to piety, in order that God may remain his Guest.[16] Accordingly, it is clear that when Brenz speaks of God's indwelling, he is thinking of a real change in the empirical-psychic make-up of the believer. Nothing "magical" is to be found in it. Yet this is not only a moral incentive. On the contrary, here a new life is born – a life that takes possession of man's psyche in such a way that it holds its ground even against the onslaught of death.

But to what extent is this union with Christ's nature a receiving of divine majesty? Here the knowledge that the indwelling takes place through faith and in faith stands the test. The union brings it about "that we are made sharers in the divine nature" *(ut efficeremur consortes divinae naturae)* (869). If we share in the divine nature, we also share in the destiny which the divine nature had in Christ. Only then are we actually "sharers" *(consortes)* with Christ. God's majesty stood the test in His humiliation. If we want to be where Christ is in the everlasting future, we must also be as He was and where He was in this present life. We have Christ's divine majesty only in faith like His and in enduring the same suffering (p. 873; cf. 373).

The frequently made charge that the thought of the "imitation of Christ" *(imitatio Christi)* crops up in the doctrine of the "mystical union" *(unio mystica)* just as it does in the mysticism of the Middle Ages is certainly true. And even in Philipp Nicolai one can observe that this leads to the danger of quietism, which is not in harmony with the Reformation. Yet only the danger. For what Brenz sets forth shows two things just as clearly. First, that here the sphere of faith is by no means necessarily abandoned. One can only *believe* in the indwelling of Christ,

[16] P. 742: "Therefore let us flee every unholy baseness and devote all our care to zeal for piety and respectability, in order that God may remain in our lodging and preserve us in all dangers, with true and perpetual safety, through Jesus Christ" *(Fugiamus igitur omnem prophanam turpitudinem et conferamus omnem curam nostram in studium pietatis et honestatis, ut Deus maneat in nostro hospitio et conservet nos in omnibus periculis, vera et perpetua salute, per Jesum Christum).*

because the empirical state of affairs – the world about us and in us, suffering, the necessity to die – speaks against it. Secondly, however, Brenz declares that the imitation of Christ can by no means be an external imitation but grows out of the necessity immanent in faith itself. For, as has already been set forth, the subject as psyche cannot be unaffected by the function performed by the faith of the transcendental subject. For faith Christ always remains the Other One, whose righteousness is imputed to us. At the same time He also becomes a psychic content. Accordingly, He "dwells" in us as "God's concealed majesty" and thus creates in us a life just as obedient in doing and in suffering, therefore just as activistic and as quietistic, as His own. Here Brenz preserves the boundaries drawn by the doctrine of justification. Nicolai, too, observes them, although in the *Freudenspiegel* this seems to be obscured because he begins with a detailed description of "eternal life" and does not develop the doctrine of justification until he comes to his discussion of the blessings with which God prepares for eternal life.[17]

3. If from this point one looks back to Luther, the Reformer emerges in this connection too as the founder of Lutheranism. To be sure, he went through German mysticism, and thoughts entertained by Gerson and, above all, by Bernard accompanied him throughout his life.[18] Accordingly, the "entrance of medieval mysticism into Lutheranism" begins neither with the adoption of medieval and Jesuitical subject matter by way of Lutheran prayer literature [19] nor particularly with Johann Arndt; it begins with Luther. But Luther has Biblical grounds for repeating again and again the pictures of the nuptial relationship of Christ to the Christian and of the "temple" of God in the saints; what is said about the union, the association, and the communion of Christ with the believers; and about "making Our abode." Furthermore, everything – at least in our connection – depends on how he shaped these ideas after his doctrine of justification had been completely evolved.

[17] Cf. *T. Schr.* I b, pp. 86 ff. Here Nicolai anticipated the analytical method of the later dogmaticians.

[18] H. Hering, *Die Mystik Luthers im Zusammenhange seiner Theologie und in ihrem Verhältnis zur älteren* Mystik, 1879. — Gottschick, *Luthers Lehre v. d. Lebensgemeinschaft d. Gläubigen mit Christus, ZThK,* 1898, pp. 407 ff. — M. Rade, *Luthers De libertate Christiana mystisch?*, op. cit., 1913, pp. 266 ff. — A. V. Müller, *Luther und Tauler,* 1918. — O. Scheel, *Taulers Mystik u. Luthers reformatorische Entdeckung,* 1920. — Ernst Wolf, *Staupitz und Luther,* 1927. — Erich Seeberg, *Luthers Theologie* I, 1929, pp. 107 ff.

[19] Paul Althaus the Elder in his Leipzig university program, which has become famous: *Zur Charakteristik der evangelischen Gebetsliteratur, im Reformationsjahrhundert,* 1914, now in *Forschungen zur evangelischen Gebetsliteratur,* 1927, with a continuation concerning the literature of prayer up to the eighteenth century.

It is self-evident that in Luther too one finds all those safeguards with which Melanchthon seeks to bring the thought of "God's indwelling" into harmony with justification. Christ comes to us in the Holy Spirit, that is, in His Word. He dwells in us "through faith" in this Word. The union with Christ consists in this, that we receive His righteousness and that He takes our sin upon Himself – in the sense of the later doctrine of "commutative imputation" *(imputatio commutativa).* These are fundamental thoughts contained in Luther's first commentary on Galatians.[20] And where a sermon delivered in 1528 and then printed employs the expression which Luther himself used elsewhere – that Christians and Christ become "one cake" *(ein kuchen)* – the transcript confines itself to the statement that faith is the "clamp" *(Klammer)* by means of which the hearts are held together and joined in Christ (WA 28, 188, 9 and 28). But Luther would have been a poor interpreter of the Gospel According to St. John if he had let it go at that.

If it is an essential requirement of mysticism – at least of German mysticism – that man, by means of a special technique of thinking, reduce his consciousness to "nothingness" in order then to find God in the lowest depth of his inner self, Luther, after he had arrived at clarity with regard to righteousness by faith, surely was and remained the opposite of a mystic. He turns against mysticism as early as the appearance of his treatise on freedom. And when expounding Gal. 2:20 in his large commentary on Galatians – the passage which even Gottschick calls the "real basis *(sedes)* for the connection between Christ's indwelling and justification" – he continues to demand in the strongest terms that faith in no case look into itself but only to Christ.[21] Without this basic demand every doctrine of the indwelling, no matter how it may look otherwise, would necessarily not only endanger but would actually destroy justification. The necessity for "self-accusation" *(accusatio sui),* without which there is no justification, holds true of the whole natural

[20] WA 2, 490, 502, 504, 531, 548; but still in the *Lectures on Genesis,* WA 43, 582, 21 ff.

[21] Luther's warning against "mystical theology" *(theologia mystica)* (Drews, *Disp.,* p. 294), which is quoted by Paul Althaus the Elder (*Forschungen,* p. 62) according to Loofs (*Dogmengesch.,* 4th ed., 1906, p. 724), belongs here. Luther bases this warning on the fact that there is speculation there "concerning the exposed majesty of God" *(de majestate Dei nuda)* (p. 294), that the fanatics want "to deal and speak with the exposed God" *(cum nudo Deo agere et loqui).* His polemics against the "nuptial" relationship of the soul are directed expressly against this, that the fanatics "have fashioned God Himself as the bridegroom, the soul as the bride" *(Deum ipsum sponsum, animam sponsam finxerunt),* that men believe they are able to associate "with the inscrutable and eternal majesty of God without a mediator" *(cum majestate Dei inscrutabili ac aeterna sine medio)* (p. 296). As will be seen, the Christ mysticism connected with Bernard is not affected by this.

and moral "inwardness," including what the mystics call the "depth of the psyche" *(Seelengrund)*. This Luther hammered out clearly in the 1520's in his polemical writings against the fanatics.

But if the concept of indwelling is to have any special meaning at all, it is self-evident that one must keep an "inwardness" of man in mind. In no circumstances, however, can this consideration of an "inwardness" account for knowledge of God and union with God. Therefore it cannot account for justification either. The "inner man," who alone comes into question, does not exist until there is faith; he is the man of faith. "Where there is no faith, there is no inner man" *(Ubi fides non est, ibi non internus homo)* (WA 28, 180, 2). Faith, however, clings constantly only to the other Person – the Person who I am not – to Christ. If it is right for us to speak of *having* Christ, this always has the primal meaning *(Ursinn)* that we have become partakers of His righteousness – in faith (189, 18 ff.). The "looking at Christ" *(Anschauen Christi)* which Luther – like Bernard – often demands means "that you be transferred outside yourself into Christ and be transplanted from a wild olive tree, to speak with Paul, and from the world into Christ" *(ut transferaris extra te in Christum et transplanteris ex oleastro, ut cum Paulo loquar, et ex mundo in Christum)* (WA 25, 331, 5). From this it follows that the "inner man" per se can neither account for knowledge of God and union with God nor ever bear Christ in himself in such a way that faith directs itself to a "Christ in us." [22]

Nor does Luther overstep these bounds when he speaks of a union of the believer with Christ – a union which consists in faith and comes about through faith. For apart from the fact that here there is nearly always an "as it were" *(quasi)* – we become "one body, as it were, in the Spirit" *(quasi unum corpus in spiritu)* (WA 40 I, 284, 7), faith makes of you and Christ "one person, as it were" *(quasi unam personam)* (285, 5) – it is first of all and above all righteousness that unites the believer with Christ. Therefore it is the faith-righteousness of "commutative imputation" *(imputatio commutativa)* (*Lectures on Hebrews*, 195, 8 ff.). This Luther emphasizes even where he describes the sharing of all goods by Christ and the Christian in accordance with the picture of the nuptial relationship (WA 41, 554, 5; 556, 1 ff.; WA 42, 174, 6 ff.). Nevertheless, he does not stop with this. It is true that the concepts he often coordinates with righteousness – "life" *(vita)*, "salvation" *(salus)*, "glory" *(gloria)*, etc. – are still to be understood in an imputative sense (WA 28, 188, 4; WA 40 I, 284, 6). But this is no longer

[22] Cf. *Lectures on Hebrews*, 131, 11, and Enders 1, 29, 40: "Christ dwells only in sinners" *(Christus non nisi in peccatoribus habitat)*.

true when he says with pride that the heart is consoled when Christ enters it (WA 11, 112, 20), that the Holy Spirit writes flames of fire in the heart (WA 12, 570, 12), that Christ is a joy and a delight for the terrified and distracted heart (WA 40 I, 299, 5), yes, that the man who could see how Christ became his flesh and blood would certainly not be able to endure the glory and the joy (WA 41, 554, 2 ff.; WA 20, 229, 11). These patent emotional effects show that Luther does not believe that the "inward man" *(internus homo)*, who as such always remains the man of faith, is not affected in his psyche by the union with Christ.

Another thing must be considered. Later in his life Luther fought vigorously against the thought of the "imitation of Christ" *(imitatio Christi)* in the sense of medieval mysticism — the thought which he recommends when he is a monk (WA 1, 175, 20; WA 2, 138, 19) and then also praises the "passive life" *(vita passiva)* as the perfect achievement of the state of being a Christian (WA 5, 166, 11 ff.). The "putting on of Christ," he says with reference to Gal. 3:27, does not mean, as Jerome wants it to be understood, to do and suffer the same things Christ did and suffered. No, it means to be clothed with His righteousness, with salvation, might, and life. But in this very way the new man is born. And this includes "that new emotions come about, a new will, that a new light arises, a new flame in the heart" *(novos fieri affectus, voluntatem, novam exsurgere lucem, flammam in corde novam)* (WA 40 I, 539, 10 ff. and 540, 6). Thus the putting on of Christ, which is described here as corresponding to the "cementing together and the adhering of faith" *(conglutinatio et inhaesio fidei)* in Gal. 2:20 (284, 6), brings about a renewal of the whole psychic make-up of the believer. If one is led here to the concept of regeneration, which has already been mentioned, nevertheless Luther takes us beyond this by making Christ or God or the Holy Spirit the subject of the "new emotions, the new will, the rising light" in us. Christ governs, so he says with reference to Gal. 2:20, with His Holy Spirit, who now sees, hears, speaks, suffers, and does everything in me (WA 40 I, 290, 10).[23] Here, therefore, Luther has preserved the thought which he emphasized so strongly at the outset and adhered to in common with the mystics: that God, who dwells in men, "does everything together with me" (WA 10 III, 159, 14 ff.; cf. WA 1, 215, 28 f.; 363, 31). When the believer loves God

[23] Melanchthon, in the *Loci* of 1522 (!), Plitt-Kolde, p. 217: "Because their will is the will of the Holy Spirit, it is not possible for them not to want what the Holy Spirit wants. For with God we are one spirit." *(Quia voluntas eorum spiritus sancti voluntas est, non possunt non id velle, quod vult spiritus sanctus. Nam unus spiritus cum deo sumus.)*

and does what God wants, this is "nothing else than the Holy Spirit Himself or rather the work that He Himself does in the heart" (WA 12, 570, 10 ff.). The indwelling of the Spirit is "nothing else than that man is the house of God with his body and his soul." All his members are God the Father's. His tongue is God's tongue; his hand is God's hand, which does nothing but good to everyone else; his eyes can see only "sheer courtesy, friendliness, love" *(Eytel zucht, freundlichkeit, lieb);* his ears can no longer bear obscene things but can hear only God's Word. True, this dwelling place of God in us is not yet finished; but He is building at it "that it may be ready on the Last Day" *(das sie sol gerust sein in extremo die)* (WA 28, 191, 20).

Here one could give consideration to the thought of God's omnipotence — the thought which Luther stressed in his treatise against Erasmus. In more than one respect, however, something fundamentally different is in question here. For one thing, this knowledge of the indwelling and the working of God actually presupposes the overcoming of the "feeling of absolute dependence." For Luther this leads logically to the conclusion that predestination is absolute, even to evil — a conclusion which is out of keeping with faith in God's revelation of Christ. It rests on a conception of man's relationship to God which corresponds exactly to the view held by the German mystics. From a moral viewpoint, therefore, it can end only in "imperturbability" *(Gelassenheit).* But in Luther's sense the indwelling of God signifies the strongest inducement to moral activity. Furthermore and finally, the indwelling by no means does away with the I-you relationship. And this is what is decisive.

This aspect of the indwelling is set forth in the first instance when Luther illustrates it with the relationship of bride and bridegroom or husband and wife. Even though in the beginning Augustine and Bernard may have led him to this (WA 3, 142, 28; 218, 35; WA 31 II, 628, 26, etc.), still as early as his treatise on freedom he had applied the illustration to "commutative imputation" *(imputatio commutativa)* (WA 7, 25, 38; 26, 4). In a sermon delivered in 1522 he uses it to make clear that between Christ and Christians there is just as little need of a mediator as there is between husband and wife (WA 10 III, 357, 28 ff.). He applied it most extensively later on in the wedding sermon he preached for Caspar Cruciger (1536). It is the text from Eph. 5 which induces him — as it induced the later dogmaticians when they dealt with the doctrine of the "mystical union" *(unio mystica)* — to illustrate the "great mystery" *(mysterium magnum)* of the union between Christ and the believers with the relationship in marriage (WA 41, 547–562).[24] Here, to be sure, he calls the church the bride of Christ (only in WA 42, 174, 6 ff.). But here the church's relationship to Christ is also automatically individualized: "The one who believes and is baptized becomes a bride" *(Qui crediderit et baptisatus, is fit sponsa)* (WA 41, 552, 10; WA 45, 176, 19). Here, too, the thoughts of "commutative imputation" *(imputatio commutativa)* recur (WA 41, 556, 3). But justification appears here only as a primary element of the union. The apostles, who preach to the bride of the cleansing and sanctification which Christ brought about by His suffering and His resurrection (551, 1), are the groomsmen who lead us to Him through the Word and Baptism (550; 551, 10). Where Luther then speaks of the Pauline "great mystery" *(mysterium magnum)* itself, of "becoming one flesh," of the "hidden wedding" (553, 6; 9; 554, 2; 558, 3; WA 45, 178, 10), there words fail him: "I am unable to find words" *(Ego non possum eloqui)* (WA 41, 553, 7). It is true that he always speaks in the first instance of righteousness as the bride's "hidden glory" *(occulta gloria)*. And Christ, as my flesh and blood, "approaches" me as the Groom through Word and sacrament (554, 4). The goods we share with Him (554, 5) are everlasting life, truth, strength, sheer grace, "and incomprehensible eternity" *(et eternum incomprehensibile)* (553, 3; WA 45, 178, 8). Nevertheless, here he must see another element not yet contained at any rate in the *concept* of justification. It is the element of *love*. Christ wants to be called the Bridegroom because He comes, not as lord and judge, neither as father or mother, but with the greatest love (553, 1; WA 45, 178, 35). Everything He gives to the bride springs from His love (556, 8). Conversely, just as in marriage the wife cannot be obedient and respectful if there is no love, so the church cannot be obedient and respectful if there is no love (559, 5).

Luther can use no more intimate way of expressing the relationship between Christ and the believer than the simile of the nuptial relationship. It is clear that as he understands it this relationship comes about only through faith and imputed righteousness – this is the essential and permanent difference between what he teaches and the mysticism of Bernard.[25] But it is no less clear that in the doctrine of satisfaction and imputation per se he would lack the element that is essential in this

[24] The parallel passages stem from a sermon delivered in 1537 on Matt. 22:1 ff. (WA 45, 175—180). Cf. the extensive printed comments (WA 22, 333—345; in addition, WA, 1, 701, 30; WA 31 I, 341; WA 39 I, 498, 16).

[25] How energetically Luther departed from Bernard's purely psychological mysticism is shown with particular impressiveness in his lectures on the Song of Songs, into which the Weimar edition has finally given a pertinent insight (WA 31 II, 586—769). The earlier editions contain only an extract from an old printing.

connection. On Christ's part that relationship means a sacrifice not only for mankind in general but also for me personally. Faith, which, of course, always means the application "for me" *(pro me)*, knows this. But the participation in righteousness, which could be misunderstood as a participation merely in goods, does not become an actual personal participation until the believer knows that Christ also means him personally, knows him personally, and loves him personally. Luther — particularly as an expositor of the Gospel According to St. John — could not easily overlook the motif of love in God's nature. If you look to God, he says, "there are sheer flames and fire of love in God" *(sind eytel flammen und feur charitatis in deo)* (WA 36, 426, 5). "In the depths of His divine nature there is nothing else than a fire and a burning, which is called love for men" *(In abgrund seiner Gottlichen natur nihil aliud est quam ein feur und brunst, quae dicitur lieb zun leuten)* (424, 3). God is "in Himself pure love" *(an yhm selber mera charitas)* (428, 3). And in the same way Christ does His work "out of the greatest love" *(summa charitate)* (WA 40 I, 296, 11), "out of pure love" *(mera charitate)* (297, 8). But when Christ uses the simile of the wedding, He wants to give "an example of true union and love" *(exemplum verae unionis et dilectionis)*, because at this wedding "groom and bride are united in the most intimate manner" *(conjunctissime et sponsus et sponsa conjunguntur)*. On the part of the bridegroom this means: "He desires her herself, her herself" *(ipsam, ipsam vult)*, namely, the bride in a wholly personal way (WA 10 III, 415, 8 ff.). Thus the realization of divine love necessarily includes the reference "for me" *(pro me)*. Therefore it is identical with faith. "Accordingly, faith brings it about that Christ is ours, and His love brings it about that we are His. He loves; we believe. The result is one cake." *(Also macht der glawb, das Christus unser ist unnd seyne liebe macht, das wir seyn sind. Er liebt, sso glewben wyr, da wirt eyn kuch auss.)* (WA 10 I, p. 74, 16.)

But the effect of God's love is not exhausted in faith, which receives it and refers it to itself. Neither is it exhausted in the fact that God's love engenders our love for Him (WA 10 III, 157, 9 ff.); that our love for God expresses itself in our keeping of His Word, His commandments (158, 24), and proves by love for one's neighbor (157, 19) that there is no true obedience to God without love (WA 41, 559, 5), likewise that one does not honor Christ without love (20, 398 f.). All these statements could give the impression that God's love and our love have a cause-and-effect relationship. To be sure, Luther asserts emphatically in this connection that they do have a cause-and-effect relationship. But he states just as clearly that here it is a matter of an actual love relationship in which the element of reciprocity is contained. "Thus the Lord loves me; I, in turn, shall love Him" *(Sic me diligit dominus, ego vicissim eum diligam)* (WA 45, 178, 36). "Thus I am toward and with Christ, so that I do not doubt that His heart is mine. On the other hand, He does not doubt that my heart is His heart" *(Sic ego gegen et cum Christo, ut non dubitem, quod suum cor est meum, econtra non dubitat, quod cor meum cor suum)* (177, 24). One could hardly find a stronger way to express the fact that according to Luther, too, faith has a "private relationship to Christ" *(Privatverhältnis zu Christo)* – a relationship derided by Ritschl as specifically pietistic – namely, the relationship of reciprocal love between the "I" and the "you" in the most personal sense of all. And Luther said this in a sermon he delivered in the year 1537![26]

[26] Even Zinzendorf's illustration — with which many find fault and which certainly should not be approved of — that because of our relationship God is "our father-in-law, so to speak," has its prototype in this sermon of Luther's: ". . . that I should be a heavenly lady, the daughter-in-law of our Lord God and the wife of the Son of God" *(ut sim himelfraw, unsers Herr Gottes schnur et dei filii uxor)* (WA 45, 179, 23). But here, too, Luther regularly refers the illustration of the nuptial or marriage relationship directly to God: "God is my Bridegroom" *(Gott ist mein sponsus)* (178, 15). "God wants me as His bride" *(Deus wil mich zur braud)* (179, 25). Next to this, "I am the bride of Christ" *(Ego Christi sponsa)* (178, 35). Cf. "bride of God and of the Son of God" *(Sponsa dei et dei filii sponsa)* (WA 41, 455, 1). — On the other hand, Karl Holl declares with his customary certainty that "although Luther said often enough that the believer becomes 'one cake' *(ein Kuche)* with Christ, he never applied this expression to the relationship to God" (*Luther,* 4th and 5th ed., p. 81). In a footnote this is also expressed by saying that Luther, like Paul, "recognizes only a Christ mysticism, not a God mysticism." The passages just adduced show, as do hundreds of others, that this is a distinction which Luther did *not* make.

Furthermore, it is necessary to ask where Luther actually used the expression "one cake" *(ein Kuche)* "often enough" for the relationship in question. Here Holl, who, in his time, found such serious fault with the aged Wilh. Walther for continuing to make use of the Erlangen edition, departs from his custom by complying indiscriminately with a tradition to which the older editions of Luther's works gave rise. An examination of all the quotations adduced by Theod. Harnack, Köstlin, Hering, and Gottschick in support of the aforementioned expression leads to the following conclusions:

Obviously, here all those passages in which the expression "one cake" *(ein Kuche)* is used to describe the relationship of men to one another (WA 10 II, 54, 20; 10 III, 218, 15; 15, 607, 22; 28, 149, 1, where *kuchen* should be read instead of *kirchen*) should drop out. But even in WA 38, 564, 23, it is very doubtful whether the expression refers to the relationship to the individual. Here the Gospel, resp. Christ, is designated as the leaven that penetrates "the whole mass of those to be saved" *(totam massam salvandorum).* For this reason it is impossible "for Christians to be taken hold of by Christ, because Christ has been incorporated in them as a leaven in such a way that there is one body, one mass, one cake, one bread, etc." *(rapi Christianos a Christo, quia in eis Christus fermentum ita incorporatus, ut unum sit corpus, una massa, ein kuche, ein brod, usw.)* Cf. also the following section. — In most of the rest of the proofs adduced by the aforementioned investigators the expression occurs only in the printed sermons, not in the transcripts.

But if a reciprocal relationship of love is actually the point in question here, one understands both the importance and the limitations of the statements in which Luther speaks of God's or Christ's indwelling in words that recall the older mysticism and still have a different meaning when he uses them. This is already clear in a sermon of 1520, where he says that God remains in those who love Him – "those who without a doubt are never unaware of God's presence" *(nimirum nunquam non sentientes dei praesentiam)* (WA 9, 464, 10 f.).[27] For according to the context this whole feeling of presence can refer only to God's indwelling in man. "For you who love Me the Father will not only have regard down from heaven that you may live; He will dwell in your inmost

Thus in all these cases this is due to the editor, not to Luther. This is certainly true in WA 28, 188, 28; 36, 423, 26; 429, 34; WA 45, 667, 33 (here the transcript is missing); possibly in 28, 149, 10; 22 (see above); perhaps also in WA 12, 583, 17, where only the printed version is extant (cf. the same sermon in Roth's edition, 17 II, 440, 12). But what is said here does not lead beyond imputation either. Here, too, the more extensive remarks concerning the "incorporation" *(Einleibung)* are found for the first time in the version printed in the Erlangen edition, 1st ed., 15, 338—347. In addition to the passage in WA 10 I, 1, p. 74, 16, which is quoted above in the text, only the passages in the sermon on Holy Communion on Maundy Thursday 1523 are left (WA 12, 485, 3 and 7; 486, 8; 488, 9; 490, 3). But this sermon is found only in print. Besides, it is found in two decidedly different versions. Furthermore, here the expression, at least in the main passage (486, 8 ff.), signifies as clearly as possible the "commutative imputation" *(imputatio commutativa)*. This does not call in question the possibility that the expression "one cake" *(ein Kuche)* may occur in other passages — passages which escaped the notice of the investigators mentioned or could not yet have been known to them (e. g., WA 37, 236, 2). But it could scarcely be possible to use it as a cardinal proof of Luther's "Christ mysticism."

But if Holl wanted to accept printed versions of sermons at all, he had no right to write that it is "significant that Luther, on his part, did not take over the expression 'friendship' for the relationship to God — the expression that stems from Augustine and was retained in scholasticism" (op. cit.). To our knowledge, the expression stems from John 15, even though there it signifies the relationship to Christ. But Luther uses it again to refer to the relationship to God, at least in the printed versions of the sermons on the fourteenth and fifteenth chapters of St. John (1538) — the versions edited by C. Cruciger (WA 45, 691, 31; 695, 30). Cf. WA 20, 227, 27.

When the editors of Luther's sermons — in this case especially Aurifaber, Roth, Cruciger, and Poach — use the expression "one cake" *(ein Kuche)* with special fondness and frequently elaborate on it, this shows, so far as our context is concerned, that the sphere of ideas which, in the later doctrine, referred to the "mystical union" *(unio mystica)* was considered important and "Lutheran" even in Luther's time. But in order to avoid renewed confusion in connection with the interpretation of Luther, we refrain here from making additional use of this fact.

[27] Cf. the "genuine presence" *(rechtschaffene gegenwertigkeit)* in the weekday sermons on John 6—8 (WA 33, 227, 12) and the entire context in WA 33, 223—230, in Aurifaber's version. — At the place mentioned above (WA 9, 464, 2 ff., in connection with 466, 5 ff.) one could even find again the doctrine of the later dogmaticians of the "mystical union" *(unio mystica)* with the Trinity!

hearts and will never be absent from you" *(Non solum pater e celo deorsum ad vos respiciet, qui me amatis, viveretis, in intimis cordibus vestris habitabit et nunquam non presens erit vobis)* (WA 9, 466, 6). To us God is not only the object of loving remembrance but a party to the contract of the reciprocal love which binds us to Him in an inseparable union and is therefore both in Him and in us. For us He always remains the You. The line of thought is similar when Luther bases the statement that "God works with me and continues to look after me" on the sure knowledge of the Father's love bestowed on us through Christ. He says: "Thus my heart becomes a still, humble dwelling place of God" (WA 10 III, 158 f.; 1522). He also says: "We are at least a little spark of the divine fire and light; He is the fire of which the heavens and the earth are full" (221, 12). In any case, therefore, we are a little spark of the divine fire! Or: "Therefore God can be nothing else than love and a burning. Therefore see to it that you love. Then God will be in you" (WA 36, 429, 4; 1532). Some might think at first that this is a slip of Rörer's pen. But this is not the case; for the following statement precedes it: "Love is such a thing that it is not human, angelic, but divine, yes, God Himself. Therefore see to it that you love." *(Lieb est talis res, ut non humana, angelica, sed Gottlich, ja Gott selber. Ideo agite ut diligatis.)* (424, 4.) And when it is stated in the same place that God "in the depths of His divine nature is nothing else than a fire and burning, which is called love," one is standing directly before the "mystical union" *(unio mystica)* of Philipp Nicolai![28] No editor would have had the audacity to add on his own responsibility the statements that are found in a sermon delivered in 1526 and have been handed down only in a printed version: that "God pours out His dear Son on us, lets Himself flow into us, and draws us into Himself, so that He becomes altogether human and we altogether divine . . . it is all one thing, God, Christ, and you" *(Christum seynen lieben son ausschuttet uber uns und sich ynn uns geust und uns ynn sich zeucht, das er gantz und gar ver-*

[28] Here we again pass over the passages in Luther that speak of a union of the natures, because they occur only in printed versions of sermons: WA 10 III, 419, 8; WA 45, 667, 30; WA 14, 19, 1 ff. (on 2 Peter 1:4, where the fact that the transcript is missing is particularly deplorable). Even these passages are significant to the highest degree for the view of Luther's closest younger associates. One is reminded especially of the later dogmaticians when Cruciger's version speaks of the "dwelling place, the pleasure grounds, or the Paradise of the heavenly Majesty, yes, of the kingdom of heaven" (WA 45, 605, 33; WA 21, 457, 21 ff.; cf. WA 12, 487, 2). — In the printed version of the lecture on Ps. 51 (1532) one finds, as has already been stated, the expression of substance that was interpreted by the later dogmaticians as "materialistic": "Therefore the true Spirit dwells not only through gifts but also as to His substance" *(Habitat ergo verus Spiritus non tantum per dona, sed quoad substantiam suam)* (WA 40 II, 421, 37).

menschet wird und wyr gantz und gar vergottet werden . . . und alles mit eyander eyn ding ist, Gott, Christus und du) (WA 20, 229, 30 ff.; 230, 10) – if Luther himself had not said this. One is almost reminded of the later demarcations between the "union of the essences" *(unio substantiarum)* and the "essential union" *(unio substantialis)* when Luther says about the relationship of God, Christ, and Christianity: "The natures are diverse, and still both are a whole essence; although the nature of the Deity is different from that of Christianity, nevertheless, just as the Father and the Son are one divine essence, so Christ is one Christian essence with His Christianity" *(Variae sunt naturae et tamen quaeque sind totum wesen, quamquam natura alia deitatis quam Christianitatis, tamen sicut pater et filius unum divinum wesen sind, sic Christus cum sua christianitate ist ein Christlich wesen)* (WA 28, 187, 18 ff).

Accordingly, the later doctrine of the "mystical union" *(unio mystica)* has been traced back to Luther with good reason. If one wanted to adduce Luther's printed sermons, there is no element of the later doctrine that could not be found in them. At any rate, they prove that Luther's own listeners found these thoughts in his writings and that these thoughts were already operative in Lutheranism in Luther's time. Nor was there any interruption. For, as has been pointed out, in the age of the Formula of Concord the same thoughts are found both among the Württembergians and in Lower Saxony. The concentration of what Luther taught about the "mystical union" *(unio mystica)* on the relationship of the love union gives the key to the solution of the problem which at first makes one mistrustful. The love of God is received in faith just as everything that comes from God is received. So far there is no overstepping of the bounds of the doctrine of justification. But the love of God as such is perceived not only as a statement made by God. It calls the heart of the believer into union with itself. It calls the psyche. And the psyche answers. God remains the Other One. He is not the depth of the soul, as the mystics teach. He always remains the You – otherwise there could be no love relationship. But God's You and the I of the psyche are connected through love, which makes of man and God "one thing."

PART TWO

Dogma and the Church

Chapter Three

DOGMA

14. Holy Scripture [1]

What was so far set forth as the impact of the Gospel *(evangelischer Ansatz)* in Lutheranism appears as a great spiritual upheaval, as a psychic occurrence that is experienced with elemental force first of all by the great individual and is experienced together with him and in the same way by others, but at the same time is "recognized" and expressed in theological formulae that become firmer and firmer. Among those affected no one, however, would have hesitated for a moment to give an answer if he had been asked what the driving dynamic of the mighty upheaval is. The answer is and could only be: the Gospel. This dynamic was not experienced as an emergence of inner powers, as an automatic relaxing of tensions in the psyche; it was heard as a Word from another world.[2] In his *Loci* of 1521 Melanchthon had given the definition: "The Gospel is a promise" *(Evangelium est promissio).* Here lay the decisive break with the Gospel as a "heavenly philosophy" *(philosophia coelestis)* or as the "law of Christ" *(lex Christi).* Nor is it by any means merely a historical report. It is this too. But it is Gospel only because it contains a compelling "today," and even more because it is a "promise," because it reveals the potentiality of what is to come – the potentiality that always points beyond the "now" and the "here."

Consequently, no catchword was as suitable as this one for com-

[1] A. W. Dieckhoff, *Luthers Lehre in ihrer ersten Gestalt,* 1887, pp. 177 ff. — R. Otto, *Die Anschauung vom h. Geist b. Luther,* 1898. — W. Walther, *Das Zeugnis d. Geistes nach Luther,* 1899. — R. H. Grützmacher, *Wort und Geist,* 1902. — L. Ihmels, *Die christliche Wahrheitsgewissheit,* 3d ed., 1914, ch. 1. — Additional literature in the text.

[2] Hafenreffer, *Loci,* p. 137: "The Sacred Scriptures . . . are nothing else than epistles transmitted to us concerning the eternal fatherland" *(Scripturae sacrae . . . nihil aliud sunt quam epistolae de patria aeterna nobis transmissae).*

pressing the whole propulsive power of the Lutheran Reformation into a single concept. For all those who heard it expressed with Luther's new emphasis it was the announcement of a beginning and the incentive to action. The rebellion of the peasants seemed to put this to a test. All the ardor of the movement is centered in the concept of the Gospel. On April 17, 1525, the "whole assembly of the Christian brothers at Altdorf" wrote to the council of the city of Strassburg: "Since the holy Gospel has dawned among you in Strassburg but is not yet permanently established among us, our whole assembly addresses to you as highly intelligent and gracious Christian and evangelical gentlemen the humble, obedient, and friendly petition and wish that you give us poor, thirsty people a drink and help us in our troubles."[3] To be sure, something else results quickly from this "humble petition"; and only three days later the assembly at Neuenburg demands in the name of Christ, "who redeemed and purchased us at a high cost with His red blood," the abolition of serfdom, a reduction of taxes, and the right to hunt and gather wood. And once again, three days later, the butchers' guild of Strassburg is asked to provide powder, spears, and field guns, "because we want to help protect and activate the Gospel."[4]

Here the explosive dynamic connected with the emphasis on the Gospel appears in a glaring light. It is true that at this place one need say no more about the fact that to Luther the "promise" of the Gospel meant something different from all tribute in blood and produce. Nor was Luther a Zwingli; he did not think of spears and field guns as offensive arms of the Gospel. But the final break with Zwingli did not come until later. Besides, in his treatise to the Christian nobility Luther himself had projected a program of reform which reached deep into social conditions. Even in matters pertaining to the church hotspurs had attached themselves to the coattails of the Reformer of the church. Decisions of the utmost importance had to be made here. Differences were unavoidable. In the Peasants' War the decision came about through the sword. After the peasants themselves had taken up the sword, Luther was neither able nor willing to prevent this. But before matters took this course, he appealed to another court — a court to which the peasants, too, had appealed. In his *An Admonition to Peace: A Reply to the Twelve Articles of the Peasants in Swabia* he calls attention to the fact that the peasants give proof of their grievances "with a number of Scripture passages" and that he himself "is, of course, also counted

[3] *Politische Korrespondenz d. Stadt Strassburg,* ed. by Hans Virck, Vol. I, 1882, p. 112.

[4] Ibid., pp. 117 and 122.

among those who deal with Divine Scripture here on earth" (WA 18, 291, 17; 292, 19). But anyone expecting an examination of the peasants' demands exclusively on the basis of the Bible is disappointed. Not one authority is invoked, but two: the Gospel and — the state and its right. Jurists should hand down decisions concerning the "freedom of game, birds, fish, wood, forests; concerning services, tithes, the exacting of interest, times, death, etc." "For it is not proper for me as an evangelist to hand down an opinion and to judge in these matters. I must instruct and teach consciences what pertains to divine and Christian matters. There are books enough about the other things in the laws of the empire." (327, 28 ff.) Here the Gospel is rejected as a court of decision; with regard to the question of serfdom — and here the peasants had appealed to the Gospel in particular — it is used against them (326, 28). "Suffering, suffering, cross, cross is the right of Christians; that's all there is to it" (310, 28).

Here the practical aspect of this discussion is not yet in question. The only thing that matters now is that here Luther, in making an altogether concrete decision, avoids slipping from a strictly soteriological knowledge of the Gospel into a formalistic "Scripture principle" in the sense of later dogmatics. Among men there is a domain with which "the Gospel" has nothing to do — with this exception, that in this domain too it holds forgiveness of sins in readiness. The confessions have expressed this limitation — which, of course, is unavoidable because of the impact of the Gospel *(evangelischer Ansatz)* — with the greatest clarity. "For the nature and righteousness of the heart taught by the Gospel is not external and temporal; it is internal and everlasting," says the Augsburg Confession (XVI). But this does not preclude the fact that another part of Holy Scripture, the "Law," is the court of absolute instance for that worldly domain. But even if it were possible to identify the Law, concerning which the confessions say that it has a manifold "use" even for the Christian, with a definite, outwardly marked part of Scripture, this would not do away with that limitation. For this would not spare the Christian the decision as to when one part of Scripture and when another part pertains to him. For the knowledge that the Law does not apply to the believer as a believer is one of the fundamental postulates of the impact of the Gospel *(evangelischer Ansatz)*. But since this decision cannot be understood as an arbitrary choice but is made by God Himself in what He says in the Gospel concerning the believing sinner, the evangelical content of Scripture continues to have for the believer an authority with which its legal content can no longer interfere. Even though many problems are still awaiting settlement here, nevertheless, according to this, an indiscriminate authority of Scripture completely in conformity in all details is out of the question.

If one wants to understand why Lutheranism, in its incipient stage, was cautious so far as a theoretical formulation was concerned, one dare not lose sight of this inner complexity of the Scriptural principle. Naturally, Scripture was the authority – but not only for Luther. All his opponents accepted Scripture as authoritative. Thomas Aquinas did so too, and especially the school of Occam. And from Friedrich Kropatscheck's presentation one gets an impression of its authoritative significance for the life of the pious in the Middle Ages.[5] It certainly was important in the highest degree that for Luther the other pillars of authority in matters of faith had been shattered since 1519 – finally pope, fathers, and councils. Hans Preuss has shown how hard Luther struggled to achieve this.[6] The break with the Roman Church was irrevocably determined by what he had done. But the return to the exclusive validity of the authority of Scripture certainly did not mean that the necessary reconstruction was complete. It was not even assured. There followed the controversy with the fanatics, with the peasants, with Erasmus, with the Swiss. They all shared the "Scriptural principle" in one way or another. But what a multiplicity of possible ways this presents! If Luther finally took, and could take, only one of them, the ultimate motives are not to be found in the formal recognition of the authority of Scripture. Yes, one can say that at all events Luther's relationship to the fanatics is determined by the fact that he actually fights against the formal emphasis they place on the authority of Scripture. In their indiscriminate extension of its obligating character to the sum total of the content of Scripture Luther sees a main source of their errors.[7]

Accordingly, the state of affairs would not have been clarified by merely placing the formal Scriptural principle ahead of everything else

[5] Fr. Kropatscheck, *Das Schriftprinzip der lutherischen Kirche. I. Die Vorgeschichte. Das Erbe des Mittelalters,* 1904.

[6] Hans Preuss, *Die Entwicklung des Schriftprinzips bei Luther bis zur Leipziger Disputation,* 1901.

[7] Above all, in the sermons on Genesis, 1527 (WA 24, 1—16; e. g., 12, 14 ff.): "One must deal and proceed carefully with Scripture. From the beginning the Word came about in many ways. One must not only look to see whether it is God's Word, but one must rather look to see to whom it was spoken, whether it pertains to you or to someone else. For here there is a difference as between summer and winter. . . . There is a twofold Word in Scripture: the one does not concern me or pertain to me; the other does pertain to me. And on that which concerns me I can wager boldly, and I can rely on it as on a firm rock. . . . False prophets rush up and say: 'Dear people, this is God's Word.' It is true, and we cannot deny it; but we are not the people to whom He is speaking."

in the confessions. Many theologians of the nineteenth century deplored the fact that this had not been done. But had it been done, confusion rather than clarity would have resulted. It is true that the *Copenhagen Articles* of 1530 begin with the statement that the *Canonica Scriptura* is the sole rule and law according to which all those who want to receive grace and salvation from God must live and be governed. But that this did not yet answer the question which arose here can be seen, for example, in the fact that in the fourth article – cf. the eleventh – the doctrine of the Trinity comes up, therefore a dogma which the ancient church, in addition to Scripture, presupposes as a source. And in the same way the right of the state to make laws on its own authority is recognized in the thirty-seventh article.

But internal uncertainties with regard to the Scriptural principle had already made themselves felt in the *Ansbach Counsel* of 1524, which also gives it first place. Here the preamble has the heading: "Against Those Who Consider the Gospels Credible on the Basis of Human Confirmation" *(Fränkische Bekenntnisse,* p. 184). Thus in the first instance the emphasis lies where, when discussing this question, one must look for it on the basis of the impact of the Gospel *(evangelischer Ansatz).* The authority of the Gospel is at stake! In the opinion of the opponents the church and the church councils had originally conferred this authority on the Gospel. But this would mean "exalting the daughter above the mother, placing first things last, and, in short, making something completely wrong out of a divine arrangement, since, according to the words of Christ (Matt. 16), the church is built and founded on the Gospel, not the Gospel on the churches." If, strictly speaking, this line of reasoning applies only to the unwritten Gospel of the beginning, still immediately afterwards there is further discussion of the majority of the gospels. The church or the Christians of the earliest time would never have accepted these gospels "to confirm them and to make them credible." To be sure, the gospels were "accepted through divine, infused faith," but only by "Christians who hear the voice of their true Shepherd and flee from a stranger." The Old Testament also comes up in this connection. As the reason for accepting the gospels it is stated "that they saw and found that the Gospels were in complete agreement with Scripture and the prophets, who prophesied of Christ long before" *(dass sie die selben der schrifft und den Propheten, so von Christo lange zeyt davor geweyssagt, einhellig gleich und gemess haben gesehen und erfunden).* In like manner, the early Christians rejected pseudo gospels that wanted to creep in. For them it was decisive when they discovered that these writings were internally out of harmony with the Old Testament. But even the Old Testament did not owe its authority to councils or the official church. For according to the testimony of the prophets, the councils themselves and the official church had often opposed the divine Word. And since the New Testament shared this fate with the Old Testament, it would be altogether wrong to say that the gospels were not declared to be authoritative until the official church had come into being.

Later on the third article deals "with the expounding of Divine Scripture." It inveighs against the claim of councils and bishops that they alone have the right to give an authentic interpretation. In opposition to this pretension it declares "that it is in the province of no man's reason or power to expound Divine Scripture in any other way than by interpreting one text of Divine Scripture with another text in such a way that no text contradicts the other and that every passage of Divine Scripture can have validity everywhere" *(das in keines menschen vernunfft oder gewalt stee, götliche schrifft anderst, dann einen text götlicher schrifft mit dem andern dermassen ausszulegen, das keiner dem andern widerwertig sey und die götlich schrifft an allen orten besteen kan)* (p. 217). Human reason is incapable of knowing the divine content — out of weakness, blindness, and obduracy over against the Word of God. A "supernatural light" (219) is needed to bring about this knowledge. But since there is no such supernatural light outside Scripture, it follows that one can always explain and "judge" "Scripture only with Scripture, and one text of the Bible by means of and with the other" (223). With this declaration one must also refute the objection that Scripture in itself is obscure and therefore in need of authentic interpretation on the part of the church. On the contrary, Scripture is "in itself lucid and clear" *(an jr selbs hell und klar)*; and to him who exposes himself without reservation to the divine Word it gives proof of its illuminating power (222).

As has been said, the conclusion of the preamble on the "Gospel" was in conformity with what is meant by the impact of the Gospel *(evangelischer Ansatz)*. But in finding its way from here to Scripture as a whole *(zum Schriftganzen)* the counsel proceeds altogether too fast. Equating *the* Gospel with "the gospels" and the whole New Testament, and then making a similar deduction regarding the authority of the Old Testament, could lead to a conception of Scripture which did not take into account the understanding which ripened for Luther in the controversy with the peasants. In agreement with Luther, Melanchthon had already emphasized in the *Loci* of 1521 that Gospel is by no means synonymous with the New Testament but is already to be found in the Old Testament. Something similar was true of the well-expressed statements in the *Ansbach Counsel* concerning the "sufficiency" *(sufficientia)* of Scripture and Scripture's "perspicuity and ability to interpret itself" *(perspicuitas et facultas semetipsam interpretandi)* – as the later dogmaticians said. These statements repeat what Luther had contended for from the beginning until 1519. In the controversy with Carlstadt, who denied the sufficiency and the autogenous clarity of Scripture, Luther stated very sharply that the Spirit works only through the external Word and that it is precisely this externality of the Word which protects faith from the suspicion of illusionism (WA 18, 135 ff.; WA 25, 336, 33). This was an essential element in relation to the impact of the Gospel *(evangelischer Ansatz)* and was also clearly expressed by the Ansbachians. But now it strengthened the tendency to underscore the very externality of the divine Word, therefore the wording fixed in writing. After this one could have expected a Biblicism of Lutheranism that would become stronger and stronger. But it is one of the decisive facts of the early history of Lutheranism that it did not pursue this course. That it did not do so with respect to ethics – sociology, the church, culture, politics – can be seen from the aforementioned criticism directed against the "Biblicism" of the rebellious peasants. This will be dealt with again later. But that Lutheranism did not pursue this course with respect to dogmatics either is shown by the very development of those first doctrinal "counsels" up to the time of the Augsburg Confession.

This is when the dogma of the Evangelical Lutheran Church came into being. That dogma is actually the point at issue here is illustrated most strikingly by the acceptance of the Trinitarian and Christological dogma – the acceptance that appears in the first article of the Augsburg Confession as an acceptance of the formal "decree of the Nicene Synod" *(decretum Nicaenae synodi)*. The first of the *Schwabach Articles* still adduces only Scripture passages as authority for the doctrine of the Trinity.[8] Nevertheless, it is wrong to derive the Augsburg Confession's reference to the Nicene Creed from the conciliatory bent of Melanchthon, who wanted to point to the common ground which the early church shared with the Church of Rome. It is true that this tendency is characteristic of the Augsburg Confession. But the reference to the Nicene Creed is already found in the first of the *Marburg Articles,* in connection with which one cannot speak of this tendency (WA 30 III, 160). Consequently, for this acceptance as well as for the origin of the evangelical

[8] John 1:1 f.; Matt. 28:19; "and many similar verses, especially in the Gospel of St. John" (WA 30 III, 86, 11 ff.).

dogma there must be other reasons than the aforementioned bent of Melanchthon. Whatever they may have been, they can in no case be derived from a Biblicism of this or that nature. On the contrary, it is very clear that the whole procedure goes much further. This is not yet the place to investigate whether a departure in substance from the principle of the sufficiency of Scripture was included. Viewed purely from the outside, it *was* a departure. For anyone who interpreted that principle externally, that is, formalistically, could demand that, in order to keep out every human admixture, one should make use only of the canonical wording of Holy Scripture in all public, didactic, polemical, and apologetical expositions.

This demand was actually made while the evangelical confessions were being formulated. And it was made by Bucer. He begins the opinion he handed down concerning the *Schwabach Articles* with the statement that "faith must rest on the sole, certain Word of God." [9] This was the principle of the Reformation with regard to the sufficiency of Scripture. But then Bucer goes on to say that it is advisable to use nothing but Biblical words when formulating the articles.[10] This seems to be only a result of that principle. But when Bucer demands this, he points to two purposes: it would further unity and prevent errors. It is self-evident that the hope of furthering unity was utopian from the very start. For the evangelical principle of the sufficiency of Scripture from which he derived his demand was in itself, of course, an element of the unbridgeable antithesis to the Roman opponents. How could unity be furthered if one now insisted with special emphasis on this principle? But even the belief that one is immune from errors if one uses nothing but Biblical words bears witness of very naive notions concerning the causes of controversies in the field of dogma. Bucer

[9] Reprinted in W. Gussmann, *Quellen* II, pp. 289 ff. and in H. v. Schubert, *Bekenntnisbildung und Religionspolitik 1529—30*, 1910, pp. 169 ff. — We are quoting according to the text in Gussmann.

[10] In Gussmann: "Therefore although some articles could be taken in the right sense, yet, because one should be a believer in God and should take great pains to avoid human wavering, it would be advisable, wherever this is possible, that all the articles be expressed in Biblical words and in the clearest and briefest manner. This would further unity to a marked degree and would make it sincere, if everyone saw that he is united with the one Christ purely and simply; and then the window would not be opened to any error." — It is in keeping with the character of Bucer, to whom Brenz ascribed "the cunning of a fox" *(calliditas vulpina)* after the Marburg Colloquy, that at the decisive moment he himself could do otherwise. In the first article of the *Confessio Tetrapolitana* of 1530 he himself uses the expressions to which he takes exception here, even the expressions of the *Chalcedonense;* and he bases his action on what the "holy fathers" did. German in K. Müller, *Ref. Bek.*, pp. 55 ff.; Latin in Niemeyer, *Coll. Conf.*, 1840, p. 745.

points to Luther's own scruples with regard to the expression "Trinity" and believes it is also better to avoid the expression "Person" in the doctrine concerning God. To this Conrad Sam remarks in the margin: "This would seem to be too Arianistic. I agree with Luther, regardless of all the Jews, who take offense at this." (P. 290.) Here Sam perceives very correctly that even the emphasized abandonment of a concept that has become controversial in the history of dogma amounts to taking a position in this dispute. It is possible, of course, that in such a controversy a simple Biblical expression can prove the incorrectness of an expression that has come up and does not occur in Scripture. But then the use of the Biblical expression does not, as Bucer believes, indicate a position above party lines; it means that a definite blow is administered to the opponent. If the controversy is actually to be settled in this way, a thoroughgoing critical examination of the non-biblical expression is necessary. This means that the Biblicist in agreement with Bucer also takes part in the controversy concerning dogma – the controversy in which he cannot do without his own logic in using and relating his Scripture passages and therefore is also exposed to error.[11] In the controversy with the fanatics Luther had found confirmation for old Vincent of Lerin's experience that all false teachers appeal to Scripture. After this he went even further. He stated emphatically that the very time to use expressions that do not occur in Scripture is when one struggles against error (WA 18, 141, 11 ff.).

Bucer's critical examination touches on something of the greatest significance for all Lutheranism: the positive relating of the nascent evangelical dogma to the preceding history of dogma. It has been necessary to give it preliminary consideration at this point because it can clarify the Lutheran Scriptural principle negatively at least in one respect: Scripture is not a codex from which one gets church doctrine merely by quoting.

The realization of this fact is confirmed by the only theoretical discussion of the Scriptural principle to be found in the confessions that have been accepted – by what the Formula of Concord sets forth "Concerning the Summary Concept, Rule, and Guide, etc." Here the Formula of Concord designates Holy Scripture as "judge, rule, and guide according to which, as the only touchstone, all doctrines should and must be discerned and judged as to whether they are good or bad, right or wrong." Accordingly, the Formula of Concord ascribes to Scripture

[11] Here one may recall Spurgeon's illustration of using nothing but Scriptural expressions and yet saying something that is absurd: "God's Word says, 'Judas went and hanged himself' and 'Go and do likewise.'"

critical or regulative significance for doctrine. And to the expression "pure, unadulterated well of Israel," which means that Scripture is the source of knowledge, there is the immediate addition: ". . . which alone is the one true guide according to which all teachers and doctrine are to be judged." Here, therefore, "doctrine" is considered at least a relatively independent factor alongside Scripture. — In this way one of the first specific definitions of the statement concerning the sole authority of Scripture has been arrived at. Scripture is a norm for all church doctrine without being identical with it.

The actual acknowledgment of the relative independence of church doctrine alongside Scripture has great weight — all the greater because the attack on the Roman principle of tradition, which is also a matter of consequence for the confessions, could apparently have been carried out much more consistently on the basis of Bucer's point of view. For from a distance it could seem that here a new authority had to enter into competition with the authority of Holy Scripture. If, however, one exposed oneself to this appearance of evil, a good conscience is taken for granted, namely, a stability of the sole authority of Scripture founded on perspicuity that cannot be the subject of debate. This stability actually exists. For the "Scriptural principle" is anchored exactly where, and exactly as, all the conviction of the Reformation is anchored.

The connection between the conviction faith has and the Gospel and its proclamation has been developed as a necessary component of the doctrine of justification. This connection has also been taken into account sufficiently by means of *oral* proclamation. Luther even found that it is "not at all in conformity with the New Testament to write books about Christian doctrine" *(gar nicht new testamentisch, bucher schreyben von Christlicher lehre).* "Before they wrote," he said, the apostles had "previously preached to and converted the people with the physical voice, which was also their real apostolic and New Testament work" (WA 10 I, 1, p. 625, 15 ff.). "But since it became necessary to write books, there is already a great loss, and there is uncertainty as to what is meant" *(Da man aber hatt mussen bucher schreyben, ist schon eyn grosser abbruch and eyn geprechen des geystes).* The writing of books became necessary because false teachers and various errors had arisen (627, 1 ff.). Even though fixation in writing is of the highest value because it establishes authenticity, nevertheless oral proclamation always has certain advantages (WA 40 I, 651, 4 ff.). The word heard from the pulpit works more fruitfully and more powerfully than the word read at home (WA 36, 220, 23 ff.). Among the hundreds of expressions Luther used to describe the Gospel not a single one occurs more frequently than "preaching." It is preaching about Christ. But this is also true, and especially true, of the written Gospel (WA 10 I, 1, p. 13, 20). The Gospel is "a chronicle, a history, a biography of Christ, who He is, what He did, said, and suffered, which one has described briefly, the other at length, one in this way, the other in another way" *(eyn Chronica, historia, legende von Christo, wer der sey, was er than, geredt und erlitten habe, wilchs eyner kurtz, der ander lang, eyner ssonst der ander sso beschrieben hatt)* (p. 9, 16). Luther goes on to underscore this historical character of the Gospel by saying that he compares this account of Christ to books on profane history – books which deal with the life, the deeds, and the sufferings of kings and princes. This Gospel of Christ is contained in the New Testament not only in a fourfold way; it is there in a manifold manner. In their epistles Paul and Peter are also evangelists. The Gospel is to be found in the Old Testament too. "Since the gospels and the epistles have been written because they themselves want to be such pointers *[tzeyger]* and direct us to what the prophets and Moses wrote in the Old Testament, that there we ourselves should read and see how Christ was wrapped in swaddling clothes and laid in a manger, that is, how He is presented beforehand in the writings of the prophets" (p. 15, 1 ff.). But the account of Christ actually becomes Gospel when you "accept and recognize Him as a gift and a present given to you by your God and as your own" (p. 11, 13). And herein it establishes its character as "a book of divine promises" (13, 4).

Thus, therefore, the Book, which comprises the Old and the New Testament, gains our faith. It also proclaims the Law to us, and without the demand and the judgment of the Law there can be no penitence and therefore no faith. But he who does not find Christ in this Book engages in superfluous reading, even if he reads it carefully (WA 51, 4, 8). Only he who seeks and finds Him in this Book is the real master of Scripture (p. 2, 23). One should "refer the Bible to Christ . . . nothing but Christ should be proclaimed" *(die Bibel auf Christum ziehen . . . nihil nisi Christus praedicandus)* (WA 16, 113, 5 ff.). Basically, therefore, the Bible offers nothing more than could be said in a single sentence. But in His mercy God – in order to give us all the more certainty – lets the Bible speak in greater detail and has added many concrete examples of faith (WA 24, 17, 14 ff.). Scripture is evidence of all the articles about Christ: "This is the point that compels us to value Scripture so highly" (WA 32, 56, 21 ff.).[12] These and similar statements,

[12] This is expressed in an excellent manner when Jac. Heerbrand begins his *Kompendium* with the words: "What is the goal of theology and of all Holy Scrip-

which could be multiplied by the hundreds, show that for Luther the content of Scripture and the proof of its authority coincide, as do the content and the basis of faith. In giving this proof the statements about "sufficiency" *(sufficientia)* and "perspicuity" *(perspicuitas)* have nothing essentially new to say. All salvation is contained in Christ – "and all Holy Scripture points to Him. If now someone else comes and brings another teacher than Christ, say: 'God did not put the stamp of His approval on such a thing; He means Jesus alone.'" (WA 33, 19, 24; 33.) Saving faith looks confidently to Christ. If one does this, one is looking into the sun and sees nothing else (WA 36, 306, 2 ff.; 12). For this very reason it is also true "that nothing is brighter than the sun, that is, Scripture. But if a cloud has come in front of the sun, still there is nothing else behind it than the same sun. Therefore if there is a dark passage in Scripture, do not despair; surely the same truth is behind it that is clear in another place. And he who cannot understand what is dark should stay with what is clear." (WA 8, 239, 16.)

In Luther, therefore, the interrelationship of the authority, the sufficiency, and the perspicuity of Scripture is inseparable because Scripture, as he reads it, is strictly Christocentric. Accordingly, one can say that the doctrine of justification is the key to his "Scriptural principle." This explains early Lutheranism's initial stand with regard to the Scriptural principle. The fact that the Augsburg Confession says nothing about this principle shows that it recognizes Luther's position with respect to Scripture. Had it begun with special statements about Scripture – say, that Scripture is God's Word, that it is inspired, that it is necessary for the knowledge of God and salvation – this would have been wasted effort over against the Roman opposition. Rome did not question any of these statements. The declaration "Nothing but Christ should be preached" *(Nihil nisi Christus praedicandus)* was what gave the Scriptural principle as defined by Lutheranism its truly reformational character. On the other hand, it was not possible to formulate this as if it were in opposition to the conception of Scripture as this conception, expressed in the aforementioned statements, was the common property of medieval theology. Objectively speaking, it was not in opposition. Nor were the

ture? Christ, the Son of God and man, born of the Virgin Mary, crucified, died on account of our sins, who rose again for the sake of our justification." *(Quid est scopus Theologiae et totius s. Scripturae? Christus, Dei et hominis Filius, ex Maria virgine natus, crucifixus, mortuus propter peccata nostra, qui resurrexit propter justificationem nostram.)* Thus in the edition of 1575. In the later editions — e. g., of 1585 — a detailed doctrine concerning Scripture precedes this sentence. — Even in the beginning Rurer, for example (Gussmann, *Quellen* I, 2, p. 7), could write: "One should hear, accept, and believe only the divine Word in matters that pertain to consciences and to the salvation of the soul."

writers of the confessions convinced that it was. Consequently, it was necessary to presuppose the traditional Scriptural principle as a self-evident, common basis and, by means of a Christological treatment in all details, to establish what was specifically reformational. This was done in the whole soteriological position of the Augsburg Confession, in the Apology, and, in addition, in Luther's Smalcald Articles.

One could say that here "the Gospel" was and remained the only valid standard. From another point of view this makes the aforementioned limitation of the authority of Scripture understandable, namely, that it is the norm of church doctrine without being identical with church doctrine. A mere string of statements from Scripture does not yet guard against vagaries – it is even sure to lead to vagaries if the Gospel's point of emphasis and reference is not found and preserved. But it must be the task of church doctrine to find the central point of the Gospel. Actually an authentic form of the Gospel existed only in Scripture – of the Old and the New Testament. Therefore if one wanted to put "the Gospel" on the scales, one could quote only "Scripture." It is true that in the recognition of the inner relationship between Law and Gospel, of "history," "examples," and "preaching," there lay the realization that Scripture is a whole. But the inevitable need of a guarantee of authenticity led necessarily from the proof which the contents of Scripture – it is Christocentric – gives of its authority to the formal proof. This question demanded an answer: Why is it that among all writings only the so-called canonical books have validity as Holy Scripture?

15. Canon, Inspiration, Means of Grace, Apologetics

To determine what the canon of the Holy Scriptures comprised, Roman theology adduced the actual use in the church (*Trid. Sess.* IV). Was it unevangelical to be in agreement with this? Even for the evangelicals a more careful deliberation could lead to no other result. What one held in one's hand as a "sacred volume" (*volumen sacrum*) one owed to what the church had done to put it there – unless one wanted to give credit for it to the bookbinder. But after this simple state of affairs – the admission of the evangelicals that Scripture has its authority from the church [1] – had been exploited by Roman polemics against the evangelical doctrine of the sufficiency of Scripture, this dependence had to be more precisely defined. For no evangelical would think of placing the weight of the church's verdict on a par with the authority of Scripture itself.

[1] Wilh. Herbst, *Das Regensburger Religionsgespräch von 1601*, 1928; Especially *Rückblick*, pp. 176 ff.

Dependence on the church in connection with the fixing of the canon was defined more accurately in three stages. For one thing, it was emphasized that in this matter the church has no other function than that of a witness – and its testimony has weight only because, by acknowledging the canonical character of the Holy Scriptures themselves, it has bowed to their divine authority.[2] This implied that in addition to the testimony of the church there had to be another criterion of canonicity; and this criterion was found in the internal harmony which, in the case of doubtful writings, would have to be established by those writings that were canonical beyond doubt.[3] But then the corresponding hallmark of the canonicity of this nuclear group of the Holy Scriptures was still missing. Later this hallmark was designated as the "internal testimony of the Holy Spirit" *(testimonium spiritus sancti internum).*[4] Thus the way to certainty with regard to the canon leads back to the path to certainty with regard to the authority of Scripture. For dogmaticians understood the "internal testimony of the Holy Spirit" *(testimonium spiritus sancti internum)* to mean exactly what the self-testimony of the content of Scripture for faith in Christ meant to Luther.

To be sure, another line of thought now runs alongside this one. The constantly intensified retreat to an internal criterion should by no means cancel the testimony of the church. The later dogmaticians, who

[2] Selnecker, *Examen Ordin.* I, 120: "The church has declared by its testimony that certain books are canonical, not because it rendered or made them canonical by its own authority, but because they were already canonical books and had authority from themselves because of God, the Author, and the majesty of the teaching. The church does not make the books canonical, but it merely recognizes them and distinguishes the voice of its Shepherd from the voice of a hireling and from the writings of other men." *(Ecclesia declaravit sua testificatione certos libros esse canonicos, non quod autoritate sua redderet et efficeret illos canonicos, sed quod iam canonici libri essent et autoritatem a se ipsis haberent propter Deum autorem et doctrinae majestatem. Ecclesia non facit libros canonicos, sed tantum agnoscit et discernit vocem pastoris sui a voce mercenarii et a scriptis aliorum hominum.)*

[3] Hafenreffer, *Loci,* 141: "On what basis, however, is it possible for us to be in agreement concerning this distinction between canonical and apocryphal books? Not only on the basis of the weightiest testimony of the church, which at first had the original of each book, recognized it, put forth a whole of the canonical books and always passed it on to posterity with faithful care, but also on the basis of the surest and weightiest internal criteria of every canonical writing and on the basis of the harmonious agreement and analogy with the rest of Scripture." *(Unde vero de discrimine hoc canonicorum et Apocryphorum librorum constare nobis potest? Non tantum ex gravissimo ecclesiae testimonio, quae primitus singulorum librorum Originalia habuit, recognovit, Systema Canonicorum edidit et fideli semper cura propagavit ad posteritatem, verum etiam ex internis cuiusque Canonici scripti certissimis atque gravissimis kriteriois et cum reliqua Scriptura harmonica consensione et analogia.)* — Christof Jordan (from Wundsiedel), *Disp. de sacra script. canonica, praes. Aeg. Hunnio,* Wittenberg, 1601.

[4] Baier, *Comp.,* 120.

place the testimony of the Spirit side by side with the church's testimony, protest only against treating what the church says as a "divine testimony" *(testimonium divinum)*. In accordance with the precedent set by Chemnitz, however, they find a second difference – one that is in opposition to basing canonicity on the testimony of the church as the Roman Catholic opponents do. It is not the testimony of the church of today that guarantees canonicity; it is the testimony of the "primitive church" *(ecclesia primitiva)*. This testimony – so Chemniz argues – has special weight because (1) the primitive church knew the authors and could therefore vouch for their apostolic character, (2) was still close enough to the happenings that were reported, and (3) was qualified to judge whether the writings actually tallied with the oral preaching of the apostles – the preaching that was still vividly remembered *(Ex. Conc. Trid.* I, 85). In this sense dogmaticians like Johann Gerhard and Abraham Calov then provide proofs of the canonicity of the individual books from the literature of the early church – proofs corresponding in what they accomplish to those that modern Biblical isagogics gives of the authenticity of these books.

Here the change of the direction in which one looks is of great importance. When establishing the authority of Scripture one looks first only at the contents, and this finally remains decisive when the canon as a whole is determined. Yet one looks just as definitely at the authors of the Biblical books. The line of investigation becomes historical. This, of course, does not have the result that the number of critically contested books might have become larger if the historical method of considering them had been used than it would have become if the other method had been employed. One could sooner prove the opposite. At any rate, since Chemnitz' time theologians have become ever more timid in the critical position they take over against the antilegomena. The frankest statements about this stem from Luther, above all from his forewords to the Biblical books. Without any qualification Hafenreffer designates 2 Peter, 2 and 3 John, Hebrews, James, Jude, and the Apocalypse as apocryphal. Johann Gerhard, however, begins to retreat along the whole line. He does so on the basis of history – even though by no means all the later theologians have gone along with him.[5]

Even though the whole question pertaining to the demarcation of the canon may seem to be unimportant – because, after all, there was agreement with regard to the preponderant make-up of the Old and the New Testament – still this turning to the historical method of con-

[5] Chr. Matthias is still in agreement with Hafenreffer in designating the same books as "apocryphal," *Syst.*, p. 12.

sideration was related in principle to a corresponding way of establishing the authority of Scripture itself – a way that had consequences much more important: the constantly stronger emphasis placed on the doctrine of inspiration.

The doctrine of inspiration is also concerned with the authors. It proceeds from the possibility that doubt as to the reliability of the Biblical writers endangers faith. It has the tendency to contest responsible or even only coresponsible authorship of human writers, and in a strict sense to present God as the sole Author. If this has been successfully established, Holy Scripture, in its entire compass, contains only words of God – words which, in their entirety and in the same measure, present binding "doctrine." This doctrine, given by God Himself, is then identical with revelation. Implicit in the inner structure of this doctrine is the basic fact that it does not rest until actually every word is regarded as "inspired." For only then does the Scriptural proof based on this concept of revelation become irrefutable from the first.[6] In the inner context of the impact of the Gospel *(evangelischer Ansatz)* no point can be seen at which this doctrine could be anchored as a necessary element. On the contrary, there is danger that it may abandon the Gospel impact *(evangelischer Ansatz)* at critical points. This could be illustrated by the concepts of revelation, faith, and the Word of God. But it is sufficient to point to the last of the "qualities" *(affectiones)* which, in essential agreement with Luther and the confessions, are ascribed to Scripture: "efficacy" *(efficacia)*.[7]

The later dogmaticians take this to mean the efficacy belonging to

[6] The development of the doctrine of inspiration in early Protestantism is presented by O. Ritschl, *Dogmengesch, d. Prot.* I, 1908, pp. 55—192. — Important are especially the proofs that the doctrine of inspiration, in its fully developed form, is of Reformed origin, that it is advocated above all by Calvin since 1543 (in opposition to Heppe), that neither Melanchthon nor the Philippists present it, and that Flacius is the first advocate of verbal inspiration among the Lutherans. — In addition, cf. R. Seeberg, *DG* IV, 2d and 3d ed., pp. 322 ff. (on Luther); pp. 432 f. (on Melanchthon); pp. 566 f. (on Calvin). — On the reaction of Roman polemics cf. W. Herbst, op. cit. — Among other presentations, especially concerning Luther's doctrine of inspiration, cf. W. Rohnert, *Was lehrte Luther von der Inspiration der H. Schrift?*, 1890; Joh. Kunze, *Glaubensregel, Heil. Schrift und Taufbekenntnis*, 1899, pp. 474 ff. — O. Scheel, *Luthers Stellung zur H. Schrift*, 1902. — W. Thimme, *Luthers Stellung zur H. Schrift*, 1903 — In addition, Winter (Soest), *Die genetische Begründung der Schriftautorität bei Luther*, 1925, and Paul Althaus the Younger, *Autorität und Freiheit in Luthers Stellung zur Bibel, Theol. Aufsätze*, 1929, pp. 140 ff. Paul Schempp, *Luthers Stellung zur H. Schrift*, 1929.

Classical presentations of the fully developed doctrine of inspiration in the Lutheranism of the seventeenth century are to be found in Joh. Gerhard, *Loci*, chs. 2 and 11, and in Calov, *Syst.* I, 448 ff.

[7] The other *affectiones* are those that have already been mentioned: *auctoritas, perfectio s. sufficientia, perspicuitas.*

Holy Scripture as a necessary element in connection with illumination, conversion, and salvation (Calov, *Syst.* I, 474). This efficacy clings inseparably to Scripture "even apart from its use" *(etiam extra usum)* (Baier, 136). Therefore no one who has the Bible at hand, reads it, hears it, and meditates on it can escape this efficacy. It has its objective basis in a permanent union of the Word of God with the Holy Spirit (Hollaz, *Ex.* IV, 3). Here Holy Scripture is the instrument of the Spirit, but by no means in such a way that the Word does not become efficacious until a special act of the Spirit has taken place – an act that would have to evoke this efficacy only when application is made to the individual reader or hearer. No, the power of the Spirit of God and the power of His Word belong together inseparably as the "principal cause" *(causa principalis)* and the "instrumental cause" *(causa instrumentalis)* of the divine act of saving. Although the former is unthinkable without the latter but does not act without it, the latter is not even conceivable without the former. The Word of God is never without the Holy Spirit. And on this its efficacy *(efficacia)* depends (Baier, 144 ff.).

The more precise development of this doctrine is the fruit of long discussions with Calvinism, with George Calixt, and with Rathmann, of Danzig.[8] But there is no doubt that its core – the doctrine of the character of the Word of God as a means of grace and of the permanent union of the operation of the Spirit with the operation of the Word – belongs to the essential elements of Luther's theology and that, to prove this, the dogmaticians had the right to adduce various statements of the confessions.[9] This doctrine is connected in the closest possible manner with the impact of the Gospel, since the turning from the fear of God's wrath to faith and to the new righteousness is brought about exclusively through the proclamation of the Gospel and, in a preparatory way, through the proclamation of the Law, therefore through the "Word of God." But if, on the other hand, faith is a product of the divine Spirit, the statement about the union of the operation of the Spirit with that of the Word is unavoidable. This union is necessary because, according to the conviction of all Lutherans, an operation of the Spirit that is not brought about through the external Word is fanaticism. It is permanent because over against the Word about Christ, which compels a decision, there can be no neutrality. Therefore he who hears or reads the Word is also called to by the Spirit of God.[10] Even though it is

[8] R. H. Grützmacher, *Wort und Geist,* 1902, pp. 220 ff.

[9] *CA* V, XVIII, 3; Apol. VII, 13; XII, 70; Smalcald Articles III, 8, 3; *FC, Epit.* II, 3, 9; *SD* XI, 39 f., 69. Cf. also Luther's Catechisms.

[10] WA 29, 580, 4: "The Holy Spirit must address us with the Word of God."

possible to close one's ears, this does not make the call inoperative. For the closing of one's ears shows that judgment has been pronounced.

In itself the doctrine of inspiration is not out of keeping with this elementary conception of the relationship of the Word and the Spirit. It is self-evident that the Holy Spirit could not have eliminated the authors' own mental cooperation when dictating to them. But one must ask whether this cooperation can and should be drawn into the personal relationship of the believer to the Word of God. If the authority of the Word for the believer is to be established by it — this, of course, is the real concern of the doctrine of inspiration[11] — it puts historical reflection in the place of a direct listening to the voice of God. For Luther the Word becomes authoritative because it judges, promises, and pardons. Acknowledgment of its authority is nothing else than letting oneself be judged and pardoned. Faith has no other footing than Christ Himself, who gives and guarantees the promise and the pardon through His incarnation, His life, death, and resurrection. If this footing is not secure enough to provide a basis for faith in the promise and thus in the authority of the Word of God, there is no faith at all. In the subject of faith itself — the transcendental I — there is no room for reflections on the literary origin of the accounts. Every deliberation of this kind belongs to rational thinking, which can in no circumstances provide a basis for faith. If, therefore, together with Luther, one wants to, and must, ascribe "efficacy" *(efficacia)* to the Word of God itself, "that it is spoken truly and is the power of God for salvation for everyone who believes" *(ut vere dicatur et sit potentia Dei ad salutem omni credenti)* (Mentzer, p. 11), one cannot call on the doctrine of inspiration for help. As soon as deliberation on the activity or the inactivity of the Biblical writers is necessary, the "efficacy" *(efficacia),* the self-testimony, of the Word has been denied.

To be sure, this by no means precludes the fact that the doctrine of inspiration has its necessary place somewhere else. Altogether apart from Scripture's self-testimony about this matter — which was important for the early dogmaticians as well as for Luther — reflection on the sacred writings from which one hears the Word of God is unavoidable in the sum total of what theology teaches. But since it proceeds from the historical persons of the authors and puts them in connection with God's

[11] Joh. Winckelmann, Balth. Mentzer, and Joh. Scholl, *Propositiones de praecipuis . . . christianae religionis capitibus,* Marburg, 1602. Here *Disp. de scriptura canonica,* by Mentzer, *Th. 8:* "The authority of Holy Scripture is as great as that of the Holy Spirit, who speaks, whose amanuenses those men were" *(Tanta est S. Scripturae auctoritas, quanta est dictantis Spiritus sancti: cuius illi fuerunt amanuenses).*

work in revelation, it is an element in the interpretation of the story of salvation. In this respect it must be properly valued in another context.

Melanchthon and his closest pupils did not make use of the doctrine of inspiration to prove the authority of Scripture. In the last edition of the *Loci* the self-testimony of the Law as well as of the Gospel in the hearts of believers is still the reason on which all certainty is founded. Yet by means of another line of thought Melanchthon, too, trod a path which later became disastrous for establishing the basis of the authority of Scripture. The doctrine of the "testimonies" *(testimonia)* for Scripture which later on were the real subject of the apologetics of the Enlightenment can be traced back to him. In the preface to the fourth volume of the Latin writings of Luther (1552) Melanchthon enumerates the following evidences of the divine revelation: the miracles that accompanied it, the age of the divine doctrine, the inner superiority of the divine doctrine in comparison with what the heathen believe, the testimony of the Spirit in the hearts, the joy of the martyrs, the preservation of the church, the punishment of the enemies of the Gospel *(CR* 7, 1078 ff.).[12] For the pious these are proofs, "that they may recognize and determine that only this doctrine concerning God and the salvation of men is true which God Himself has revealed in the church and has wanted to be contained in the writings of the prophets and the apostles" *(ut agnoscant ac statuant solam hanc doctrinam de Deo et de salute hominum veram esse, quam Deus ipse in ecclesia patefecit ac in propheticis et apostolicis scriptis comprehendi voluit).* Accordingly, these are evidences of the authority of Scripture. It is true that Melanchthon did not state that they were conclusive for unbelievers. But "although evil men laugh at these steps of the testimonies, nevertheless the consideration is useful for good minds" *(quamquam homines perversi rident hos gradus testimoniorum, tamen bonis mentibus consideratio utilis est)* (1082). Above all, it was precarious to put the external evidences on the same level with the testimony of the Spirit. In this way the danger of rationalizing the authority of Scripture and thus lessening the value of Scripture's self-testimony drew tangibly near.

Hafenreffer shows that he is aware of this danger and that he tries to eliminate it. At the head of his chain of evidence for the "certainty and the authority of Holy Scripture" *(certitudo et auctoritas scripturae s.)* he refers to what is plainly irrational in what Scripture contains: "Because

[12] A similar series is given in a letter of Feb. 1, 1557, to Peter Palladius, Bishop of Roskilde: "The miracles, the antiquity, the nature of the teaching, the marvelous preservation among the ruins of empires, the steadfastness of the confessors, and the pledge in the heart" *(Miracula, antiquitas, genus doctrinae, conservatio miranda inter ruinas imperiorum, confessorum constantia et arrabo in corde)* (*CR* 9, 79 ff.).

it contains things that are most abstruse and very far removed from all human acumen, such as the mysteries of the Trinity, incarnation, redemption, resurrection, etc." *(Quia res abstrusissimas et ab omni humano acumine remotissimas continet: ut sunt mysteria trinitatis, incarnationis, redemptionis, resurrectionis, etc.)* (*Loci* 143.) With reference to 1 Cor. 2:1 the second evidence also points to what is plainly extrahuman and offensive in what Scripture contains. Next there are references to the inner harmony of Scripture, to its "efficacy and perfection" *(efficacia et perfectio)*; and not until then are the "miracles, the propagation" *(miracula, propagatio)*, and the testimonies of profane writers referred to. Hafenreffer's chain of evidence, therefore, is still dominated by the totally inexplicable nevertheless of faith.

From Johann Gerhard on a distinction is made between internal and external criteria, ahead of which Gerhard himself puts the "internal testimony of the Holy Spirit" *(testimonium spir. s. internum)*. Essentially the criteria are the Melanchthonian "evidences" with a few others.[13] But in Gerhard's writings Hafenreffer's "most abstruse things" *(abstrusissimae res)* have become the "majesty of things" *(rerum majestas)*. The offense which Hafenreffer regards as the most important characteristic of Scripture begins to be smoothed over. Soon the nevertheless of faith becomes mere supranaturalism. In his criticism of the *Catechismus Racoviensis* Frederick Balduin enumerates a similar series to prove that 2 Tim. 3:16 may be referred to the canonical writings: the divine call of the prophets and the apostles, their miracles and prophecies, the wide dissemination of Scripture, the blood testimony of the martyrs, the plagiarisms of heathen authors, etc. He includes the statement: ". . . because they treat of divine mysteries which transcend understanding and reason, and are not found in other books" *(quod de mysteriis divinis agunt, quae sensum et rationem superant nec in aliis libris reperiuntur)*.[14] Here one already seems to be aware of the supranaturalism of a later time. The revelation contained in Scripture is characterized by information concerning things that go "beyond reason" and therefore beyond human inventiveness. "By means of revelation," writes George Frederick Seiler, of Erlangen, in the following century, "unknown and future things were made known to the holy men." But "by means of inspiration

13 In Aegidius Hunnius the number of the arguments has already increased to 21. *Tractatus de ss. majestate, auctoritate, fide ac certitudine scripturae*, Lübeck, 1593. More than a third of the whole book is concerned with the *XVIII. argumentum ab universali populorum testimoniis, quod populi Dei rebus gestis perhibent*, pp. 81 to 142.

14 Frid. Balduin, *Solida refutatio Catechismi Ariani, qui Rachoviae in Polonia anno 1608 excusus . . .* , Wittenberg, 1620, p. 14.

[θεοπνευστία] God kept them from mingling falsehood with truth, from overlooking anything because of forgetfulness or negligence, and from expressing anything incorrectly by using improper words."[15]

This, therefore, is what revelation means: unknown and future things. Scripture was needed to tell men more than they could know without being told. And this is why the authors of the Bible had to be inspired. To its opponents this "genuinely Biblical supernaturalism" *(ächt biblischer Supernaturalismus)* presented an open flank on three sides. What was once unknown and could be made known only through "inspiration" *(Eingebung)* has meantime become known to mankind. Consequently, one can expect "that the new covenant has to become just as antiquated as the old" – so Lessing argued. Or – because the concept of what is unknown is oriented by what is known and therefore also by what is acknowledged as known – one could use the contrast that has been established between what is unknown and what is known to discredit Scripture because of the very fact that some things are unknown. In Wegscheider the "most abstruse things" *(res abstrusissimae)* of Hafenreffer have become the "most obscure things" *(res obscurissimae)* – things which compel one to charge this very darkness, not to God but to the authors *(Instit.,* p. 166). Or in the supposed or the actual interest of the authority of Scripture one could deny that there are any obscurities at all, as the older Socinians had already done. In this way supranatural Biblicism was stripped of its strongest argument. For what had now happened to the "internal testimony of the Holy Spirit," which the older dogmaticians had declared to be the only actually evangelical criterion for the authority of Scripture? "Finally," says Seiler, "the last argument is still left. By using it we cannot, of course, convince others of the truth of the Christian religion. But we can convince ourselves, and we can strengthen our hearts in faith. It is founded on a sure inner feeling" (ibid., p. 14.).[16]

In opposition to this conception of the testimony of the Spirit, Mos-

[15] G. F. Seiler, *Ausführliche Vorstellung der Christlichen Religion,* Giessen, 1781, p. 36.

[16] The statement is then developed in greater detail: "With this dark feeling of truth there is connected an unquestionable reasoning to this effect: by the power and the help of this evangelical doctrine I have been freed from the anxieties of an evil conscience, improved in my sentiments, equipped with powers to conquer evil lusts and to practice virtues of every kind, and enabled to bear the sufferings of this life patiently and with exalted courage. Thus through my own feeling I experience the healing power and effectiveness of this doctrine. . . . How indeed could it be possible for me still to doubt that the Christian religion has been given to the human race by God, since through it I have been equipped with new powers and have partaken of so many and such great benefits?" (P. 15.)

heim had asked the pertinent question: "Can anyone feel pious impulses and still be in error?" *(Potest aliquis pios motus sentire et tamen errare?)*[17] It is certain that Seiler and those who shared his views want "to prove only this, that Jesus of Nazareth was an envoy from God and that His doctrine is true." Furthermore, the authority of Scripture should be guaranteed by "historical proofs."[18] This is the general theme of the extensive apologetics of the eighteenth century, which, according to English examples, mustered the sum total of the learning of the times in the domains of history, natural sciences, and philosophy to prove that Scripture is "still trustworthy" and that, as a result, "Christianity is still tenable." The end is the loss of sovereignty and the loss of certainty – losses which characterize evangelical Christianity in the first years of the nineteenth century.[19] Nicolaus Selnecker's simple statement had been forgotten: "Scripture is read with the necessity to believe – the writings of others are read with the freedom to pass judgment" *(Scriptura legitur cum credendi necessitate – aliorum scripta leguntur cum iudicandi libertate)* (*Ex. Ord.* I, 117). This statement could no longer be understood, because a whole flood of "testimonies" *(testimonia)*, "criteria" *(kriteria)*, "arguments" *(argumenta)*, evidences, and proofs had come streaming between faith and the Word of Scriptures – a flood which finally reached its crest in Lilienthal's *The Good Cause of Revelation (Gute Sache der Offenbarung)* in sixteen volumes (third edition, 1779 ff.). To speak of "necessity" *(necessitas)* in connection with a faith which gathered crutches in this thicket of encyclopedic wisdom would not be superreasonable; it would be unreasonable. Biblicism severed from the impact of the Gospel *(evangelischer Ansatz)* had destroyed evangelical Christianity.

16. The Acceptance of the Old Creeds[1]

The origin of the first Lutheran confessions is connected in the closest possible manner with the carrying-out of the Reformation in

[17] According to Wegscheider, ibid., p. 153. I have not been able to find this passage in Mosheim. Wegscheider specifies *Dogm.*, 142; but the sentence does not occur there.

[18] The "credibility" of the evangelists and the apostles is proved: "1. The ambassadors of Jesus of Nazareth were honest men and had the reputation of leading a blameless life. 2. Nor did they lack the ability to pass judgment on what they saw Jesus do. 3. They preached to the human race an efficacious and powerful teaching for the improvement of the heart. 4. They testified . . . publicly before the judgment seats of their enemies, etc."

[19] I refer here to the first chapter of my book *Der Kampf um das Christentum seit Schleiermacher und Hegel*, 1921.

[1] R. Seeberg, *Melanchthons Stellung in der Geschichte des Dogmas und der Dogmatik, NKZ*, 1897, pp. 126 ff. — Walther Köhler, *Luther und die Kirchengeschichte* I, 1900, pp. 76 ff., 98 ff. — L. Ihmels, *Das Dogma in der Predigt Luthers*

independent new church formations. Insofar as the confessions deal with the establishment of the "doctrine" that is publicly valid, they have become the expression of an evangelical dogma. One cannot speak of the character and the measure of their validity until there is clarity with regard to the church in the evangelical sense. As soon as the Gospel is understood in the sense of its impact *(Ansatz)*, it is not necessary to prove that in the church of the Gospel doctrine must really be of decisive significance. As preacher and as professor Luther himself is living proof that what the church teaches cannot consist in a reciting of Scripture passages. When he says: "Let the preacher teach only the Word of God" *(Concionator doceat tantum verbum Dei)* (WA 47, 771, 26), he means anything but such reciting. He demands that "all sermons in Christendom must refer and point to the one and only Christ" *(alle predigten in der Christenheit auff den einigen Christum gehen und zeigen müssen)* (WA 45, 521, 10). For him this is the same thing as the oft-repeated distinction between true and false teachers that should be made with reference to their position regarding justification, faith, and works. Therefore he demands of preachers that they employ the right accent, emphasize the center, and put the periphery into the background. This presupposes theological work which bears practical fruit in preaching but must also be shown in disputes about dogma. Luther's own exegetical works, however, show how the exegete who is really concerned with understanding the Gospel inevitably becomes a dogmatician.

Naturally, this certainly does not mean that the product of theological work should or need be brought into tight dogmatic formulae as they were actually stabilized in the confessions. "Doctrine" in this sense is something different from what it is when Luther speaks of the "doctrine of the Gospel" and means the preaching of the church. In itself, however, the difference is merely formal. Furthermore, the impact of the Gospel *(evangelischer Ansatz)* provides no reason why central thoughts should not occur again and again in the thousandfold variety of preaching. *Then church doctrine is the stable element in the preaching of the church.* The only condition is that the Word of God remain the "rule and guide" for the one as well as for the other, as the confessions, in Luther's sense, demanded. At the same time this is a guarantee that church doctrine as such can claim no "faith" for itself, just as evangelical sermons do not lay claim to "faith" for themselves. On the contrary, they all "must

(Leipziger Univ.-Programm), 1912. — Heinr. Schmid, *Geschichte der synkretistischen Streitigkeiten*, 1846. — E. L. Th. Henke, *Calixt und seine Zeit*, 1853—56. — Kattenbusch, *Luthers Stellung zu den ökumenischen Symbolen*, Giessen, 1883. — Johannes Meyer, *Luther und d. Apostolikum*, 1918.

refer and point to the one and only Christ" *(auf den einigen Christum gehen und zeigen müssen)* and should, therefore, only awaken faith in Christ.

At the very outset the Augsburg Confession seems to put itself in opposition to this self-evident demand.[2] In the first article we read: "That the decree of the Nicene Synod concerning the unity of the divine essence and concerning the three Persons is true and must be believed without any doubting" *(Decretum Nicaenae Synodi de unitate essentiae divinae et de tribus personis verum et sine ulla dubitatione credendum esse).* In the first place, the words "must be believed" *(credendum esse)* give one pause. Here a law of faith *(Glaubensgesetz)* seems to be proclaimed. A contradiction in itself! How can one still speak of "believing gladly" *(libenter credere)* – as Luther had done (WA 18, 714, 9; Enders 3, 312, 26) – in connection with a compulsion to believe *(Glaubenszwang)*? But, much worse than this, here the decree of a synod is designated as something to be believed. Here the ship of the Reformation, which has just recently departed from land, seems to be sailing back into the harbor of the medieval church, which produced laws of faith and demanded obedience to them. Faith itself, the most precious treasure, seems to be betrayed!

One must say that here of all places it was a mistake to combine the concept of the "decree" *(decretum)* with the "must be believed" *(credendum)* in the Latin text.[3] How dangerous this mistake could become is to be seen in the fact that by using the concepts "norm of faith" *(norma fidei),* "agreeing with the Roman Church" *(concordare cum romana ecclesia),* "defining" *(definire),* etc., the papal confutation tried to interpret the appeal to the Nicene Creed entirely in accordance with its own meaning. But this is actually an isolated mistake on the part of the Augsburg Confession. For when it causes one to prick up one's ears, one notes that the upholding and the carrying-through of the impact of the Gospel *(evangelischer Ansatz),* to which it is in opposition, is one of the main concerns of the Augsburg Confession. How could it have

[2] With regard to what follows cf. my lecture in Copenhagen, *Glaube und Bekenntnis der Kirche im Lichte von Marburg und Augsburg, Denkschrift üb. d. Lutherischen Weltkonvent zu Kopenhagen,* 1929, pp. 41 ff.

[3] The German text contains nothing corresponding to this, not even the word "faith" at this place. On the other hand, in Hier. Baumgartner's translation into German of the oldest draft of the Augsburg Confession — the draft that is not retained in the Latin original (end of May 1530) — it is stated: ". . . to keep and to believe . . . the decision of the Council of Nicaea." The text in Kolde, *Die älteste Redaktion der Augsb. Konfession,* 1906, p. 11. — It has been pointed out that the *Schwabach Articles* have a Scriptural proof, but that the *Marburg Articles* already have a reference to the Nicene Creed.

been otherwise after the false conception of faith had been so emphatically assailed in the *Counsel of Ansbach* and every halfway instructed layman was able, by using this very criterion, to distinguish between what was evangelical and what was Roman? The second article of the Augsburg Confession begins with a fundamental element of the impact of the Gospel *(evangelischer Ansatz)*, and up to the end this impact of the Gospel is never again lost sight of. It has been pointed out that the rest of the confessions up to the Formula of Concord established the essential elements of Luther's doctrine of justification. All their articles on penitence, on faith and good works – but also on free will, on original sin, on monastic vows, on the saints, and on the Mass – serve, in the final analysis, to safeguard the purity of evangelical faith. Thus it holds true of the Augsburg Confession as well as of the later confessions that here the general theme of evangelical preaching was stabilized in theological discussion and formulation.

This is also the firm position on the basis of which the Roman Church is criticized. This is a matter of the greatest importance for the self-assessment of the new church formations that came into being with the confessions. It is not the founding of a new church that is striven for; neither is it – at least not primarily – a substitution of the previous church ideal for one that is new. It is the reformation of the Catholic Church, of which the confessors themselves profess that they are members within the limits demanded by the impact of the Gospel *(evangelischer Ansatz)* and guided by the principles of this point of departure. To be sure, the intentional limiting of the demand for reform to the specifically evangelical concern is now underscored by the frequently emphasized tendency, especially of the Augsburg Confession, to point out the relationship of the evangelical church to the ancient church even in the domain of dogmatics. At the very beginning the emphasis on the common doctrine of the Trinity serves this purpose. Here God is spoken of in words that do not differ at all from the dogma of the ancient church. The same thing is true of the third article (on the Son of God). Consequently, both articles were accepted by the papal confutation, which also let the fifth article stand with reservations, in connection with which it emphasized that here the activity of the Holy Spirit is discussed. In the Apology, Melanchthon emphasized once more the agreement that was established here. Furthermore, in the Smalcald Articles, Luther placed the "high articles on the divine majesty" *(die hohen Artikel der göttlichen Majestät)* ahead of all the rest as beyond controversy and dispute.

At this point there crops up in early Lutheranism an element that does not show its relationship to the impact of the Gospel *(evangelischer Ansatz)* without further ado, yes, an element that can seem to be a break with it. Everything else in the Augsburg Confession is "doctrine of faith" *(Glaubenslehre)*, is referred in the strict sense to the faith which "God wants to regard and account as righteousness before Himself" *(Gott will für Gerechtigkeit für ihm halten und zurechnen)*. Even the sacraments achieve their purpose in faith (Art. 13). Only the article on the second coming of Christ is an exception. It, too, speaks of transcendental things, the relationship of which to justifying faith is lacking at first. The decisive difference between both lines of thought consists in this, that the one has its organizing principle in the subjective function of faith, the other, however, embraces a sphere of transhuman relationships the organizing principle of which, if it exists at all, must not be transcendental in nature, like faith, but transcendent.

But Luther's Smalcald Articles immediately give a positive reference to the relationship that exists in spite of this. Here Luther begins the second chief part with a series of Scripture statements which "pertain to the office and the work of Jesus Christ or to our redemption." Then he goes on: "Now since this must be believed and otherwise cannot be grasped with any work, law, or merit, it is clear and certain that only such a faith justifies us" (Rom. 3:28). Here again we are confronted at once and with all clarity by the faith with which the evangelical doctrine of justification deals. It is true that faith is a subjective function. But nothing subjective could engender or even characterize it. It lives only because of the forgiveness of sins or — what amounts to the same thing — because of the righteousness of Christ. Again, however, this is not something of which man takes possession; it is identical with Christ Himself, His birth, life, suffering, and resurrection. When the Gospel, that is, information concerning Christ, is designated again and again as a promise, the "offering" *(offerre)* and the "promising" *(promittere)* are not something that is then added to the historical information. No, this information itself is the Gospel. The historical indicative becomes a promise by being announced to me. When it turns to me, I hear the "for me" which makes of the "historical faith" *(fides historica)* a "saving faith" *(fides salvifica)*.

Accordingly, one could conceive of a "confession" which speaks in the historical indicative exclusively, like the Second Article of the Apostles' Creed, let us say, where it makes no difference if the introductory formula reads "I believe that" or "The church teaches that" or "I confess that." For he who actually speaks, confesses, and teaches about Christ as is done there has faith and is justified, even if he does not use the expressions "faith" and "justification" at all.

That is the way Luther viewed the Apostles' Creed. Using medieval German, he calls it *Der Glaube,* not because it offers an analysis of the concept or the function of faith but because to man "it shows God and His mercy, revealed and offered in Christ" (WA 7, 204, 27), because it expresses the one thing by which faith in the evangelical sense can be characterized: its basis and content. Viewed in this way, it is neither a supplement to nor in competition with Holy Scripture. Furthermore, it does not present a development of the teaching of Scripture; "but, just as a bee gathers honey from many beautiful and happy little flowers, so this creed is gathered from the books of the dear prophets and apostles, that is, from all Holy Writ; it is a fine and brief summary for children and simple Christians" (WA 41, 275, 30). It is superior to the rest of the creeds because it "expresses the articles of faith in a very fine manner, briefly and correctly" *(kurtz und richtig die Artickel des glaubens gar fein fasset)* (WA 50, 262, 17). The so-called Athanasian Creed, to which Luther refers in the first part of the Smalcald Articles, is for him "a protective creed for the first creed" *(ein schutz Symbolen des ersten Symboli).* It emphasizes one particular article more extensively because of the Arians, namely, that Jesus Christ is God's only Son and our Lord. In Him we believe with the same faith with which we believe in the Father." Furthermore, Luther puts the so-called Ambrosian Hymn of Praise on the same plane with these two creeds; it has the advantage of "not only confessing the true faith but also of praising and thanking God" (263, 10). Luther's Catechisms prove that he succeeded in establishing in detail the relationship of the "objective" content of the old creeds, at least of the Apostles' Creed, to justifying faith. When in the Large Catechism he defines the difference between the first chief part and the second by stating that the former teaches "that we can do what, according to the Ten Commandments, we should do" *(das wir dasselbige thuen können, so wir lauts der zehen gepot thuen sollen)* (WA 30 I, 182, 22) or "that the Ten Commandments teach what we should do," but that "faith" teaches "what God does for us and gives us" (192, 18) – it becomes clear that the "must be believed" *(credendum)* in the first article of the Augsburg Confession can be understood evangelically in only one way. A *law* of faith is out of the question. Then faith, too, would belong in the framework of the first chief part. In reality "faith" always means a deed and a gift of God. Accordingly, what is obligatory in the concept "must be believed" *(credendum)* can always be understood to refer only to the compelling power which the content of faith *(Glaubensinhalt)* exerts on the believer.

Therefore the emergence of a dogmatic Christology in the confessions — an emergence which at first can strike evangelical faith as strange — is by no means inconsistent with the primary task of dogma — to define the stable element in preaching — since preaching must carry out the Gospel's aforementioned "offering" *(offerre)* and "promising" *(promittere)*. The "offering" *(offerre)* takes place in the most elementary manner through preaching about Christ Himself, about His Person and His work. On the other hand, preaching about *faith* in Christ — as it was stabilized in the doctrine of justification — is the second step and has become necessary only because the inner relationship between the "objective" content of the evangelical announcement and faith was contested by the opposition or declared to be insufficient for justification. For that which groups itself around the thought of justification in the confessions does not have as its purpose the addition of several new articles of faith to the theme of Christ *(Christusthema)* contained in the Gospel and in dogma. On the contrary, it must prove the sufficiency of this theme. Therefore the Augsburg Confession — for example, in its article on monastic vows — says that the monastic doctrine that satisfaction for sin is merited by piety militates against the glory of Christ (XXVII, 38). And in all other confessions there are related references to the fact that everything that is stated about faith and justification is said to the glory of Christ. If the glory of Christ had never been called in question, the matter could actually have ended with the confession of the content of faith *(Glaubensinhalt)*. Luther established something similar with regard to the old confessions, the Athanasian as well as the Nicene Creed. Both are concerned with insurance against the false doctrine of the Arians, with the polemical stabilization of the knowledge that "Jesus Christ is God's only Son and our Lord" (WA 50, 262, 20; 551, 12 ff.).

Now, to be sure, the sphere of dogmatic ideas contained in the Nicene Creed, to which the Augsburg Confession refers, and in the Athanasian Creed, to which the Smalcald Articles refer, goes beyond the Apostles' Creed in more than one direction. When, in connection with the Athanasian Creed, Luther emphasizes the Christological interest, this corresponds, of course, to the elementary relationship which he establishes between the "high articles of the divine majesty" and the doctrine of justification. Nevertheless, in his explanation of the creed, he must, in conformity with its content, proceed from Christology to the doctrine of the Trinity (WA 50, 273, 22 ff.). But when Melanchthon wrote about the Nicene Creed, he started from the doctrine of the Trinity; he built Christology into the creed.[4] It is clear that by doing so he was more in conformity with the old creeds than Luther was. But then this also postulated a different point of contact. In both of his writings Melanchthon assigns first place to the doctrine of God. In doing so he refers to the First Commandment and to the necessary correspondence of the knowledge or invoking of God and revelation *(CR* 23, 210, 357). In the later editions of the *Loci* he had given a similar reason for the same point of departure. But he had referred to "faith" *(fides),* which corresponds to revelation, and had immediately called attention to the specifically reformational interest in salvation (WA 21, 255, 605). To be sure, here he understands "faith" *(fides)* to be nothing more than "knowledge" *(notitia)* and "assent" *(assensus).* Melanchthon, therefore, had the feeling that it was not possible to derive the doctrine of the Trinity contained in the old creeds from the doctrine of justification, even if this doctrine included the Gospel as a "promise" *(promissio),* that is, as an announcement concerning Christ's Person and work. Now his concept of revelation is expressed in such a way that he can also include in it the testimonies of Scripture "concerning the essence of God" *(de essentia Dei).*[5] Only in this way is the soil really prepared for an inner appropriation of the old creeds. For these know nothing about a connection with the doctrine of justification. On the contrary, the Athanasian Creed speaks of faith as if its saving power depended on the knowledge and the acknowledgment of the dogmas "concerning the essence of God" *(de essentia Dei).*

Thanks to the reformational confessions, the old creeds have found a permanent place in the dogma of the evangelical churches and, since Melanchthon, have gained and retained decisive influence. Therefore it is important to know what position was assigned to them among the norms of dogma. The Formula of Concord distinguished its authority sharply from the authority of Scripture. The latter binds one unconditionally. With regard to "the other creeds, however, and quoted writings" historical relativity is established. They are "only a testimony and an explanation of faith, how in articles concerning which there was controversy in any period Holy Scripture was understood and expounded by those who were living at that time, and doctrine contrary to it was rejected and condemned" (Intr. 8). Accordingly, here — in contrast with Scripture — a voluntary explanation of one's position with respect to

[4] *Enarratio symboli Niceni* (1550), *CR* 23, 197 ff., and *Explicatio symboli Niceni* (1557, edition of 1561), 23, 247 ff.

[5] *CR* 21, 609; cf. also *Examen Ordinandorum* 23, XXXVII f.

these creeds is necessary. "We declare that we embrace them" *(profitemur nos illa amplecti),* that is, we pledge ourselves to them (3). Melanchthon, too, used the expression "to embrace" *(amplecti)* for the old creeds (*CR* 9, 279; 23, 195). *Scripture is obeyed. The old creeds are accepted.*

This acceptance confronted reformational theology with very difficult problems pertaining to methods and materials. Provided that it found roads to the dogma of the ancient church that could be trod without harm to the impact of the Gospel *(evangelischer Ansatz)* – Luther's explanation of the Athanasian Creed is an attempt in this direction – it would be altogether out of place to see in the acceptance nothing but an encumbrance. On this assumption it was even a liberation. For it broadened the prospect of other possibilities of approach. It led into the great stream of theological thinking which, after all, did not have its beginning in Wittenberg. For its part it also kept dogma from running wild. The development of sectarianism, even that which took place in the age of the Reformation, shows that the authority of Scripture alone does not yet guard against this. By accepting the dogma of the ancient church, reformational theology, if one still disregards its material content, submitted voluntarily, so to speak, to control on the part of an unquestionably classical period of thinking in the matter of dogma. That period should not be regarded as formal authority. This was sharply expressed in the struggle against the Roman principle of tradition. No, the fundamental thought in connection with this was the fact that those dogmas wanted to be an acceptance of a revelation identical with the reformational doctrine of justification. By taking this acceptance seriously – subject to criticism in detail on the basis of the authority of Scripture – and thinking it out anew from the standpoint of reformational knowledge one subjected oneself to the high discipline of the dogmatic thought which distinguished the theology of the ancient church. Since the "embracing" *(amplecti)* actually resulted from this, Lutheranism had entered into a great partnership in knowledge with the ancient church – a partnership which, at least in this matter, confirmed the claim to genuine catholicity.

The dangers connected with the acceptance on the other side came glaringly to light in the syncretistic controversies of the seventeenth century. They consisted above all in the fact that the acceptance was not understood as an assignment presented anew to every generation on condition that the authority of Scripture be maintained but was taken into account as an accomplished fact – a fact which one can use in debate as though it were an established book of laws, as was done at that time with the accepted Roman law. For George Calixt it was not so much the central content of the old creeds and synodical decrees as their great age and their – supposed – universal acceptance that should give them their definitive authority. His criteria for the truth and the divine origin of a religion – criteria which place the main emphasis on "antiquity" *(antiquitas)* and "perpetuity" *(perpetuitas)* – were a mockery of the Reformation.[6] Here the previous argumentation was stood on its head. Johann Gerhard deduced the catholicity of the evangelicals from their catholic faith. He said that the faith which adheres to the teaching of the prophets and the apostles is catholic *(Loci* XI, 216 ff., 219, 229). With respect to the dogma of the Trinity, Hülsemann wanted to acknowledge the authority of the Nicene Creed, not because it interprets Scripture aright but only "inasmuch as it is in agreement with that dogma of the church which passes over from an interpretation of the Scriptures that was taken for granted before" *(ut consentiens cum illo Ecclesiae dogmate, quod ex praesupposita scripturarum interpretatione transit)*.[7] But Calixt wanted the old creeds to be accepted because, according to the well-known canon of Vincent, they are catholic! It was only consistent when in his irenic *Tractate on the New Art [of Nihusius] (Tractatus de arte nova [Nihusii])* he declared the whole Augsburg Confession to be superfluous and decided that in Augsburg the evangelicals should rather have confined themselves to the acceptance of the old creeds and synodical decrees up to the time of the Council of Chalcedon.[8] It really takes a goodly amount of prejudice based on church politics to cause old and new accounts of Calixt's plans for union to have nothing but contempt for this man's Saxon opponents and their undeniably blunt polemics. When Hülsemann wrote with respect to Calixt's disavowal of the Augsburg Confession that it must "indeed be deeply painful" *(ja hertzlich wehe tun)* that in this

[6] Georg Calixt, *De veritate unicae religionis Christianae, ed. Fr. Ulr. Calixt,* Helmstedt, 1658, pp. 22 ff.

[7] Joh. Hülsemann, *Manuale Augustanae confessionis,* Wittenberg, 1631, p. 25. Compare this with Luther's principle, Enders 3, 196, 46 ff.

[8] Georg Calixt, *Tractatus (Digressio) de arte nova, Frankfurt,* 1652 (reprint), p. 286: "But they could have proceeded more briefly if they had said that their confession concerning the doctrine of faith was the Apostles' Creed, the Nicene Creed, the Constantinopolitan Creed, the articles formulated at Ephesus, the Chalcedonian statement, and whatever the old universal church had professed with unanimous consent" *(Potuissent autem sese brevius expediisse, si dixissent, suam de doctrina fidei confessionem esse Symbolum Apostolicum, Nicaenum, Constantinopolitanum, Ephesinos articulos, Calchedonensem ekthesin et quidquid unanimi consensu vetus universa ecclesia professa esset).*

way "no one or few may be taught what Law or Gospel is, what penitence or faith is, or what Christ's benefactions are," he actually hit the antireformational romanticism of Calixt in the right place.[9] For in the event of an exclusive return to the old councils this essential part of reformational theology would surely be lost again.

It is true that Calixt stood up for a time-honored Lutheran principle when he argued against the founding of a new church by means of the Reformation. He took the concept "reformation" in its strict sense. For his part he also advocates the historical way of thinking characteristic of Lutheranism as a whole. Yet his plans, which were based on church politics, prevented him from being in earnest about the idea of development in the matter of the history of dogma. But it was this idea which had to be considered when the old confessions were accepted, if indeed these confessions and those of the Reformation were not to be merely tautological in character. It was precisely in connection with the syncretistic controversies that the opponents of Calixt kept a sharp lookout for everything that is not expressed in the old creeds and yet from the evangelical standpoint, is "necessary for salvation" *(heilsnotwendig)*.[10] If they appealed to the reformational confessions as authoritative – above all, to the Augsburg Confession[11] – still they did not forget that according to the testimony of the Formula of Concord the Augsburg Confession, too, wanted to be and was meant to be merely a "testimony of those living at that time" *(Zeugnis der damals Lebenden)*. Even Leonhard Hutter, who claimed that the Augsburg Confession was inspired, illustrated its distinction in rank from Holy Scripture by saying that it is "like one who merits faith and assent in the church, not because he is trustworthy of himself but insofar as he is completely in agreement with that sacred and inspired canon" *(ut qui non* αὐτόπιστος, *sed eatenus fidem et assensum in Ecclesia meretur, quatenus cum sacro illo ac* θεοπνεύστῳ *Canone per omnia concordat)*.[12] If the confession and Scripture were actually supposed to have the same author, this was inconsistent. But it shows the seriousness with which the relativity of the dogma of the church had to be maintained.

[9] Hülsemann, *Calixtinischer Gewissenswurm*, Leipzig, 1654, pp. 1451 ff.

[10] Cf. O. Ritschl, *DG des Prot.* IV, 430 ff.

[11] In a reply to the men of Leipzig the University of Helmstedt resented being referred to the Formula of Concord, which had no legal validity in Brunswick. To the university this was almost an affront (May 30, 1649). Cf. G. Calixt's *Briefwechsel*, ed. by E. L. Th. Henke, 1833, p. 189.

[12] L. Hutter, *Aug. Conf. Analysis methodica*, Wittenberg, 1602, p. 43. Concerning the Holy Spirit as the author of the confession see p. 6.

17. The Doctrine of God [1]

According to Luther, all "natural knowledge of God" comes to an end before the "hidden God" *(Deus absconditus)*. Melanchthon thought he could give it a friendlier assignment. The dogmaticians of the seventeenth century followed him in this. The upshot was the Enlightenment. This difference seems to refer only to the assumptions of the knowledge of God, not to its content. But in accordance with the impact of the Gospel *(evangelischer Ansatz)*, all knowledge of God depends on revelation. Consequently, it is possible only in faith. But according to everything that has been said about revelation, the knowledge of God resulting from faith must take a different course from that which results from rational meditation. "Faith is the creator of a divine quality," says Luther, "not in the Person but in us. Apart from faith God loses His justice, glory, power, etc., and there is no majesty or divine quality where there is no faith." *(Fides est creatrix divinitatis, non in persona sed in nobis. Extra fidem amittit deus suam iustitiam, gloriam, opes, etc., et nihil majestatis, divinitatis, ubi non fides.)* (WA 40 I, 360, 5.) This really says everything. What at first seems to be a monstrous power – the power to be the creator of a divine quality in us – Luther may ascribe to faith without being misunderstood, because to him faith itself is nothing vis-à-vis God. After all, it lives only because God invokes it and calls it into being. God is in us only in such a way that we hear His call. According to Luther, knowledge of God is possible only in this reciprocal relation, this dialog between the God who calls and the faith which hears. The explanation Luther gives of the Apostles' Creed in his Large Catechism can be summarized in these words: "This is my God" (WA 30 I, 183, 24); "that Jesus Christ is my Lord" (186, 11); "I believe that the Holy Spirit makes me holy as His name is holy" (188, 21). For him every confession, every dogma, takes on the character of a personal answer to God's revelation. He extols the so-called Ambrosian Hymn of Praise, which he counts among the "three creeds or confessions of the faith of Christ," because it teaches "not only to confess the true faith but also to praise and thank God in this faith" (WA 50, 263, 10). And

[1] In addition to the presentations of Luther's theology mentioned previously cf. E. Hirsch, *Luthers Gottesanschuung*, 1918. — Friedr. Wilh. Schmidt, *Der Gottesgedanke in Luthers Römervorlesung, ThStKr*, 1920—21, pp. 117 ff. — G. Aulén, *Das christl. Gottesbild in Vergangenheit und Gegenwart*, 1930, pp. 158 ff. — T. Bohlin, *Gudstro och Kristustro hos Luther*, 1927. — Carl Stange, *Der christl. Gottesglaube im Sinne d. Reformation, Studien z. Theologie Luthers* I, pp. 235 ff. — Concerning Luther's reticence over against the expressions "Trinity" and "Person" cf. R. Seeberg, *DG* IV, pp. 184 ff. It is not possible to give further particulars about this in the following paragraphs. — Ph. Bachmann, *Luthers Kl. Katechismus als Aufgabe f. d. Gegenwart*, 1929, p. 49.

he counts the Apostles' Creed among the "prayers" a Christian should say (WA 38, 373 ff.).

Luther's whole theology appears as the answer of a man with whom God Himself has spoken. To him the fact that God is a Person is no problem and cannot be a problem, because his faith has a personal relationship to God. Therefore everything to be said about God is said with reference to the responsibility which this relationship demands. It is true that Luther must speak about God's wrath with reference to his own evangelical relationship to God and as one who is under the earnestness of the divine Law. But to him, who is a believer, who owes his knowledge of God to the righteousness of God that has been given as a gift, the consequences of this wrath appear as "alien works" *(opera aliena)* of God. This is the sharpest expression for his refusal to balance in a speculative way the wrath of God against the mercy of God. In connection with Christ's work it has been established that he does not think of denying the terrible reality of God's wrath. For he describes Christ's suffering itself as an "alien work of God" *(opus alienum Dei)* (WA 1, 112, 39; *Lectures on Hebrews* 130, 10 ff.); he says of it that the Gospel has to perform an "alien work" *(opus alienum)* when it reveals the sins of sinners (113, 16), that by condemning the righteousness of the Law Christ Himself performs an "alien work" *(opus alienum)* (WA 25, 190, 17). How would all this appear to him as the consequence of something that is unreal? But faith knows, of course, that the Son has appeased the wrath of the Father and therefore that God, by imputing the righteousness of the Son, lets His mercy be victorious over His wrath. This is the case over against the believer. Therefore faith views "doing good and saving" *(benefacere et servare)* (WA 25, 190, 2) as the "proper office of God" *(officium proprium Dei)*. For this reason it seems to faith as if God were angry when "death, hell, and sin reproach the conscience" *(todt, hell und sund das gewissen strafft)* (WA 6, 208, 35). In His attitude toward the believer God seems to be angry (WA 43, 203, 7). When God threatens death while wrestling with Jacob or while dealing with Abraham, this is only "play" *(ludus)* (WA 14, 298, 22!; WA 44, 97, 1). Yes, because God, by means of the revelation in Christ, lets one look into His heart, Luther can say that the "alien work" *(opus alienum)* goes "against His nature" *(contra naturam suam)* (WA 42, 356, 23). For it goes against His "nature" exactly as sin, which compels Him to wrath, does, "because," as he adds, "thus the wickedness of men compels" *(cogente ita malicia hominum)*.

Nowhere is what appears to be the completely anthropomorphic character of Luther's conception of God as evident as it is here. But this character has not only been taken from the usage of the Bible; it is also the only possible way to do justice to the fact that faith is addressed by a divine "You" *(Du)*. Every attempt to construct God's "essence" *(Wesen)* hypothetically from His "attributes" *(Eigenschaften)* must run aground on the diastasis of wrath and mercy. Since a chronological detaching of the one by means of the other is unthinkable, the potentiality of both in God would have to be accepted. For Luther, of course, the efficaciousness of mercy is actually bound to the historical work of redemption. But, in the first place, this points back to an eternal decree which already presupposes the reality of God's love. In the second place, however, the efficaciousness of mercy has become a reality in what resulted from His wrath on the cross of Christ – an event which likewise has eternal significance. Therefore the only superordinate characteristic applicable to God's wrath as well as to His mercy is His freedom, which is the general theme of the treatise titled *On the Bondage of the Will (De servo arbitrio)*. To be sure, this is a definitive expression of the fact that God is a Person. But it is merely formal; and, strictly speaking, it designates only the border of the knowledge of God. It leads necessarily to the thought of predestination, and any desire to go to the bottom of this is equivalent to a battle against God (WA 18, 690, 26).

At the same time, however, there is an essential difference between the knowledge of God with respect to His wrath and the knowledge of God with respect to His mercy. For the wrath of God a human cause is discernible. God is angry "because the wickedness of men compels Him" *(cogente malicia hominum)* to be. The potentiality of wrath in God Himself is indiscernible in any case. We know only the effects of His wrath. The mercy of God, on the other hand, has no human cause whatever. It can have its cause only in God's "nature." For this reason it is His "proper work" *(opus proprium)*. It is revealed in Christ and only in Christ, and in Him it has its effect. Here, therefore, the knowledge of God has its real footing (WA 36, 331, 4 ff.). "He who denies Christ denies God" *(Qui negat Christum, negat Deum)*, says Luther as early as the time of his *Lessons on the Psalter (Dictata super psalterium)* (WA 3, 99, 25). For he who denies Christ denies the God with whom alone faith is concerned (WA 18, 685, 12).

It is true that when the transcendental I receives pardon, it has faith. But faith knows that God's verdict means the empirical I – with the concrete fullness of what the empirical I contains. It means man in his relationship to God. No less, however, in his relationship to his human and cosmic environment. On account of sin all these relationships are in the shadow of death. But what is said about Christ causes them to step into the brightly gleaming light of the teleology of divine grace. Therefore Luther cannot eliminate faith's experience of salvation when he speaks of God in relation to man's environment or to the cosmos in general. His doctrine of God's effective work in man is emphasized in a distinctively soteriological manner. From the standpoint of predestinarian thinking the goal of this work is determined by the destruction or the salvation of men. It is altogether from the standpoint of faith that God performs His works in the service of love for His creatures. Of course, Christ's work gives us the certainty of divine love (WA 20, 402, 31 ff.). But it is not restricted to this; it also determines all the externals of our life. "If you look at God even physically, there are sheer flames and fire of love in God" *(Si inspicis deum etiam leiplich, sind eytel flammen und feur charitatis in deo)* (WA 36, 426, 4). All God's works in nature are a "blessing" *(Segnen)*, for the purpose of making men happy, as Luther sets forth with wonderful vividness in his Dessau sermon on Psalm 65 (WA 37, 425; esp. 446 ff.). And just as for faith in Christ in particular everything depends on the "for you," so in connection with the knowledge of God in general the "great emphasis" *(magna emphasis)* is on the "your" of the First Commandment.[2] Therefore "to know God aright is to know that with Him there is sheer goodness and grace" (WA 18, 520, 27). Then to believe means nothing short of "expecting and looking for sheer goodness from Him" *(eitel guts zu yhm versehen und von yhm gewarten)*, in which Luther here (in the Large Catechism) includes the sum total of external conditions. The creatures are "merely the hand, the channels, and the means by which God gives everything" *(nur die hand, rohre und mittel, dadurch Gott alles gibt)* (WA 30 I, 136, 8).[3]

To be sure, Luther knows that "reason" *(Vernunft)*, too, must trace everything that is good back to God. But he knows that reason lacks two things. In the first place, trust in God's good will. It permits misfortune to divert it from this trust.[4] In the second place, reason is not capable of "properly ascribing or attributing divinity to the only One

2 WA 16, 432, 7: "The chief emphasis is on the word 'your.' With this emphasis He addresses the individual, as if He wanted only you, as if there were no one else on earth, in order that a man may reflect [on this] as if God were speaking with him alone." *(In "tuus" maxima emphasis, qua alloquitur singularem, quasi te velit in singulari, quasi alius non sit in terra, ut homo cogitet, quasi secum loquatur solo.)*

3 Further particulars in *God and the World* and in what follows.

4 WA 19, 206, 14: "In the first place, it [reason] believes that God can do this and knows how to do it, to help and to give. But that He desires or is willing to do this for it too — this it cannot believe. Therefore it does not remain firm in its opinion. For it believes and knows that God has the power; but it is in doubt about the desire, because it feels the opposite when there is adversity."

to whom it is due" *(die gotheyt recht aus teylen noch recht zu eygen, dem sie alleyne geburt).* It plays "blindman's buff with God" *(der blinden kue mit Gott);* when it reaches for Him, it always misses. It touches "the devil every time, or its own notion, which the devil rules" *(allewege den teuffel odder yhr eygen dunckel, den der teuffel regirt).* It knows, of course, that there is a God. But "what or who God is . . . the Holy Spirit alone teaches" *(was odder wer Gott ist . . . leret alleine der heylige geyst)* (WA 16, 206 f.). There is also a revelation of God in nature, in the creation and preservation of the world. But in themselves man's relationships do not let God be known as the One He is. It is not until the Divine Spirit has done His work that the connection between revelation and faith is established here. This work assures you, the human being, that the Creator and Preserver of the world is *your* Creator and Preserver, that He is your Father. "But this is much more comforting: that my God, my Lord, is a Father, from whose name the whole Godhead springs and bursts forth; that He must give in abundance everything I pray for in His name. Here there is sheer help and grace; He wants to place me above everything that is temporal and eternal. . . . But reason can never look at it in this way, and nobody can feel it in his heart unless the Holy Spirit Himself brings it about." (WA 17 I, 430, 26; 38 ff.)

Wherever – for the purpose of defining Luther's doctrine of God – one begins in this way, one invariably runs into Luther's faith in God as it is directed toward the salvation of the I. Without the "for you" there is no faith. As a result, there is no right knowledge either, no matter whether one thinks of God's power or His omnipresence, His righteousness or His love. All this is a confirmation of that bold statement: "Faith is the creator of a divine quality in us" *(Fides est creatrix divinitatis in nobis).* This means, in the first place, that God Himself must prove His existence to man by revelation if He wants to be known. In the second place, He must bear witness that there is no other knowledge of God than that which is personal. This knowledge is personal both because here the believer must always give consideration to his own person and because here one is always face to face with God as a personal "You" *(Du).* Luther is merely using another expression for this personal character of the knowledge of God that springs from faith when he distinguishes it from the knowledge of God that springs from reason by stating that the latter has its doubts about God's will (WA 19, 206, 14 ff.). For the call of God which faith hears is, of course, the desire His love has to bring about the salvation of man. In itself the fact that God has this desire does not say any more than is contained in what is stated about His absolute freedom. But the statement about His freedom can hurl one into all the abysses of the idea of predestination. God's freedom is the content of faith *(Glaubensinhalt)* only inasmuch as, in a specific sense, it is "bound by no law" *(exlex):* as Lord of the "kingdom of grace" *(regnum gratiae)* He is not bound to the "kingdom of the Law" *(regnum legis)* (WA 44, 704, 5 ff.). At the same time, however, this freedom is the obligation He assumed vis-à-vis faith by means of His deeds: "In Himself God is pure love, and this is seen in His works" *(Deus an yhm selber est mera charitas et hoc videtur in suis operibus)* (WA 36, 428, 3). This is the personality of God in its ultimate depth: the union of freedom and the obligation of the will—a union in His love.

These were the principles that guided Luther when he accepted the doctrine of the Trinity as taught by the early church. "On the outside the works of the Trinity are undivided" *(Opera trinitatis ad extra sunt indivisa)* (WA 54, 57, 35, and frequently). Luther traced this statement back to St. Augustine. What it says was self-evident to him. Over against His creatures God is absolutely One (WA 37, 291, 7). Luther is equally certain of the revelation of three Persons.[5] Here the personality *(Personalität)* is assured above all by the name "Father"; that of the Son, by the historical Person of Christ (cf. *The Doctrine of the Two Natures*); that of the Spirit, by the fact that He "speaks" to me and performs in me God's personal work of sanctification through the forgiveness of sins (WA 54, 41, 5; WA 38, 374, 35). It is true that whenever Luther speaks of the doctrine of the Trinity as such, he puts the strongest emphasis on the "oneness" *(Einheit)* of God; but he does not let this tone down the "threeness" *(Dreiheit)* to a mere Trinity of revelation *(zu einer blossen Offenbarungstrinität)*. On the contrary, he adopts the doctrine of im-

[5] Above all, in the expositions of the Apostles' Creed. For these and later for Luther's doctrine of the Trinity the following presentations, which go into greater detail, should receive special consideration: *A Brief Form of the Ten Commandments,* 1520, WA 7, 204 ff.; *A Simple Way to Pray, Written for a Good Friend,* 1535, WA 38, 358 ff.; the Smalcald house sermon on the articles of the Creed, 1537, WA 45, 11 ff.; the sermon for Trinity Sunday in the same year, WA 45, 89 ff.; *The Three Creeds or Confessions of Christian Faith,* 1538, WA 50, 262 ff.; *Concerning the Last Words of David,* 1543, WA 54, 28 ff.; and the Catechisms. For Luther's view concerning the development of the Trinitarian dogma also *On the Councils and the Churches,* 1539, WA 50, 509 ff. — About the writing *Concerning the Last Words of David* Gregorius Joestel wrote from Wittenberg: "As long as the world has stood, no book has been written that extolled the article of the Trinity more than this one does." WA 54, 21. — In addition, cf. the *Disp. de divin. et humanit. Christi* of Feb. 28, 1540; Drews, *Disp.*, pp. 585 ff., as well as all the disputations of 1541—45. EA *var. arg.* 4, 458 ff.

manent relationships.[6] It is true that he makes no attempt to penetrate it on the basis of the understanding he has because of faith *(Glaubensverständnis)*. The connecting link is the concept of substance *(Wesen)*; the traditional "works on the inside" *(opera ad intra)* constitute the immanently distinguishing factor. Of course, Luther adduces ample proof from Scripture, even from the Old Testament; and he makes use of the old analogies from nature and psychology, particularly those of Saint Augustine. In general, however, the doctrine of the Trinity came to a standstill in his theology like an erratic boulder. But one cannot say that he was unaware of its significance prior to the emergence of opposition on the part of fanaticism *(Schwärmertum)* with its unitarian tendencies. As early as 1520 he calls this doctrine the "highest article in faith – the article on which all the others depend" *(höchst artickell ym glauben darynnen die andern alle hangen)* (WA 7, 214, 27). When later, on the other hand, he says in his explanation of the Trinitarian creeds of the "main article, the one concerning Jesus Christ" *(heubtartickel von Jhesu Christo)* that "all the others attach themselves to it and firmly support it" *(dem fallen alle artickel zu und stehen jm fest bey)* (WA 50, 266, 37), one can sooner conclude from this that he recognized more and more the Christological approach to the doctrine of the Trinity as the only one that was compatible with his theology.

Subsequently Melanchthon provided the systematic program. In the Augsburg Confession the article "On God" was put ahead of all the other articles. It retained this position throughout early Lutheran dogmatics – if one leaves out of account the prolegomena, which, to be sure, were gradually inflated to an enormous degree.[7] Nor did the analytical method bring about a change. Perhaps a reason for this is to be sought in the fact that since Melanchthon's *Loci* of 1535 the natural knowledge of God was treated in connection with the doctrine of God in general, as well as in the fact that here every reader could find a door, so to speak, leading to the inner mysteries of Christian doctrine. But the entire doctrine of the Trinity is also treated in this article. As a result, early dogmatics likewise succeeded only to a slight extent in actually fructifying the new outlooks presented by the impact of the Gospel *(evangelischer Ansatz)* for the doctrine of the Trinity as well as for the general doctrine of God, which preceded what was taught about the Trinity. Melanchthon himself was the only one to make an exception. In the

[6] Cf. the argument, WA 45, 91, 5 ff.

[7] Of course, it is completely missing in the *Loci Theologici* of Urban Rhegius as edited in 1545 by Johann Freder. In the main this book observes the procedure of Melanchthon's first *Loci*.

final edition of the *Loci* he finds in the doctrine of the Trinity a place for Christology in its entirety. His closest pupils followed him in this. Here at least a focal point of the doctrine of the Trinity had been found – a focal point which could have provided a sure foundation for the entire conception of God. But this possibility did not materialize either; for the arrangement still kept Christology separated from the real doctrine of salvation, which would have had to be its starting point if the impact of the Gospel *(evangelischer Ansatz)* was to come into its own at all.

Apart from subtler turns of expression, like the sharply individualizing way in which Melanchthon worded the Trinitarian concept of Person,[8] the doctrine of the Trinity as taught by the early church was reproduced to a greater extent at first than it was really thought through anew. Melanchthon himself made cautious attempts to understand it in a speculative manner, in accordance with Augustinian and medieval patterns. While thinking about Himself – so he argued in the *Loci* of 1535 – the Father begets a thought which becomes His image, and into this image he pours His essence *(Wesen)*. This is the "Word." With respect to the Spirit, of course, Melanchthon merely adds that He is an impulse or a driving, moving, and life-giving force (21, 258). In the final edition of the *Loci* this is explained by saying that just as the Son was begotten by means of the Father's thinking, so the Holy Spirit proceeds from the will of the Father and the Son; for to impel and to love are matters of the will (21, 616). And in the *Explanation of the Nicene Creed* the Spirit is designated as "substantial love and coeternal joy between the Father and the Son, of the same essence as the Father and the Son" *(substantialis amor et laetitia coaeterna inter Patrem et Filium, homoousios Patri et Filio)*. It is the purpose of the revelation of the Spirit, he wrote, to call forth in believers emotions identical with Him: love and peace that rests in God (23, 360). In the gradually stronger emphasis placed on love one could see progress toward the explanation of the intra-Trinitarian relationship, even in the sense of a stronger adjustment to the belief in God *(Gottesglauben)* as understood by the Reformation. In this sense the Lutheran theologians of the nineteenth century again resorted to Richard of St. Victor's attempt to deduce the immanent necessity of the three Persons in God from the general concept of love.[9] His manner of deduction asserted itself even in the smaller

[8] *CR* 21, 1076, in connection with 21, 614.

[9] E. Sartorius, *Die Lehre von der heiligen Liebe*, 4th ed., 1861, Part One. — L. Fr. Schöberlein, *Die Grundlehren des Heils, entwickelt aus dem Prinzip der Liebe*, 1848, and *Geheimnisse des Glaubens*, 1872. — With reference to Melanchthon also Kahnis, *Luth. Dogmatik*, 2d ed., 1874, I, 401. Concerning Richard of St. Victor: R. Seeberg, *DG* III, 2d and 3d ed., p. 372.

school of Melanchthon.[10] But the later dogmaticians of the seventeenth century would have nothing to do with it.[11] They were suspicious of the philosophical backgrounds, and here they were strengthened by the very fact that Melanchthon had put the Platonic definition of God as the "eternal mind" *(mens aeterna)* ahead of everything else.

Yet one surely should not interpret the reticence of the early dogmaticians over against a speculative development of the doctrine of the Trinity as mere incompetence. Early Lutheranism as a whole regarded this doctrine not only as an inheritance which one dared not leave to others to preserve. No, this teaching was recognized as the expression of a truth which the reformational approach *(der reformatorische Ansatz)* itself did not let them evade. In its final article the Formula of Concord inveighed sharply against the Unitarianism which cropped up anew in the century of the Reformation or was revived (*Epit.* XII, 29; *SD* XII, 37). In the defensive action which all the churches of that time took against the anti-Trinitarian theology of the Socinians, the Lutheran dogmaticians stood in the very front rank. Wherever they scented approaches to this theology in Calvinism, they attacked. Rome's insinuations that neither they nor the Lutheran confessions took the doctrine of the Trinity seriously but had accepted it merely for reasons of prestige were indignantly rejected.[12] The reason for their certainty in this matter was by no means their formal agreement with the old creeds; it was their conviction that they were standing on unimpeachably Biblical ground.[13] They devoted an enormous amount of work to the Scriptural proof of the Trinity. *And this is the contribution which early Lutheranism actually made to a real appropriation of the doctrine of the Trinity in the Western World.* At that time this was undertaken largely with insufficient exegetical resources. Nevertheless, the dogmaticians stated the basic question correctly in the evangelical sense. It was not a question of formal differences in rank between church doctrine and Scripture

[10] E. g., Nic. Selnecker, *Examen ordin.*, 2d ed., 1593, p. 179.

[11] E. g., Quenstedt, *Theol. did.-pol.* I, 389.

[12] Against what the Socinians had to say in opposition: Joh. Gerhard, *Loci* III, 322 ff. — Fr. Balduin, *Sol. Refutatio Catechismi Ariani, qui Rackoviae, etc.*, 1620, pp. 49 ff. — Against the supposed or actual weakening: Äg. Hunnius, *Calvinus, Judaizans,* Wittenberg, 1593. — Against the insinuations on the part of Rome: L. Hutter, *Aug. Conf. . . . Analysis methodica,* Wittenberg, 1602, pp. 51 ff. — Joh. Hülsemann, *Manuale Aug. Conf.*, Wittenberg, 1631, pp. 1 ff.

[13] Cf. especially Abr. Calov, *Exegema Aug. Confessionis,* Wittenberg, 1665. — Sebastian Schmidt, *Collegium biblicum prius, in quo Dicta Veteris Testamenti . . . , Argentor,* 1676. *L. III, de s. Trinitate.* Cf. also Schmidt's *Exercitationes theologicae de Deo et eius attributis item de Theologia naturali cum clave Jobaea, Guelpherbyti* (Lüneburg), 1690.

doctrine; it was a question of what gave rise to the doctrine of the Trinity. The struggle for Scriptural proof caused them to realize that it was not the historical heresies which gave rise to this doctrine, as Luther still believed, but the economy of divine revelation itself. If they did not know how to make more of it dogmatically, the reason is to be found, in the first place — as stated — in the arrangement of their dogmatics, which began with the doctrine of the Trinity instead of letting this doctrine arise in and with the doctrine of salvation, but, in the second place, in the doctrinaire abridgment of the concept of revelation.

Nevertheless, they were by no means entirely without the feeling for the right approach *(Ansatz)*. Balthasar Mentzer makes this statement after speaking highly of the large number of doctrinal testimonies to be found in the Bible for the "threeness" *(Dreiheit)* of the Persons: "It is clear above all that the Son was made flesh, which cannot be said about the Father and the Holy Spirit" *(Imprimis illustre est illud, quod filius factus est caro, quod de Patre et Spiritu sancto dici non potest)*.[14] Here one is farthest away from Melanchthon's speculative attempts at giving proof. The fact that God is personally revealed in Christ compels one to recognize the divine Son side by side with the Father. And — in addition to citing the doctrinal testimonies of Scripture as well as Luther's thought that the Spirit performs God's personal work of sanctification in us — Melanchthon had already given evidence of the personality *(Personalität)* of the Spirit by pointing out that through Him the Father and the Son "unite the church with Themselves in the friendliest embrace" *(dulcissimo complexu sibi copulant Ecclesiam)* (23, 235 f.); that the church of God "will always remain, and will remain there where the Word of the Gospel is heard, and that the Holy Spirit does His work in conjunction with that Word" *(semper mansuram et ibi mansuram esse, ubi sonat vox Evangelii et cum ea voce efficacem esse Spiritum sanctum)* (21, 632). Or, as Hunnius expressed it, that He "is present in the whole church, which is scattered throughout the whole world, and governs it" *(toti Ecclesiae per universum terrarum orbem dispersae praesens adesse, eamque gubernare)* — according to John 14.[15] If this is proof not only of the traditional thought of a homogeneousness *(Zusammengehörigkeit)* of the Spirit and the church but of His personality *(Personalität)* itself, one may conclude correctly that it is the immediate reality of the Word of God preached by the church, and thus the church itself, which presents

[14] B. Mentzer, *Exegesis Aug. Confessionis,* Giessen, 1615, p. 32; cf. Luther in WA 45, 91, 9.

[15] Äg. Hunnius, *Articulus de Trinitate,* Frankfurt am Main, 1592, p. 135. Cf. Melanchthon's polemics against Origen's view of the Spirit, *CR* 15, 468.

God to faith as a new Personality *(Personalität)* – a Personality distinguished from the Father and the Son.

Finally the Formula of Concord, too, had the courage to take a firm step for the purpose of bringing the doctrine of the Trinity into positive connection with the impact of the Gospel *(evangelischer Ansatz).* In its article on God's eternal providence and election it sets forth "that the entire Holy Trinity – God the Father, Son, and Holy Spirit – directs all men to Christ as to the Book of Life in which they should seek the Father's eternal election" (*SD* XI, 66). Christ Himself, it continues, proclaimed our eternal election to everlasting life (Mark 1:15; John 6, 40; 3:16). The Father wants this proclamation to be heard and accepted by all men (John 6:37). "And in order that we may come to Christ, the Holy Spirit works the true faith through the hearing of the Word" (Rom. 10:17). If one adds to this that the Formula of Concord, by strictly preserving the bounds of revelation, confines the thought of predestination to election to life, here an attempt is made both to show revelation as a unit in its central content on the basis of the impact of the Gospel *(evangelischer Ansatz)* and at the same time to arrange it with reference to the Trinity.

To be sure, all this did not yet overstep the bounds of the Trinity as it is revealed. Yet by confining itself to this, by speaking of the immanent relationships only in the formulae of the early church – not counting Melanchthon and his disciples – early Lutheranism probably pointed only to the limits set to the impact of the Gospel *(evangelischer Ansatz)* itself. This delimitation, however, reveals the very magnitude of early Lutheranism's mission in the history of dogma; and in the conscientiousness with which this delimitation was adhered to one sees loyalty to the mission. When the concept of God was neutralized in the writings of the dogmaticians of the seventeenth century – Melanchthon had already made a start in this direction – the terrifyingly great distance from Luther's knowledge of God as a living Person became evident. This delimitation lessened the distance. Melanchthon's speculative attempt is based on the Platonic concept of the "eternal mind" *(mens aeterna).* If, in accordance with this example, the later dogmaticians had been in earnest in the doctrine of the Trinity about their definitions of God as the "infinite Being" *(ens infinitum),* the "spiritual Being" *(ens spirituale),* etc., the idea of revelation maintained by the Reformation – but at the same time the impact of the Gospel *(evangelischer Ansatz)* itself – would in all probability have quickly vanished.

But the fact that early Lutheranism, in its work in the field of dogmatics, did not succumb to this danger does not become completely evident until one examines its treatment of the Christological dogma. Only on the basis of this treatment is it possible to arrive at a conclusive judgment concerning Lutheranism's belief in God *(Gottesglaube).*

18. The Doctrine of the Two Natures [1]

"Take Christ out of Scripture, [and] what more will you find in them?" *(Tolle Christum e scripturis, quid amplius in illis invenies?)* Luther asked Erasmus (WA 18, 606, 29). One could also apply these words to Luther's own writings. "Nothing but Christ is to be preached" *(Nihil nisi Christus praedicandus)* is his maxim. Preaching about Christ

[1] The quotations adduced in what is discussed under this heading refer to the following writings: M. Flacius Ill., *Refutatio vanissimi Adiaphoristarum commenti de Logo,* Jena, 1558; in German: *Verantwortung vom Logo . . . ,* 1561. — *Bekendtnis der Prediger in der Graffschaft Mansfeldt,* Eisleben, 1560 *(Mansfelder Bek.).* — J. Brenz, *De personali unione duarum naturarum in Christo,* Tübingen, 1561, and *De majestate Domini nostri Jesu Christi ad dextram Dei Patris et de vera praesentia Corporis et sanguinis eius in Coena,* Frankfurt, 1562. — *Von der Person und Menschwerdung unsers Herrn Jhesu Christi, Der waren Christlichen Kirchen Grundfest, wider die newen Marcioniten, Samosatener, Sabellianer, Arianer, Nestorianer, Eutychianer und Monotheleten Unter dem Flacianischen hauffen. Durch die Theologen zu Wittemberg . . . ,* Wittenberg, 1571 *(Grundfest).* — *Ausschreiben Decani und Doctoren, Professoren der Theologen Facultet zu Wittenberg . . . von wegen der Aufflagen und verleumbdung wider den neulicher zeit zu Wittemberg aussgegangnen Catechismum . . . ,* Wittenberg, 1571 *(Ausschreiben).* — *Christliche Fragstück Von dem unterschied der zweyen Artickel des Apostolischen Glaubens Bekenntnis, Das Christus gen Himmel auffgefaren sey und nun sitze zur Rechten Gottes des Allmechtigen Vaters. . . . Gestellet Durch die Theologen in der Universitet Wittemberg,* 1571, *Mense Augusto (Fragstück).* — *Wiederholete Christliche Gemeine Confession und Erklerung. Wie in den Sechsischen Kirchen, vermöge der heiligen Schrifft und Augsb. Confession, nach der alten Grundtfest D. Lutheri, wider die Sacramentierer gelehret wird . . . ,* Königsberg, 1572. *(Bekenntnis der Theologen in den Fürstentümern Braunschweig beiderteils, Lüneburg, Grubenhagen, Mecklenburg, in der Universität u. Kirche zu Rostock, in den Kirchen zu Lübeck, Hamburg, Hildesheim, Göttingen, Hannover, Einbeck, Hameln, Braunschweig, Goslar, Halberstadt und Königsberg i. Pr. (Bekenntnis d. Niedersachsen).* — *Kurtz Bekentnis und Artickel vom Abendmal des Leibs u. Bluts Christi, daraus klar zu sehen, was hievon in beiden Universitäten Leipzig und Wittenberg und sonst in allen Kirchen und Schulen des Churfürsten zu Sachsen bisher öffentlich geleret, gegleubt und bekant worden . . . ,* Jena, 1574 *(Bek. d. Univ. Leipz. und Wittenberg).* — *Von der Geburt und waren Menschwerdung unsers lieben Herrn J. Chr. Wider Newe Schwermerey Illyrici Und seines Manicheischen Anhanges, Die da vertheidigen Christum assumpsisse Carnem alterius specie etc. Durch M. Hier. Mencel, Der Graffschafft Mansfelt Superintendenten,* 1575. — *Articuli de Coena Dominica ministris Ecclesiarum et scholarum Marchiticarum mandato ac jussu . . . Joh. Georgii Marchitic. Brandeburgensis, Electoris etc. proponendi. . . . Ad eosdem brevis et necessaria piorum et orthodoxorum virorum responsio,* 1576 (anonymous and without mention of the place of publication; quoted from *Gegner von A. Musculus.*) — Jac. Andreä, *Predigten zu Esslingen gehalten, wider die Schwenckfeldianer,* 1576. — M. Chemnitz, *De duabus naturis in Christo, den. recogn. Lips.;* 1580 (the first edition is not available to me). — Jac. Andreä, *Von den Spaltungen, so sich zwischen den Theologen Augspurgischer Confession von A. 1548 bis auff das 1573. Jar nach und nach*

is the basis and the content of the doctrine of justification. It is the answer to our anxious questioning about God. It overcomes the fear of wrath and presents faith with forgiveness. Faith, of course, is the relationship: "Christ for me" *(Christus pro me).* Yet it is an actual relationship between me and One who is not the product of my heart. Therefore the receiving of Christ's work cannot be separated from the question about His Person. "He who wants to discuss sin and grace, Law and Gospel, Christ and man, in a manner befitting a Christian must for the most part, discuss nothing else than God and man in Christ" *(Qui de peccato et gratia, de lege et evangelio, de Christo et homine volet Christianiter disserere, oportet ferme non aliter quam de deo et homine in Christo disserere).* Thus Luther wrote against Latomus (WA 8, 126, 31). And he clung to this belief throughout his life. Rescue from God's wrath depends on this, that Christ "is a Brother, a Friend" *(sit frater, amicus)* (WA 16, 419, 12), that He is a human being like us. And it depends no less on this, that Christ "is simply God" *(sit simpliciter Deus)* (WA 18, 707, 28). With these statements Luther, as the passage just quoted shows, sees himself involved in the doctrinal disputes of the early church; he sees himself fighting in the front lines against Arians and Manichaeans, whom he names. The impact of the Gospel *(evangelischer Ansatz)* stood in a much more direct relationship to the Christology of the early church, that is, to the doctrine of the two natures in Christ, than it did to the early church's doctrine of the Trinity.

For Luther it is entirely out of the question to think that it is faith

erhaben . . . , reprinted in Tübingen, 1580. — Friedr. Petri, *Num fides possit supra coelos evolare et illic ipsam carnem Christi comprehendere,* Wittenberg, 1584. — Stephan Gerlach, *Assertio piae sanaeque doctrinae de div. majestate Christi hominis,* Tübingen, 1585. — *Acta Colloquii Montis Belligartensis, quod habitum est A. Chr. 1586 . . . Praeside Illustrissimo Principe . . . Friderico, Comite Wirttembergico et Mompelgartensi etc. inter clarissimos viros D. Jacobum Andreae, Praepositum et Cancellarium Academiae Tubingensis et D. Theodorum Bezam, Professorem et Pastorem Genevensem* . . . , Tübingen, 1587. — Aegidius Hunnius, *Bestendige Widerlegung des unwarhafftigen Berichts von dem streit des Heiligen Abendmals, in welchem etliche Calvinische Predicanten zu Embden . . . verkeret haben,* Wittenberg, 1597. — Joh. Winkelmann, *Propositiones de praecip. quibusdam Christ. religionis Capitibus. . . . Tom. III,* Marburg, 1602 (together with B. Mentzer and Joh. Scholl). — *Solida verboque Dei & Libro Concordiae Christianae congrua Decisio quatuor illorum inter aliquos Theologorum Aug. Confessionis nuperrime Controversorum capitum principaliorum. . . . Cum mandato Serenissimi . . . Princip. Johannis Georgii I., Electoris & Ducis Saxoniae* . . . , 1624, reprinted in Leipzig, 1663 *(Decisio Saxonica).* — Nic. Hunnius, *Epitome Credendorum,* 1625, reprinted in Frankfurt and Leipzig, 1702.

In addition, cf. Otto Fricke, *Die Christologie d. Joh. Brenz,* 1927. — Erich Vogelsang, *Die Anfänge d. Christologie Luthers nach d. ersten Psalmenvorlesung,* 1929. — Paul Wilh. Gennrich, *Die Christologie Luthers im Abendmahlsstreit 1524 bis 1529,* 1929. — Gottfr. Noth, *Grundlinien der Theologie des Martin Chemnitz,* 1930.

which is induced by the "cross of Christ" to *interpret* this "central point of the history of the world" as a deed of God and thus to be led to the necessity of a Christology. This contradicts not only his conception of faith, which engenders nothing but is always engendered; it also contradicts his whole conception of revelation, which took place in Christ. For him the Christological problem begins with the birth of Christ. It is in this very point that he is closest to the early church. For him as well as for the early church Christ's birth is the incarnation of God. This is implicit in the fact that he equates the "revealed God" *(Deus revelatus)* with the "incarnate God" *(Deus incarnatus)*. For him the fact – basic to his doctrine of salvation – that Christ fulfilled the Law of His own free will begins with the incarnation. This very use of His free will points to a transhuman initiative of the will that forms His Person. Here Luther is confronted by the question of pre-existence. If in this way the Pauline thought of the salutary fulfillment of the Law through Christ brought him of necessity to the Johannine doctrine of the Logos, this immediately placed him in the midst of the uncertainties of the early church. For the transhuman initiative of the Logos is the initiative of the eternal Son of God. But the will of the Son of God is the same will that induces the man Christ to fulfill the Law even in suffering and in death. For Luther, therefore, the revelation of God in Christ certainly does not mean that God dealt so and so with the man Christ, that He let Him die and be raised from the dead. No, the works of Christ are, in the strict sense, the works of God. Therefore "I must believe that He is true God, just as high, powerful, eternal, almighty as the Father" (WA 37, 41, 1 ff.). He who looks into the heart of Christ looks into the heart of God (WA 2, 140, 36). The fact that Christ was put under the Law is proof of His true humanity. But the fact that at the same time He conquered the destructive power of the Law causes Luther to conclude that "therefore He is the Son of God" *(ergo est filius Dei)* (WA 40 I, 569, 7).

This starting point of Luther's Christology is reminiscent of one aspect of Anselm's explanation: the Redeemer had to be man because mankind was obligated to render satisfaction for sin. He had to be God because only the Son of God was capable of doing this. Actually, many of the early Lutheran theologians made this consideration the basis of the doctrine of the two natures.[2] But even though the relationship of

[2] Urban Rhegius, op. cit. (see *The Doctrine of God*), 31 a: "No one but God can render satisfaction, no one but man should, etc." *(Satisfacere nemo potest nisi Deus, nemo debet nisi homo etc.)*. With these words, of course, Rhegius is attacking the mediatory activity of the saints. — In addition, Winckelmann, *Disp.* VI, theses 4 and 10.

the work of redemption to the problem of Christ's Person is entirely in conformity with Luther's way of understanding it, yet the difference between the two men is apparent at once. Anselm asks about the why of God's incarnation and finds the reason in the fact that the work was necessary. Luther asks about the sufficient reason for the validity of the work and finds it in the incarnation. Thus here, too, Luther proceeds from the impact of the Gospel *(evangelischer Ansatz).* In fact, judgment concerning the Christology of Lutheranism depends on whether and how this procedure was adhered to.

To this one must immediately add a second consideration. Early Lutheranism's contribution to the doctrine of the Trinity consisted in its struggle for Scriptural proof. The same thing is true of Christology, even though in another form and to another degree. The so-called historico-critical theology of the last generation counted Luther and – self-evidently then more than ever – later Lutheranism among the advocates of a "dogma concerning Christ" *(Christusdogma)* which, as they said, had no inner relationship to the picture of the historical Jesus as it is presented by the Synoptic Gospels. A one-sided dependence on Paul was held primarily responsible for this. This is wrong in the first place because, as is shown by quotations from Scripture adduced by Luther and the later dogmaticians, the strongest supports for the "metaphysical" character – this is the charge that is stressed above all – of the aforementioned "dogma concerning Christ" *(Christusdogma)* are to be found in the Gospel According to St. John, at the beginning of the Epistle to the Hebrews, and perhaps also in the Epistle to the Colossians. Concerning the Pauline origin of the Epistle to the Colossians, however, the advocates of that historico-critical theology were at least divided in their opinion. But it is also wrong to speak of one-sided Paulinism, because in the very doctrine which gave him a special inducement to round out his Christology, namely, in the doctrine of Holy Communion, Luther did not adduce Pauline statements about Christ but quoted the words of the "historical" Jesus. To be sure, these words are handed down by Paul; but this is no reason for denying that they are contained in the Synoptic Gospels. In addition, it will become evident that and how the historical words referring to Holy Communion – at all events, Luther held them to be historical – are connected with the innermost concerns of his whole theology. Furthermore, the statement contained in Mark 1:15 was the starting point for what he did in the year 1517. And this was not an external and isolated connection; it led to the most deeply seated contrast with the medieval church in general. Jesus, who proclaimed "repentance and Gospel," gave to Lutheranism as a whole the problem to which, to be sure, the solution was then found in the writings of Paul. And one cannot say that the confessions finally substantiated this fact. Because the problem cannot be separated from the solution, Luther was able again and again to express his opposition to the Roman Church in the formula which stated that in the Roman Church Christ was made the Lawgiver, the "angry Judge," although in reality He is something entirely different. But one need read only a few of Luther's nearly 1,200 sermons on texts from the Gospels to realize that although he let Paul sharpen his view of Christ dogmatically, he took the picture of Christ Himself from the Gospels and on the basis of this picture brought proof that Christ was something different from the "angry Judge."

But what has already been said about the disputability of the long-held conception of the Scriptural principle of Lutheranism is apparent here too. The Socinians, among others, championed this Scriptural principle; and it is well known what kind of Christology resulted. They made use of this very "Scriptural principle" when they attacked the Lutheran Christology and the Christology of the church in general.[3] In Luther, and certainly in what the authors of the Formula of Concord wrote, "Scriptural proof" applies to Christology and to faith, which here, as always, is, in the strict sense, faith in Christ, not faith in a doctrine, not even in a Scriptural doctrine concerning Christ. Even a man like Flacius, in whose writings the "Scriptural principle" as the later dogmaticians understood it has already moved forward a long distance in another respect, had to submit to reproaches for his reticence over against the doctrine of the Logos – and because he allegedly likened the Holy Spirit to "a parrot" *(einem Papagoi)*.[4] He, too, not only rejected Melanchthon's speculative approach *(Ansatz)* to a Christology; but he knew as well as Luther did that the doctrine of the Logos stands only at the border of a Christology which, in the strict sense, must be based on faith.

But this approach *(Ansatz)* points immediately to the decisive concern of Lutheran Christology: to preserve the unity of Christ's Person in all

3 Ostorodt, op. cit. (see *Justification in the Confessions*), p. 50: "From this argument [that the divine nature is derived from the expression 'Son of God'] to which the Trinitarians ordinarily attach very great importance, one can see on what basis their cause rests, namely . . . on 'chains of reasoning' *[consequentiis]* and *not on the definite Word of God.*"

4 Flacius, *Refutatio.* — Cf. the correspondence between Pastor Werner in Barby and Melanchthon, *CR* 8, 922 ff. — Flacius had attacked Melanchthon's doctrine that the Son was born through the Father's contemplation or thinking *(von der Geburt des Sons durch des Vaters anschawen oder gedencken).* Cf. *The Doctrine of God.*

circumstances.[5] In the *Schwabach Articles* it is emphatically stated that "one should not believe or teach that Jesus Christ suffered for us as a man or as mankind; but because here God and man are not two persons but one indivisible Person, one must hold and teach that God and man or the Son of God truly suffered for us" (WA 30 III, 87, 16). On one side this struck the very nerve center of the Christological problem; it struck the most sensitive spot. Today, of course, it is felt that there is primarily something else, namely, the picture of Christ as it is presented in the Gospels, which compels one to maintain emphatically the unity of the Person. In the early church the significance of this thought receded entirely. For the battle which the early church fought for the wholeness of the human nature turns against Docetism. The modern interest in the psychological unity of the historical personality is lacking. One may not take it for granted even in the writings of men like Lucian and Arius. Nor does early Lutheranism feel it in all its significance. But the fundamental change of direction which took place – the change toward control of the dogma concerning Christ *(Christusdogma)* also in the light of the picture of Christ as it is presented in the Gospels – had certainly fixed a focal point which modern Christology as a whole has never since abandoned. – But an entirely different interest in the unity of the Person becomes apparent in the pivotal statement just quoted from the *Schwabach Articles.* God and man are said to be so inseparably united in Christ that the suffering is true of the whole Person. The validity of Christ's work presupposes the personal union. According to what has been said before about the work of Christ, there can be no doubt that this knowledge is intrinsically right. Here it is not the psychological unity that is under consideration; it is the unity of God and man in the Person. The question arises to what degree one can let God participate in the work of Christ by virtue of the personal union. In special measure the *suffering* of Christ is indeed a part of this work. Did God suffer in Christ? Are we not in the midst of Patripassianism?

Of course, the acceptance of the doctrine of the Trinity had provided immunity against this danger of Modalism. The security it gives is expressed in the fact that the suffering of the *Son* of God is spoken of. But from the very connection with the doctrine of the Trinity – the connection that was accepted – it follows that the Son is essentially God; and if it was said that He actually became man in the historical Christ, the suffering of Christ was also inconceivable without the participation

[5] Luther: "These two natures in Christ should not be separated; they should be united as much as possible" *(Hae duae naturae in Christo non debent separari, sed uniri, quantum possent).* Drews, *Disp.,* p. 512.

of God. In fact, this was maintained in early Lutheranism, and in view of Christology as set forth by the opposition it is important to make this clear. It is self-evident that here Brenz did not waver for a moment, even though he, too, was unwilling to tamper with the *Chalcedonense*. It is true, he says, that in His nature God can neither suffer nor die. But because of the personal union with Christ He was present when Christ suffered and died as if He Himself were suffering and dying. And He is not affected by it in any other way.[6] Martin Chemnitz defined this more cautiously and at the same time more exactly by saying that although suffering and death happen only to the human nature of Christ, one should not let this cause one to think that the divine nature is inactive. On the contrary, by virtue of the unity of the Person the divine nature participates insofar as it *wills* the suffering of the human nature, does not avert it, permits it, strengthens and preserves it in such a way that it is able to bear the enormous burden of the sin of the world and of all the wrath of God, and in such a way that it makes the suffering precious in the sight of God and salutary for the world *(De duabus naturis,* 218). And Nicolaus Selnecker gave the assurance that "the suffering of Christ in the flesh is truly and in reality the suffering of God because of the personal union of the flesh with the Person of the Son of God" *(passio Christi in carne vere et realiter sit Dei passio propter personalem unionem carnis ad personam Filii Dei) (Ex. Ord.* I, 383). The Formula of Concord confines itself exclusively to quotations from Luther and summarizes their meaning by saying that "it is not right to say . . . that the aforementioned statements [God suffered, God died] are only verbal declarations *[praedicatio verbalis]*, that is, mere words, and that this is not so in fact. For our simple Christian faith proves that the Son of God, who became man, suffered for us, died, and redeemed us with His blood."[7] Here at least there is a return to the still undeveloped statement made in the *Schwabach Articles*.

The reason for the great caution exercised by the authors of the Formula of Concord and, in addition, by the later dogmaticians in connection with this question is to be found, not so much in psychological difficulties – in the writings of Chemnitz and Selnecker one can clearly

[6] Brenz, *De pers. unione,* pp. 22 f. — Concerning the *Chalcedonense: De maj.*, pp. 17 ff.

[7] *FC, SD* VIII, 45. — Luther: WA 26, 319, 29 ff.; 321, 19 ff.; 324, 25 ff.; WA 50, 590, 11 ff. — Among the more recent theologians no one reflected more earnestly on this thought than Hermann Bezzel. It is in keeping with the central significance which he ascribed to the condescension of God that he "surely did not recoil from a *genus tapeinoticon* [the assumption that the divine nature was capable of suffering]." Rupprecht, *Herm. Bezzel als Theologe,* 1925, p. 60.

observe the attempt to psychologize — as in the consideration of the complicated and therefore particularly delicate structure they had erected out of the "personal representations" *(propositiones personales),* out of "uniting" *(unitio),* "union" *(unio),* participation" *(communio),* "communication of attributes" *(communicatio idiomatum),* and their three "kinds" *(genera),* above the ancient doctrine of the two natures. This structure is the most splendid memorial to the architectonics of the generation that brought the Formula of Concord into being. Even the work in the field of the history of dogma — the work that was done by drawing on and interpreting the ancient church doctrine — is astounding. Again and again the reader will also be sharply aware of the impact of the Gospel *(evangelischer Ansatz).* Yet the doctrine of the two natures, as it was accepted, was an obstacle which barred the way to the end of the road that was taken when the question was discussed.

The obstacle did not lie in the fundamental thesis: that divine and human nature are united to form the Person of Christ. This statement was certainly burdened with the early church's conception of nature — the conception which, as an expression for something that is material and foreign to the idea conveyed by the word "person," rebels against the modern conception of personality. In the first place, however, the accepted statement about the enhypostasis of the human nature, according to which the Logos forms the Person in Christ, had softened the impression that it is a combination of materials where it had not done away with this impression. In the second place, there is also an effort to make the concept "nature" so general that in itself it is not burdened with any of the categories foreign to Christology but serves merely as the point of contact for the content that should be put into it for the purpose of Christology.[8] This is to be seen particularly in connection with the definition of the divine nature. When the Formula of Concord expresses this definition by saying that "to be almighty, eternal, infinite, everywhere at the same time naturally, that is, of itself to be present according to the property of the nature and its natural essence, and to know everything, are essential attributes of the divine nature" *(SD* VIII, 9) — it could cite as evidence the precedent set by Luther (WA 50, 587, 29). Here, however, there is lacking that very side of the divine essence on the revelation of which in Christ everything depended, namely, His mercy, His love, His will to pardon. It is true that all this cannot be separated from the "attributes" *(Eigenschaften)* enumerated

[8] Hafenreffer, *Loci,* p. 305: ". . . by nature are understood the two elements or parts, so to speak, that constitute the Person of Christ" *(. . . per naturam ambo principia seu partes [ut ita loquamur] intelliguntur, quibus persona Christi constituta est).*

there; but these attributes themselves are equally applicable to the "hidden God" *(Deus absconditus)*.[9] To a certain extent the doctrine of the God-man's participation in the works of God was a substitute. But this meant that the problem of the essential union of the natures had, strictly speaking, already been abandoned. In what an altogether different manner one could have met the attack on the "finite capable of containing the infinite" *(finitum infiniti capax)* if in accordance with the impact of the Gospel *(evangelischer Ansatz)* God's inexhaustible will to confer grace *(der unerschöpfliche Gnadenwille Gottes)* had been made, not the cause but the decisive content of the "assumption of the human nature" *(assumptio naturae humanae)!* Instead, the Reformed opponents, who represented a totally different belief in God *(Gottesglaube)*, brought about involvement in the struggle for the rational concepts of the infiniteness and the absoluteness of God, although in the development of the doctrine of predestination it had been correctly realized that these rational concepts are foreign to the evangelical idea of revelation.[10]

The shilly-shallying that took place in connection with the pursuit of the aforementioned idea that God participates directly in the suffering of the Son is a result of what has been mentioned as lacking. Even though it was correct to say that the "suffering" as such took place only in the human nature, yet the basic thought could be carried out in such a way that in the very act of voluntarily bearing the curse of sin through His Son God limited Himself, namely, His right to punish, to His wrath, but that in doing so He also limited His very "majesty as the Lord" *(Herrenmajestät.)* What thus appears to be a breakdown of the "absolute" omnipotence of God is, on the other hand, the *revealed* omnipotence of His mercy. It has already been pointed out how important this knowledge is for the impact of the Gospel *(evangelischer Ansatz)*, and that it is the center of interest in the Lutheran doctrine of salvation.

[9] M. Chemnitz enumerates "eternity, immeasurableness, majesty, omnipotence, all-sufficiency, wisdom, goodness, righteousness, immutability, immortality, invisibility, incapacity for suffering" *(aeternitas, immensitas, majestas, omnipotentia, omnisufficientia, sapientia, bonitas, justicia, immutabilitas, immortalitas, invisibilitas, impassibilitas)* (*De duab. nat.*, p. 23). It is clear that the concepts "goodness" *(bonitas)* and "righteousness" *(justicia)* that are added here cannot replace what is missed above. Nor did later dogmatics bring a change here. Cf. Baier, *Comp.*, pp. 598 f. In the context of the doctrine of the two natures Buddeus mentions only "omniscience, wisdom, omnipotence, immeasurableless, omnipresence, eternity" *(Omniscientia, sapientia, omnipotentia, immensitas, omnipraesentia, aerternitas)* (*Instit.*, 1741, pp. 270 f.). — J. Lor. v. Mosheim, *Elem. Theol. Dogm.*, 1758, p. 321: "infinite wisdom and knowledge, eternity, aseity and independence, infinite power" *(infinita sapientia et scientia, aeternitas, aseitas et independentia, infinita potentia)*.

[10] H. Lauerer, *Die Kondeszendenz Gottes, Festchrift f. Ihmels*, 1928, pp. 258 ff.

Yet this knowledge was brought to bear emphatically on the other aspect of Christology. For the whole dispute with regard to Christology had its origin in the doctrine of Holy Communion. The violent polemical writings of the opposition were directed against the teaching that Christ's divine attributes are communicated to His human nature *(genus auchematicum)*, and the contesting of this belief was calculated to shake the Lutheran doctrine of the "communication of attributes" *(communicatio idiomatum) to its foundations.*[11] But the fact that it was the doctrine of Holy Communion which caused Lutheran theology to formulate this teaching is no proof that this was also done in the interest of the Sacrament. If this were the case, the idea of Christ's omnipresence, which, of course, forms the bridge between the doctrine of Holy Communion and the doctrine of the "communication of attributes" *(communicatio idiomatum)*, would also have constitutive significance for the latter. This is out of the question.

The omnipresence of the body of Christ certainly was one of the essential points in the dispute concerning Holy Communion so far as this dispute touched on Christology at all. But that it cannot be the reason for Christology as taught by the Formula of Concord is clearly shown by the fact that although this confession quotes words of Luther which state without question that Christ is omnipresent "even according to His human nature," as for the rest it confines itself to the definitions which originated among the opponents of the omnipresence. For although it teaches at the critical place that Christ is present in the church even according to His human nature and that He instituted Holy Communion to give assurance of this presence, it bases this teach-

[11] The Formula of Concord expresses the essential content of this *genus* in a somewhat complicated sentence: "For the Holy Scriptures, and the ancient fathers, on the basis of Scripture [in which they were fully trained], testify forcefully that, for the reason and because of the fact that it has been personally united with the divine nature in Christ, the human nature in Christ, when it was glorified and exalted to the right hand of the majesty and power of God, after the form of a servant, and humiliation had been laid aside, did receive in addition to and above its natural, essential, permanent properties also special, high, great, supernatural, inscrutable, ineffable, heavenly prerogatives and advantages in majesty, glory, power, and might above everything that can be named, not only in this world but also in that which is to come [Eph. 1:21]; and that, accordingly, in the operations of the office of Christ, the human nature in Christ, in its measure and mode, is equally employed [at the same time], and also has its efficacy, that is, its power and effect not only from and according to its natural, essential attributes, or only so far as their ability extends, but chiefly from and according to the majesty, glory, power, and might which it has received through the personal union, glorification, and exaltation." (*SD* VIII, 51). — Cf. Luther's *Disp. de communicatione idiomatum* (the subtitle in the older editions) of 1540, Drews, *Disp.*, pp. 585 ff., as well as the letter to Franz Gross, Enders 14, 131 ff.

ing, not on the omnipresence in general – as Luther, Brenz, and Andreä do – but on the statement that He "can be and actually is present where He wills." Accordingly, it confines itself to multipresence or, as it is expressed even more terribly by the dogmaticians, to multivolipresence (*SD* VIII, 79). Thus it restricts itself to the wording of such statements as dispute the "ubiquity of the flesh of Christ" *(ubiquitas carnis Christi)* more or less explicitly.[12] And where Chemnitz makes a sharp distinction between "proper attributes of the divine nature" *(attributa divinae naturae propria)* given to Christ by virtue of the hypostatic union and the "spiritual gifts, heavenly and divine" *(dona spiritualia, coelestia et divina),* conferred on Him as proof that His divine attributes are communicated to His human nature *(genus majestaticum),* he enumerates only the omnipotence, the "quickening life" *(vita vivificans),* the "power to pronounce judgment" *(potestas judicium faciendi),* the "glory of God" *(gloria Dei),* and the "cleansing from or the destruction of sins" *(mundare seu delere peccata);* but he says nothing here about omnipresence *(De duabus naturis,* ch. 21, esp. pp. 267 ff.). From this it follows that the concept of the omnipresence of the body of Christ which was in controversy in the doctrine of the Sacrament was by no means felt to be an integral part of the "communication of attributes" *(communicatio idiomatum)* and that therefore interest in this concept cannot be the real reason for the doctrine.

Then, however, the formulation with which the Formula of Concord, in its first summary, circumscribed the "divine properties" *(proprietates divinae)* communicated to the human nature is all the more important: "For to quicken, to have all judgment and all power in heaven and on earth, to have all things in subjection under His feet, to cleanse from sin, etc., are not created gifts, but divine, infinite properties; yet, according to the statement of Scripture, these have been given and communicated to the man Christ" (*SD* VIII, 55). It is clear that this summary, which corresponds exactly to the one given by Chemnitz, confines itself to what is absolutely in agreement with Scripture. But it is equally clear that this way of wording it has the closest connection with the impact of the Gospel *(evangelischer Ansatz).* For one dare not overlook the fact that it is the purpose of the *genus auchematicum* to point

[12] *Bekenntnis der Niedersachsen* and *FC, SD* VIII, 79. On the other hand, there is the statement: ". . . that we should not mix this extensive disputation concerning ubiquity into the treatment of the Lord's Supper" *(. . . das wir diese weitleufftige disputationem de ubiquitate nicht einmengen in den handel vom Abendmal).* – Even more sharply in the confession of the universities of Leipzig and Wittenberg (after the collapse of the Philippists!): "Nor do we invent any ubiquity of the flesh" *(Wir erdichten auch nicht einige ubiquitatem carnis).*

out the real communication of those "attributes" *(Eigenschaften)* to the human nature of Christ.[13] Then, however, this means that, according to this way of presenting the matter, God bound to the man Christ the power over life and death essential to Him Himself, His absolute authority, His will to cleanse mankind from sin. And this is a fundamental point of Luther's understanding of the "incarnate God" *(Deus incarnatus)* – the point that is also indispensable for the doctrine of justification.

The decisive concern of the doctrine of the *genus auchematicum* becomes altogether clear when one considers the doctrine of Christ's omnipresence from this viewpoint. Luther expressed this doctrine in the formula: "Where you are able to say, 'Here is God,' you must also say, 'Therefore Christ the man is also there' " (WA 26, 332, 31). Or shortly before even more sharply: "But now that He is a man who, in a supernatural manner, is one Person with God, and there is no God besides this man, it must follow that in the third [namely, the repletive] supernatural manner too He is and can be wherever God is, and that everything is altogether full of Christ, even according to the human nature" (ll. 18 ff.).[14] Thus Luther spoke in the large confession concerning Holy Communion. He declared almost more defiantly in the *Sermon on the Sacrament:* "For although He is everywhere, and I could find Him in a stone, in fire, in water, or even in a rope, just as He is truly there, yet He does not want me to seek Him without the Word and to cast myself into fire or water, or to hang myself with a rope. He is everywhere; but He does not want you to grope for Him everywhere; but grope where the Word is, and you will take hold of Him in the right way. Otherwise you tempt God and are guilty of idolatry." (WA 19, 492, 19 ff.) If for the time being we disregard the final way of putting it, which leads back to the idea of the real presence in Holy Communion (cf. *The Sacrament of the Altar)*, it is clear that here Luther is predicating an omnipresence of Christ such as cannot be taught more comprehensively even about God. But one dare not misunderstand this. Luther is not speaking of God's omnipresence as pantheistic. Just as he says here concerning Christ that it is idolatry to look for Him in the things themselves, so he says that for the senses "even God Himself is

[13] As early as 1518 Luther says: "Thus that all power should be given to Christ according to His humanity" (WA 1, 691, 13; 693, 1).

[14] Cf. Brenz, *De person. Un.*, p. 13: "It is necessary . . . that wherever the Deity is, there the humanity should also be" *(necessarium . . . ut ubicunque est Deitas, ibi etiam sit humanitas).* — A defense of the two quotations from Luther is found in N. Selnecker, *Ex. Ord.*, I, 348. — The second: *FC, SD* VIII, 81. — A defense against the attacks of the Jesuits is found in Stephan Gerlach, *Assertio*, ch. VII.

not where He is, even if He is everywhere or somewhere" *(ist auch Gott selbs nicht, wo er auch ist, er sey an allen enden odder an etlichen enden)* (WA 26, 318, 20). As Tycho Brahe put it later in Luther's sense, God is "everywhere and nowhere" *(ubique et nullibi)* (cf. *God and the World)*. Christ participates in this "everywhere and nowhere" *(ubique et nullibi)*; "for you must put this essence of Christ, that He is the one Person with God, very far, far outside the creatures, as far as God is outside them; on the other hand, it must be as deep and as near in all creatures as God is in them" (336, 15).

If Luther unquestionably goes beyond the compulsions that grew out of the doctrine of the real presence, something else must have motivated him. He expressed it on the occasion of the Marburg Colloquy.[15] There Oecolampadius conceded the presence of Christ according to His divine nature. But the man Christ, he said, is above the stars. Luther, however, should not cling to the human nature of Christ; he should lift up his thoughts to the divine nature. To this Luther replied that he "neither knew nor worshiped another God than the God who had become man, that he wanted no other God than this one. For there is no other God who can save. Therefore he could not bear to see the human nature of Christ dealt with in such a derogatory and degrading manner." (WA 30 III, 132, 23 ff.) Here the idea of revelation implicit in the impact of the Gospel *(evangelischer Ansatz)* stands before us in all its clarity. Without Christ, God is the God of wrath; in Christ, He is the God of grace. In Him — but Luther understands this only in the strict sense of the "incarnate God" *(Deus incarnatus)*. To think the man Christ out of existence in this connection is nothing else than to think of God as the "exposed God" *(Deus nudus)*, therefore to have no faith and to surrender oneself to wrath. The Christian can take comfort in God's presence only when he may believe that this presence, too, is the presence of the "incarnate God" *(Deus incarnatus)*, and that this includes the presence of the man Christ.[16]

The Jesuit opponents of Lutheranism could not understand this train of thought. They did not need the idea of the omnipresence of Christ, for they believed that they had Him in the Host. The Lutherans rejected this kind of real presence, just as they called it slander when Luther's

[15] Cf. my essay *Luther in Marburg, Zeitwende*, 1929, No. 10.

[16] Stephan Gerlach, *Assertio*, p. 380: "And therefore He is called Immanuel because not the exposed God but the God who became incarnate and was made man is now with us and helps our wretchedness" *(Et ideo Immanuel dicitur, quod Deus non nudus, sed incarnatus et homo factus iam nobiscum sit et nostrae miseriae auxiliatur)*. Thus with reference to "the omnipresence of Christ the man" *(omnipraesentia Christi hominis)*.

conception of the omnipresence was understood by his Calvinistic opponents as a doctrine of an "inclusive omnipresence" *(omnipraesentia inclusiva).* The embittered antagonism of the Calvinists was understandable. There it was the God of absolute predestination – in Luther's sense, therefore, the "hidden God" *(Deus absconditus)* – who demands the obedience of faith. Self-evidently, this caused the certainty that faith can have God only in Christ to slip away. To be sure, the Calvinists also taught that there is a presence of Christ, but, as Beza said at the Mömpelgard Colloquy, "in the mind" *(in mente).* Although it sounded entirely Lutheran when he added, "Which presence faith itself does not make, but the power and Word of God" *(Quam praesentiam non ipsa fides, sed virtus et verbum Dei faciat)* *(Acta,* p. 75), the Württembergians were not for one moment deluded into believing that this addition made the slightest change in the statement of the Calvinists that Christ is present only "in the mind of man" *(in mente hominis).* But the contrast is missed entirely if, because the Würtembergians looked upon this statement as a denial of their faith, one reproached them with a coarser conception, namely, one attaching to the "flesh." For the reverse of the high spirituality on the part of the Calvinists was their conception that the body of Christ is in heaven and for this reason cannot be on earth. Only in this way can one understand the Calvinistic demand that faith should raise itself to heaven in order to find the man Christ there. This heaven was certainly not to mean the "heaven that is everywhere" *(coelum ubiquitarium)* of the Lutherans, but a "definite place that can be seen above this whole world" *(locum certum, qui supra hunc omnem mundum aspectabilem sit).* This definite place was meant when Andreas Musculus was asked: "Why is Dr. Andreas afraid to include the body of Christ in heaven?" *(Quid timet D. Andreas Christi corpus coelo includere?)*[17] But for the Lutherans nothing could have been more out of the question; for to them the right hand of God to which Christ has ascended could not be a circumscribed place, as Luther had emphatically asserted over against Zwingli. Here the question reaches over into the domain of the philosophy of life *(Weltanschauung),* and there it will be pursued further (cf. *The Relativity of the World Picture).* Even here, however, it is clear that the doctrine of the omnipresence of Christ is connected with the question concerning God's relationship to the world in general and that for this reason – let it be repeated – it reaches out far beyond the interest in Holy Communion.

If this taught Lutheranism joyfully to affirm God's creation, the reason lay in the belief that the Creator, who is close to the world,

[17] *Gegner von A. Musculus,* pp. 38 and 6. — Cf. the discussion by Friedr. Petri.

is also the "incarnate God" *(Deus incarnatus)*.[18] And this was why Martin Chemnitz could speak of the "very sweet comforts" *(dulcissimae consolationes)* of the doctrine of the two natures. Nowhere perhaps does the fundamental idea of the impact of the Gospel *(evangelischer Ansatz)* come into its own more clearly than in the statements contained in the confession laid down in Lower Saxony in 1572: "Now the modern theologians want to have only one half of Christ in His church on earth, namely, only His divine nature. From us, who are and live in this world, in the Christian church, they want to remove, take away, and separate His human nature – according to which He, as our Brother, is most closely related to us – farther than heaven is from earth. For us poor human beings the divine nature is much too high. Furthermore, through sin we are estranged and separated from God so far as grace and life are concerned [Is. 5:9; Eph. 4]. When the divine nature takes direct action against us, it is like a consuming fire. Therefore the Son of God, as a Mediator, united Himself with our nature, in order that with the nature and through the nature according to which He is closest to us, devoted and related to us as our Brother, and according to which we are also flesh of His flesh and bone of His bone, the divine nature may deal with us in grace to give us life. This beautiful, necessary comfort is taken and stolen from us when one teaches that Christ is present in His church on earth and acts only according to and with His divine nature and not at the same time according to and with His human nature."[19]

19. The States and Offices of Christ[1]

It was not only the recollection of Phil. 2:5 ff. which compelled the formulation of the doctrine of the two states of Christ. The inner reason lay in the necessity to bring the doctrine of the "communication of attributes" *(communicatio idiomatum)* into harmony with the historical picture presented in the Gospels. For even though the "exalted" Christ was the starting point for the doctrine of the two natures, faith was concerned with the "exalted" Christ only because He was said to be iden-

[18] Again this is a basic thought of Bezzel's doctrine of condescension. Cf. Rupprecht, op. cit., pp. 13 f.

[19] In my essay titled *Wirkungen der lutherischen Abendmahlslehre, AELKZ*, 1927, Nos. 32—34, I erroneously attributed the statements quoted to Chemnitz. — *FC, SD* VIII, 87, reminds one of the same statements.

[1] See the writings mentioned in footnote 1, p. 236 f. — Joh. Huswedel (from Hamburg), *Diss. de duarum naturarum Christi unione personali eiusque effectis, praes. David Rungio* (a detailed connection with the early history of dogma), Wittenberg, 1600. — Joh. Victor (from Alsfeld), *Disp. de Logo s. Filio Dei, praes. St. Gerlach*, Tübingen, 1598. — Samuel Kefel (from Strassburg), *Theses de persona Dom. et Serv. Jesu Christi, praes. Joh. Pappo, Argentor*, 1600.

tical in person with the man who, as history records, was born and crucified. For this reason Jacob Andreä – in the last of the six sermons of the year 1573, in which he wants to make the meaning of the doctrine of the two natures plain to "simple Christian faith," that is, to the layman – quotes the Second Article of the Apostles' Creed in its entirety and then proceeds: "Here you have only one Christ and not two Christs in such a way that the one is the Son of God, the other is the Son of Man; that the one is born of God, the other is born of Mary; that the one suffered, the other did not suffer; that the one was raised from the dead, the other was not raised; that the one is in majesty, the other is not. But there is only one Christ, the Son of God and of Mary." Here one sees that although Lutheran theology, in the controversy in which it was engaged concerning the oneness of Christ's Person, is guided first of all by the question posed by the doctrine of the two natures, it is for this reason by no means indifferent to the question concerning the oneness of the historical Person. For the peculiarity of the Second Article of the Apostles' Creed, which Andreä adduces here, consists in this, that it presents as a historical series of events the very thing which the doctrine of the two natures seeks to solve in the form of a problem in relationship. It is true that in the middle there is the part stating that the Redeemer was born, suffered, and died; but the conception by the Holy Spirit, the sitting at the right hand of God the Father Almighty, and the eschatological outlook in the conclusion give it a place identical with the one which the doctrine of the two natures tries to give it in its way. And since the Apostles' Creed does not provide the slightest support for the belief that the "sitting at the right hand" *(sessio ad dextram)* brought about an essential change in Him who was born and Him who died – in the sense of a separation, let us say, of the divine from the human – Andreä had every right to make use of the Second Article for the general doctrine of the "communication of attributes" *(communicatio idiomatum)*. Here the identity of the Son of God with the man Christ is expressed so obviously and unreservedly that one can understand Andreä well not only on the basis of what his faith presupposes but also from the standpoint of theological purity when he says, "A great shame!" *(Pfuy Teuffel!)* to the Philippists of his time, who revived Zwingli's *alloeosis* and were willing to concede the communication of the divine properties to the man Christ only "as a way of expressing it and a manner of speaking" *(per phrasin et modum loquendi)*.

On the other hand, the Apostles' Creed now puts the animating character of historical movement into the relationship of the divine and the human side of Christ's Person – the relationship which at first gives the impression of being rigidly static in the doctrine of the two natures. Here the broad sketch is identical with the one in the second chapter of the Epistle to the Philippians: from above to below and from below to above. For this reason early Lutheran theology — in agreement with the church of all times — has good reason to apply the concepts of humiliation and exaltation employed in the passage in Philippians to what the Apostles' Creed means when it states the superhistorically historical series of events. In doing so it was easy to refer the kenosis taught in Phil. 2:5 to the act of incarnation and thus to designate "the Logos without the flesh" (λόγος ἄσαρκος) as its subject. In their effort to find room for the development of the man Jesus and, in general, for the genuine humanness *(Menschlichkeit)* of His consciousness and His actions, the "kenoticists" of the nineteenth century — Gottfried Thomasius, Sartorius, Gess, Hofmann, Frank — actually proceeded in this direction. When they strove to answer the question how such a divesting *(Entäusserung)* of the Logos is compatible with the unchangeableness of His position in the Trinity, they saw a problem where there really was no problem. For there can be no objection to Schöberlein's statement that for God the period of Christ's life on earth is merely a mathematical point and therefore that what for our discursive thinking is unfolded as a sequence in time is, when seen from the viewpoint of the Logos Himself, merely a timeless act, not a time span.[2]

This very consideration, however, makes it possible to understand the totally different character of the doctrine of humiliation in early Lutheranism. For the early dogmaticians the thought that the incarnation could mean that God or His Son was changed into a man was altogether out of the question. In the doctrinal disputes which led to the Formula of Concord the contrast with Schwenckfeld gave occasion again and again to establish this.[3] The early dogmaticians regarded as intolerable, both from the standpoint of soteriology and with respect to the unchangeableness of God, a kenosis doctrine of the kind taught by the kenoticists of the nineteenth century, according to which the Logos

[2] Ludwig Schöberlein, *Die Geheimnisse des Glaubens,* 1872. Here the essay, *Die Einheit von Gott und Mensch in Christo,* p. 64. Cf. Luther: "Christ has a twofold nature, and according to this one and the other one He was born without time, against time, and before the times" *(Christus habet duplicem naturam et secundum hanc et alteram natus est sine tempore, contra tempus et ante tempora),* Drews, *Disp.,* p. 518.

[3] E. g., *Mansfelder Bek.,* pp. 136 ff. — Andreä, *Esslinger Pred. wider die Schw.,* p. 12. — Chemnitz, *De duab. nat.,* p. 286. — *FC, SD* VIII, 89. — Nevertheless, it was cast into the teeth of this group by the Philippists that in their writings there were "very many things entirely similar to and in accordance with Schwenckfeld's allegations" *(Grundfest).*

actually lays aside the properties which to them seemed essential. For Brenz this was intolerable because it contradicted the statement that the incarnation was a "receiving of man into the divine majesty" *(assumptio hominis in majestatem divinam).* If for the time being one postpones asking what the difference is between this exaltation and the exaltation Paul means in Phil. 2, it becomes clear that for Brenz only "the Logos in the flesh" [λόγος ἔνσαρκος] – to use the terminology of Johann Gerhard – could be the subject of the divesting *(Entäusserung).* It is true that Brenz himself, in his detailed paraphrase of Phil. 2, always names only Christ as subject *(De majestate Domini,* 82 ff.); but here one must keep in mind his view that the Son of God takes the form of a Person only in Christ. Thus Christ, who is not united but identical with the Logos, divests Himself. This means, as Brenz sets forth in exact accordance with the passage in Philippians, that "although He possessed this majesty [namely, of God], He nevertheless covered and overspread it with the form of a servant" *(quamquam possideret eam majestatem [scil. Dei], tamen texit et obduxit eam forma servi).* Brenz, exactly like the modern kenoticists, includes the development not only of the body but also of the intellect among the necessary characteristics of genuine humanness *(Menschlichkeit).*[4] Of course, the humiliation to the form of a servant becomes complete in His obedience unto death. In precisely this way He, the other Adam, becomes the antitype of the first Adam, who "aspired to equality even with God" *(affectavit etiam Dei aequalitatem)* and became disobedient. On the other hand, Christ, who actually was equal to God, took the form of a servant and became obedient like a servant. In this way Brenz finds the bridge from the passage in Philippians to Rom. 5:19 and thus from the Person of Christ, as he sees it, to Christ's work of salvation. When Brenz, even though he also ascribes intellectual growth to the man Christ, states that the fullness of the Godhead dwells in Him and accords to this fullness the sum total of the divine properties, the humiliation, viewed from the standpoint of the Son of God, is not just a temporary loss of the Godhead; for – and here

[4] Brenz, *De maj. Dom.*, p. 83: "Therefore this is said, not because Christ was not a true man, who is made up of a body and a rational soul, but because after the fashion of men He endured all kinds of human weaknesses, by being born, by growing, by increasing in bodily strength and mental perception, by needing drink and food, by being hungry, by being thirsty, by sitting, by walking from place to place, and whatever there is of these infirmities" *(Hoc idcirco dicitur non quod Christus non fuerit verus homo, qui corpore et anima rationali constat, sed quod in modum hominum sustinuit omnia humanarum imbecillitatum genera, nascendo, increscendo, robore corporis et intellectu mentis augescendo, potu et cibo indigendo, esuriendo, sitiendo, sedendo, de loco in locum ambulando et quicquid est harum infirmitatum).*

one may get help from Schöberlein's thought – the chronology of the earth is but a moment of eternity. "For the Godhead is something absolute to the highest degree, and wherever it is, there it is completely" *(Divinitas enim res est simplicissima et ubicunque est, ibi Tota est)* (p. 28). This inviolable totality of God, in which Brenz includes omnipotence, etc., is also true of God's relationship to time. Even over against time the Godhead is absolutely one thing and no more; it cannot be divided into a sequence of events in time.

The other groups of Lutherans proceeded from Luther's statement: "Everything that is said about Christ's humiliation and exaltation must be stated of the man, for divine nature can neither be humbled nor exalted." [5] It is true that when this statement is made use of, it appears at times that the human nature is said to be the subject of the humiliation. And nineteenth-century theology often designates this as what early Lutheranism really meant. But Nicolaus Selnecker, whose writings cause one to get such an impression, includes even the act of incarnation – not the state resulting from this act – in the humiliation. Yes, he even limits the statement that the divine nature does not humble itself with an "insofar as" *(quatenus)*: insofar as the assumption of human nature does not mean that humiliation must be stated of the Logos as the Son of God.[6] Therefore when he sometimes makes the human nature the subject of the humiliation, this can be meant only in the sense of the later distinction, according to which the Person of the Logos is designated as "the subject which" *(subjectum quod)*, but the human nature is designated as "the subject by which" *(subjectum quo)*,[7] or, as Baier expresses it, in such a way that the humiliation "pertains to the human nature"

[5] Epistle for Christmas, WA 10 I, 1, p. 150, 8 (1522). — *Bekenntnis der Niedersachsen.*

[6] *Ex. Ord.* I, 313 f. The human nature as the subject: "Then there is exinanition, because after the human nature of the Logos had been assumed, as if it had not partaken personally of any godhood . . . it was subject to infirmities" *(Deinde exinanitio est, quod assumta natura humana τοῦ λόγου, quasi nullius deitatis personaliter particeps facta esset . . . infirmitatibus subjecta fuit* (314). The act of incarnation as humiliation: "But this annihilation, so to speak, evacuation, or exinanition of the Son of God embraces these three things: In the first place, the incarnation itself, by which the Son of God . . . was made man" *(Comprehendit autem haec quasi annihilatio, evacuatio seu exinanitio Filii Dei haec tria: Primum ipsam incarnationem, qua Filius Dei . . . homo factus est)* (313). The divine nature: "The divine nature is not emptied except insofar as the Logos, the Son of God, is said to be emptied, because He Himself alone — not the Father, not the Holy Spirit — deigned to assume the human nature into the oneness of His Person" *(Divina natura non exinanitur, nisi quatenus Logos Filius Dei exinaniri dicitur, quod solus ipse, non Pater, non Spir. S., dignatus est assumere humanam naturam in unitatem suae personae)* (314).

[7] König, *Theol. pos.*, p. 160. — Hollaz, *Ex.* III, 282.

(ad humanam naturam pertinet) (*Compendium*, p. 605). This and nothing else was also the meaning of the aforementioned statement in Luther's sermon. According to the general Christological assumptions, one could teach that the humiliation takes place in the human nature alone only if the Godhead of the Logos was said to have undergone a change, that is, a loss of the Godhead of the Logos. And one had to predicate the humiliation of the human nature because, of course, in the doctrine of the two natures it is stated that the divine properties are communicated to it.

But this final necessity shows that in early Lutheranism the doctrine of the humiliation has a purpose identical with that of the kenosis doctrine of the nineteenth century. For the latter, like the former, was meant to make room for the historical picture of the man Christ – the picture which seems to contradict the doctrine of the "communication of attributes" *(communicatio idiomatum).* And, like Luther, both Brenz and the theologians in Lower Saxony stress the point that the inner essence is also part of the genuine humanness *(Menschlichkeit).* "The increase of the gifts in His human nature also belongs to this. Concerning the Gospel for the day after Christmas Luther writes about this as follows:[8] 'Although He was always full of the Spirit and grace, yet the Spirit did not always move Him but aroused Him sometimes to this, sometimes to that. Therefore even though the Spirit was in Him ever since He was conceived, yet it grew just as His body grew, and His intellect increased in a natural way just as in other men. Thus the Spirit settled in Him more and more,[9] and moved Him, the longer, the more, etc., until after laying aside weakness all this became perfect.'"[10] Here the statement that the Logos assumed human nature and made it His perfect organ without being changed into it is taken seriously. He retains full freedom in shaping and using His organ but at the same time remains in full possession of His divine properties. For if in the historical man one can observe weakness and, according to His own words, a limitation of His knowledge, these limitations of the man, who is bound to time, are not true of the Logos, who Himself is not bound and therefore

[8] Cf. WA 10 I, 1, pp. 446 ff. (1522).

[9] Op. cit., 447, 18: . . . *ynn yhn.*

[10] *Bek. d. Niedersachsen.* Cf. Chemnitz, *De duab. nat.*, p. 258: ". . . whence He did not know some things, learned, made progress in wisdom, [there was] the desire that the cup be removed, the strength of the body dried up, blood flowed out through His sweat, etc." *(. . . unde quaedam ignoravit, didicit, profecit sapientia, voluntas transferri calicem, corporis virtus exaruit, sanguis per sudorem effluxit etc.)* Similarly, Selnecker, Aeg. Hunnius, and the later dogmaticians.

can undergo no growth and experiences the life of the man in time as a single moment, so to speak, without time.

But when, within the framework of their doctrine of the two natures, those theologians predicated the possession of the divine properties of the man too, they certainly had reason for this in the historical picture presented by the Gospels, because the Gospels also know of a shining forth of that which is extrahuman in what is human: "not in such a way that it [that which is extrahuman] dwells in it [what is human] by itself or alone, or works separately, merely being present in the assumed nature, but in such a way that it shines in the assumed nature, comes into view with and through it" *(non ut absoluta aut nuda tantum praesentia in assumpta natura illa inhabitent aut seorsim operentur, sed ita, ut in assumpta natura luceant, cum illa et per illam se exerant).* Thus Chemnitz (*De duabus naturis,* 309). If, in addition to numerous statements of Paul, he also cites as proof of this, for example, Matt. 8:27; 11:27; 17:2; 18:20; 24:35; Luke 10:22, etc., and many related words of Christ in the Gospel of John, likewise the miracles of Jesus and the forgiveness of sins bestowed by Him, it is, of course, very easy to declare that all this is unhistorical; but one cannot deny that Chemnitz and those who shared his belief had reason to find the congruity of that doctrine verified in the historical picture they had before them.

But since, as has been said, they did not deny the existence of the limitations which are attested there and which they based on the free use of His human organ through the Logos, and since they still could not concede that the union of the Logos with the human nature is imperfect, it was imperative to answer the question how the essential possession of the divine properties can be reconciled with the limited extent to which these properties shone forth in the life of Christ. For this Hafenreffer had already used the picture of the incognito [11] which was later employed by Kierkegaard too – a picture which the prince's son, for whom his *Loci* were primarily intended, certainly understood very well. It is meant primarily in this sense when the statement is made concerning Christ that He kept His majesty "secret" or "hidden." [12]

[11] Hafenreffer, *Loci,* 400: "Why is it called the state of exinanition? Not because Christ the man had no majesty — for He had it through and because of the personal union — but this is what princes are sometimes wont to do even on their travels; while they do services for their servants, they are and remain masters in spite of this." *(Quare vocatur status exinanitionis? Non quod Christus homo nullam majestatem haberet, habuit enim per et propter unionem personalem: sed quod interdum principes etiam in peregrinationibus facere solent: qui dum ministris suis famulitia praestant, nihilominus tamen domini sunt et manent.)*

[12] Brenz, *De maj.,* p. 82. — Chemnitz, *De duab. nat.,* p. 353: ". . . He emptied Himself; that is, He concealed the use and manifestation of His divine glory and

To be sure, Chemnitz says of this hiding that it took place not only "in the flesh" *(in carne)* but also "by means of the flesh" *(per carnem)*. Here one can find a contradiction of Luther's idea of revelation, according to which it is really in and through the "incarnate God" *(Deus incarnatus)* that the revelation takes place. According to what Chemnitz says, it can seem that the flesh as such should, on the other hand, serve as a covering *(Verhüllung)*. Brenz, however, saw the covering of the majesty not in the flesh as such but in the form of a *servant* and in the work of a *servant* that was done by Him who had become man. In this way he came to the conviction held by Luther. This is the only view of covering with which one can reconcile the thought that the divine majesty shines forth occasionally, namely, "when it pleases Him" (*FC, Epit.* VIII, 16). But, as has been said, this corresponds only to the historical picture presented in the New Testament. Then what appears to be the psychological difficulty of predicating of Christ the possession, say, of omniscience and then reconciling with this the lack of knowledge He occasionally admitted – this apparent difficulty does not exist if one actually lets the man be the perfect organ of the Logos, who communicates Himself entirely to the "human nature," it is true, but influences this nature at His discretion and thus imposes upon it the limitations necessarily connected with His will to have the form of a servant and to do the work of a servant. A more serious difficulty seems to consist in this, that the occasional shining-forth of the divine majesty in Christ threatens to destroy the essence of faith, to which indeed the "reconciling of opposites" *(mediatio contrariorum)* belongs: it should see the completion of the revelation of salvation *(Heilsoffenbarung)* in the deepest humiliation, namely, on the cross. From this "should" faith seems to have a dispensation to a certain extent when it finds support in those manifestations of God that are visible, so to speak. But this danger would exist only if these manifestations had to be the basis of faith. This is the case, however, neither in the writings of Luther nor in those of Brenz. Furthermore, it is not the case in the writings of Chemnitz.

The Christological dispute in which the Württembergians engaged in the following century with the Giessen camp concerning the question whether Christ took part in the universal rule of God even while He lived on earth was waged by both sides on the basis of false conclusions

power, and concealed it through the flesh, withdrew it, and made it rest . . ." (*. . . exinanivit se, hoc est, usurpationem et ostensionem divinae suae gloriae et potentiae in carne et per carnem occultavit, retraxit et quiescere fecit . . .*). — *Bek. d. Niedersachsen.* — *FC, SD* VIII, 26, 65, 85. — Luther, *Lectures on Romans* II, 10, 18: "The divinity was emptied and was concealed in the flesh" *(Exinanita est divinitas et in carnem abscondita)*.

drawn from the doctrine of the two natures.[13] There was unity with respect to the statement that because of the unchangeableness *(Unveränderlichkeit)* of God the humiliation could hold true only "so far as the human nature was concerned" *(quoad naturam humanam)* and that "so far as the divine nature was concerned" *(quoad naturam divinam),* there was no diminution of the participation of the Son of God in the rule of God even during His life on earth. When the Giessen camp expressed this by saying that the Son of God exercised divine rule according to the one nature but not according to the other, they were open to the criticism of the Tübingen camp, which took this to be the fatal "Calvinistic outside" *(Extra Calvinisticum),* which means that because the Logos, who dwells in the human nature, is infinite, He is at the same time "outside it" *(extra eam).* For if this is true, the communication of Christ's divine attributes to His human nature *(genus auchematicum)* was actually done away with while Christ dwelt on earth. In reality the Saxonian Decision *(Decisio Saxonica),* through which the Giessen Christology was accepted, refers expressly to the teaching that the attributes of each nature are ascribed to the entire Person of Christ *(genus idiomaticum).*[14] When, on the other hand, the Tübingen camp maintained that there was a "hidden" participation of the human nature in the divine rule while Christ dwelt on earth, it seemed to be defenseless against the objection of the opponents, who questioned the humiliation and thus the whole saving work *(Heilswerk)* of Christ. For how, the *Decisio Saxonica* asks emphatically, shall one make head or tail of this, that "according to the flesh" *(secundum carnem)* Christ had to lament the fact that He was forsaken by God and at the same time could still be Lord over angels and principalities? (P. 40.) In this way His life became a mere delusion, and then one could conclude that just as the suffering was an actual suffering only in the eyes of men, so it is valid only in the eyes of men, not in the eyes of God (41).

These conclusions, drawn from the doctrine of the two natures which was taken for granted by both sides, show the weakness of this doctrine or, at all events, the weakness of the form it had assumed in the meantime. According to it, the essence of the divine as well as of the human nature consists in an aggregate of attributes that can be combined now in this way, now in another way, and, strictly speaking, differ from one another merely quantitatively: the human nature knows something, the

[13] We omit the details and refer to Quenstedt's presentation (*Theol. did.-pol.* III, 389 ff.). — The problem is discussed by Luther as early as the time of the *Lectures on Romans* (II, 10).

[14] *Decisio Saxonica,* p. 74.

divine nature knows everything; the former is bound to a place, the latter is everywhere at the same time, etc. There had been an involuntary adjustment to the Calvinistic contrasting of the finite with the infinite, which, according to Calvinistic doctrine, are mutually exclusive for quantitative reasons. Therefore the Württembergians immediately scented the "Calvinistic outside" *(Extra Calvinisticum)* where the Giessen camp refused to admit that the human nature participated in the divine rule *(Gottesherrschaft)* of the divine nature – the rule about which there could be no doubt. And here, as has been said, they were by no means wrong. But it would have been better to remember the statements in which Luther disputed the fragmentary parallelism of the finite and the infinite. "Nothing is so small," he had said in his large confession concerning Holy Communion, "that God is not still smaller. Nothing is so large that God is not still larger. Nothing is so short that God is not still shorter. Nothing is so long that God is not still longer. Nothing is so wide that God is not still wider. Nothing is so narrow that God is not still narrower, etc."[15] True, God is "greater" than the greatest among the creatures. But this is not a quantitative superiority, for He is also smaller than the smallest thing of all. When taken to be the measure of extent, the concepts "large" and "small" are altogether unusable with reference to God. The difference is qualitative in nature. But something else must be considered.

If it was correct to view the incarnation as "an assumption of the human nature" *(assumptio naturae hominis)*, the actual consequence of this, as was stated by the Tübingen camp, was the assumption of the man into the majesty of God or – the thing that was important here – God's will to exercise His rule through the man Christ. But the new element which this puts into the rule of God as exercised before the incarnation can really be understood only in the light of the incarnation: in Christ God's omnipotence, His omnipresence, and His omniscience are combined in the will to bring about a reconciliation; they enter the service of that will. In this divine rule *(Gottesherrschaft)*, characterized

[15] WA 26, 339, 39 ff. Cf. WA 23, 139, 12, and on the following pages the application to Christology. — In addition, *Disp. de unitate essentiae divinae II* of 1545, EA *var. arg.* 4, 476 ff. Here Thesis 18: "After the article of the Trinity the most important is the article concerning the incarnation of the Son of God, where — which was impossible — the comparative relation of the finite and the infinite came about" *(Post Articulum Trinitatis summus est ille de incarnatione Filii Dei, ubi finiti et infiniti [quod erat impossibile] facta est proportio).* Thesis 19: "This Person, at once finite and infinite, became the Servant of sinners and the newest and lowest of all things, which is incredible; but to those who believe it is most pleasing" *(Haec persona finita simul et infinita facta est peccatorum serva, et omnium rerum novissima et infima, quod est incredibile, sed credentibus iucundissimum).*

as just stated, the man Christ has an integrant share. So far there is no "Calvinistic outside" *(Extra Calvinisticum)* here. For just as it is impossible here to separate Christ's humanity from the Logos, so one cannot separate the will to bring about a reconciliation and God's work of reconciliation from His omnipotence. "The attributes of God," Balthasar Mentzer himself, one of the main participants in the aforementioned dispute, had written a few years previously, "that are essential and are united reciprocally with the divine essence, and in God, with respect to Himself, are absolutely one" *(Attributa Dei, quae sunt essentialia et cum essentia divina reciprocantur: et in Deo, respectu ipsius, sunt simpliciter unum)* (*Exeg. Aug. Conf.*, 29). The aforementioned question of the *Decisio Saxonica* – how the participation of the man Christ in the divine rule *(Gottesherrschaft)* can be reconciled with the fact of His death – was, therefore, outweighed by the statement that it was in His death that this participation was brought to completion.

Then, however, the fact of the humiliation is not inconsistent with participation in the rule of God *(Gottesherrschaft)*. For the Logos born of God takes the form of a servant and renders the obedience of a servant unto death for the very purpose of carrying out the new rule of God that begins in the revelation of salvation *(Heilsoffenbarung)*. Here the question whether the man Christ was omnipotent or omniscient cannot be put in earnest, because it makes sense only if one separates the man from the Logos, who reveals Himself in Him and reaches His goal through Him. To be sure, the man's knowledge is small, and His place is narrow. But – "God is still smaller, God is still narrower, etc." In spite of this smallness and narrowness of God in the eyes of men, He exercises His rule over all things. Just as it is absurd to ascribe omnipotence to the man Christ separated from God, so, conversely, He is Lord over all things because He is the Son of God; and He rules because God has bound His own rule to Him.

Ultimately, however, here it is not merely a matter of dogmatic theories and academic conclusions. Ultimately the reality of the statement "The Word was made flesh" *(Verbum caro factum est)* is at stake. When at the Mömpelgard Colloquy the Württembergians concluded from this that the majesty of God was imparted to the Child while He was still in His mother's womb, because the incarnation begins here (*Acta*, 197 f.), Beza replied that the Word had to be understood metaphorically *(tropice)*. He did not know a better answer (367 f.). The Christmas sermons delivered by Luther, both when he was young and when he was old, had something different to say. To Luther the Word made flesh is the "only Son of God, who has all the glory that the Father has" (WA 10 I, 245, 8); and for faith the government of the Child of which Isaiah spoke rests on the shoulders of the Child of Mary (WA 34 II, 511, 20 ff.). For Luther, therefore, faith in the birth of Christ was "the faith exceedingly rich in grace" *(der recht gnadenreych glaub)* (WA 10 I, 1, 71, 6).[16] And not only do the dogmaticians agree with him, but as often as the Christmas Gospel rings out, the church also sings with him:

He is become an infant small
Who by His might upholdeth all.

Certainly "the Jews also saw His glory, and yet they did not consider it glory as of the only-begotten Son of God" – "one must not refer the seeing to physical vision only" *(das sehen muss man nit alleyn auff das leyplich gesicht tzihen)* (245, 16 ff.). Only faith sees the majesty of God in the Child of Mary. But one would have to turn everything Luther knew and taught upside down if one wanted to define faith as the art of understanding the Word of the Gospel metaphorically *(tropice)*. Here there is nothing to explain. "The Word was made flesh," says Luther in a disputation in 1539; "that is, God's promise was fulfilled" *(Verbum caro factum est, id est, promissio Dei est impleta)* (Drews, *Disp.* 509). Here the relationship to the impact of the Gospel *(evangelischer Ansatz)* flashes forth again. As always, here, too, faith is not merely the receiving of the promise. Faith does not make a revelation out of the historical fact *(Geschichtstatsache)*, but the fact of the revelation *(Offenbarungstatsache)* recorded by history engenders faith.

Now at last it is possible to answer the question how the exaltation imparted to the man Christ through the incarnation differs from the exaltation which Paul means in Phil. 2. Brenz, whose doctrine of the humiliation distinctly provokes this question, adheres in detail to Phil. 2:9 ff. Consequently, he puts the emphasis on the giving of the "name," which, according to the context of the following verses, can be no other than the name of God and signifies the quintessence of the divine majesty. But since this majesty was already imparted to Christ by means of the incarnation, Brenz must add that the statement about the exaltation is "a way of speaking, because a thing is said to take place when it becomes known" *(phrasis loquendi, quod tunc res dicatur fieri, cum innotescit)* (*De majestate Domini,* 85). A statement dangerous to his theology! For ordinarily he inveighs bitterly against understanding concrete statements of Scripture "by means of a way of speaking" *(per*

[16] From the *Church Postil* of 1522 cf. WA 10 I, 1, pp. 142 ff. and 180 ff. In addition, the dissertation of Joh. Victor.

phrasim loquendi). In effect, however, the North Germans are in agreement with him when in connection with the exaltation they put the emphasis on the "manifestation" *(manifestatio)* of the divine majesty which was hidden in Christ when He had the form of a servant.[17] But Chemnitz and all the later dogmaticians again set forth the doctrine of the exaltation in the light of the Apostles' Creed. Accordingly, they direct their attention less to the "state" *(status)* than to the "act of exaltation" *(actus exaltationis).* According to everything they taught about the humiliation, it is self-evident that they all, like Brenz, say that only the human nature was exalted.

Now, however, a consideration of the individual acts mentioned in the Apostles' Creed shows that the exaltation is by no means supposed to be a mere manifestation. Nor is it supposed to be merely a rising from a lower world into a higher one. On the contrary, every single act is viewed as a "victory," a subduing of the enemies. In Luther this is especially true of Christ's resurrection. When he mentions death, sin, hell, and devil again and again in connection with the resurrection, the relationship he constantly stresses leads him to Christ's work of salvation *(Heilswerk),* that is, to the real basis and content of faith. It is not the historical account itself which moves us to celebrate the "victory" *(victoria)* and the "glory of the resurrection" *(gloria resurrectionis);* it is the certainty that "Christ wants to be our Comfort . . . because he teaches that this victory and the glorious resurrection of this excellent Person have been given to all who believe in it, that opposed to my death I am to have Christ's resurrection, which is greater than heaven and earth" (WA 37, 30, 20; *Lectures on Hebrews* 131, 23). As the master of sin and death, the devil makes heaven and earth narrow for me. But "my death is a spark, Christ's resurrection is the great sea" *(mea mors est scintilla, Christi resurrectio das grosse meer)* (31, 3 ff., 15). Christ arose as our Head; we are about to follow Him. The Word and Baptism make it possible for us to take part in His resurrection: "And only the husks must still arise; the grain has already arisen" *(Et tantum die hulssen sol noch aufferstehen, der kern schon aufferstanden).* Only the body, "a shabby, lousy cloak" *(ein schebichter lausichter beltz),* is buried – "the best part is already in heaven, Christ and also the better portion, namely, my soul" *(das beste stück ist schon im himel, Christus et etiam potior pars, mea scilicet anima)* (36, 162). And it is self-evident that Luther makes Paul's thought his own – the thought that Christ was raised for

17 Selnecker, *Ex. Ord.* II, 321; *Instit.* I, 165 ff. — M. Chemnitz, *De duab. nat.*, p. 353.

our justification.[18] The Easter hymns of the Lutheran Church prove that it was the soteriological, not the metaphysical, significance of Christ which it, like Luther, constantly had at heart.[19]

It was only logical for this real concern of the saving faith *(Heilsglaube)* to be emphasized and preserved in connection with the so-called "descent into hell" *(descensus ad inferos)*, which was not included in the series of saving acts *(Heilsakte)* until the Apostles' Creed was formulated. And since Scriptural reasons for the descent into hell are exceedingly meager, there was always the temptation to give free rein to speculation. For a time Luther thought that this act meant that Christ "tasted" *(geschmecket)* hell[20] – a view which Calvin, too, advocated, even though he did not insist on the relationship to 1 Peter 3:18 ff.[21] This view was included in the confessional writings of the Reformed Church. The ninth article of the Formula of Concord[22] attacks Johann Aepin, of Hamburg, who likewise advocated this view and, in doing so, won the approval of a man like Joachim Westphal but at first received only evasive answers from Melanchthon and Bugenhagen. This particular article is distinctive because it limits the descent into hell completely to the concern of faith, which is the only thing that comes into consideration here. Citing Luther's Torgau sermon of 1533 (WA 37, 62 ff.) – to which Melanchthon and Bugenhagen, by the way, had already referred in the opinion they had handed down – it declares that one should confine oneself to the established fact "that Christ descended into hell, destroyed hell for all believers, and redeemed them from the power of death, devil, and the eternal damnation of the jaws of hell" (*Epit.* IX, 4). "But we should not trouble ourselves with high, sharp thoughts as to how this took place" (*SD* IX, 2). It was scarcely possible to speak with greater reserve and yet more soteriologically. Later Frank, referring with true consistency to the Biblical distinction between the first and the second death, characterizes the doctrine that Christ also suffered the pun-

18 WA 40 I, 65: "Christ certainly rose for the sake of our righteousness; His victory is the victory over the Law, sin, our flesh, death, and hell" *(Christus resurrexit certe propter justitiam nostram, sua victoria est victoria legis, peccati, carnis nostrae, mortis, inferorum).*

19 Cf. *End of the World.*

20 Proofs in Theod. Harnack, *Luthers Theologie* II, 180 f.

21 Calvin, *Institutio* II, 16, 8 f. *Opp.* 2 (*CR* 30), 375 ff.

22 On the whole controversy cf. Frank, *Theol. d. Konkordienf.* III, 397 ff. We refrain from going into details, since here everything essential is said that can be said after becoming acquainted with the presentations of Aepin's side that were examined by Frank in manuscript. — The first opinion which the Wittenbergians handed down to the senate of Hamburg (*CR* VII 7, 666 ff.).

ishments of hell for us as "a way of speaking about God that is not found in Scripture" *(schriftloses Theologumenon)*.[23]

Among the acts included in the concept of exaltation not one is as closely bound up with the confessional disputes of the century of the Reformation as Christ's ascension. From the time of Zwingli until well into the eighteenth century the Reformed Church used the ascension as its strongest argument against the Lutheran doctrine of Holy Communion. If Christ ascended into heaven, He cannot be omnipresent; for heaven is a definite place above the stars, and Christ's disciples could testify that He had begun the spatial journey to heaven. But nothing proves the power of Luther's faith more forcefully than the fact that he completely brushed aside this "Biblical" argumentation and, as a result, also the limitations set by the world as it is pictured – limitations that were set for him too. In what he wrote against the Swiss he denied the spatial nature of heaven with all the clarity one could desire. Accordingly, he also denied the local character of the ascension. The Lutheran theologians of the sixteenth century followed in his footsteps. It was not until the eighteenth century that some dogmaticians, influenced by the Scriptural principle of the Reformed Church, made a partial retreat.[24]

23 All the malice — determined by very transparent motives — with which the Formula of Concord was attacked on the basis of certain lines of thought can probably not be seen more clearly anywhere than in the treatment Fr. Loofs accorded the ninth article. Cf. his *Leitfaden zum Studium der Dogmengeschichte,* 4th ed., 1906, p. 924: "Finally it is noteworthy in the third place that the Formula of Concord dogmatizes a comment which Luther had not meant 'dogmatically' [δογματικῶς] at all but had meant only figuratively. For in the very sermon Luther delivered in Torgau he said that Christ's descent actually *did not take place physically,* since He remained in the grave during the three days. . . . The epigones have let that which was new and valuable in the old wineskins spoil and have dogmatized the monstrosities — even those which, in what Luther said, were nothing but popular figures." — Since the essential contents of the ninth article, which comprises only a half column in both parts of the *FC,* are to be found in the sentences quoted above, the charge of monstrousness made by Loofs can refer only to the formula which the article has in common with the Apostles' Creed. For Loofs cannot have been unaware of the fact that the concept *Höllenfahrt* is nothing more than a translation of *descensus ad inferos* (descent into hell). But when he emphasizes Luther's words "did not take place physically" by means of italics and thus creates the false impression that the Formula of Concord taught the opposite, this is poisoning of the worst kind.

24 In opposition to the ascension into a spatial heaven: *Bekenntnis der Niedersachsen.* — Tilemann Hesshusius, *Kurtze u. einfeltige Anleitung, wie die wahre gegenwertigkeit des Leibs und Bluts Jhesu Christi im Abentmal . . . zubeweisen sey,* Königsberg, 1569. — Jac. Andreä, *Esslinger Predigten,* Part II, 1579, pp. 32 ff. — Steph. Gerlach, *Assertio,* pp. 483, 486. — N. Selnecker, *Ex. Ord.* II, 322, 589. — Aegid. Hunnius, *Bestendige Widerlegung,* pp. 305, 480 ff. — On Brenz's doctrine of the ascension. which is identical with Luther's doctrine, cf. O. Fricke, op. cit.,

Luther's break with the spatial conceptions of heaven had the utmost significance for the history of the philosophy of life *(Weltanschauung)*. Consequently, special consideration will be given to this subject in another context (cf. *The Relativity of the World Picture*). Here, however, the doctrine of the Swiss received a severe blow so far as both the philosophy of life and Christology were concerned. From the Lutheran standpoint one must even say that the blow was mortal. For if they

52, 191. — Joh. Pappus, *Confessio fidei (Kommentar zur Augsb. Konf.)* Frankfurt, 1589, p. 71.

The *Grundfest* of the Philippists at Wittenberg *(Bl. Mff.)* and the *Ausschreiben* of the faculty in that city obviously speak against the unspatial conceptions of heaven and of the ascent into heaven. Likewise the opponents of A. Musculus (1576), who describe (p. 27) the heaven into which Christ ascended in the strongest words as "a definite place very far removed from this earth and the whole visible world" *(certum locum ab hac terra et toto conspicuo mundo remotissimum)* in which the man Christ "is contained" *(contineatur)* (54), while the heaven of the Lutheran opponents is designated (38) as "a placeless or ubiquitarian heaven that is everywhere or is nowhere" *(coelum utopicum aut ubiquitarium, quod sit ubique aut nusquam sit)*. — Melanchthon, too, had taught the spatiality of heaven and of the ascent into heaven (*CR* 7, 884). Cf. also the letters of Duke Christoph of Württemberg to Melanchthon and Melanchthon's evasive answer *(Anecdota Brentiana,* 1868, CCLXII and CCXIX) as well as the letters to the Elector of Saxony (CCLXIII).

Proofs adduced by the Reformed Church for the spatial conceptions of heaven and of the ascent into heaven are to be found under *The Sacrament of the Altar* and *The Relativity of the World Picture.*

In Lutheran territory the preachers in the seventeenth century are the first to retreat — perhaps in order to avoid being accused before their congregations of a lack of faithfulness to Scripture. E. g., Martin Moller, who, to be sure, was characterized by Salomon Gessner, of Wittenberg, as "a Calvinist and a Sacramentarian" (*Praxis Evangeliorum* II, 1601, 401 ff.). — Later, however, also dogmaticians like König, who, according to Calvinistic models, says that the ascent into heaven came to an end in the "airy and starry heaven" *(coelum aereum et siderium)* (*Theol. pos.*, p. 177). — But Calov still points out that the Biblical account speaks only of an ascent up to the clouds. He comments: "But the heaven which He occupied is not situated locally above the stars, as the Calvinists prattle. Scripture knows nothing about this heaven. No, it is a majestic and glorious heaven, which, like God Himself, is everywhere." *(Coelum vero, quod occupabat, non est localiter supra stellas, ut Calviniani nugantur, constitutum, quo de nihil Scriptura novit, sed coelum Majestaticum et gloriosum, quod ut Deus ipse ubique est.)* Ironically he then adds: "The mathematical calculation we leave to the Calvinists themselves, who have certainly busied themselves with this very noble science" *(Calculum mathematicum relinquimus ipsis Calvinianis in ea scientia nobilissima utique versatis)* (*Syst.* VII, 706 f.). — It is self-evident that a man like Phil. Nicolai rejects the massive picture of heaven. He attacks both the Calvinistic and the Roman view (*Teutsche Schriften* I, 217). — But although Nicolaus Hunnius, whose popular *Epitome Credendorum* was constantly reprinted — in German — during the seventeenth century, says, in the words of Acts 1:9, that Christ "betook Himself on high spatially" and that "a cloud took Him away before the eyes of the disciples," he then expresses the ascent into heaven as "a departure into the hidden glory of God" (pp. 220 f.). — An excellent illustration of the introduction of children into Luther's unspatial conceptions of heaven is to be found in the catechism of the Holstein pastor Franziskus Alardus (Wilster) of 1568 (Reu, *Quellen* III, 1, pp. 555, 47 ff.).

were unwilling to give up the doctrine of the resurrection — and they could not do so without surrendering their Biblical presuppositions — the separation of the two natures in Christ, which they taught, could be set forth only by according the exalted man a particular spatial dwelling place. If this were not done, the decisive bulwark against the Lutheran doctrine would fall. The Lutherans declared that since Christ was unconfined in every respect, He was also unconfined with respect to space. Had the Reformed Church agreed, it would no longer have had its supposed protection against the hated doctrine of the omnipresence of the entire God-man.

For this reason the Reformed Church clung to the account of the ascension and believed that by accusing Luther of making the ascension a mere demonstration it showed that his doctrine of salvation *(Heilslehre)* was wrong (cf. *The Sacrament of the Altar*). In his disputes with Zwingli, Luther had actually used the expression "token" *(Wahrzeichen)* for the ascension (WA 19, 491, 10). The context, however, is: "But what Christ's ascension into heaven and His sitting are, they do not know. It is not like climbing into a house by means of a ladder; but it means that He is above all creatures and in and outside all creatures. His bodily ascension, however, took place as a token."[25] Thus the concept of a token is by no means an evasion, as if Luther were unable to ascribe specific significance to the ascension. On the contrary, he looks upon it as the expression for the final act of liberation from the limitations to which the humiliation had subjected Christ within the created world. He ascended into heaven, that is, He is now "above all creatures, in and outside all creatures." Therefore what is true of God in general is true of Him. This is the beginning of the "sitting at the right hand of the Father" *(sessio ad dextram patris)*, that last but one of the acts of redemption listed in the Apostles' Creed. Early Lutheranism as a whole understood this to mean that Christ's connection with the majesty of God is inseparable and freed from the limitations imposed by the humiliation.[26]

If one leaves Christ's second coming out of account for the time being — it will be discussed in connection with eschatology (cf. *End of the World*) — the doctrine of the states *(Ständelehre)* has now been virtually exhausted. It is true that the Apostles' Creed led to the formulation of this doctrine, but it was not the only cause. A deeper necessity

[25] This in *A Treatise Concerning the Sacrament (Sermon von dem Sacrament)*, 1526 (WA 19, 491, 26 ff.), which was compiled by someone else but at this place agrees exactly with Rörer's transcript.

[26] *FC, SD* VIII, 27 f. — Joh. Gerhard, *Loci* III, 509 ff. — As early as the time of the *Lectures on Hebrews* Luther advocates the view of the "right hand of God" that is known from his writings on Holy Communion (p. 114, 5 ff.).

sprang from the need to bring the doctrine of the two natures into agreement with the Biblical picture of Christ. But this Biblical picture did not consist in the conception of a historical Jesus who had to be discovered behind the Gospels. No, it was the picture of Christ with which the Gospel is concerned in the sense of Paul, which – at least in this respect – is in agreement with the Johannine literature, the First Epistle of Peter, and the Epistle to the Hebrews. Thus it is the picture of faith, as it was derived from "Christ's work," which is the basis of faith. The early dogmaticians devoted to Christ's work a special section on the threefold office of Christ. In doing so they distinguished between the work of the historical Christ and that of the exalted Christ in all three "offices." The work of the historical Christ has been discussed in another context; that of the exalted Christ will be dealt with in connection with the doctrines of the church, the Sacraments, and the "kingdom of Christ." To be sure, this separation means that there is danger of losing sight of the identity of the historical Christ with the exalted Christ or of getting a false impression of it. The safeguards against this will be discussed above all in connection with the doctrine of Holy Communion.

Chapter Four

THE CHURCH

20. The Dogma of the Church [1]

For a time it could seem that the Reformation in Luther's sense meant the destruction or abolition of the church. Three acts seemed to give support to this thought. The first was the smashing of ecclesiastical authorities, finally of the authority of the pope and the general councils. In this way the existing form of the church had been affected. The answer of the church with which Luther was concerned exclusively at that time was the great anathema.[2] It would be conceivable to bring the decisive factors of the existing church into a new relationship with one another by means of a constitutional change and thus to supplant the old form with a new one – perhaps as was done and justified by the imperial publicists at the time of Ludwig the Bavarian (1314–47). But Luther consigns to the flames both the bull which threatens him with

[1] W. Löhe, *Drei Bücher v. d. Kirche,* 1845; 6th ed., 1928. — Franz Delitzsch, *Vier Bücher v. d. Kirche,* 1847. — Kliefoth, *Acht Bücher v. d. Kirche,* 1854. — Kahnis, *Christentum und Luthertum,* 1871. — K. Trebitz, *Das Wesen der Kirche nach h. Schr. u. Bekenntnis, insbesondere Art. VII der CA,* 1870. — A. Ritschl, *Die Entstehung der lutherischen Kirche, ZKG,* 1876 (quoted according to *Ges. Augs.* I, 1893). — Dieckhoff, *Die Stellung Luthers zur Kirche und ihrer Reformation in der Zeit vor dem Ablassstreit,* 1883. — R. Seeberg, *Der Begriff der Kirche* I, 1885. — H. v. Schubert, *Bekenntnisbildung u. Religionspolitik 1529—30,* 1910. — W. Walther, *Das Erbe der Reformation* IV, 1917. — K. Holl, *Ges. Aufs.* I, 288. — E. Vurpillot, *De la necessité d'une Doctrine Protestante de l'Eglise,* Montbeliard, 1926. — Elert, *D. Botschaft d. VII. Art. der A. K. Verhdl. d. XIX, Haupttag. d. Allg. Ev.-luth. Konf. 1927, and "Societas" bei Melanchthon, Festschr. f. L. Ihmels,* 1928. — J. L. Neve, "The Faith of Lutheranism," *Luth. Ch. Quarterly,* 1928. — F. Kattenbusch, *Die Doppelschichtigkeit in Luthers Kirchenbegriff,* 1928. — E. Kohlmeyer, *Die Bedeutung der Kirche f. Luther, ZKG,* 1928, pp. 466 ff. — P. Althaus, *Communio sanctorum. Die Gemeinde im lutherischen Kirchengedanken* I, 1929. — H. Sasse, *Kirche und Kirchen,* and Karl Winter, *D. Lehre von der Kirche in den ev.-luth. Bekenntnisschriften* in *Credo Ecclesiam, Festschr. f. Zöllner,* 1930.

[2] Cf. the statements 25—30 of the bull *Exsurge Domine,* Denzinger, nos. 765 ff.

excommunication and the book of canon law. This is the second act. At this moment he repudiates not only the existing form but any legally constituted form of the church. Thus he not only interferes to a deep-going extent with the existing social order, but he also deprives himself of the source from which all thoughts of reform had been nourished for more than a thousand years: the conception that behind or over the church there is an "objective," ideal order which can be realized approximately if not absolutely in the concrete organization of ecclesiastical factors. This costs him the sympathy of those among the friends of reform who think "legally." [3] Even the Wittenberg jurists thought that in their later teaching they had to ignore Luther's break with canon law. Luther's exhortation – *To the Christian Nobility* – to undertake a reorganization of ecclesiastical affairs could, of course, seem to be a revocation of this second act. For if there is still anything at all to be regulated ecclesiastically, there has to be a "church" in some sense. To be sure, this appeal also deprived the church of an element which up to this time seemed to be essential. The sacred character of the organization is profaned by the surrender to "worldly" powers. But what now seems to be left of the "church" is affected and destroyed by the third act, by the proclamation of the "priesthood of all believers," which abolishes on principle every organizational element without which the church cannot exist as a unit above the individual. The church is broken up into a mass of coordinated individuals who, at best, can be combined according to national or territorial or communal points of view.

Nevertheless, over against this the fact that Luther did not lose sight of "the church" at any stage of his theological development could still be explained by saying that from a practical standpoint it was impossible for him to escape it. For it always stands about him as a living organism; and through its veins he, the Doctor of Theology certificated by the church, guides the stream of his own theology to the most distant parts. It stands before him as the gigantic historical figure which speaks to

[3] Cf., e. g., the letter of the Basle jurist Zasius to Luther in the fall of 1520. Zasius disapproves of Luther's attitude at the Leipzig Disputation: "To shake the authority of so many generations that speak for the power of the Bishop of Rome and of so many saintly men is imprudent and dangerous unless it is done on the basis of the weightiest reasons. If our law had any authority in your estimation, it would be impossible for you to give any consideration to such a purpose. For we regard it as wrong to want to overturn a state of affairs that from time immemorial has been acknowledged as law." (According to R. Stintzing, *Ulrich Zasius, Beitr. z. Gesch. d. Rechtswiss. im Zeitalter d. Reformation, Basle,* 1857, pp. 225 f.) — Here, behind the existing concrete organization, common law appears as the most sacred thing of all. On no account dare it be infringed on so far as the principle is concerned.

him through the mouth of Augustine, Bernard, and many more of its teachers. But it also stands before him clothed in sacred dignity as the content of "God's Word." Therefore it cannot be overlooked. Yet Luther appears to be the man who destroyed the church. Consequently, there must be a gap here. For he must either actually set as his goal the complete destruction of the supraindividual unity of Christians, as one of whom he became what he is — but he never thought seriously of doing this — or he must prove that the impression that he destroyed the church is altogether false.

Taken all in all, however, this impression arises in the perspective of the impact of the Gospel *(evangelischer Ansatz)*. We have developed it in the background of "fear," conscience, the Law, the wrath of God. This is the atmosphere of loneliness. The judged person stands before God completely alone and lost. And this loneliness, this total feeling of abandonment, is essential to the experiencing of the judgment. Luther became conscious of it when he realized that here there are no helpers in distress — because there are no "saints" who would be able to give help. Yet there *are* saints. If there are, the reason for loneliness is eliminated — just as the reason for the feeling of being lost is eliminated in another way. But who and where are the saints? According to the canon of faith, Luther says later against Erasmus, only those are holy who are holy in accordance with the verdict of God. This means that I know of no one that he is holy. According to the canon of love, however, I call every baptized person a saint — at the risk of being disappointed when I do so. Both kinds of saints I call church (WA 18, 651, 25 — 652, 23). If I may be sure in faith that I belong among the saints by virtue of a divine verdict, I, as a believer, am no longer alone. I am in the "communion of saints" *(Gemeinde der Heiligen)* (WA 30 I, 190, 8). And the Creed *(Glaube)*, that is, the Apostles' Creed, calls this communion of saints the church (189, 6).

Thus Luther seems to come by the shortest way from the destruction of the organism of the church as it existed to a new organism or at least to a church as a supraindividual communion *(Gemeinsamkeit)*. But appearances are deceptive. For if this new unity were to be characterized and organized according to the canon of love, it would stand on a very shaky foundation — "because it is characteristic of love to be deceived" *(quia charitatis est falli)* (WA 18, 652, 4). To be sure, I can make the attempt to establish a common relationship *(Gemeinschaftsverhältnis)* with my love. In fact, the desire for communion *(Gemeinschaft)* can be fulfilled. On principle, however, the communion *(Gemeinschaft)* remains within the sphere of what is merely possible.

But if I cling to the canon of faith, there is, of course, a communion *(Gemeinsamkeit)* – a homogeneity in faith which includes a communion *(Gemeinsamkeit)* of the possessions of faith, yes, a communion which at one point also has an energizing center: Christ, who dwells in all believers, as has been developed earlier in connection with the doctrine of the "mystical union" *(unio mystica)* (cf. *The Mystical Union)*, where, in the writings of Brenz and Nicolai as well as in those of Luther, we constantly came across the "church" as the real seat of God's and Christ's indwelling. But this makes the supraindividual unity altogether otherworldly. For I do not know them, the saints. "No one sees who is holy or believes" (WA 6, 301, 2). In this sense the church always remains "invisible" (WA 7, 722, 6). "The church is hidden, the saints are concealed" *(Abscondita est Ecclesia, latent sancti)* (WA 18, 652, 23). Therefore this whole way of looking at the matter cannot bring much more to light than the historical way can: Luther, it is true, did not absolutely destroy the church as a supraindividual unity; but he spiritualized it in such a way that when one pursues these thoughts to their logical conclusion, it is eliminated as a formative energy of history.

It is understandable that these spiritualizing thoughts are uppermost in Luther's mind as he inveighs against the Roman Catholic conception of the church. In Leipzig he had let Eck make him an advocate of the Wyclif-Huss conception of the church: the church is "the whole body of the elect" *(praedestinatorum universitas)* (WA 2, 287, 35 ff.). When, as he had a right to do, he traced this definition back to Augustine, this calls to mind the relationship that actually exists. But in Augustine this spiritual concept is bound up with a totally different way of looking at the matter – a way which is decisively affected by the whole upheaval set in motion by Luther. And according to everything that was said about Luther's further position with regard to the thought of predestination, this definition could by no means solve the problem permanently in such a way that the fundamental thoughts of the doctrine of justification were preserved. On the contrary, from the doctrine of justification there follow the statements which emphasize faith, the believers, the Spirit, the "inwardness" *(Innerlichkeit)* and "spirituality" *(Geistlichkeit)* as elements of the church (WA 6, 296, 5 ff.; 303, 5; WA 7, 634, 23; 686, 34; 709, 26, etc.). And it is clear that when Luther contrasts the "spiritual communion" *(geistliche Gemeine)* with the "physical assembly" *(leibliche Versammlung)*, as he finds the church defined by his opponents, he wants the former to be regarded as the "natural, real, true, essential Christendom" *(naturlich, eygentlich, rechte, wesentliche Christenheit)* (WA 6, 296, 7). But it is just as clear that all the aforementioned elements are emphasized and grouped together primarily for the sake of the antithesis. The church can only be believed — it is not a piece of the world, "not bound to any place, person, or time" *(nit an yrgend eyne statt, person odder zeytt gehafftet).* It is made up of the believers — not of the prelates and the clergy as such. It "exists in the Spirit" *(steht im Geist)* — not in canon law. It is a spiritual — not a political — assembly (WA 7, 684, 20; 719, 26 ff.; 721, 30, etc.).

But it is the connection with the doctrine of justification which causes Luther to attack the problem of the church from a totally different side. It is true that faith includes the transcendency of its content. In this respect the believers as such are also an otherworldly people. But this transcendency consists in the fact that for us it is something "different" only in the Word spoken to us about Christ — something that we ourselves are not. Believers can never be separated from this Word in such a way that they would exist in pure "inwardness" *(Innerlichkeit).* If Christ is the Head of all believers, He is their Head only because and when He speaks to them in the Word. "The kingdom of Christ is governed by the firm and simple Word of the Gospel" *(Regnum Christi solido simplicique Evangelii verbo regitur)* (WA 7, 743, 7). "The entire life and substance of the church is in the Word of God" *(Tota vita et substantia Ecclesiae est in verbo dei)* (721, 12). It is not the believers who form the "substance" *(Substanz)* of the church; it is the Gospel. The Gospel is the real organizing principle of the church. It begets the believers, gathers them, and combines them into a supra-individual unity.[4] On the basis of this fundamental thought Luther, in his defense against Ambrosius Catharinus, develops a conception of the church which must be regarded as an exact anticipation of the seventh article of the Augsburg Confession (1521: 7, 705–778). The church is built on the Rock Christ alone. With Him it will remain in the Spirit (709, 25 ff., 33). "It will remain perpetually" *(perpetuo mansura),* says the Augsburg Confession. It is the "communion of saints" *(communio sanctorum)* (712, 39) — "congregation of saints" *(congregatio sanctorum)* says the confession. Or the "holy congregation of the believers" *(sancta fidelium congregatio)* (742, 34) — the "assembly of all believers" *(Versammlung aller Gläubigen).* How can it be recognized?

[4] How here, too, for Luther the concept of the Word of God concentrates on soteriology is to be seen in the fact that in a letter to Brenz (1530) he says about the "righteousness of faith" *(justitia fidei):* "For this passage is the chief point and the cornerstone, which alone begets, nourishes, builds, preserves, and defends the church of God; and without it the church of God cannot continue for a single hour" *(Hic locus enim caput et angularis lapis est, qui solus ecclesiam Dei gignit, nutrit, aedificat, servat, defendit, ac sine eo ecclesia Dei non potest una hora subsistere)* (Enders 8, 224, 51 ff.).

"For some visible sign must be given by which we are to be gathered into one body for the purpose of hearing the Word of God" *(oportet enim aliquod visibile signum dari, quo congregemur in unum ad audiendum verbum dei).* Such signs are Baptism, the bread, and, above all, the Gospel. "These are the three symbols, tokens, and marks of Christians. . . . For in these Christ wants us to be in agreement" *(Triae haec sunt Christianorum symbola, tessare et caracteres. . . . In his enim vult nos Christus concordare.)* (720, 32 ff.) – "And for true unity of the church it is enough to be in agreement concerning the teaching of the Gospel and the administration of the sacraments" *(Et ad veram unitatem ecclesiae satis est consentire de doctrina evangelii et administratione sacramentorum).* And here Luther, exactly like the Augsburg Confession, cites Eph. 4:5 f. as evidence (720, 39). But it is one of the fundamental thoughts of all Scripture that agreement with respect to ceremonies is not necessary. It is not likely that anyone will be able to maintain that here – in 1521 – Luther was misled by Melanchthon.

It is self-evident that among the three "tokens of the church" *(tessarae ecclesiae)* Luther grants pre-eminence to the Gospel.[5] Where the Gospel does not resound, there even Baptism and Holy Communion cannot stimulate the church. But this is true only of the *preaching* of the Gospel. "I am speaking, not about the written but about the spoken Gospel" *(Non de Evangelio scripto sed vocali loquor)* (721, 15). Here it becomes completely clear that Luther is actually seeking and finding the bridge from the spiritualizing "spiritual communion" *(geistliche Gemein)* to the "visible church" *(ecclesia visibilis)* in the sense of Melanchthon in his later period. For the former the private reading of Scripture would have to suffice – the latter needs the proclamation before many. But shortly after this he says that, conversely, he is by no means thinking only of the "physical assembly" *(leibliche Versammlung):* by the oral and public voice of the Gospel one can know "where the church is and the mystery of the kingdom of heaven" *(ubi sit Ecclesia et mysterium regni caelorum)* (722, 3; WA 1, 694, 17). And just as Melanchthon – in the Apology – wards off the thought that the Evan-

[5] 721, 9: "For before the bread and Baptism the Gospel is the sole, the most certain, and the noblest token of the church, since through the Gospel alone it is conceived, formed, nourished, begotten, brought up, fed, clothed, adorned, strengthened, armed, and preserved; in short, the whole life and essence of the church is in the Word of God, as Christ says: 'Man lives by every word that proceeds from the mouth of God'" *(Evangelium enim prae pane et Baptismo unicum, certissimum et nobilissimum Ecclesiae symbolum est, cum per solum Evangelium concipiatur, formetur, alatur, generetur, educetur, pascatur, vestiatur, ornetur, roboretur, armetur, servetur, breviter tota vita et substantia Ecclesiae est in verbo dei, sicut Christus dicit: In omni verbo, quod procedit de ore dei, vivit homo).* — Cf. WA 11, 108, 8 ff.

gelicals understood the church to be "a Platonic state" *(Platonicam civitatem)* (IV, 20), so Luther defends himself against Murner's accusation that he wants "to build a church as Plato wants to build a state, which would be nowhere" *(ein kirch bawen wie Plato ein statt, die nyndert were)* (WA 7, 683, 11). In his treatise *On the Papacy at Rome* (1520) he had already explained that the two kinds of church, the "real" *(eigentliche)* spiritual and the physical, should not be separated from each other (WA 6, 297, 3). Now he is certain that this separation is also impossible in the abstract or at least misleading, since the *same* church is discussed in both instances.

Accordingly, the statements in which "invisibility" is predicated of the church cannot mean that the church is a "pure communion in spirit" *(Geistesgemeinschaft)*, which is not visible because the spirit is not visible. To employ modern usage, it is a spiritual *(geistlich)* unity, not one that is mental *(geistig)*. But in this way one also finds the meaning which Luther attaches to the concept "spiritual." For him it is the expression for everything "that is done in the Word and in faith" *(das im Wort und Glauben gehet)*.[6] The church, which, as he demands again and again, should be believed, is "invisible" in exactly the same sense as all the other constituents of faith are invisible. It must be believed contrary to all appearances. Therefore it is not "invisible" in the Platonic-idealistic sense, but in the evangelical-realistic sense it is "hidden" *(abscondita)*. "Therefore in Psalm 9 the church is called *Almuth*, hidden, and the article of faith which believes in the holy catholic church confesses that the church is never visible anywhere and takes away from it every place and person" *(Inde Ecclesia psal. IX vocatur Almuth, abscondita, et articulus fidei credens Ecclesiam sanctam Catholicam confitetur, eam nusquam nunquam apparere aufertque ab ea omnem locum et personam)* (WA 7, 722, 8). When here and often[7] Luther says that the church is not bound to a definite place, to definite times, not even to "persons," this, of course, cannot mean that no persons at all

[6] WA 23, 189, 8: ". . . everything that our body does externally and physically: if God's Word is added and it is done through faith, it is and is called spiritually done. Therefore nothing can be so physical, fleshly, or external that it does not become spiritual when it is done in the Word and in faith. Therefore spiritual is nothing else than what is done in and through us through the spirit and faith, no matter whether the thing with which we busy ourselves is physical or spiritual. For the spirit is in the use, not in the object, whether it be seeing, hearing, speaking, touching, conduct, carrying, eating, drinking, or whatever it may be. For he who serves his neighbor and does so physically — this does not profit him. For the flesh avails nothing. But if he does it spiritually, that is, if his heart does it out of faith in God's Word, it is life and salvation." (1527.)

[7] Cf. the entire context, beginning on p. 719, 26.

belong to it. What he denies is that the church "is seen" *(apparere)* in these persons. I should not cling to places and times as such, that is, as objects of "perception" *(sensus)* and "experience" *(experientia)* when I look for the church — this is the sense of the polemics against Catharinus, Emser, and Murner. But just as the church is not without persons, it is also "not without a place and a body" *(non sine loco et corpore)* (720, 2). Here it is always only "spiritual" *(geistlich)*, that is, where and when the Word of God is preached and heard in faith. Therefore Luther says of the church exactly what he says of other constituents of faith: it is "hidden, lest the ungodly person see the glory of God" *(abscondita, ne impius gloriam videat Dei)*.[8] What can be seen *(das Augenscheinliche)* of the church is anything but "glory" *(gloria)*. "The Christian Church cannot be without suffering, persecution, and dying, yes, not without sin either" (WA 7, 684, 9). "The face of the church is the face of one who is a sinner, troubled, forsaken, dying, and full of distress" *(Facies ecclesiae est facies peccatricis, vexatae, desertae, morientis et contristatae)* (Erlangen edition *ex. lat.* 18, 213). Nevertheless, faith sees the opposite, the saint, the "glory of God" *(gloria dei)*, the "glory of the Christian brotherhood" *(gloria Christianae fraternitatis)*. Faith knows "that the love and the communion of Christ and all the saints are hidden, invisible, and spiritual" *(das die lieb und gemeynschafft Christi und aller heyligen verborgen, unsichtbar und geystlich gescheh)* — here the three concepts "invisible," "spiritual," and "hidden" *(abscondita)* just explained are obviously used synonymously — "and only a physical, visible, and external sign of them is given to us" *(und nur eyn leyplich, sichtlich, eusserlich zeychen derselben unss geben werde)* (WA 2, 752, 36). When he speaks here of the external sign, he means Holy Communion, just as in the passage quoted earlier he means the sacraments and the publicly proclaimed Word.

Whether the church in Luther's sense is also a sociological structure like other human "communities" *(Gemeinschaften)* need not be determined at this juncture. If it is, then this is certainly the case in spite of its spiritual character, just as it is a communion of saints in spite of the sinfulness of its members. If one wanted to look for the holiness of Christians — because of which their community *(Gemeinschaft)* is a "communion of saints" *(communio sanctorum)* — in their mutual love, let us say, this would not only turn upside down the concept of holiness as understood by the Reformation; it would also twist those clear-cut

[8] Thus in *De servo arbitrio*, WA 18, 651, 27. — But cf. also *De captivitate*, WA 6, 548, 14, where the "glory of the Christian brotherhood" *(gloria Christianae fraternitatis)* is contrasted with being bound to "places, days, and persons."

statements of Luther concerning the "tokens, symbols, and marks" *(tessarae, symbola et caracteres)* of the church into the opposite of what they say. It would mean the profanation of the church, and it would attach a wrong meaning to Luther's idea of the church. Even if one disregards Luther's conception of the sacraments at this point, still for him the "Word," as the organ and transmitter of the Holy Spirit, as the "life and substance of the church" *(vita et substantia ecclesiae)*, is, in the strict sense, a sacred element of the church.[9] As a word spoken by human beings it is a piece of the world – and yet not the word of the world, but God's Word. It not only consecrates the acts of Baptism and Holy Communion, but it also imparts a spiritual character to all "worldly things" with which it has to do *(umgeht)*. Accordingly, it gives them a character that is *not* worldly. By constantly re-creating and preserving the church it impresses on it a sacred character. Faith's knowledge concerning the divine nature of the church, which is *in* the world even though it is not *of* the world, is discernible in all the statements made by Luther, even where – and precisely where – he calls the church the "communion of saints" *(communio sanctorum)*. In his use – the use which he prefers – of the concept "saints" *(sancti)* for the members of the church one discerns something of the humble pride of the "church triumphant" *(ecclesia triumphans)*, which, of course, is the "church triumphant" *(ecclesia triumphans)* only as the "church militant" *(ecclesia militans)*, as the church which has "the face of a sinner" *(facies peccatricis)*. "How could one ascend higher than to become a member of Christendom, which is queen and empress above heaven and earth, which speaks the Word and is preserved, and I come into such a communion when I become a Christian through faith?" *(Wie kund einer hoher kommen, quam quod fit membrum Christianitatis, quae est regina et keyserin uber himel und erden, quae dicit verbum und ist gehalten et in talem communionem venio, quando fio Christianus per fidem?)* (WA 28, 182, 11). Even Luther is unable and unwilling to get away from the joyful realization of the catholicity of the church. Like his opponents, he calls it the "universal church" *(universalis ecclesia)*. To be sure, he conceives of it as the "communion of saints" *(communio sanctorum)*, which is diametrically opposed to the hierarchical thought of universality (WA 6, 505, 31; 606, 34). He, too, believes that when Christ speaks about the church in Matt. 16, He is speaking "about holy things" *(de rebus sanctis)* (WA 7, 719, 3). He even calls the cemetery "an

[9] Kohlmeyer says, not without good reason, that in Luther it took the place of the medieval sacraments, that it is a "spiritualized sacrament" *(vergeistigtes Sakrament)*, op. cit., pp. 473 ff.

honorable, yes, almost a holy place, so that one could walk there with fear and all reverence, because doubtless some saints are lying there" (WA 23, 375, 31).[10]

When the Lutheran Church was formed, there were elements at work in connection with which one can ask whether they are compatible with Luther's idea of the church. But when the dogma of the church was formulated, Luther's basic convictions were never lost sight of in the course of the framing of the confessions. In its first article – "On the Church" – the *Ansbach Counsel* of 1524 really takes everything from Luther's great polemical writings. Purely linguistically, it points out, "church" *(ecclesia)* is to be rendered with the Latin *concio,* in German with "assembly or communion" *(Versammlung oder Gemein).* In this general sense the "councils and physical assemblies" can also be called church. "In reality, and speaking according to what Scripture says" *(Aygentlich und nach inhalt der schrifft zu reden),* it is the number of those whom God chose in eternity for redemption through Christ *(zur Erlösung durch Christum von ewigkait hat fürgenommen),* according to Eph. 1. Yet no further weight is attached to the thought of predestination as such, for there is the following definition: "The Christian Church is the multitude or assembly of all who believe in Christ, who live and will continue to live in unity of spirit, faith, hope, and love. And because of this unity the believers are called a communion of saints." This church is born of the living Word of God. It cannot err, because Christ has promised to be with it until the end of the world. He teaches and governs it through His Word and His Spirit. It is spiritual and invisible, because no one knows "who are actually members of the Christian church *(welche von der Christlichen kirchen aygentlich sind).* Therefore it is an "article of faith" *(Artickel des Glaubens).* It is – as is set forth further with words and quotations from Scripture which Luther had used above all in his writings against Emser and Catharinus – "bound neither to a person, place, time nor any kind of external thing" *(weder an person, stat, zeyt noch eynicherley eusserliche ding gebunden).* "Although it cannot exist or live without these, yet it must not be viewed or judged according to them" *(Wiewol sy on die selben nit sein noch leben kan, so sol sy doch nach den selben nit geacht oder geurteilt werden).* Therefore it cannot be equated either with the Roman Church or with the councils. The words of Christ in Matt. 16 state in particular "that Christ meant and promised to build His holy general church, not on Peter or anyone else, but on Himself and on St. Peter's public confession of Christ, which not flesh and blood but God the heavenly Father

[10] Enders 10, 144, 23 ff.; 14, 182, 20. WA 31 I, 232, 34 ff.

inspired in him and told him" *(das Christus sein heylige gemaine Kirchen nit auff Petrum oder yemant anders sunder auff sich selbs und auff sant Peters offentliche bekantnuss von Christo, die jm nit fleysch und plut, sunder Got der hymlisch vater eingeben und gesagt, zu bawen gemaint und versprochen hat) (Fränkische Bekenntnisse,* pp. 192 f.). Strictly speaking, the emphasis on the public nature of Peter's confession leads beyond the definition of the "invisible" church. Furthermore, when Christ's words in Matt. 18 are explained, it must be established that they refer to "the external, physical, and particular church or assembly" *(von der eusserlichen, leyblichen und sunderlichen kirchen oder versammlung).* For Christ's demand "to point out the sin" *(die sündt an zuzaygen)* can be fulfilled only before a "particular" *(sunderlichen),* that is, a small, circle, which is known externally as a church (p. 191). It almost seems that here the physical church and the church which "is assembled only in unity of faith" *(allein in eynigkeit des glaubens versamlet ist)* should be contrasted as a local congregation *(Ortsgemeinde)* and the "church in general" *(allgemeine Kirche)* are contrasted.

The whole *Ansbach Counsel* — as was ordered — is oriented toward the opposite of the traditional conception of church affairs. Therefore one can understand why, like Luther's polemical writings, it places special emphasis on the spiritual aspect. According to the wording, the "external, physical" *(äussere, leibliche)* church and the church of faith are separated from each other in a manner that is almost abrupt. Nevertheless, one senses an internal relationship. This is shown by what is said about the feeding of Christ's sheep, about the appointment of "pastors" *(Seelsorger)* (p. 234), about the obligation of the "Christian congregations" *(Christlichen gemaynen)* — therefore not only of individual believers — to "examine and verify" *(examinieren und probieren)* every doctrine (p. 231), and about the administration of the sacraments. To be sure, Luther's thought about the "symbols, tokens, and marks" *(symbola, tessarae et caracteres)* of the church, which in his writings have not only heuristic but constitutive significance, is not expressed directly; but at the very beginning it is stated that the church is built and founded on the Gospel and that the Gospel is not built and founded on the church (p. 184). And that this is meant in a sense which is not merely historical can be seen from the later statement that the Christian church "is born of the living Word of God" *(wird geborn aus dem lebendigen Wort gots)* (p. 188). The same thing is stated in the twenty-three *Frageartikel* of Nürnberg of the year 1528 (p. 469). And in the opinion which Johann Beham, pastor in Bayreuth, handed down in 1530 the realization that there is a functional connection is added to what is said about the causal relationship: "Where there is such a Christian Church, there is forgiveness of all sins; for such a Christian assembly is the kingdom of Christ in which He takes pride before Pilate . . . a spiritual kingdom of grace and true indulgence, which is distributed through the holy sacraments, also through sundry passages of comfort in the whole Gospel" (p. 571). Later the Hungarian *Confessio montana* expressed the divine dynamic of the concrete church boldly but correctly when it defined the church as "the visible assembly of those who hear, believe, and embrace the pure and uncorrupted doctrine of the Gospel and use the sacraments" *(coetus visibilis audientium, credentium et amplectentium puram et incorruptam doctrinam Evangelii et utentium Sacramentis)* and added: "in which assembly God works through the ministry and regenerates many to eternal life, to which in this life are joined many who have not been born again but nevertheless are in agreement with respect to doctrine" *(in quo coetu Deus per ministerium est efficax et multos ad vitam aeternam regenerat, cui in hac vita adjuncti sunt multi non renati, sed tamen de doctrina consentientes)* (Art. 8). Luther's conception of the "communion of saints" *(communio sanctorum)* is expressed from another angle when the *Copenhagen Articles* define the "holy church" as the congregation "of all men who are justified" *(aller gerechtfertigten Menschen)*.[11] The definition which states that the church is made up of those who are predestinated now recedes. Later it vanishes completely.[12]

Although the *Marburg Articles* say nothing about the church, the twelfth article of the *Schwabach Articles* already contains all the elements of the seventh article of the Augsburg Confession.[13] It is different

[11] *Malmö-Beretningen (Copenhagen Articles)*, p. 22. Erik Pontoppidan's translation — ". . . which is the congregation of all righteous men" — made known by Jörgensen (*NKZ*, 1930, p. 376), is decidedly erroneous!

[12] In his opinion of 1530 Caspar Löner (Hof), like the *Counsel of Ansbach* of 1524, still proceeds from Eph. 1 and says accordingly: "All elect true servants of God are the universal Christian church. . . ." (Gussmann, *Quellen* I, 2, p. 97.) Where later the church is still designated as the congregation of the elect, the passage in Ephesians is always the source. — U. Rhegius, *Loci* (ed. Freder), 1545, 176 b, places side by side "the certain number of the elect" *(certus numerus electorum)* and "the multitude of those who have been baptized" *(multitudo baptizatorum)* (177). — Hafenreffer even gives proof that "the assembly of the elect" *(coetus electorum)* is not only invisible but also visible: "for the elect are visible insofar as they dwell in the external, visible assembly of the church and make use of the external ministry of the Word and the sacraments" *(nam visibiles sunt electi, quatenus in externo visibili coetu ecclesiae versantur, atque externo verbi et sacramentorum utuntur ministerio)* (Loci, 496). — The reasons for the subsequent withdrawal are given in Joh. Gerhard, *Loci* XI, 13.

[13] "That there is no doubt that there remains and is on earth a Holy Christian Church till the end of the world, as Christ says . . . this church is nothing other

from this one because it proceeds from Christ's promise to be present (Matt. 28), and it is preferable because in this matter it also expresses the Christocentric emphasis contained in the evangelical dogma. Its concluding statement shows that what is said in the Augsburg Confession – for which, as was well known, it served as a pattern – about the elements necessary for "unity of the church" has its origin in Luther's assertions that the church is not bound to place, person, and time.[14] The characterization of those who believe in Christ as those who "believe and teach the aforementioned articles and statements" has been called "a narrowing of the concept 'church' which certainly departs emphatically from the basic reformational thoughts of Luther." [15] These words thus criticized actually bring to the fore an element of the idea of the church which took on special significance for its further development. It is the element of "pure doctrine" in the sense of later orthodoxy.

But before it can be fully appreciated, one must call attention once again to the fact that the seventh article of the Augsburg Confession does not lead beyond Luther's view as he developed it against Catharinus. That the eighth article is to be an integral part of the doctrine of the church can be seen from what Melanchthon sets forth in the Apology.[16] The anti-Donatistic statements it contains – that false Christians and hypocrites are always found in the church and that Word and sacraments are efficacious even when administered by those who are not pious – also corresponds to Luther's conviction.[17] It could not be

than the believers in Christ, who believe and teach the aforementioned articles and statements, and are persecuted and martyred because of them in the world; for where the Gospel is proclaimed and the sacraments are used rightly, there the Holy Christian Church is; and it is not bound by laws and external splendor to place and time, to person or appearance" (WA 30 III, 89 f.).

[14] The opinion advocated by Kolde (*Textausg. d. Augsb. Konf.*, 2d ed., pp. 37 f., and *Die älteste Redaktion*, p. 51) that Art. VII must really have the heading "On the Unity of the Church" *(De unitate ecclesiae)* is not in accord with the facts. His opinion is contradicted by the complete objective agreement of the seventh article of the Augsburg Confession with the twelfth article of the *Schwabach Articles*, where as yet not a single word is said about oneness or unity. Only the newly added emphasis which the Augsburg Confession, not the entire twelfth article, places on unity aims at the rejection of the charge indirectly made in the announcement of the diet that unity was being destroyed.

[15] By the editor of the *Schwabach Articles* in WA (30 III, 85). Similarly, Albr. Ritschl, *Ges. Aufs.* I, 177.

[16] The misunderstanding of the *Confutatio Pontificia*, as though this had not been the opinion of the evangelicals, would have been prevented if the eighth article had never been separated from the seventh, as was the case in the earliest version of the Augsburg Confession.

[17] For the time before 1530 cf. perhaps WA 1, 697 (9, 188); WA 17 II, 124; WA 14, 190 f.

otherwise if, when treating of the "communion of saints" *(communio sanctorum)* and of the congregation, which has the Word and the sacraments as its "marks" *(caracteres)*, the same church is meant in both instances. What Melanchthon sets forth in the Apology concerning the church is, in the main, merely a sharper continuation of the polemics against the externally valid *(äusserlich-rechtlich)* view of the nature of the church – but also against the Donatists (among whom even Wyclif is here included). Three points, however, are worthy of note. In the first place, the conclusion contains a warning against "godless teachers" *(impii doctores)* (IV, 48). That the godlessness *(Unfrömmigkeit)* of these teachers is not meant to refer to their personal quality can be seen from the sharp rejection of Donatism. Therefore the translation reads: "false teachers." Melanchthon demands that these "must be abandoned" *(deserendi sunt)*. Thus he demands separation for the sake of doctrine. This is indirectly confirmed when, in the second place, in connection with the express discussion of the possible reasons for separation, he opposes only those who have given rise to schisms because of the worldly property of priests (IV, 49 f.). In the third place, however, one must note that here Melanchthon's conception of association *(Sozietätsbegriff)* crops up. The church, he says, is not "an association of external things and rites as are other states, but it is principally an association of faith and the Holy Spirit in the hearts, which nevertheless has external marks" *(societas externarum rerum ac rituum sicut aliae politiae, sed principaliter est societas fidei et Spir. S. in cordibus, quae tamen habet externas notas)* (IV, 5). Even though a parallelism to political structures is rejected, the concept "association" *(societas)* makes the church analogous to them. And if here only the "association in spirit" *(Verbundenheit im Geiste)* seems to be thought of, yet shortly after this the same thing is expressed as follows: "the association of the same Gospel or doctrine and the same Holy Spirit" *(societas eiusdem evangelii seu doctrinae et eiusdem Spiritus Sancti)* (8). Accordingly, even at that time Melanchthon looked upon "doctrine" and the sacraments not only – as it could seem in view of *CA* VII – as "marks" *(notae)* of the church and its unity but also as means of binding together the members of the church in a sociological respect. This is confirmed by that other statement that the "godless teachers must be abandoned" *(impii doctores deserendi)*.

Then, however, those critical words in the *Schwabach Articles* take on totally different importance. There the believers are designated as those who "believe and teach the aforementioned articles and statements." Naturally, the same thing is true of this way of putting it that was said earlier – in *CA* I – of the connection of the "must be believed" *(credendum esse)* with the decree promulgated at Nicaea. The expression as such cannot be sanctioned, because it makes faith appear to be the acceptance of a number of doctrines. But the fifth and sixth of the *Schwabach Articles* prove that this is not at all what is meant. Still the concept "teaching" remains in the twelfth article. That this is not a mere error in expression either can be seen from the further characterization of the believers: ". . . for this they will be persecuted and tormented in the world." Persecution by the world can take place only when faith becomes known, therefore when it emerges from the stage of "invisibility." But the twelfth article mentions only one thing that can be interpreted in this way: the "teaching," which is then divided into the elements of the preaching of the Gospel and the right use of the sacraments. "The aforementioned articles," that is, articles one to eleven of the *Schwabach Articles,* are designated here altogether unequivocally as the content of the doctrine necessary for faith and essential to the church. In the matter of content they correspond to, say, articles one to six, nine to eleven, and article thirteen of the Augsburg Confession. Concerning doctrine one has every right to say that, unlike faith, its content is made up of a series of articles and statements.

From the fact that there is no related formula in the seventh article of the Augsburg Confession, Albrecht Ritschl concluded that Melanchthon purposely refrained from taking it over from the original draft because at that time he did not yet confuse the "purely religious" *(rein religiöse)* proclamation of the Gospel with an understanding of dogmatics. This confusion, said Ritschl, did not become noticeable until after 1537. To be sure, from this time on Melanchthon elevated pure doctrine, the "theological concept of teaching" *(theologischer Lehrbegriff)* or the "true articles of faith" *(rechte Glaubensartikel),* more and more to the point where they were the chief mark of the true church and in this way transferred the church itself out of the ideality that is meant in *CA* VII into the empirical world. But this shifting, said Ritschl (op. cit., pp. 186 ff.), signified a departure from the concept "church" as defined in the main evangelical confession, in which the "doctrine of the Gospel" *(doctrina E v a n g e l i i),* not the — theologically standardized — "*doctrine* of the Gospel" *(d o c t r i n a Evangelii),* is called the mark of the church. Since here others, too, have found the critical point at which the failure of Lutheranism to develop in the direction of doctrinal orthodoxy is said to have begun, the question of the significance of "doctrine" in the main evangelical confession must be examined somewhat more closely.

The proof adduced by Ritschl is ill-founded in that he himself must concede "that in semiprivate statements of Melanchthon one notices very soon the inaccuracy that he is fond of making the articles of faith the immediate subject of preaching in place of the Word of God or the Gospel." [18] Since the best sources actually prove that this was true at the time of the Diet of Augsburg, it follows that Melanchthon's failure to include the incriminated formula of the *Schwabach Articles* in *CA* VII can by no means be accounted for by stating that he considered it to be incompatible with the concept "church" which he developed at that time in *CA* VII. In the second place, the *Schwabach Articles* are themselves a product of negotiations in which the Wittenberg theologians co-operated to a decisive extent. Luther, it is true, denied that he was the sole author; but in the preface he wrote when the articles were printed, he conceded his coauthorship (WA 30 III, 194, 19). True, it cannot be proved that he wrote the questionable formula in the twelfth article. Perhaps it is even unlikely that he did so. If Luther was not the author, then it was written by Melanchthon or by one of the other collaborators from Wittenberg or Franconia.[19] But Luther's and Melanchthon's coresponsibility for it consists by no means only in this, that they did not object when the so-called *Schwabach Articles* were formulated and that later Luther published them with his own preface. On the contrary, this coresponsibility also lies – and lies primarily – in the fact that they, too, acceded to the demand to compile all the doctrinal articles or to assist those who did so. For it was their avowed purpose to bring about a basis of church unity *(Gemeinsamkeit)* for the proposed political alliance between Saxony and Brandenburg-Ansbach. The Saxon reply to the challenge of Margrave George in the summer of 1529 declares that "as Margrave George of Brandenburg has intended, it is necessary first of all to confess to one another the articles on which the unity of faith and Christianity under discussion rests" *(wil nit sein, wie Markgraf Jorg von Brandenburg bedacht hat, die artickel, darauf berurte aynigkait des glaubens und christenthumbs rughet, erstlich gegeneinander zu bekennen)*.[20] And in the margrave's reply we read: "When anyone departs from the articles accepted, and this is discovered, that he, if he

[18] Op. cit., p. 191. For this Ritschl quotes even *CR* 2, 182, 282, 298.

[19] H. v. Schubert (op. cit., pp. 43 ff.) considers it a product of the Saxons. Since "unlearned" (secular) councilors had a hand in drawing up the writing — provided that v. Schubert's reasoning is correct — the formula in question could have been written even by one of them. Perhaps it could be credited to Brück in particular. Cf. Brück's objection to association with the Zwinglian positions of November and December 1529. Reprinted by v. Schubert, pp. 144 ff., especially p. 148. But this by no means alters the state of affairs outlined above.

[20] Quoted by v. Schubert, p. 49. On the historical state of affairs cf. Schornbaum, *Zur Politik des Markgrafen Georg*, 1906, pp. 84 ff.

refuses to listen to reason and persists in his defection, shall not be a party to this agreement" *(Wo ainer von den bekanten artickeln abfallen und desselbigen erfunden, das er, wo er sich nit weisen lassen und uff seinem abfall verharren ward, dieses verstantnus nit teilhaftig sein soll).*[21] With respect to church politics this is the same view that Melanchthon expressed in the Apology in the more general formula that "godless teachers must be abandoned" *(impii doctores deserendi).*[22] When Saxony, on the other hand, rejected the establishment of a uniform ritual *(Kirchenordnung),* the two principles contained in the seventh article of the Augsburg Confession (unity in doctrine but freedom in external matters) were, therefore, operative for the Saxon-Franconian alliance. But this unity in doctrine was expressly formulated in the so-called *Schwabach Articles,* and with the cooperation of the Wittenberg reformers. Accordingly, the questionable words in the twelfth of the *Schwabach Articles* are not a foreign substance *(Fremdkörper);* they correspond to the total view of the church on which these articles are based.

If at this time Melanchthon took part in the doctrinal discussions for the purpose of bringing about church unity *(Gemeinsamkeit)* – the *Franconian Confessions,* now published, as well as the discussions in Copenhagen in 1530 show that here he was merely in the current of something that had to take place – it is misleading at the very outset to look for a reason why he was said to have disavowed the basic concept of the church in the Augsburg Confession. On the contrary, it is an elementary demand of historical method to interpret his statements in the Augsburg Confession in the light of his positive general attitude with respect to this question. In his own preface – even though this preface was not accepted – he explains at the end: "Now we shall speak of doctrine and first enumerate all the principal articles of faith, from which His Imperial Majesty can conclude that the Elector of Saxony permits nothing unchristian to be preached in his domain but has adhered with all diligence to the common, pure, Christian faith."[23] There-

[21] V. Schubert, p. 50. Even if these words, as v. Schubert supposes, do not yet refer to the already completed *Schwabach Articles,* they point out the principles that carried weight among the participants during the months in question.

[22] Cf. Brück's objection, which has been mentioned — the objection that brings purely religious reasons to bear for excluding the Swiss because of their doctrine of Holy Communion: "For as long as they stand up for the article against their conscience and Christ's plain words, they do not absolve the other articles of disloyalty; for all the same they are disloyal in that article and should be considered disloyal according to the aforementioned words of St. Paul . . ." (op. cit., p. 148).

[23] According to Baumgartner's translation for the Council of Nürnberg (p. 11) — the translation published by Kolde (*Die älteste Redaktion der Augsb. Konf.,* 1906, pp. 4 ff.).

fore the articles that follow propose to prove what is certain for other reasons too: that in the Electorate of Saxony "doctrine" corresponds to the "common" *(gemein)* faith of Christians. And after all twenty-one articles of the first part have been introduced by pointing out that they are the content of doctrine, it is established at the conclusion of the twenty-first article concerning the "sum of the doctrine" *(Summa der Lehre)* that it contains nothing "that is at variance with Scripture or with the catholic church or with the Roman Church, so far as what is known from the writers" *(quod discrepet a scripturis vel ab ecclesia catholica vel ab ecclesia romana, quatenus ex scriptoribus nota est).* It is impossible to express more sharply than is done in the introductory statement and in this concluding statement that the doctrinal articles of the Augsburg Confession propose to formulate just what, according to the seventh article, true church unity requires, namely, "agreement with respect to doctrine" *(consensus de doctrina).* Only the partner with whom there is the desire to be in agreement is no longer the Margrave of Brandenburg; it is the "catholic church" *(ecclesia catholica).*

But that Melanchthon was by no means willing or able to let a general promise to preach the Gospel be what was required to establish agreement – as Ritschl declared – can be seen from the fact that although his first draft of the seventh article contained a formula that could be interpreted in this way, he gave an exact definition of this formula in the final version. The first draft states that it is "sufficient for unity of the church to reach agreement with regard to the Gospel and the sacraments" *(zu einickeit der kirchen genug, das man des evangeliums und der sakrament halben uberein kom)* (Baumgartner, p. 13). Accordingly, in the preceding definition of the church it is stated that the church is "an assembly of the saints in which the Gospel is preached and the sacraments are administered" *(ein versammlung der heiligen, darin das evangelium gepredigt und die sacrament gereicht werden).* In the final version a "rightly" *(recte)* is added, in the first place, to "teaching" *(docere)* and "administering" *(administrare);* in the second place, the word "true" *(vera)* is added to the concept "unity" *(unitas).* It is not until these words are added that the entire enumeration of the doctrinal articles in the Augsburg Confession becomes significant. Even the opponents claimed that their doctrine "agreed with the Gospel" *(cum evangelio consentire).*[24] Therefore it was important that – as this

[24] Thus in the prolog to the *Confutatio Pontificia.* — Cf. also *Trid. Sessio* IV: ". . . the synod . . . placing this perpetually before its eyes, in order that after the errors have been removed, the purity itself of the Gospel may be preserved in the church" (*. . . Synodus . . . hoc sibi perpetuo ante oculos proponens, ut sublatis erroribus puritas ipsa Evangelii in ecclesia conservetur*) (Denzinger, p. 261).

was expressed in a council meeting in Nürnberg on May 7, 1530 – "the holy Gospel . . . should be proclaimed freely and purely as it has been accepted and expounded by the doctrines of the Holy Christian Church."[25] No mere reciting of the Gospel contained in Holy Scripture gives one assurance with regard to the basis of church unity; this must be done by the "exposition" *(Auslegung)*, the understanding of the Gospel which can be recognized when the doctrine of the church is examined. This is what the aforementioned additions – "rightly" *(recte)* and "true" *(vera)* – express. And the Augsburg Confession formulates what the evangelicals mean by the right doctrine of the Gospel.

Thus the Augsburg Confession itself proposed to set up the standard for what constitutes the right doctrine of the Gospel and accordingly to be a bond of unity for all those whom the *right* preaching of the Gospel has brought together into the *true* unity of the church. That Luther, too, knew many points which he regarded as essential for the doctrine of the church can be seen from his *Exhortation to the Clergy*, which was issued from the Feste Coburg at this same time. Here he enumerates "the points that must be treated in the true Christian Church – the points with which we are concerned" *(die stuck so nottig sind ynn der rechten Christlichen kirchen zu handeln, da wir mit umb gehen)* (WA 30 II, 345). And why should he not have set store by "pure" doctrine when, after all, his whole battle *in the church* was a *theological* battle? Whether the formulation in the Augsburg Confession was successful or unsuccessful – in any case it remains the great accomplishment of Melanchthon and those who told him what to do, the great accomplishment of those who on June 25, 1530, made this theological work their "confession." This confession is not a revelation of God. But it proposes to be an answer – an answer given by those who heard the Gospel in faith and professed the "doctrine" that was proclaimed among them. Things could have taken an entirely different turn. The urging of the Landgrave of Hessia in the preceding years, like that of the Swiss, aimed at a political alliance of the evangelicals. Such a purely political alliance of "Protestantism as a whole" *(Gesamtprotestantismus)* might, at the moment, have had greater practical success. But this would have disappeared together with the political constellation under which it was born. An electoral-Saxon, a landgrave-Hessian, a margrave-Ansbach, a Reutling, a Henneberg church would have remained. But it was the great success of the formulation of a confession that a supraterritorial

[25] Gussmann, *Quellen* I, 2, p. 208. — Bugenhagen's *Braunschweiger Kirchenordnung* of 1528 (ed. by H. Lietzmann, p. 38) demands that the superattendant see to it "that the doctrine of Christ remain pure among us."

unity of the evangelicals was brought into being as a dynamic in the church – not as the "invisible church" *(ecclesia invisibilis)*. As unity in the matter of confession this unity was ideal. Brought into being by means of the same preaching of the Gospel – "for only doctrine gives birth to and preserves the church" *(dan allein aus der leer wird die christlich kirch geboren und erhalten)*, as Melanchthon wrote in the preface which was not accepted – and recognized by reason of the unity *(Gemeinsamkeit)* of its profession of the "pure doctrine of the Gospel" *(pura evangelii doctrina)* (Apology IV, 5). It is not a uniform ethos, not unity in administration, and, least of all, not a common political policy that shows the unity which alone is in keeping with the nature of the church; it is unity in doctrine. "The manifest truth must make us one, not obstinacy" *(Es muss unns die offentliche warheit eynis machen unnd nit die eygensinnigckeit)*, Luther had said in what he wrote to the nobility (WA 6, 455, 14).[26] The church that is one in "manifest truth" *(öffentliche Wahrheit)* – this is the church which Luther did not destroy but reformed.

21. Catholicity

The claim of the Augsburg Confession that it contained nothing that deviated from the catholic church[1] was certainly founded on reasons which, first of all, were practical and apologetic. Here it was a matter of the evidence found in "evangelical doctrine" *(doctrina evangelica)*, which, since the imperial edict of 380 and together with "apostolic instruction" *(apostolica disciplina)*, was regarded as the prerequisite of the "name 'catholic Christians'" *(nomen Christianorum Catholicorum)*.[2]

[26] Cf. from a later time (1535): "The catholic church is more than holy enough if it is unanimous in faith and doctrine; necessity itself compels customs and forms to vary" *(Abunde satis sancta est ecclesia catholica, si fide et doctrina sit unanimis, mores et ritus ipsa necessitas cogit esse diversos)* (Enders 10, 144, 23). — This is exactly *CA* VII!

[1] The *Augustana-Sonderheft* of *Hochkirche*, 1930, pp. 169 ff., contains Fr. Heiler's detailed investigation of this claim and of the criticism to which it was subjected.

[2] The Justinian *Codex jur. civ.* begins with this edict: "It is our will that all the peoples which the realm of our clemency rules remain in the kind of religion of which the religion made known up to this time by the divine apostle Peter himself declares that he handed it down to the Romans . . . that is, that according to the apostolic instruction and the evangelical doctrine of the Father and the Son and the Holy Spirit, we should believe in one Deity under like majesty and under the blessed Trinity. Those who comply with this law we command to take the name 'catholic Christians' . . ." *(Cunctos populos, quos Clementiae nostrae regit imperium, in tali volumus religione versari quam divum Petrum Apostolum tradidisse Romanis, religio usque adhuc ab ipso insinuata declarat . . . hoc est, ut secundum Apostolicam disciplinam Evangelicamque doctrinam Patris et Filii et Spir. S. unam*

In accordance with the belief that agreement in doctrine is the mark of catholicity, Brenz signed the Augsburg Confession and the Apology at the convention at Smalcald (1537). He appended the following note: "Unimportant as I am, I conclude that all these things are in agreement with Holy Scripture and with the opinion of the true and genuine catholic church" *(Pro mediocritate mea judico haec omnia convenire cum sacra scriptura et cum sententia verae* καὶ γνησίης *catholicae ecclesiae).* But it is evident in the Apology that value is attached to the mark of catholicity per se. In the German translation we read that the opponents boasted "of being the Christian church and believe what the 'catholic' *(catholica),* universal *(gemeinsame)* church believes. But here, in our cause and in our most important article, Peter, the apostle, states that there is also a 'catholic' *(catholica),* universal *(gemeine)* church when he says: 'To Jesus all the prophets bear witness that we obtain forgiveness of sin through His name.'" Such a consensus of all the prophets must also "be a decree, a voice, and a unanimously emphatic decision of the universal, catholic, Christian, holy church and justly be regarded as such" (V, 66 f.). What does the word "catholic" mean? This seems to be the matter at issue here. But that catholicity *(das Katholische)* per se is a mark of the church is admitted indirectly even by the evangelicals. With regard to this there has never been a different opinion in Lutheranism. Luther himself never gave up the idea of the universality of the church. At a critical time he attached importance to the fact that he had never done violence to the "pure and catholic faith" *(synceram et catholicam fidem)* (WA 5, 597, 28; 8, 96, 11). If he does not use the expression "catholic" often, this is in accord with his desire to express for "simple folk" *(die Einfältigen)* the reality of the church as simply as possible in their own language. For the same reason he would like to replace the expression "church" with a German word and designate the church as "a Christian communion or assembly, best and clearest of all, as 'a holy Christendom'" *(ein christlich gemein odder samlung, aufs aller beste und klarste 'ein heilige Christenheit' bezeichen)* (WA 30 I, 189, 6 ff.). Conversely, however, he strengthens the expression "a Christian, holy people" *(ein christlich heilig Volk)* with the appended statement: "This is the holy and catholic church" *(Das ist sancta et catholica ecclesia)* (WA 50, 625, 15). Even in his *Wider Hans Worst* (1541), in which he points out the irreconcilable, confessional contrast in the sharpest possible manner, he demands recognition of the fact that we have

deitatem sub pari majestate et sub pia Trinitate credamus. Hanc legem sequentes Christianorum Catholicorum nomen jubemus amplecti. . . .) All the rest shall "bear the infamy of heretical dogma" *(haeretici dogmatis infamiam sustinere).*

the same Baptism that the old (as we read in the Creed, "catholic," that is, universal) Christian church has (WA 51, 479, 25). Melanchthon demanded: "We should all be catholics" *(Omnes esse debemus Catholici)* (*CR* 24, 399). Jacob Heerbrand objected indignantly when the opponents of the catholic church made the accusation: "For not at any time has anything been written, said, and done by me against the catholic church. Far be this, far be, I say, from me such impiety!" *(Non enim unquam quicquam contra Catholicam Ecclesiam a me scriptum, dictum, factum est. Absit hoc, absit, inquam, a me impietas ista.)* [3] And although a man like Balthasar Mentzer, resorting to Biblicism that is somewhat pedantic, calls attention to the fact that the word "catholic" is unbiblical, he himself makes use of this word.[4] Scarcely anything different is meant when in the theses which he published in conjunction with his colleagues, Johann Winckelmann and Johann Scholl, the "universal church" *(universa ecclesia)* or the "whole church" *(tota ecclesia)* is spoken of.[5] Certainly the disputations that took place at the same time under Leonhard Hutter, of Wittenberg, demanded emphatically that the name "catholic" should in no circumstances be surrendered.[6] In George Calixt all the romantic attachments bound up with the concept of catholicity again come to life. Although his Saxon opponents understood this to mean something else, they likewise had no thought of giving up the idea of catholicity. Among the evangelicals it found its spokesman in the nineteenth century in Wilhelm Löhe; in the twentieth century it came to life anew under the leadership of Lutheranism in Scandinavia.[7]

[3] *Defensio Jac. Heerbrandi adversus G. Gotthardi calumnias,* Tübingen, 1587, 10. — The Wittenberg testimonials of ordination regularly certify that the candidate is in agreement with the teaching of the catholic church (Enders 7, 13; 11, 227, 278; 12, 173; 13, 35; 14, 286; 17, 357). — In the *Catech. min.* of Urb. Rhegius of 1535 the spreading of the "catholic church" throughout the earth is prayed for (Reu, *Quellen* III, 2, p. 619, 25). — The Dane Nik. Hemming points out in the foreword to his postil of 1562 that "the doctrine of the catholic church" *(doctrina Catholicae Ecclesiae)* "has so far been sincerely observed for more than forty years" *(ultra 40 annos adhuc sincere tuetur)* both at the University of Wittenberg and in the church of his native land. He mentions Joh. Palladius, Joh. Sening, Olaus Chrysostomus.

[4] B. Mentzer, *Exegesis August. Confessionis,* Giessen, 1615, p. 296.

[5] The title is given in note 1 under *The Doctrine of the Two Natures.*

[6] *August. Confessionis Symboli analysis methodica in Disp. XXIV distributa . . . praes. et autore L. Huttero,* Wittenberg, 1602, 432.

[7] Cf. Olaf Moe, *Die drei Hauptzweige der lutherischen Kirche, AELKZ,* 1927, pp. 182 ff., 207 ff., 225 ff., especially p. 227. Furthermore, the activity of Archbishop Soederbloem in the ecumenical movement and Per Pehrson, *Das lutherische Einigungswerk,* 1929, and Bishop Stadener, *Die ökumenische Bedeutung des Augsburger Bekenntnisses für das Luthertum der Welt, Verhandlungen der 21. Allg. Ev.-luth.*

It was in keeping with the initial emphasis on the spirituality of the church — the emphasis determined by opposition to hierarchism — that its universality or catholicity was likewise found in the sphere of non-empirical spirituality. This is what was meant when the *Ansbach Counsel* of 1524 gave the following definition: "The Christian church is the multitude or assembly of all those who believe in Christ, who live and will continue to live in unity of spirit, faith, hope, and love. And because of this unity the believers are called a communion of saints." (*Fränkische Bekenntnisse,* 187.) The church is an inner unity that encompasses all believers. After all, this says more than is contained in the statement which Luther took over from Huss: that the church is "the whole body of the elect" *(universitas praedestinatorum).* For here the only thing that must bind the individuals to one another is the "absolute decree of God" *(decretum absolutum Dei).* After all, the purely spiritual aspect of the idea of universality prevented Lutheranism from confining membership in the "catholic church" *(ecclesia catholica)* to its own confessional church. Luther, too, knew that, just as always, there have been "holy people" even under the papacy — "holy people" who were saved solely by the grace of Christ (WA 50, 563, 17). And even Aegidius Hunnius declared that "the church was in the midst of the papacy, even though the papacy itself was not the church" *(in medio Papatu fuisse Ecclesiam etiamsi Papatus ipse non esset Ecclesia).*[8]

But theological discussions were carried on in proportion to the occurrences of external separation. For why, it was necessary to ask, why must there be separation if one can belong to the "true" church even within the fold of the papal church? It was pointed out how the concept "church" as developed by the Augsburg Confession overcame the purely spiritual way of expressing this matter. Separation results from the demand of "evangelical doctrine" *(doctrina evangelica)* — the demand that is essential to the church — and from the corresponding administration of the sacraments. Within these bounds the evangelicals were ready to maintain external unity. In an opinion handed down in 1530 the Wittenbergians demand recognition of the fact that "even though there are differences among us, we are not for this reason separated from the church; nor are the sacraments for this reason without efficacy among us" *(ob wir schon vngleiche Ordnung gegen einander halten, wir darumb nicht abgeschnittene gelider von der kirchen sind,*

Konferenz in Augsburg, Leipzig, 1930. — On the German side: L. Ihmels, *Die Ökumenizität der lutherischen Kirche, Denkschr. d. luth. Weltkonvents zu Eisenach,* 1925, pp. 52 ff.

[8] Aegid. Hunnius, *Articulus de Ecclesia . . . ,* Frankfurt am Main, 1592, 36.

auch darumb die hailigen Sacrament bey vns nicht vntuchtig sind).[9] Melanchthon's treatise *On the Power and the Primacy of the Pope (De potestate et primatu papae),* which states that there is readiness to recognize papal primacy "according to human law" *(de jure humano),* was included in the Book of Concord. Participation in numerous religious discussions resulted from the desire to restore the ruptured external union by gaining unity in doctrine. And in view of the separation from the Swiss, which resulted at the same time and for similar reasons, Brenz declared: "I do not condemn their churches . . . but I do condemn their pernicious dogma" *(Non damno ecclesias eorum . . . sed damno perniciosum dogma eorum).*[10]

From the realization of the constitutive significance of pure evangelical doctrine and the corresponding administration of the sacraments there followed, with inner logic, the application to the mark of catholicity. Melanchthon draws this conclusion in the Apology. The church is called catholic, he says here, not because it unites definite peoples into an "external state" *(politia externa),* but rather because it unites people who are scattered over the whole world yet are in agreement in the Gospel, have the same Christ, the same Holy Spirit, the same sacraments, regardless of differences in human traditions (IV, 10). Luther expresses almost the same verdict in his treatise on councils and churches (1539): "Now where you hear or see this Word preached, confessed, and practiced, have no doubt that in that place there certainly must be a true 'holy catholic church' *(Ecclesia sancta Catholica)*" (WA 50, 629, 28; Enders 10, 144, 23). But where does one find "agreement concerning the doctrine of the Gospel" *(consentire de doctrina evangelii),* about which Melanchthon speaks here as well as in the Augsburg Confession? Must a Christian wander from one preacher to another in order to establish this from one case to another, from one Sunday to another? This was neither Melanchthon's nor Luther's intention. For this very reason the "great consensus" *(magnus consensus)* is established in the first article of the Augsburg Confession – the consensus that obtains in the domains of those who signed the confession. It is one of the essential purposes of the document to establish the fact that this consensus exists. Here a new aspect of the fundamental significance of the confession for the evangelical church is revealed. The

9 *CR* 26, 173. It is the writing hitherto regarded as the *Torgau Articles* and also reprinted as such by Kolde in his text edition of the *CA*. Joh. v. Walter (*Festschrift der Coburgia,* Göttingen, 1930, pp. 35 ff.) has now shown that it cannot be the *Torgau Articles* — after Gussmann had already proposed instead of it another of the writings first published by Förstemann and later printed in *CR* 26, pp. 171 ff.

10 Brenz, *De majestate Domini,* 181.

Augsburg Confession gives expression not only to the supraterritorial unity of the church; it is also the guide followed by the individual when he looks for unity *(Gemeinschaft)* with respect to evangelical preaching and the evangelical sacraments. "For the confession is a sure sign by which one must recognize the church," the preachers at Mansfeld declared in 1560.[11] This is nothing but the practical application of the principle of the Augsburg Confession. Here one must note that the very concept of the confession excludes every notion of an authoritative compulsion to believe. The individual who looks for the church in which the Gospel is proclaimed looks for it, not as something strange but as the communion *(Gemeinde)* of which he himself is a member. If he is a member by virtue of unity in faith, he also realizes the necessity of entering into unity in the matter of confession. For this very reason Luther, in the passage just quoted, places confessing and believing side by side. "For faith without confession is nothing." This is the brief and succinct statement made in the counsel of the clergy of Culmbach in 1530.[12]

Unity *(Gemeinsamkeit)* in confession always made the evangelicals conscious of the universality of the church. "So far as religion is concerned," says Flacius, "the evangelicals are only one kind of people *(nur einerley Volck).*"[13] To be sure, when making this statement they were thinking by no means only of their theologically well-considered confessional writings. When in the aforementioned passage in the Apology Melanchthon illustrates the "universal church" *(universalis ecclesia)* – Justus Jonas translates this with "catholic" *(catholica)* – with Peter's words that all the prophets testify that we obtain forgiveness of sins in the name of Jesus (Acts 10:43), he is stating, in the first place, that the doctrine determined by the impact of the Gospel *(evangelischer Ansatz)* must be the doctrine of the catholic church. In the second place, however, he means that this doctrine and consequently the catholic church existed when there were only promises concerning Christ – therefore when there was not yet a formulated confession.[14] The same applica-

11 *Bekenntnis der Prediger in der Grafschaft Mansfelt, unter den jungen Herren gesessen, gedr. im Schloss zu Eisleben,* 1560, 165.

12 Reprinted in Gussmann, *Quellen und Forschungen* I, 2, p. 53.

13 Matt. Fla. Illyricus, *Von einigkeit und uneinigkeit der evangelischen und Papisten gegen einander, und jedes theils unter sich selbs in fürnemen Artickeln Christlicher Lehre (Flugschrift o. J.).*

14 Cf. the Hungarian *Conf. Montana,* Art. 8: "Another description of the church. We teach and believe that since the beginning of the world there has been, has always remained, and will forever remain only one catholic or universal church — although it is sometimes obscured by many errors." *(Alia descriptio ecclesiae.*

tion of the passage in the Book of Acts then permeates nearly everything the later dogmaticians have to say about the concept of catholicity. Here, of course, the apostles regularly stand alongside the prophets. But after the confessional dispute had broken out, the confession that was formulated naturally took on the special significance that was meant by the preachers at Mansfeld. It confronts one plainly in Melanchthon's correspondence. Thus he speaks, for example, of the union with the Swedes because of the "doctrine of God which both the Swedes and our churches profess in one spirit and with one voice with the catholic church of Christ" *(doctrina ecclesiae Dei, quam et Suedicae et nostrae ecclesiae uno spiritu et una voce cum catholica ecclesia Christi profitentur)* (*CR* 7, 723). Or the Wittenbergians write to the clergy of Nürnberg: "There are in existence your religious instruction and our churches, in which the sum total of doctrine is handed down, which testify not obscurely that we truly embrace and guard the consensus of the catholic church of Christ concerning doctrine" *(Extant Catacheses vestrae et nostrae Ecclesiae, in quibus doctrinae summa traditur, quae non obscure testantur nos vere consensum Catholicae Ecclesiae Christi de doctrina amplecti et tueri).*[15]

To be sure, this unity in faith and confession, which made itself felt beyond all national boundaries, seems to be counterbalanced by the external separations which befall Lutheranism, united as it was in doctrine and in the administration of the sacraments, and which were upheld by Lutheranism with conscious consistency. The doctrinal contrast vis-à-vis the Swiss was regarded by Luther and to no smaller extent by those associated with the Augsburg Confession as so radical that external church association with the Swiss seemed to them to be intolerable. In the well-considered words he addressed in 1533 to those in Frankfurt am Main, Luther demanded: "Whoever knows that his pastor teaches as Zwingli does should avoid him and sooner do without the Sacrament throughout his life than receive it from him, yes, sooner die for this and suffer everything" (WA 30 III, 561, 13). He condemns the "jugglers" *(Gaukelspieler),* who, for the sake of external unity, speak equivocally with reference to crucial points. Above all, however, "it

Docemus et credimus unam tantum Catholicam sive universalem Ecclesiam ab exordio mundi fuisse, semper mansisse mansuramque esse in perpetuum [quamquam aliquando multis erroribus obscuratur].)

[15] Enders 12, 389, 127; cf. the entire letter (pp. 385 ff.). Furthermore, the letter which the King of Sweden wrote to Luther on Oct. 16, 1540 (Enders 13, 158 ff.). — In the aforementioned essay in the *Ihmels-Festschrift* I have compiled additional proofs of Melanchthon's extranational correspondence (to Denmark, Livonia, Poland, Hungary, England) on the basis of confessional unity.

frightens me to hear that in one church or at one altar both groups should seek and receive one Sacrament, and one group should believe that it receives only bread and wine, but the other group should believe that it receives the true body and blood of Christ. And I often doubt that it is credible that a preacher or pastor could be so obdurate and wicked as to keep silence in this matter and let both groups go along in this way, each in its own opinion." (564, 35 ff.) In itself it is self-evident that very profound internal reasons, not the external authority of the Augsburg Confession, determined Luther's position in this matter. But his doctrine of the Lord's Supper will make this especially clear (cf. *The Sacrament of the Altar*). The position which Luther and the church of the Augsburg Confession took was a thorn in the side of all those who wanted to achieve church unity by means of ecclesiastical policy instead of doctrinal unity. It becomes intelligible only if one has understood the evangelical character of church unity on the basis of the impact of the Gospel *(evangelischer Ansatz)*. The other camp acted in the same way when the internal state of its own church affairs, not high politics, was at stake. This is shown by the example of Bonifacius Amerbach, a jurist in Basle. In 1520 Luther's writings brought Amerbach to the side of the Reformation. The manner in which the Reformation was carried out in Basle and the connection with politics caused him and the other professors at the university to practice reserve. But the doctrine of Holy Communion as taught by Oecolampadius offended him most of all. In opposition to it he addressed a statement of confession to the council and advocated Luther's doctrine of Holy Communion. Because this led him to refrain from attending the Zwinglian church services and from partaking of Holy Communion, he was exposed to constant vexations and was threatened with excommunication. A counterpart to this would scarcely be conceivable in the Wittenberg of that time! In a letter written in 1529 to J. Montaigne in Avignon, Amerbach expresses the hope that he might be permitted to live in Basle as the Jews live in Avignon, "namely, as one out of sympathy with the things recently put into practice by us" *(nempe ab nostris nuper institutis prophanus)*. Otherwise he would have to emigrate to Freiburg. This, of course, was not understood at all in Basle.[16]

[16] Th. Burckhardt-Biedermann, *Bonifacius Amerbach und die Reformation*, Basle, 1894. There the confession concerning Holy Communion (pp. 395 f., especially theses 5 and 8). The letter to Montaigne (p. 232). Cantiuncula, Amerbach's friend in Metz, also considered the intention to live as "one out of sympathy" *(profanus)*, that is, legally as a dissident, practically impossible. It was said that he was free to emigrate (op. cit., p. 71). — Not until after 1534 was Amerbach, because of the influence of Bucer, persuaded to partake of Holy Communion in Basle.

The insistence with which Calvinism constantly pressed union later on is properly illuminated when one considers that wherever Calvinism attempted to hammer the "unity of Protestantism" *(Einheit des Protestantismus)* into Lutheranism, it had made its way into areas of the church that were originally Lutheran. That its "irenical theology" *(Irenik)* was a concealed form of agitation for itself one can study with special profit in the case of Johann a Lasco, the Polish agitator who, as a "poor emigrant," traversed the Lutheran lands from Denmark to Württemberg with an entourage of two other preachers and 170 souls. He always insisted on debating with the Lutheran clergyman. But if after this he was not regarded and treated as one of their own, he would fill the world with his complaints about the intolerance of the Lutherans.[17] Hans Leube has likewise shown impressively as well as incontrovertibly that the Reformed "irenical theology" *(Irenik)* in the seventeenth century was often a concealed agitation for its own idea and its own political right, and certainly by no means a waiving of its own confessional position.[18]

Meanwhile the problem of external separation and, together with it, that of catholicity was felt more acutely over against the Roman Church, which claimed the mark of catholicity for itself and for itself alone. The more clearly the general picture of Christianity shifted to the disadvantage of the Roman Church, and the less the external make-up of the Roman Church justified the claim, the more strongly this church emphasized the mark of catholicity. In the translation of the Apology, Justus Jonas complains that the opponents "call the dear, holy Gospel Lutheran" (VIII, 44).[19] Conversely, Luther called the papacy a sect (WA 7, 753, 27). And in 1530 Lazarus Spengler, the Nürnberg town clerk, distinguished without hesitation between those Augsburgians who were "Christians" and those who were "papistic" *(babstisch)*.[20] But this

[17] Cf. H. Schmid, *Der Kampf der lutherischen Kirche um Luthers Lehre vom Abendmahl im Reformationszeitalter*, Leipzig, 1868, pp. 152 ff., 176 ff. — C. H. W. Sillem, *Briefsammlung des Hamburgischen Superintendenten Joachim Westphal (a. d. Jahren 1530—75)*, 2 vols., Hamburg, 1903; e. g., pp. 190 f., 196, 205, 284, 362, 519. This collection of letters also provides insights into Calvinism's infiltration of the Netherlands. — Concerning the disputation in Stuttgart cf. Brenz's letters to P. Brubach and to Hartm. Beyer (July 14, 1556), and Sept. 2, 1556), *Anecdota Brentiana*, 1868, nos. CCXXXVIII and CCXXXIX. — In spite of these and similar reports Laski continued to be praised in our day as a "prophet and herald of a later, better time" (by Dalton, *PRE* 11, 295, 60).

[18] Hans Leube, *Kalvinismus und Luthertum im Zeitalter der Orthodoxie*. Vol. I, *Der Kampf um die Herrschaft im protestantischen Deutschland*, Leipzig, 1928.

[19] As early as 1524 Melanchthon speaks about "Lutherans" *(Lutherani)*, *CR* 1, 658.

[20] To Conrad Rehlinger, a councilor in Augsburg. In Gussmann, op. cit., p. 218.

is the period in which the evangelical state churches came into being. The attachment of the mark of catholicity to one's own church became a claim involving ecclesiastical policy. This was almost unavoidable. The estates of the realm who made a confession at Augsburg in 1530 put forth this claim in the sense of the edict of 380. They were guided by the fictitious idea that the empire of the old Caesars was continued in the German Empire. They did not want to be regarded as having left the catholic church, of which the Roman opponents were members too. Even in the religious peace concluded at Augsburg in 1555 – the peace that was established between those who confessed "the old religion and the estates of the realm who are associated with the Augsburg Confession" – they were able to see to it that the application of the expression "catholic" to the Roman party was avoided. But in the theological discussion there is further reference to the edict of 380. Thus it is adduced by George Dalmatinus in a disputation which took place in Tübingen under Heerbrand.[21] But at this very point it becomes clear that one cannot put the question on the basis of ecclesiastical policy. Perhaps it was right to ignore the fact that the edict designates Damasus, the Roman bishop, and Peter, the Alexandrian, as guarantors of the apostolic religion. For what was true of Damasus was not necessarily true of all his successors. Although the Roman Church of the Middle Ages had considered this self-evident, the church in the realm of the real assigns of Justinian had contested it again and again since Photius. But when – in order to substantiate the claim of the evangelicals that this name should be applied to them – Dalmatinus and others after his time made use of the statements of the edict in which the name "catholic" is reserved for those who adhere to the doctrine of the Trinity but at the same time treated the claim of the Roman opponents as a usurpation, they entered an area in which theology has to end. For here they subjected themselves indirectly to the power of the empire in matters pertaining to ecclesiastical law. This presupposed not only the mistaken idea that there was a continuity of the law of the old Roman and German empires – the mistaken idea of which Luther was aware (Vol. II, *Rechtsgeschichte*) – but, particularly after the religious peace that was concluded in Augsburg, it was an anachronism. In 1530 the estates of the realm could still argue this way. In doing so, however, they acknowledged tacitly that even the opponents belonged to the same catholic

[21] *De Catholica et Catholicis Disputatio . . . praeside . . . D. Jac. Heerbrando . . . M. Georgius Dalmatinus Gurgfeldianus . . .* , Tübingen, 1572, theses 9 ff. But scholars of a later period also did so.

church. But now this was to be contested. And after the Roman Church had refused to accept the evangelical reform, it had to be contested.

Luther had already drawn this painful conclusion. "Because they boast of being the church, they have the obligation to prove this. . . . But if they are unable to prove it, they must confess . . . that they are not the church and that we cannot be heretics because we fall away from the church that amounts to nothing *[nichtig]*. Yes, since there is no middle ground, we must be the church of Christ, and they must be the church of the devil, or the other way round . . . for from the beginning of the world to the end there are two churches. St. Augustine calls them Cain and Abel." (WA 51, 477, 19 ff.) And later he adds correctly: "But because on earth there is no judge in this matter – for those who formerly made themselves the chief judges have become a party, and their judgment is worthless according to all laws, just as judgment given by us, who are the other party, is worthless among them – we must let it be so and await the true Judge" (524, 20).

These statements of Luther say more than that the evangelicals and their opponents are two parties in the same church. On the contrary, they prove that both parts want to be the church. If Luther is thinking here (1541) of church bodies that are also separated externally and no longer have a common worldly judge, then the bottom has been knocked out of the argument taken from the edict of 380. In fact, from now on two completely separated churches are opposed to each other. But the aforementioned argument is now obsolete for another reason. Not, of course, because it would have to be to the disadvantage of the evangelicals. So far as the German Empire is concerned, the church adhering to Rome at the time of the religious peace concluded at Augsburg has the emperor on its side, but only about one tenth of the population. But the church of the Augsburg Confession has behind it about seven tenths of the Germans,[22] represented by a considerable number of the estates of the realm. Although the question as to who holds real sovereignty in the German Empire – the emperor or the estates of the realm – is not ventilated in terms of the law until the seventeenth century, it has its root in the actual disarrangement of legal matters which reaches at least into the beginning of the era of the Reformation. Therefore an analogous application of the edict of 380 could be to the advantage of the evangelicals. For if the German Empire was actually the heir of the empire of the Caesars – which, of course, was not really the case – the estates of the realm could now avail themselves of the same right to determine the public validity of a definite religion that had been

[22] The remaining two tenths belong to the smaller groups.

claimed for the emperor in the empire of Theodosius I and Justinian. This right is given to them for the first time at the Diet of Speyer in 1526, even though only provisionally; but in the peace concluded at Augsburg in 1555 it is granted to them conclusively. It makes possible the external existence of the evangelical church bodies and is therefore of the greatest practical significance. But since its validity is always confined within narrow and the narrowest territorial boundaries, there is danger that it will lead to a tremendous forfeiture of ideals. For who would still dare give the mark of catholicity to the church of the Count of Mansfeld or to the church of the free imperial city of Alen as such?

But for the evangelicals the claim to this mark was not merely a question of prestige. The only ones always indifferent to it were the fanatical adherents of "building the church from below" or "building the church on the congregation." This principle had its origin in sectarianism. It openly contradicts the evangelical conception of the church. The nature of the church demands that it be founded, built, and preserved "from above." Of course, this "above" is not represented by bishops and councils, not even by general superintendents or synods. It is a transcendental "above," but an "above" that works within the world by means of the proclamation of the Word and the administration of the sacraments. It is not the "congregation," that is, a number of adherents, that makes up the church. No, it is the Word of God spoken into the world "from above." This principle, to which Luther clung throughout his life in spite of his occasional calls for such "as want to be Christians in earnest," is the point of departure for three trains of thought in which the idea of catholicity was pursued further (cf. *Church Government*).

1. If the church is constantly brought into being anew and preserved through the Word, the Word is always first, and the church is second – not the other way around. "The church does not make the Word, but it comes into being from the Word" (WA 8, 491, 34). This antithesis of Luther's occurs in many variations throughout all subsequent theology. The church, which wants to be conscious of itself, constantly looks at its origin. To be sure, its origin in the Word of God is transcendental in nature. But since this Word, like all divine revelation in time, constantly appears in an innerworldly garb, the look at its origin is at the same time a looking back at history. It is now characteristic of all Lutheran theology that in doing so it did not remain entangled in the primeval history of the church and elevate this history "in faith into the sphere of contemporaneity." On the contrary, it was constantly conscious of the distance that separated it from the primeval church, not only with respect to a comparison as to value but also in a purely historical respect.

It knew that the primeval church cannot be brought back. Nor did it by any means regard the interim development as a mere misdevelopment. On the contrary, it sought and wanted continuity (cf. *History*). This is the deeper reason for its love of the "old" church – the love which is conspicuous at first. The "old" church is by no means understood to be only the primeval church. Even Luther wants to prove that "we remained with the true old church, that we are the true old church" (WA 51, 479, 17). When, as evidence for this, he also adduces adherence to the Apostles' Creed (482, 17), this proves that for him continuity with the old church means more than formal acknowledgment of its canonical writings. And in the letter he sent in 1532 to Duke Albrecht of Prussia on the doctrine of Holy Communion he attaches importance to the fact that this article "has been believed and held harmoniously in all the world ever since the beginning of the Christian church up to this hour, as the books and writings of the dear fathers, both in Greek and in Latin, prove. . . . For it is dangerous and terrible to hear or to believe anything against the harmonious testimony, faith, and doctrine of the entire Holy Christian Church, which has now endured harmoniously in the whole world for more than 1,500 years." (WA 30 III, 552, 5 ff.) These words express a consciousness of continuity that has nothing in common with the interest of ecclesiastical-political prestige. In his treatise on the authority of the antiquity of the church George Calixt was later able to place side by side with this testimony of Luther's numerous statements by Melanchthon, Martin Chemnitz, Johann Gerhard, J. G. Dorsch, Johann Scharf, and even by Hülsemann, his embittered opponent, who had an excellent knowledge especially of medieval theology.[23] Among the writings which give historical evidence of this continuity are, for example, Melanchthon's tract *On the Church and the Authority of the Word of God (De ecclesia et de auctoritate verbi Dei)*, what he wrote about the Nicene Creed, Selnecker's *Catalog of the Principal Ecumenical and National Councils from the Time of the Apostles to Our Times (Catalogus praecipuorum conciliorum oecum. et nationalium a tempore apostolorum usque ad nostra tempora)* (1564), and the works on church history by Flacius and his collaborators (cf. *History*). But Martin Chemnitz' *Examen Concilii Tridentini* also serves this purpose. For this work Chemnitz received the title "the most villainous Lutheran" *(sceleratissimus Lutheranus)* from Count Bartholomäus v. Portia, the papal

[23] *G. Calixti, De veritate unicae Religionis Christianae et Authoritate antiquitatis ecclesiasticae Dissertationes (ed. Frid. Ulr. Calixt)*, Helmstedt, 1658, pp. 119 ff. — Cf. also the quotation from the book of forms of Duke Julius, pp. 82 f.: "We are by no means minded to put aside the ancient, true, catholic, Christian religion . . ."

nuncio.[24] In Strassburg, Johann Pappus made a collection of statements from Augustine which paralleled all the statements of the Augsburg Confession.[25] Although this consciousness of the historical bond which holds the church of all ages together is something different from the certainty of faith that there have always been true believers, it cannot be separated from this certainty. For this certainty rests on the other certainty that the voice of the Gospel was never completely silent. Therefore the consciousness of continuity is also a necessary element in the idea of the catholicity of the church. But it is in need of a corrective. For the statement of Luther's quoted last calls to mind very seriously what, as stated before (cf. *The Dogma of the Church*), even Zasius had cast into his teeth. But this had made no impression on Luther.

2. This corrective lies in the fact that the church was founded from above through the Word of God. Catholicity, too, must be understood from above. "And so far as unity is concerned," says Heerbrand, "not any [church] whatever is pleasing to God. For robbers and thieves agree, and rebels conspire, as do the chief priests, the scribes, and the Pharisees against Christ." *(Et quod ad unitatem attinet, non quaevis [ecclesia] Deo grata est. Consentiunt enim et latrones et fures et seditiosi conspirant, sicut Pontificii, Scribae et Pharisaei contra Christum.)*[26] Therefore a critical standard is needed over against historical continuity. Jacob Andreä states very vividly that this means a revolution, not a complete breaking-down, when he says: "The papists have forgotten these [old] landmarks and have set up new landmarks." Luther, however, "did not tear out or remove the old landmarks or set up new ones in their place; he merely restored the old landmarks."[27] Andreä, too, is concerned with proving that "we have not fallen away from the right, true, catholic, Christian church." But what, then, are the landmarks of genuine catholicity? Later Calixt referred to the famous definition of Vincent of Lérins. To be sure, in doing so he gives preference to "universality" *(universitas)* and "antiquity" *(antiquitas)* rather than to "agreement" *(consensio)* when he mentions the three marks of catholicity. But as early as the sixteenth century Heerbrand, for example, and Dalmatinus,

[24] *Nuntiaturberichte aus Deutschland* III, 3, Berlin, 1896, p. 217.

[25] Joh. Pappus, *Confessionis Augustanae et Augustinianae Parallela, quibus liquido demonstratur, magnum illum ecclesiae doctorem D. Aurel. Augustinum cum omnibus Augustanae Confessionis Articulis consensisse,* Frankfurt am Main, 1591.

[26] Op. cit., p. 39. — Cf., e. g., also Calov, *Exegema Aug. Conf.*, 2d ed., 1665, on Art. VII on "the reasons for unity" *(rationes unitatis)*.

[27] Jac. Andreä, *Drey und dreissig Predigten Von den fürnemsten Spaltungen in der christlichen Religion . . .* , Tübingen, 1589, pp. 503 and 505.

but especially Chemnitz, quote the man from Lérins. It is clear that here there is danger of reversion to the purely formalistic principle of tradition. But it is significant to observe how Chemnitz seeks to meet this danger. The words of Vincent – "which has been believed always, everywhere, and by all" *(quod semper, quod ubique, quod ab omnibus creditum est)* – he varies as follows: "which has been received consistently from Scripture, always, everywhere, and by all believers" *(quod semper, quod ubique et ab omnibus fidelibus ex Scriptura constanter receptum fuit)*.[28] Here, therefore, the synthesis of the consciousness of continuity and the Scriptural principle is sought and found. The consensus of the believers has its marks in Scripture, to which, for this reason, the mark of catholicity is primarily attached.[29] But this, on the other hand, is no different from finding the catholicity of the church in the fact that unity is founded on Christ as the Head of the church. For the consensus of the believers finds the application of this catholicity in the fact that the church does and teaches nothing but what Christ has directed it to do and teach. To this "catholic" church belong all those who hear the voice of their Shepherd.[30] Here the coauthor of the Formula of Concord is protected against the threat that catholicity will evaporate into the air of pure spirituality. This requires no further proof. For he regards "unity of faith" *(unitas fidei)* and "purity of doctrine" *(synceritas doctrinae)* as belonging together of necessity. Johann Gerhard's conception of the "catholic confession" *(Confessio Catholica)* corresponds

[28] *Ex. Conc. Trid.* III, 331, 51. On the other hand, II, 161, 45: ". . . has been observed by all in like manner" *(ab omnibus similiter observatum fuit)*. In II, 421, 54, even the "in like manner" *(similiter)* has been dropped.

[29] Chemnitz, op. cit., I, 87, 49. According to Eusebius the ὁμολογούμενα of the New Testament are "the legitimate catholic writings" *(scripta legitima catholica)*. — Cf. C. C. Brochmand, *Lychnos . . . oppositus veritatis pontificiae speculo, h. e. . . . causarum, quibus inductus Ill. Dux Christianus Wilhelmus Marchio Brandenburgensis a Lutherana Ecclesia defecit et se Eccl. Pontificiae mancipavit, Refutatio,* Rostock, 1640. — There, on p. 155, after enumerating the opposing marks of catholicity: "We add that above all the church is called catholic because of the whole body of the prophetic and apostolic doctrine" *(Nos addimus: Ecclesiam potissimum vocari Catholicam ob doctrinae Propheticae et Apostolicae universitatem)*.

[30] II, 161 ff. Thus Dalmatinus, too, can summarize his disputation in the statement: "Therefore from all this it manifestly appears and follows that in name and in fact we also do not lack what is embraced in the most respectable words 'catholic church' and 'catholics,' since in unity of faith we are in agreement with the true, prophetic, apostolic, catholic, canonical church of all times in all parts of the Christian doctrine" *(Ex his igitur omnibus manifeste apparet et sequitur, nec nos carere nomine ac re honestissimo vocabulo Catholicae Ecclesiae et Catholicorum comprae-henso: cum sentiamus in fidei unitate cum omnium temporum vera, Prophetica, Apostolica, Catholica, Canonica Ecclesia in omnibus partibus doctrinae Christianae)* (thesis 89).

exactly to the purpose of Chemnitz and Melanchthon.[31] Catholicity also appears in the acceptance of the old creeds. It has already been shown that this included and did not exclude examining these creeds according to Scripture. Furthermore, catholicity appears when the evangelical confessions make the rejections expressed by the old creeds their own. In the third place, however, it appears, above all, in the evangelical confessions themselves, since in doctrines that are contested these confessions are in earnest about the sole authority of the "catholic canonical writings" *(scripta catholica canonica)*, Holy Scripture, which is acknowledged by all Christians.

3. Of course, it is precisely because of this last purpose of the confessions that those who formulated them were accused of destroying the unity of the church. Objectively this reproach is certainly wrong if it is attached to the confessions themselves. The confessions did not cause the divisions; they merely stated that there was dissension with regard to doctrine, and in doing so they gave the reasons for their own position. The Roman Church, above all, forfeited the claim to be more in this respect than the evangelical church, since the Council of Trent made it a "particular church" *(Partikularkirche)* to the same degree and in the same sense as their evangelical opponents were. Still the statement that there was dissension did not remain the last word in early Lutheranism. What led beyond this was Melanchthon's definition of the church as the "assembly of those who have been called" *(coetus vocatorum)* (*CR* 21, 825). Only those who distorted his statements about the "visible church" *(ecclesia visibilis)* could maintain that this contradicted the definition given in the Augsburg Confession. He who reads without prejudice what Melanchthon sets forth in the *Loci* or in the *Examen Ordinandorum* will be convinced of the opposite. Here the Gospel and the sacraments are constitutive.[32] Consequently, here, too, Melanchthon remains true to the founding of the church "from above"; and this must be emphasized over against misrepresentations by the other side. But if both he and Luther believed that Christians are called to be members of the body of Christ primarily by Baptism, the statement about the "assembly of those who have been called" *(coetus vocatorum)* is a new point of departure *(Ansatz)* for the idea of catholicity. In his vehement polemical treatise *Wider Hans Worst* Luther had written that no one will "be able to deny that we as well as the papists are descended

[31] Joh. Gerhard, *Confessio Catholica, in qua doctrina catholica et evangelica, quam Ecclesiae Augustanae Confessioni addictae profitentur, ex Romano-Catholicorum Scriptorum Suffragiis confirmatur . . .*, Frankfurt and Leipzig, 1679.

[32] Cf. the definition given by the Hungarian *Confessio montana*, Art. 8.

from holy Baptism and are called Christians because of this" (WA 51, 479, 20). To be sure, he sees that the validity of Baptism among his opponents is questioned. But it is not the act as such that is questioned – the act that they have performed (WA 50, 630, 21 ff.); it is the certainty that the Christian has been called. And this certainty is founded on Baptism. In spite of all, therefore, Baptism is a unifying bond even with the "papists." For this reason Luther could also designate the "Christian church" *(ecclesia christiana)* as the "multitude of those who have been baptized and called" *(multitudo eorum, qui baptizati sunt et vocati)* (WA 14, 190, 20). And Urban Rhegius calls attention to the fact that in Scripture it is the usual thing to understand "the church to be the whole multitude of those who have been baptized" *(ecclesia pro tota multitudine baptizatorum)* *(Loci,* p. 177). Consequently, the later usage of the "assembly of those who have been baptized" *(coetus baptizatorum)* is not Melanchthon's special property; it is common to Lutheranism. Of course, it was meant to be a criticism of the Roman Church's claim to sole universality when this church was confronted again and again with the statement that it was only a "particular church" *(ecclesia particularis).*[33] Indirectly, however, this included the acknowledgment of a supraconfessional unity of Christians. And even though Leonhard Hutter does not understand the "particular churches" *(ecclesiae particulares)* to be the individual confessional churches, yet he expresses the idea of genuine catholicity in this context: "For nevertheless there remains only one catholic church, which embraces all those particular churches within its periphery as a mother embraces her daughters. For my dove is one, my perfect [dove] is one." *(Manet enim nihilominus una tantum Catholica Ecclesia, particulares illas omnes ceu mater filias suo ambitu complectens. Una enim est columba mea, una est perfecta mea.)* (P. 431.)

This enables one to understand why early Lutheranism looked again and again to the East in order to give practical expression to the idea of supraconfessional unity. In his writing *Against the Highly Renowned Romanist in Leipzig (Wider den hochberühmten Romanisten zu Leipzig)* (1520) Luther believed that he could say of "the Muscovites, the White Russians, the Greeks, the Bohemians, and many other great lands in the world" (which were not united with Rome) that "all these believe as we do, baptize as we do, preach as we do, live as we do. . . ." (WA 6, 287, 9 ff.) In 1559 Melanchthon expresses to the Patriarch of Constan-

33 Hunnius, op. cit., p. 33. — Heinrich Meier, *Pfeiler der Evangelischen Wahrheit. . . . Darinnen zwar kurtz, doch gründlich erwiesen, dass die Evangelische (sonst Lutherisch genannte) Kirche die wahre, uhralte, Catholische und Apostolische Kirche sey,* 1662, I, 44.

tinople the conviction that in the Eastern Church God "is preserving for Himself an assembly which rightly worships and calls on His own dear Son, Jesus Christ" *(sibi servat coetum, qui Filium ipsius Jesum Christum recte colit atque invocat)* (*CR* 9, 923). Accordingly, he is not thinking of an "invisible church" *(ecclesia invisibilis)* here either. Hunnius, too, cites the "indisputable example of the Eastern Church" *(irrefragabile exemplum Orientalis Ecclesiae)* to show that a particular church *(Partikularkirche)* can be catholic even without affiliation with Rome.[34] Jacob Andreä and Lukas Osiander, the Tübingen theologians, sought contact in a practical way with Constantinople.[35] And the delegation which Count Ernest the Pious sent to the Ethiopian Church of Abyssinia was a result of the same ecumenical pull toward the East.

Even though all this had no practical effect, still it gives expression to the desire to preserve one's own territorial churches from parochial induration. This desire was born of the certainty of belonging to the "one holy catholic church" *(Una Sancta Catholica)*.

22. The Sacrament of Baptism [1]

The ecumenical significance attached to Baptism in early Lutheranism leads to the question whether merely an external, ritual unity *(Gemeinsamkeit)* or a deeper connection of another kind is thought of

[34] Hunnius, op. cit., p. 34. — L. Hutter, op. cit., p. 434. — H. Meier, op. cit., p. 44. — Kromayer, *Theol.*, pp. 791 ff. — Cf. also the Wittenberg testimonials for Michael (1534), the Ethiopian (Enders 10, 61), and for Georgiewitz (1544), the Armenian (Enders 16, 66 f.).

[35] J. Schall, *Tübingen und Konstantinopel, Bl. f. Württemb. KG*, VII, 1892, 33 ff. — Cf. the criticism of the Jesuits: *Gewisse und Wahrhaffte Zeytung auss Constantinopel vom Hieremia jetzigem Patriarchen daselbsten, was sein und aller Griechischen und Orientalischen Kirchen Urtheil und Meynung sey von allen Articuln der Augspurgerischen Confession, Ingolstadt*, 1583. — On the other hand, Jacob Heerbrand, *Ableinnung Unnd Abfertigung der newen Zeitung auss Constantinopel, so diss 83. jars zu Wien von einem Jesuiter wider die Christliche Augspurgische Confession aussgesprengt*, Tübingen, 1583. There, on p. 81, a protest against the insinuation that the people of Tübingen wanted to force themselves on the patriarch: "Nor have we yet desired that he accept us as his children; but . . . we have hoped (as love hopes for everything) that — since in some articles he is closer to us than the pope at Rome is — when he, together with his people, has been better instructed out of God's Word, he will also come close to us in other articles and join us in unanimity of doctrine and unity of the church, as we heartily desire to be at one with everybody in the right and true faith and are also intent, so far as is humanly possible, on winning many for the Lord Christ for eternal life; and we are loath to neglect any opportunity if we are aware of it. . ."

[1] J. W. Fr. Höfling, *Das Sakrament der Taufe nebst den andern damit zusammenhängenden Akten der Initiation*, 2 vols., 1859. — Paul Althaus the Elder, *Die historischen und dogmatischen Grundlagen der lutherischen Taufliturgie*, 1893. — Additional literature of the nineteenth century in Al. v. Oettingen, *Dogmatik*, II, 2,

here. One can think of the former when Luther gives special emphasis to the external character of Baptism — the character which enables one to recognize Christians as the people of God (1523; WA 12, 695, 6). But when the Formula of Concord likewise points to the "great difference between baptized and unbaptized persons," it quotes Gal. 3:27 and concludes from this passage that all baptized persons "have put on Christ and thus are truly reborn" *(SD* II, 67). Here, therefore, an essential, internal significance is attached to Baptism. Self-evidently, this was also Luther's view. Then the question can be answered by saying that although the rite of Baptism is in itself merely an external bond for the churches as such, at the same time the effect of Baptism can bring about internal unity *(Gemeinsamkeit)* of the individuals. This is also confirmed by the fact that Lutheranism, exactly like the Roman Church and the Eastern Church, makes the validity of Baptism independent of the personal quality of the person who baptizes (WA 37, 279, 7; 300, 18) and recognizes not only Baptism performed by the laity [2] but also infant Baptism.

The scruples which crop up because of this proximity to churches that lay special stress on ceremonies are even intensified when the Augsburg Confession declares "that Baptism is necessary for salvation" *(quod baptismus sit necessarius ad salutem),* and when the Apology adds that Baptism is not only necessary for children but "also efficacious for salvation" *(et efficax ad salutem).* The statement that the act of Baptism is necessary for salvation — the act which must be thought of as merely external — seems to be diametrically in opposition to the impact of the Gospel *(evangelischer Ansatz),* according to which salvation comes about through the Gospel and faith exclusively.

Now it is true that the sacraments have already come up in another connection, namely — like the Gospel — as "symbols, tokens, and marks of the church" *(symbola, tesserae et caracteres ecclesiae)* in Luther; as "signs of the fellowship of the church" *(signa societatis ecclesiae)* in Melanchthon *(CR* 23, 39); as "marks of the church" *(notae ecclesiae)* in the later dogmaticians. Actually it is only within the frame of the church that one can speak meaningfully of Baptism at least, for indi-

435 ff. — Furthermore, O. Scheel, *Die dogmatische Behandlung der Tauflehre in der modernen positiven Theologie,* 1906. — J. Gottschick, *Die Lehre der Reformation von der Taufe (Hefte z. ChrW, No. 56),* 1906. — P. Graff, *Gesch. d. Auflösung der alten gottesdienstlichen Formen in der evangelischen Kirche Deutschlands,* 1921. — Carl Stange, *Die Bedeutung der Sakramente,* 2d ed., 1927, and *Zur Tauflehre Luthers, Studien zur Theol. Luthers* I, 1928, 345 ff. — Joh. Meyer, *Histor. Kommentar zu Luthers Kl. Katechismus,* 1929, pp. 445 ff.

[2] In the rituals, e. g., Sehling, *KO* I, pp. 267, 568; IV, 34, 230, etc.

viduals cannot baptize themselves. But since the church baptizes, it is no longer "purely a speaking church" *(reine Wortkirche);* it is at the same time a church that performs acts. Although the *Ansbach Counsel* of 1524 declared that the name "sacrament," like the number "seven," "was invented only by men" *(allain durch die Menschen erdicht worden ist)* and for this reason wanted the use of the word "sacrament" prohibited,[3] yet in the course of time the name "sacrament" ceased to be attacked. And the traditional essential connection between church and sacrament was accepted along with the name. Later it will be necessary to discuss the fact that as a result of this connection – brought about especially by *CA* XIV – even the evangelicals accorded to the ministry a position which, with certain limitations, runs parallel to the position of the clergy in the Latin and in the Greek church.

If, then, the fact that the external picture of the Lutheran Church conforms in large measure to those other particular churches *(Partikularkirchen)* is due in the final analysis to the doctrine of the sacraments, the question concerning the basis of this doctrine has decisive importance. But early Lutheranism in its entirety knows no other basis than the "institution" *(Einsetzung)* by Christ. This is something different from basing the doctrine on the authority of Scripture. In his treatise *On the Babylonian Captivity (De Captivitate Babylonica)* Luther explains in connection with the "sacrament" of extreme unction that the Epistle of James, even if it had been written by an apostle – which he doubts even as early as this – can never institute a sacrament: "an apostle may not institute a sacrament on his own authority, that is, give a divine promise together with an attached sign. For this pertained to Christ alone." *(non licere Apostolum sua auctoritate sacramentum instituere, id est, divinam promissionem cum adjuncto signo dare. Hoc enim ad Christum solum pertinebat.)* (WA 6, 568, 12.) Luther points out that even Paul declares expressly that he received the Sacrament of the Eucharist from the Lord. Therefore it is strictly historical to base the sacraments on the institution by Christ. In view of everything that was set forth about Christology and about the doctrine of the church in Lutheranism, this cannot strike one as strange. As seen from the viewpoint of the world, the mark of historical contingency is attached to the whole story of salvation. This does not contradict the nature of faith; it is a prerequisite. If it were necessary to think about what God did and offers, this would be the content of "reason" *(ratio),* not of

[3] *Fränk. Bek.,* p. 232. But the printing of 1525 already adds: "But in order not to begin and wage a needless war of words, we will drop the word (as the papists use it) . . ."

faith. It is true that here faith, too, sees a necessity. But this is not rational-causal in character; it is teleological. And even that which is teleological is not to be understood in the sense of innerworldly definiteness of purpose; it is to be understood eschatologically. Faith in the divine teleology is identical with the certainty that I am not the one who decides for or against my salvation in my now and my here, but that it is God who makes the decision.

"This is also the case with Baptism. The water is Baptism, and the Holy Spirit is in Baptism. Here you might say, 'Why is it necessary to baptize with water?' But the Holy Spirit speaks this way, 'Are you listening? Here are God's will and Word; remain with these, and let your own opinion go.'" (WA 19, 496, 20.) This positivistic basis contains a protest against every assessment of the sacraments that is merely symbolical. For as the correspondence of a picturesque representation to an idea the mere symbol bears its significance within itself. But for the sacrament in the purpose of Lutheranism it is essential that the significance be attached to the "symbolical" act through the Word of Christ. Without this Word the significance of the same act could be entirely different. Luther compares Christian Baptism with the baptism of the Law – with the washing of the members of the body, of clothing, of vessels – and with the baptism of John, the "baptism of repentance" *(baptisma poenitentiae)*. But: "Because of the Word, which is operative in it and not in the others, only the Baptism of Christ is a sacrament" *(Solius Christi baptisma sacramentum est propter verbum, quod in illo et non in aliis operatur)* (WA 6, 473, 7). Here, however, as always, Christ's Word was the "Word of life or of promise." If the fundamental agreement of the doctrine of the sacraments with the rest of the doctrine of salvation is established here, the contrast with the Roman Catholic conception of the sacraments is apparent at the same time. For according to our previous conclusions, the concept of promise found here as the essential content of the Word of God that constitutes Baptism [4] is sharply distinguished from the concept of the "grace" *(gratia)* which the sacraments impart according to the way the Roman Catholic Church understands them. For this reason a stand is made against the Roman Catholic doctrine that Baptism no longer has any validity for the sins committed after Baptism, but that the sacrament of penance must then take its place.[5]

Of course, when the question about the content of the divine promise

[4] *CA* XIII (Latin text); Apol. XII, 18. — Melanchthon, *Loci, CR* 21, 871: "The sacraments 'are signs and marks of the promises in which God shows us something'" *(Sacramenta "sunt signa et notae promissionum, in quibus Deus nobis aliquid exhibet")*.

[5] Luther (1519): WA 2, 733, 7 ff.; cf. WA 37, 288, 27. — Melanchthon, *CR* 23, 42 f.

is answered, now – in addition to the words of Christ that institute Baptism – the other New Testament statements, which interpret those words, are adduced. Luther's Small Catechism is the classical example of this. From what Christ says in Mark 16:16 that content is only "will be saved" *(salvus erit)*. But from Titus 3:5 one concludes that this takes place by means of the "new birth in the Holy Spirit." From Rom. 6:4, however, one concludes what Baptism signifies: that together with Christ we are buried into death, and, corresponding to His resurrection, "we also should walk in newness of life." These three trains of thought unfold the preceding answer to the question about the "benefit": forgiveness of sins, deliverance from death and the devil, eternal salvation. It is clear how this whole plan is determined by the fundamental idea of the doctrine of justification. And this is expressed even more sharply in the Smalcald Articles when an attack is launched both against the belief that a "spiritual power" is inherent in the water *alone* – this belief does not attach enough value to the significance of the "Word" – and against the Scotistic-voluntaristic devaluation of the connection between the Word and the water as such (III, 5).[6] Finally one must consider the emphasis on faith – "to all who believe this" – especially when opposing the statement that the effect results "from the performance of the work" *(ex opere operato)*: "For where there is no faith, Baptism is of no avail" *(Denn wo der glawb nit ist, hilfft die tauffe nit)* (WA 7, 321, 10; *CA* XIII).

In the frame of this train of thought it is the function of Baptism to give assurance. For it is necessary "that faith must have something to believe, that it hold to this, stand on it, and be based on it. Now, therefore, faith clings to the water and believes that in Baptism there is sheer salvation and life, not because of the water . . . but because it is connected *(verleibet)* with God's Word and arrangement *(ordnung)*, and His name[7] is attached to it *(daryn klebet.)*" (WA 30 I, 215, 24; cf. WA 2, 732, 19 ff.; WA 37, 262, 10.) Thus Baptism becomes exactly analogous to the Word, on which faith relies. But it differs from it (1) because Baptism is a concrete act, therefore the "visible Word" *(verbum visibile)*, and (2) because here the Christian is addressed by God in a wholly personal way, is called by name, and is accepted personally as a child.[8]

[6] Cf. Large Catechism (WA 30 I, 214, 34 ff.).

[7] Even baptizing in the name of Christ (instead of in the name of the Trinity) should — according to the example of the earliest church — be permitted, at least as a general principle. Buchwald, *Ungedr. Predigten Bugenhagens*, p. 209, 27 ff. But the rituals, books of forms, etc., make no use of this.

[8] Cf. in this sense Melanchthon on the sacraments in general, *CR* 31, 468—470.

But this attesting and assuring significance of Baptism would scarcely justify according it so important a place beside the preaching of the Gospel, as is done in the doctrine of the church and is also expressed in the accepted name of the sacrament. The fact that the function of the act of initiation is ascribed to Baptism makes this more understandable. Through Baptism we are "received into Christendom" *(in die Christenheit genommen)* (WA 30 I, 212, 8), "that in this way we may be recognized as a people of Christ our Duke" *(das wir dar bey erkennet werden eyn volck Christi unssers hertzogen)* (WA 2, 727, 22; WA 37, 263, 2). Through Baptism we enter the congregation of those to whom the promises of God are spoken and who, therefore, belong to the church (Melanchthon *CR* 21, 474; 860). But inasmuch as this entrance takes place through the act of Baptism, it is emphatically stated that the church is not a spiritual communion *(Gemeinschaft)* to which one works up by virtue of one's own spiritual activity. On the contrary, one is called to this communion. One is received into it through an act for which a purely receptive attitude on the part of the person received is essential. This act, therefore, not only separates Christians from non-Christians; it also separates the Christian chapter of our life from the pre-Christian. And it precludes the delusion that our status as Christians is something different from a gift of God. But if the external procedure is "God's arrangement" *(Gottes Ordnung)*, if Christ has "bound" us to this procedure (WA 30 I, 216, 4), then an "external thing" gets a value which distinguishes it definitely from all other externals. True, it gets this value only because of the Word. But this Word connected with it gives to Baptism the character of a "water rich in grace," which becomes something different from "simple water." The name of God spoken at Baptism makes the water a "divine" *(durchgottet)*, "spiritual" *(durchgeistet)*, "divine, heavenly water" *(Gottlich, himelisch Wasser)* (WA 37, 264, 27; 265, 24; 266, 3). Lutheran rituals demand that this sacred character of the act of Baptism should not lead to a superstitious veneration of the water.[9]

But the act of initiation is not merely a portal through which the Christian enters the church in order to leave that portal behind. Lutheranism has a different view. This is shown by its conception of infant baptism. The acceptance of infant baptism is emphatically pointed

[9] E. g., the directive issued by Duke August of Saxony in 1580: "Since in some places what has still remained of the papistic magic induces the sextons to sell the baptismal water that is left, just as some also traffic in the hosts which are left and which are afterwards used for magical purposes, the pastors should earnestly admonish the sextons to do away with this; and if it happens again, they should be severely punished." (Sehling, *KO* I, 1, p. 426). — Cf. Joh. Gerhard, *Loci* IX, 210 f.

out and substantiated in the confessions. And the controversy with the Baptists gave definite accents to the whole treatment of the doctrine of Baptism. For the church infant baptism is actually not an exception; it is the rule. Therefore the doctrine of Baptism should not treat of it on the periphery; if it is to be justified at all, infant baptism must become conspicuous in the center. Here Roman Catholic theology has no difficulty; it teaches that the efficacy of the sacrament does not depend at all on the attitude of the person who receives it. For the evangelicals this was impossible because, particularly in the case of Baptism, it seemed impossible to limit the efficacy to the act itself. But Zwingli's conception was equally unsatisfactory to them. According to what he taught, Baptism is primarily a sign for others and affects the baptized person only insofar as it imposes an obligation on him.[10] But this would have minimized the value of everything else the New Testament says about Baptism.

The question — answered in the negative by the Anabaptists — whether it is right to baptize infants had been stated in a better way when this problem was posed. It was said that one should rather ask whether the church has a right to exclude infants from Baptism. But this way of putting the question presupposes as the chief principle that Baptism is primarily and above all a gift, a present from God, which does not depend on the worthiness of the recipient but, on the contrary, includes his need. After clarity had been established with regard to original sin, there could be just as little uncertainty in Lutheranism about the need of infants as there could be about the statement that Baptism is a gift. "For it is most certain," as we read in the Apology, "that the promise of salvation also pertains to little children" *(Certissimum enim est, quod promissio salutis pertinet etiam ad parvulos).* In another place Melanchthon gave proof of this by citing Matt. 19:14. Luther does the same thing. He constantly refers above all to the command of God, who demands unqualifiedly that all nations be baptized and does not impose the condition that faith must precede Baptism. Accordingly, he does not argue from the standpoint of the child; he argues from the standpoint of the church, by which children, as we read in the Augsburg Confession, are "offered to God . . . and received into His grace."[11]

[10] Zwingli, *Sämtl. Werke,* IV, 217, 20; 226, 31 ff.; 231, 24.

[11] On infant baptism especially *CA* IX and Apol. IV, 51 ff. Furthermore, Melanchthon, *Loci, CR* 21, 474 ff. (Matt. 18:14!), 856 ff., and the opinions concerning the Anabaptists, 1, 931 ff., 955 ff. In the other opinions and in the dealings with the Anabaptists, Baptism plays only a subordinate role (2, 997, 1003; 3, 17, 28, 195; 4, 737). — Luther, especially *A Letter on Anabaptism to Two Clergymen (Von der*

But when, in connection with Baptism, Lutheranism attached all the importance to the Word, to the promise, to pardon, to the "receiving" *(acceptatio)*, and to the "adoption" *(adoptio)*, the question whether one had a right to grant Baptism to infants had to become sharper. For in the analogy to the doctrine of justification faith must be demanded as that which receives. Therefore the attempt has been made again and again to ascribe faith even to infants – an "unconscious" *(unbewusst)* faith, the possibility of which should be proved by referring to God's power as the Creator. In what he wrote to the Waldensians and the Bohemians (1523) Luther declared emphatically: "It would be better never to baptize a single child anywhere than to baptize without faith" *(Es were besser, gar uberall keyn kind teuffen denn on glawben teuffen)* (WA 11, 452, 30). Among other things, he adds as proof that "through the faith and the prayer of the church the young children are cleansed from unbelief and the devil, endowed with faith, and thus baptized . . ." (453, 3). But in the Large Catechism and elsewhere he definitely refuses to make Baptism conditional on faith. Furthermore, he relates the faith of children to Baptism only with the words "that they may believe" *(ut credant)*, not "because they believe" *(quia credunt)*. Here – also like Melanchthon and the later dogmaticians – he is thinking of psychological effects.[12]

But the question concerning the faith of children loses importance not only because the validity of Baptism should in no case be made conditional on it as on something already in existence; it is also apt to prove detrimental to the weightiest concern of the Lutheran doctrine of Baptism, namely, that the significance of Baptism should extend throughout one's whole life. And this is true not only of the chronological passing of one's lifetime; it is true of the totality of life – the

Wiedertaufe an zwei Pfarherrn) (1528), WA 26, 144 ff. Furthermore, the Large Catechism (WA 30 I, 218 ff.) and the letters adduced in the next footnote. — Bugenhagen, *Predigt über Mrc. 7: 31 ff.* Buchwald, *Ungedr. Predigten Bugenhagens*, pp. 25 ff. *Braunschweiger KO*, ed. by Hans Lietzmann, pp. 7 ff.

[12] WA 30 I, 219, 15 ff.; WA 26, 164, 23 ff.; WA 37, 279, 23. ". . . that the Lord may give him faith" *(. . . ut det ei dominus fidem)*: WA 15, 710, 11. Cf. 709, 39 ff. It is significant that the statement "the child itself must believe" has been added by the editor. Cf. the deviations in WA 10 I, 2, p. 411. Furthermore, WA 26, 156, 18 ff., WA 46, 687, 21 (Aurifaber's version); Enders 3, 274 ff.; 377 ff.; 4, 51; 10, 1 ff. — Lazarus Spengler's confession of faith (1533, reprinted in Th. Pressel, *L. Spengler*, Elberfeld, 1862, pp. 93 ff.): ". . . therefore I also flatly contradict the heresy of the factious spirits and Anabaptists, who presume to base this salutary token and sacrament on the faith of men, which, of course, is a direct gift of God, and not on His divine promise . . ." (P. 97). — Melanchthon, *CR* 3, 33. — Joh. Pappus, *Commentarius in August. Confessionem*, Frankfurt am Main, 1589, pp. 146 ff.

totality which always comes into question when man deals with God. The whole man must die with Christ; the whole man must rise again with Him — "daily," that is, without interruption. According to Paul, Baptism is the burying of the dying man; but at the same time it is the sacrament of the hope of eternal life. In this way we are "incorporated" *(eingeleibet)* into Christ.[13] "The whole Christian life," said Melanchthon in the *Loci* of 1521, "is a mortification of the flesh and a renewing of the Spirit, and that which Baptism signifies takes place until we rise straight from the dead . . . and for this long a time Baptism is a sacrament of repentance" *(Tota vita christiana, est mortificatio carnis et renovatio spiritus et res, quam significat baptismus, geritur tantisper, dum prorsus a mortuis resurgamus . . . adeoque sacramentum poenitentiae baptismus est)* (Plitt-Kolde, pp. 230 ff.). Here it is necessary to mention that evangelical repentance must embrace judgment concerning sin and faith. For this reason Luther can say in the Large Catechism that Baptism includes the "third sacrament," "penitence, as something that is nothing else than Baptism" (WA 30 I, 221, 13). Not until then does the conception of Baptism as "rebirth" get its deepest meaning. Faith is not without the psyche. Faith receives; the psyche comes into being. To receive Baptism is the first thing; to live in Baptism is the second. "Therefore if you live in penitence, you are walking in Baptism, which not only signifies but also works, begins, and carries on such newness of life . . ." "Therefore Baptism always retains its validity, and even if someone falls from it and sins, still we always have access to it, in order to subdue the old man again." (221, 16 ff.) Rebirth is an event that embraces man's whole life. It is the coming forth of the new man. "Thus this life is not piety; it is the process of becoming pious. It is not health; it is the process of becoming healthy. It is not being; it is becoming. It is not rest; it is activity. As yet we are not; we are becoming. It is not yet done and has not yet taken place; it is in the process of becoming. It is not the end; it is the way. As yet every-

[13] Nowhere are these thoughts, which Luther emphasizes particularly in his early period, expressed more briefly and more strikingly than in the *Nürnberger 23 Frageartikeln* of 1528 (reprinted in Joh. Wilh. v. d. Lith, *Erläuterung der Reformationshistorie vom 1524. bis zum 28. Jahr,* Schwabach, 1733, p. 253): "On Baptism (1) that Baptism is a washing of regeneration in which we put on Christ and are incorporated *(eingeleibt)* into Him and obtain forgiveness of sin; (2) that in Baptism we are planted with Christ unto the same death and through suffering and dying become free from the sinful flesh; (3) that in addition we have the promise and the hope that we, like Christ, will rise again; (4) that all nations should be baptized in the name of the Father and of the Son and of the Holy Spirit; (5) that infant baptism is efficacious and is not to be rejected; (6) that those who have been baptized are resigned to suffering and death in order that they may be rid of the sinful flesh." Cf. also *Fränk. Bek.*, p. 165.

thing does not glow and glisten; but everything is getting better." (WA 7, 337, 30.) This is true of the effect faith has on the psyche.

In Baptism, however, faith receives the first thing, which at the same time is also the whole thing and the last thing: "eternal holiness" *(aeternam sanctitatem)* (WA 37, 266, 37). No child of man should be excluded from receiving this; for, after all, it is merely a receiving. The child *must* consent to being given into death through Baptism, just as it *must* consent to being "conceived and born in sin." But that God promises it "eternal holiness" and eternal life — this it *may* consent to. And not even from an adult does God demand more than that we consent to this.[14]

23. The Sacrament of the Altar [1]

As in the case of Baptism, the protagonists of Lutheranism in the sixteenth century had no thought of making a breach in the principle of catholicity when they dealt with Holy Communion. They knew as

[14] The more recent presentations concerning the later development of the doctrine of Baptism are all based on Baier's *Compendium* and on the literature quoted by him. Even Baier points out that the later comments on the "heavenly material" *(materia coelestis)* were only provoked by the question put by the Mömpelgard Religious Colloquy (*Comp.*, p. 879). Therefore this can be disregarded here. — Concerning the questions pertaining to the ritual of Baptism, especially the practice of having sponsors, cf. the works of Höfling and P. Graff that have been mentioned.

[1] Note 1 under *The Doctrine of the Two Natures* gives the exact titles of the following writings: *Mansfelder Bekenntnis,* 1560; *Bekenntnis der Niedersachsen,* 1572; *Bekenntnis der Universitäten Leipzig und Wittenberg,* 1574. In addition, Brenz, *De majestate,* 1562; *Gegner v. A. Musculus,* 1576; F. Petri, *Num fides,* 1584; *Acta Coll. Montis Bell.,* 1586; Aeg. Hunnius, *Bestendige Widerlegung,* 1597. Furthermore, Ph. Nicolai, *Sacrosanctum mysterium,* 1602; L. Hutter, *Analysis,* 1602; B. Mentzer, *Exegesis,* 1615; Hülsemann, *Manuale,* 1631.

In addition, the following: The *Swabian Syngramma,* quoted according to a later printing: *Clarissimorum virorum, qui a. 1526 Halae Svevorum convenerunt, Syngramma et pium et eruditum super verbis Coenae Dominicae,* Frankfurt am Main, 1561. — *Die Wittenberger Konkordie,* according to *CR* 3, 75 ff. — *Confessio et Apologia pastorum et reliquorum ministrorum Ecclesiae Magdeburgensis,* Magdeburg, 1550 *(Magdeburger Bek.).* — Joachim Westphal, *Farrago consentanearum et inter se dissidentium opinionum de coena Domini, ex Sacramentariorum libris congesta,* 1552. — The same writer, *Epistola, qua breviter respondet ad convicia Joh. Calvini, item Responsio ad scriptum Johannis a Lasco, in quo Augustanam Confessionem in Cinglianismum transformat, Ursellis,* 1557. — *Johannis Brentii Confession, Lehr und Bekandtnuss vom Streit uber den worten des H. Nachtmals Christi, die er sammt andern Theologen in Schwaben wider Zwinglium, Oecolampaden und Carolstaden im Jar 25 und 29 geschrieben und geführt. Item D. Pauli Eberi, Wittembergischen Pfarrherrns erste Confession und erklärung,* Heidelberg, 1556 (by anonymous opponents). — Martin Chemnitz, *Anatome propositionum Alberti Hardenbergii de Coena Domini. Adjuncta sunt alia quaedam eiusdem argumenti a D. Joachimo Morlino* (contains, among other things, the *Sententia concionatorum Bremensium de prioribus propositionibus D. A. Hardenbergii* and the *Sententia D. A. Hardenbergii de propos. Conc. Brem.*), Eisleben, 1561. — N. Selnecker, *Christliche, Wahrhafftige Widerlegung und Ableinung der fürnembsten ungegründten Auflagen, mit welchen die*

well as their opponents did that according to Paul the Sacrament of the Altar should be a meal of communion *(Gemeinschaft)*, not of strife. "For who denies that the Sacrament of the Supper is a symbol and a protestation of communion?" *(Sacramentum enim coenae symbolum esse et communionis protestationem quis negat?)* The *Swabian Syngramma* put this question to Oecolampadius. At that time Melanchthon declared that he wanted to hold with the early teachers (*CR* 1, 830). He said that he had no desire to originate a new dogma in the church, that he did not want to deviate from the "consensus of the church" (1, 901). And in the year of the Augsburg Confession he published *Opinions of Some Early Writers Concerning the Lord's Supper (Sententiae veterum aliquot scriptorum de coena Domini)* (23, 733 ff.). The confession drawn up in 1572 by the Lower Saxonians considered it to be its task to refute the charge that "new, strange opinions were being taught" *(newe frembde opiniones getrieben)* in their church. Brenz wanted to make use of the statements of the fathers with the necessary respect, provided, of course, that they were understood "with great promptitude of the heart according to the analogy of the faith" *(magna animi promptitudine iuxta analogiam fidei)* (*De div. maj.*, 96). Luther was ready to acknowledge that in spite of all misuses the Sacrament of the Lord's Supper had also been preserved in the Roman Church.[2] The conviction that there

Sacramentirer die reine Kirchen zu beschweren sich unterstehen . . ., Dresden, 1576. — M. Chemnitz, *Repetitio sanae doctrinae de vera praesentia corporis et sanguinis in coena*, 1561. — N. Selnecker, *Libellus brevis et utilis de Coena Domini*, Leipzig, 1561. — *Summa purioris Doctrinae de sacrosancta Coena Domini . . . ad nascentem Ecclesiam Galliae missa a ministris verbi, qui sunt in ditione Comitum Mansfeldensium*, Eisleben, 1562. — Tiliman Hesshusius, *Kurtze und einfeltige Anleitung, Wie die wahre gegenwertigkeit des Leibs und Bluts Jhesu Christi im heiligen Abentmal aus unwiderleglichem Grund Göttlichen Worts zubeweisen sey*, Königsberg, 1569. — Joh. Wigand, *Causae, cur in coenae Dominicae verbis* τὸ ῥητὸν *sit retinendum*, Jena, 1571. — Aegid. Hunnius, *Articulus sive Locus de Sacramentis vet. et novi Testamenti, praecipue de Baptismo et Coena Domini*, Frankfurt am Main, 1595. — From the next century I mention only the Biblicist Sebastian Schmidt, *Tract. de principiis s. fundamentis praesentiae corporis*, 3d ed., *Argent.*, 1711.

Heinr. Schmid, *Der Kampf der Luth. Kirche um Luthers Lehre vom Abendmahl im Reformationszeitalter*, 1868. — R. Rocholl, *Die Realpräsenz*, 1875, and *Altiora quaero*, 1899. — W. Köhler, *Zwingli und Luther* I, 1924. — K. Barth, *Ansatz und Absicht in Luthers Abendmahlslehre, ZZ*, 1923, No. 4. — L. Ihmels, *Das lutherische Verständnis des Abendmahls, AELKZ*, 1928, pp. 464 ff. — Paul Althaus the Younger, *Luthers Abendmahlslehre, Luther-Jahrbuch*, 1929, pp. 1 ff. — E. Sommerlath, *Der Sinn des Abendmahls nach Luthers Gedanken über das Abendmahl 1527—1529*, 1929. — Y. Brilioth, *The Eucharist in the Lutheran Church, The Review of the Churches*, 1929, pp. 188 ff.

[2] In *A Letter of Dr. Martin Luther Concerning His Book About Private Mass (Ein Brief D. Martin Luthers von seinem Buch der Winkelmesse)* (1534), in which Luther stresses as strongly as possible the contrast with the Roman Mass and protests emphatically against placing the church and the fathers above Christ: "Here-

was agreement with the past was so strong that in 1560 the preachers of Mansfeld expressed the opinion "that from times of old really no article [pertaining to matters of religion] has been attacked less than the doctrine of the venerable Sacrament of the Body and the Blood of Christ" (*Mansfeld Confession,* p. 173). Even with reference to the use of the round Host, Aegidius Hunnius cited the example of the "early church," which one has the "Christian liberty" to follow (*Bestendige Widerlegung,* p. 18).[3] Because of this conservative position the Reformed Church, which held to a different belief and was accused of depriving the Sacrament of the Altar of the content it has in accordance with its institution, characterized the Lutheran doctrine of the Lord's Supper as "Catholic" – naturally, in the evil sense of the word. At the Marburg Colloquy, Zwingli had accused Luther of giving support to "the papacy" (WA 30 III, 159, 36). And in the resolution he addressed to the states assembled in Berlin on March 28, 1614, Johann Sigismund, Elector of Brandenburg, censured Luther for having remained stuck "very deep in the darknesses of the papacy" so far as his doctrine of the Lord's Supper was concerned.[4]

It was impudent on the part of the elector to say that Luther himself

with, therefore, I now confess again before God and the whole world . . . that where Mass is celebrated according to Christ's directive, whether it be among us Lutherans or in the papacy or in Greece or in India, although there is only the one form — which, of course, is wrong and a misuse, as is done in the papacy at Eastertime and at other times of the year when they commune the people — that there under the form of the bread there is the true body of Christ, given for us on the cross; under the wine, the true blood of Christ, shed for us . . ." (WA 38, 264, 26 ff.; 266, 5 ff.). — Cf. Apol. IV, 55.

[3] The most extensive discussion of this question of ritual is found in the dissertation by Ernst Zephyrius (from Celle), *De fractione panis, praes. Georgio Mylio, Wittenberg,* 1605.

[4] "Finally, as for Mr. Luther, we acknowledge him as a chosen vessel of God through whom very much that is good has happened to the church. And we would be sorry to think or believe anything else about him. On the other hand, you will agree with us when we say that he has stuck very deep in the darknesses of the papacy. For this reason it is not surprising that he will not be able completely to extricate himself and make his way out of all the teachings of men. In his own writings he firmly attests that he has studied and learned the doctrine of the Lord's Supper as it now continues to be practiced in the Lutheran churches — namely, that in, with, and under the bread and the wine the body and the blood are physically present in an invisible manner — not from the Holy Spirit or out of divine Scripture but from Cardinal de Aliaco, whose doctrine has long since been rejected by the papists." Quoted according to L. Hutter, *Calvinista Aulico-Politicus, Alter, Wittenberg,* 1614, p. 47. — The same charge in the little controversial writing *Responsum ad Epistolam cuiusdam Anonymi Calviani, qua Theses Jacobi Schopperi . . . de s. coena ab ipso publice defensas oppugnare conatus fuit,* Wittenberg, 1605. — Jac. Schopper the Younger was a professor at Altdorf. He had written *De s. Coena* in 1594.

confessed that he did not get his doctrine of the Lord's Supper from Holy Scripture. Nevertheless, it was more honest than the attempts to read the Reformed doctrine of the Lord's Supper into the public statements of the evangelical church – the attempts about which the Lutherans constantly complained ever since Luther's letter to the citizens of Frankfurt. For the elector's statement contained at least an acknowledgment that here an unbridgeable ditch had been dug. Luther could counter the foolish charge that he was giving support to the papacy with the well-founded declaration that he had "tussled" *(herumgeräuft)* enough with the papacy itself even with regard to the Lord's Supper. Consequently, the question arises to what extent one had to admit that the medieval church had the Sacrament of the Altar and to what extent one had to deny that the Reformed Church had it. Nowhere is this expressed more briefly, and nowhere more pertinently, than in the tenth article of the Unaltered Augsburg Confession: ". . . that in the Lord's Supper the body and the blood of Christ are truly present and distributed to those who partake of it" *(quod corpus et sanguis Christi vere adsint et distribuantur vescentibus in coena Domini).* Here the real presence and the receiving of the body and the blood of Christ in the Lord's Supper are dealt with – and above all what was taught about this.

It is significant that the Lutheran confessions – in contradistinction to many Reformed confessions – never derived their doctrine of the Lord's Supper from a general definition of the sacraments.[5] This would only have obscured the fact to which the greatest importance is constantly attached: that Christ's words of institution are "extraordinary" *(inusitata),* without analogy of any kind (*FC, SD* VII, 38). Just as Christian Baptism – of which, after all, pre-Christian analogies were acknowledged – so the celebration of the Lord's Supper is based, first of all in a purely positivistic manner, on the institution by Christ. What Luther said about Baptism should also be true of the Lord's Supper: that when the question is asked "whether it is necessary or not," all creatures must keep silence if God directs that it be done (WA 19, 496, 3 ff.).[6] If the importance due Christ's words per se can still be in-

[5] Even though the general definitions are by no means lacking: *CA* XIII; Apol. V, 42; VII, 1; 3 ff.; 14; XII, 49, 69. Smalcald Articles III, 5. *Magdeburger Bek.* of 1550, *Bl.* C 3. — M. Chemnitz, *Ex. Conc. Trid.* II, 3 ff.; Anton Haggenbusch (from Laubach), *De sacramentis in genere,* Giessen, 1608, and all later dogmaticians.

[6] Joh. Wigand, *Causae, Bl.* C 3: "In this Supper there is a special arrangement, a special decree, a special will of God. . . . The reason is that Christ Himself spoke. Thus He ordained, thus He willed, thus the evangelists wrote through the Holy Spirit, thus the words sound, thus they speak, thus they testify." *(In hac Coena est peculiaris constitutio, peculiare decretum, peculiaris voluntas Dei. . . . Causa est, quia Christus ipse dixit, Sic sancivit, sic voluit, sic Evangelistae per*

creased, this can be done by the fact that they should have validity as His testament. Here He instituted the sacrament "with great deliberation and earnestness" *(mit grossem Bedacht und Ernst)* – the sacrament "which was to be a constant memorial of His bitter suffering and death, and of all His benefactions; a seal of the new covenant; a comfort for all troubled hearts; and a constant bond and union of Christian with Christ, their Head, and among one another" *(SD* VII, 44, 50). He who violates Christ's last will severs the tie that binds him to Christ as well as to Christians. But by directing that the act be repeated and by attaching His promise to it He gave the guarantee that at later celebrations there would be no less and that no less would be given than at the first one. "Because it is not contrary to Scripture or faith that Christ's words, as we understand them, give Christ's body at the first celebration of the Lord's Supper, we see no reason why this should be contrary to Scripture and faith at other celebrations of the Lord's Supper" (WA 26, 286, 29). And Brenz declares that when we celebrate the Lord's Supper, we receive Christ's body and blood with no other veneration, no other faith, no other obedience "than if we had reclined at that first supper, which Christ celebrated while He was still on earth and was visibly present" *(quam si accubuissemus in prima illa coena, quam Christus adhuc in terra coram visibili praesentia celebravit)* (*De div. Maj.*, p. 171; *SD* VII, 75).[7]

According to the account of the institution, there can be no doubt that Christ wanted a definite act to be repeated. Against the Roman Mass the Formula of Concord remarked: "But Christ's command, 'This do,' embraces the whole action or administration of this sacrament – that in a Christian assembly we take, consecrate, distribute, receive, eat, and drink bread and wine, and by so doing proclaim the Lord's death – must be kept complete and unchanged" (*SD* VII, 83 f.). On this assumption we may be certain that Christ fulfills His promise, that we receive His body and His blood when we receive the bread and the wine. These words of promise, the "proper basis" *(propria sedes)* of the doctrine of the Lord's Supper *(Bekenntnis der Niedersachsen)*, tolerate no special interpretation; for they need none. For, as Chemnitz sets forth

Spiritum s. scripserunt, sic verba sonant, sic loquuntur, sic testificantur.) — The people of Mansfeld to the Gallic church, *Bl. D* 5 (4): ". . . for if there is no other reason for the necessity, the reason of the institution and the will of the Son of God is alone sufficient for Christians" *(. . . si enim nulla sit alia ratio necessitatis, sola sufficit Christianis ratio institutionis ac voluntatis filii Dei).* — Melanchthon, *CR* 1, 948 f.

[7] Cf. Claus Harms in the theses of 1817: "If the body and blood of Christ were in the bread and wine at the Marburg Colloquy in 1529, they are still there in 1817."

against Hardenberg, when Christ says that what is present, distributed, and received in Holy Communion is His body, which is given for us, He is speaking "of the substance of His body" *(de substantia sui corporis)*. For concerning *this substance* there is the certainty that it is given for us.[8] But since this real presence of the body of Christ is bound to the act itself, it follows that a lasting union of the body and the blood with the elements "apart from the use" *(extra usum)* cannot be meant. The establishment of this fact affects not only the "private Masses" *(Winkelmessen)*. No, in this way the bottom is knocked out of certain calumnies on the part of the Reformed Church. And for a time Melanchthon was not proof against these calumnies.[9]

Accordingly, the formula that the body and the blood of Christ are distributed and received "in, with, and under the bread and the wine" is used for the purpose of excluding every other "union" *(conjunctio)* and to express in a positive way nothing else than simultaneity.[10] All definitions of the manner in which the elements are united with the body and the blood of Christ as well as of the manner in which the body and the blood of Christ are received together with the bread and the wine have only limitative significance. This is true first of all of the rejection of the doctrine of transubstantiation. As the Formula of Concord expressly states, the formula "in, with, and under" is directed primarily against this doctrine (*SD* VII, 35).[11] In his *On the Captivity (De captivitate)* Luther had attacked the doctrine of transubstantiation because, as he set forth, it is merely a product of scholastic theology and therefore cannot be made an article of faith.[12] He is happy "that among the people there is left the simple faith in this sacrament . . . they believe

8 The Hungarian *Conf. Montana,* Art. X: "We teach and believe that at the Supper of the Lord the true and substantial body and blood of the Lord that was born of a virgin and suffered on the cross is taken by the church" *(In coena Domini docemus et credimus, verum et substantiale corpus et sanguinem Domini, de virgine natum et in cruce passum, sumi ab Ecclesia).*

9 *Bekenntnis d. Niedersachsen, Bl. Cij* (7). — *Bekenntn. d. Univ. Leipzig und Witt.* of 1574, *Bl. Diiij.* — Luther, *Von der Winkelmesse* (1533), WA 38, 195 ff.; Enders 15, 182, 16. — *Wittenberger Konkordie, CR* 3, 75. — *Magdeburger Bekennt. gegen die Billigung der Messe ohne Kommunion durch d. Interim, Bl. C 3 b.* — Chemnitz, op. cit., *Bl. B 2,* against "mixing" *(commixtio)* and "inclusion" *(inclusio).*

10 Proof in L. Hutter, *Analysis,* pp. 538 ff. — Luther to Paul Speratus (1522), Enders 3, 399.

11 Cf. Selnecker, *Libellus IX.*

12 WA 6, 508 ff. Here Luther tells that Cardinal de Aliaco was the first to call his attention to the questionableness of the doctrine of transubstantiation. Elector John Sigismund's statement that Luther admitted that he "learned" his doctrine of Holy Communion from the cardinal is correctly clarified by the fact that here the rejection of the specifically Roman dogma is discussed.

simply in faith that Christ's body and blood are truly contained there" *(apud vulgum relictam esse simplicem fidem sacramenti huius . . . simpliciter fide Christi corpus et sanguinem veraciter ibi contineri credunt)* (WA 6, 510, 20 ff.). Thus Luther demands that no theory interpose itself between the act of Holy Communion and faith. For this reason the Confession of the Lower Saxonians also mentions "local inclusion, natural mixture, joining" *(localem inclusionem, naturalem permixtionem, affixionem)* among the "ways" *(modi)* that are to be rejected in addition to transubstantiation. When it is then stated of the presence of the body of Christ that it is invisible and incapable of being perceived, this simply establishes the empirical state of affairs. But that the body of Christ "is truly and essentially present, this we commend to Him who instituted the sacrament" *(wahrhafftig und wesentlich gegenwertig sey, das befehlen wir dem Stiffter)*. In agreement with Luther the theory is rejected that Christ descends from and ascends to the right hand of God every time the Lord's Supper is celebrated. And Brenz adds that when the Roman Catholic theory ascribes the descending to the power of the words of consecration, "This is magic" *(Haec est magia)* *(De maj.*, 165).

The same thing is true of what the other side said about the manner of the presence. When, in opposition to Zwingli and the fanatics, the "metaphorically" *(tropice)*, the "signifies" *(Bedeuten)*, and the *alloeosis* are rejected, the contrast again is: "that they [the body and the blood of Christ] are simply but truly present and received" *(simpliciter sed vere adesse et sumi)*. In the age of Calvin it is important above all to refute the misinterpretations which state that the presence of Christ is understood "quantitatively" *(quantitative)*, "qualitatively" *(qualitative)*, or "locally" *(localiter)*; that a "crude, carnal, local, or physical mixture" *(crassam, carnalem, localem seu physicam commixtionem)* is taught. Thus Chemnitz against Hardenberg. But it is equally true that the concepts "substantially and corporally" *(substantialiter et corporaliter)*, which recur frequently among the Lutherans, do not propose to give an accurate definition of the way and the manner. On the contrary, they are meant to express opposition to the teaching represented by those who said that "only the vigor or the efficacy of the absent body is present, the substance of which is as far removed from the Supper that is celebrated on earth as heaven is from the earth" *(adsit tantum vigor sive efficacia corporis absentis, cuius substantia a coena, quae in terra celebratur, tam procul remota sit quam distat coelum a terra)*. It is self-evident that the formula "sacramental union" *(unio sacramentalis)* — which is supposed to say everything there is to be said (*SD* VII, 37) — signifies nothing more than that those who used it did not give an exact definition of the way and the manner. Bucer's explanation of the *Wittenberg Concord* states: "It is a heavenly matter, it is exhibited in a heavenly manner" *(Res coelestis est, coelesti ratione exhibetur)*. In this way – so it was said here – the statement is to be rejected "that Doctor Luther, together with his associates, teaches that Christ is united with the elements 'bread' and 'wine' in a natural manner or that these things are exhibited in any way to the present age" *(nec D. Lutherum cum suis docere Christum cum elementis panis et vini uniri naturaliter aut exhiberi ea ulla ratione seculo praesenti)*.[13]

The same thing is true of the definitions that are given of the manner of receiving. Materially not a single statement made by the Lutherans goes beyond the way the Augsburg Confession expresses this: "is truly distributed and received" *(wahrhaftiglich ausgeteilt und genommen wird)*. In the controversy everything centers in the "oral" receiving. This was the one point of the Lutheran doctrine that was attacked indefatigably by the Reformed Church. Yet there can be no earnest doubt that the receiving means the eating – if, according to Him who instituted the sacrament, it is the act itself that matters. For this the Formula of Concord also refers to Paul: ". . . that all who receive the blessed bread also partake of the body of Christ. Therefore he certainly cannot be speaking of a spiritual eating; but he is speaking of a sacramental or oral eating of the body of Christ, in which both the pious and the godless Christians participate." (*SD* VII, 56.) Here, too, the definitions are either merely limitative or negative in nature: ". . . not, however, in a coarse, carnal, Capernaitic manner, but in a supernatural, incomprehensible manner" (64).[14] Nor did the later dogmaticians go beyond this.[15] Actually the "oral eating" *(manducatio oralis)* is merely the simple application of the statement concerning the real presence of the body of Christ. Whether the real presence was taught was at the same time the test of honesty in this matter. Since this doctrine was disputed by the opposition, one also knew what to think of likening Calvin's way of speaking to the Lu-

[13] *CR* 3, 79. — Cf. the later limitations of the "in, with, and under" *(in, sub et cum)*. E. g., in Hafenreffer, *Loci*, 612 f.

[14] Somewhat differently in the *Bek. d. Niedersachsen:* ". . . not in a visible, natural, fleshly, perceptible manner but in an invisible, hidden, imperceptible, and inscrutable manner" *(Bl. Ciijb)*.

[15] Heerbrand, *Comp.* of 1585, p. 588. — Joh. Gerhard, *Loci* X, 301 ff. — Ph. Nicolai, *Sacros. omnipraes. myst.*, 562. — König, *Theol. pos.*, 247. — Quenstedt, *Theol.* IV, 204. — Baier, *Comp.*, 920. — Against the repulsive chicanery on the part of Reformed theologians with regard to consistency cf. Chemnitz, *De coena*, 20. — Hafrenreffer, *Loci*, 616 ff., speaks only of the "sacramental eating" *(manducatio sacramentalis);* but he, like the others, contrasts it in an especially sharp manner with the "spiritual eating" *(manducatio spiritualis)*, of which John 6 speaks.

theran way. Chemnitz is right when he says: "For as the union or the presence of the body of Christ is in the Supper, so the eating is" *(Qualis enim est unio seu praesentia corporis Christi in coena, talis etiam est manducatio)* (*De coena,* 20).

The other point of attack for the polemics carried on by the Reformed Church was the doctrine concerning the partaking of the sacrament by those who are unworthy, the "excrement of Satan" *(excrementum Satanae)* accepted by the Lutherans, as Beza expressed it with particularly good taste. Luther had enunciated this doctrine unambiguously in his *A Confession Concerning the Lord's Supper* (1528; WA 26, 491, 4 ff.). The Oberlanders had recognized it in the *Wittenberg Concord* of 1536. Likewise Brenz.[16] It had been repeated in the Smalcald Articles (III, 6), and Luther's Large Catechism had made it common property. Naturally, the crypto-Calvinists rejected it. Finally the Formula of Concord defended it with special emphasis.[17] On the Lutheran side the cardinal passage was to be found in the words of Paul, 1 Cor. 11:29, which Luther had also employed indirectly and allusively in the Small Catechism. But it is clear that the exegesis applied here had its basis in the total conception of the Lord's Supper as this conception had been brought about by the account of the institution. Now, of course, the question was whether it is faith that produces the real presence of Christ. This thought was not very remote when the *Swabian Syngramma* put all the emphasis on the Word of Christ and added: "But the symbol of the Supper confirms faith, not on account of the act but on account of the Word" *(Coenae autem symbolum confirmat fidem, non propter factum sed propter verbum),* or when Luther declares in the Small Catechism that it is faith, not the eating and the drinking, which obtains what the words of Christ promise. For from the analogy to the doctrine of justification one could conclude that the good of salvation *(das Heilsgut)* is received by faith, but that unbelief goes away empty. Even the *Syngramma,* however, is as far away as anything could be from a spiritual volatilization of the real presence. It is precisely the real presence of "the physical body of Christ given for us" *(corpus Christi corporale pro nobis traditum)* which the Word is said to guarantee. Therefore the formal analogy to the doctrine of justification must lead to the opposite result. Just as unbelief never does away with the efficacy of the Word of God, so it does not do away with the efficacy of the Word of Christ which guarantees His real presence. But just as – likewise according to Luther – unbelief in the face of the Word of promise is the gravest sin, so it is also the real

[16] Cf., e. g., Brenz, *Exegesis in Joh. Ev.,* Hagenow, 1528, pp. 125(b) f.

[17] *SD* VII, 8; 16; 27; 32; 63; 68; 88; 123.

mark of "unworthiness" at the Lord's Supper. Luther's conviction is accurately reproduced when the Formula of Concord wants this concept applied, not to "Christians weak in faith, timid, and sorrowful" but to those who "go to the sacrament without true contrition and sorrow for their sins, without true faith, and without the good intention to improve their life" (*SD* VII, 68 f.; cf. Enders 13, 153). If impenitence in the face of the Word of promise has fatal consequences, it leads to the same result, inasmuch as it is "unworthiness" at Holy Communion. But the special thing in connection with Holy Communion is the fact that here the power of the Word which compels a decision is exercised by Christ, who is present by virtue of the Word. Over against an unworthy person, however, this presence can be no different from what it is for one who has faith. For it is this presence that compels the decision. But if at the Lord's Supper, as has been said, everything depends on the act, to which the eating necessarily belongs, unworthy persons despise the body of Christ not only when the Word is heard but also with the "oral eating" *(manducatio oralis).* It is perfectly logical when the Lutherans substantiate the transsubjective real presence of Christ in the same way by declaring that it is not done away with either by the unworthiness of the clergyman who distributes the sacrament or by the unworthiness of the person who receives the sacrament.[18] "In the same way I also speak of and confess the Sacrament of the Altar, that here the body and the blood are truly eaten and drunk orally in the bread and the wine, even if the priests who distribute the sacrament did not believe or were guilty of other misuses. For this does not rest on the faith or the unbelief of men; it rests on God's Word and on what He has ordained" (WA 26, 506, 21).

The most vehemently contested statements of the Lutheran doctrine of the "oral eating" *(manducatio oralis)* and the eating "of the unworthy" *(indignorum)* are hard but inevitable results of the doctrine of the real presence. They were the standard by which one could measure whether this doctrine was taken seriously. Now they also enable one to understand why Luther recognized the sacrament in the Roman Church but denied that the Swiss had it. If we still postpone the question about the relationship to justification as well as about the "profit" *(Nutzen)* of the sacrament, it is clear first of all in what respect there was an awareness of being related to the Roman Church with regard to the Sacrament of the Altar. In spite of the untenable doctrine of transubstantiation, in spite of the withholding of the cup from the laity, in spite of

[18] Luther in the Large Catechism V, 15. — *Bek. d. Univ. Leipzig und Wittenberg, Bl. Eij.* — *SD* VII, 16.

the sacrificial act of the priest which is almost blasphemous to evangelical ears, in spite of many absolutely unacceptable details of the rite of the Mass that result from this, and in spite of the fact that "this dragon's tail, the Mass, has begotten much vermin and dung of many kinds of idolatry" *(dieser Drachenschwanz, die Messe, viel Ungeziefers und Geschmeiss mancherlei Abgötterei gezeuget)* – as Luther says in the Smalcald Articles – in spite of all this it could not be denied that even according to what the Roman Church teaches "the body and the blood of Christ are truly present in the Lord's Supper and are distributed to those who partake [of the sacrament]" *(corpus et sanguis Christi vere adsint et distribuantur vescentibus in coena Domini).* One had to acknowledge that here the receiving of His body guaranteed by the Word of Him who instituted the sacrament was emphatically assessed as a gift of transsubjective origin and transsubjective reality. It is true that further pursuit of this sharing *(Gemeinsamkeit)* threatened to hurl the evangelical side back into the doctrine of efficacy "resulting from the work performed" *(ex opere operato).* But against this the Augsburg Confession (XIII) had already erected a frontier wall by rejecting this doctrine in no uncertain terms and by speaking in the German text of the *true* faith. In this way the antithesis had been marked correctly and sufficiently. At the same time, however, the doctrine concerning the "eating of the unworthy" *(manducatio indignorum)* had left room for the acknowledgment of the transsubjective reality of the presence of Christ.

The state of affairs was totally different vis-à-vis the doctrine of the Reformed Church. Here the deductions concerning the "oral eating and the eating of the unworthy" *(manducatio oralis et indignorum)* also challenged their basic assumption – the real presence and the real receiving of the body of Christ – in which the Lutherans saw the meaning of the whole act. Perhaps the external relationship to the Lutheran rite of Holy Communion was greater than it was between that of the Lutherans and that of the Roman Catholics. But this could not gloss over the fact that although the act desired by Christ was repeated, this was done with the firm determination on no account to let belief in the real presence come up. Indeed, Pareus, of Heidelberg, who was widely praised because of his "irenics," even justified the Reformed rite of breaking the bread by stating expressly that in this way the "idolatry" of Lutheran Holy Communion is broken down in the most radical way and that the "idol" of Christ present in the bread is cast down in the hearts of the people.[19] The Lutheran doctrine of Holy Communion is

[19] David Pareus, *Tractatus de Sacra Eucharistia succinctus quidem et absolutissimus (coll. Joach. Ursinus),* Amberg, 1612, p. 222.

spoken of again and again in this "irenic" style. The consensus which Calvin arrived at with Zurich in 1549 placed the Lutheran teaching on a level with the Roman doctrine of transubstantiation because, as they said, it was equally absurd.[20] The Reformed preachers in Emden stated that on account of the "idolatrous doings" *(Götzenwerk)* in the Lutheran rite of Holy Communion there was "no difference whatever between them [the Lutherans] and the papists."[21] When in spite of heaped-up charges of Roman doctrine and Roman idolatry pressure was constantly brought to bear on Lutheranism to induce it to disavow the "differences" and to unite with the Reformed Church – is it any wonder that finally the opponents were taken at their word with the statement that actually Lutheranism was closer to the "papists" (with the exception of the Jesuits) than to the "Calvinists"?[22]

It would have been fairer if the *Consensus Tigurinus* had charged that the Lutheran doctrine of Holy Communion was even more absurd than the Roman doctrine. For in the doctrine of transubstantiation Luther had already seen an attempt at rationalization – an attempt by means of which the possibility of the real presence was to be made understandable. Conversely, however, it was in the way of putting the question – the way presupposed here – that Reformed theology found itself in agree-

[20] *Bek. d. RK,* p. 163, 13: "For neither do we consider it less absurd to put Christ under the bread or to join Him with the bread than to transubstantiate the bread into His body" *(Neque enim minus absurdum iudicamus, Christum sub pane locare vel cum pane copulare quam panem transsubstantiare in eius corpus).*

[21] *Historischer Warhafftiger bericht unnd Lehre Göttlichen Worts von dem gantzen Streit und handel dess heiligen Abendmals . . . Durch die Prediger der Christlichen Gemeine zu Emden. Mit angefügter Vorrede Christophori Pezelij . . . ,* Amberg, 1591, p. 4.

[22] Polyk. Leyser, *Christianismus, Papismus et Calvinismus, das ist drey unterschiedliche Auslegung des Catechismi Lutheri, 1595, Vorrede.* — On the other hand, *Erwegung Deren Theologen meynung, die sich nicht schewen, Evangelische Herrschafften zu bereden, dass sie lieber mit den Papisten und dem Römischen Antichristen, als mit den Reformierten Evangelischen, die sie auss Hass Calvinisch nennen, Gemeinschafft haben sollen. Aus dem in A. 1614 gedruckten Irenico D. Parei gezogen . . . ,* Amberg, 1620.

The charge that the Reformed were called "Calvinistic" "out of hatred" is illustrated by the fact that the book itself always speaks of the "Lutherans." "What is permissible to Jove . . ." *(Quod licet Jovi . . .).* At the end of this book there is also a defense against the reproaches of "Turkish religion" that were made since 1574 by the Lutherans — by Ph. Nicolai, among others *(Fundamenta sectae Calvinisticae communia cum Nestorianis, Arianis, Mahometanis . . .).* On this account Nicolai is always called the "Nicolaite" (Rev. 2:6). In a quotation from a refutation written in 1597 by the preachers in Zurich it is stated of Nicolai: "And although we . . . this miserable fellow who lays about him and bites like another wild hog, without any reason and Christian modesty . . ." This was spoken in the style of the aristocratic Calvin, who heaped expressions like "calf," "mad dog," and the like, on Joachim Westphal to such an extent that even for Bullinger this was too much.

ment with Roman Catholic theology. But it arrived at opposite conclusions. It stated that the real presence of the body of Christ was *impossible.* One can scarcely find fault with Luther and the Lutheran theologians for asserting in opposition to this statement that "impossibility" is out of the question when, as here, the promise and the doing of God are concerned. But they could not stop with this either if they did not want to subject themselves to the accusation of forcing a solution. If, however, they asked why the real presence was impossible, it was cast into their teeth – as was done at the Marburg Colloquy and later at the Mömpelgard Colloquy – that in connection with the body of Christ, as in connection with every other body, only a "circumscribed," that is, a spatially limited, way of being is conceivable. From the Biblical statements concerning Christ's sitting at the right hand of God and His ascension into heaven, said the Reformed theologians, it is evident that the place to which Christ ascended is a spatially defined and spatially limited place above the stars. "They were enchanted," says Brenz of the Swiss, "by their dream of an empyrean heaven in which Christ now sits, now stands, now walks, and of the condition of a body which cannot be a true body unless it is circumscribed by a place" *(Fascinati sunt suo somnio de coelo Empyraeo, in quo Christus nunc sedeat, nunc stet, nunc ambulet, et de conditione corporis, quod non possit esse verum corpus nisi loco circumscribatur).*[23] Because of the impression made by Luther's doctrine of Holy Communion the spatial interpretation of the "sitting at the right hand of God" was given up in part, but the spatial limitation in a place called heaven was adhered to all the more firmly on the basis of the account of Christ's ascension. Naturally, on this assumption the presence of Christ was "impossible." For then there is a distance in space. In refutation of the Lutheran doctrine of Holy Communion not only Zwingli but also the *Consensus Tigurinus* inspired by Calvin declares with regard to the body of Christ that "it has to be as far away from us as heaven is from the earth" *(necesse est a nobis tanto locorum intervallo distare quantum coelum abest a terra).*[24] It re-

[23] Brenz, *De majestate,* p. 93. — On this contrast in the conceptions of heaven cf. *The States and Offices of Christ* and *The Relativity of the World Picture.*

[24] *Bek. d. RK,* 163, 20. — Among Reformed confessions cf. also the *Erlauthaler Bekenntnis* of 1562: "According to the nature and property of the human flesh, Christ ascends into heaven spatially, by changing the place, sits in one definite place, on the right hand of God according to the flesh, occupies a distinct place" *(Secundum carnis humanae naturam et proprietatem localiter, mutatione loci ascendit in coelum, sedet in uno certo loco, in dextera Dei Christus iuxta carnem, locum definitum occupat* (300, 16 ff.). — *Schottisches Bekenntnis* of 1560, 259, 35. — *Conf. Tarczal-Tordaensis* of 1562, 420, 20 ff. — *Böhmisches Bekenntnis* of 1609, 467, 8: "in which place" *(quo in loco).* — The *Consensus Bremensis* of 1595 calls it "an abominable

mains to be seen whether, in view of this argument, one has the right to praise the Reformed doctrine for being more "spiritual," as has been done up to our time. But it is easy to understand that Brenz was speaking of "carnal dreams of the Zwinglians" *(carnalia somnia Cinglianorum)* (op. cit., p. 165).

In opposition to this, Luther and the Württembergians maintained the doctrine of the "omnipresence" *(Allenthalbenheit)* of the whole Christ. They could do so on the basis of their Christology, which did not permit any kind of separation of Christ from the omnipresent Father; and they could do so on the basis of their conception of the spacelessness *(Unräumlichkeit)* of heaven. Another group in early Lutheranism spoke out against this. In 1572 the confession of the universities of Leipzig and Wittenberg rejected it on the ground that otherwise there would be a violation of the principle that one should make no statement whatever about the "manner of the presence" *(modus praesentiae)*. The *Confession of the Lower Saxonians* in 1572 calls attention to the fact that according to Luther's advice the doctrine of ubiquity should not be divisive. It confined itself to the statement that Christ could be where and when He wants to be, but that this does not mean that He has to be everywhere. Even Brenz advised Duke Christoph not to bother Matthäus Alber, the chaplain who had spoken out against ubiquity. "He is a good, pious man; and he works most industriously in the consistory. Besides, he is a dear colleague of mine." [25] It has already been pointed out that the doctrine of the omnipresence was a necessary result of the impact of the Gospel *(evangelischer Ansatz)*. In addition, this doctrine made it easy for Luther as well as for Brenz to arrive at what they taught concerning Holy Communion. But it also confronted them with certain difficulties.

error" "that the heaven into which Christ ascended is not a place different from the earth and from hell but is merely the heavenly kingdom and is everywhere" (749, 6 ff.).

Joh. Heinr. Heidegger, *Corpus Theol. Christ., Tig.*, 1700, II, 66: "For [Christ] crossed the heavens, namely, the first, in which the air is, and the second, in which are the stars, the sun, and the constellations, Heb. 4:14, and thus was made higher than the heavens, higher than the lower heavens . . ." *(Transiit [Christus] enim coelos, puta primum, in quo aer est, et secundum, in quo stellae, sol et sidera sunt, Hebr. 4, 14, atque sic factus* ὑψηλότερος τῶν οὐρανῶν, *sublimior coelis inferioribus . . .)*. After the omnipresence has been assailed by citing this as the reason, there is the further statement: "Therefore since Christ has left the earth, which is a place, and has gained heaven, a new place, and the movement from that place to this one has been a translating, what is a true, spatial ascension if this one is not?" *(Cum igitur et terram, quae locus est, Christus reliquerit et coelum, novum locum, acquisiverit et ex illo in hunc locum motus translatus fuerit, quid ascensio vera, localis est, si haec non est?)*

[25] Hartmann, in *Württemberg. Kirchengeschichte,* 1893, p. 393.

Indeed, the Reformed objection that according to this doctrine the body of Christ has to be spread out over all space is too unintelligible to be taken seriously. It was right to point out that all those who advocated the doctrine of ubiquity had rejected the "inclusive omnipresence" *(omnipraesentia inclusiva).* In conscious opposition to the "carnal dreams of the Zwinglians" *(carnalia somnia Cinglianorum)* the body of Christ was to be thought of as being outside the barriers of time and space.[26] Against the Zwinglians Brenz also maintained that the divinity in which Christ shares is "absolute: wherever it is, it is in its entirety" *(simplicissima: ubicunque est, tota est).*[27] The real complication which the idea of ubiquity caused for the doctrine of Holy Communion consisted in the fact that Christ's special real presence in Holy Communion seemed to be overlooked. With regard to this Brenz declared that although the whole Christ is always present in His church, His body and His blood are *distributed* in Holy Communion by virtue of His Word. Luther expressed this better: "There is a difference between His presence and your taking. He (namely, God) is free and unbound wherever He is and does not have to stand there like a knave put in a pillory or with an iron collar around his neck. . . . The same thing is true of Christ. Even though He is present everywhere, He does not let you take hold of Him or reach for Him. He can divest Himself of His shell, so that you get the shell and do not take hold of the kernel. Why? Because there is a difference when God is present and when He is present *for you.* But He is present *for you* when He adds His Word, binds Himself with it, and says: 'Here you shall find Me.' Now when you have the Word, you can be certain that you are taking hold of Him and have Him. And you can say: 'Here I have You, just as You say.'" (WA 23, 151, 3 ff.) No matter what stand individuals took with respect to the doctrine of ubiquity, they were all unanimous in holding to the conviction which Hülsemann, in reply to the question that had been raised, later reduced to the formula: "To what extent or in what way Christ is present in the Sacrament of the

[26] This was the main subject of discussion in the East Frisian controversy concerning Holy Communion. In addition to *Historischer Wahrhafftiger bericht,* etc. (mentioned in note 21), cf. *Wahrhafftiger Gegenbericht der rechtgleubigen Predicanten in Ostfrisslandt, auff des D. Petzels Vorrede uber das Embdische Buch vom handel des Abendmals, A. 1590 zu Bremen aussgangen. Erstlich gedruckt zu Embden bey Johan von Oldersum unter das alte Rathaus, A. 1594.* Furthermore, Aegid. Hunnius, *Bestendige Widerlegung,* pp. 306 ff. and 489 ff. — Cf. also Samuel Kefel, *Theses de persona Dom. et Serv. Jesu Christi, praes. Joh. Pappo,* Argentor., 1600, pp. 14 f.

[27] Brenz, op. cit., p. 97. — The statement which the Mansfeldians addressed to the Gallic church in 1562 also quoted the old jingle: *Sumit unus, sumunt nulle, quantum isti, tantum ille. Nec sumptus absumitur.*

Supper, all this must be taken from the institution alone, which determines the whole nature of the sacrament" *(In quantum et quomodo Christus in Sacramento coenae adest, id omne ex sola instiutione sumendum est, quae totam sacramenti naturam limitat)* (*Manuale,* p. 291).

It has already been stated why Luther could not yield to the challenge of Oecolampadius in Marburg to be content with the divinity of Christ — the presence of which was willingly admitted — and not to cling to His humanity. Luther's answer was elucidated in the *Confession of the Lower Saxonians* by the statement that outside the revelation in Christ the divine nature is a "consuming fire." But the method of teaching employed by Calvin and many Reformed confessions — according to which faith was said to be able to fly up to that place in heaven and in this way to overcome the interval of space between it and Christ — was also unacceptable to Lutheran theology in more than one respect.[28] For, in the first place, Lutheran theology's own nonspatial conception of heaven would have necessitated a rejection of the whole spatial approach. In the second place, such a teaching would have made it necessary to hold to the view that although God is present in an immediate manner, He is present without Christ. This was impossible because of the ultimate compulsions of faith. In the third place, it would have been a denial of the decisive realization that in Holy Communion it is not man who is to come to Christ but, conversely, that it is Christ who is to come to man.[29]

But there was another reason for clinging to this very point. In connection with Holy Communion as well as in connection with the impact of the Gospel *(evangelischer Ansatz)* the subject of discussion was faith. If the whole Sacrament of Holy Communion — not only what was taught

[28] *Conf. Tarczal-Tordaensis* of 1562: "For so great is the power of faith or rather of God, whose Word and sacraments faith believes, not that it brings Christ's flesh out of the heavens [for there it is going to remain until He Himself comes to judge the quick and the dead, as Scripture, which faith neither wants to nor can resist], but, on the contrary, that it, relying on the promises of God, constantly bears itself aloft to heaven and there joins them truly and efficaciously to Christ and, to put it this way, incorporates into Him those in whose hearts it itself [in another way, He Himself] is" *(Tanta enim est fidei virtus aut Dei potius cuius verbo et Sacramentis fides credit, non ut Christi carnem e caelis eliciat [ibi enim mansura est, donec ipse veniat judicaturus vivos et mortuos, sicut scriptura testatur, cui fides reluctari nec vult, nec potest] sed e contrario sese in coelum usque subvehat, promissionibus Dei freta, ibique vere et efficaciter Christo illos uniat, et ut ita loquar, incorporet, in quorum animis ipsa [alias: ipse] inest)* (*Bek. d. RK,* 420, 21 ff.) — Cf. *Gr. Westminster-Katechismus* of 1647: ". . . that it might constantly elevate our affections to that place" *(. . . ut affectus nostros eo usque elevaret),* 618, 41.

[29] Andreä at the Mömpelgard Religious Colloquy, *Acta,* p. 166. — In addition, cf. the entire discussion by F. Petri, *Num fides possit supra coelos evolare et illic ipsam carnem Christi comprehendere,* Wittenberg, 1584. — *FC, SD,* VII, 122.

about it but also the use itself — was not to run counter to the impact of the Gospel *(evangelischer Ansatz)* in a most dangerous manner, the relationship to what is promised here cannot be different from what it is in the act of justification. Thus here, too, it was not right to take faith to be anything else than pure receiving. Accordingly, one could not speak seriously here about a flight of faith toward heaven. At best, one could have let this pass as a mere figure of speech, which, however, could not have contributed anything at all to the solution of the problem of Holy Communion. But this then leads to the question concerning the place of Holy Communion in the total doctrine of salvation *(Heilslehre),* which, after all, is determined altogether unambiguously by justification.

If one wanted to take this to be the question concerning the "profit" *(Nutzen),* Lutheran theology conducted itself with a goodly amount of reserve over against this matter. In answer to the charge that the real presence of Christ is neither profitable nor necessary the theologians of Mansfeld replied in what they wrote to the Reformed Church in France that even if this were really the case, still the will of Him who instituted the sacrament would be sufficient. Luther had replied in a similar vein to objections of the same kind. Since this was the fundamental position, the conclusions concerning the "profit" *(Nutzen)* could justify neither the act of Holy Communion nor what had been said about the real presence. If for this reason it is more correct to speak about the effects than about the profit, it is possible to differentiate four groups of ideas. In the first place, the celebration involves "communion, a gathering" *(communio, synaxis).* Luther had emphasized this in his first writings on Holy Communion.[30] But if the real presence was taken for granted, this "communion" *(communio)* — according to the statements of Paul (1 Cor. 10:16 f.) — could be understood only on the basis of the "participation in the body of Christ" *(communicatio corporis Christi)* (*FC, SD* VII, 57 f.). It is not the unity of action and believing on the part of those who partake of the sacrament that engenders this communion; it is Christ, who offers Himself. Therefore the communion at the Lord's Supper is genuine church communion, because the church is not a society but a communion that has been instituted. Looking back from this point, one understands again how impossible it must have seemed to

30 Cf. especially *A Treatise Concerning the Most Holy Sacrament of the True Body of Christ and Concerning the Brotherhoods (Ein Sermon von dem hochwürdigen Sakrament des wahren Leichnams Christi und von den Brüderschaften)* (1519). When in this writing Luther calls the sacrament a "sure sign of this union with and incorporation into Christ" (WA 2, 743, 21), one must note that here he still clings to the doctrine of transubstantiation (749, 10 ff.). — Cf. also the previously quoted question from the *Swabian Syngramma.*

fall in with the aforementioned "ascent of faith." For then the Lord's Supper would change from a communion of receiving into a unity of activity. It is self-evident that on the subjective side participation in the body of Christ results in participation in the mutual love of those who partake of the sacrament.[31]

In the second place, every celebration of Holy Communion in accordance with the will of Him who instituted the sacrament is a renewal of the remembrance of the death of Christ and of all His benefactions. This is emphatically underscored especially by the Formula of Concord (*SD* VII, 44). If the fundamental character of all Christian proclamation is not to be violated here, the decisive point in connection with the "remembrance" *(Gedenken)* is the Word, not the thought of man — the thought that hears this *(nicht der dieses vernehmende Gedanke des Menschen)*. Therefore the words of institution should be "distinctly and clearly spoken or sung publicly before the assembly" at every celebration (79). And here, no less than at other times, the proclamation of the Word should not be a mere demonstration. "The faith of the hearers is awakened, strengthened, and confirmed by Christ's Word" (81).[32]

In the third place, there is, in addition, something special about the strengthening and the assuring that takes place in Holy Communion. The thirteenth article of the Augsburg Confession stated about the sacraments in general that they are signs and a testimony of the divine will toward us, in order to awaken and strengthen our faith. Thus the efficacy of the sacrament, like that of the Word, rests on the fact that it is a means in the hand of God. But the distinctiveness of the sacrament vis-à-vis the Word consists not only in the fact that here the good of salvation *(das Heilsgut)* is symbolized and illustrated but above all in the fact that it is individualized in an unambiguous manner. When Luther demanded: "You must believe not only that Christ is present with His body and His blood but also that here He is given to you as a gift" — this, of course, reminds one that individualization is indeed a specific function of faith. But when the sacrament is dispensed to the individual, every thought that the "for me" *(pro me)* relationship of faith could be a usurpation is out of the question. "For even though in the sermon there is the very thing that there is in the sacrament and vice versa, yet there is the advantage that here [in the sacrament] it points to a particular person. There [in the sermon] one does not point to or specify a person. Here [in the sacrament], however, it is given to you and to me in particular, that the sermon may apply specifically to us."

[31] Luther, WA 2, 754, 9. — Brenz, *De majestate,* 180 f.

[32] Cf. *CA* XXIV, 30 ff. — *Copenhagen Articles* XXVI.

(Denn wiewol ynn der predigt eben das ist, das da ist ym Sacrament und widderumb, ist doch daruber das vorteil, das es hie auff gewisse person deutet. Dort deutet und malet man keine person abe, aber hie wird es dir und mir ynn sonderheit geben, das die predigt uns zu eigen kompt.) (WA 19, 504, 27 ff.) This is also the basic thought of that part of the Small Catechism which deals with Holy Communion.[33] On the basis of his exegesis of John 6, which he shares with the others, as well as on the basis of what he teaches about the "mystical union" *(unio mystica)*, Brenz can even say that Christ is truly present in the believer with His body and blood even at other times. In Holy Communion, however, He *feeds* the believer with His body and blood, "that He may bestow on him those gifts that are salutary for the strengthening of faith and for the assurance of divine mercy" *(ut conferat in ipsum ea dona, quae ad fidei confirmationem et ad certitudinem de divina clementia sunt salutaria)*.[34]

But the individualization that takes place when the sacrament is dispensed to the individual would be entirely meaningless if it did not actually transmit the good in question. For only then is it really a pledge. It not only attests, but it also "*gives* forgiveness of sins, life, and salvation." Christ's work of salvation is appropriated when there is forgiveness of sins. If this was settled when Christ's body was broken and His blood was shed, forgiveness is also an appropriation of His body and blood. Or conversely: the receiving of His body and blood in faith is forgiveness of sins. But just as the atoning power of the death of

[33] Cf. also WA 23, 150, 13 ff. — The Mansfeldians to the Gallic church: "In the first place, you should believe that the body and blood of Christ are given and received in the Supper. In the second place, you should also believe that the body of Christ suffered for you on the cross, that the blood of Christ was shed for you on the cross for your redemption. In the third place, you should also believe that because of that body, which was crucified, and that blood, which was shed, you have remission of sins, life, and eternal salvation; and the spiritual eating is strengthened through that physical eating." *(Initio credas, corpus et sanguinem Christi in coena dari et accipi. Deinde credas quoque, corpus Christi pro te in cruce passum, sanguinem Christi pro te in cruce effusum in redemptionem tuam. Tertio credas etiam, te propter corpus illud crucifixum et sanguinem illum effusum habere remissionem peccatorum, vitam et salutem aeternam ac spiritualis manducatio per illam corporalem confirmatur).* (*Bl. E* 3.)

[34] *De dispensatione corporis et sangu. Christi in coena,* appendix to *De maj.*, p. 169. — Concerning the assuring significance of Holy Communion cf. *Bek. d. Univ. Leipzig und Wittenberg, Bl. Eiij.* — As opposed to Baptism, the "sacrament of initiation" *(sacramentum initiationis)*, L. Hutter does not hesitate to call Holy Communion the "sacrament of assurance" *(sacramentum confirmationis)*, *Analysis,* p. 517. — Joh. Albr. Bengel: "Now if I receive my Savior with my soul's desire and my heart's joy as Him whose body was given for the forgiveness of my sins and therefore for my reconciliation and union with God, I eat His flesh" (O. Wächter, *Bengel,* p. 270).

Christ is dependent on the fact that He was one of us, a true human being "with flesh and blood," so the promise attached to Holy Communion can be fulfilled only if Christ is present here not only according to His divinity, as Oecolampadius maintained, but if "the body and the blood of Christ are truly present and are distributed to those who partake" [of the sacrament] *(corpus et sanguis Christi vere adsunt et distribuuntur vescentibus)*, as the Augsburg Confession taught. "For in His body," says Brenz, "and in His blood, which He expended for the expiation of our sins before God the Father, He bequeathed to us the remission of sins" *(In corpore enim et sanguine suo, quae ad expianda peccata nostra coram Deo patre impendit, legavit nobis remissionem peccatorum)* (op. cit., p. 177).[35]

Finally there is a fourth series of thoughts. Brenz adopts the old concept of the viaticum; others refer to the "medicine of immortality" (φάρμακον ἀθανασίας) of Ignatius.[36] Selnecker calls attention to the words of Cyril: "that Christ is, dwells, and wants to remain in us not only spiritually, as through the Word and the Holy Spirit, but also physically or by a natural participation, and that now we can and should receive a living hope of the resurrection of our bodies and of salvation and life and eternal glory" *(quod Christus in nobis non tantum spiritualiter sicut per verbum et S. S., sed etiam corporaliter seu participatione naturali sit, habitet et manere velit et quod iam vivam spem de resurrectione nostrorum corporum et de salute et vita ac gloria aeterna concipere possimus et debeamus)*. It cannot be denied that the danger of superstitious conceptions crops up here. The theologians just mentioned did not fall pray to them. It is equally impossible to deny that, like the idea of justification, the forgiveness of sins received in Holy Communion with the body and the blood of Christ has to have an eschatological culmination. "For where there is forgiveness of sins there is also life and salvation." One could let these thoughts flow into the "mystical union" *(unio mystica)*, as is the case in the writings of Philipp Nicolai (e. g., *De omnipraesentia*, 691 f.). Yet even in his writings, or rather precisely in his writings, the meaning of the "mystical union" *(unio mystica)* is eternal life. Or one can recall the words of Luther: "Thus for us the sacrament is a street, a bridge, a door, a ship, and a stretcher, on which and by means of which we journey from this world into eternal life" *(Also ist unss das sakrament eyn furt, eyn bruck, eyn thur, eyn schiff*

[35] Cf. *Copenhagen Articles* XXVI.

[36] E. g., the fourteenth reason in *Funfftzig erhebliche Ursachen, darum die lutherischen (wie man sie nennt) . . . zu den Sakramentierern oder Calvinisten nicht tretten sollen*, by Johann Schütz, pastor at Rhiestedt. The year is not given.

und tragbar, yn wilcher und durch wilch wir von disser welt faren ynss ewige leben) (WA 2, 753, 17).

This is the Lutheran doctrine of the Sacrament of the Altar. It was hated, maligned, and made fun of by its opponents. "Their lying tears the rafters asunder" *(Sie lügen, dass die Balken krachen),* Luther had to declare about those who were opposed to his doctrine of Holy Communion (WA 26, 565, 27). This doctrine was substantiated and tended earnestly and carefully by our early theology. Because of its decisive concern it has become popular as perhaps only justification by faith alone has become popular. But did it not contradict the doctrine of justification by faith alone? If one emphasizes the "by faith alone" *(sola fide),* Melanchthon gave the correct answer in the Apology. He says of "the exclusive little word 'alone': 'We rule out the thought of merit. We do not rule out the Word or the sacraments, as our opponents falsely charge.'" *(particula exclusiva "Sola": Excludimus opinionem meriti. Non excludimus verbum aut sacramenta, ut calumniantur adversarii.)* (II, 73.) It is clear how this is meant. But if one emphasizes faith and the forgiveness of sins, the discussions of the effects of Holy Communion have shown what great pains were taken not to deviate from the basic principles of the impact of the Gospel *(evangelischer Ansatz).* It is not the doctrine of Holy Communion that can work like a foreign substance here; it is the use of the sacrament itself. But for this our church can be held no more responsible than any other church. From even the most ancient documents of Christianity the Sacrament of the Altar towers like a cliff that can always be seen. This doctrine is set forth in its entirety in the First Epistle to the Corinthians. It is neither capable of nor in need of further development. It mocks every effort at spiritualization. If it actually were a hindrance in the path of the doctrine of justification, the question would be whether the latter would not sooner founder on it than be able to push it aside. If there were actually a contradiction here, one could not understand how Paul, the first dogmatician who treated the doctrine of justification, could have overlooked it. And whoever stands on the ground of Lutheranism will be convinced that here our theology, like our church with its practice, has walked most faithfully in the paths pointed out by Paul.

Naturally, one could go still further and find that this sacrament points beyond Christianity in general to most extensive religio-historical associations. No one familiar with history will deny this. But even if one divides early Christianity into single elements, which of them would be different? If in spite of this our faith sees no essential syncretism here, but the most perfect inner unity of origin, this certainty is connected exclusively with the "incarnate God" *(Deus incarnatus)*. It is none other than the Christ of the New Testament. If He is the promise that justifies the concept of the Gospel, He is also the promise that makes Holy Communion a sacrament. The fact that I, freed from the limits of *His* historical moment and *His* geographical location, may refer Him to *my* historical moment, to my today and my here – this is the doctrine of the real presence of the "exalted Christ."

24. Worship [1]

The doctrine of the sacraments did not run counter to the principles of the impact of the Gospel *(evangelischer Ansatz)*. But it leads beyond them. Theologically understood, the impact of the Gospel *(evangelischer Ansatz)* has its place in the individual. It frees him from all alleged human helpers and representatives, from all sociological ties, and places him in complete loneliness before God. This loneliness, however, is transcendental in nature, not empirical. On God's part the dialog between faith and God is carried on through the medium of the "Word." In this way the individual immediately enters a new, even though a totally different, kind of supraindividual unity. For the Word of God is proclaimed exclusively through men: through the apostle who wrote the Gospel, through the preacher who proclaims it, through the brother who gives comfort and absolution. If one can conclude even from this that the church which thus comes into being has no similarity to Plato's utopian state, every attempt at its one-sided spiritualization is checked by means of the sacraments. No matter to what extent all importance is attached to the "invisible heavenly good of grace" *(das unsichtbare himmlische Gnadengut)* in Baptism and Holy Communion – in any case the sacraments are also ceremonies. Both, however, owe their origin

[1] J. Gottschick, *Luthers Anschauungen vom christlichen Gottesdienst und seine tatsächliche Reform derselben*, 1887. — Joh. Wolf, *Luther und die musikalische Liturgie des ev. Hauptgottesdienstes*, 1902. — Paul Althaus the Elder, *Zur Einführung in die Quellengeschichte der kirchlichen Kollekten in den lutherischen Agenden des 16. Jahrhunderts (Leip-Univ. Programm*, 1914, now in *Forschungen zur ev. Gebetsliteratur)*. — Hans Preuss, *Die deutsche Frömmigkeit im Spiegel der bildenden Kunst*, 1926, pp. 156 ff. and 221 ff. — Ad. Allwohn, *Gottesdienst und Rechtfertigungsglaube, Luthers Grundlegung evangelischer Liturgik*, 1926. — Heinr. Frick and Ad. Allwohn, *Evangelische Liturgie*, 1926 (*Das Heilige und d. Form, Beihefte z. Monatsschrift für Gottesdienst u. kirchl. Kunst* I). — Gerh. Hilbert, *Luthers liturgische Grundsätze*, 1927. — Friedr. Gebhardt, *Die musikalischen Grundlagen zu Luthers Deutscher Messe, Luther-Jahrbuch*, 1928, pp. 56 ff. — Theod. Knolle, *Luthers Deutche Messe u. d. Rechtfertigungslehre*, ibid., pp. 170 ff. (additional writings here). — E. Strasser, *Das Wesen der lutherischen Kirchenkunst, Festschrift f. Ihmels*, 1928, pp. 428 ff. — J. Fr. Krüger, "The Lutheran Liturgy and Life," *Wittenberg Bulletin*, 1930, No. 8.

to the fact that they were instituted by the same Christ who is the basis and the content of faith. This means that they go beyond the impact of the Gospel *(evangelischer Ansatz)* in three ways. In the first place, Christ seems to be changed here from Him who reconciles into Him who commands. In the second place, here definite ceremonies take on a sacred character. In the third place, the church is compelled to settle empirical questions of form.

But the objection that must come up in connection with the first of these three factors can now be raised even in connection with the proclamation of the Word. For it, too, is based on Christ's will. Just as this does not cause Christ to lose His character as the One who overcomes the Law, so it does not do so when He institutes the sacraments. For the sacraments are meant to strengthen the pardon that takes the place of the Law and judgment. But even though this precludes confusing Christ with a new lawgiver, still the question remains whether an unevangelical element does not come into the attitude of the believer because he thinks that by performing the sacramental act he is observing a command given by Him who instituted the sacraments. At any rate, this would be unevangelical if a special ethical value were attached to the performance as compliance with this command. This danger comes to light in the fact that the administration of the sacraments, together with the proclamation of the Word, is designated as "divine service" *(Gottesdienst).* It is one of Luther's most important realizations that he freed the concept of divine service basically from the performance of what is ceremonial.[2] The counsel of the clergy of Culmbach in 1530 is an excellent echo of everything Luther had stated positively about this matter. It begins with the question: "What is right, true divine service?" It cites numerous proofs from Scripture for the following answers: to know God, to fear and honor God, to believe and trust in God, to love God, to call upon God in trouble, to confess God, to serve one's neighbor.[3] Here apparently there is really no room at all for fulfillment by means of ceremonial service. The last thing mentioned is particularily in accord with Luther's purpose: perfect divine service is service to one's neighbor. But this does not mean — as some ethicists of the nineteenth and the twentieth century suppose — that man should

[2] I refer here once for all to the exhaustive presentation in Allwohn's *Gottesdienst und Rechtfertigungslehre.* Allwohn deals with the development up to 1523. For Luther's later period it is sufficient in this connection to refer to his discussions in the Large Catechism as well as to his debate with Melanchthon (Enders 8, 165 f.; 170). In addition, *FC, SD* X, 8, and *KO* of Duke August of Saxony of 1580 (Sehling, *KO* I, 1, p. 364).

[3] Gussmann, *Quellen* I, 2, pp. 48—55.

look exclusively at his neighbor, that is, at the world. Divine service is service to one's neighbor only because it is performed "for God's sake" *(um Gottes willen)*, that is, by one who fears, loves, and trusts in God. The Culmbachians are right when they include knowledge of God and prayer as definitive parts of divine service. Consequently, there is no reason why the proclamation of the Gospel as preaching before an assembled congregation in order to awaken and strengthen faith, or why gathering for the purpose of common prayer should be excluded from the concept of divine service. This would be unevangelical only if a "value" before God were attached to the performance of the one or the other per se. Therefore the same thing is true of services to one's neighbor. The evangelicals had no such value in mind in connection with any other act. Nor did they have such a thought when the sacraments were administered. Naturally, in connection with the sacraments they were compelled to give special emphasis to their performance of the act over against the totally different doctrine of the Roman Church. They did so by rejecting the validity "as a result of the work performed" *(ex opere operato)* – which, of course, was condemned for other reasons – and by pointing out that the meaning of the sacraments consists, not at all in what man does but in the receiving of the divine promise.[4] From this it follows that Christ orders the administration of the sacraments only in order to offer Himself, and that for this reason the observance of His command represents, not a moral achievement but merely the readiness to receive. Naturally, this way of reasoning could be employed only on the basis of the Lutheran conception of the sacraments.

If, then, we may observe ordinary usage and, in its narrower sense, apply the concept of divine service *(Gottesdienst)* to church worship

[4] *Torgau Articles, De missa,* concerning the "proper use" of the Sacrament of the Altar: "Now the new testament is not our work; it is God's work. God offers and gives us something, as one is wont to make a will. Thus grace and the forgiveness of sin are offered and given." (*CR* 26, 177.) — *CA* XXIV (Latin text). — Apol. XXIV, 70: ". . . a ceremony is useless without faith" *(. . . inutilis est ceremonia, nisi fides accedat);* 72, concerning the "use of the sacrament" *(usus sacramenti):* ". . . to remember Christ is not the idle celebration of a show or a celebration instituted for the sake of an example . . . but it is to remember the benefits of Christ and to receive them through faith, in order that we may be quickened by them" *(. . . meminisse Christi non est otiosa spectaculi celebratio aut exempli causa instituta . . . sed est meminisse beneficia Christi, eaque fide accipere, ut per ea vivificemur);* 88, on the meaning of the Greek "canon": ". . . although it speaks of the entire worship, and, in opposition to the *opus operatum,* Paul [Rom. 12:1] has spoken of λογικὴ λατρεία [reasonable service], namely, of the worship of the mind, of fear, of prayer, of the giving of thanks, etc." *(. . . cum loquatur de toto cultu et* λογικὴ λατρεία *a Paulo [Rom. 12:1] dicta sit contra opus operatum, videlicit de cultu mentis, de timore, de fide, de invocatione, de gratiarum actione etc.)*

(Kultus) without contradicting Luther's ethic, there is the further result that it is not the "desire for sociability" *(Trieb zu Geselligkeit)* which, as Schleiermacher maintained, is the formative principle; it is the call of God, which wants to be heard in the Word and in the sacraments. The people do not unite with one another as is done in a society or a circle; God unites them by letting the same Word be proclaimed to many at the same time, and Christ, by bringing the individual disciples together into the communion *(Gemeinschaft)* of His body and blood. On the basis of similar considerations Luther, in his *On the Captivity (De captivitate),* wanted prayer to be sharply separated from the act of the Mass. Prayer presupposes faith, which receives the "testament." Therefore it cannot be essential for the sacrament (WA 6, 522, 14 ff; esp. ll. 30 ff.). Accordingly, this means that the activity of those who take part in divine service – the activity which manifests itself in prayer – is the second thing; it does not occur until the divine call has provided the initiative. And later – for example, in the Large Catechism, in connection with the Third Commandment – Luther speaks so one-sidedly of the pedagogical function of divine service – the function to be carried out by means of instructive preaching – that there seems to be no room at all in divine service for activity on the part of the "congregation." If Melanchthon was charged with being in error when he occasionally designated the church as a school,[5] the man primarily responsible for this is Luther, who speaks here and elsewhere about divine service as if he were thinking of an instruction period in a school in which the teacher is the only one who does the talking.

This impression is correct to the extent that according to Luther "the preaching and teaching of God's Word is the main part of all divine service" (WA 19, 78, 26). Accordingly, in his *The German Mass and the Order of Divine Service (Deutsche Messe und Ordnung Gottesdiensts)* he places the desire for a good catechism ahead of the order of divine service. If there is no good catechism, he says, it happens that many a person hears sermons for three or four years and still can give no answer concerning any article of faith. In view of this admission it would be bad if Luther had limited divine service to the pedagogical function – a function which, as he knew from experience, could by no means be performed satisfactorily! In reality, however, his liturgical directions or counsels teach something totally different. It is primarily the sacraments that compel him to acknowledge that ceremonies have a rightful and necessary place. In his *Formula of the Mass (Formula missae)* he declares that he never thought of doing away with the "wor-

[5] Albr. Ritschl, *Ges. Aufsätze,* 1893, pp. 201 ff.

ship of God" *(cultus dei)* altogether, and he gives his reason for this when he says: "For this we cannot deny, that Masses and the Communion of the bread and the wine are a rite instituted by Christ by divine direction" *(Nam hoc negare non possumus, Missas et communionem panis et vini ritum esse a Christo divinitus institutum)* (WA 12, 206, 17). No matter how strongly he emphasizes Christian freedom in connection with the form of this rite, no matter how much he deviates from the form handed down at the end of the Middle Ages, no matter how earnestly he warns against the belief that external customs could commend us to God, still there are certain ceremonial elements that he, too, regards as indispensable. Thus when he emphasizes the freedom to arrange various ways, he still demands that the words of the blessing remain as they are *(modo benedictionis verba sinant integra)* (214, 16). Furthermore, his whole struggle for the distribution of Holy Communion in both kinds could not be understood if he had not, on principle, held this aspect of the rite to be necessary. The struggle against the Mass without communicants also confirms this. And he never deviated from this position later on. Yes, in *The German Mass and the Order of Divine Service (Deutsche Messe und Ordnung Gottesdiensts)* he finds that it "is in accord with Holy Communion to pass and give the sacrament immediately after the consecration of the bread, before the cup is blessed" (WA 19, 99, 5). This, too, is a purely ceremonial requirement. Nor can one see to what extent he could have refrained from insisting on this if he had been able to put into practice the divine services in the home – the services concerning which he stated in the *Deutsche Messe* that they are valuable to those "who earnestly want to be Christians." [6]

[6] The question would still remain whether this whole plan can ever be brought into harmony with Luther's other principles pertaining to worship. One should bear in mind that in the *Formula missae* Luther had demanded that those who partake of Holy Communion assemble around the altar ". . . that they should be plainly seen and recognized by those who are communing as well as by those who are not communing, in order that then their life may be seen, approved of, and made known in a better way. For participation in this Supper is part of the confession by which they confess before God, the angels, and men that they are Christians." *(. . . quod oporteat eos palam videri et nosci tam ab iis, qui communicant, quam iis, qui non communicant, quo deinde eorum vita quoque melius videri et probari et prodi possit. Nam huius communio caenae est pars confessionis, qua coram deo, angelis et hominibus sese confitentur esse Christianos.)* When he adds that this is not a law but is "honorable and proper" *(honestum ac decorum)* WA 12, 216, 20 ff., his reference to the character Holy Communion has as a public confession is closely connected with his conception of the sacrament and of the church. Therefore it is hard to understand how he can concede the use of the sacrament to the house congregation mentioned in the *Deutsche Messe*. For this actually means the function of public confession. In this connection one must always note that this plan is

No one who agreed with Luther in the matter of the doctrine of the sacraments could fail to acknowledge the relative necessity for ceremonies in divine service. To a sharp criticism of the ceremonies of the medieval church the *Ansbach Counsel* of 1524 adds the statement: "On the other hand, there are in use some ceremonies that are partly an ornament of Christian churches, in order not to treat the sacraments of the church in a manner so empty and plain, and in order that there may be a difference between sacred and profane things *[inter sacra et prophana]*. But some are a sign of a spiritual and divine thing" (*Fränkische Bekenntnisse,* p. 316). Among these are meant the two ceremonies that Christ Himself instituted and the laying-on of hands, which the apostles used "when they imparted the Holy Spirit to someone or ordained a priest." It is true that the *Copenhagen Articles* of 1530 emphasize – altogether in Luther's sense – that true divine service does not consist in external singing and reading, in the Mass, in ceremonies, in beautiful temples, in cowls, and in anointing or other external holiness (*Malmö-Beretningen,* p. 26, Art. XXVI, interchanged in Erik Pontoppidan's translation with the following article). But immediately after this they demand that the language of the country be used for the sacraments, the Gospel, the reading of Scripture, and all hymns of the congregation (Art. XXX). Thus they, too, presuppose as self-evident that the congregation is assembled for the purpose of worship *(Kultus)*. It cannot be denied that the Ansbach demand for a ceremonial differentiation "between sacred and profane things" *(inter sacra et prophana)* carries with it the threat of a new hypostatization of what is "holy." The Lutheran rituals did everything in their power to obviate this danger. On the other hand, it was felt – and rightly so – that even the most cautious acknowledgment of what is ceremonial brings one face to face with the problem of external form. This is now true of worship *(Kultus)* in general. The form of worship is formally conditioned by artistic taste.

To be sure, the principles expressed in connection with the consolidation of Lutheran worship *(Kultus)* are now anything but aesthetic in character. But this would be decisive only if the purpose had been to bring a new form of worship into being. Although even on Lutheran soil there was here and there the thought of a reduction to the worship of the primitive church or of a limitation to what is directly specified

concerned, not with an emergency, which obviously justifies the waiving of publicity, but with an ideal state of affairs! — On partaking of the sacrament as a confession cf. also WA 41, 614, 23; on necessary "externals" *(externa)* in the worship cf. the words of the Wittenbergians to the Nürnbergians (1540), Enders 12, 389.

in Scripture – as was self-evident in most Reformed churches [7] – still, as in the domain of dogma, the principle by far predominant in Lutheranism was to recognize previous development even with respect to worship. Scripture must be normative only for what is to be *weeded out.*[8] To be sure, even this conservative position required the elimination of no small amount of what the Roman Catholic Church had handed down in the matter of worship. In the Smalcald Articles, Luther listed a large number of acts and customs which, together with the Mass, were to be done away with because they had come into being directly or indirectly as a result of the sacrificial character of the Mass: private Masses, vigils, pilgrimages, "and other alms," brotherhoods, the adoration of relics, and "the beloved indulgences," but also the invocation of saints and, in addition, "the baptism of bells and altar stones, and the practice of asking for sponsors on such occasions . . . the consecration of lights, palms, cakes, oats, the consecration of spices, etc." Insofar as all this was not a direct result of the Roman Mass, he rejected it as idolatry or because it was incompatible with justification. But in these points of view there then lay the basic limitations for what was to be avoided in the future. When, for example, Bugenhagen's church ritual of 1531 speaks of "unnecessary ceremonies" and declares categorically: "These we do not want" (Emil Sehling, *Die evangelischen Kirchenordnungen des 16. Jahrhunderts,* V, 338), *this* point of view played no role for Luther in the purging of what had been handed down. Of course,

[7] *Westminster Confession* of 1647, XXI, 1: "But He Himself has instituted the acceptable manner of worshiping God, and by His will He has defined it in such a way that one should not worship Him according to the fancies and inventions of men or the suggestions of Satan under any visible form or in any way that Sacred Scripture does not prescribe" *(At rationem Deum colendi acceptabilem ipse instituit, itaque voluntate sua definivit, ut coli non debeat secundum imaginationes ac inventa hominum aut suggestiones Satanae sub specie quavis visibili aut alia via quaviscunque quam scriptura sacra non praescripsit). Bek. d. RK,* p. 99.

[8] WA 26, 167, 11 ff.: "For one should not overthrow or change what cannot be overthrown or changed on the basis of clear Scripture. God is wonderful in His works. What He does not want, this He points out exhaustively in Scripture. What He does not point out there, this one should let stand as His work. We are excused. He will not mislead us." (1528.) — M. Chemnitz, *Examen* I, 135: "Christian liberty regulates the apostolic rites" *(Ritus apostolicos moderatur christiana libertas).* — *Copenhagen Articles* X: "Yet we do not despise all the outward ceremonies or old customs that are observed freely and may be dispensed with as the occasion requires. But we are opposed to those that are at variance with God's Word and are dangerous to simple hearts, because these simple hearts think that through them they become wise and holy." The Hungarian *Confessio montana,* Art. XV: "We keep the ceremonies in the church, and we think that they should be kept. They adorn the ministry and can be kept with a good conscience." *(Caerimonias in Ecclesia servamus et servandas esse sentimus, quae ornant ministerium, possuntque bona conscientia servari.)*

this church ritual, too, wants it to be understood that the unnecessary ceremonies are such as "cannot exist side by side with God's Word and the Christian faith" *(mit gades worde unde dem chistenen loven nicht könen bestahn).*[9]

For the *positive* form, of course, all the more emphasis is placed on reference to the "profit" *(Nutzen)* or at least to definite purposes. External customs are to provide an external incentive primarily for those whose faith is still weak; they are to stimulate "devotion" *(Andacht),* especially when the sacraments are administered, but also to give indirect support to the proclamation of the Word.[10] Although this might seem to give full scope to utilitarian arbitrariness, such a view is destroyed by pointing to the "discipline" *(Zucht)* that is to be promoted by means of external worship.[11] This is more than a mere repetition of the pedagogical motive. It expresses the realization that the congregation assembled around the Word and the sacraments needs other forms than an individual needs when reading the Word or praying by himself. Unity demands that the individual refrain from being arbitrary and autocratic. It demands the individual's regard for the whole. Conversely, however, it also demands that the whole have regard for the

9 Only rarely does one encounter the principle that ceremonies should be limited to a minimum. E. g., *Mansfelder Bek.* of 1560, p. 333 b: ". . . not to overload and burden the church with adiaphora." — *Henebergische KO* of 1582: ". . . as few ceremonies as possible should be instituted and used in connection with the sermons and the administering of the sacrament" (Sehling, *KO* I, 2. p. 301).

10 *Artikel der ceremonien und ander kirchen ordnung der Bischöfe von Samland und Pomesanien von 1525:* ". . . serviceable and necessary for the good and outward stimulation of childlike and weak Christians, as the majority are" (Sehling, *KO* IV, 30). — *Rigaische KO* of 1530 (ibid., V, 12). — *Brandenb. KO* of 1540 (ibid., III, 52). — *Kurländ. KO* of 1570 (ibid., V, 82).

11 *Merseburger Synodalunterricht* of 1544: "But some are not at variance with God's command but have been instituted for the purpose of good discipline and order, such as holidays, singing, reading, organ-playing, etc., which are adiaphora and voluntary per se" (Sehling, *KO* I, 2, p. 17). — *Pommersche KO* of 1569: ". . . for the furthering of proper Christian discipline and practice" (ibid., IV, 381). — When the *Mansfelder Bekenntnis* of 1560 (p. 333) speaks of adiaphora that "serve the purpose of discipline," and when the Formula of Concord declares that the congregation of God has the right to exercise control over the external worship "for the purpose of good order, Christian training, and discipline," one is reminded here, too, of the imperial edict of 380, where, in addition to the "evangelical doctrine" *(doctrina evangelica),* the "apostolic discipline" *(apostolica disciplina)* was demanded as a mark of catholicity. To be sure, the statement that has been quoted (*SD* X, 9) contradicts this demand to the extent that it speaks of the intentional waiving of uniformity. But the dissertation by G. Dalmatinus (cf. *Catholicity*) believes it can prove that the administering of the sacraments in accordance with their institution completely satisfies the edict's demand that the "apostolic discipline" *(disciplina apostolica)* be retained.

individual. It demands regard for the "weak" – a demand which, in accordance with what Luther requires, is emphasized in many church rituals.

But discipline in the external sense is not the only purpose served by unity of form. In addition, the Formula of Concord mentions "good order," "evangelical decorum" *(evangelischer Wohlstand* [εὐταξία]), and "edification of the church" *(SD* X, 9). It is clear that here, where public worship is concerned, the concept of "edification" *(aedificatio)* cannot be meant as pietistic-individualistic. According to New Testament usage, the Formula of Concord is also thinking of the church building as such (Eph. 2:20 ff.; 4:12; Col. 2:7), the whole aim of which, of course, is to be "a habitation of God in the Spirit," but which, as "the assembly of those who have been baptized" *(coetus baptizatorum)*, needs an external feeling for design *(Formensprache)* in order to find expression in time. The Word and the sacraments serve this churchly building by calling Christ to mind not only as the Reconciler and Redeemer of the individual but also as the Head of the church, as the Cornerstone of the church building. Thus in the preface to the Hamburg church ritual of 1529 Bugenhagen calls attention to the Word of Christ, "This do in remembrance of Me," and says: ". . . that is, as Paul states, proclaim My death and the purpose for which I have been given to you by My heavenly Father." Then he continues: "Where indeed can the laity and, together with them, those who are learned do this better than when we assemble and sing, read, preach, and hear from Holy Scripture about Christ our Savior in words that can be understood, to comfort and better ourselves, to praise God, and to give thanks?" (Sehling, *Die evangelischen Kirchenordnungen des 16. Jahrhunderts,* V, 491.) When he adds that this is not limited to the church building – because everyone, together with his servants and others, could do the same thing – still here the viewpoints for the feeling for design *(Formensprache)* of the "assembling" are expressed in an excellent manner. Although the representation of Christ is merely a new way of stating that Christ Himself calls the congregation together, at the same time Christ induces them to search for a way of giving expression to that which motivates them. But the given form for expressing our common feelings, which bind the individual into the whole without coercion, is common song and common prayer. In melody and in rhythm the evangelical chorale found adequate expression for the response of the congregation to the call of God in the Law and in the Gospel, for its hymn to Christ as He is present now and as He will be in the future. Like the chorale, the rhythmical language of the text gives expression to the aesthetic taste which satisfies the *Ansbach Counsel's* demand for sacred dignity. For the right to include congregational singing in worship the church rituals refer to Eph. 5:19. And the *Merseburg Synodical Instruction (Merseburger Synodalunterricht)* of 1544 shows that soon there was critical sifting, which warned against the hymns of the Sacramentarians and the Anabaptists but recommended Luther's *Little Hymn Book (sangbüchlein)* and "Spangenberg's Latin and German church hymns *(canciones ecclesiasticae)*" (Sehling, *Die evangelischen Kirchordnungen,* I, 2, p. 17).

For Luther common prayer is one of the most elementary components of worship. Although in 1520, as has been said, he wanted it separated from the sacramental act as such, yet in 1523 he demands that a Christian congregation should never assemble without preaching and prayer. After the lection and the exposition "one should then thank God in common, praise Him, and ask for the fruit of the Word."[12] Even when worship is concentrated strictly on the Word and the sacraments – as Jacob Andreä later advocates in his Esslingen sermons in accordance with the special Württembergian custom that had been established in the meantime – still he does not fail to include, in addition to the Word and the sacraments, "invocation" of God (IV, 69). When Luther emphasizes thanks and praise as Bugenhagen stresses glorification and thanks, he sees common prayer as a result of the proclamation of the Word. For praise of God can come only from faith, which is not aroused until the Word has been proclaimed.[13] In this way the whole act of worship takes on the character of honor paid to God. And this is the most important supplementation of the pedagogical purpose so far as content is concerned. In the church rituals "honor to God and the improvement and salvation of the wretched people" are coordinated.[14] Common prayer is the profession of the congregation that Christ is present; it is a profession in the form of adoration.[15] And just as the representation of Christ stands in the center of worship so far as content is concerned,

12 *Von ordenung gottis diensts,* WA 12, 35, 20 and 36, 12.

13 WA 16, 472, 4: "When His Word is rightly proclaimed and rightly heard . . . then the name of God is rightly honored, then He can also be rightly called upon" *(Quando recte praedicatur et recte eius verbum auditur . . . tunc recte honoratur nomen dei, tunc eciam recte invocari potest).* Cf. also Knolle, pp. 189 ff.

14 Thus the *KO für die St. Wenzelskirche zu Naumburg, 1537—38* (Sehling, *KO* I, 2, p. 61).

15 *Pommersche Agende* of 1569: "Where the divine Word is preached, sung, read, and prayed in this way, there God the Lord is present and mighty with his holy angels, so that we sing praises to the name of the Lord together with all God's angels and with all His elect" (Sehling, *KO* IV, 434). — On the "adoration of God" *(adoratio Dei)* cf. the letter of the Hamburgians to Melanchthon of 1549 (*CR* 7, 372).

so the adoration also pertains to Him.[16] It is self-evident that this does not preclude the common prayer of supplication. God is honored even when one calls upon His name in need. Common need also leads to gatherings for the purpose of common prayer. Thus, says Rechtenbach, we should "pray with one accord" *(unanimiter)* when danger of war is imminent, altogether unanimously; we should assemble and have public hours of prayer. For it is a great advantage over against the enemy when Christians gather and call to God, not out of many hearts and mouths but out of one, and in mass battle formation, as it were, hold together, and all stand as one man."[17] On the basis of similar considerations Luther renewed the litany when the Turks were threatening (WA 30 II, 119, 2). Here common prayer's restriction as to form is especially apparent. But this is also true in the case of the collects and, as is self-evident, in the case of the prayerlike chorales.

The elder Paul Althaus praises the collects contained in the Lutheran books of liturgical forms of the century of the Reformation for "a beautiful continuity, a tenacious adherence to the common property handed down" *(Zur Einführung,* pp. 70 f.) – even though there is freedom in details, and even though there is a tactful accommodation to the evangelical doctrine. Actually it was precisely in the liturgy that the Lutheran Reformation proved that it was in earnest when it affirmed that things become appropriate for use in the church. But the very fact that within these boundaries progress was generally conservative, not revolutionary, must be regarded as genuine artistic taste so far as appropriateness for use in the church is concerned. For the feeling of church unity extends not only to those who happen to gather at one place and at the same moment; it goes back to the time of the primitive church. The determination to foster this historico-liturgical connection is expressed in the church rituals as a principle, and Luther was the first to set an example by putting this determination into practice.[18] Apart from all variations in details, he took over the liturgical chants of the clergymen and the congregation; the position of the clergyman at the

[16] N. Selnecker, *Ex. Ord.* I, 627 f. Even more sharply the Württembergians at the Mömpelgard Religious Colloquy (*Acta,* pp. 345 ff.).

[17] Ludw. Rechtenbach, *Militia Christiana. . . . Das ist Christlicher und Heilsamer Heerzug. Bericht von Krieg und Kriegswesen* II, 1619, p. 32.

[18] The *Artikel der Zeremonien u. ander KO der preussischen Bischöfe* of 1525 say that part of the external customs are "of a blameless ancient origin" (Sehling, *KO* IV, 30). — The *KO für das Gericht Wintzingerode* (the year is not known) demands observance of the ceremonies "that have been in Christian customary use in our churches from time immemorial" (Sehling I, 2, p. 254). — The Wittenberg reformation of 1545 refers to the "accounts of the old churches that for almost three hundred years after the time of the apostles . . ." (*CR* 5, 591.)

altar; numerous set formulas, especially the collects; the confession of faith (which now, of course, is to be sung by the congregation); the fixed pericopes; the Aaronitic blessing, etc. After taking this path in the matter of acceptance of the liturgy the Lutheran books of forms frequently went further. What Luther says about "admonition" before Holy Communion applies to the fixed formulas of the liturgy and also to the liturgical prayers: "But it is my wish that for the sake of the people this paraphrase *(paraphrasis)* and admonition be put in carefully formulated or prescribed words *(conceptis seu prescriptis verbis)* or in a special manner, to keep one person from stating them one way today and another from stating them another way tomorrow, and to prevent anyone from proving his skill in leading people astray, with the result that they can neither learn nor retain anything" *(Deutsche Messe,* WA 19, 97, 2 ff.).

Even though here the pedagogical purpose is again discernible, yet the restriction of forms was a self-evident consequence of the fundamental idea of unity in worship. To justify worship in general most church rituals call attention to 1 Cor. 14:40, where it it said that everything should be done "decently and in order" *(decenter et secundum ordinem).*[19] Worship is order. But this brings up the problem of uniformity in the ceremonies. The reference to "Christian freedom" is constantly repeated in the confessions and in the church rituals because one must differentiate strictly between the concept of order and that of church law. The idea of a legal obligation was out of the question – not only in order to forestall confusing the command of the church with the command of God but also to cut off every thought of meritorious fulfillment. Consequently, the ethical element attached to the concept of order could be understood only as voluntary "subordination" *(Unterordnung).* In this sense an appeal is again made to consideration for the weak and, more generally, to love. Certainly the statement contained in the church ritual for the Duchy of Prussia of 1544 held true: "Such church customs, rites, gestures, and ceremonies should serve us Christians; but we should not serve them" (Sehling, IV, 63).[20] But one

[19] Thus the *Visit-Instr. f. d. Erzbistum Magdeburg* of 1562 (Sehling I, 2, p. 409). — On the concept "order" — "fine and orderly," "proper and orderly," "respectable and orderly," "orderly and beautiful" — see Sehling, *KO* I, 1, p. 430; I, 2, pp. 17, 253; III, 52, 440; IV, 62, 381, 434; V, 7, 467, 556; in addition, *FC, SD* X, 9; Chemnitz, *Examen* I 135; *Mansfelder Bek.* of 1560, p. 333.

[20] Luther to A. Lauterbach (1543): ". . . in order that we may show that we are masters of the ceremonies, not their slaves" *(. . . ut esse nos dominos ceremoniarum, non servos ostenderemus)* (Enders 15,131). — In view of the attitude of many "weak persons" Luther could become hot under the collar, even though he constantly showed consideration for these persons (Enders 4, 347, 30 ff.).

could not expect this submissiveness from the customs associated with worship if an individual tyrannized the others with his Christian freedom. Pastors in particular were exposed to the temptation to do this. Accordingly, arbitrariness on their part had to be curbed in a special way by referring to the need for order.[21] On the other hand, it was not right to violate the principle that uniformity in the ceremonies is not necessary for true unity of the church. Brenz even regarded a lack of uniformity as an advantage. For he declares that "a lack of uniformity in the ceremonies cannot help being profitable and has been particularly useful because it leads to the realization that there is Christian freedom in unnecessary church customs." [22]

This was certainly not incorrect. But there was another side. In spite of what can be said about the advantage afforded by a lack of uniformity, it was primarily the territorial rulers who felt and satisfied the need to bring about uniformity of worship within the boundaries of their lands. What this could lead to is shown by the controversies concerning the Interim and especially by Melanchthon's attitude toward this question. The Formula of Concord rendered a service by combating the idea that by bringing about unity in the ceremonies "these two opposing religions" could be "brought into agreement and become one body" *(SD* X, 5). For the time being, however, the principle expressed by the Formula of Concord – "that the community of God in every place and at every time [that is, in every local congregation] has the right, authority, and power to change, reduce, or increase" external customs (X, 9) – remained merely platonic. Even though there can be no objection to this, still it is impossible to understand why what was demanded of the individual in relationship to his local congregation – namely, voluntary submission to order – should not be true in the same degree of an individual congregation in relationship to a larger whole. The measures taken by the ruling princes show that there was need of this. But there was also the wish not to destroy uniformity in worship by means of territorial boundaries. Thus the church ritual of Riga of 1530 expresses the wish "that so far as is possible and helpful to our people, we may agree not only with our people here in Livonia but also with our neighbors and other states in the German lands in which the Gospel of Christ

[21] It was necessary to check the demoralization that had spread chiefly in Courland and Livonia. Cf. the letters Luther, Bugenhagen, and Melchior Hofmann (1525!) addressed to the Christians in Livonia (WA 18, 417 ff.). Furthermore, the *Rigaische KO* of 1530 (Sehling V, 12 f.) — *Verhandlungen auf dem Landtage zu Wolmar,* 1533 (Sehling V, 7), and, in addition, the *Kurländ. KO* of 1570 (ibid., p. 83).

[22] To Duke Christoph, July 18, 1551, *Anecdota Brentiana,* p. 312.

is also proclaimed clearly and richly — especially in the principal matters pertaining to outward divine service or ceremonies" (Sehling, *KO* V, 13). In the foreword to the Hamburg church ritual of the preceding year Bugenhagen declared that if a way of "commemoration" *(commemoratie)* — that is, the aforementioned representation of Christ in the divine service — can come about throughout "the whole German land," "This we will gladly and heartily accept" (ibid., p. 491). And even the church ritual of Duke August of Saxony of 1580 would "have liked to see nothing more" than that a completely uniform order were maintained in "all churches of the Augsburg Confession" (Sehling, I, 1, p. 364). These wishes stem from the very same desire for form that demands order in an individual congregation. It is self-evident that in this connection the special differences resulting from history and nationality have to be taken into account. The best example of this is the agreement as well as the difference in the Lutheran churches of Scandinavia. But it was not necessary for the country of Henneberg to have an order different from that of the bordering country of Schwarzburg or for the land of Hadeln to have one different from that of Dithmarschen on the other bank of the Elbe. This disruption of forms was born of egoism. It was by no means restricted to the customs observed in worship, and it was a disintegrating element for all artistic taste with reference to the church.

A great church style can flourish only in the soil of a common appreciation of what is fitting for a great church. According to the persuasion of the evangelicals, it was the sense of the seventh article of the Augsburg Confession — the article on ceremonies — that the latter cannot rest on the former. And in Lutheranism it was actually based on the fact that the "doctrine of the Gospel" *(doctrina evangelii)* was a common possession. Therefore there was an evangelical basis for community of style. This basis could express itself in a style-forming manner provided that ideal community of possession *(die ideelle Gemeinsamkeit)* was felt in the longitudinal axis of history. On this the distinctive mark of the Swedish church in the matter of worship is based. This church successfully resisted the radical changes which the "ultrareformational Germans," especially Georg Normann, the "learned and upright" Pomeranian, attempted to bring about there.[23] Up to the present time it has retained the forms of the traditional church customs that were cleansed exclusively according to dogmatical viewpoints. In Germany, on the other hand, there arose a disruption and an impoverishment which kept increasing until well into the eighteenth century. Paul Graff has de-

[23] Hjalmar Holmquist, *PRE*[3], 18, 27, 60.

scribed this in detail. The number of services decreased steadily. For the most part independent liturgical celebrations, matins, and vespers disappeared. There is a belief that within the services the church is obligated to increase the "Protestantizing" of the liturgy. The alb, which is certainly not many-colored, must yield sole dominion to the puritanical darkness of the everlastingly black clerical robe. Even the beauty of the green branches at the festival of Pentecost is forbidden – in Gotha because it leads to sleeping in church, in Bayreuth and in Reuss Younger Line because it leads to violation of the forest laws (Graff, p. 105). The ruler of the land, not what the church wants in the matter of form, is the master of style. The pattern had a downward effect. The time came when the nobility no longer wanted to partake of the Lord's Supper together with the commoners; when, like the rulers of the land, it withdrew to the "authentically Protestant" boxes in the church; when the servile breed of parsons in the state church granted it private baptisms, private marriages, and "entombments" *(Beisetzungen)* instead of public funerals. Pietism demands that in this way religious life be made private for the "believers." But assaults were made on the only institution for which the church had created the form in which the individual could find expression – on private confession. To take the place of this, Zinzendorf then created his own style for worship, his pretty things *(Niedlichkeiten)* and his societies for the promotion of Christian intimacy *(Schätzelgesellschaften).* That was the end in this field. Not until the nineteenth century was there a reawakening of early Lutheranism's sense of the forms appropriate to the church. This reawakening took place when the writings of Rudelbach, Löhe, Kliefoth, and others showed that there was a renewed understanding of the impact of the Gospel *(evangelischer Ansatz).*

Lutheranism's contacts with the Reformed Church hastened the dissolution of the liturgical sense and its impregnation with motifs characteristic of the Enlightenment. The Swiss-Reformed influence is clearest in Württemberg, where, at the instigation of Schnepf and Blarer, the altar service disappeared completely. The Slovak Lutheran Church has retained the rich liturgy of the age of the Reformation up to the present time; but the Hungarian Lutheran Church, which has many contacts with the Reformed Church, is liturgically impoverished.[24] Frederick William I, as the Reformed "chief bishop" *(summus episcopus),* compelled the Lutheran Church of his land to do away with all the church

[24] The synod held at Silein in 1610 had already exempted the Magyar Lutheran clerics — as distinguished from those of other nationalities — from wearing the alb (K. Kuzmany, *Urkundenbuch zum österreichisch-evangelischen Kirchenrecht,* 1856, p. 191, *can.* VI).

vestments, altar decorations, and liturgical singing that remained. He found pastors to his liking. "Here I have got rid of everything immediately," wrote Pastor Grenzel at Nienburg. "I have also cut up my clerical robe and have had a coat made out of it." Frederick William also found men who resisted.[25] The Reformed Church enriched divine service only to the extent of providing hymn boards. But the Enlightenment and its disintegrating influence began as early as the age of orthodoxy. Not as though in the seventeenth century the one-sided emphasis on preaching had not in itself already destroyed the sense of form. The most eminent preachers of the seventeenth century still follow unconsciously the organic desire for form which comes about as the result of the ministerial office. Others, however, make use of baroque rhetoric; they speak like schoolmasters or public prosecutors. In the eighteenth century the content of preaching aims more and more at the utilitarianism of later rationalism. To the same degree preaching almost achieves autocratic rule. Divine service itself is subordinated to the one-sided viewpoint of benefit *(Nutzen)*. For all practical purposes the old contrast between the clergy and the laity returns in a most terrifying form. Divine service means being preached to by morning preachers, afternoon preachers, main preachers, court preachers, university preachers, and prison preachers.

But had not the reformers themselves and the first Lutheran church rituals spoken about the "benefit" of divine service? Yet there could be no talk of a formative or even of a determining effect of this motive. Once Luther himself had made the complaint that Bugenhagen's sermons were too long.[26] To him something essentially different was the important thing in divine service. The contemplative element — which in Luther's case cannot be thought out of existence — is opposed to a one-sided definiteness of purpose. It has practically nothing to do with the "contemplative way" *(via contemplativa)*, which he challenges. This "contemplative way" is a form of the ethos or of ethical inaction. To Luther, therefore, it is impossible of realization. Even though the later "sacred meditations" *(meditationes sacrae)* may have been dependent on Roman Catholic patterns so far as content is concerned, still one

[25] R. Rocholl, *Gesch. d. evang. Kirche in Deutschland,* 1897, p. 117. — O. Mehl, *Des Soldatenkönigs Kampf gegen die Zeremonien, Hochkirche,* 1928, No. 1.

[26] WA TR 4, 5171 f. and 2, 2643; 3, 3419, 3637; 5, 5200, 6400. Cf also Herm. Hering, *Doktor Pomeranus, Joh. Bugenhagen, Schr. VRG,* No. 22, 1888, p. 138. — Later, for example, the council of the city of Windsheim complains about the "excessively long sermons" of the pietistic vesper preacher Rhein, who had made a "good" impression at first "in spite of the catarrh he had contracted, even though" he spoke "in a voice that was somewhat soft." Paul Schaudig, *Der Pietismus und Separatismus im Aischgrund, Schwäbisch Gmünd,* 1925, p. 17 and p. 6.

cannot deny Luther the psychological form of meditation. This finds expression in the confession that Christ is present in Holy Communion. Under the impression of the Word Luther says of the perceptibility of His nearness in the heart: "But your heart feels Him well, that He is certainly present, by the experience of faith" (WA 19, 489, 15). Luther needs no proof that this feeling of the heart should not be confused with faith itself. Not only Luther the monk but also Luther the preacher at a congregation exhorts to "remembrance" of the Passion of Christ and instructs his hearers to be absorbed in every detail of Christ's Passion.[27] Even in the *Magnificat* (1521) he declares "that the greater the devotion is, the fewer words it uses" (WA 7, 521, 21). In connection with the doctrine of the "mystical union" *(unio mystica)* it has been shown that his attack on Areopagitic mysticism is not in conflict with this. To some extent – in the writings of Johann Arndt and Johann Gerhard – the contemplative element subsequently took on forms that run counter to the idea of a congregation. To some extent – for even though preachers like Scriver cast it in a subjectivistic form, still this cannot do away with the fact that his preaching has the character of genuine preaching to a congregation.[28] Or would Luther not have been able to join in the singing of Paul Gerhardt's Passion hymns, which have obvious contemplative characteristics? And should these hymns have induced Jacob Andreä to retract to some extent his proud statement that "if the apostles St. Peter and St. Paul themselves were to rise from the dead and see and hear our Christian congregation and what is done there, they would certainly conclude and acknowledge that our assembly is a Christian congregation"? (P. 69.)

But the contemplative element is not a separate part of divine service, something that at times can be lacking. No, it is an essential feature; it specifically distinguishes the proclamation of the Word in worship from the indoctrination imparted in religious instruction. It makes demands of form on the way worship is constituted and on the way

[27] WA 2, 139, 11 ff. Cf. in addition, the later Lenten sermons; for example, in the *House Postil* (WA 52, 226 ff.), or, if Dietrich's preface and the entire *Passio* (pp. 734 ff.) are really spurious, perhaps the Lenten sermons in Rörer's transcript of the year 1534 (WA 37, 322 ff., 333 ff., 338 ff., 347 ff., 352 ff.). Certainly here, as always, the listener is exhorted to establish the reference "for me" *(Pro me)*, thus to let himself be won for faith. But this cannot obscure the fact that here Luther urges and leads his hearers to give consideration to the details of the "great Passion" *(passio magna)* — consideration that leads beyond the mere statement of the facts, as is given, for example, in the writings of Paul.

[28] Now at last Scriver has also found appreciation on the part of the Germans. Cf. Fritz Becker, *Christian Scriver und sein literarisches Werk. Ein Beitrag z. Gesch. u. relig. Prosa im 17. Jhrhdt.* (dissertation), Münster, 1929.

it is put into practice – demands that find expression in its solemnity and in its emotional content. These are demands of style and tact. They can be fulfilled only when the value of the act to be formed is contained in the act itself, therefore when the meaning of divine service is not determined by a purpose based on heterogeneous laws. Not until this is the case can one understand the strong emphasis on the musical aspect of Lutheran divine service. Music is always "purposeless." The high opinion Luther had of it can certainly not be traced to a pedagogical purpose. But with music he opened up a path which led to the heights attained by Bach. A similar situation obtains with regard to architecture in the domain of Lutheranism. To be sure, the *Frauenkirche* in Dresden and the *Michaeliskirche* in Hamburg are "churches for preaching" *(Predigtkirchen).* But only puritanical fanaticism can overlook, or find fault with, the artistic expression of form which is discernible in the vaulted space as well as in the baroque details. These spaces generate a solemnity which reflects their purpose. And this corresponded to what the Reformer had in mind. "Today we have in the churches an altar because of the communion of the Eucharist; we have platforms or pulpits for the purpose of teaching the people. This has been done, not only for the sake of necessity but also for the sake of solemnity." *(Hodie in templis habemus altare propter communionem Eucharistiae, habemus suggesta seu cathedras ad docendum populum. Haec non necessitatis tantum causa, sed etiam solemnitatis facta sunt.)* (WA 42, 72, 12.)

Measured by the other standards of expediency, praise of God itself, which was mentioned as the "purpose" of worship, is purposeless. Nothing is to be accomplished by it either before God or among men. The teleology of Lutheran divine service, like that in the primitive church, is eschatological in nature. With respect to worship the aforementioned representation of Christ has found its completed form in the church year. "The church year," says Ludwig Jacobskötter, "is our dome that has been resolved from visible space and built into the movement of invisible time." [29] In adhering voluntarily to this way of expressing the fact that faith and the story of salvation are contemporaneous – a way of expression that came into being in the early church – Lutheranism retained something that is genuinely catholic.[30] But the church

[29] L. Jacobskötter, *Zivilisation und Kirche,* 1922, p. 249.

[30] On the historical events in the church year cf., e. g., an anonymous "Sermon on the Wonderful Birth of Our Savior Jesus Christ . . . ," Wittenberg, 1550: "For although many things belong together, so that one must say something about many things at the same time, yet God Himself divided the things into time. On every occasion, therefore, one should give a rather long report of a special happening."

year is constantly neutralized by flowing into the idea of the end of all things, which to us neither is nor can be contemporaneous. "It ends with what all time ends, with death; but because it is the church year, it does not end as time and every year end; it comes to an end when it sees fulfillment, the new heaven and the new earth, where there will be no more death. The towers of the dome become the pinnacles of the eternal city." (Jacobskötter, p. 258.) The Christ who is to come, the Christ who means the end of all things, is the cancellation of time – just as His presence in Holy Communion is the cancellation of space. Therefore the establishment of His presence in divine service always means only the Crucified One, because He is the One who rose from the dead and was exalted – exalted, not into the "definite place" *(locum definitivum)* of the confessions of the Reformed Church but outside space and time. The purer the form in which the establishment of Christ's presence takes place, the more the encumbrance of time becomes submerged. To be sure, here, too, there is only an approximation. But perhaps nowhere do we come so close to the spaceless form which at the same time guards against "aloneness of the spirit" *(Beisichselbstsein des Geistes)* as we do in music. Therefore music has for us primarily the characteristic of what is "beautiful and glorious" – the characteristic of which the Pomeranian book of forms of the year 1569 speaks: "Such assemblies in the house of the Lord of those who believe in Christ are very pleasant, beautiful, and glorious; they should be held in the highest honor, love, and esteem. Then we Christians see in them an image of the everlasting, glorious assembly of all the elect, who will appear on the Last Day before the Son of Man, our Lord Jesus." (Sehling, *KO* IV, 434.) [31]

25. The Office of the Ministry [1]

The Augsburg Confession bases the need for the office of preaching directly on its doctrine of justification. "In order that we may attain this faith, the ministry of teaching the Gospel and administering the sacraments has been instituted" *(Ut hanc fidem consequamur institutum est*

[31] N. Selnecker, *Chr. Psalmen, Lieder und Kirchengesenge,* Leipzig, 1587. In the foreword Selnecker says: "Christian music on earth is nothing but a foretaste of or a prelude to everlasting life, since here we only intone and sing the antiphons until through temporal death we sing the introit and the sequence, and in everlasting life the true completory and the hymns in all eternity."

[1] W. Löhe, *Kirche und Amt,* 1851, and *Der evang. Geistliche,* 3d ed., 1876. — Ad. Harless, *Kirche und Amt nach lutherischer Lehre,* 1853. — E. Huschke, *Die streitigen Lehren von der Kirche, dem Kirchenamt, dem Kirchenregiment und der Kirchenordnung,* 1863. — Th. F. D. Kliefoth, *Liturgische Abhandlungen* I, 2d ed., 1869. — A. Vilmar, *Die Lehre vom geistlichen Amt,* 1870. — Karl Köhler, *Die Lehre der luth. Bekenntnisschriften über Kirche, Kirchenamt und Kirchenregiment, Jahrb.*

ministerium docendi evangelii et porrigendi sacramenta) (V). It is impossible to give sharper and clearer expression to the fact that the impact of the Gospel *(evangelischer Ansatz)* does not isolate the Christian but puts him into the church – the church that proclaims the Word and administers the sacraments. This was not altogether self-evident. For it could just as well have been said that God gave Holy Scripture to be read by everyone for himself. When, in spite of this, immediate reference is made to the office of preaching, this calls to mind, in the first place, those statements from Luther's early period which put the oral Word ahead of the written Word.[2] In the second place, however, here the realization holds true that the operation of the Word leads to the formation of a congregation and of worship. For concerning Christians who themselves have come to faith through the Word Luther says that they "are in duty bound to proclaim, teach, and disseminate it [the Word]" (WA 11, 412, 6). Every Christian placed into a circle of non-Christians must "preach to the erring heathen or non-Christians and must teach the Gospel because brotherly love makes it his duty to do so" (412, 18).

But if a Christian is in duty bound to do this, he must also be fundamentally justified in doing so. For this duty is intrinsic in the very fact that he is a Christian. Therefore it is out of the question for his right to do so to be based on a special classification of Christians. But since Baptism, confession, and Holy Communion are "sheer Gospel" *(eitel Evangelium)* (WA 10 III, 395, 14), what is true of binding and loosing (Matt. 18:18) – which Christ has committed to all Christians, not to certain individuals – is also true of the sacraments. Luther bases this on the priesthood of all believers (WA 11, 411, 31; WA 12, 180, 17 ff.; WA 15, 720, 26 ff.). "Now he who has faith and is a Christian also has Christ; now if he has Christ, so that everything Christ has is his, he also

f. deutsche Theol., 1871, pp. 381 ff. — Ferd. Walther, *Die Stimme unserer Kirche über die Fragen von Kirche und Amt*, 4th ed., 1894. — G. Rietschel, *Luther und die Ordination*, 2d ed., 1889, and *Lehrb. d. Liturgik* II, 1909, pp. 405 ff. — H. A. Köstlin, *Die Lehre von der Seelsorge nach evangelischen Grundsätzen*, 1895. — P. Drews, *Ordination und Lehrverpflichtung der Ordinanden in Wittenberg, Deutsche Zeitschr. für Kirchenrecht*, 1905, pp. 66 ff., and *Einleitung zum Ordin.-Formular*, WA 38, 401 ff. On the other hand, Paul Vetter, *ARG* 12, 1915, pp. 64 ff. — W. Caspari, *Die geschichtl. Grundlage des gegenwärtigen Gemeindelebens*, 2d ed., 1908, pp. 243 ff. — M. G. G. Scherer, *Das geistliche Amt, Amtl. Bericht der Weltkirchenkonferenz für Glauben und Kirchenverfassung von H. Sasse*, Berlin, 1929, pp. 312 ff.

[2] This connection is even clearer in the seventh of the *Schwabach Articles* — the article which served as the pattern for *CA* V: "To attain such faith or to give it to men God instituted the office of preaching or the oral Word, namely, the Gospel . . ."

has the power to forgive sins" (WA 10 III, 394, 27). But the forgiveness of sins is the real content of the Gospel. The abolition of the division into clergy and laity follows as a corollary from the priesthood of all believers. Luther was convinced that this abolition caused one of the essential principles of canonic law to fall to the ground (WA 10 III, 396, 24). Unfortunately for him, the Wittenberg jurists were unable to go along with him in this matter (cf. *Rechtsgeschichte,* Vol. II).

Even though Luther emphasizes again and again that it is the duty of Christians to proclaim the Word not only to non-Christians but also within the church, still the right given to all Christians seems to leave a special office of preaching completely unjustifiable. Nevertheless, Luther never doubted that in the sense of the Augsburg Confession this office was necessary. But he is confronted with what appear to be two wholly contradictory series of thoughts, which seek to understand why this is the case. In the first place, there is an aspect which seems to be purely practical. One could almost call it utilitarian. The proclamation of the Word is a public matter. For this reason some persons — e. g., women, children, and "unqualified persons" *(untüchtige Leute)* — are excluded without further ado (WA 10 III, 171, 5 ff.; WA 50, 633, 12). But since the apostle says that everything should be done "in order" *(secundum ordinem)* (WA 12, 189, 24), it is impossible for all the others to speak. "If we were all to preach, it would be like women going to market; then no one would want to listen to the other person, and all would want to speak" (WA 10 III, 397, 17) — "then there would be a confused bawling such as one hears nowadays among frogs" (WA 10 I, 2, p. 239, 25). But since only one can speak at a time, we have "ordained pastors and priests to perform this service for us and in our stead" (WA 10 III, 395, 40 ff.). For this, however, the aesthetic principle of "order" is by no means the only standard. It is precisely because all have the right to proclaim the Word that an individual dare not claim this right at the expense of the others — which would be the case if he were to exercise this right without the consent of the others. "For without common consent and command one may not take upon oneself that which is common to all" (WA 6, 408, 14). Here the aesthetic concept of order is transferred immediately into the realm of what is ethical. One could almost say that it is transferred into the realm of ecclesiastical law. Above all, it is important that according to this the right to proclaim the Word, which is originally given to all individuals, should devolve on the "congregation" *(gemeine),* therefore on the whole group, which is more than the sum of its members. Consequently, the office of preaching established in this way is a function of the "congregation," that is, not of a number of individuals who unite as if they were forming a club. According to everything set forth concerning Luther's conception of the church, this cannot be otherwise. If one recalls here what the imperial publicists of the fourteenth century – e. g., Marsilius of Padua (1270 to 1342) – had to say about the derivation of the office of the ministry, Luther, too, seems to remain completely within the framework of a democratic congregational ideal in conformity with secular law.

But a totally different series of thoughts stands in opposition to this practical one.[3] The aforementioned statement of the Augsburg Confession traces the office of preaching back to divine institution. Melanchthon was never in doubt about this. For him the idea of the universal priesthood had only minor significance.[4] It would, of course, be a mistake if one wanted to conclude from this that he had a more conservative position than Luther. In what he taught about society Melanchthon conceded an important place to the idea of fellowship. We saw this cropping up in his doctrine of the church. Conversely, if Luther, in his view of the nature of the church, never disowned the idea of divine institution, it would be beyond comprehension if he had proceeded in a purely sociological manner in connection with the establishment of the office of preaching. To be sure, it seems to be a conscious abandonment of the idea of institution when he declares in his *On the Captivity (De captivitate):* "The priests whom we call are chosen from among us to do everything in our name, and the priesthood is nothing else than the ministry" *(Sacerdotes, quos vocamus, ministri sunt ex nobis electi, qui nostro nomine omnia faciant, et sacerdotium aliud nihil est quam ministerium)* (WA 6, 564, 12). But he turns against the statement that the priesthood is established by the words of institution of Holy Communion and by the differentiation between priests and the laity which results from this statement. He finds that this teaching destroys the "Christian brotherhood" *(fraternitas Christiana),* which, of course, is an essential element of his doctrine of Holy Communion. But this objection to a status distinguishing the office-bearer is immediately weakened by the fact that he wants the office to be understood in the strict sense as a service.[5] In itself this is not yet a contradiction of the idea of insti-

3 Here one can dispense with a discussion of the trains of thought pertaining to natural right that are found even in Luther's writings. For the establishment of the office of preaching as such they are overcome by the idea of institution.

4 Proof in Herrlinger, *Die Theologie Melanchthons,* 1879, pp. 268 f. — In the sense of Luther's first series of thoughts the *Copenhagen Articles* (Art. 40) derive the office from the universal priesthood.

5 *Lectures on Hebrews* 175, 7 ff.; Enders 2, 385, 14 ff.; WA 7, 753, 28; WA 12, 190, 24. — The *Hungarian Conf. montana,* Art. 8: "For the Lord does not appoint

tution; there is merely an insurance against claims that the status is divine in its origin. In what he wrote to the nobility there is already a clear-cut distinction between office and status (WA 6, 408, 26).

As early as the time of that very writing, however, Luther traces the assigning of the "pastorate" *(Pfarramt)* to an individual back to apostolic direction (440, 31). According to his Scriptural principle, this, of course, is not yet "divine institution." The later dogmaticians also differentiated the apostolic establishment of the office from the divine institution, even though in effect they coordinated the former with the latter.[6] Yet the reference to the authority of the apostles undermines the purely practical principle of necessity. But as early as his stay at the Wartburg, Luther declares with regard to Ps. 68:23: "The foot of Christ is the office of preaching." Then he goes on to point out that after the apostles had died as martyrs, "other preachers were raised up" (WA 8, 24, 13 ff.). In this way the initiative in connection with the preaching of individuals is ascribed to Christ, even though an institution of the office as such is not yet being discussed. In the exposition of the prophet Jonah (1526) a distinction is then made between the office and the Word, "that, therefore, both the office and the Word of the office must be contained in God's command." Referring to 1 Peter 4:11, he states that the preacher should be certain "that both the Word and the office are divine and are commanded by God" (WA 19, 233, 6 ff.). The idea that God "instituted" the office of preaching then recurs frequently (e. g., WA 30 II, 598, 33; WA 37, 269, 18; WA 47, 191, 38; 192, 5; WA 50, 647, 6 ff.). Since it is usually expressed only in passing, one must conclude from this that Luther regarded this view as self-evident. Consequently, he must not have felt that it was out of harmony with the practical reason.

Yes, precisely where Luther declares expressly that the office of preaching was founded, instituted, commanded, and established by Christ, the statement recurs that this pertains to *all* Christians. With regard to John 20:21, for example, he says of Christ: "There He com-

magistrates and masters in its [the church's] midst; He appoints ministers who are to serve it with the Word and the sacraments" *(Neque enim magistratus ac dominos sed ministros constituit in medio eius [ecclesiae], qui serviant ei verbo et sacramentis).* Later the Dane Brochmand has a different view (*Syst.* II, 263): "Therefore there is no doubt that just as in any well-established state there are found people who command and people who obey, so also in the house of God, which is surely a state that is best-ordered by far, the same thing happens" *(Dubium ergo nullum est, quin velut in quavis Republica bene constituta inveniuntur, qui imperent et imperantibus pareant, ita etiam in domo Dei, quippe Republica longe ordinatissima idem usu veniat).*

[6] L. Hutter, *Gründtlicher Bericht von Ordentlichen und recht Apostolischen Beruff, Ordination und kräfftigem Ampt der Lutherischen-Evangelischen Prediger,* Wittenberg, 1608, p. 27.

mands the office, which includes the preaching of the Gospel" *(Ibi befihlt er das ampt, quod est praedicare et Evangelium).* And with reference to John 20:22 he states that here Christ commanded "His apostles and their successors to exercise rule over sin" *(suis Apostolis et successoribus eorum das Regiment über die sünde)* (1531; WA 30 I, 318, 15; 320, 5). But just as he declared in 1523 with regard to the same passage that "this power was given not only to the clergy" *(haec potestas non solum data clericis),* and that "although the apostles were addressed, nevertheless all Christians were addressed" *(quamquam apostolis dictum, tamen omnibus Christianis)* (WA 11, 96, 24; 97, 24; WA 12, 521, 15 ff.), so in 1540 he paraphrases the same statement as follows: "I am not speaking only of those who are ministers; I am speaking of all Christians" *(Non loquor tantum de illis, qui ministri, sed omnibus Christianis)* (WA 49, 139, 6). From this it is clear that Luther does not feel that there is a contrast between the founding of the office through Christ and the practical reason that prompts the congregation to delegate to an individual the right to preach. This is understandable only if in connection with the concept "office" he is thinking on principle merely of the functional aspect, not of the personnel of the parochial organization. Here, too, Luther preserves the idea that the Word and the sacraments, not the individual Christians, constitute the "substance of the church" *(substantia ecclesiae).* Here the last remainder of the static condition of medieval ecclesiasticism is overcome.

But now the fact that Luther says anything at all about the institution of the office through Christ has all the more significance. In this respect he puts the office completely on a par with the Gospel and the sacraments.[7] By doing so he traces the functions of the church back to the historical Christ and subordinates them to Christ's express command. Thus this positivistic derivation of the office, exactly like the derivation of the sacraments, immediately takes on a meaning that binds it firmly to the impact of the Gospel *(evangelischer Ansatz).* By reason of Christ's command "the Passion and the resurrection of Christ come into use."

[7] *On Private Mass and the Consecration of Priests (Von der Winkelmesse und Pfaffenweihe)* (1533): "For this we must believe and be certain of, that Baptism is not ours, but Christ's; that the Gospel is not ours, but Christ's; that the office of preaching is not ours, but Christ's; that the Sacrament is not ours, but Christ's; that the Keys or forgiveness and retention of sins are not ours, but Christ's. In brief, the office and the sacraments are not ours, but Christ's. For He has ordained and bequeathed all this in the church, to practice and use it until the end of the world. And He does not lie. Nor does He deceive us." (WA 38, 240, 24.) — In addition to the passages adduced, cf. WA 34 II, 296, 7; WA 37, 136, 13 ff.; WA 41, 543, 17; and the sermons printed in WA 41, 123, 34; WA 52, 567, 28 ff.; WA 28, 466—479.

He says: "I am sending you." This means that they "should bring the resurrection into use and practice" (WA 34 I, 318, 15 ff.). Here Christ commands His apostles and their successors "to rule over sin" (320, 5). The sins of the others are "subject to our power when they bite you in your conscience *(nostrae potestati subjecta, quando vos beissen in conscientia).* A preacher, a pastor, has this power." (323, 7.) The "rule" of the pastor consists in this, that he *serves* the sinner with the Word of promise, with the forgiveness of sins. Therefore Christ established the office because, as He who was crucified and was raised from the dead, He wanted to bestow forgiveness, and because after His exaltation it is necessary for others to proclaim the fact that He bestows forgiveness. Here, too, one sees again that and how the forgiveness of sins works to form the church. It is not only practical-pedagogical considerations that lead Luther to refer the troubled sinner to the comforting Brother (WA 41, 543, 31). No, in order to preclude every thought of one's own initiative, the Word should be *heard* on principle, and as the Word that is *heard* it should ask for and find faith. The kingdom of the forgiveness of sins is actually in those who proclaim it. Here, of course, one should not look at the person as such but at Him who gave the command to proclaim.[8]

But one cannot pass over in silence the considerations that speak in favor of delegating the office to an individual. The explanation of John 20:23 in the *Contiunculae* of 1534 leaves no doubt that Luther also traces the exercise of the Power of the Keys through the "ministers" *(ministri)* back to Christ's special will as the Founder (WA 45, 461, 13 ff.). In the dispute with the "sneaks and unqualified preachers" *(Schleicher und Winkelprediger)* even the expressions "clergy" and "laity" crop up again. Here, of course, *Kleros* should not be understood as meaning the estate; it means "parts, that to each one his part of the people is en-

[8] Cf. the entire context of the sermon delivered on April 23, 1536, WA 41, 541 ff., especially p. 544, 32 ff. and 545, 2: "God has established a kingdom to which He has sent forth His disciples . . . that He might help men from their sins . . ." *(Gott hat ein reich gesetzt, ad quod emisit discipulos . . . ut homines helfft a peccatis. . . .)* L. 27: "Christ establishes a kingdom in which they [sins] are pardoned and retained. The person should have no influence at all. But one should look to Him who gave the commission." *(Christus stifft regnum, in quo condonantur et retinentur. Nihil moveat persona. Sed inspiciatur is, qui commisit.)* 546, 10: "Do not stare toward heaven when you want your sins remitted. But you have it here below. . . . Go to the minister. In an emergency tell your neighbor to declare absolution in the name of Jesus Christ. Then you have the Word. When they do so, Christ has done so." *(Non gaff ghen caelum, quando vis remitti peccata. Sed hie unden hastus. . . . Ito ad parochum, inn not dic ad proximum, ut recitet absolutionem in nomine Jesu Christi, tum habes verbum, quando ipsi faciunt, Christus fecit.)*

trusted, as St. Paul also writes to Titus, where without his knowledge or consent no other person or a stranger should dare teach his parishioners either secretly or in public" (WA 31 I, 211, 5; cf. WA 10 III, 120, 20). Yet immediately after this Luther opposes basing the right to preach on the universal priesthood.[9] And with reference to 1 Cor. 14 he remarks that Paul "here commands the congregation to hear and to improve, not to teach or to exercise the office of preaching. Then he makes a clear distinction and calls the congregation the laity."[10] Here the danger of a reversal comes tangibly close. Yet later on, as the quotation from the year 1540 proves (WA 49, 139, 6), Luther was unwilling to retract any part of the statement that the office is entrusted to the whole congregation and that for this reason it is delegated to the individual only by the congregation. Then, however, one must ask how, in the first place, the official activity of the pastor can be dependent on the will of the congregation and yet, in the second place, should be respected as a divine arrangement. The decision is given by the answer to the question whether the pastor receives his distinctive status by ordination – in the later sense – or by a call. In the first instance the distinction pertains to his person in itself. Then it makes him a cleric in the old sense. In the second instance it pertains only to his relationship to the congregation.

Luther took the term "ordination" from the medieval church. But what does he mean by it? By designating it as an "ecclesiastical rite" *(ritus ecclesiasticus)* in his *On the Captivity (De captivitate)* (WA 6, 561, 27) he denies that it has a sacramental character. He means that the traditional distinction between clergy and laity is done away with altogether (563, 27 ff.). In 1523 he recommends to the Bohemians that they procure ministers *(Amtsträger)* in the following manner: assemble; select from their midst by vote one or, if necessary, several qualified men; recommend and endorse them to the whole congregation *(universitati)* with prayer and the laying on of hands; and then acknowledge and honor them as duly appointed bishops and ministers *(ministri)*.[11] Here two acts are distinguished: the election and another act, the essential elements of which are, apart from the rites of prayer and the laying on of hands, the "recommending and the confirming" *(commendare et con-*

[9] "Nor does it help them to plead that all Christians are priests. It is true that all Christians are priests. But not all are pastors."

[10] The word ἰδιώτης is used in 1 Cor. 14:16. WA 30 III, 525, 19 ff.

[11] WA 12, 191, 22. Cf. 193, 35 ff. Here it is stated more precisely that the laying on of hands should be done by those who are more competent *(potiores)*, but that the recommendation should be made to the people and the church or the whole congregation *(populo et Ecclesiae seu universitati)*.

firmare). The inner relationship to the congregation is implicit in both acts. The bishop is elected *by* the congregation, is recommended *to* the congregation. But the confirmation also takes place *through* the congregation, for it contains the acknowledgment that the rights belonging to all have now been delegated to the individual. This threefold relationship to the congregation, however, is also essential insofar as it follows from the participation of all the believers and confessors that the act of installation has been guided and carried out by God.[12] A sermon for the Twenty-first Sunday after Trinity in the year 1524 speaks more explicitly about the concept "ordination." Ordination is not consecration. Through Baptism we have all been consecrated as priests. To ordain means to select an individual for the sake of order and to confer on him the right to preach and to administer the sacraments – the right which we all have. *What we give him today we can take away from him tomorrow.*[13]

According to this, it is clear that Luther does not recognize an act of ordination which confers on the ordained person per se a right that has validity without being dependent on his service to the congregation. On the contrary, later he also uses the concepts "to ordain" and "to call" synonymously.[14] From this, however, one also gets the answer to the question to what extent the status that distinguishes a pastor is conferred by divine right even though it is given by the congregation. This

[12] P. 191, 25: ". . . by believing with a sure faith that what the common agreement of the faithful, those who acknowledge and profess the Gospel, has directed and done in this way has been done and directed by God" *(. . . indubitata fide credendo, a deo gestum et factum esse, quod hac ratione gesserit et foecerit consensus communis fidelium, Euangelion agnoscentium ac profitentium).*

[13] WA 15, 721, 3: "To ordain is not to consecrate. Therefore if we know a pious man, we bring him forward, and, by the power of the Word which we have, we give him the authority to preach the Word and to give the sacraments. This is to ordain. . . . On the basis of ordination it is established as a result of the election that, for the sake of retaining order, not everyone should have the desire to preach. Thus they have the obligation to perform their ministry, but not perpetually. Today we can commit it to him, tomorrow we can take it away again. The priesthood which we have received from Christ is perpetual. The former is the ministry." *(Ordinare non est consecrare. Si ergo scimus pium hominem, extrahimus eum et damus in virtute verbi quod habemus, auctoritatem praedicandi verbum et dandi sacramenta. Hoc est ordinare . . . Ex ordinatione constituitur auss der wal, ut maneat ordo, ne quisque velit praedicare. Item debent ministerium suum agere, sed non perpetuo: possumus ei hodie commendare, cras iterum adimere. Perpetuum est sacerdotium, quod a Christo accepimus. Illud est ministerium.)*

[14] WA 38, 221, 1: ". . . to ordain or the call to the public Christian office of preaching and the ministry"; likewise l. 20. — WA 38, 238, 7: "For to ordain should be termed and should be to call and to commit the ministry." Still in 1539: ". . . that it consecrates or calls servants of the church" (WA 50, 632, 36).

distinction comes to him by virtue of the call. The pastor's calling is exactly analogous to worldly callings, as Luther sets forth in his exposition of Ps. 32 (WA 31 I, 189–218; 1530). Every performance of what a calling requires is a service to God. But only when it is actually done because of "a call and a command." Such a call and command – apart from the extraordinary instances in which God steps in directly, as in the case of the Old Testament prophets – is always given to us through men and is therefore bound up with life in a community made up of men, and is designed for the purpose of preserving and shaping this community. In such a call – one that takes place through men – we may and should see a *divine* call if those who extend the call are authorized by God to do so. These are, for example, the persons to whom we owe obedience according to the Fourth Commandment, therefore parents, the government, the worldly "lords." But God has also conferred on the church of Christ such authorization to extend a call.[15] The obligation implicit in the call applies to our readiness to love our neighbor. To him who is called it gives the necessary certainty that he has a call.[16] Conversely, it imposes on the congregation that extends the call the obligation to honor its pastor and to hear his word as the Word of Christ.[17] For this reason the office of preaching is the highest office in Christendom (WA 11, 415, 30).

It is still necessary to clear up the question whether it is Luther's understanding that the congregation which extends a call is limited to the local congregation which the ordinand is obligated to serve. Practically, such a view would amount to a refusal to give this right to a church organization made up of several congregations. It is not necessary to prove that such a principle of independence, if it ever existed,

[15] WA 16, 34, 1: "This is a calling through man; but it is confirmed through God, because it has its foundation in Scripture" *(Haec est vocatio per hominem, sed per deum bestetiget, quod habet fundamentum in scriptura)* (1524). Cf. WA 38, 252, 18 ff. (1533).

[16] WA 17 I, 362, 1: "It is a calling of love, not the one that proceeds from faith, because I, you, and everyone are obligated to one another, because the Word of God says: 'Love your neighbor.' If it calls, I am certain that I must go, and I am as certain as if God were calling me." *(Vocatio est charitatis, non celestis, quae ex fide proficiscitur, quia ego, tu et quisque ists eim andern schuldig, quia verbum dei: Dilige proximum. Si vocat, certus sum, quod debeo ire et adeo certus, quasi deus vocaret me.)* (1525.) Cf. WA 16, 35, 1; WA 20, 412, 21; WA 30 III, 519, 29.

[17] WA 10 III, 398, 19; WA 37, 381, 14: ". . . that the mouth of every pastor is the mouth of Christ." WA 49, 140, 8: "Therefore you should not hear the pastor as a man, but as God" *(Ideo non debes pfarherr audire ut hominem, sed ut deum).* Cf. WA 11, 99, 2; WA 12, 531, 7.

was broken down at the latest when the practice of visitation began. For it is self-evident that these visitations presuppose the recognition of a larger whole's responsibility for the individual local congregation. Of course, numerous statements are to be found in which the procedure of calling is clearly transferred to the individual congregation (e. g., WA 6, 440, 21 ff.; WA 11, 411, 28; WA 12, 191, 22). In accordance with this, the treatise on sneaks and unqualified preachers *(Schleicher und Winkelprediger)* demands that the *Kleros,* the exact delimitation of the parish, be observed (WA 30 III, 518 ff.). Luther himself applies this principle when in 1524 he states emphatically in his letter to the citizens of Frankfurt: "Now, my very dear friends, I am not your preacher. Nor is anyone obligated to believe me." (WA 15, 393, 6.) And yet the independence of the individual congregation is unknown to Luther from the very beginning and remained unknown to him. As early as the time of his writing to the Christian nobility he wants to arouse consciousness of a larger whole's responsibility for the individual congregation. But the aforementioned principle is also broken down when he recognizes the necessity of calling several pastors through the agency of the same body (WA 12, 191, 23; Enders 11, 40, 18); when he designates "the city" as this body (WA 6, 440, 31); or when, in substantiation of the right to call through the congregation – with public approval – he calls attention to the fact that "in several places even the secular rulers, such as councilors and princes, have installed, and paid salaries to, preachers for themselves" (WA 11, 415, 19). For when a body, like a city which, because of the number of its inhabitants, is not able to manage with one pastor, for this reason installs several, there is no reason why this city should not divide the work to be done there among several of its sections. Besides, this was self-evident because of the existence of several parish churches. This does no violence whatever to the principle of calling through the "congregation" – although this congregation is larger than the audience of the individual pastor. Therefore it is nothing fundamentally new when later on Luther counts the installation of pastors among the marks of the church of Christ, which, as he believes, is a larger circle than the individual congregation (WA 50, 635, 35 ff.; cf. WA 38, 221, 20–32). As early as his *On the Installation of Ministers (De instituendis ministris)* (1523) he envisions the possibility that once "many cities" *(multae civitates)* in Bohemia had chosen bishops for themselves in the prescribed manner, these bishops could have a meeting of their own and choose one or several from their midst "who would be their superiors, that is, would serve and visit them, just as in the Acts of the

Apostles Peter visited the churches, until Bohemia should return to the lawful and evangelical archiepiscopate, which would be rich, not in much property and power but in many services and visits to the churches" *(qui maiores illorum sint, id est, qui illis ministrent et visitent illos, sicut Petrus visitavit ecclesias in actis Apostolorum, donec Boemia redeat ad legitimum rursus et Evangelicum archiepiscopatum, qui non multis censibus et ditionibus, sed multis ministeriis et visitandis Ecclesiis dives sit)* (WA 12, 194, 14 ff.). This outlook for Bohemia would be just as incomprehensible as the appeal to the Christian nobility would be for Germany if what Luther demanded on principle had meant that every single local congregation had to be left to its own devices. Otherwise one would have to accuse him — and this would be a false charge — of believing that the church consciousness of Christians should end at the boundaries of a locality and that the individuals are held together as a church either by the pastor or by the boundaries of a locality. But this would be openly out of keeping with the struggle he waged against binding the church to a specific place or to a specific person.

But the telling effect this has on the relationship of the individual congregation to the pastor whom the congregation itself has chosen — the relationship which at first seems to be totally independent — results from the delegation of the right of visitation to the future "superiors" *(maiores)* among the Bohemian bishops, with the proposed archbishop at their head. The prerequisite of the congregation's right to call — or even the opposite of this right — is the right and the duty of the congregation to determine whether the person to be chosen is qualified, to watch over what he teaches, and to depose him if he openly contradicts the "true doctrine." Luther demands this with special emphasis in the same year (1523) in which he makes the aforementioned proposals to the Bohemians.[18] But examination as to doctrine is an essential element of the right of visitation. If this right is given to the "superiors" *(maiores)* and to the archbishop, a basic restriction of the right of examination to the local congregation is out of the question. Practical experiences taught the Wittenbergians very quickly that the individual congregations were frequently altogether incapable of doing this. In rural areas especially they scarcely had the necessary amount of judgment in matters pertaining to doctrine. And even if they had it, they did not always have at

[18] *The Reason Why a Christian Assembly or Congregation Has the Right and Authority to Judge All Doctrine, to Call, Install, and Dismiss Teachers: Proved from Scripture (Das eyn Christliche versamlung odder gemeyne recht und macht habe, alle lere tzu urteylen und lerer tzu berufen, eyn und abtzusetzen, Grund und ursach aus der schrifft)* (WA 11, 408—416). Cf., e. g., WA 10 I, 2, p. 290, 10 ff.; WA 10 III, 173, 27; 174, 17 ff.; 397, 31.

their disposal qualified persons whom they could choose "from their midst" and call. In fact, this was very seldom the case. Not for a moment did Luther leave out of consideration the requirement that there be specific qualification (WA 6, 440, 21; WA 12, 191, 22; 193, 39; WA 15, 721, 2; WA 50, 633, 17). When at times he states emphatically that the choice should be made in accordance with the congregation's free discretion *(aus freier Willkür)*, this, of course, implies a protest against the installation of a pastor against the will of the congregation. But in no case can arbitrary action *(Willkür)* extend to qualification as to doctrine. In this respect the congregation which really wants to be a Christian church is subject to a general norm which not only coordinates it with its sister congregations but at the same time subordinates it. Even though Melanchthon had a special part in obligating those who are ordained to accept the confessions that had appeared in the meantime, the requirement that there be an obligation with respect to doctrine in general is a self-evident application of what Luther teaches about the church. Not until this requirement was set up was the connection established between the impact of the Gospel *(evangelischer Ansatz)* and what Luther teaches about the office of the ministry and about the congregation. It is basically immaterial, of course, whether the obligation is affirmed only inwardly by the pastor or is publicly confirmed by means of a solemn declaration. The second way, however, is an appropriate manner of giving expression to the public character of the spiritual office. By it the pastor is bound to the aforementioned norm, which has validity beyond the individual congregation and thus obligates him to the larger whole with which the congregations teaching the same doctrine are united.

Luther presupposes this state of affairs when he acknowledges that a larger whole has the right of visitation. For the need of examination before a pastor is installed in office as well as the need of it in the further course of official activity is inextricably bound up with the specific duty to teach. If, on the other hand, examination as to doctrine is an essential element when a pastor is called, a basic restriction to the future congregation members of the right to call the pastor is out of the question for Luther. On the contrary, where the unity in doctrine of a larger group has been assured, the same right should be granted to the whole that is granted to one of its parts which happens to be assembled at the same place. Since, in addition to the ability to teach, the fitness of the person to be called includes characteristics concerning which a decision cannot be made without taking the local conditions into consideration, the co-operation of the local congregation is, of course, usually indispensable.

26. The Later Doctrine of the Office of the Ministry And the Nature of This Office [1]

Luther's doctrine of the office of the ministry is determined formally by two characteristics. In the first place, by his endeavor to preserve at all costs its relationship to the basic thoughts of the Gospel. This is seen, for example, in the connection it has with the priesthood of all believers or in the fixing of the functions of the ministerial office. In the second place, however, by the practical flexibility, for which the reason is to be found in the transitional character of his time. Above all, it makes itself felt when one asks where, in Luther's opinion, that which is essential for the church ends and where the practical freedom of formation begins. For since Luther clings to the distinctive character which the church and the office acquired when they were instituted, it is impossible for him to consider, say, the way preachers are to be examined or installed as essential as the existence of the office itself and the exercise of its functions. Luther is convinced that the office itself was instituted by Christ. But the theological examination is a human arrangement. One can overlook or deny this fundamental difference only if one calls

[1] Joachim Mörlin, *Vom Berufe der Prediger,* 1565 (quoted according to the collection: *Vom Beruff und Enturlaubung der Prediger, Christlicher Fürtrefflicher Lehrer Bedencken, Als nemblich D. M. Lutheris, H. Ph. Melanchthonis, Der Theologen zu Leipz., D. Joh. Brentii, D. J. Mörlini usw.,* Giessen, 1608). — Laurentius Drabitzius, *Von trewer Seelenhirten Ampt unnd jhrer zugeordneten Schafe (Einführungspred. f. Seb. Freiberger),* Leipzig, 1601. — Polyc. Leiser, *Eine christl. Predigt . . . da der Ehrw. u. Hochgel. H. Georg Mylius . . . alldar zum Pfarrer u. Superintendenten Investirt ist worden,* Wittenberg, 1603. — Joh. Rhelin, (from Nördlingen), *De ministr. eccl. vocatione,* Tübingen, 1600. — Peter Gädicke, *De jure vocandi ministros,* Giessen, 1609. — Joh. Georg Sigwart, *Ein Predigt Vom Ampt der Kirchendiener u. Zuhörer (Ordin.-Predigt für Joh. Georg Weiganmeyer),* Tübingen, 1609. — The same author, *Christl. Pred. Von dem Predigtampt, desselben Dienern u. Zuhörern (Ordin.-Pred. für G. W. Bogenritter),* Tübingen, 1610. — Nicol. Hunnius, *Ministerii Lutherani divini adeoque legitimi demonstratio etc.,* Wittenberg, 1614. — Joh. Val. Andreä, *Geistliche Kurzweil, Strassburg,* 1619 (here *Das gute Leben eines rechtschaffenen Dieners Gottes*). — Paul Tarnov, *De sacrosancto Ministerio,* Rostock, 1624. — F. Balduin, *Brevis institutio ministrorum verbi divini,* Wittenberg, 1623. — L. Schlüsselburg, *Wie und was von der Vocation, Ordination, Introduktion und Dimission der Prediger zu halten, Vier aund zwantzig Hochwichtige Fragen und Bedenken,* Rostock, 1625 (posthumous). — Joh. Bened. Carpzow, *Lutherischer Unferfälschter Apostolischer Löseschlüssel,* Leipzig, 1654. — Joh. Ludwig Hartmann, *Pastorale evangelicum s. institutio plenior ministrorum verbi,* Nürnberg, 1678 (greatly overrated so far as its treatment of practical theology is concerned, and completely dependent on the Reformed Wilhelm Zepper in Herborn!). — Quenstedt, *Ethica pastorum et instructio pastoralis,* Wittenberg, 1678.

Hans Leube, *Die Reformideen in der deutschen Lutherischen Kirche zur Zeit der Orthodoxie,* 1924. — Herm. Werdermann, *Luthers Wittenberger Gemeinde wiederhergestellt aus seinen Predigten,* 1929. — Cf. the writings mentioned in note 1 under *The Office of the Ministry.*

in question the distinctive character which the church and the office acquired when they were instituted, and if one construes both the church and the office as based on freedom of association, as, for example, is done by the Socinians and, subsequently, in the period of the Enlightenment. Luther's theological doctrine of the spiritual office flows unnoticed into the domain of sociology. This accounts in no small measure for the uncertainty and the lack of clarity that have often prevailed in Lutheranism with regard to questions pertaining to church government (cf. *Church Government*).

It is self-evident that the later dogmaticians strove to follow Luther in the matter of Scriptural proof. To be sure, in the writings of Melanchthon and his narrower circle of adherents the doctrine of the universal priesthood receded into the background; but Luther's conclusion – which was essential for the doctrine of the ministry – that the office is the property of the church as a whole was emphatically retained.[2] Accordingly, the right to examine the doctrine, to elect, and to call is ascribed to the whole congregation.[3] Mentzer declares that it is sinful *(nefas)* for an individual who has not been called by the congregation to arrogate the office to himself, and that it is wrong for the government to force an officeholder on the congregation against its will.[4] But more and more Scriptural proof is adduced for the doctrine that the office is instituted by God.[5] According to what Luther taught, there is a distinction between the direct calling of the prophets and the apostles and the call extended through men. But even in the latter case God must be considered the Author when the calling takes place properly *(recte)*, in the sense of *CA* XIV. It is Christ Himself who, as the Mecklenburg *Kirchenordnung* of 1552 says, calls the specified persons "through members of the church."[6] Like Luther, the later dogmaticians conclude – especially from John 20:21 – not only that the preachers are sent but also that the congregation is obligated to follow them. The preachers are the legates of God;

[2] *Conf. Magdeburg.*, 1550, *Bl. G.* (see note 1 under *The Sacrament of the Altar*) — B. Mentzer, *Exegesis*, pp. 642 f. — J. Hülsemann, *Manuale*, p. 469.

[3] J. G. Sigwart, *Ordinationspredigt v. 1609*, p. 41. — L. Hutter, *Gründl. Bericht* (see note 6 under *The Office of the Ministry*), p. 50.

[4] Mentzer, op. cit., p. 644.

[5] *CA* V; cf. Mörlin on Matt. 9 and Luke 10 (laborers in the harvest). — L. Hutter (*Loci*, 186) deduces the conferring on the individuals from John 20:21, Matt. 28:19 f., and Mark 16:15, as *CA* XXVIII, 7 had already done, while Luther, like others even among the later dogmaticians, had deduced from these passages the conferring of the command to baptize on the whole church. — Balduin develops his pastoral theology on the basis of the First Epistle to Timothy.

[6] Sehling, *KO*, V, 191. — Joh. Gerhard, *Loci* XII, 79.

they give light to the Christian congregation. They have "their place alongside the apostles" *(ihren Staat bei den Aposteln)*, and for this reason they are to be held in high honor.[7] Like Luther, the church regulations – especially according to the precedent established by Bugenhagen's Brunswick *Kirchenordnung* of 1528 (ed. Lietzmann, p. 40) – exhort the congregations to support or at least to help support their pastors.

But Luther's second conclusion – that the call to the office of the ministry carries with it no class distinction before God and no "indelible character" *(character indelebilis)* – is carefully observed. Although Bugenhagen declares in the Hamburg *Kirchenordnung* of 1529 that preachers "receive before the congregation the spiritual calling according to which they may be called 'ordained to the ministry of the Spirit, not of the letter'" *(vor der gemene entfangen den geestliken orden, dar van se mogen heten ordinati ad ministerium spiritus non littere)*, he adds: ". . . thus another received a worldly calling, which is nevertheless also God's, in that he is called to be a burgomaster, a civil servant, etc. His calling lasts as long as his office lasts." *(. . . alse ein ander annimpt einen weltliken orden, de doch ock gades is, dat he wert vorordent to einem borgermeister, to einem stadtknechte, usw. So lange sin ampt waret, so lange waret ock sin orden.)* Later Mentzer provides exact proof that in the New Testament the concept "priest" is never used for the New Testament officeholders. He appropriates Luther's comments on the word κλῆρος, which occurs thirteen times in the New Testament. Like Luther, Calov traces the concept *ordo* back to 1 Cor. 14:32, therefore to "order." When Hülsemann declares that the "power" *(potestas)* conferred at ordination can be withdrawn only because of a crime, it is self-evident that for him defection from pure doctrine is included and that the irrevocability of authority is to be understood only as security against dismissal on the part of the congregation.[8] It was not until later, at the time of rationalism, that the title "priest" was reintroduced or at least aimed at for the evangelical clergy.[9]

One of the first departures from Luther's fundamental thought could be found in the fact that later dogmaticians divide spiritual authority

[7] Sehling, op. cit., p. 161. — Mörlin, p. 31. — Pol. Leyser, *Pred. v. 1603, Bij.* — Sigwart, *Pred. v. 1610,* p. 25.

[8] *Hamburger KO* of 1529, in Sehling V, 502. — Mentzer, op. cit., p. 639. — Calov, *Exegema zu Art. XIV, Bl. Eeeee.* — Hülsemann, op. cit., p. 492. — Concerning the use of the word "priest" only in the sense of the universal priesthood cf. Hutter, *Gründl. Bericht, Bl. A.*

[9] But cf. the contradiction in Josias Fr. Chr. Löffler, *Kl. Schriften* II, 392 ff. and 415 ff. (1817), as well as the writings adduced by him.

into "power of the office" *(potestas ordinis)* and "power of jurisdiction" *(potestas jurisdictionis).* The so-called *Torgau Articles* still reject the validity of episcopal jurisdiction only because of its abuse in practice and try to justify the assumption of this jurisdiction by the sovereign *(CR* 26, 178 f.; cf. *Catholicity).* In the Augsburg Confession, Melanchthon attacks it on principle. Its secular aspect is completely rejected, and the authority of the bishops is limited to the Office of the Keys. This is identical with the right to preach and to administer the sacraments (XXVIII, 5). In the Apology, however, Melanchthon returns to the pre-Reformation distinction between "power of the office" *(potestas ordinis),* which embraces preaching and the sacraments, and "power of jurisdiction" *(potestas jurisdictionis),* which is defined as "the authority to excommunicate and, on the other hand, to absolve those who are liable to punishment because of public offenses, etc." *(auctoritas excommunicandi obnoxios publicis criminibus et rursus absolvendi, etc.)* (XIV, 13; likewise in the *Loci* of 1535, *CR* 21, 494, 501). Insofar as this is merely a matter of abstract differentiation, it is, of course, rather unimportant. Chemnitz is right when he sees the basic error of the Roman doctrine in the fact that here the power of jurisdiction is said to add something to the office of the ministry (*Examen* II, 363). But even in the writings of Johann Gerhard the two powers of the office are almost directly juxtaposed. It is particularly hazardous for Melanchthon to adduce the "ordination of ministers" *(ordinatio ministrorum)* and the "censorship of morals" *(censura morum)* as accessories of the "power of jurisdiction" *(potestas jurisdictionis)* (*Loci* XIII, 16). To be sure, one can offer no valid objection to the actual custom of carrying out the act of ordination only through ordained clerics (Enders 11, 40, 18 ff.); but the derivation of this custom as a right from the clergy's "power of jurisdiction" really gives to this power a content which no longer has anything to do with the Office of the Keys. The role of custodian of morals, which the "censorship of morals" *(censura morum)* ascribes to the officeholder, is a falsification of Luther's conception of the office.[10] One is not surprised when at a later time Johann Benedikt Carpzov I,[11] in spite of all

[10] Nor can one arrive at another verdict concerning Hafenreffer's doctrine of the office. Although he avoids the concept "power of jurisdiction" *(potestas jurisdictionis),* he divides the power of the office into four rights, resp., duties: preaching, the sacraments, the Keys, and "seeing to it that there is proper order in the church" *(decentem curare ordinem in ecclesia)* (Loci, 513).

[11] For the Carpzov family we are making use of the numbering proposed in *PRE*[3]. It is misleading to speak only of "Johann Benedikt C." In the seventeenth and eighteenth centuries there are five distinguished scholars with this name. Seven

his striving to cling to Luther himself, can say at times in his monograph on the key of remission that the imparting of absolution "is identical with what takes place at court" *(wie in einer Gerichts-Handlung).* The preacher, he says, "also has the power to recognize and pass judgment on the nature of the sinner" *(auch potestatem cognoscendi et judicandi super qualitatem peccatoris);* he must "recognize and judge between the pure and the impure, between the penitent and the impenitent, whether a person is to be absolved or not to be absolved" *(erkenen und richten zwischen reinen und unreinen, zwischen bussfertigen und unbussfertigen, ob einer zu absolviren oder nicht).* Even though from a practical point of view there is certainly a logical connection with the Office of the Keys, still usage shows how here the line extending from Melanchthon over Johann Gerhard leads to that clerical conception of the office in which – at least in this respect – the Roman conception and the Calvinistic conception meet.

Of course, the danger of this development is made very clear by the Office of the Keys itself, the establishment of which is similar to that of Baptism and the Lord's Supper (Matt. 16:19; 18:18; John 20:23). The connection of these words with the impact of the Gospel *(evangelischer Ansatz)* is not immediately apparent. To the general duty of Christians to forgive a brother a wrong done by him there is added here, for one thing, the assurance that this forgiveness is to be valid "in heaven" too. Nor can this assurance, according to the context, by any means be limited to the wrong done to him who forgives. It pertains to sins in general, which in their very nature are always directed against God. So far as the right to forgive sins is concerned, the connection with the impact of the Gospel *(evangelischer Ansatz)* is, of course, very clear. Basically every proclamation of the Gospel is forgiveness of sins and is always authorized by God. For this reason the right to use the key of remission is identical with the right to proclaim the Gospel – the right which, according to Luther, is basically incumbent on all believers (WA 10 III, 394, 27 ff.). This explains Luther's advice to go to a "good friend" or to a "pious man" when there are qualms of conscience, to make a confession to him, and to be absolved by him (395, 25; 398, 35); it also explains the statement of the Augsburg Confession which makes the proclamation of the Gospel and the Power of the Keys identical (XXVIII, 5). It is self-evident that the delegation of the Office of the

other members of the family likewise have the Christian name Benedikt. The enumeration in *PRE* is not even complete. For example, David Benedikt, the eldest son of Johann Benedikt I, is missing.

Keys is connected with the delegation to the officeholder of the right to preach and to administer the sacraments.

On the other hand, a different situation obtains with respect to the power of binding. This power is the opposite of the forgiveness of sins. For this reason it seems to contradict not only the impact of the Gospel *(evangelischer Ansatz)* but also the doctrine of the office of the ministry as so far developed. It seems to contradict the former insofar as here the exclusion of the impenitent person from the forgiveness to which he submits *ipso facto* is said to become a ritualistic or at least a ritual-like human act; it seems to contradict the latter because the office which "preaches reconciliation" is made to serve the divine Law. To be sure, the ritualistic element per se can, like Baptism and the Lord's Supper, be founded positivistically on the institution by Christ; but whereas it is carried out in complete agreement with the idea of justification when Baptism and the Lord's Supper are administered, here it has a content directly opposed to justification. Baptism signifies incorporation into the church as into the body of Christ. On the other hand, the declaration that sins are "retained" signifies exclusion from the body of Christ. Although the ritualistic element is understandable when the right and the duty to exclude were designated as jurisdiction, it still cannot be sanctioned.

When Luther explained the power of binding in his *Concerning the Keys (Von den Schlüsseln)* (1530), he had left some things unclear. On the one hand, he finds that binding in Christ's sense is "directed toward a desire to deliver the sinner from sins and by its binding seeks nothing else than this, that the sinner's conscience may be free and rid of sins. For he punishes and binds in order that the sinner may stop sinning, make amends for it, and avoid it." (WA 30 II, 467, 23.) Here Luther's purpose is obviously pedagogical. Binding has only a provisory significance. At any rate, it is subordinated to loosing so far as the idea is concerned. This is perhaps in conformity with the way Luther, who had learned something from the opposite position taken by the antinomians, also ascribes to the office of the ministry in general the duty to preach the Law. Acknowledgment of the Law belongs to the inner presuppositions of evangelical penitence. Nor dare the office which preaches reconciliation pass this over in silence. In the same writing, however, we also find this definition: "The key of binding is the power or office to punish the sinner who is unwilling to make amends, to punish with a public condemnation to eternal death by segregation from Christendom. And if he remains in this state, he is certainly damned eternally"[12] (503, 18.). Here what was provisory becomes definitive. For even though the Novatian error, which denies reacceptance to a penitent sinner, is rejected, here the binding itself actually becomes a judicial act. A "verdict" is pronounced, and its legal validity is confirmed by the punishment, which follows without fail.

At first blush the thought of "binding" can appear to be a wholly foreign body in the "Gospel." Nevertheless, as an idea it is merely a new way of giving expression to the critical significance normally ascribed to the Person of Christ. The stone which God made to be the foundation of the church is rejected by a part of mankind. In doing so this part of mankind excludes itself. Yet it is something else if this exclusion is to result from unbelief per se or if it is made dependent on the judicial discretion of an especially qualified person. The Reformers had no doubt concerning the necessity of giving consideration to the words of Christ from which the Office of the Keys was derived and which have their completely valid analogy in the writings of Paul. "For he who wants to live like a heathen or a dog and does not publicly repent of this, to him we do not want to administer the Sacrament; nor do we want to accept him as belonging to the Christians. Let him die as he has lived and see for himself. For we should not cast pearls before the swine or that which is holy to the dogs."[13] Here the elementary feeling of the Christian congregation is speaking. Luther's *Directives of the Visitors (Unterricht der Visitatoren)* (1528) deals in completely different places with confession and excommunication, both of which belong to the Office of the Keys. Concerning confession it is explicitly stated that the pastor should not admit to the Sacrament anyone who is not "worthy" *(geschickt)* – in order not to make himself an accessory to an unworthy reception (WA 26, 220, 7 ff.). Later it is stated that "it would also be a good thing not to let punishment by means of true and Christian excommunication go out of use." After previous repeated admonitions the Sacrament should be denied to openly great and impenitent sinners, and then the verdict of excommunication should be announced to them. It is not stated what role the pastor must play in connection with this procedure (233, 25 ff.). But the Augsburg Confession counts exclusion "from the communion of the church" *(e communione ecclesiae)* among the specific functions of the spiritual office (XXVIII, 21; Apology XIV, 13).

[12] This definition does not occur in the first draft, which has been handed down only in manuscript. On the contrary, the first draft restricts itself to the pedagogical interpretation (WA 30 II, 435—464).

[13] *Whether One May Flee from Death (Ob man vor dem Sterben fliehen möge)* (1527) (WA 23, 371, 16).

Basically this was unavoidable after the exercise of the rights given to the whole congregation had been assigned to the spiritual office. Nevertheless, one can understand that most church constitutions as well as Luther himself prescribed definite restrictions with regard to this very point. Of course, if one confines excommunication to nonadmittance to the Sacrament — of which the Smalcald Articles speak (III, 9) — the "binding" could be carried out by the pastor without hesitation. For one could consider this a part of his obligation to administer the sacraments "properly" *(recte)*. But as soon as one proceeded to announce the exclusion from the church in a solemn manner — if possible, by using Paul's statements concerning "handing over to Satan" — there was imposed on him who made the announcement a responsibility which, from a practical point of view, it was impossible for him to bear. It would be bearable for him only if he had been appointed a custodian of morals or rather a judge of morals. This contradicts the Lutheran conception of the office. Naturally, he cannot be relieved of the act of announcing the excommunication; for he bears the power of the office. But he can make this announcement only if he knows that in this terrible, special case he is in agreement with the verdict of the congregation. For this reason the *Artickel der ceremonien* of the evangelical bishops of Samland and Pomesania (1525) specify that "the Christian congregation should make use of its right to use the Christian punishments of excommunication against such great public evils"[14] (Sehling IV, 34). The *Hamburger Kirchenordnung* of 1529, which, by the way, regards the whole procedure of excommunication as merely provisional, demands at least that "the verdict of the preacher" be issued "in the name of the congregation" *(der predicanten ordell in dem Namen der gemeene)* — which presupposes, of course, that in individual cases the preachers are sure of assent (Sehling V, 509). A similar statement is made in the *Copenhagen Articles (Confessio Hafnica)*, where we read that excommunication should be carried out *aff guds ordz tiener eller sogne prest* but *medt menige christen forsamlings samtycke* (XVII). And in connection with his *Invocavit* sermon in 1539 Luther had expressly made cooperation on the part of the congregation a condition.[15] Naturally, it was not easy to determine how this was to be carried out. It is scarcely imaginable that in such cases the congregation should reach a decision on the basis of the prin-

[14] Primarily the custom of "choking babies to death."

[15] WA 47, 669, 1 ff.: "The rumor has reached you that I want to excommunicate some. Concerning this there is a great outcry. But not as the officials [do]. [It is rumored] that I had wanted to apply the ban of which Matt. 18 speaks.

ciple that the majority rules. Therefore everything depends on whether there are other ways of making the decision of the congregation known. But this is no longer a theological question. It belongs in the domain of sociology. At all events, however, it should be recognized as properly disburdening the pastor of judicial functions in Luther's sense when, for example, the regulation of the Mecklenburg consistory of 1570 demands the cooperation of the consistory. Excommunication should not be threatened or carried out until the consistory "regards and recognizes" the public sin "as widely known *(notoria)*, manifest, public, and undeniable, and decides concerning it that by it the whole church is offended either by false doctrine or an evil life" *(vor notoria, kundbar, öffentlich und unverneinlich helt und erkennt, auch davon urteilt, dass die ganze kirchen dadurch entweder mit falscher lehre oder bösem leben geergert wird)* (Sehling V, 243). The other side of cooperation on the part of the congregation is the demand that there be a public apology before the assembled congregation. The possibility of doing this is constantly held open to the penitent sinner even by Luther, just as in any case the person who is still excommunicated is allowed to attend the services that are devoted to preaching. A precedent established in the early church forbids him to be present when Holy Communion is celebrated, and this prohibition is prescribed by many church constitutions. The public apology is regarded as reacceptance, not as a punishment.

Nor did the endeavor to guard the evangelical pastor against the position of having to serve as a judge disappear in the Lutheranism of the seventeenth century. Where the opposite is the case, there are aftereffects of Melanchthon. Although in the *Tractate on the Power of the*

I for my person do not excommunicate anyone. But all Christians must act in this matter, with your prayer, as Paul says 1 Cor. 5 — we, too, with your spirit. An Our Father should be spoken against someone. And if he makes amends, another Our Father should be spoken, that he may be received again. 1. Therefore the ban must take place altogether publicly, not in private confession. . . ." L. 24: "I know nothing else than that acts of adultery and other manifest disgraceful deeds are punished. If the opposite is true, you must help ban, and you must pray, must contribute your spirit and your prayer. . . ." "1. I should send two of the elders and deacons, and deal with him, in order that he may desist. Then I should proceed. There I should declare that he has been excommunicated, because he has been warned in accordance with the command of Christ, as you properly see. Now help to advise and pray, kneel down, give your spirit and an Our Father, and hand him over to the devil. . . . The ban is not a tyrant; but it is the earnest rebuke of the church, to sweep out what is unclean and to cleanse sin." — Cf. WA *TR* 4, 4381 a and b. — As early as 1522: "Therefore if the congregation does not know, one should not accept the excommunication, and one should show the messenger the door" (WA 10 III, 122, 1).

Pope (Tractatus de potestate Papae) he gives assurance that "the keys pertain to the church, not to the person of one specific man" *(quod claves non ad personam unius certi hominis, sed ad ecclesiam pertineant)* (24, 68), elsewhere he assigns the exercise of the Power of the Keys unconditionally to the spiritual office and says that it is an expression of the "rule of the church" *(regimen ecclesiae).* And where in spite of this he speaks of calling in other persons, he characterizes these, together with the pastor, as judges.[16] It is significant that in a letter to Nürnberg, in which he recommends that the government invite a number of pastors to give their opinion when public criminals are punished, he sings a hymn of high praise to Farel (*CR* 3, 1249 f.). This can no longer be called cooperation on the part of the congregation when the Power of the Keys is exercised. It is the beginning of theocracy or, what amounts to the same thing, the beginning of the end of Lutheranism. Yet one should not forget that at least in connection with confession Melanchthon kept away from the thought of punishment. Like Luther, he wants confession to be understood as consolation for consciences (*CR* 21, 494).

Luther's endeavor to shield the person of the pastor from the position of having to be a judge cannot be separated from his conception of the office. The pastor's entire efficiency rests on the power of the Word of God. The Word forgives, and the Word judges. The application to the individuality of the hearer must be made by the hearer himself, not by the pastor. The more selflessly the human being in the pastor withdraws behind the sole validity of the Word, the more confidently he may hope to be the mouthpiece of God. This led to the completely self-evident result that fitness to be called as a pastor was made dependent, first of all, on his position with respect to "doctrine" and that his preparatory education and his examination were planned accordingly. Melanchthon's efforts, which culminate in his *Examination of Those to Be Ordained (Examen ordinandorum),* have no other purpose than the

[16] *CR* 14, 894, 973; 21, 494. Without reference to the office: 14, 429; 15, 1074. On the other hand, 14, 915: "through the pastor and other judges who have been appointed in the church" *(per pastorem et alios judices in ecclesia ordinatos).* Furthermore, in the most extensive treatise "on excommunication" *(de excommunicatione),* 16, 482 ff.: ". . . after summoning witnesses before the church. . . . That the highest verdict in this visible church is neither in the possession of one tyrant nor in the possession of a promiscuous crowd but in the possession of the church, that is, of knowing persons chosen from many for the purpose of passing judgment" *(. . . adhibitis testibus apud ecclesiam. . . . Summum judicium in hac visibili ecclesia neque penes unum aliquem tyrannum esse neque penes promiscuum vulgus, sed penes ecclesiam, id est, electos ex multis peritos ad iudicandum)* (486 f.). — Among the later dogmaticians cf., e. g., Quenstedt, *Theol. did.-pol.* IV, 403b.

practical execution. As early as 1526 the *Kirchenordnung* of Hadeln prescribes the selection of a man "who has good testimony of a good life, is learned and adept in Scripture, is sure of what he teaches, and has from God the gift of speaking and expounding Scripture according to the spirit and truth" *(de dar hefft ein gudt getuchenisse eines guden levendes und de dar gelehret und geschicket is in der schrifft und de siner lehre gewisse iss und hebbe van godt de gave tho redende und de schrifft na dem geiste und warheit uth tho leggende)* (Sehling V, 473). Nor did Luther ever doubt that the efficiency of an evangelical pastor presupposes knowledge, understanding, and confession of the evangelical truth. In his numerous sermons on John 10 this fact constantly recurs as the mark which distinguishes a genuine shepherd from hirelings and wolves. No matter what the case may be with respect to the significance formulated confessions have for the church (cf. *The Acceptance of the Old Creeds, The Doctrine of God, Catholicity*) — obligation to them does not mean that a foreign yoke is imposed on the pastor; it means that he has completed a period of conscientious study which the congregation entrusting itself to him can demand of him.[17] The prescriptions of many church regulations which obligate the pastor to continue his studies, and pastoral conferences to occupy themselves with theological matters, show that the knowledge and understanding demonstrated in the examination should not be dragged along as a dead deposit.

By giving primacy to the officeholder's duty to teach, which is one of the essential elements of the Lutheran Reformation, the pastoral profession *(Pfarrerstand)* was made the "teaching profession" *(Lehrstand)*, which has been the object of violent attacks since the days of pietism. That the flowering of evangelical theology — even in the nineteenth century — and, indirectly, very many other far-reaching cultural results are due to the fact that first place was given to the officeholder's duty to teach could, of course, not be an excuse for the dangers that are said to have arisen for evangelical churchdom on this account. Nor, on the other hand, can the judgment concerning the Lutheran office of the ministry be substantiated by pointing to these damages themselves. Either way the mistake is the same. In both cases a goal which is immediately rejected when there is clear understanding is falsely attributed to the Lutheran Reformation and the churchdom which arose from it.

[17] Cf. the excellent comments of Jac. Andreä in *Esslinger Predigten* IV, 72 ff. — What he points out here in opposition to the criticism of the Anabaptists and in defense of studying at a university, especially the study of the original languages of the Bible (pp. 82 ff.), is nothing more than a recognition of Luther's well-known demands.

When such false charges are made, it is presupposed that the church should be, or wants to be, a disciplinary institution or – to speak in terms of the Enlightenment – an association for moral purposes. This was Calvin's goal, but it was not Luther's. Only sinners belong to the Lutheran Church; not willful sinners, to be sure, but penitent sinners – yet always only sinners, who in this life can never be anything else. On principle the Lutheran Church has nothing to offer to the righteous people whose saintliness one can observe in the cut of their clothes, in their bill of fare, and in the "language of Canaan." What its members do or do not do, miss or do not neglect, in an ethical respect belongs in the domain of sociology and has nothing at all to do with the nature of the church. The evangelical human being is answerable for this, not the evangelical church. At best the evangelical church is answerable indirectly, insofar as it owes the individual the Gospel, which engenders his faith and thus becomes indirectly perceptible in the ethical dynamic.

Only in view of this indirect connection can one justify the fact that in the Lutheranism of the seventeenth century a still further shifting of the conception of the office took place – a shifting that perhaps could lead even farther away from Luther's original conception than the jurisdictional conception. It consists in the revival of the medieval conception of the "care of souls" *(cura animarum, Seelsorge)* as one of the duties of the pastor. Of course, if in this connection one thinks only of the self-evident Christian duty to be concerned about one's brother and the welfare of his soul *(Seelenheil)*, one may count Luther among the advocates of the "care of souls." No one impressed the duty to care for souls as emphatically on the consciences of the heads of families as Luther did. When in recent times naive critics regard the patriarchal element as the main thing in this connection, this can be explained only by the fact that in spite of their extensive works on the problems presented by the overestimation of historical development *(Historismus)* they were blind to history. The achievements in the matter of the "care of souls" *(Seelsorge)* within the compass of that patriarchal regimen in the domain of Lutheranism – and, indirectly, also in the matter of ethical training – could, in the light of the sources, be illustrated only by individual examples, say, by individual parsonages and residences of rulers; but again this would lead into the domain of sociology. It cannot be denied, however, that in the sense of the Lutheran Reformation the pastor as such is motivated by the duty to care for souls. True, Luther uses the expression *Seelsorger* only rarely.[18] And when it is used at all in his *The Arrangement of a General Treasury (Ordnung eines gemeinen Kastens),* which had to do with the systematization of the finances of the parish at Leisnig (1523), precisely here the pastor's sphere of duties is described only as proclaiming the Word of God and administering the sacraments (WA 12, 16, 19). But as early as 1520 Luther opposes "feeding the sheep of Christ" in the medieval sense of "governing" with the statement: "Where there is no love, there is no feeding" *(Wo nit lieb ist, da ist keyn weyden)* (WA 6, 319, 3). This is the demand made by the inner and personal relationship of the pastor to his parishioners *(Pfarrkinder).* And in *Whether One May Flee from Death (Ob man vor dem Sterben fliehen möge),* addressed to Johann Hess, pastor at Breslau, in 1527, it is precisely the "carer for souls" *(Seelsorger)* whom Luther calls upon to care for the individual, also by "visiting" him, even though he declares that it is impossible to have at every sick person's "bedside a daily pulpit and altar, because they have so despised the common pulpit and altar to which God has called them and which He has demanded" *(vor ihrem bette einen teglichen predigtstuel und altar halte, weil sie den gemeinen predigtstuel und altar so haben verachtet, dazu sie Gott beruffen und gefoddert hat)* (WA 23, 371, 34).

Accordingly, most church regulations make it the pastor's duty to visit the sick.[19] To those who seek advice he should give comfort from God's Word (Sehling I, 5; I, 1, p. 190); as "shepherd of souls" *(Seelhirt)* and "carer for souls" *(Seelsorger)* he should pray, give thanks, and sing with his parishioners *(Pfarrkinder)* (264). It is not likely that church regulations would fail to state that he should avoid anything that could give offense; for example — as the general articles for Albertine Saxony of 1557 demand — he should abstain from "drinking, taking strolls, and other offensive frivolities" *(saufens, spacirengehens und anderer ergerlichen leichtfertigkeit)* "and thus stimulate everyone to hear God's Word diligently and to receive the sacred, venerable Sacrament frequently" *(und also menniglich zu fleissiger anhörunge gottes wort und ofter entfahunge des heiligen hochwirdigen sacraments reizen)* (322). It goes without saying that when the pastor is installed, special reference is made to his personal relationship to the members of his future congregation.[20] Above all, however, this relationship makes itself felt in

[18] E. g., WA 30 III, 519, 3: "For the pastor, of course, has the pulpit, Baptism, and the Sacrament, and all care of souls is entrusted to him." Cf. *Seelwärter, Seelväter* (*TR* 5, p. 574, 19; 578, 15).

[19] E. g., Sehling, *KO* I, 1, 199, 323, 349 ff., 437, 511, 516, 568, 572, 579, 646 ff.; III, 417; IV, 98, 363, etc.

[20] Cf., e. g., Sigwart's *Ordinationspredigten.*

private confession and in the personal announcement that takes place before partaking of the Lord's Supper. Like Melanchthon and the confessions, Luther distinguished private confession — which, according to *CA* IX, should be retained — sharply from auricular confession and the Roman sacrament of penance in general. On principle Luther put the Office of the Keys, where private confession belongs, on the same level with the "mutual conversation" *(mutuum colloquium)* and the "consolation of the brethren" *(consolatio fratrum)* (Smalcald Articles III, 4). Precisely here one sees that the pastor is a "carer for souls" *(Seelsorger),* not what one would call a judge. When — especially in accordance with Melanchthon's intention, which is echoed in many church regulations — the personal interview before partaking of Holy Communion takes on the character of an examination on the basis of the Catechism, one can, of course, find here again an overestimation of doctrine; but here it becomes incontrovertibly evident how earnestly the care of every single member of the congregation was made the pastor's duty.

Nevertheless, here something remains — something that rises in opposition to the whole later, pietistic ideal of a carer for souls. Theophil Grossgebauer demands — as Spener does later on — that the pastor satisfy himself as to whether the individual in his congregation has been "born again." The office of shepherd *(Hirtenamt),* he says, is something different from the office of preaching *(Predigtamt).* The former demands "special supervision of every sheep" *(absonderliche Aufsicht auf ein jegliches Schaf).* Every individual is to be pressed "in every way" until "we notice that they have been born again" *(wir mercken, dass sie wiedergeboren).* Yes, the pastors *(Kirchen-Diener)* were designated as those who must "feed and regenerate souls" *(Seelen zu weiden und wiederzugebähren haben).*[21] The office of shepherd becomes an office for the guidance and the investigation of individual souls, just as it does in the contemporary moral theology of the Jesuits. It is no accident that at the same time there arises an evangelical casuistry that is altogether on a par with that of the Jesuits. Ludwig Dunte could compile as many as 1,006 decisions of cases of conscience *(Decisiones casuum conscientiae).*[22] The *Consistorial Decrees (Definitiones consistoriales)* of Benedikt Carpzov II, which are approximately equal in number to the *Decisiones casuum conscientiae,* are formally in contrast with them only because of the greater precision of the jurists. To be sure, the dyed-

[21] Th. Grossgebauer, *Treuer Unterricht v. d. Wiedergeburt,* in *Drei geistreiche Schriften,* Rostock, 1667, pp. 472 f. Cf. the entire treatise and *Wächterstimme,* ch. 6.

[22] Ludwig Dunte, *Decisiones Mille et sex Casuum etc.,* Ratzeburg, 1664.

in-the-wool pietist abominates these canonical decisions just as he abominates the school ethics of contemporary professors of theology; but what they themselves demand of the carer for souls also makes the church an ethical board of directors. Beyond this, however, it makes the carer for souls God's policeman, who questions the offender and keeps him in protective custody until he has been born again and has become ripe for the little wreath of pietism. In the territory of Ernest the Pious special "keepers of morals" *(Sittenmeister)* and in Württemberg – after Johann Valentin Andreä had bewailed the fact that the church discipline of Geneva was unknown in Lutheranism – monitors were appointed by the law of the land. It was their duty to supervise church attendance and the observance of Sunday as a holy day.[23]

Even though such measures taken by the state were comprehensible from the standpoint of the ruler, who, even according to the teaching of the Reformation, must look after the ethos of his country, still, where they are founded theologically on the nature of the church, one can recognize that a serious shifting of the Lutheran conception of the church has come about or is on the way. Luther's belief in the omnipotence of the Gospel and its proclamation is being extinguished. This always was and will be the case where one's attention is directed to man instead of to God, and this reversal of the direction of one's attention gives rise to the new ideal of a carer for souls. When Luther used the word "shepherd," he understood something different. The office of shepherd *is* the office of preaching. The food for the sheep is the Gospel, which is offered to them through the sermon (WA 10 III, 170 ff.). The good shepherd certainly knows even the weak sheep in his flock. He goes before them and takes "note of those that are sick, that are mangy or have colds" *(achtung drauff, welche krank seind, welche reudig seind oder den schnupen haben)*. It is "not enough to preach correctly, which hirelings can also do" *(nicht gnug, das man recht predige, welchs die miedling auch thun können)*. Good shepherds sit up with the lambs and fight against the wolves – but "with the Word of God" (WA 10 I, 2; p. 243, 18 ff.). "This is done wholly through the Gospel, because the Gospel is the pasture, the ointment, the bandage with which [the sheep] is bound up; because the Gospel does everything man needs; it edifies; it comforts" *(Hoc fit totum per Evangelium, quia illud est pascua, die salben, band, per quod ligatur, quia facit omnia, quibus homo indiget, edificat, confortat)* (WA 20, 370, 15). The "weak, sick, broken, lost – all these one must leave among the sheep, because there would be no shep-

[23] On this law for Württemberg cf. Jul. Hartmann in *Württemberg. Kirchengesch.*, 1893, p. 450.

herd who would want to cast them aside forthwith" *(schwach, kranck, zerbrochen, verloren, die muss man alzumal lassen sein unter den schaffen, quia non esset pastor, qui statim vellet abiicere eas)* (369, 17). This is the opposite of the pietistic ideal of a congregation. The rule of the shepherd "consists in feeding, that is, in preaching; there can be no higher service" *(sthet ynn der weid, i. e., Im predigen, höher kann mans nicht machen)* (WA 34 I, 329, 9). This is the opposite of the pietistic ideal of a carer for souls. Luther believed in the omnipotence of the Gospel. What this meant for the ethos will come under the heading of sociology.

27. Church Government [1]

Since both the proclamation of the Gospel and the sacraments are necessarily bound up with the nature of the church, it is evident that the church cannot exist without the spiritual office. By transmitting the proclamation of the Gospel and the administration of the sacraments to officially appointed individuals Lutheranism took over an arrangement that had been continuously in practice since the days of the apostles. As has been pointed out, Luther himself traced the fact that the official charge was given to individuals back to the will of Christ, the Founder. Thus in a formal manner the office is analogous to the scaraments. For this reason one can understand why the Apology was willing to acknowledge the sacramental character of the office on the condition that the office be regarded as the "ministry of the Word" *(ministerium verbi),* not as the office of a priest who offers sacrifices (VII, 11). As was proper, this conception did not gain general accept-

[1] See the writings mentioned under *The Dogma of the Church, The Office of the Ministry,* and *The Later Doctrine of the Office of the Ministry and the Nature of This Office.* In addition, Benedikt Carpzov (II), *Jurisprudentia Ecclesiastica* (first published in 1645), Leipzig, 1695. — J. H. Böhmer, Jus ecclesiasticum Protestantium . . ., Halle, 1714. — Aem. Ludw. Richter, *Grundlagen d. Kirchenverfassung n. d. Ansichten der sächsischen Reformatoren, Zeitschr. f. deutsches Recht u. d. Rechtswissenschaft,* 1840, pp. 1 ff. — The same author, *Gesch. d. evang. Kirchenverfassung in Deutschland,* 1851. — G. v. Zezschwitz, *Die wesentlichen Verfassungsziele d. lutherischen Reformation,* 1867. — Otto Mejer, *Lehrb. d. Deutschen Kirchenrechtes,* 3d ed., 1869. — Karl Rieker, *Die rechtl. Natur d. evangelischen Pfarramts,* 1891. — The same author, *Die rechtl. Stellung d. evang. Kirche Deutschlands in ihrer gesch. Entwicklung,* 1893. — The same author, *Sinn und Bedeutung des landesherrl. Kirchenregiments,* 1902. — Rud. Sohm, *Kirchenrecht I,* 1892. — Paul Drews, *Entsprach das Staatskirchentum dem Ideal Luthers? ZThK,* 1908, supplementary number. — Karl Müller, *Anfänge d. Konsistorialverfassung im luth. Deutschland, Histor. Zeitschr.* Vol. 4, 1909, 11 ff. — The same author, *Kirche, Gemeinde u. Obrigkeit nach Luther,* 1910. — Karl Holl, *Luther u. d. landesherrliche Kirchenregiment, Ges. Aufs.* I, 4th and 5th ed., 1927, 326 ff. — Alfr. Reuter, *Luthers u. Melanchthons Stellung zur jurisdictio episcoporum NKZ,* 1925, pp. 549 ff. — H. Steinlein, *Luthers Stellung zur Bischofsfrage, Reichsbote,* May 8, 1927. — Kurt Matthes, *Das Corpus Christianum bei Luther im Lichte seiner Erforschung,* 1929.

ance; for the assignment of a commission does not include the promise to the officeholder that he will have a specific charism. If government *(Verfassung)* means organization, one can see in the institution of the pastoral office the beginning of a definite church government; for this institution constitutes an organizing principle for all church members. Of course, it matters little if in lieu of this one sees the beginning of government in the formation of a local congregation. But since this formation does not take place according to the principle of association but comes about because all the members are called through the Gospel, and this call is bound to the efficiency of the office, the local congregation and the pastoral office are mutually dependent. Basically the one results from the other.

It is questionable, however, whether what has just been said is an exhaustive treatment of the organization of the church. Organization is necessary if an association wants to be capable of action toward the inside and toward the outside. For an association must have the means by which this activity is carried on. Government is the regulating of the activity that is carried on by prescribed means beyond specific occasions, persons, and factors. But the functions that are vital to the church – preaching, the administration of the sacraments, and the Office of the Keys – have been regulated by the institution of the pastoral office and the relationship existing between this office and the congregation. There seems to be neither room nor need for further governmental regulations.

Nevertheless, the discussion of the pastoral office itself gives rise to a number of problems that require further organizational regulation. We saw that as early as 1523 Luther considers at least two acts necessary for the appointment of a pastor and clearly distinguishes them from each other – the election and the installation. Logically the actual act of calling – as the result of the election and as a prerequisite to the installation – must come between the election and the installation. Furthermore, Luther and, as is self-evident, all the later theologians demand that the person to be called be examined. Who is to perform these acts? Here it becomes necessary to have an organization for the purpose of making inner action possible. Only in connection with the election could one, if need be, consider it possible to do without an organization, since Luther, at least in his early period, wants the "whole congregation" to act when this takes place. But even this merely appears to be the case. For an election presupposes the possibility that those who take part in it may reach various decisions. At all events, therefore, it is necessary to make a regulation that would apply when the election does not turn out to be unanimous. But in connection with this act it is also impossible to let the "whole congregation" consist of the sum of all its members. In any case, the young children must be excluded. Therefore it is necessary to establish when the age of majority is reached. But whether all church members who have reached the age of majority are capable of taking part in the election of a pastor can appear to be doubtful, even though Luther – as the church regulations did later on – considers trial sermons necessary. Passing judgment on these trial sermons presupposes capabilities – especially in the area of doctrine – with which Luther himself by no means credits every adult. The same requirements recur when the call is extended. Besides, ordination as a ceremonial act demands the organizational appointment of individuals who in this instance are authorized to act in the name of the congregation. This is government.

Furthermore, it became evident – likewise as early as 1523 – that Luther does not speak of the local congregation as being independent and self-sufficient. The practical expression of his conviction is seen in the fact that visitations were carried out. In particular, the observance of the "evangelical doctrine" *(doctrina evangelica)* is not the concern of the individual congregation; it is the concern of all those who profess this doctrine. Preparation for the pastoral office requires thorough study. For this it is necessary to have teachers of theology, and they cannot be identical with the sum total of the congregation members. The more extensive the circle is from which they have emerged as the most competent because of their accomplishments in the field of theology or because of other conspicuous qualifications, the greater will be their importance as teachers. Since every individual congregation has a vital interest in the thorough training of its future pastors, it will join Luther in demanding not only "that children be sent to school" *(dass man die Kinder zur Schule halten soll)* (1530) and also in demanding "of the councilmen of all the cities of Germany that they establish and maintain Christian schools" *(von den Ratsherren aller Städte deutschen Landes, dass sie christliche Schulen aufrichten und halten sollen)* (1524) – and here Luther means higher schools – but they will also support his appeal to the Christian nobility to maintain and reform the universities (WA 6, 457, 28 ff.; 461, 36 ff.). But only the territories are able to maintain the universities. If the individual congregation has to entrust the theological education of the pastor to the teachers who have been appointed from a larger circle – and if it is able to do this because, or insofar as, the same confession is accepted – it follows that it will also entrust the examination to the men of the larger circle who are specially qualified in theology. The qualification to examine, however, is the same as the qualification to supervise doctrine. Even though the fundamental right to examine with respect to doctrine is maintained — the right to which, according to Luther, every Christian is entitled — still provision must be made for cases in which the judgments of the congregation differ. And even when the whole congregation is unanimous in condemning the pastor because of allegedly false doctrine, the judgment of the congregation cannot without further ado be regarded as valid. For this would mean that in the case of a conflict the very person who has been especially called to proclaim the "evangelical doctrine" *(doctrina evangelica)* would be eliminated. For this reason it is in the interest of the congregation as well as of the pastor that there be a post outside the congregation but bound to the same confession — a post which takes over the settlement of differences or makes the decision. Nevertheless, the regulation of the arrangements necessary for the maintenance of the pastoral office reach beyond the individual congregation. These arrangements are no longer functions of the individual congregation; they are functions of the larger church entity. Consequently, they, too, require organization.[2]

The question that arises here and actually is often asked — whether on principle the individual congregation or the church as a whole comes first — is falsely put. It could be answered only if the one proceeded

[2] Even the *Hadelner KO* of 1526 acknowledges "authorized agents" *(volmechtige)* of the congregation in connection with the election of pastors (Sehling V, 473). — Cf. Mentzer, *Exegesis,* p. 640: "the calling negotiated through suitable men appointed for this purpose" *(vocatio mediata per homines idoneos ad id constitutos).* — On trial sermons cf. Luther, WA 16, 34, 8. — Trial sermons as well as examination before the consistory in Dresden with reference to abuses that have occurred: Many were "drilled through a student or someone else to answer a number of questions and are not admitted to ordination until they are able to answer these questions. . . . Afterwards they read to the congregation the sermons of others." (Sehling I, 1, p. 418.) — On the necessity of the study of theology cf. *Mecklenburg KO* of 1552 (Sehling V, 161). — On the special qualification for undertaking the examination: *Instruktion z. Visit. im Albertinischen Sachsen von 1539:* ". . . are questioned and examined by the learned men in Leipzig" (Sehling I, 1, p. 283). For the Lutheran Church in Hungary: *Beschlüsse d. Synode zu Silein* (1610), can. 7, in Kuzmany, *Urkundenbuch zum österreichish-evangelischen Kirchenrecht,* p. 192. — According to the Wittenberg reformation of 1555, the sovereigns are to "appoint qualified persons for the questioning (for the examination)" (*CR* V, 585). — According to the *Kurländ. KO* of 1570, the patrons can "call, place, and receive" pastors; but it is the duty of the superattendant to conduct the examination — as well as the ordination and the installation (Sehling V, 109). — Concerning the examination of those who are already in office: Once every three months the city pastors of Stendal are to order the country pastors within a radius of two miles to come to the city, let them preach there, and examine them (Sehling III, 316) (1578). A similar duty is imposed on the pastor of Bagow (ibid., p. 153) (1553). — Even for vacancies the congregation is directed to get help from outside. E. g., *Henneberg KO* (Sehling I, 2, 321).

from the other. In reality the individual congregation and the church as a whole have the same origin – in the operation of the Gospel. But if one asks about the "divine right" of both, one must say that this concept is inherent first of all in the church as a whole. For the "divine right" can be derived only from the establishment through Christ. But Christ gave the commission to preach, to baptize, etc. – the commission that makes the church what it is – neither to individual persons nor to individual congregations; He gave it to the sum total of all Christians. Luther himself emphasizes this fact untiringly. It is true that when conditions in the church as they existed at that time lead him to make this statement, he is contending above all against reserving the commission for individual persons, namely, for the bishops; but it would be a strange "improvement" of the situation if, instead, he had proclaimed the autocracy of the individual congregation at the expense of the "sum total" of all Christians, which he emphasized with such vigor. What he says about the activity of the local congregation in connection with the institution of the pastoral office cannot be misleading. It is clearly the purpose of his statements to guarantee to all individuals the right to which they are entitled on the basis of the priesthood of all believers, that is, as Luther states it, on the basis of Baptism, in which we "are anointed to be priests." But this right does not inhere in their membership in the local congregation; it inheres in the church of Christ in general. The very fact that they are members of the church of Christ gives them a divine right. The fact that they live with one another in local congregations is incident to their life on earth. Therefore all the proposals Luther makes with regard to what the local congregation has to do with the institution of the pastoral office spring from considerations of expediency. Consequently, they cannot be assessed as regulations of a divine constitutional right of the church.

Since the same thing is true of the various proposals, regulations, and customs with reference to the education, the examination, and the supervision of pastors, and since, in addition, all functions essential to the church become important, one must conclude that in the church there are only the following elements of divine right: (1) the existence of the pastoral office; (2) the functions of this office – preaching, the sacraments, the keys. This is true of the church as a whole as well as of the individual congregation. At the same time it means that there is no longer a basic difference between the two.

In a sermon delivered in 1524 Luther says that in Christ's statement "I am the Shepherd" there is "embraced His rule and Christendom, in order that we may listen to Him alone" *(verfasst sein regiment und*

Christenheit, ut solum illum audiamus). When an evangelical sermon is preached, Christians always hear the voice of Christ the Shepherd. The person of the preacher is a mattter of secondary importance. "I must look at the office; otherwise no purpose is served" *(Auff das ampt muss ich sehen, alias hilffts nichts)* (WA 15, 533). The authority of the office does not rest on the arrangement made by the individual congregation; it rests on the fact that the office makes the voice of the Archshepherd operative. This is the meaning the office properly has for the church as a whole. For the church as a whole it is always one and the same. Accordingly, the differentiation made with respect to the activity of the office in individual local pastorates takes place for practical reasons. Then, however, there is no reason why a differentiation in performance should not be made according to points of view that are not local. To be sure, Luther refused to apply the passages in which Paul speaks of a number of offices (1 Cor. 12:28; Eph. 4:11) to the ecclesiastical hierarchy (WA 50, 633, 3 ff.; 28 ff.). For him the "apostles, evangelists, prophets" are eliminated without further ado because they come to be "apostles, evangelists, prophets" as the result of a direct and extraordinary divine call. Nor does he recognize a difference between bishops and presbyters. The *Confessio Hafnica* (Art. 36) also says: "True Christian bishops or priests – they are one and the same" *(Rechte christliche Bischöfe oder Priester – das ist dasselbe).* And Melanchthon's *Tractate on the Power of the Papacy (Tractatus de potestate Papae)* definitely rejected at least the validity of a difference in rank "by divine right" *(de jure divino)* (65). The later dogmaticians followed him with respect to this matter.[3]

Nevertheless, Luther took the momentous step and – so he himself, at any rate, viewed it – told the princes that "out of Christian love" he wanted to appoint certain persons as visitors. He derives the office of the visitors from the original meaning of the terms "bishop" and "archbishop" (WA 26, 197, 17 ff.). Although here, too, he considers the bishop the pastor *(Pfarrherr),* who "should visit, look after, and supervise his parishioners" *(pfarrkinder besuchen, warten und auff sehen sol),* "the archbishop" should "visit, look after, and supervise such bishops, to see how they are teaching" *(der Erzbischof solche bischove besuchen, warten und auffsehen, wie die selbigen leren)* (196, 5 ff.). Apart from the appeal to the princes, this was nothing new, for as early as 1523 Luther had recommended this arrangement to the Bohemians. Indeed, in view of the opposition he had expressed in his *On the Councils and the Churches*

[3] L. Hutter, *Gründtl. Bericht,* pp. 42 and 47. – Hülsemann, *Manuale,* p. 493. Cf. p. 463. Titus was not archbishop in the sense of canon law. – Calov, *Exegema zu Art. XIV.* – Sigwart, *Ordin.-Pred. von 1610,* p. 6.

(Von den Konzilien und Kirchen) (1539) it is altogether unthinkable that by doing this he was sanctioning the hierarchical principle. No matter what arrangements are made here, they are made "by human law" *(de jure humano)*. But this is also true of the local division of the church into parishes. With the same qualification there was a readiness to recognize even the bishops of the hitherto existing church, provided that they held their office in the sense of the Gospel (Apology VII, 24; Smalcald Articles III, 10). And according to this principle it was actually possible to deal with the new Duchy of Prussia. But the office of the archbishop – according to Luther's preface to his *Directives of the Visitors (Unterricht der Visitatoren)*, they could be designated as such – is no longer an office of the individual congregation; in its specific sense it is an office of the church as a whole.

But this office of visitation contains nothing that, on principle, would go beyond the purport of the office of bishop or the office of pastor. It is merely a necessary result of dividing into local pastoral offices the one office with which the church is charged. The same spiritual office must be exercised by the entire church as such in the form of the right to visit, because the local congregation is and should be merely a member of the whole. It is basically as well as practically immaterial whether one argues here from the bottom – as Luther does in what he wrote to the Bohemians, that is, with a view to the interest of the individual congregations – or – as the later dogmaticians do – from the top, that is, from the point of view that an orderly arrangement of the whole is necessary.

Things do not take a new turn until the right of visitation or the right of supervision – into which, as was understandable, the right of visitation had to develop – was viewed as a function of "church government" *(Kirchenregiment)* in a special sense. But this is justifiable only as long as one does not understand church government differently from the way it is understood by Luther and the confessions, namely, that it is the "spiritual power" *(geistliche Gewalt)*, "which is called teaching, that is, the Gospel" *(die heist leren, das ist das Evangelium)* or the pastoral office.[4] For only then is the basic identity of the one office preserved. It is scarcely necessary to say that this is not undermined when Luther also illustrates the meaning of "spiritual government" *(geistliche Obrigkeit)* with the Power of the Keys (WA 10 III, 121, 20). For this very power is an integral part of every pastorate. Nor is this view of church government broken asunder when church regulations transfer the examination of future pastors to the superintendents appointed for the exercise

[4] Luther, WA 10 III, 122, 20. Cf. the entire sermon and the usage in *CA* XIV.

of the right to inspect, or even to the consistories, or especially when they transfer to the former the ordination and installation or to both the supervision of the orderly administration through the pastors of preaching, the sacraments, and the keys. For the only purpose all this has is the upholding of the one office of the church as a whole. Supervision over the conduct of pastors is also to be mentioned in this connection; likewise supervision over general order in the congregations when this is understood to be merely the orderly exercise of specific church functions.

It is something entirely different, however, when church government is taken to be a special "governing office" *(Regieramt)* of the church and thus powers that, on principle, go beyond the purely pastoral functions are conceded to it. For this we have been prepared by the previously mentioned definition of the "power of jurisdiction" *(potestas jurisdictionis)*, the consequence of which Johann Gerhard designated not only as the right to ordain but also as the "censorship of morals" *(censura morum)* (cf. *The Later Doctrine of the Office of the Ministry and the Nature of This Office)*. To be sure, it is completely in conformity with Luther's purpose when his *Directives of the Visitors (Unterricht der Visitatoren)* makes it the duty of pastors to "exhort the people to fear" *(die leute zur forcht vermanen)* (WA 26, 227, 20) and urges them to obey the laws of the state and to do other "Christian works." For Luther no longer had any doubt that a preacher of the Gospel dare not dispense with the Law. At any rate, the doubt he had entertained with respect to this matter had come to an end after the first controversy with the antinomians. Melanchthon had long since ceased to be in doubt about the matter. But this does not mean that the pastor should exercise "church discipline" *(Kirchenzucht)* in the sense of a "censorship of morals" *(censura morum)*. Only when a burdened conscience wants to be freed or when offense has been given to the congregation is there occasion to exercise the Power of the Keys. It is true that Luther, too, recognizes a "censorship of morals" *(censura morum)*, that is, not only a right to supervise the conduct of Christians but even a right to punish. But this is the business of the government.[5] The notion that church government is something different from the pastoral office of the church as a whole and, in any case, that it has special governmental functions comes about as the result of combining it with state government.

Yet until a short time ago this combination – above all, in the form of church government by the princes – passes, or passed, for a specific

[5] This is developed with special sharpness in the *Braunschweiger KO* of 1528 (Lietzmann's edition, pp. 53 f.).

mark of Lutheran church government, even though there was no lack of opposition to this view. Judgment concerning the matter depends on the question whether specific Lutheran theology finds expression in such a combination. This would be the case if the combination were intrinsically connected with the Lutheran concept of the church. Luther's appeal to the princes arose from actual requirements of the reformation of the church. The princes, as he sets forth in his writing to the nobility, are under obligation to make reparation for the harm which, in his opinion, the hitherto existing church had done to national and state property. This demand had a previous history that was centuries old. Nor would anyone who was not bound to canonical law be likely to oppose it. Furthermore, it lay in the nature of the circumstances that in evangelical areas the jurisdiction of the bishops – to the extent that it belonged in the purely civil sphere and for this reason was denied to them by the confessions – be exercised henceforth by the princes. This is particularly true of jurisdiction over marriage, which, in part, could have far-reaching consequences for families and the right of inheritance. The fact that this jurisdiction was taken over by the state certainly did not mean that there was church government by the princes. At all events, this was not Luther's intention. Confusion with respect to this matter did not arise until the consistories entrusted with it also received specific church functions. The handling of matrimonial matters as "mixed cases" *(causae mixtae)* – that is, as the business of the church and the secular authorities – by the same board can be regarded as a classical example for the mingling of church and state that came later.[6] But this has nothing to do with the Lutheran concept of the church. In fact, it is in opposition to this concept. Even the obligation which Luther places on the government vis-à-vis "conflicting doctrines or heresies" *(widderwertigen leren odder ketzereyen)* is regarded as an obligation of the state, not of the church, and is defined accordingly. Luther distinguishes between those who are "seditious" *(auffrürisch)* and thus threaten the state itself and those who "teach contrary to a manifest article of faith" *(leren widder einen offentlichen artickel des glaubens)* and by doing so "blaspheme the name of God" *(den namen Gottes lestern)*. The government should take action against both categories, but only for its own protection and for the protection of its subjects. It is important to note that only the "teaching and blaspheming" *(leren und lestern)* of the second category should be stopped. "For in this way no one is forced to believe, for he can still believe what he wants to believe"

[6] Cf. Benedikt Carpzov (II), *Jurispr. eccl. L. II, T. I, def. 1.* In addition, the chapter on matrimony in the second volume.

(Denn hie mit wird nemand zum glauben gedrungen, denn er kan dennoch wol glauben was er wil).[7] Even though Luther regards the appropriate protective and punitive measures as belonging purely to the state, still vis-à-vis the second category there is a tacit presupposition that the government itself — at least in general — is standing on the ground of Christian faith. Finally, the same thing is true of the analogous administration of the church and cloister property taken over by the state. The request that this be done is an appeal to the administration of the princes vis-à-vis the church — without taking for granted that the princes rule the church.

But as early as Luther's *To the Christian Nobility (An den christlichen Adel)* (1520) it is suggested to the princes that they arrange a council for the reorganization of church affairs. And the visitations were supposed to accomplish at least for the individual territories what could not be achieved for "Christendom" as a whole, not even for the German Empire. Thus there is included among the duties of the government a very far-reaching influence both on worship — at least negatively by doing away with the existing "abuses" — and on doctrine, the actual practice of which through the pastors is a main subject of visitation. Of course, to these requirements, which had grown out of the internal situation of the territories, an external requirement had been added, one that had long since ceased to resemble them. The demand of the Edict of Worms that the princes take measures against the Lutheran heresy presupposed that this "heresy" was notorious. The estates that refused to take measures assumed a grave responsibility — a responsibility that could be borne only if it was untenable to base the edict on notorious heresy. In this consciousness of responsibility one finds the final reason for the formation of the confessions, which began in the

[7] Somewhat more sharply after the disturbance in Münster, where the punishment of the Anabaptists was demanded because they "bring" the children "to damnation and establish two kinds of people among us, the baptized and the unbaptized" (WA 50, 14, 1. Enders 6, 299 ff.; 7, 150). — The seven mountain cities in Upper Hungary confess in the *Conf. Montana* of 1558 (Art. 9) that "we have compelled the Anabaptists who could be cured to recant, but have driven those who were incurable from our fields and borders; and if this had not been done by our most learned pastors and preachers, who were assisted by divine grace and care as well as by the diligence of the senates, there would have been danger that all the cities would have been devastated by this breed of pestiferous men" *(nos Anabaptistas sanabiles ad revocationem coegisse, insanabiles vero agris et finibus nostris eiecisse et nisi hoc factum fuisset a doctissimis nostris pastoribus et concionatoribus adjutis divina gratia et cura ac diligentia Senatuum, periculum fuisset, ne omnes civitates per hoc genus hominum pestiferorum fuissent devastatae)* (Borbis, p. 26).

year 1524 in the Margraviate of Brandenburg-Ansbach and in the imperial city of Nürnberg, not in Electoral Saxony.[8] The dismissal of the Diet of Speyer in 1526, which is commonly designated as the starting point of the state church, can be regarded as such only insofar as here a provisional sanctioning on the part of the empire took place. The deeper reason for this is to be found in the Edict of Worms, that is, in the legal regulation it took for granted, since here the estates were called upon to assume or share responsibility for the doctrine proclaimed in their domains. For if they were expected to persecute heresy there, a right to exercise supervision was implicitly *(implicite)* conferred on them. All the estates – including the spiritual estates – adopted this view by complaining in the *100 Grievances (gravamina)* of the Diet of Nürnberg of 1523 – grievances that were approved by all – "that the pastors who were hired for money and were generally uneducated recite smut and fables that are similar to the fables of the heathen, and in this way the common people are led away from the true Christian faith and trust in God to superstition and dreams." [9] Of course, these complaints are made to the man who was called "the head of Christendom" at that time. But they take for granted that the estates have already concerned themselves with the actual doctrine in their domains. In 1522 the government of Württemberg – at that time it was Austrian – had meddled sharply in church affairs *(Württemberger Kirchenordnung,* p. 266). No matter what the previous history may be, it will not do to treat as a usurpation the fact that later the evangelical estates saw to it that, from the standpoint of imperial law, the evangelical doctrine was taught in their domains. The Edict of Worms had made this care their duty. The objection that the edict actually demanded the persecution of this doctrine would be untenable. Naturally, this persecution was intended to protect the "evangelical doctrine" *(doctrina evangelica),* which had been recognized by the Roman Empire since 380. In the aforementioned imperial edict this doctrine was designated as being substantially what the Nicene Creed had taught about the Trinity (cf. *Catholicity).* First, therefore, it would have been necessary for the empire to prove that the evangelical estates were in opposition to the teaching of the Nicene Creed. But the evangelicals, as has been

[8] As early as May 2, 1525, Nik. Hausmann in Zwickau, referring to the Franconian pattern, urges Duke John Frederick of Saxony to intervene in the affairs of the church (synod, visitation). Burckhardt, *Geschichte d. sächsischen Kirchen- und Schulvisitation,* 1879, pp. 5 ff.

[9] Quoted according to Seckendorf, *Historie des Luthertums,* German edition, 1714, col. 562.

pointed out earlier, had anticipated this in the Augsburg Confession. Here, on the contrary, it is proved that the doctrine accepted by them was the "evangelical doctrine" *(doctrina evangelica)* and that for this reason the term "catholic" could not be denied them. If this was not acknowledged by the opposite side, it was because there was no theologically impartial judge to make the decision. In any case, the decision of the Augsburg Religious Peace in 1555 did not insist on getting a theological decision from the empire. But the right of the estates – which was acknowledged here – to render a decision with regard to the doctrine accepted in their domains is only a final inference from the responsibility for this that was expected of them as early as 1521.

This is the recognition by imperial law of the "government of the church by the sovereigns" *(das landesherrliche Kirchenregiment).* From the state of affairs that has been described it follows that it is not possible to derive this government solely from the emergency measures demanded by Luther. On the contrary, it was based to an equal degree on the religious interdict demanded by the German Empire. The fact that now the territorial sovereigns could avail themselves of this interdict to a special extent – even against the emperor – is related to the strengthening of the empire's intermediary powers, which the popes in the Middle Ages and as late as the fifteenth century had furthered by means of special concordats. But the necessity for the evangelical estates to avail themselves of the interdict resulted from the attitude of the emperor, who ever since 1521 had let himself be committed unilaterally and prematurely to the Roman party. This is a direct application of the medieval idea of the sociological unity of Christendom to the new situation that had been brought about by the schism. If there is a mistake here on the part of the evangelicals, it can consist only in the share they had in the schism itself. It is not possible here to reach a decision about the matter. The medieval idea of unity links the political and the ecclesiastical factors together into a homogeneous organism. Yet only the general distribution of the forces is debatable. The same idea still forms the basis of the evangelical state church.

Accordingly, the state church is an inheritance from the Middle Ages. It is true that the forces are now distributed in a different way; but that – exactly in accordance with the view held throughout the Middle Ages – they do not constitute "Christendom" until they work together is the assumption both for what Luther wrote to the Christian nobility and for what he taught about the three estates – the teaching that is the concrete starting point of his sociology. Luther's conception of the congregation fits perfectly into this pattern. If one leaves out of account the wish to gather those who earnestly desire to be Christians [10] – which was and remained merely an episode – the congregation is only a miniature image of Christendom. Luther's preface to *The Arrangement of a General Treasury (Anordnung eines gemeinen Kasten)*, which deals with what had been done at Leisnig, recommends to all congregations that they make a similar arrangement, and actually there were innumerable arrangements of this kind. They were decided on and introduced by councils, burghers, and peasants. These representatives of the middle-class community regulate the ethos of the congregation as well as its social conditions and the maintenance of the pastoral office (WA 12, 16–30). Even if one could see in the ruler of the land only the representative of his subjects, his concern for the worldly as well as the spiritual welfare of his land would, on the other hand, be merely a transferring of this regulation of the congregation to the conditions of the territory.

The classical expression for the inseparable knitting-together of the civil and the church community has always been found in Melanchthon's statement that the sovereign is "custodian of both Tables" *(custos utriusque tabulae)* and thus must look after "external discipline" *(externa disciplina)* as well as "true worship of God" *(verus cultus Dei)*, that is, pure doctrine (e. g., *CR* 2, 710; 3, 224; 16, 87). But the treasury arrangement of Leisnig shows that at least in the smaller sphere Luther actually also expects "custodianship of the First Table" *(custodia prioris tabulae)* from the civil factors. It is misleading to infer, as has been done up to the present time, that at the very start there is a fundamental difference between Luther and Melanchthon with regard to government of the church by the sovereigns. It is correct that Luther and Brenz appealed to the Christian love of the princes when they asked that the latter use their influence, which, in fact, was particularly great, to bring about the evangelical formation of the church.[11] But it is wrong when the later representatives of the so-called territorial system – with the approval of all students of canonical law, theologians, and historians who based their conclusions on Ä. J. Richter – say that Melanchthon derived the government of the church by the sovereigns from the rights of the sovereigns. For the sovereigns the obligation over against God and their subjects is placed unequivocally above their powers as sovereigns, which differ very greatly from the seventeenth-century idea of sovereignty. So far as the idea of the state is concerned, there is, of course, a considerable difference vis-à-vis Luther when even in this connection

[10] Gerhard Hilbert, *Ecclesiola in ecclesia*, 2d ed., 1924.

[11] Luther, WA 6, 413, 27 ff.; WA 26, 197, 25. — Brenz, *Anecdota* XV.

Melanchthon bases it on natural rights.[12] But here this reference is merely an auxiliary thought. In the same connection it is preceded by the reminder that there is the "duty to communicate doctrine" *(officium communicandae doctrinae)* as "part of the confession" *(pars confessionis)* (16, 86) – the duty which arises from the Gospel – which, exactly as in Luther, belongs in a special measure to the princes as "the principal members of the church" *(praecipua membra ecclesiae)* (89). Nor does the difference between Melanchthon and Luther consist as yet in the latter's greater skepticism with respect to the "Christian character" *(Christlichkeit)* of the princes. For in this respect Luther, in spite of his critical remarks about the princes in general, had almost blind confidence in his own sovereigns.

On the contrary, the difference does not begin until it is determined how the aforementioned governmental obligation is to be carried out. Not until then do the special powers of the sovereigns make themselves felt. According to Melanchthon, they keep within the bounds of the obligation placed on them from without – which is obviously in contradiction to the modern idea of sovereignty and utterly in opposition to the absolutist idea.[13] For according to Melanchthon, the powers of the government over against the church are the powers of the executor. Naturally, the government has no judgment of its own in doctrinal matters and, as a result, is directed with regard to these matters to the judgment of authorities in the field of theology, even though this statement was attacked by one of Melanchthon's students (*CR* 10, 852). Nevertheless, this statement was taken into account when the consistories were formed. But Melanchthon goes far beyond this when, in general,

[12] *CR* 16, 91: "It is the special and principal purpose of human society that God become known. The government is the guardian of human society, therefore . . ." *(Finis societatis humanae proprius et praecipuus est, ut Deus innotescat. Magistratus est custos societatis humanae, ergo . . .)* More in Vol. II.

[13] Naturally, Melanchthon and his pupils do not deny the government the right to make its own laws. But the government's relationship to its own laws is clearly distinguished from its relationship to the Decalog. Cf., e. g., Nik. Selnecker, *Institutio* III, 105: "In the state, however, when one asks about the duties of the government, it is right to enumerate these six duties: (1) The government should foster the churches and the schools; (2) it should also be the guardian of the entire Decalog of the First and the Second Table; (3) it should be the guardian of its own positive laws; (4) it should be the executor of the Decalog and of its own laws; (5) it should be the guardian of peace; (6) it should be the father, the nourisher, and the cultivator of the land and its subjects." *(In Politia vero cum de officiis magistratus quaritur, recte haec sex officia numerantur: 1. magistratus sit nutritius ecclesiarum et scholarum; 2. sit custos totius Decalogi primae et secundae tabulae; 3. sit etiam suarum legum positivarum custos; 4. sit executor decalogi et legum suarum; 5. sit custos pacis; 6. sit pater et nutritor et cultor terrae et subditorum.)* — More about this in Vol. II.

he ascribes to the government an obligation over against the church and obedience to the office of the church. "For we must all obey the ministry of the Word; thus a magistrate in the state is the servant and executor of the church" *(Omnes enim debemus obedire ministerio verbi; sic magistratus in republica minister et executor ecclesiae est)* (WA 16, 124; WA 3, 472). Here the obligation over against the church becomes obedience over against the spiritual office. And, of course, "for the sake of order" *(propter disciplinam)!* There is no longer reciprocal help on the part of the factors of Christendom – the help that Luther had in mind. This is theocracy pure and simple.

For what is here made incumbent on the government does not apply only to, let us say, the private life of the sovereign and his officials as personal members of the church. No, according to Melanchthon, it is a principle for the exercise of their official duties. Indeed, the government should not only see to it "that there continue to be an assured dwelling place of the church, where the heavenly doctrine is to be propagated" *(ut certa sedes maneret ecclesiae, ubi propagaretur doctrina coelestis)*[14] and should not only "protect the churches and the schools" *(ecclesias et scholas tueri)*, guarantee external existence to the structure of the pastoral office, and supervise the pastors in the exercise of their duties. No, as the "Wittenberg Reformation," which was written by Melanchthon in 1545, prescribes, it should also establish "ecclesiastical courts" *(Kirchengerichte)*. These are the consistories. They are by no means mere administrative organs. On the contrary, they are also criminal courts in the strict sense of the term. Their judgment, it is true, "does not put man to death with the sword; but it punishes with the Word of God and with separation or ejection from the church." Thus when the key of binding is used, they support the pastor on the basis of the judgment of the church as a whole – the support which he really needs (cf. *The Later Doctrine of the Office and the Nature of This Office*). But even when the powers are delimited, there arises a point of view that cannot be derived from the Office of the Keys itself. This ecclesiastical court is competent as a penal court in cases "which the secular government does not want to consider."[15] Thus it is a lengthen-

[14] Thus Laurentius Zoch, *CR* 11, 435. It is one of Melanchthon's favorite thoughts that the state grants the church a "home" *(domicilium)* or "hospitality" *(hospitium)*. Cf. Vol. II.

[15] *CR* 5, 604. P. 639 in the Latin text: "which the secular power neglects" *(quas profana potestas negligit)*. The following cases of this nature are enumerated: "If someone teaches false doctrine; if someone despises the Christian religion or the sacraments; if someone does not confess and does not commune in the course of a year; likewise, if someone commits an act of violence or a crime against the preacher or other servants of the church; likewise, if someone keeps an indecent

ing, so to speak, of the punishing arm of the government – a lengthening that makes it possible in this area to proceed against those who are outside its jurisdiction because of the natural limitation of the established criminal law of the state. But this is not enough. After the judges of the consistory have imposed the penalty of excommunication, this is published by the authorized pastor. Then, however, the Latin text goes on to say: *Est autem contemtor excommunicationis pro facti atrocitate et a potestate gladium gerente coercendus. Nam potestas politica Ecclesiam in tuenda pia disciplina iuvare debet, ut Rom. 13. scriptum est.*[16] ("But he who despises excommunication is to be restrained in accordance with the hideousness of the deed and by the power that bears the sword. For the political power must assist the church in maintaining good order, as is written in Rom. 13.") It can remain to be seen whether those who despise excommunication are to be regarded as the main offenders – they despised the threat of excommunication when they committed their misdeed – or those who "want to draw" an excommunicated person "to Baptism or similar Christian company" *(zur Tauf und dergleichen christlichen Gesellschaften ziehen wollen)*, which is also forbidden. Here it becomes clear in every case that according to Melanchthon the state should be of service to the church in one of its own (the state's) most special areas, namely, in the area of the administration of criminal law. For not only the punishment imposed by the "ecclesiastical court" *(Kirchengericht)* but also the punishment imposed by the secular court serves the moral discipline of the church.

Not until now does it become clearly apparent what Melanchthon expects of the state church. At the same time one sees how he differs from Luther. The hundreds of references to the usefulness of the church for the state, for its "tranquility" *(tranquillitas)*, for the "public welfare" *(salus publica)*, cannot obscure the actuality of his theocratic ideal. At best this is counterbalanced theoretically by the fact that he subsumes state and church under the concept "human society" *(societas humana)*. Practically, however, this society becomes effective only in church and state. And then the state receives its sphere of duties from the hand of the church, not, as Luther says, directly from God. Nor does it mat-

woman; likewise, if someone is reputed to be guilty of adultery, so that there are strong suspicions against him; likewise the usurers; likewise, young people who practice open rebellion against their parents or against others to whom they have been entrusted, and refuse to give up their forbidden amusements and their drinking" (pp. 604 f.) The canonical pattern is clearly apparent!

16 Cf. the commentary on 1 Cor. of 1551 (*CR* 15, 1073). On the other hand, there is nothing like this in the *Quaest. aliquot ethicae* of 1552 (16, 482—488: "on excommunication" *[de excommunicatione]*).

ter much that in theory Melanchthon takes the church to mean not only the "spiritual estate" but, like Luther, all the estates. Actually, as has been shown, he derives the executive duty of the government from its obedience over against the "ministry of the Word" *(ministerium verbi)*. Only one necessary safeguard is in place. It is true that the duty to inflict civil punishment on a person who despises excommunication arises out of the judgment of the consistorial ecclesiastical court; but this is a board of the sovereign.[17] To this extent the most dangerous edge of the theocracy is blunted. So far as the ecclesiastical court is concerned, one could, of course, still ask whether for Melanchthon the emphasis is not on the church.

It is not necessary to demonstrate how far we have departed from the Lutheran idea of the church when we speak of Melanchthon's theocratic ideal. The basic mistake lies in the fact that "discipline with respect to morals" *(disciplina morum)* is transferred to the church. This is something different from what Luther means when he, too, makes it the duty of the church to preach the Law. For when he does so, the church still remains the church of the Word, yes, the church of the Gospel – the church which also has need of the preaching of the Law in order to lead to repentance. Even the power to bind *(Bindegewalt)* does not mean a "censorship of morals" *(censura morum)*; it means only the exclusion of a person who inwardly no longer belongs to the church at all and confirms this by being openly impenitent. It is proper for the government to exercise the right to supervise and the right to punish Christians – not, however, in the service of the church but because of a direct obligation toward God.

The upshot was different from what Melanchthon desired. No theocracy came into being. Instead, there was government of the church by the sovereigns. In the end the power of the church became an appendage of the sovereignty of the princes, and the church became a department of the state. The closer the development approached this stage, the easier it was for the jurists to be reconciled to it. For the dogmaticians it became ever more difficult to do so.[18] It is not surprising that the

[17] In opposition to Rieker's teaching that the consistories, as successors of the episcopal office according to the understanding of their contemporaries, are to be viewed as *church* boards Sehling asserted justifiably that *actually* they were arrangements made by the sovereigns. — Rieker, *Die rechtl. Stellung,* pp. 166 ff.; *Sehling, KO,* I, 1, p. 58. — Cf. also the first two discussions in Otto Mejer's *Zum Kirchenrecht des Reformationsjahrhunderts,* 1891.

[18] Cf., e. g., Abraham Calov's comments on the employment of secular power for the purpose of enforcing discipline (*Syst.* XI, *qu.* II ff.) — a test case for the consequences of the confusion created by Melanchthon. All under the general title "On Love of One's Neighbor" *(De dilectione proximi)!*

theologians wanted to cling to the idea of the church as this idea was expressed in the Augsburg Confession (VII)! But neither is it surprising that there was an increase in the number of cases in which Roman Catholic or Reformed sovereigns claimed, by virtue of their rights as sovereigns, to be chief bishops of Evangelical Lutheran churches. Nor was the grotesque element in this state of affairs softened by the fact that the sovereigns turned over the exercise of their episcopal right to evangelical boards. An evangelical pastor as such became an official of a Roman Catholic sovereign. "Other things being equal," the college of privy councilors of Dresden wrote in August 1720 to Valentin Ernst Löscher, who had acted contrary to the religion of the sovereign, "a clergyman is gladly permitted to be a servant of God. But he is also a servant of the congregation and of the sovereign who pays his salary." And Count Seebach added to the documents: "The superintendent excuses himself by referring to his conscience. In many other cases this is usually the excuse when one is unwilling to obey the government."[19] What fruits this government of the church by the sovereigns bore for the attitude of the people toward the evangelical pastors and the church in general is evident today to everyone. Or at least it should be.

For Luther this was really an emergency measure. But just as Melanchthon did not create the state church, so Luther's appeal to the princes did not bring it into being. In what Melanchthon says it becomes incontrovertibly clear that the state church has its roots in the world of thought that was current in the Middle Ages. Naturally, this does not excuse the fact that he, too, like Calvin, also revived the ancient theocratic ideas of the church. But one dare not hold the Lutheran idea of the church responsible for this. From the Lutheran idea, only an organizing principle follows: the duty and the right of the pastoral office – the office that belongs to the whole church. Therefore the extent of the divine right the government of the church has is determined by the episcopal character of the church. It is immaterial whether the episcopal office is exercised only by the pastors of individual congregations or also by those who perform episcopal functions for a larger circle, whether one calls the former pastors and the latter bishops or the former bishops and the latter archbishops. What was said in connection with worship about artistic taste with reference to the church holds true here too. But what goes beyond this – the demarcation of parishes; questions about preparatory training, examination, election, support, the disciplining of pastors; questions concerning representation

[19] Blanckmeister, *Val. Ernst Löscher und seine Zeit*, 1920, pp. 87 and 91.

toward the outside; the question whether for these and other external matters congregational representation and synodical arrangements are useful or necessary — all this must be arranged and answered differently today from the way it was done at the time of Luther and perhaps differently tomorrow from the way it is done today. Here Christian liberty is the other side of the Lutheran idea of the church.

28. Missions [1]

The attitude of early Lutheranism toward missions is closely connected with the state church, which has its basis in the government of the church by the sovereigns. Even if there were no evidences to the contrary, a moderately well-intentioned person would not assume that the church of the Gospel, which, like the Lutheran Church, lives in and by the Gospel, would not have thought of proclaiming the Gospel among non-Christians. Indeed, as Gustav Warneck pointed out, Luther was not "a man of missions in our sense of the word" *(Missionsmann in unserm Sinne).* The poor man! Instead of founding a missionary society, accompanying Cortez to Mexico, or at least assuring for himself a professorship of missionary science, he devoted himself, of all things, to the reformation of the church! In him Warneck misses not only "missionary activity" *(Missionstat)* but also the "idea of missions" *(Missionsgedanke).* If one tries to think of the idea of missions on the basis of the impact of the Gospel *(evangelischer Ansatz)* and does not take it to be a theory that has to do with engaging in an undertaking, it can mean only two things: (1) faith in the omnipotence and the universal teleology of the Gospel and (2) the affirmation of the mission to proclaim the Gospel.

[1] J. Ferd. Fenger, *Gesch. d. Trankebarschen Mission* (translated from the Danish by E. Francke), 1845. — R. Bückmann, *Die Stellung d. luth. Kirche des 16. und 17. Jahrh. zur Heidenmission u. d. gemeinsamen Bestrebungen von Leibniz u. A. H. Francke zu ihrer Belebung, Zeitschr. f. kirchl. Wiss. u. kirchl. Leb.*, 1881, pp. 362 ff. — G. Plitt — O. Hardeland, *Gesch. d. luth. Mission*, 2d ed., 1894—95. — P. Drews, *Die Anschauungen reformatorischer Theologen über die Heidenmission, Zeitschr. f. prakt. Theologie*, 1897, pp. 1 ff. — W. Grössel, *Die Mission und die evang. Kirche im 17. Jahrh.*, 1897. — Josef Pindor, *Die evang. Kirche Kroatien-Slavoniens in d. Vergangenheit u. Gegenwart*, 1902. — G. Warneck, *Abriss einer Gesch. d. protestantischen Missionen*, 10th ed., 1913. — E. Mirbt, *Die ev. Mission in ihrer Gesch. u. Eigenart*, 1917. — Franz Rud. Merkel, *G. W. v. Leibniz u. die China-Mission*, 1920. — Heinr. Frick, *Die evang. Mission, Ursprung, Geschichte, Ziel*, 1922. — The same author, *Giessener u. Frankfurter Orthodoxie über d. Mission, Allg. Miss.-Zeitschr.*, 1923, pp. 7 ff., and *Vom Pietismus zum "Volkskirchentum," Neue Allg. Miss.-Zeitschr.*, 1924, pp. 196 ff. — Karl Holl, *Luther u. d. Mission, Ges. Aufs.* III, 234 ff. — E. Strasser, *Die Taufe in d. Gesch. d. deutschen ev.-luth. Mission*, 1925. — Jul. Richter, *Ev. Missionskunde*, 2d ed., 1927. — Mart. Richter, *Der Missionsgedanke im ev. Deutschland d. 18. Jahrh.*, 1928. — Friedr. Langenfass, *Von der Reformation zur Mission*, in *Missionspraxis in der Heimat*, 1930.

After all that has been said, there is no further need to speak about Luther's and early Lutheranism's belief in the omnipotence of the Gospel. And how could Luther, who expounded the Psalms, the Prophets, and Paul, have overlooked or doubted the universal purpose of the mission of Christ and of His Gospel? From Col. 1:23 and Mark 16:15 he concludes that the Gospel is not to be kept in a corner but should fill the whole globe; from Ps. 117, that "the Gospel and Baptism must traverse the whole world" *(das Evangelium und die Tauffe müssen durch die gantze wellt komen);* from Hag. 2, that it will be a precious treasure for all nations. God wants to bless, "not two or three nations but the whole world" *(nicht zwey odder drey volck, sondern die gantze welt).*[2] Neither Melanchthon nor any of the later dogmaticians subtracted anything at all from this universal task of the Gospel. This was not entirely self-evident, for it presupposed the realization that there is an absolute need of salvation for all mankind. Here both Zwingli and the later Socinians had a different opinion.[3] Indeed, even Melanchthon had to point out that some of his contemporaries – like Voltaire later on – had a predilection for the religion of the Turks because they had grown tired of their own religion (*CR* 11, 145). But for him as for Luther and all the later dogmaticians there was no belief in Christ that would not have included criticism of all other religions.[4] Even though Luther cannot believe that the heathen longed for the Gospel (WA 13, 541, 17), he does not doubt that they are in need of it. The very promise of the blessing for the heathen "bears witness that all nations are under a curse and the power of the devil" *(testatur omnes gentes esse sub maledictione et potestate diaboli)* (WA 43, 252, 13).

When Luther sometimes speaks as though the Gospel had already fulfilled its mission in all nations – which has been cited again and again as proof of his lack of understanding of the idea of missions – this is for him the simple conclusion drawn from the universal validity of the Gospel. If the Gospel is proclaimed at all, it is proclaimed "for all." Of course, Luther sometimes mentions geographical details when he speaks of this. The Gospel has been in Egypt, in Greece, in Italy, in Spain, and in France. But contempt for the divine promise causes it to come again and again to other nations. "Now it is in Germany. Who knows for how long?" He also believes "that in Armenia, Ethiopia,

[2] WA 31 I, 339, 18 ff.; 285, 9 ff.; 232, 29; WA 37, 435, 27; WA 13, 525, 4; WA 24, 392, 13.

[3] Joh. Musäus, *Diss., an Gentiles absque fide in Christum per extraordinariam Dei gratiam ad salutem pertingere . . . possint,* 1670 — against the Arminian Curcellaeus.

[4] Herbert Vossberg, *Luthers Kritik aller Religion,* 1922.

Mauritania, India, and the lands toward the east there are still many Christians; but in Asia Minor they are all under the Turks." But he emphasizes this belief in order to prove that the church of Christ is not bound to a particular locality. The idea of many later theologians – that the church of the present time is no longer obligated to preach among the heathen, because the apostles have already reached all – is totally foreign to him, just as it is to Melanchthon. Furthermore, it would be opposed to the dynamic view of the Gospel and the church. It is self-evident that Luther knows that no apostle came to the Germans. He had also heard of the newly discovered "islands," "which are heathen, and no one has preached to them." [5]

Accordingly, the course of the Gospel to all nations is not in the perfect tense; it is an act in progress – an act that took place and takes place without interruption. "The kingdom of Christ passes through the whole world" *(Christi regnum per totum mundum transit)*, says Luther in the present tense (WA 41, 594, 22; WA 31 I, 285, 12). In the very place in which he points out that "many heathen of high nobility and rank have become Christians" *(viel von hohem adell und stand der heydenschafft Christen worden)* he adds, as though it were self-evident, that "the Gospel wants to be taught and preached always and always, in order that it may always appear above the horizon" *(das Euangelium ymer und ymer will getrieben und gepredigt sein, das es ymer ym auff-gang sey)* (WA 10 I, 1, 540, 5 and 12 ff.). The blessing of the promise has gone out "throughout the length and breadth of the world, has come among both heathen and Jews, and keeps on going farther" *(so weit die welt ist, komen beyde unter Heyden und Jüden, und gehet noch ymer weiter)* (WA 24, 392, 28). The preaching of the Gospel "was begun through the apostles and continues, and is carried farther through the preachers here and there in the world, is driven out and persecuted; yet it is made known farther and farther to those who have never heard it before. . . . Or, as the saying goes, when someone sends out a message, the message has gone out, even though it has not yet come to the intended place or the specified location but is still under way." *(ist durch die Apostel angefangen und geedt ymmerdar fürt und wirt durch die prediger weiter getrieben hin und her in der welt, veryagt und verfolget, doch ymmer weyter denen, die sy zuvor nit gehöret haben, kund gemacht. . . . Ader wie man spricht, wann ainer ain bottschafft lasst*

[5] WA 23, 533, 10; WA 12, 540, 3 ff.; WA 47, 565, 18; WA 20, 526, 7 ff.; WA 5, 547, 28; WA 10 III, 139, 21; WA 10 I, 1, 21 and 14 ff.; WA TR 5, 6035. – Karl Holl calls attention to WA 2, 476, 33, from which he concludes justifiably that Luther actually attacks the ancient legend of the division of the world (op. cit., p. 234).

aussgon, die bottschafft ist aussgegangen, wie wol sie noch nit in das vorgenomen ordt oder bestympte stelle komen ist, sonder noch underwegen.) (WA 10 III, 140, 6.) "For the church is in constant use to convert others to faith and to call them to penitence" *(Est enim Ecclesia in perpetuo usu convertendi alios ad fidem et vocandi ad poenitentiam)* (WA 25, 365, 17). The Gospel keeps on advancing against those who do not want to hear it. "For the Lord does not want a flatterer as a preacher, since He does not say: 'Go around the village or past it.' No, do not go around or past; go in; approach them boldly, and tell them what they do not like to hear." *(Denn der herr will keynen schmeychler tzum prediger haben, dieweyl er nit sagt: Gehet umb das dorff oder neben hynn. Neyn, nit umbhyn oder neben hyn, hyneyn geht, frisch an sie und sagt yhn, was sie nit gern horen.)* (WA 10, I, 2, 50, 10.)

Here one feels all the earnestness of Luther's proclamation. Here there is no trace of a satiated resting from the Christianizing of the world. The Gospel always appears above the horizon, is always under way, is always on the attack. It must come to all nations. But just as it was taken away from some, so Luther is not under the delusion that its proclamation must have positive success. God has promised the Gospel to all the heathen, but "He does not say that all will accept it" (WA 24, 392, 23). In Luther, however, this view of the Gospel is not a "view." In the strict sense it is the "idea of missions" – which reminds us that Luther also holds himself responsible for his "thoughts." He who speaks about the Gospel in this way also proclaims it. The thought is at the same time the realization. This would be true even if Luther had not thought at all of "heathen" in our sense. For the eager attention the Gospel pays to its proclamation is independent of the kind of people we have before us. Only from the dynamic of the Gospel itself can the "idea of missions," which should be evangelical, get its obligating power, not from reflecting on this or that kind of people.

But the statements that have been adduced show that Luther does not think of the idea of missions as individualistic. He thinks of it as pertaining to the church; that is, he thinks in terms of "Christendom" as a whole as well as of the world of nations and its history. It is self-evident that as he does so, he also looks at the people and the nations that have not yet heard the Gospel. Exactly like the missionary preaching of today, he refers to the "heathen" as we understand the word that Christ the Shepherd speaks about the "other sheep" or about those whose invitation to the great wedding came late and who were brought from the highway (WA 12, 540, 2 ff.; 600, 12; WA 37, 181, 11; 342, 1). In conformity with the evangelical text he certainly takes the word "heathen" as referring, above all, to the non-Jews in general. As a result, he can also say that this is meant for us heathen or that accordingly the apostles came to the heathen. Yet in the same connection he continues: "This has not yet been done. This time is in progress, inasmuch as the servants are going into the highway; the apostles made a beginning and are still calling us together." *(Hoc nondum factum. Hoc tempus ghet, quod servi gehn auff der strassen, apostoli inceperunt et nos adhuc ruffen zu samen.)* (WA 17 I, 442, 36.) Thus this means that the apostolic mission to the heathen is continuing in us today. And Luther thinks this thought out in a practical way.

We are not to be satisfied with preaching before Christians. "It is necessary always to proceed to those to whom no preaching has been done, in order that the number [of Christians] may become greater" *(Oportet semper progredi ad eos quibus non praedicatum, ut plures fiant)* (WA 16, 216, 1). This obligation rests on all Christians. "In addition, Christians should also bring forth much fruit among all the heathen by means of the Word, should convert and save many by eating about themselves like a fire that burns amid dry wood or straw; thus the fire of the Holy Spirit should consume the heathen according to the flesh and make room everywhere for the Gospel and the kingdom of Christ" (WA 23, 645, 30). Practically, this obligation to do missionary work confronts the prisoner of war who, by means of his Christian conduct, should "adorn and praise the Gospel and the name of Christ" in Turkish surroundings. By doing this you would "disgrace the faith of the Turks, and perhaps you would convert many" (WA 30 II, 194, 28 ff.).[6] And not only conduct should make an impression. In heathen surroundings every Christian, not only the prisoner of war, should be a missionary. Here the "duly called" *(rite vocatus)* of the church organization at home carries no weight. A Christian not only has "the right and the power to teach the Word of God but is under the obligation to do this; otherwise he runs the risk of losing his soul and of incurring the disfavor of God" *(recht und macht, das gottis wort tzu leren, sondern ist das selbige schuldig tzuthun bey seyner seelen verlust und gottis ungnaden).* But, Luther objects, must one, then, not first be called to do this? Certainly – in Christian surroundings. But when the Christian is at a place "where there are no Christians, there he needs no other call than that he is a Christian who is inwardly called and anointed by God. There it is his obligation to preach to the erring heathen and non-Christians, and to teach the Gospel as a duty of Christian love, even though no one calls

[6] Likewise Melanchthon, *CR* 5, 735; 14, 891.

him to do this." *(da keyn Christen sind, da darff er keyns anders beruffs, denn das er eyn Christen ist ynwendig von gott beruffen und gesalbet. Do ist er schuldig, den yrrenden heyden odder unchristen tzu predigen und tzu leren das Euangelion aus pflicht bruderlicher liebe, ob yhn schon keyn mensch datzu berufft.)* (WA 11, 412, 11 ff.)

But if one wanted to interpose that here the exercise of the duty to do missionary work is made dependent on chance, Luther declares elsewhere that it must become a sending. "For if all the heathen are to praise God, it must first be established that He has become their God. If He is to be their God, they must know Him and believe in Him. . . . If they are to believe, they must first hear His Word. . . . If they are to hear His Word, preachers who proclaim God's Word to them must be sent to them." (WA 31 I, 228, 33 ff.) And finally a word about how highly Luther esteemed missionary work among the heathen: "Thus it is the best work of all that the heathen have been led out of idolatry to the knowledge of God" (WA 47, 466, 5). Not one of these statements contains a theory of missions. They are simply applications of the impact of the Gospel *(evangelischer Ansatz)* to the fact that the Gospel has not yet reached all mankind. Here the modern mission theorist misses questions of sociology – questions that no longer have anything directly to do with the "idea of missions."

This is particularly true of the constantly repeated reproach that Luther neither demanded nor undertook any "special arrangements for missions" *(besondere Veranstaltungen zur Mission).* This reproach – as it is usually meant – belongs in the technical high schools, where the science of business is taught. But if it has a deeper significance and rests on the view of many dogmaticians of the seventeenth century, who rejected "special arrangements" where or because there was no special call to make them and who thought that here, too, they had to apply the "duly called" *(rite vocatus)* from *CA* XIV, it has been shown that in any case Luther does not know of this barrier vis-à-vis the heathen.

"Missions," says Wilhelm Löhe, who perhaps also knew something about this, "is nothing but the one church of God in its motion – the realization of a universal, catholic church" (*Drei Bücher,* p. 18). This is exactly what Luther thought. The motion of the one church – church *is* motion, for it merely expresses the endless dynamic of the Gospel. There is a state-church system that is static or, to use Hegel's expression, "slow and careful" *(statarisch).* Here "special arrangements" for missions are necessary. But basically it is the church itself which, because it proclaims the Gospel, moves in the direction of all nations – and is kept moving by them. A theory of missions which takes missions to mean the enlargement of the body of "Christian" nations by a few new ones is itself "slow and careful" *(statarisch)* in its thinking. As has been shown, Luther also knew that many nations were forsaken by the Gospel. In answer to a letter of Lutheran missionaries in Trankebar, Johann Albrecht Bengel wrote: "The message concerning the course of the Word and the growth of the kingdom of God in the East and in the West call forth thanks and praise among all those who love the salvation of God; but in addition to joy they also give rise to worry that, just as dark places become light, so light but ungrateful places may become dark." [7] This, too, is spoken exactly in accordance with what Luther believed. The "church in its motion" is a going, a power, a proceeding — but not a growing heap. Every missionary endeavor that is not proud of the fact that it is a "special arrangement" but wants to be nothing else than the church in its motion should add to the statistics of its successes a category in which there is a report about the simultaneous loss in the church at home. For the "special arrangement" is meaningful only when it is supported by responsibility for the whole church.

For many mission theorists missionary work does not begin until it goes overseas. This is where Luther and his contemporaneous fellow believers naturally "broke down" completely. Maybe Luther's statement that he surely would not go far in a skiff on the Elbe, which the Wittenbergians could perhaps have equipped, contributed to this. In addition, however, there were inadequate conceptions of the spread of the Gospel up to that time. The statement of the later dogmaticians that the apostles had already offered the Gospel to all nations is commonly put down as a poor excuse. In reality the reason for this statement lay in the religio-geographical knowledge of the age. From Philipp Nicolai we have a survey that goes into great details and was often made use of by later theologians. From it one can gather with certainty that there was a firm belief that no land and no nation was without Christians.[8]

[7] O. Wächter, *Joh. Albr. Bengel,* 1865, p. 196.

[8] *Commentarii de regno Christi,* 1597, in *Opp. omnia latina* II, 1 ff. (the translation in *Alle Teutschen Schriften,* I, 1 ff., is shortened). — Since Nicolai's survey, which is based on the most careful studies, is typical of the views held during that entire age, it is advisable to give a brief sketch of it. I. In the north he enumerates the following areas as already Christianized: The Orkney Islands, with an episcopal see in Kirkwall; the Shetland Islands; the Faero Islands, with their own bishopric; Iceland below the sixty-third parallel, with four parishes, now evangelical, thanks to the efforts of the Danish-Norwegian kings; Greenland and Grockland, with two bishops under the Archbishop of Nidaros. Farther north in Sweden the Lapps, who are hard to reach but, at the instigation of the King of Sweden, have been provided with the Gospel by the pastors of the adjacent provinces, which are enumerated in detail. Next to Finland there is the great realm of the Muscovites. Its boundaries, provinces, relationship to the ecumenical patriarchate, and ecclesiastical organization

This presentation explains Luther's frequently quoted statement that when the message of the Gospel is proclaimed, this is "as if one threw a stone into the water; the stone causes ripples, circles, and streams round about it; and the ripples always roll them farther and farther; one

are described correctly. Then there are the khanates of Kasan and Astrakhan; and there is reference to a German colony in the city of Nelewki which has called an evangelical pastor from Thuringia. Finally there are the Circassians on the Black Sea; and in the northeast there is Great Tartary, whose inhabitants live in extensive areas as nomads, formerly were Christians, but were again subdued by Islam.

II. In the east there is the realm of the Turks. But here the Eastern Church lingers on. In addition to the Greek Orthodox Church, with its four patriarchates, the *Armenii*, the *Jacobiti*, the *Nestoriani*, the *Cadurci*, the *Suriani*, the *Maroniti*, and the *Aethiopici* are accurately described and correctly marked off from one another, both geographically and confessionally. The various attempts on the part of the evangelicals to associate with them are also enumerated. In praise of the Armenians it is stated that as merchants they spread Christianity all the way to the farthest parts of the east. In Turkey the ratio of the Mohammedans to the Christians is estimated to be three to one. In the east the Curds are adjacent to the Armenians. They are described as being Nestorians. Although Islam rules in Persia, yet the Christians enjoy freedom of religion. According to reliable reports, the Christian faith, albeit in the form of Nestorianism, is making progress there. Some Thomas Christians are still to be found in India. But even the religion of the Brahmins shows clear traces of Christian influences. The Jesuits are now at work there. But their errors are rejected by the Thomas Christians (historical details are adduced). For the characterization of China, Nicolai refers to the Venetian Marcus and to Johannes Mendoza, who found Armenian books and traces of the activity of the apostle Thomas among the Chinese. Then there is a survey of Japan and other parts of East Asia, in which the Jesuits have thirteen residences. These residences are mentioned by name. In order to gain entrance there, the Jesuits proclaim the Christian religion as it is taught at home by the Lutherans, whom they so vehemently attack. To begin with, they are silent about the primacy of the pope, the traditions of men, the Mass, purgatory, the doctrine of merits, and indulgences. Instead, they proclaim the doctrine of the fall and condemnation of the first human beings, of the redemption through Christ, of faith, and of Baptism. To prove this, a report sent from Japan in the year 1564 by the Jesuit Joh. Baptista Montius is made known. Then there are reports about Arabia, the island of Socotra (in the Gulf of Aden), to which special attention is paid because Christians living there also call themselves Thomas Christians; about Palestine; and about the islands in the Aegean Sea, on which Christian churches are pointed out everywhere.

III. In the south the state of the Christians in Egypt is presented first, both geographically and confessionally. The missionary activity of the Jesuits and their encounter with the hitherto existing church is described. Then, toward the south, there are the adjacent areas of Malindi, Kilo, Mozambique, and Sofala. But the reports about these areas are scanty. Here, too, says Nicolai, missionary activity is successfully carried on by the Jesuits. After rounding the Cape of Good Hope one arrives at the territory of the Congo, where the Portuguese have done missionary work with great success. An attempt to reach the sources of the Nile from there miscarried, says Nicolai. "But I should not doubt that a union of the Congolese and the Ethiopians could do much for the propagation of Christianity in the inland regions of Africa if their realms bordered on each other or the intermediate nations were subdued with equal concern on the part of both and with the resort to arms" *(Non autem dubitarim, quin ad Christianismi propagationem in mediterraneis Afri-*

drives the other until they come to the shore. Although the water becomes calm in the center, the ripples do not rest but keep on flowing." (WA 10 III, 140, 6 ff.) For Luther the mobilization of the idea of missions is a summons to Christians to proclaim the Gospel to those who live near them and have not yet heard it. If there are Christians in every nation, this was not only correct from an ethical point of view but was also based on practical thinking. But since Christians, to a great extent, have been misled, the proclamation among them of the pure Gospel must itself always be the starting point. The fact that in reality the religio-geographical picture that was painted was partly incorrect and partly inadequate is probably of no consequence for the critical estimate of the Lutheran idea of missions!

This picture is reflected in the attempts at missionary work that were undertaken in early Lutheranism. For even though the reformation of the church at home and the consolidation of the new church setup completely occupied the thoughts and the actions of an entire century, early Lutheranism never forgot Luther's ideas about the motion of the church

canarum regionum partibus multum facere posset Congensium et Aethiopum coniunctio, si istorum regna finibus cohaererent vel gentes intermediae pari utrorumque cura et armorum studio perdomarentur). Then there is the northwestern part of Africa, with its Spanish ecclesiastical organization. From Mauritania, especially from Morocco, there are reports about conflicts in which the Christians living there are engaged with the papal church.

Finally IV. In the west lies the New World *(Novus orbis)* called America. The following areas are known to Nicolai: Labrador, the Bahamas, *Chicora Jordane fluvio insignis* (?), Florida, *Panucium* (?), Jamaica, Mexico, Cuba, Yucatan, Haiti, Baragua, and Darien (isthmus). Furthermore — in South America — *Cumana* (?), *Paria* (a coastal region of Venezuela), Quito, Chile, Peru, and Brazil. He is in error when he says that Nicaragua and Guatemala are also in South America. It is said that in these lands there were — in addition to much superstition and irreligion — traces of what was originally a pure knowledge of God. These are enumerated. The Spaniards created an ecclesiastical organization with three archbishops. The Archbishop of Santo Domingo is at the head of these. The Jesuits carry on missionary work in South America, and their residences and staffs of teachers are mentioned individually.

When G. Warneck states about Johann Gerhard's religio-geographical survey, which reproduces the one made by Nicolai, that it is "not only indiscriminatingly naive but also dogmatically biased," it is difficult to refrain from quoting certain passages from *Faust.* Had Warneck taken the trouble to read Nicolai, whom Gerhard quotes, he would — so one hopes — at least have been wary of using the expression "indiscriminatingly"; for Nicolai's survey is based step by step on reports of travels and missionary activity. Every reader who is not "dogmatically biased" and who has any notion of the possibilities of passing judgment at that time on the geographical and ethnographical sources, and then compares Nicolai's statements with, let us say, the world as mapped during that same period, will acknowledge that what Nicolai accomplished was extraordinary in every respect. — It is certainly not surprising that the picture is already totally different in the writings of a man like Joh. Alb. Fabricus (1731), who lived in the eighteenth century and whom Warneck praises!

and about the boundless dynamic of the Gospel. We, "too," wrote Jacob Heerbrand, "are intent, so far as is humanly possible, on winning for the Lord Christ many for eternal life, and we do not want to neglect any opportunity of which we are aware." [9] But where and how? At three points Lutheranism was in contact with notorious non-Christians: with the Jews at home, with the Turks in the Balkans, and with the heathen Laplanders in Scandinavia.

It is known that from Württemberg Primus Truber and Baron Ungnad von Sonegg sought to win the southern Slavs for the Gospel in their homeland. They undertook to do so with Bibles and other literature. But at the same time they gave thought to missionary work among the Turks. The translation of the Slovenian New Testament into Glagolite by Stefan Consul of Pinguente was submitted in 1559 to a committee of clerical and secular experts. In the opinion handed down by these men it is stated, among other things, that "by this means, so we hope, the right Christian religion and the true saving Gospel will be promoted throughout Turkey, that the heart and the disposition of the Turks will be renewed to the holy faith . . . and that in time our Savior Jesus Christ will be made known in Turkey" (Josef Pindor, p. 24). Baron von Ungnad himself directs an appeal for help to the German princes, "in order that thus the pure doctrine of the divine Word may also be brought to Turkey, since it is to be expected that by this means and in this way almighty God will smite the Turks with the sword of His strength, just as He has exposed and smitten the papacy in its entirety" (op. cit., p. 30). Ambrosius Fröhlich, the Viennese book dealer, wishes that the Catechism, too, be translated. With such a translation one would "with God's help confer a great blessing and do a great deal of good" not only among the Slavic nations but also "at the court of the Turkish emperor" (p. 27). The preacher Vlahovic gave the advice to recruit Turkish printers. "Provided that the priests of the Uskoks get the printing press, I would like to have printed for the Turkish emperor a little book which would tell

[9] Cf. the title of the book and the quotation in note 35 under *Catholicity*. — In Urban Rhegius' *Catech. minor* of 1535 we read: "Grant, I beseech Thee, almighty Father, according to Thy prophetic promises, that from the rising of the sun to its setting Thy name may be extolled in all nations under heaven, that through the Gospel Thy fatherly goodness may become known and be extolled everywhere, in order that the inheritance of Christ, the kingdom of grace, and the holy catholic church may grow throughout the world. . . ." *(Fac obsecro omnipotens pater, iuxta promissiones tuas Propheticas, ut ab ortu solis usque ad occasum magnum fiat nomen tuum in Gentibus universis sub coelo, ut per Evangelium tua paterna bonitas ubique innotescat et magnifiat, quo crescat haereditas Christi, regnum gratiae, sancta Ecclesia catholica per orbem. . . .)* (Reu, *Quellen* III, 2, p. 619.)

how all the prophets prophesied and preached concerning the world that the Lord Jesus Christ is the Son of God, that Mohammed led the Turks astray, and that the pope misled all Christendom. We would like to convert the Turks if there were assistants and such books." (P. 34.)

These statements and plans express not only complete confidence in the omnipotence of the Gospel but also the passionate purpose to do missionary work. Nor did the summons remain without an echo. It is true that the Elector of Brandenburg excused himself by saying that because he had to provide a daughter with a dower, he could do nothing; but Elector August of Saxony, Duke Christoph of Württemberg, and others made considerable sacrifices. According to Philipp Nicolai's report, a copy of the Augsburg Confession in translation is said to have reached Georgia in Transcaucasia and there to have been translated "into the Iberian language" *(in sermonem Ibericum)* (p. 10). "For this reason I certainly pray for the Georgians with all my heart," Nicolai adds, "just as if I had nothing else to pray for than that the uncorrupted doctrine of the Gospel might be spread far and wide throughout Asia and the whole globe" *(Quod certe toto pectore Georgianis precor, nihil perinde in votis habens, quam ut Evangelii doctrina incorrupta longe lateque per Asiam et universum terrarum orbem diffundatur).* True, the 25,000 books that were printed in Urach and Tübingen ended up at the stake of the Counter Reformation. Later on the irreplaceable printing press fell into the hands of the Jesuits. But even though no tangible success was achieved here, one dare not deny that here sixteenth-century Lutheranism made a determined effort to put Luther's idea of missions into action.

So far as the Jews are concerned, Luther, filled with his heroic faith in the compelling power of the Gospel, had not doubted at first that they would be responsive to the evangelical proclamation. He believed that before this they had not been treated properly — "as though they were dogs and not human beings." He hoped that if they "were carefully instructed" *(seuberlich unterweysset)* from Holy Scripture, "many of them would become true Christians" *(es sollen yhr viel rechte Christen werden)* (WA 11, 315, 3 ff.). Later, however, the experiences he himself had with them, the knowledge of their own efforts to induce Christians to fall away from their faith and of their blasphemous statements against Christ, not only exasperated him violently but also made him skeptical with regard to the success of any attempts to convert them. "To debate with a Jew" is "like striking an anvil with a blade of straw" *(mit eim Juden disputirn alls mit einem strohalm auff ein ambos schlagen).*[10] Nor was Luther wrong when he pointed to the fact that the Jews had lived among Christians for 1,500 years and were very well acquainted with what was known about Christ. For this reason missions among the Jews cannot actually be placed on the same level with missionary work among the heathen and the Mohammedans. Nevertheless, in early Lutheranism there was no lack of attempts to convert the Jews. It was especially in Hesse in the sixteenth and seventeenth centuries that these attempts met with some success. Here it was the sovereign who repeatedly authorized and organized missionary activity of the church among the Jews.[11]

Perhaps the Hessian landgraves had an especially great interest in the winning of the Jews. But in their attitude there was also a concrete and analogous application of the government of the church by the sovereigns to missions. It could not be the business of the individual pastor, says Dannhauer, to convert the Jews. No, this was the task of "all Christendom" *(totius christianismi).* For this reason the government had to take the necessary measures. It is true that the Jews could be won for the Christian faith only by divine grace, not by political power. But – as had been done in Hesse – they surely could be compelled to take part in colloquies arranged for the purpose of converting them.[12] Because the conversion of unbelievers is the business of all Christendom, it must be taken in hand by the sovereign. Here there is an application to a special occasion of the view Melanchthon had concerning the executive duty of the government in the service of the church (cf. *Church Government*). Melanchthon himself keeps within the limits thus specified. It is the chief purpose of human society that the people instruct one another, "that the knowledge of God be propagated" *(ut notitia Dei propagetur)* – this is the duty of missions. But then there is the further statement that the government is the "chief guardian of society" *(praecipuus custos societatis)* and consequently has to see to it that this task of society is carried out (*CR* 16, 118). "For this reason God has established states, that it may be possible for the Gospel to be propagated" *(Propter hanc causam Deus ordinavit politias, ut Evangelium propagari possit)* (16, 87).

10 WA 50, 312 ff.; WA 53, 417 ff.; WA TR 1, p. 161, 5. — The Weimar edition of the *Table Talk* adduces approximately 350 statements Luther made about the Jews. — R. Lewin, *Luthers Stellung zu den Juden,* 1911. — O. v. Harling, *Luthers Bedeutung f. d. Judenmission, Jahrb. d. sächs. Missionskonferenz,* 1917, pp. 82 ff. — W. Walther, *Luther und die Juden und die Antisemiten,* 1921. — Ed. Lamparter, *Evangelische Kirche und Judentum,* 1928. — H. Steinlein, *Luthers Stellung zum Judentum,* 1929. — Melanchthon's skeptical statement about a universal conversion of the Jews before the end of the world (*CR* 15, 700).

11 H. Frick, op. cit., pp. 118 f.

12 Dannhauer, *Theologia casualis,* ed. by Fr. Mayer, Greifswald, 1706, p. 464.

The King of Sweden is congratulated "because he has undertaken to see to it that the churches are equipped and that the Gospel is propagated" *(quod curam Ecclesiarum ornandarum et propagandi Evangelii suscepit)* (4, 567). Although Melanchthon emphasizes again and again that the church of Christ is "scattered" among all nations, that it can live in freedom in only a few states but is oppressed in most states (12, 25; 14, 908, etc.), he did not ask himself the technical question what the attitude should be *there* with respect to the "propagation of the Gospel" *(propagatio Evangelii).* For him as for Luther it was enough to be confident that the Word will find hearers and belief wherever it resounds. For Duke Johann Ernst of Saxony, Veit Dietrich unfolds the picture of the "propagation of the church" *(propagatio ecclesiae)* as it develops, not into a secular kingdom but into "scattered assemblings, yet not hidden but spreading the divine Word around in public and respectable gatherings as in the schools, sharing it with kings, princes, and states, and drawing many everywhere to the true invocation of God, even if meanwhile they were laughed at, hissed, and expelled by tyrants and by the majority of the people" *(coetus dispersos, non tamen obscuros sed circumferentes vocem divinam et in congressibus publicis ac honestis ut in scholis, impertientes eam regibus, principibus, civitatibus et multos passim ad veram invocationem Dei pertrahentes, etiamsi interim riderentur, exploderentur, pellerentur a tyrannis et a maxima parte hominum)* – an excellent picture of the church carrying on missionary work! (*CR* 5, 262.) Accordingly, the idea of missions was present in Melanchthon's school as well as in Luther's. But the church becomes capable of action toward the outside – as toward the inside (cf. *Church Government*) – only through the government of the church – the government that had now been placed in the hands of the sovereigns.

It is incorrect to say that the Lutheran princes were not conscious of this missionary duty that had been added to their obligations. On the aforementioned third front, where the church of the Gospel came into direct contact with ancient heathenism in the northern part of Scandinavia, King Gustavus Vasa stepped in immediately. It is true that the mission among the Laplanders, which he began, has no recognition in the histories of missions. In view of the meagerness of the sources no one should have the courage to say that it was unsuccessful. That it was on a small scale is clear from the fact that the work was undertaken again under Gustavus Adolphus. Gustav Warneck, of course, expresses the following judgment: "This state-church mission was a reformational act of territorial church power, not really mission work among the heathen, since it consisted only (!) in the sending of pastors and in the establishment of parishes" (p. 23). Yet one must ask what the difference was between a "mission" among people who are designated by Warneck himself as "heathen through and through" and "real missionary work among the heathen." Is it *no* missionary sending when pastors are sent among heathen? Besides, the statement that only pastors were sent is not even correct. In the diary of the Vadstena monastery there is the entry in the year 1525: "In the same year, on the Day of St. Gereon, in accordance with the command of our king, the lord Gustavus, Brother Benedictus Petri went forth to lead the people of the Lapps to the divine worship" *(Eodem anno die S. Gereonis ex mandato Regis nostri Dni Gostavi exivit frater Benedictus Petri ad inducendum populum lapponicum ad divum cultum).*[13] This first emissary among the Laplanders at the time of the Reformation was not a pastor! To be sure, the sovereign stood behind him – the sovereign who also took in hand the reformation of the church of his land. But the sending to the heathen on the borders of his country was not reformation; it was missionary work "in the strict sense of the word."

If this was not to be missionary work, then the Danish mission in Trankebar could not be regarded as missionary work either. As early as 1670 the royal endorsement of the East India Company specified that the company should always maintain priests for the purpose of converting the heathen "Indians" (Fenger, p. 11). And it is known that the mission in that place, as it actually came into being, was due to the initiative of King Frederick IV. When the Swedes settled on the Delaware, Gustavus Adolphus had given instructions to bring the Gospel to the Indians. In contrast with the cruelties of the Puritans, the Swedes treated the natives in a friendly manner. As a result, the Indians attended divine services. And Pastor Johann Campanius translated Luther's Catechism into their language. Liljenbladt, the royal secretary, wrote the preface to this translation.[14] Leibniz' much-praised missionary plans for China also rested on the expected initiative of the princes. This employment of the sovereigns for missions corresponded entirely to the actual conditions in the evangelical state churches. But it also coincides with the prevailing conceptions of the church, which is scattered in all nations. Denmark was the first Lutheran country to have an opportunity to colonize overseas. Here, therefore – to speak with Luther – a stone had been thrown into the water – a stone that had to and could cause "ripples, circles, and streams." Veit Ludwig von Seckendorff, whom the advocates of pietism claim as one who was in agreement with their prin-

[13] *Scriptores rerum Svedicarum medii aevi* I, 1, p. 219.

[14] Gottfr. Fritschel, *Gesch. d. christl. Mission under den Indianern,* 1870, p. 149.

ciples and practices, still shared the view widely circulated in the seventeenth century that it would be tempting God to "send out people who should teach publicly in heathen and Turkish countries and even lose their lives on this account." Yet he continues: "But the high governments and states that have the means and the opportunity to bring the Christian doctrine in an honest, holy, and good way into such countries sin when they fail to do so."[15] Seckendorff had been the chancellor of Duke Ernest the Pious of Gotha and Altenburg. According to Warneck, one may not record this attempt to have the Gospel proclaimed in Abyssinia as a missionary attempt either. Of course, there is, in addition, a much earlier attempt of a Lutheran sovereign to carry on missionary work among heathen. In 1583 Duke Ludwig of Württemberg had Magister Valentin Class of Knittlingen "journey to the kingdom of Fezzan beyond Spain to learn the Arabian language and what kind of teachings these nations have, and in order that by this means our saving religion might be propagated among these barbarian people."[16] This Lutheran missionary undertaking has been suppressed by the histories of missions, which, as is self-evident, mention every Englishman who went on a missionary journey. For on no account should the picture of "missionless" Lutheranism be muddied.

It was not indolence on the part of the Lutheran princes that hampered the missionary energy of early Lutheranism; it was the state church as such that did so. Grössel has shown how the idea of missions actuated our early theology, even though many statements in his presentation would have to be corrected. Among the early dogmaticians there is no one who, on principle, would have denied that there was an obligation to preach the Gospel among the heathen.[17] What prevented them from

[15] Seckendorff, *Christenstaat,* Leipzig, 1686, pp. 716 and 718.

[16] *Württemb. KG.,* 1893, p. 385.

[17] Conceptions of this duty frequently vary in this or that detail. Instead of presenting them here, I refer to what Grössel says about them. The information he gives is supplemented in part by Drews and Frick. — Johann Gerhard is always the parade horse trotted out to show that orthodox theologians have no understanding of missions. Consequently, Warneck, too, presents him to his readers in this light. Unfortunately, Jul. Richter does the same thing. Here the reader is amused at first by Gerhard's presentation of history, which Warneck characterizes as "not only indiscriminatingly naive but also dogmatically biased" (cf. note 8). Then, however, the reader is horrified when he hears that Gerhard says that "the power of the apostles to preach in the whole world, the power that is combined with a direct call, the gift of miracles, authority, and the prerogative of infallibility — the prerogative that is credible in itself" *(potestas apostolorum praedicandi in toto orbe cum immediata vocatione, dono miraculorum,* ὑπεροχῇ *ac* αὐτοπιστῷ *privilegio infallibilitatis coniuncta)* is extinct. "With scholastic doctrinarianism . . . all the pleas that are brought to bear for a continuing duty of the church to carry on missionary

insisting on "special arrangements" for missionary work among the heathen or influenced them even to refuse to accept such arrangements was the notion that the religio-geographical situation as well as the political partition of the globe was stable, as it were. They believed that there are centers of the Christian church everywhere. If there are centers of evangelical churchdom, then the administration of the church must attend to preaching among non-Christians just as it must attend

activity are then refuted as 'absurd.'" In this way Gerhard, the enemy of missions, is sufficiently stigmatized.

Gerhard's comments, as he himself states and Warneck, too, correctly remarks, are directed against Hadrian Savaria. Anyone who has the slightest idea of Gerhard's precise dialectic sees at once that here everything depends for him on the adverbial modifiers with which he seeks to refute Savaria's derivation of the duty to carry on missionary work from the continuing apostolate, and that, here, too, as always, in the care with which he discusses the concept of "the succession of the apostles" *(successio apostolorum)*, he gives expression to his direct opposition to Bellarmine. He has already presented his own conception of the apostolic succession in an entirely different place (XI, 288 ff.). Obviously, it is the conception common to Lutheranism, namely, that all "legitimate ministers of the Gospel are true successors of the apostles" *(ministri Evangelii legitimi sunt veri apostolorum successores)* (XI, 323). — Gerhard's conclusion with regard to the calling of the heathen through the Gospel is identical with Luther's: that it has not come to an end but continues at the present time. "That universal calling of the nations did not begin at the time of the birth of Christ, but it continues to this very day through the preaching of the apostles and in the same way" *(universalis illa vocatio gentium non coepit tempore nativitatis Christi, sed per praedicationem apostolorum eademque adhuc hodie durat)* (XIV, 191). In opposition to Bellarmine, who points to the successes the Roman Church has had in its missionary activity, he does *not* assert that missionary work among non-Christians is no longer in place today. On the contrary, he states that the Lutheran Church also has successes in its missionary activity. Concerning the conversion of Jews and Turks he says that "many such [conversions] take place in our churches too, in various places through some grace of God" *(quales etiam in nostris ecclesiis per Dei gratiam aliquam multae in diversis locis fiunt)* (XII, 59). And in answer to the question about the missionary activity carried on among the heathen by "missionless" Lutheranism — the question with respect to which the modern historian of missions and the Roman polemicist are in agreement — he replies: "But if Bellarmine demands of us by all means that we show that conversion to our churches has taken place, we refer him to Iceland, Greenland, Lapland, Livonia, etc., in which regions many thousands of persons have been converted from heathenish idolatry to the true God through the preaching of the Gospel" *(Quodsi omnino a nobis exigat Bellarminus, ut gentilium conversionem ad nostras ecclesias factam esse monstremus remittimus illum ad Islandiam, Grönlandiam, Laponiam, Livoniam etc., in quibus regionibus evangelii praedicatione multa hominum milia ab ethnica idolatria ad verum Deum sunt conversa)* (XII, 60). Yes, Gerhard can even cast into the teeth of his Roman opponent the very words that were used when the latter complained that the Lutheran sect even "had the audacity to sail to the Greeks, to the Indians, and to the New World itself" *(ad Graecos, ad Indos, ad ipsum novum orbem navigare ausa est)* (XI, 287). — A man who speaks in this way about the successes of evangelical preaching among Jews, Turks, and heathen, at home and abroad, should not be stigmatized as an enemy of missions. Here we are not taking the basic position into consideration. It is identical with Luther's.

to preaching in general – this had been the practice in northern Europe and in the first colonies of Lutheran states. But if those centers are in the hands of nonevangelical churches, the Gospel goes to the heathen by way of the reformation of these Christian but still nonevangelical churches. As always, here, too, the obligation and the right to proclaim are conditional on the "proper call" or, what is identical, on the "proper sending" *(ordentliche Sendung)*. But only the "government of the church," which was in the hands of the sovereigns, came into question as the agency that sends. The example of Duke Ludwig of Württemberg in the sixteenth century showed that this was not necessarily an unqualified hindrance to transterritorial sending to non-Christians. But it became a hindrance when the government of the church was combined more and more emphatically with the idea of sovereignty. In the soil of the views that are basic here the idea of missions and its practical application in the seventeenth century made progress for this reason in connection with the overseas colonization carried on by the Protestant states. But to the same degree – to the extent that the thinking was strictly in terms of a state church – free missionary activity on the part of circles that were not sanctioned by the government was hampered inwardly.

The latent impulse to carry on missionary work was released by two factors. In the first place, by the improvement of the knowledge of the political and religio-geographical state of affairs in the countries overseas. What Philipp Nicolai and Johann Gerhard did not and could not know, Scriver already knew when in a frequently quoted passage in his *Seelenschatz* he pointed out that one sixth of the globe had been converted to Christianity. And a man like Leibniz was acquainted with the political and colonizing possibilities in East Asia in a way that was totally different from the way those men knew these possibilities at the turn of the seventeenth century. In the second place, however, excessive emphasis on the government of the church by the sovereigns – the emphasis which the seventeenth century had brought with it or inaugurated – at the same time provoked in an increasing measure the criticism that culminates in pietism without having been invented by pietism. Even Seckendorff, who advocates government of the church by the sovereigns, knows no dangers. But for a person living at the time of the Enlightenment the cohesion with the politico-ecclesiastical union – the cohesion which in the sixteenth century is felt to be predetermined by fate – emerges ever more clearly as a political matter. External freedom vis-à-vis the sovereign is limited more and more by the police and by legislation. Internal freedom vis-à-vis the sovereign, on the other hand, becomes all the greater. In the sixteenth century the opposite had been the case – a reciprocal relationship that has always repeated itself in history. This internal freedom vis-à-vis cohesion with the inherent political and ecclesiastical union is the presuppostion on the basis of which individuals went forth overseas to carry on missionary work among the heathen. A man like Peter Heiling, of Lübeck, who went to Abyssinia in 1634 for the purpose of doing missionary work, had been inspired in Paris by Hugo Grotius. Of course, there is the question whether one may regard this as a "Reformed" inspiration – as is done in the histories of missions – or not rather as an inspiration due to the Enlightenment. Even the idea of the much-praised Baron Justinian of Welz to found a "society" *(Gesellschaft)* of orthodox Christians of the Augsburg Confession (1664) is typically in conformity with the Enlightenment. But these questions belong in the domain of sociology.

Even if one wants to attribute the Danish missionary work in East India to pietism and for this reason wants to deny that the Lutheran Church was responsible for it – which is incorrect historically as well as so far as the idea itself is concerned – Lutheranism of the nineteenth century, at the latest, has proved that it neither was nor is "missionless." Lutheran missionary work of the past century is not a product of Reformed stimuli; it is the definite breakthrough of Luther's idea of missions in the part of Christendom that is named for him – which can be recognized even in the criticism directed against the special missionary character of Lutheran missions. It is no accident that protagonists of missions like Rudelbach, Scheibel, Löhe, L. A. Petri, Louis Harms, and Graul were at the same time restorers of the confessional consciousness of the church. For to the same degree to which the confessional – therefore the ideal – reason for church membership outweighed the territorial reason which the state church had, the view became freer for the relationships and the tasks of the church at large. Also for missions.

PART THREE

Philosophy of Life

Chapter Five

THE WORLD AS SPACE

29. Justification and Philosophy of Life

As early as 1586, when the colloquy on religion took place at Mömpelgard, a number of questions pertaining to the philosophy of life *(Weltanschauung)* were drawn into the confessional discussions. In connection with the debate on the doctrine of Holy Communion and on Christology there were the general questions relating to space — the questions which had already come up in Luther's doctrine of Holy Communion. In addition, the relationship of the kingdom of Christ to the world was touched on. As had already happened in Luther's time, the account of the ascension gave rise to discussions concerning the hereafter and the present world. Finally the predestination problem led to the subject of "necessity" *(necessitas)* and thus to God's relationship to world affairs in general. The *Saxon Decision (Decisio Saxonica)* of 1624 marks the end of the Christological discussions inside Lutheranism. Although its attempt to distinguish various kinds or degrees of God's presence among creatures makes a decidedly wooden impression, still the necessity to come to an understanding with regard to God's relationship to the world according to its physical aspect is at least perceptible. And the Christological motive in evidence here is a point of departure for the application of a specifically Christian perspective. But it is no more than this. Here, if anywhere, the failure of the later dogmaticians makes itself felt in a manner that is painful. Their whole effort is directed toward the outward retention, not of the ideal bases but of the statements formulated with reference to man's cosmic position — questions that had grown out of the doctrines of Holy Communion, Christ, and predestination.

The starting point for a second and third series of thoughts is found in Melanchthon's *Loci.* From time immemorial one of these two — the eschatological — was part of the permanent stock of every honest treatise on dogmatics. Here a specifically Christian manner of treatment comes about as a matter of course. And one may say in praise of early Lutheran treatises on dogmatics that they kept themselves free at least from the vagaries of modern apologists with respect to natural science. Here they follow New Testament trains of thought with special scrupulousness. It is true that in the writings of Melanchthon concrete eschatology plays only a subordinate role; but so far as the manner of treatment was concerned, Melanchthon became a model for the later dogmaticians. He also stated the theme for the third train of thought when in the last edition of the *Loci* he gave one section the following heading: "On Disasters, on the Cross, and on True Comforts" *(De calamitatibus et de cruce et de veris consolationibus).* This very heading shows that here Melanchthon took over into dogmatics Luther's firmly held conclusions that the suffering of a Christian is a "cross" which God's will requires him to bear and that it is also one of the distinctions conferred on the church. The evaluation of suffering is an essential part of the qualitative view of the world and is indirectly connected with eschatology. Of course, its great significance, especially for early Lutheranism, is less perceptible in treatises on dogmatics than it is in hymns, in sermons, and in prayers.

It is self-evident, however, that among the dogmaticians the doctrine of God is, in general, the main incentive to the discussion of questions pertaining to the philosophy of life. What those who follow the lead of Melanchthon repeat about the creation, the preservation, and the governing of the world; about the various kinds of causality; about God's operation, cooperation, and permission; about the possibility, the origin, and the reality of evil in the world; about miracles, angels, and devils – all this, in spite of all modifications with respect to details, does not lead in an appreciable measure beyond the subject matter of dogmatics and the treatment of this subject matter in medieval scholasticism. The same thing is true of exegetical theology, which found a special incentive to speak about these questions in commentaries on Genesis. Here, of course, the transformation of the world picture becomes discernible in the course of the seventeenth century. The possibility of a "multitude" of worlds, which was a direct consequence of the Copernican astronomical system, calls in question the unique character of the history of mankind; but in doing so it also calls in question the central significance of Christ. Paleontology, as an independent branch of learning, threatens the position of what the Bible calls the first human being. It does so when it speaks about "preadamites." Just as these and similar "problems" are played out against the official dogmatics of the church by "free thinkers" who are more or less daring, so the dogmaticians derive an apologetic of the "Biblical philosophy of life" from the traditionally Aristotelian treatment of questions pertaining to the philosophy of life. And he who examines one of the early treatises on dogmatics – since Calov and Quenstedt, let us say – with this in view gets the impression that they do indeed contain very much about the philosophy of life; but at the same time he gets the other impression, namely, that here Lutheranism in general is helplessly enmeshed in a philosophy of life that is at the brink of death and is struggling convulsively for air.

In the seventeenth century this enmeshment grew rapidly worse after the time of Johann Gerhard. Of course, it is not an exclusive possession of Lutheranism. Nor does Lutheranism have sole possession of the systems of dogmatics as they were constructed by the scholastics. No, this enmeshment is but a separate occurrence in the history of knowledge in general. One finds an exact repetition among the Roman Catholics and among the Calvinists. Furthermore, it has complete counterparts – for example, in the field of contemporaneous jurisprudence. Yes, here – at least in the domain of Biblical exegesis – Lutheran theology follows examples that are clearly Reformed in character. And just as the "free-thinking" mentioned in the preceding paragraphs had its beginning, not in Germany but this time in bigoted England, so England is also the land in which the aforementioned Biblicistic apologetic originated.

All things considered, early Lutheranism occupied itself at the most varied points with questions pertaining to the philosophy of life. And it did so to such an extent in a definite direction that one can understand the verdict according to which it is said to have been, in its entire attitude, merely a last deep groan of the medieval philosophy of life – perhaps in the direction of nominalism – and for this reason to have perished with finality in the Enlightenment. This verdict, which – thanks primarily to Ernst Troeltsch, who followed the lead of Wilhelm Dilthey – has almost become a popular saying, goes back to the assessment of orthodoxy by the early Enlightenment itself, and for this reason it is suspect when viewed from a greater distance. Here Hegel's totally different assessment of the Reformation and its theology could have advised caution, even if one must reject it together with its historico-philosophical presuppositions. Hegel attempted to understand the nature of Lutheranism on the basis of a central point. He found this in the correspondence of the subjectivity and the certainty of the individual to the objective truth of the spirit, especially in the fact that here man has a "direct spiritual relationship" to Christ. Proceeding from this, he also found a positive relationship to the Lutheran doctrine of Holy

Communion. In spite of all its lack of certainty as to content this conception had the advantage of being a homogeneous total aspect of reality on the basis of which justice could be done the epoch-making significance of the Reformation. Troeltsch's assessment of the Reformation breaks down not only because of his insufficient knowledge of the sources – his accurate acquaintance with Lutheranism was limited to Johann Gerhard and Melanchthon – but also because of his inability to find in the Reformation a dominating central point. But this, in turn, is connected with the efforts of certain schools of theological thought to minimize as much as possible the theological difference between Luther and Calvin. For in doing this one has to disregard the central significance of what has been developed as the impact of the Gospel *(evangelischer Ansatz).* This very impact *(Ansatz)* of Lutheranism is incompatible with the basic idea of the theology of Calvin. In fact, the two are in irreconcilable opposition to each other. Because Troeltsch did not take Luther's doctrine of justification seriously enough – perhaps also because he had no correct knowledge of it – he considered it merely a variety of the "medieval doctrine of justification." In reality Luther's doctrine of justification is not only the dominating central point of Lutheranism but also the rising of the "modern philosophy of life" – provided that one can speak about such a rising at all. The philosophy of life of the nineteenth century is a chaos in which not only Kant and Spinoza, Goethe and Buddha, but also Augustine and Thomas, Plato and Aristotle whirl in utter confusion. Here, however, we understand "modern" to mean neither what is chronologically postmedieval nor, as Troeltsch does, the Enlightenment, but that philosophy of life which has gone through Kant's critique of knowledge or at least has been schooled in his way of questioning – even if it arrives at contradictory answers. From this nothing at all results for the "truth" or the "right" of Lutheranism. For the decision with regard to this stands or falls with the impact of the Gospel *(evangelischer Ansatz).* On the contrary, here – just as in the domain of sociology – it is merely a matter of pointing out the dynamics, which tomorrow can produce results altogether different from those it produced yesterday or produces today.

2. The place from which one gains a perspective of Luther's philosophy of life is to be found in the central point of the impact of the Gospel *(evangelischer Ansatz).*

It is based above all on the concentric combination of the entire content of knowledge with the conception of "reason" *(ratio).* Here Luther combines the series of thoughts that proceed from the causal view of the world and also reason a posteriori to "God the Creator" with the ethical view of the world — the view that culminates in the idea of the "highest good." As long as he keeps within rational epistemology — which he does only hypothetically since the breakthrough of the Reformation — this combination lets him appear as an uncompromising predestinarian, that is, a determinist. All his predecessors, whose battle against the official Pelagianism of the church he continues — Gregor von Rimini, Bradwardina, Wycliffe — seek in one way or another to preserve the qualitative independence of man's empirical ethos in the doctrine of freedom, in the doctrine of sin, and in the doctrine of grace. For in spite of this even the strict voluntarists among them, who also let the ethical sphere be founded contingently on God's absoluteness and thus apparently deprive it of every rational basis, then operate with ethical concepts in such a way that its inner-worldly fulfillment of man's actions split into something that is empirically good and something that is empirically bad. But because this splitting is empirical, it is perceived and recognized as "rational." Thus within the immanent knowledge of the world there is singled out a domain which, on the one hand, is said to be actually immanent but, on the other hand, is to be considered as a realization of the ethical idea or of the transcendent will of God. The reverse of this is the doctrine of "infused grace" *(gratia infusa)* — the doctrine which they all have in common in spite of its more or less close approach to a purely imputative version of the concept of grace. This doctrine — again in spite of modifications with respect to details — they all share with the second period of scholasticism *(Hochscholastik)*. From this there then results a general supranaturalism which is oriented to the immanent-causal view of the world, namely, that another relationship is operative in the elemental relationship of the affairs of the world. Although this other relationship overlaps the elemental relationship, cuts it up, or at least pierces it at definite points, it is conceived of as being just as causal and, in its effect at least, just as empirical as the elemental relationship.

Basically the whole philosophy of life expressed in and connected with this comes to an end in Luther's "primal experience" *(Urerlebnis)*. Above all, this experience contains the radical thinking-through-to-the-end of the causal-deterministic view of the world. In this way Luther demolishes Pelagianism, which confronts him in the "moderns" of the fifteenth century in a manner that is even more terrifying than it is in classical Thomism. So far as this is concerned, he can appear to be a simple disciple of the strict predestinarians. But what distinguishes him from these is the conscious and conclusive abstention from every attempt to put the idea of predestination into a positive relationship to an ethical conception of God, no matter what the nature of this conception may be. To be sure, in his writing against Erasmus there are references to the old Augustinian solution — the solution that was revived by Bradwardina — according to which an empirical scope for the human will is left within the "necessity" *(necessitas)* decreed by God. For this reason he can say: "We are not such unwilling persons" *(Non inviti tales sumus)* when it is a matter of substantiating man's guilt in spite of the deterministic basic thought. But the incentive to this is not, as in Augustine and all later dogmaticians, the intention to make room for an ethical theodicy. It is one of the main purposes of the writing against Erasmus to prove that this is impossible. For although the aforementioned statement concerns man and makes him responsible, it concerns God to no lesser degree — God, who prescribes to man an obligation and thus makes him responsible in such a way that he is fatefully prevented from fulfilling the obligation.

Accordingly, for Luther this whole way of thinking ends in three conclusions.

In the first place, the "world" is a homogeneous whole in which no factor is subtracted from the only causal connection which constitutes it and in which — what is most important of all — no point is conceivable at which human freedom could break out.

In the second place, although man's responsibility, which is attested in his conscience, promises a realm of freedom that could elevate above the empirico-causal misfortune, there is no fulfillment of this promise in the world.

In the third place, every attempt to bring the experience of the causal relationship of the world into agreement with the ethical — unfulfillable — demand in the idea of God is a failure. It leads to nothing else than to the "hidden God" *(Deus absconditus)*, that is, to the unrecognizableness of God.[1] Accordingly, the product of the rational-causal view of the world and the acknowledgment of the ethical demands is for Luther a logical agnostic determinism. From here no way out presents itself. There is not even a glimpse of any other reality.

Luther had a clear understanding of this in his struggle against every form of Pelagianism. Yet by emphasizing it he hit not only one particu-

[1] In the context of the philosophy of life the concept of the "hidden God" *(Deus absconditus)* can be taken into account only as a borderland concept. When Luther goes beyond this and gives it a specific content by means of the idea of divine wrath, one cannot yet regard this as an invalidation of the entire approach that is presupposed here. For Luther divine wrath manifests itself in the concrete situation of man, in the demonic character of destiny. Although destiny demands from man what is good, at the same time it subjects him to the necessity of doing what is evil.

lar statement of Erasmus, but he hit humanism as a principle of the philosophy of life — as this principle later reached classical consummation in the writings of Kant. According to it, in all knowledge of the world our reason is the lawgiver of nature, and in the genuine ethos our reason is its own lawgiver. Man is the measure of all things. This statement is correct if, like Kant, one lets the knowledge of nature and the ethos stand side by side dualistically. The two thwart each other if one refers them to each other. The principle of freedom of autonomous ethics and the causal principle of the knowledge of nature are mutually exclusive. Not even Kant's doctrine of the intelligibility of freedom can delude one as to this. For even lawgiving reason is intelligible. It would be possible to believe that one escaped the indissoluble contradiction between necessity and freedom expressed by Luther in the idea of the "hidden God" *(Deus absconditus)* only if one connected the doctrine of intelligible freedom with a naive empiricism which does not understand the apriority of the concept of causality. Only he who looks at the causal nexus of things as a fact "per se" can, by virtue of his intelligible freedom, consider himself independent vis-à-vis this causal nexus of things. But Kant put an end once for all to such naive empiricism. On the contrary, it is the same transcendental I that must apply the concept of cause to the knowledge of the world and adds its own freedom to its ethical self-assertion. Both statements are unavoidable, but they remain in indissoluble contradiction. This contradiction can appear to be bearable as long as the idea of God is kept out. For Luther as well as for Erasmus it was unavoidable. But one could object by saying that here Luther and Erasmus simply did not know how to keep themselves free from the tradition of the church. Actually this contradiction has a necessary place for Luther even here. It is not yet possible to make this clear by resorting to a formal contrasting of the approach according to natural law with the ethical approach.

3. Luther did not draw the final conclusions of agnostic determinism until after he, like Kant, had learned to separate the empirical I from the transcendental I. But the road by which he arrived at this was totally different from the road taken by Kant. Kant's predecessors are the German mystics of the Middle Ages, who, like him, find the a priori by means of a reduction of consciousness (cf. *Luther on Justification*). The result is the pure aloneness of the spirit. For the mystic this is redemption from the empirical I — the I that is satiated with experience. Luther, too, demands "that you should come out of and away from yourself" *(dass du aus dir und von dir kommen mögest)*. But this redemption he experiences in the Gospel. Of course, the Word about Christ confirms

the indissoluble contradiction between necessity and freedom, between destiny and guilt. In the scope of the immanent approach God becomes the "hidden God" *(Deus absconditus)* in the cross of Christ. But by directing itself to me this same Word about Christ pertains to me too. Christ's righteousness is my righteousness because the Word pertains to me. But it pertains to me only if this righteousness remains unentangled with my empirical existence. Faith, which hears this Word, has no other function than this hearing and exists only by hearing. If in spite of this it is my I that hears and believes, it can be only the "pure" I, that is, the I that cannot be further qualified in an empirico-psychological manner, therefore the transcendental I. In connection with the doctrine of justification it was shown that for Luther the logical presupposition for the idea of the transcendental I is not the reduction of thinking to what is categorical, but that it is self-judgment, which, together with faith, constitutes penitence.

But since faith in the Word about Christ receives forgiveness of sins, the "hidden God" *(Deus absconditus)* becomes the "revealed God" *(Deus revelatus)* in this same cross of Christ. Thus Luther stands before the "hereafter." This "hereafter" is "totally different" from the world of agnostic determinism, in which the combination of "theoretical" and "practical reason" comes to an end. Faith is addressed by God – the abolition of agnosticism. It receives forgiveness – the abolition of determinism. For determinism means fateful unfulfillability of the ethical and therefore also invincibility of guilt. In the forgiveness of sins, the "other righteousness," the ethical has been fulfilled, and guilt has been overcome. Later the Enlightenment understood the hearing of the Word of God to be a correction of errors of knowledge. But Luther's concept of revelation is no error; it is the only possible and the only correct interpretation of the reality of the world, inclusive of the ethical demand. The hearing of the Gospel does not do away with this reality in such a way that this reality would thus be declared to be an error. On the contrary, the hereafter of God reveals itself only when the rational view of the world has been brought "to a mathematical point" *(ad punctum mathematicum)* and has achieved its final success in the realization of death. Nor does the forgiveness of sins by any means invalidate the importance of the ethical demand. If the demand were unimportant, there would be no sin and consequently no forgiveness either.

Here, too, three conclusions result.

In the first place, the relationship between the present and the hereafter is not identical with the relationship between the beginning and the continuation of the same reality. On the contrary, God's hereafter makes the present of our world-reality a whole in itself, that is, it confirms not only the correctness but also the completeness of our knowledge of the world. Here we do not understand completeness to mean that the content of knowledge is exhausted. No, we understand it to be the appearance of the limits within which all knowledge of the world must remain, no matter whether we have already exhausted it or not.

In the second place, the present and the hereafter are not duplicated. The impact of the Gospel *(evangelischer Ansatz)* only puts the present and the hereafter into a relationship that is purely functional. It is true that we can see the present, but this view cannot be made use of to gain a position with respect to the hereafter. The relationship of the present to the hereafter is purely negative. Conversely, the relationship of faith to God's hereafter is, of course, purely positive; but we cannot see this hereafter. The impact of the Gospel *(evangelischer Ansatz)* does not compare a conception of the hereafter with a conception of the present. Nor, as a matter of fact, is it merely a simple point of intersection of which one could think in connection with Luther's emphatic statement that the definitive knowledge of the world, like justification, is a point. If the revelation of the hereafter does not enable one to see the hereafter, it is for this reason by no means without content. On the contrary, it may be compared to the geometrical locus of a system of coordinates which shows a plurality of points, or rather many points, at which the one whole can be referred to the other whole.

In the third place, even though, according to what has been stated, the present and the hereafter are in different dimensions, still both ultimately have one thing in common, one thing that is set above them: that which is "valid." Rational knowledge of the world is valid, the ethical demand is valid – but the forgiveness of sins is also valid. The threat of death is valid. The promise of life is valid. If one leaves out of account the differentiation as to the content of what is valid, one can understand this to be a transsubjective arrangement which we cannot escape in one way or another. This would make it nothing more than a new abstraction of determinism. Actually it can always be defined only as to content, that is, by differentiation. The authority it has for us is not the authority of an impersonal arrangement. The forgiveness of sins is valid only because of the personal authority of God, who pronounces it. The same divine authority stands behind the ethical demand, at least for faith, which sees precisely this ethical demand confirmed in the forgiveness of sins. But since forgiveness at the same time contains the decision with regard to death and life, it also becomes clear that the power destiny has over our existence lies in the same hand. The same state of affairs, which can be understood in an immanently deterministic manner without the Gospel, moves the forgiveness of sins into the light of the divine purpose. Therefore if our involvement in the causality of the world is in the power of God, our knowledge of the world is likewise under the power of God. Accordingly, for faith the forgiveness of sins, the ethical demand, and the knowledge of the world are valid because of the personal authority of God. Therefore that which is valid actually has a homogeneous origin in spite of its differentiation as to content. But this origin is strictly personal in nature. Only if it is personal in nature – or rather because it is personal – are this homogeneity of the origin and the differentiation as to content in compatibility. An impersonal arrangement, an impersonal moral law, can either only demand or only forgive. Only a person is able both to conceal and to reveal, is able both to determine and to set a goal.

In this way the homogeneousness of the present and the hereafter – the homogeneousness which at first seems to fall apart into dualism – is made secure for faith. But it can no more be inferred from the empirical state of affairs of the world than it can be inferred from the ethical demand. All postulates of God are and remain mere question marks. Not even the forgiveness of sins can be postulated. But for faith it exists. For this reason only faith also knows about the power of the personal God over the world and destiny. But it really does have this knowledge.

This is the relationship between justification and the philosophy of life. Lutheranism's philosophy of life is unthinkable without faith in God. But this faith in God does not imply that the great facts of the natural knowledge of the world fall to pieces one by one. On the contrary, it takes these facts into itself as a whole and affirms their validity. At the same time, however, it points out their relativity by letting them be kept in the power of God – at once affirmed and overcome.

30. The Relativity of the World Picture [1]

The Lutheran doctrine of Holy Communion is one of the first tests to be applied to the start developed in the direction of a philosophy of life. Luther's writings on Holy Communion contain various statements about the relationship between God and the world. Consequently, one could get the impression that it was precisely his interest in Holy

[1] Some of the relationships established in the following paragraphs have already been set forth in my essay *Wirkungen der lutherischen Abendmahlslehre usw.*, *AELKZ,* 1927, Nos. 32 ff.

Communion that provided the actual start toward his philosophy of life. And since in connection with this he also makes use of Occamistic concepts, his critics believed that they could easily prove that so far as his philosophy of life was concerned, he remained completely tied to the Middle Ages. Then there was but one step to the opposite conclusion: that his doctrine of Holy Communion actually had its origin in the medieval philosophy of life. That this is not correct was proved when the Sacrament of the Altar was discussed. Here the very opposite was shown, namely, that for the Lutheran doctrine of Holy Communion points of view entirely different from those pertaining to the philosophy of life were decisive. And it also became clear that at least at one point the Lutheran doctrine of Holy Communion actually exercised a liberating influence so far as the philosophy of life was concerned. This also became evident in the field of Christology. For Luther it was the story of Christ's ascension – which was cited by the Reformed opponents against the Lutheran doctrine of Holy Communion – that gave him the incentive to free the relationship between the present and the hereafter in a basic manner from the world picture of his time (cf. *The States and Offices of Christ* and *The Sacrament of the Altar*). "Heaven," as God's place, is not a place in a spatial sense. If the doctrine of Holy Communion had no other significance than that it helped Luther reach clarity with regard to this matter and induced him to insist emphatically on this in theology in spite of all accusations of heresy on the part of the Reformed Church, it would indeed be great enough on this account. For the effects on the whole development of the modern world picture are almost incalculable.

That the Lutheran doctrine of Holy Communion and the Christology connected with it actually had an epoch-making effect here can be seen from two facts: (1) that the "omnipresent heaven" *(coelum ubiquitarium)* of the Lutherans was attacked not only by the Reformed Church with every "Scriptural proof" the Reformed Church could employ and with an overbearing "scientific method" *(Wissenschaftlichkeit)* but (2) that crypto-Calvinism in German territory also combined the return to the spatial conceptions of heaven with the abandonment of Luther's doctrine of Holy Communion. Here a simple example shows how completely misleading it is to bring the Protestant denominations into a gradual change which, as is self-evident, would leave Lutheranism entirely in the Middle Ages but would make Calvinism the "more modern" denomination, which at the most is still outstripped only by the type that is fanatical *(Schwärmertypus)*. Just as genuine Calvinism repristinates the medieval ideal of a theocracy in a sociological respect, so in the domain of the philosophy of life it clings to the old world picture. And it adduces theological reasons for doing so. Instead of the free and simple faith in Christ, which substantiates Luther's "Scriptural principle" *(Schriftprinzip)* but at the same time also limits it, there is that narrow-minded Biblicism which confuses "obedience to Scripture" with faith and therefore canonizes the hare that chews the cud and has the hoof cloven just as it canonizes the "Biblical government" *(biblische Verfassung)* of the church. It is self-evident that because of its apparent consistency this Biblicism had something that was attractive to all evangelicals. And for the development of Lutheranism it was ominous that here, too, this Biblicism could gain ground before the struggle between the old and the new world picture had been settled. At that time it was still barely possible to realize its effects on the world picture in all their impossibility. But where one yielded to it, the break of Luther's conception of heaven with the old world picture could no longer be maintained. The end was the moss-grown apologetic of the nineteenth (and the twentieth) century, which burdened evangelical Christendom with a curse of ridiculousness. Luther himself, of course, had nothing to do with this. The mother of this apologetic was the English apologetic of the Age of Enlightenment, and its grandmother was Calvinism's "modern philosophy of life." [2]

[2] In order to understand the impression which the "Biblical" substantiation of the ancient world picture by Reformed clergymen could make, it is necessary to think back to the condition of the congregations in the sixteenth century. Cf., e. g., the following polemical statements in opposition to the Lutheran conceptions of an unspatial heaven — statements made by the Reformed preacher Georg Spindler, who lived in the Upper Palatinate (*Postilla, Auslegung der Evangelien,* Herborn, 1594, II, 121): "You should retain this true and incontestable doctrine concerning the ascension of Christ, for it is useful against the papists and other teachers who want to have Christ essentially present with His body in the bread of Holy Communion. And since this article stands in their way, they devise a different and strange explanation of it and say that Christ's ascension was mere make-believe and only an illusion [the argument against Luther's 'tokens'], when the Lord rose into the clouds and thus became invisible, incomprehensible, infinite, and present everywhere with His body. For to them ascending must be tantamount to becoming invisible and being everywhere. And they euphemize this with Christ's statement that He is going to the Father. The Father, they say, is everywhere. Now ascending into heaven and going to the Father are one and the same thing. Therefore ascending into heaven is tantamount to being everywhere, since, of course, going to the Father does not mean to come to the essence of the Father, because He always was with the Father, and the Father always was with Him, but to come where God's throne is. — In addition, they maintain that heaven, into which Christ ascended and wants to take us to Himself, is everywhere too and extends through heaven, earth, and hell, and that for this reason the Lord did not need to ascend a hairbreadth from earth in order to come to the Father with His body [the argument against Andreä, who had used this expression]. For in their heaven [the heaven of the Lutherans], which is everywhere, angels and devils run around higgledy-piggledy, and the

Luther's position with regard to the questions concerning the world picture had been established unambiguously by the impact of the Gospel *(evangelischer Ansatz).* As such, all knowledge of nature remains within the bounds of the "world." It can neither produce nor supplant the revelation by which faith lives. It cannot even postulate this revelation. But knowledge of nature cannot impede this revelation either. In Lutheranism, therefore, the fact that the church limits itself, in Luther's sense, to the preaching of the Gospel had to result in complete freedom of research and complete freedom of teaching in the field of natural science. Luther's own attitude toward astrology affords sure proof of his own tolerance in these matters. Like many other humanists, Melanchthon was swayed by a magical world picture. He believed that the stars influence the temperament and the character of men. He cast horoscopes. Luther was a sworn enemy of astrology, and at times he even characterized it as idolatry. For this reason he often made fun of Melanchthon and even reproved him. In general, however, he let him have his way, since the Gospel remained untouched by astrology.[3]

Here, to be sure, every shifting of the impact of the Gospel *(evangelischer Ansatz)* could again immediately bring dangers. In Melanchthon's case this shifting occurred when he ascribed to the "natural" knowledge of God a positive significance for faith that was completely different from the significance Luther ascribed to it (cf. *Natural Theology*). This assessment of the knowledge of the world will always give rise to the tendency to regard the findings of natural science as conclusive. Otherwise the natural substructure brings into theology a factor of uncertainty – a factor which can become fatal precisely because of its dependence on the knowledge of the world into which it has entered. In Melanchthon's case there are the additional considerations that he

angels carry their heaven around with them, just as the devils carry their hell around with them. This is horrible to hear."

I repeat only one of the quotations adduced by R. Rocholl (*Realpräsenz,* 1875, pp. 120 ff.) from the literature of the seventeenth and the eighteenth century. From it one can see how long the conceptions of heaven that were maintained by the Reformed Church in its polemics against Lutheranism were retained. In his *Aussichten in die Ewigkeit* (1769 ff.) Lavater declared: "A cannon ball would have more than a trillion years . . . to hurry away to the nearest fixed star. . . . One can imagine with what speed Jesus ascended into heaven."

[3] Melanchthon, especially in *Initia Doctr. Physicae,* in the section *De Fato Physico* (*CR* 13, 331 ff.; also 322 ff. and 392 ff.). Furthermore, the preface *in libr. de judic. nativitatum Joh. Schoneri* (*CR* 5, 817 ff.) and the letters to Schoner (3, 115 ff.) and Simon Grynäus (2, 814 ff.).

Luther against astrology: WA 1, 404, 1 ff.; WA TR, 1, 678; 855 ff.; 1026; 3, 2824; 4, 4705 (astronomy against astrology!); 4846; especially against Melanchthon, WA TR 2, 1480; 3, 2892; 2952b; 3520; 5, 5538; 5573; 6250 (astrology is "reason" *[ratio]!*)

regarded himself as an authority in the field of natural science and that for his time he actually was an authority. It is understandable that when the world picture of Copernicus came into view, he regarded it with hostile eyes. What he, as a teacher and an organizer, accomplished in Wittenberg even for the teaching of natural science is excelled by no one of his contemporaries and became a model for other universities. But here, too, the basis for this was the reading of the ancient teachers. He knew how antiquity had struggled for a satisfactory explanation of the orbits of the planets. He knew the account which Archimedes gave concerning the "paradox" of the immobility of the sun and the movement of the earth – the "paradox" enunciated by Aristarchus of Samos (*CR* 13, 216). He also saw the indubitably great achievement of Ptolemy with the eyes of antiquity (WA 11, 292; 7, 405). It is self-evident that his attitude toward Copernicus is part of this whole sphere of ideas, which characterizes Melanchthon as a genuine humanist but has nothing at all to do with his evangelical theology. One could imagine a connection with his theology only if the Copernican world picture either had to or could be found to carry with it a factor of uncertainty for his "natural" theology.[4]

[4] Two reasons induce us to investigate somewhat more closely the position of early Lutheranism with respect to the new world picture. For one thing, this illustrates the relativity of the world picture best. Then, however, it also seems necessary to contradict the assessment made of the attitude of the Wittenberg reformers toward the great transformation of the world picture. This assessment is totally false in spite of the fact that it is deeply rooted in the general history of science and still has aftereffects in the writings of Troeltsch and even in what "Luther scholars" of the present time state. It goes back to a number of Catholic scholars who made it their business to blame the Wittenberg reformers and thus to erase the fatal impression created by the official condemnation of the Copernican world picture on the part of their own church.

The foundations of this house of cards were laid in Franz Beckmann's essays titled *Zur Geschichte des Kopernikanischen Systems* in the second and third volume of the *Ermländische Zeitschrift* and in Franz Hipler's *Nik. Kopernicus und Martin Luther* (Braunsberg, 1868). In Hipler's *Spicilegium Copernicanum* (Braunsberg, 1873) a number of documentary sources were disclosed from which all later historians of astronomy, and especially of Copernicus, have drawn. The building was crowned by Adolf Müller, S. J., professor of astronomy at the Gregorian University and director of the observatory on the Janiculum in Rome, in *Nicolaus Copernicus*, Supplement No. 7 to *Stimmen aus Maria Laach* (Freiburg, 1898).

In the matter of this construction of history J. H. v. Mädler (*Geschichte der Himmelskunde*, 2 vols., Braunschweig, 1873) is dependent on Beckmann. He says that the "fervent spirit of ecclesiastical fanaticism" rages against Copernicus. For example, he has totally false views concerning Rhaeticus' relationship to Wittenberg. And he spread these views. Even Leop. Prowe, who, in his extensive monograph on Nic. Copernicus (2 vols., Berlin, 1883—84), rectifies, or at least tries to tone down, many details, has, on the whole, not entirely escaped the influence of Beckmann and Hipler. — Cf. finally R. Wolf, *Geschichte der Astronomie* (Munich, 1877) and, on Copernicus, L. Lohmeyer, in Heinrich von Sybel's *Historische Zeitschrift*, Vol. 57, 1887. Up to the present time an incalculable number of writings that have not advanced farther toward the sources are based on these learned presentations.

Melanchthon speaks in greatest detail about the Copernican system in the section of the *Initia doctrinae physicae* of 1549 which deals with the movement of the world (*CR* 13, 216 ff.). Here he opposes this system with two kinds of reasons. In the first place, with Scriptural reasons. Psalm 45, he says, proves that the sun moves; Ps. 78:69 and Eccl. 1:4 prove that the earth is stationary. And it is designated as a miracle when on one occasion (in the story of Joshua) God wanted the sun to stand still. No one will maintain that this "Scriptural proof" touches the center of evangelical theology at any place. Besides, Melanchthon continues as follows: "Strengthened by these divine proofs, let us embrace the truth, and let us not permit ourselves to be led away from it by the deceptions of those who think it is an ornament of the intellect to throw the arts into confusion" *(His divinis testimoniis confirmati, veritatem amplectamur nec praestigiis eorum, qui decus ingenii esse putant conturbare artes, abduci nos ab ea sinamus)* (217). Thus the Scriptural proof should deter one from throwing the "liberal arts" *(artes liberales)* into confusion. Accordingly, there now follows a far more extensive compilation of the "physical arguments" *(argumenta physica).* From these it is concluded that the earth is situated in the center and is immobile. For Melanchthon these arguments are decisive. If he wanted to decide the Copernican question theologically, he had to be satisfied with the Biblical reasons. At a later place he even finds the theory of Copernicus concerning the movement of the moon acceptable; but he prefers to follow the traditional teaching of Ptolemy, "in order that in some way we may attract studious persons to the common teaching accepted in the schools" *(ut aliquomodo studiosos invitemus ad communem doctrinam in scholis receptam)* (244). The only question remaining would be whether here there is not an instance in which specific knowledge of natural science should support the knowledge of God in the sense of "natural theology." This is not the case. At any rate, Melanchthon does not give the slightest indication of it. The aforementioned place in his discussion of physical science is followed by another section – a section dealing with the question: Is there only one world, or are there several worlds? But Mädler's statement that in this connection Melanchthon is writing against Copernicus is a falsification. For Melanchthon expressly names the opponents he is attacking here: Empedocles and Democritus as well as a fable in the writings of Aelian. Thus he keeps within the sphere of the humanistic-ancient outlook.[5]

[5] Mädler I, 176. — Furthermore, Mädler states that Melanchthon called on the Christian authorities to root out the blasphemous and anti-Scriptural teaching of Copernicus. This reference has been taken over from Mädler by others, manifestly without having been verified. The passage is found in a letter written to Burkard

But now the way the Wittenberg reformers treated Joachim Rhaeticus is cited as convincing proof of their fanatical hostility toward the new world picture.[6] Actually the significance of Rhaeticus for the dissemination of the Copernican teaching is great enough to make this attack on Wittenberg understandable.[7] The reformers are said to have made it impossible for him, the outspoken disciple of Copernicus, to work at their university, to have prevented him from carrying out the plan he projected in Wittenberg to have the chief work of Copernicus printed, and finally to have induced him to leave the city. The facts of the case are as follows:

Mithobius on Oct. 16, 1541 (*CR* 4, 679). The conclusion of the letter reads as follows: "So far some have raged against the churches, others have fashioned corruptions of doctrine, have contended by means of offensive pamphlets, have fashioned absurd dialogs, have taken delight in the pleasures of Venus, have neglected the churches and the schools, have contended by currying favor. Now Nemesis brings on an enemy who is not to be despised. But let us pray God that He may protect the churches and may also stir up our people to the true duties of the fear of God. I have seen the dialog and have opposed the publication. The story will gradually abate of itself; but some believe that it is an outstanding virtue to adorn such an absurd matter, as the well-known Sarmatian astronomer who moves the earth and makes the sun stationary does. Surely wise rulers should restrain the impudence of clever persons. Keep well." *(Hactenus alii saevierunt in Ecclesias, alii finxerunt corruptelas doctrinae, certarunt obscoenis libellis, finxerunt insulsos dialogos, oblectarunt se Veneris voluptatibus, neglexerunt Ecclesias et scholas, certarunt ambitione. Nunc Nemesis attrahit non contemnendum hostem. Sed oremus Deum, ut tegat Ecclesias et nostros etiam ad vera* τῆς θεοσεβίας *officia exuscitet. Vidi dialogum et fui dissuasor editionis. Fabula per sese paulatim consilescet; sed quidam putant esse egregium* κατόρθωμα *rem tam absurdam ornare, sicut ille Sarmaticus Astronomus, qui movet terram et figit solem. Profecto sapientes gubernatores deberent ingeniorum petulantiam cohercere. Bene vale.)* — From the context it is seen (1) that the Copernican teaching is not meant until the Sarmatian astronomer is mentioned, and (2) that the request addressed to the rulers is directed against all the previously mentioned improprieties. But this request is the opposite of a complaint in the first part of the letter: "Even before this time most of the princes have been much more attentive to the destruction of monasteries than to the establishment of parishes and schools" *(Plerique Principes etiam ante hoc tempus multo fuerunt in diripiendis monasteriis diligentiores quam in constituendis* παροικίαις *et scholis).* From this it follows that here Melanchthon is by no means appealing to the government as the possessor of ecclesiastical power — thus to the right to punish heretics — but to the protectors of education. Entirely apart from the fact that Copernicus is mentioned here at all, and mentioned only incidentally, his teaching appears again here at best as a disturbance of the humanistic curriculum. The princes are obligated to prevent this.

As will be shown, Melanchthon, for all practical purposes, also conducted himself altogether differently from the way this incidental remark could perhaps lead one to expect. Rhaeticus did not return from Copernicus until the autumn of 1541!

6 Mädler I, 180. — Adolf Müller, p. 86. More literature here.

7 It is due to Prowe that this significance is pointed out in detail. Most of the facts mentioned about Rhaeticus in the following paragraphs have been substantiated on the basis of documentary evidence.

Through the instrumentality of Melanchthon, Rhaeticus, twenty-three years of age, had been called to Wittenberg in 1537 as a mathematician. In 1539 he goes to Copernicus long after it had become known in Wittenberg what this man taught.[8] But no obstacle was put in his way. His position is kept open for him. In the following year the public gets the first reliable information about the new system.[9] On his return journey in the autumn of 1541 Rhaeticus receives a letter of recommendation from Duke Albrecht of Prussia to the Elector of Saxony, resumes the Wittenberg professorship at once, and immediately after this – in spite of the fact that the Copernican teaching had just been made public through him – becomes dean of the faculty of arts. At the end of the year he appears as professor in Leipzig, which even at that time was Lutheran. Absolutely nothing can be ascertained about the reasons for his change of residence. The only thing certain is the fact that in between he was repeatedly in Nürnberg to supervise the printing of Copernicus' chief work, which the Lutheran theologian Andreas Osiander published in Lutheran Nürnberg.[10] For these journeys Melanchthon gave him letters of recommendation to his Nürnberg friends. In the letter to Veit Dietrich, dated May 2, 1542, Melanchthon calls Rhaeticus "a man who is learned and capable of teaching this most pleasing knowledge of the movements of the heavenly bodies" *(virum eruditum et ad docendas has dulcissimas artes motuum coelestium idoneum)* (*CR* 4, 810); in the letter to Erasmus Ebner, dated July 7, it is stated that Rhaeticus is "born to search out learning" *(natum ad Mathemata pervestiganda)* (839). It is only in the letter to Joachim Camerarius, dated July 25, that one can read a criticism between the lines. But since Melanchthon hopes that Rhaeticus' "enthusiasm" will give

8 Luther's (only) derogatory remark about Copernicus is made in June 1539 (WA TR 1, 855; 4, 4638).

9 *De libris revolutionum Nicolai Copernici Narratio prima,* 1540, reprinted in Prowe II, 293 ff. The book has the form of a report to Schoner, who had resigned from his spiritual office in Bamberg and, at the advice of Melanchthon, had become mathematician at the gymnasium in Nürnberg.

10 Osiander's famous preface, reprinted last in E. Hirsch, *Die Theologie des A. Osiander,* 1919, p. 290; cf. p. 120. — Adolf Müller, S. J., managed to make this preface of Osiander's responsible for the condemnation of the Copernican work by the papal Congregation of the Index (Mirbt, *Quellen,* No. 510, p. 367) — the condemnation which took place sixty-three years later — because in it the new system was designated as a hypothesis. "It was this man who . . . first laid the 'cuckoo's egg' of dissension in Copernicus' beautiful work by branding it as suicidal as soon as it appeared, reduced it to the level of an arithmetical hypothesis without claim to validity, and transferred it to the domain of religious scruples" (p. 105). Thus the Lutheran editor of the Copernican work is responsible for the fact that the teaching concerning the movement of the earth was forbidden in the Roman Church until the year 1757!

way to the Socratic philosophy as soon as he has become the father of a family, one will scarcely think of his Copernican teaching in this connection.[11] The whole letter shows how much Melanchthon misses Rhaeticus; and in an earlier letter to Camerarius, dated May 11, it is stated that Rhaeticus left Wittenberg reluctantly.[12] Accordingly, all this may be taken as sufficient evidence that the historically important journeys of Rhaeticus to Nürnberg – the journeys that pertained to the printing of the work of Copernicus – do not presuppose a break with Melanchthon. But that the transfer of the printing to Nürnberg did not take place because of censorship exercised by the Wittenbergians is clear from the fact that in the same year a shorter writing of Copernicus was issued in Wittenberg by Rhaeticus and was printed by Hans Lufft, who printed Luther's translation of the Bible.

But it is really altogether out of place to ascribe to Melanchthon in these matters a papal role in the domain of Lutheranism. The authority he enjoys in this respect is the authority of the prominent humanist. For the attitude of Lutheran theology toward Copernicus the open-mindedness of Osiander has at least the same symptomatic significance that the ancient-humanistic prejudice of Melanchthon has. And did Melanchthon actually cling to this prejudice? In the commemorative address in honor of Kaspar Cruciger, which was delivered in 1549, he says: "Moved by these and similar observations, we have begun to admire and love Copernicus more" *(His et similibus observationibus moti Copernicum magis admirari et amare coepimus)* (*CR* 11, 839). The address was recited by Erasmus Reinhold, about whom there will be more to say later. One need not place special emphasis on Melanchthon's authorship. Even if one assumes that he wanted to make everything as palatable as possible for the mathematician who was to deliver the address, here it is attested in a solemn academic ceremony that Cruciger – who was a professor of theology at Wittenberg, had long been one of Luther's co-workers, and had even cooperated with Luther in the translation of the Bible – was one of Copernicus' admirers.

[11] *CR* 4, 847: "I have been indulgent to the age of our Rhaeticus, in order that his inclination, which has been stirred up by a certain enthusiasm, so to speak, might move on to this part of philosophy with which he occupies himself. But at various times I have said to myself that I desire in him a little more of the Socratic philosophy, which he is likely to add when he is the father of a family." *(Indulsi aetati nostri Rhetici, ut ingenium quasi quodam Enthusiasmo incitatum ad hanc philosophiae partem, in qua versatur, proveheretur. Sed aliquoties ipsi dixi, me in eo plusculum socraticae philosophiae desiderare, quam fortassis adiunget cum erit paterfamilias.)*

[12] *CR* 4, 815. Cf. also the letters to Camerarius of November 1542 (*CR* 4, 896 and 898). From a letter to him dated May 25, 1550 (*CR* 7, 601), it is evident that at that time Melanchthon was still corresponding with Rhaeticus!

As to the princes from whom Melanchthon is alleged to have called for help against Copernicus, Duke Albrecht of Prussia, in identical letters to the University of Wittenberg and to the Elector of Saxony, asked that Rhaeticus be permitted, "for the accomplishment of his projected work, to go for a time, without a discontinuance of his salary as a lecturer, to the place where he had decided to have his book printed" *(das ehr sich zu volfurung solches seines vorhabenden werckes an die ort, da ehr sein Buch trucken zu lassen entschlossen, eine zeitlang ohn abbruch seiner besoldung der lectur begeben moge).*[13] That this concerned the printing of the work of Copernicus is clear from the fact that Rhaeticus had asked for the duke's letters of recommendation for this very purpose. One can scarcely go wrong if one connects the journeys of Rhaeticus to Nürnberg with a temporary leave in the sense of the duke's letter. It is certain that Copernicus himself was and remained a faithful son of the Roman Church. But no historian will cover up the facts that a Lutheran prince subsidized the publication of his work, that a Lutheran theologian arranged for the printing, and that a Lutheran mathematician supervised the printing – a Lutheran mathematician who was second to none in working for the introduction of the new world picture and did not forfeit the friendship of Melanchthon by doing so.

The new world picture is a product neither of the Roman nor of the Lutheran spirit. On the contrary, it is the triumph of an exact knowledge of nature – a knowledge that is free from all theological and ecclesiastical prejudices. To this extent one can regard it, at best, as a product of the German Renaissance. Yet it is not accidental that it was enthusiastically accepted first of all in Wittenberg and Nürnberg, and that it started its triumphal march from these cities. In the Rome of the time of the Renaissance the profane branches of knowledge had been temporarily emancipated from the supervision of the church. Post-Tridentine Catholicism thoroughly made up for what had been neglected. But at the central points of Lutheranism the emancipation was basic in character. The church, which derives its mission from the Gospel and knows that the proclamation of the Gospel exhausts this mission, has no interest in the various world pictures. Had Luther claimed authority in the field of the knowledge of nature similar to that claimed by the pope, this authority would probably have been recognized. There are examples to show where jurisdiction that has nothing to do with his theological mission was conceded to him – not always for the good of our church. His influence on a number of princes was great enough to make it appear then that a suppression of the Copernican teaching was possible in the

[13] Reprinted in Prowe I, 2, pp. 403 ff.

Lutheran territories. In reality Luther was far from doing this. The isolated derogatory remark he made about Copernicus has been completely overestimated in recent literature. A statement of this kind, made at table, is no authoritative *(ex cathedra)* decision. It was made in the year 1539, therefore before anything by Copernicus had been printed; and it did not become publicly known until Aurifaber's first edition of the *Table Talk* had appeared! This was in 1566.[14] Because of this statement Luther may be considered narrow-minded in matters pertaining to natural science — as narrow-minded as, let us say, a theological professor of today who, like numerous representatives of other branches of knowledge, also of the natural sciences, has not yet become acquainted with Einstein's theory of relativity. *But that his theological authority hampered the spread of the new world picture — this is a palpable falsification of history.*

The University of Wittenberg at the time of the Reformation deserves credit for having opened up an academic career for Rhaeticus, who was the first man to propagate the new astronomy, and for having preserved this career for him after he had turned to Copernicus. But the university did more than this. Melanchthon placed the greatest emphasis on the encouragement of mathematics. Since 1525 two lectureships were devoted to this subject. Rhaeticus lectured on lower mathematics.

[14] In Lauterbach's version, which is not revised, as Aurifaber's is, the remark reads as follows: "Mention was made of a certain new astrologer who proved that the earth moves, not the heaven, the sun, and the moon; and if anyone moves in a vehicle or a ship, he thinks that he is stationary and that the earth and the trees are moving. But now things happen this way: He who wants to be clever should not accept anything that others think; he must make something of his own, as that man does who wants to turn all astrology (also called astronomy) topsy-turvy. Nevertheless, I believe even those confused statements of Sacred Scripture; for Joshua commanded the sun to stand still, not the earth." *(De novo quodam astrologo fiebat mentio, qui probaret terram moveri et non coelum, solem et lunam, ac si quis in curru aut navi moveretur, putaret se quiescere et terram et arbores moveri. Aber es gehet jtzunder also: Wer do wil klug sein, der sol ihme nichts lassen gefallen, das andere achten, er mus ihme etwas eigenmachen, sicut ille facit, qui totam astrologiam [alias astronomiam] invertere vult. Etiam illa confusa tamen ego credo sacrae scripturae, nam Josua iussit solem stare non terram.)* (WA TR 4, 4638.)

How little emphasis one may place on this reference which Luther makes to the story of Joshua is evident from the fact that on another occasion he expressly acknowledged that the use of the Bible accommodates itself to appearances: "To this day philosophers debate where the earth stands. Scripture says that it was founded on the waters and speaks according to what the eyes see. For the earth is in the waters, so to speak, as Genesis states: 'Let the dry land appear,' which is what we see before our eyes." *(Philosophi adhuc hodie disputant, in quo subsistat terra. Scriptura dicit fundatam esse super aquas et loquitur secundum visionem oculorum. Terra enim quasi in aquis est, sicut in Genesi dicit: Appareat arida, id quod videmus ad oculum.)* (The first twenty-five psalms expounded at Coburg, 1530; on Ps. 24:2, WA 31 I, 370, 15.)

Astronomy came within the sphere of higher mathematics. For the filling of these positions only the best scientific fitness and the best aptitude for teaching were taken into consideration.[15] When in the year 1545 the professorship of lower mathematics had to be filled anew once more, the university, in its proposal to the elector with regard to an appointment, could point with pride to the fact that the universities of Tübingen, Leipzig, Greifswald, and Rostock had followed the example of Wittenberg with respect to the encouragement of mathematics.[16] Erasmus Reinhold, who lectured on higher mathematics and in whose company Luther observed the comet seen on January 13, 1538, also became an enthusiastic Copernican. In the foreword to his edition of Georg von Peurbach's theory of the planets Reinhold points to the revolutionary theory of Copernicus, "whose divine intellect all posterity will have good reason to admire" *(cuius divinum ingenium tota posteritas non immerito admirabitur).*[17] There is no trace of any obstacles in the way of his activity as a teacher in Wittenberg. In 1546 he, together with the entire university, left the city because of the Smalcald War. At the beginning of 1547 he returned with Melanchthon. In the summer of this year he is dean of the faculty of arts. From 1549 to 1550 he is rector of the university. In 1553 he leaves Wittenberg on account of the plague, and soon after this he dies in Saalfeld, his native city. When in the *Prutenic Tables (Tabulae Prutenicae),* which he publishes under the eyes of Melanchthon while he is a professor at Wittenberg, he continues not only to praise Copernicus as a learned man but also to give particular praise to Copernicus' book *On the Revolutions (De revolutionibus)* and thus makes known to the whole world that he himself has written a com-

[15] Cf., e. g., Melanchthon's deliberations after Rhaeticus' departure (*CR* 4, 847).

[16] Quoted in Walter Friedensburg, *Geschichte d. Univers. Wittenberg,* 1917, p. 231. — On the other hand, at this time the cultivation of mathematics at the young evangelical University of Marburg was in a miserable condition. Cf. H. Hermelink (and S. A. Kähler), *Die Philipps-Univers. zu Marburg,* 1927, p. 157.

[17] Quoted according to Prowe I, 2, p. 279. — Prowe's remark that Reinhold purposely refrained from mentioning Copernicus' name because this name was "not heard with pleasure" in Wittenberg is based on false notions concerning the state of the sciences at Wittenberg, which is the matter under discussion here. All those who knew about the new theory realized why Copernicus was called "the most distinguished master . . . from Prussia" *(praestantissimus artifex . . . ex Prussia).* Copernicus' main work, which made his name known to the whole world, is *announced* by Reinhold: "and now he is preparing to have the results of his labors published" *(et iam adornat editionem suorum laborum).* Furthermore, it is necessary to call attention to the fact that even when Luther and Melanchthon do not mention Copernicus' name in the statements that are held against them, their modern accusers are never in doubt as to who is meant!

mentary on this book,[18] this is proof that at the University of Wittenberg one could embrace the teachings of Copernicus without fear of ecclesiastical censorship. For the *Prutenic Tables (Tabulae Prutenicae)* Melanchthon procured for Reinhold the support of Duke Albrecht of Prussia *(CR* 5, 444), and after Reinhold's death he praised him with enthusiastic words both as a man of learning and as an evangelical Christian (10, 616).

It is easy to understand that even at the Lutheran universities the struggle for the new system was not settled at one sweep. What role Wittenberg played in this connection can probably be seen from the fact that Rud. Wolf, who wrote a history of astronomy, concludes that after Rhaeticus had become "bogged down" *(verrant)* in his trigonometrical research, one "actually had to regard Reinhold as the sole apostle" of the Copernican system. Lucas Valentin Otho – who studied there later, visited the aging Rhaeticus in Hungary, and completed the latter's trigonometrical tables – praises Wittenberg in his foreword to these tables because the study of mathematics was flourishing there and adds: "There were evidences of Ptolemy, likewise evidences of Copernicus" *(Erant in promptu Ptolemaica, erant etiam Copernica).*[19] If the teaching of Copernicus was fostered at the universities at all, this took place in the domain of Lutheranism. In Tübingen it was championed by Michael Maestlin, who formerly had been a pastor in Württemberg. He was the teacher of Kepler, who edited his *Prodrome (Prodromus)* and, in connection with this, reprinted the *First Account (Narratio prima)* of Rhaeticus and acknowledged his enthusiastic allegiance to Copernicus. "For 1577 to 1590" he also wrote an "astronomical almanac based wholly

[18] *Er. Reinhold Salveldensis, Prutenicae Tabulae coelestium Motuum,* Tübingen, 1551. In the preface, which contains views and expressions that are entirely Melanchthonian in character, we read: "The very learned man, whom we can mention as an Atlas or a second Ptolemy, Copernicus . . ." *(Vir doctissimus, quem ut Atlantem vel Ptolemaeum alterum nominare possumus, Copernicus . . .)* — "We are greatly indebted to the most eminent man Nicolaus Copernicus because he not only freely shared his observations . . . with studious men but also, by publishing his work on the revolutions, restored and recalled to light the teaching concerning the movements, which had almost collapsed. . . . But in fact I have set forth the causes and the method of each composition in our commentaries which I have written on Copernicus' work dealing with the revolutions." *(Magnam igitur gratiam debemus summo viro Nicolao Copernico, quod et observationes suas . . . studiosis liberaliter communicavit et collapsam pene motuum doctrinam restituit atque in lucem revocavit edito opere suo revolutionum. . . . Causas vero et rationem singularum compositionum exposui in commentariis nostris, quos scripsi in opus revolutionum Copernici.)*

[19] Quoted in Prowe II, 399. — Only *Valentinus Otto Magdeburgen.,* who is mentioned in *Alb. Ac. Vit.,* II, 16a (Halle, 1894) and matriculated in April 1561, could come into question.

on the Copernican system."[20] At the very time the new world picture had to pass through the gravest crisis as a result of the papal index of 1612 Wilhelm Schickard was teaching the Copernican system at Tübingen in addition to Maestlin, his fellow countryman; Ambrosius Rhodius was teaching it at Wittenberg; Origanus, the Silesian, was teaching it at Frankfurt an der Oder; Bernegger, the zealous Lutheran who came from Austria, and, somewhat later, Nikolaus Reimers, from Dithmarschen, were teaching it at Strassburg; and Peter Crüger, the Prussian, was teaching it at Danzig.[21] Here and there this was certainly embarrassing to their theological colleagues, who for a long time probably still understood no more about the astronomical bases of the Copernican system than Luther did. But if the Copernican teaching had been regarded as heresy in the Lutheranism of that time, the practice of the time guarantees that exactly the same measures would have been taken against it that were taken by Rome.

To be sure, there is a widespread notion that a Lutheran heresy trial of this nature was undertaken in the case of a great astronomer because he had embraced the Copernican system – in the case of Kepler. He had been brought up at the foundation in Tübingen and had studied theology. Then, like Maestlin, his teacher, he turned to mathematics and became a professor of mathematics at Graz.[22] Here, while the evan-

[20] *ADB* 20, 575; 22, 795; 45, 669. Therefore Maestlin did not, as J. Hartmann states in *Württemb. KG* (p. 401), "refrain for the love of peace from mentioning his conviction that the Copernican astronomical system was correct."

[21] Concerning those who are named here cf. the respective articles in *ADB*. — On the other hand, the distinguished astronomers from Catholic areas who lived at this time and adhered to the old system are Adriano Romano, in Louvain; Manuel de Figueiredo, in Lisbon; Andrea Argoli, in Padua. Scipione Chiaramonti, in Pisa, who bitterly attacks Tycho Brahe, Galileo, and Kepler, declares that it is a crime ever to go beyond Aristotle. Cf. Mädler I, 181, 211 f. Christoph Clavius († 1612), the erudite man who collaborated with Gregory XIII in the reform of the calendar, was an adherent of the Ptolemaic astronomical system. In addition, it is necessary to state that the aforementioned *Prutenic Tables* by Reinhold, the Wittenberg professor, had to serve as the basis of the great papal calendar reform. — Didacus a Stunica and the Carmelite Foscarini, who were Catholic adherents of Copernicus, were condemned together with Copernicus' work (Mirbt, op. cit.). Galileo's fate is known.

[22] Here the construction begins. Adolf Müller, S. J., writes in his biography of Copernicus: "It is known that Kepler, too, partly because of his adherence to the Copernican teaching, had to leave Württemberg and seek the protection of Catholic princes, and that in spite of fervent entreaties he never again got a position in his homeland." — Actually Kepler was *proposed* by the chancellor of the University of Tübingen for the professorship of mathematics at the provincial foundation school in Graz, and was "apparently" released with all honors. Later the same Adolf Müller, S. J., has to admit this in his monograph titled *Johann Kepler, der Gesetzgeber der neueren Astronomie*, Supplement 83 to *Stimmen aus Maria Laach*, 1903, p. 9.

gelicals are being persecuted and expelled, he resolutely professes his allegiance to the Augsburg Confession. At first he is tolerated by the Jesuits — presumably because they had no substitute from their own ranks — but then he has to leave Steiermark too. He comes to Prague, works for a short time with Tycho Brahe, the Danish Lutheran, and in 1601 succeeds Brahe as court astronomer of Emperor Rudolf II. After the emperor's death he goes to Linz, has to live from hand to mouth during the Thirty Years' War, and dies in 1630 while on his way to Regensburg. Repeatedly he tried to find a position in his native Württemberg. He was rejected because he could not make up his mind to subscribe to the Formula of Concord. As the reason for this — and as the only reason — he states in a letter to the theologian Matthias Hafenreffer, who had been his teacher in Tübingen, that he could not confess the omnipresence of the body of Christ.[23] The narrow-mindedness shown by the people of Tübingen and by those who managed the affairs of the church in Stuttgart when they refused for this reason to give a man of his rank a position is no credit to Lutheranism in Württemberg at his time. For, in the first place, the doctrine of the omnipresence was by no means a common possession of Lutheranism (cf. *The Doctrine of the Two Natures)*; and, in the second place, Kepler could rightly point out in the same letter that subscription to the Formula of Concord was usually not demanded of the laity. It was particularly reprehensible to deny ecclesiastical unimpeachability to this man, who had lost his position in Steiermark because of his profession of allegiance to the Augsburg Confession and, wherever he was, had always stayed with his church.[24]

[23] A letter written to Hafenreffer on April 11, 1619 (Kepler, *Opp. Omnia*, ed. by Chr. Frisch, Frankfurt am Main, 1858, VIII, 863): "In the matter of the Holy Supper I hope that you will hold nothing that you would not desire in me; in all the other articles I agree with the Augsburg Confession and the Formula of Concord; only in the article concerning the general presence of the body am I unable to condemn those who speak with the fathers cited above, and so far I myself use those phrases, if it is permitted to except this; I am ready to subscribe to [the Formula of] Concord as a layman and as one who confesses that here and there he is uncertain with respect to the construction and the pertinent words of a relation that is not clear" *(In negotio S. Coenae spero vos nihil habituros, quod in me desideretis; in articulis ceteris omnibus acquiesco Augustanae confessioni et Formulae Concordiae; in solo articulo de generali praesentia carnis non possum damnare illos, qui loquuntur cum phrasibus supra citatis, ipseque adeo illis phrasibus utor si hoc licet excipere, paratus sum subscribere Concordiae ut laicus et qui fateatur se hinc inde haesitare circa constructionem et relativa vocabula non liquidae relationis).*

[24] In a writing that unfortunately has been lost Kepler declared that he was in agreement with Luther's doctrine of predestination. On the Lutheran statement that "the finite is capable of containing the infinite" *(finitum infiniti capax)* he comments in the following words: "This whole Word, not one part, because it cannot be divided, is the whole quantum that is everywhere in His presence; not giving up the things by which He was present, He nevertheless let Himself down into the

But one dare not forget that Kepler also wrote very much about theological matters, and that once he had been employed in Tübingen, he could not have been forbidden to do this. Therefore if there was concern in this respect over the "pure doctrine" of the Swabian university, this is wholly in keeping with the theological approach of the entire age. On the other hand, it is wrong to say that Kepler was kept out because of his world picture, as is stated again and again. One can easily believe that this was distasteful to the theologians at Tübingen. They did not share this attitude. But for the very reason that Maestlin, his teacher, was publicly teaching the Copernican system it could not be a cause of his disqualification as a professor in Tübingen. Unlike Kepler, however, this man, you see, was regarded as orthodox even in theological matters.

That theology in Tübingen also wanted the freedom of the natural sciences preserved is shown by a repeatedly mentioned letter which Hafenreffer wrote on April 15, 1598. Here he asks Kepler in the friendliest words to confine himself to the interpretation of the external world but to let the Bible alone when doing this. Kepler's attempts to bring the astronomical findings into agreement with the statements of the Bible, he said, were unnecessarily disturbing the public.[25] Here Hafenreffer

womb of the virgin — as the Damascene [St. John of Damascus] teaches me to say, not Kepler — and in spite of this He did not make that womb be present everywhere" *(Hoc verbum totum, non pars una, quia non est partibile, totum quantum quantum est in sua ubique praesentia, non deserens ea, quibus erat praesens, sese tamen totum demisit in uterum Virginis [ut me non Keplerus sed Damascenus loqui docet] nec tamen illum uterum ubique praesentem fecit).* Hafenreffer wrote in the margin: "'You are getting to be silly with your mathematics' — obviously something happened here that is beyond my geometrical grasp, something that must be looked at with the eyes of faith, because for this work a finite womb was made capable of containing the infinite Word" *(Mathematice stultescis — accidit nempe hic aliquid ultra meum captum geometricum, quod fidei oculis intuendum est, quia finitus uterus factus est ad hoc opus infiniti verbi capax)* (*Opp.* VIII, 861).

[25] Since Hafenreffer's letter has been quoted with constantly decreasing accuracy and its meaning has thus been changed to the opposite — cf., e. g., B. O. Zöckler, *Theol. u. Naturwiss.* I, 537, and Ludw. Günther, *Kepler u. d. Theologie,* 1905, pp. 28 f. — the most important parts are given here *(Opp.* I, 37 f.): "Therefore if there is any place here for my brotherly advice, as I firmly hope, henceforth in demonstrating hypotheses of this kind you should busy yourself with mathematics pure and simple, without being concerned about whether they [the hypotheses] agree in this way with created things or otherwise. For I think that mathematics has attained its end if it presents hypotheses with which phenomena agree as exactly as possible. And I think that you yourself will yield to him who would be able to produce better ones. . . . But if — and may the very great and very good God avert this — you wanted publicly to reconcile these hypotheses with Sacred Scripture and to defend them, I certainly fear that this matter will end in dissensions and imprisonment, in which case I would wish that I had never seen these deliberations of yours, which in themselves are mathematically excellent and noble. For

unreservedly acknowledges the autonomy of research in the field of the natural sciences. In his own *Loci theologici* (1600), on the basis of which entire generations of the Württembergian and the Swedish clergy were schooled in dogmatics, he, on his part, kept within the required limits. In contrast with the dogmaticians since Calov, but in agreement with the theologians of contemporaneous Lutheranism, he refrains in this work from any discussion of the world picture as presented by the natural sciences. In a letter to Maestlin, dated June 11, 1598, Kepler even surmises that Hafenreffer himself is inclined toward the Copernican teaching – "that he is a man not hostile to Copernicus" *(non esse alienum a Copernico hominem) (Opp.* I, 38). Kepler himself, of course, was far too greatly interested theologically to be able to observe these limits. It is true that he declared his readiness to do so; but then, in spite of this, he made highly detailed attempts to bring the well-known passages of the Bible, especially the account of Joshua, into harmony with Copernicus by way of exegesis.[26]

Today no reasonable person will blame Kepler for this. But one must admit that here, on the threshold of the seventeenth century, it was the astronomer, not the theologian, who did not want to observe the limits which Hafenreffer correctly defined in the sense of the impact of the Gospel *(evangelischer Ansatz).* From this impact no point can be found at which evangelical faith would have to have a necessary relationship to Ptolemy or to Copernicus. On the contrary, the theological intolerance of the seventeenth century vis-à-vis the astronomers runs exactly parallel to the advance of an unevangelical Biblicism. The first anti-Copernican monograph in the field of Lutheranism that Adolf Müller, S. J., can mention was written by Peter Bartholinus (1632), the Danish theologian and mathematician. Since he adheres wholly to the school of Abraham Calov, it is not surprising that, in consideration of the Bible, he, too, rejects the movement of the earth. Conversely, Leonhard Hutter wanted nothing to do with the sphere theory of the

there has long since been more contention in the church of the Lord than is expedient for those who are weak." *(Proinde si fraterno meo consilio, uti firmiter spero, locus aliquis est, porro in ejusmodi demonstrandis hypothesibus nudum mathematicum agas, nihil sollicitus, utrum rebus creatis ita respondeant an secus. Mathematicum enim finem suum consequutum arbitror, si tales exhibeat hypotheses, quibus* φαινόμενα *quam exactissime respondeant; et te ipsum puto cessurum esse illi, qui proferre posset meliores. . . . Sin, quod maximus et optimus avertat Deus, publice istas hypotheses cum Scriptura s. conciliare velles et propugnare, certum metuo, ut in dissensiones et nervum res isthaec erumpat: quo casu velim ego, me istas cogitationes tuas, in se quidem et mathematice praeclaras et nobiles, nunquam vidisse. Jam dudum enim in ecclesia Domini plus contentionis est, quam infirmis expediat.)*

[26] Especially in the introduction to *Astronomia nova, Opp.* III, 146—157. Cf. Günther, op. cit., p. 31.

Ptolemaic world picture. He had similar reasons. This theory, he said, cannot be proved on the basis of the Bible. Therefore the anti-Copernicans are by no means in sympathy with the Ptolemaic world picture either.

Nevertheless, here the Bible, which Luther read as Law and Gospel, had become a canon in the field of the natural sciences. But this defection from the impact of the Gospel *(evangelischer Ansatz)* came too late to cast doubt on the great success the German Reformation achieved for the liberation of the natural sciences. Ever since Luther destroyed the Reformed fantasies concerning a delimited dwelling place of Christ above the "empyrean and starry sky" *(coelum empyraeum atque stellatum)*, there was no longer an interest of faith that could still have justified a critical attitude of the church toward exact research. Basically there certainly was no longer need of such liberation in the area of the Renaissance. But there a break with the Christian belief in God ensued simultaneously with the destruction of the scholastic world picture. Men like Tycho Brahe and Kepler, however, believed evangelically, and as investigators of our solar system and its laws they nevertheless contributed to the new knowledge of the world. And it was precisely in the history of astronomy that Maestlin as well as Kepler found a place of honor, just as Johann Fabricius († 1587) and Samuel Dörffel († 1688), who was pastor in Plauen im Vogtland, did. Fabricius was the first to observe the sunspots and the rotation of the sun; Dörffel was the first to prove the parabolic orbit of comets. Here it was not Jacob Heerbrand, with his sermon "on the comet and the peacock's tail" *(vom Kometen und Pfauenschwantz)*, who was Luther's true successor. No, it was Dörffel, this cool calculator of comets. For on one occasion, when considering the comet of 1538, Luther had declared — very pointedly in opposition to Melanchthon: "I do not want to tell Germany's fortune on the basis of the stars, but on the basis of theology I announce to Germany the wrath of God" *(Ich wil Germaniae nicht ex astris war sagen, sed ego illi iram Dei ex theologia annuntio)* *(Tischreden* 3, 3711). We shall let the Roman Church have the great Copernicus, and we shall acknowledge that after struggling for centuries it has accommodated itself to the new world picture. But there are documents to prove that up to the present time the Roman Church has preserved for itself a right to supervise even the natural sciences.

31. God and the World

The world pictures of Ptolemy and Copernicus have two things in common. Both are seen from the viewpoint of accurate observers and calculators. For this reason faith either has no relationship at all to them, or it has the same relationship to both — no relationship at all if it wanted to feel that it is supported or threatened by the one or the other; the same relationship, because those world pictures do not break down the agnostic determinism which, as the direct opposite, is the immanent supposition of faith. The struggle for those world pictures was fought out long ago. But the independence of faith also has validity over against every other world picture. Copernicus and even Kepler still believed that the planetary system is bounded by a sphere of fixed stars. Beyond this there remained for them, too, a final place of refuge for spatial conceptions of heaven. Aristotle, too, believed that heaven — that which is nearest to the "prime mover" (πρῶτον κινοῦν) — lay beyond this sphere. Historians of philosophy give Giordano Bruno credit for being the first to regard the infinity of space as immensurableness of the world and thus to banish heaven from space. We know that long before his time the doctrine of Holy Communion led Luther to the same conclusion.

But in any case the struggle that had to do with the movement of the earth — the struggle that seems naive to us today — had far-reaching results for man's impression of the world. For an unsophisticated person the earth is that which is absolutely stable — that which gives a feeling of security to everything belonging to it and clinging to it. As soon as the realization of the unceasing movement of this stable anchorage of natural life flashes up, everything that is spatial descends a few steps. It loses security. It loses dignity. A new impression of time emerges. Movement is time. Indeed, up to this point the stars also rotate to convey to men definite measures of time. Melanchthon still regards this as the purpose of the movement of the planets (*CR* 5, 818). Yet these measures of time are computed by relating the rotating stars to the absolutely stable tellurian place. Time, too, still contains this fixity.[1] Time serves that which is spatial. When the earth enters into the movement, time begins to become pure relation. For Copernicus and Kepler the sun was still stable. And for two centuries the "fixed stars" were still stable. Today our Milky Way system is only one of the nebulae that are all "nascent" — and are all subject to the second thermodynamic axiom: They constantly

[1] Nik. Selnecker, *Propositiones et Quaestiones in octo libros Physicorum Aristotelis*, Basle, 1560, p. 139: "Is the movement of heaven time, as some interpret this definition? It is not; but when time is said to be the number of the first movement, it is understood to be space, which is measured by the movement itself of heaven and the sun." *(Estne coeli motus tempus, sicut aliqui definitionem hanc interpretantur? Non est: sed quando dicitur tempus esse numerum primi motus, intelligitur esse spacium, quod mensuratur ipso motu coeli et solis.)* In his *Christliche Betrachtungen des gläntzenden Himmels* (Nürnberg, 1657) Joh. Mich. Dilherr, of Nürnberg, refers to Aristotle's definition, which is meant here. In this connection movement is thought of as relation to the stable earth (pp. 314 ff.).

give off warmth to ice-cold space. This means that their nascence is a cooling. Physics and astronomy are vying with each other in an attempt to find an exception at a single point or at least to ferret out a development in the opposite direction. In vain. This is the ultimate victory of the impression of time over space. That which is spatial submits to the fact that time cannot be turned back. For the present we shall postpone the relating of this change to faith in God.

But the realization of the movement of the earth had a further result. It was the beginning of the end of the magical philosophy of life. In contradistinction to the "modern" philosophy of life, this philosophy of life always thinks in terms of the whole. The accurate scholar of today regards it as his task to trace every occurrence in nature back to its nearest single cause. In this matter he has become the teacher of "modern man." Here, too, of course, a whole beckons as the final goal: the derivation of all individual occurrences, of all types of forces, of what is mechanical, of what is chemical, of what is biological, from a final all-controlling power *(Dynamis)*, perhaps from a very simple law of motion. If one emphasizes the concept of force, we are confronted with a new myth. In one way or another the new man exerts himself to overcome complete absorption in details. What we seek in this way comes first and is self-evident for the magical man. Every occurrence in nature is a happening in the whole contexture of the world. Agrippa von Nettesheim illustrated this with a string which begins to vibrate when it is touched at any place in its whole extent. Here, too, of course, there are various forces. But no force is isolated. If one power is actualized, the related powers sound in sympathy — actively or passively. The susceptibility common to them is sympathetic action. Astrology and alchemy as well as the practical medicine of that time are based on this fundamental view. To be sure, much genuine "superstition" is also based on it. But that astrology and alchemy themselves had their origin in superstition — this is a prejudice that fails to do justice to the grandeur of the magical philosophy of life.

Although this philosophy of life does not necessarily presuppose that the earth is a stable place, it does take for granted that the astronomical system is a whole per se. This is especially evident in astrology. But this became a thing of the past at the moment the sphere of fixed stars lost the significance of a boundary line after the other spheres had lost this significance. The vibrations that start from tellurian or planetary happenings no longer reverberate on the "firmament." They go farther into infinity. They do not return. Even the proportions have shifted. The earth is no longer the sounding board for all the mysterious sounds in the world of the stars. It itself is merely a speck of dust in the universe – a speck of dust that can gather up no more than a vanishing fraction of all the astral effects. Only in Paracelsus' conception of man as a microcosm does a part of the magical philosophy of life continue to live at the present time.[2]

Not until the seventeenth century does the struggle of the two aspects of the world reach its peak. One can observe it within early Lutheranism exactly as one can observe it throughout the Occident. Melanchthon was not the only friend astrology had. The Copernicans Rhaeticus, Reinhold, Maestlin, and even Tycho Brahe and Kepler cast horoscopes.[3] The Paracelsian relationship between the elements and man's temperaments *(Komplexionen)* continues to play an important role in the writings of Jacob Böhme. And in one of his sermons Christian Scriver uses an illustration that makes the magical sympathetic action even clearer than Melanchthon's does: If one places two identically tuned violins on a table and touches one string of one of them, the corresponding string of the other violin sounds in sympathy even though it has not been directly touched. It would be completely wrong, however, to ascribe greater enlightenment to Luther because he would have none of this. He had acquired his distaste for astrology in the medieval church, and his *Table Talk* shows how self-evident the belief of the medieval church in demons was to him. In comparison with this even Melanchthon's astrology strikes one as being an emancipation. It is very closely allied to the humanizing and secularizing of worldly knowledge. His principle that definite "forces" of the stars influence earthly affairs is capable of a development that is by no means incompatible with modern knowledge of nature. For example, his assumption that the comet of 1538 caused the great drought of that year is not altogether dissimilar to the present-

[2] On the idea of the microcosm in dogmatics cf., e. g., J. Heerbrand, *Compendium,* 1575, p. 3 (1585, p. 32).

[3] A good insight into astrology in the sixteenth century and in the seventeenth is afforded by Friedr. Braun in *Christoph Schorer von Memmingen (Einzelarbeiten a. d. KG. Bayerns,* Vol. 3), 1926, pp. 33—118. — Unfortunately, Braun, too, appropriated the commonly held opinion concerning the church's attack on Copernicus — the opinion which, in any case, is incorrect so far as Lutheranism is concerned. The only evidence he adduces is a doubt expressed by Bernegger regarding the tolerance of the theologians of the year 1634. Therefore this evidence stems from the beginning of the Biblicistic reaction (Braun, p. 97, note 4). Braun's opinion — "that the astrological belief grew up in the soil of ancient polytheism, not in the monotheistic soil of Christianity" — has validity only for relationships that no longer have any significance in the age of the Reformation. Astrology was transmitted to the Christian Middle Ages by the Arabs. They were rigidly monotheistic or pantheistic, but they were by no means polytheistic. — On E. Reinhold as a caster of horoscopes cf. E. Kroker, *Nativitäten und Konstellationen aus der Reformationszeit, Schr. d. Ver. f. d. Gesch. Leipzigs,* 1900, VI, 1 ff.

day attempt to connect droughts with the increase in the number of sunspots.[4] Johann Michael Dilherr finds that for astrologers and astronomers to consult the stars when inquiring about the temperament of man is no more "against God" than for physicians to look for this in the human body. This is entirely correct, for in any case the exploration of nature by astronomers as well as by physicians has no direct relationship to God. In one way or another earthly facts or occurrences are put into world-immanent relationships. And if here the work of magical astrology and magical medicine makes demons and witches superfluous and does not attribute changelings and monsters to an incubus or a succubus but to the sport of natural forces, no matter whether those forces are said to be of an astral or a sublunary kind, Melanchthon, the astrologer, is closer to the present-day knowledge of nature, which thinks in a purely immanent way, than Luther, who was opposed to astrology. But by letting his friend have his way Luther, too, has a part in this work of emancipation. Since the magical philosophy of life leads to a limitation of the knowledge of nature to the immanent relationships of the world, it confines itself to grasping the world picture. But in doing so it contributes to its own destruction. For the increasing elimination of extra-worldly "forces" demands proof of an inner-worldly substitute. Furthermore, this has to end in the methodical tracing of individual relationships. Thus it becomes the beginning of the scientific method of modern times.

To be sure, a long distance had to be traversed before this point was reached. But one cannot mistake the fact that Melanchthon is already embarking on this course. What cast suspicion on astrology and related arts of the medieval church was their claim to be able to predict the future. This claim appeared to be an interference in God's government of the world or at any rate a lack of submission to His power over destiny. For the attempt to calculate the future in advance on the basis of inner-worldly facts seemed to proceed from the assumption that God Himself is bound to the forces that are active in nature. First of all, therefore, Melanchthon distinguishes the mere observation of the stars and their laws sharply from conclusions with respect to the future. It is impossible for the observation of the stars and their laws to be in contradiction to the will of God. On the contrary, it serves purposes that the Creator

[4] *CR* 3, 505: "The comet brought about the drought of this time" *(Siccitatem huius temporis cometa peperit)*. Nor does it make any basic difference when Melanchthon adds: "But there is another cause, one that is less important, which nevertheless will again cause droughts in the summertime: the conjunction of Saturn and Mars" *(Sed accedit causa alia levior, quae tamen aestate siccitates rursus faciet: Coniunctio Saturni et Martis)*.

Himself has fixed for mankind. Yes, it confirms for us the fact that nature did not come into being by accident but was created "by some eternal architectural mind" *(ab aliqua aeterna mente architectatrice)* (*CR* 5, 818 f.). But in the "divining doctrine concerning the stars" *(doctrina de astris divinatrix)* there is another important difference. "Some predictions are physical, some are without natural causes" *(aliae praedictiones sunt physicae, aliae sine causis naturalibus).* It is the second kind that is forbidden in the divine Law. These "predictions" *(praedictiones),* which Melanchthon, like Ptolemy, calls "anaitiological" (ἀναιτιολόγητοι, that is, not having a natural cause), "such as auguries, oracular responses, and many magical or diabolical arts, as of those who are called soothsaying demons, that is, spirits, who dwell in frenzied persons and utter prophesies when they are questioned" *(ut auguria, sortes, sunt et multae magicae seu diabolicae, ut eorum, qui vocantur* πυθῶνες, *id est, spiritus, qui in fanaticis habitant et interrogati vaticinantur)* (13, 337). This kind of soothsaying, says Melanchthon, must be condemned. For, as he states, it seeks to eliminate the relationships in which God's own activity in nature takes place. On the other hand, precisely these natural relationships underlie the "physical predictions" *(praedictiones physicae).* The physician who reaches a conclusion concerning the condition of the heart on the basis of the pulse and prognosticates in accordance with this conclusion, says Melanchthon, proceeds from the assumption that God's arrangement is valid.[5] Nothing else is done by the astrologer who forecasts the weather on the basis of his observation of the sky and, because of the stable influence of the stars on the earthly elements and the play of their humors and forces, also predicts the future of man. This, says Melanchthon, is always a matter of the knowledge of the arrangements and the relationships that God Himself brought into being.

These comments of Melanchthon make two things clear. In the first place, here a purely scientific prognosis is peeled away from the previous connection with magical soothsaying. This is the beginning of the diagnostics of the modern physician and of the meteorology of today. In the second place, however, here the knowledge of nature comes between God and the person who seeks counsel and help. But this should not lead one to forget God. Nature's arrangement, you see, is God's arrangement. From it man can still derive the teleological argument for the existence of God. But he does not need this. The power on which, as he knows, his immediate future, his health, and his crops depend is no longer surrounded by the secrets of supramundane arbitrariness. It be-

[5] There are other reasons for Melanchthon's polemics against the "empiric physicians" *(empiricos medicos)* (*CR* 11, 202 ff.). I cannot go into these reasons here.

comes controllable. Instead of interpreting the future on the basis of a sign, one now has a rule on which to base a conclusion with respect to a special case in the future. But the rule also enables one to make preparations. Finally the natural science that is applied stands alongside accurate observation — the science which, by controlling nature, passes on to man most of what he formerly thought he had to pray for: lengthening life and preventing plagues by means of the improvement of hygiene, increasing the harvest yield by means of artificially produced nitrogen, averting "water and fire hazards" by means of dams and "up-to-date fire-fighting equipment." In this connection one can speak of a new philosophy of life only if the idea of an arrangement based on natural law lifts beyond individual experiences and brings the vital consciousness of the individual into an inner relationship to the view of the cosmic whole — or if the observed changes from one kind of energy into the other lead to belief in a world dynamic that shapes the universe. The former is the philosophy of life of Kant, Herbart, Feuerbach, and the positivists; the latter leads from Leibniz to Herder, Schelling, and Goethe.

The basis of Luther's belief in God lies beyond a philosophy of life of this or that kind. One could say that to this extent it has no closer relationship to the various philosophies of life than it has to the Ptolemaic or the Copernican world picture. But this, of course, is only conditional; or it is altogether wrong. Luther's belief in God is not without a philosophy of life either. First of all, it is the opposite of every form of pluralism. It presupposes the unity of life and the interlacement of life in the world as a whole. In this respect it is unconditionally related to the modern philosophy of life. But here the contrast with Kant's dualism also becomes immediately apparent. In Kant's view nature as a whole and the ethical world are separate. It was understandable when the neo-Kantian interpretation of Luther identified the hereafter of the Lutheran belief in God with the hereafter of the Kantian moral law. Nevertheless, this was an error. It is true that Luther, like Kant, is aware of man's claim to autonomy. But he lets this claim be thwarted. And not by the obstructions with which the natural relationship confronts it — this is the doctrine of anti-Kantian materialism. No, according to Luther, autonomy is thwarted by the realization that life and the world are a whole. This wholeness embraces nature and ethos, because it is precisely when we relate the two to each other that we encounter God, and because it is only the hereafter that enables us to recognize God's world, life, and ethos as a unity and a whole. Ethical autonomy may be successful in individual cases — ethical life as a whole is subject to the judgment of God. There may be a self-assertion of man over against nature, but not over against God, whose power is just as "valid" over against what is ethical as it is over against the laws of nature (cf. *Justification and Philosophy of Life*).

All this has been stated from the standpoint of agnostic determinism, which is the immanent supposition of Luther's doctrine of justification. We have established the fact that agnosticism is done away with in the faith God asks for and that determinism is abolished in the forgiveness of sins (cf. *Justification and Philosophy of Life*). But in this connection one must understand determinism to mean the destiny-controlled unfulfillability of what is ethical. For Luther says that this unfulfillability has been decreed against us by destiny, and this very fact is the essence of the determinism he professes before the "hidden God" *(Deus absconditus).* In addition, however, what is ethical is so deeply imbedded in our life that God's sovereignty in no case confines itself to what is ethical. On the contrary, it controls the whole, therefore the whole of the natural relationships. But then the question arises what relationship between God and nature as a whole there is for faith if determinism as well as agnosticism is to be overcome in faith.

It is self-evident that even for faith God is and remains in possession of the power over destiny. Kant mocks: "To guide to their advantage the invisible power that controls the destiny of men is a purpose they all have." [6] If this is meant to apply to a desire to meddle in God's power over destiny, Luther, of course, would have expressed himself against it with equal vehemence. He who believes, however, not only has no desire to meddle but also does not need to do so. For he is certain that the "invisible power that rules over destiny" guides everything to our advantage. Here faith again sees "everything," that is, the sum total of all separate parts, as a whole that is led through death to life. In this sense justifying faith is also faith in destiny. And this leads at the same time to its distinction from determinism. Fate, about which especially Melanchthon and his disciples speak, is not equated with predestination; it is equated with divine providence.[7] Predestination per se – when Lutheranism does not restrict it to election – is a purely deterministic concept. It deduces man's destiny from God as the first cause – the cause that continues to be operative up to the present time through the agency of a long and never-interrupted chain of causes. Nor is this deistic view of the relationship between God and the world overcome by the idea of God's omnipotence – not even when God's freedom is maintained

[6] *Religion innerh. d. Grenzen d. blossen Vern.*, Reclam edition, 191.

[7] In accordance with Augustine, e. g., in Joh. Gerhard, *Loci* IV, 135 f. — Dannhauer, *Theol. Cas.*, ed. by Fr. Mayer, 1706, p. 294.

in this connection. According to this view, God could make use of His freedom only when He fixed the first cause. For if this first cause predestines the course of the world and the destiny of man with finality, God's omnipotence must exhaust itself supervising the chain of causes. The belief in providence that follows from this is fatalism. Melanchthon calls it stoical; the later dogmaticians call it Turkish. Both Melanchthon and the later dogmaticians are right.[8] Here it is easy to think of kinship to the magical philosophy of life. Among the Arabian advocates one must assume a fatalistic consciousness of life. When discussing physics Melanchthon separates stoical fate from Aristotelian fate. The former is "the connection of the first cause with secondary natural and voluntary causes" *(connexio primae causae cum secundis naturalibus et voluntariis);* the latter is "the order of natural causes. For Aristotle, therefore, fate and nature mean the same thing" *(ordo causarum naturalium. Idem igitur Aristoteli significant fatum et natura)* (*CR* 13, 329 f.). Aristotelian nature is the sum total of the "secondary causes" *(causae secundae).* In this way Melanchthon seeks, on the one hand, to gain ground for the concept of contingency and, in his synergistic era, indirectly for human freedom.[9] But when he carries out the same distinction with respect to the freedom of God, he is influenced in dogmatics, of course, first of all by the related idea that God dare not be made the originator of sin — which would be inevitable for the stoical-deistic view (21, 650). In physics, however, he leaves no doubt that the distinction is necessary because God's freedom is not exhausted when the "first cause" *(prima causa)* is fixed. No, it is proved by the free management of the "secondary causes" *(causae secundae)* within the course of the world (13, 329). Even as strict an astronomical and astrological calculator as Tycho Brahe, who stands on the boundary line between the magical and the modern philosophy of life, maintains the freedom of God in the same sense.[10]

This is completely in accord with Luther's conviction. Concerning his relationship to the idea of predestination everything that is necessary has already been said. It is true that in his writing against Erasmus he

[8] Cf. the contrasting of the Turkish and Christian belief in providence in J. Fr. Buddeus, *Concordia religionis christ. statusque civilis,* Halle, 1712, pp. 115 ff. — Similarly Leibniz in his *Essai de Théodicée,* 1710.

[9] *CR* 21, 372: "But liberty is . . . the source of contingency in human actions" *(Est autem libertas . . . fons contingentiae in actionibus humanis).* Cf. p. 647. — Cf. Selnecker, op. cit., pp. 90 ff.

[10] *De nova stella* (*Denuo ed. Reg. Soc. Scient. Dan., Hauniae* 1901), *Blatt* A 3 c: "For the divine majesty acted with the greatest freedom. Nor was it hampered by any bonds of nature; but when it wishes, it stops the water for the rivers and turns back the stars." *(Divina enim maiestas liberrime egit, nec ullis obstricta est Naturae vinculis, sed cum vult, sistit aquam fluviis et vertit sidera retro.)*

rejects the differentiation among the various kinds of "necessity" *(necessitas)* that Melanchthon took over from scholasticism; but that he, too, does not consider God's freedom exhausted in the predisposition that takes place when the "first cause" *(prima causa)* is fixed follows from the very concept of the "hidden God" *(Deus absconditus).* If the divine will were fixed in the causal relationship between the world and the first disclosure of the "hidden God," it would be basically possible to figure out from this causal relationship what the divine will is. But God's "concealment" *(Verborgenheit)* proves that this is impossible. Therefore where Luther sings high praise to the divine freedom, he cites the statement of the psalmist: "It [the Divine Majesty] can do and does everything it wants to do in heaven and on earth" *(Ea [divina majestas] potest et facit omnia quae vult in coelo et in terra)* (WA 18, 636, 29). Luther does not want to call God's omnipotence the power which does not do much that it can do; he calls it "that active power by which He does everything mightily in all things" *(sed actualem illam, qua potenter omnia facit in omnibus)* (718, 28). From this it follows, in the first place, that God has a direct relationship even to the "secondary causes" *(causae secundae),* that is, to the world as a combination of everything that constitutes nature *(Naturzusammenhang)* and, in the second place, that in this He is free, therefore retains His identity as a Person and for this reason cannot be equated with the impersonal law of nature. In his writings on Holy Communion Luther spoke frequently about the relationship between God and the world. It is understandable that when he did so the concept of presence, that is, the space relationship, has the most conspicuous place. God *is* in the things, Luther can say here (WA 19, 492, 6); He is in every creature (WA 23, 135, 3); He is "completely" *(repletive)* present (WA 26, 329, 27). But not for a moment does he let there be doubt that this is not a matter of a passive existence *(ein ruhendes Sein).* The cue that leads to all these discussions is the Biblical metaphor "the right hand of God." Luther contends vehemently against interpreting "the right hand of God" as a place. On the contrary, God's "right hand" is "God's omnipotent power, which at one and the same time can be nowhere and yet must be everywhere. It cannot be at any one place, I say. For if it were at a particular place, one could take hold of it there, and it would be confined there. . . . But the divine power cannot be confined and restricted in this manner. For it is intangible, immeasurable, outside and above everything that is and can be. Conversely, it must be essentially present at all places, even in the smallest leaf of a tree. This is the reason: It is God who creates, does, and preserves all things through His omnipotent power and right hand, as our

Creed confesses. For He does not send out officials or angels when He creates or preserves something; all this is the work of His divine power itself. But if He is to create and preserve it, He must be there and must make and preserve His creature in all its innermost parts as well as in all its outermost parts. Therefore He Himself must, of course, be present in every creature in its innermost and outermost parts, on all sides, through and through, above and below, in front and behind, so that nothing can be present in all creatures and inside them to a greater extent than God Himself with His power." (WA 23, 133, 21 ff.)[11] In these statements three things are worthy of note: (1) the strong emphasis on God's immanence in the creatures; (2) the thoroughly dynamic wording of the statements; (3) the dialectical wording. God is present in the creature; and He is present in such a way that He creates, works, and preserves. He is *outside* the creature because, or to the extent that, it is only a creature; He is *in* it because it is God's creature.

At the same time this is the origin of the Lutheran statement that "the finite is capable of containing the infinite" *(Finitum infiniti capax).* In the later controversy concerning Holy Communion, as is easily understood, the interest continued for the most part to be confined to the question of space. Where God's presence is dealt with only as a question of space, the magical philosophy of life is speaking to us. In the preface to his book *On the New Star (De nova stella)* Tycho Brahe makes statements about God's presence — also about the "inscrutability" *(imperscrutabile)* of God and the revelation of God in Christ — that have a direct resemblance to statements made by Luther. The incorporeal, infinite, eternal, incomprehensible God is "everywhere and nowhere" *(ubique et nullibi).* God does not need the corporeal, finite, temporal, comprehensible, and spatial form of the world. But the dynamic of the divine immanence is missing. Brahe stands midway between the Ptolemaic and the Copernican world picture. Like Copernicus, he believes that the planets rotate about the sun, but that the planets, together with the sun, rotate about the earth. He cannot tear himself away from the ancient idea of the absolute steadiness of the earth. Even in this connection he calls the earth the "center of the whole universe" *(centrum totius Universitatis).* God placed man on this center "in order that from there, as from a watchtower, he may contemplate the nature and the arrangement of the universe" *(ut inde quasi ex specula universi orbis Naturam et constitutionem contemplaretur).* Here he should "constantly be engaged in the delightful consideration of the divine works that shine forth everywhere in the structure of the world" *(perpetuo in iucunda operum divi-*

[11] Cf. WA 23, 143, 10 ff.; WA 26, 339, 25 ff.

norum, quae in Mundi fabrica undique elucent, consideratione versari). The creatures he looks at are "monuments of the divine work" *(monumenta divini operis)* and should honor God as their "Maker" *(opifex).* These statements certainly do not contain anything that Luther, too, could not have written. But something is missing. Here the "everywhere and the nowhere" *(ubique et nullibi)* of God is perceived in a purely spatial manner. As in the writings of Luther, God's immanence is expressed dialectically. But the energizing factor is missing.

It is significant that this final and essential element of Luther's conception of God and the world also asserted itself where his doctrine of Holy Communion and his Christology were taken seriously. In the school of Melanchthon, Nicolaus Selnecker, for example, distinguished four stages of God's presence. Here the fourth stage, as the singular presence in the Logos, can be eliminated. The first is the "presence of preservation, by which God is present in all creatures in such a way that He preserves them as long as He wants to preserve them. . . . Here and everywhere God is present essentially, immediately, and powerfully." *(praesentia conservationis, qua Deus omnibus creaturis adest, ita ut conservet eas tantisper donec vult eas conservare. . . . Enter, praesenter Deus hic et ubique, potenter.)* The second is the presence in the angels and in man in eternal life. By virtue of the third "He is present in this life in those who are reborn, by which [stage] . . . He not only preserves their life but also brings about in them emotions that are pleasing to Him" *(adest in hac vita renatis, quo [gradu] . . . non tantum vitam eorum conservat, sed etiam efficit in eis motus sibi placentes).*[12] Thus here the dynamic element appears for the first time in the psychology of those who are reborn. The *Decisio Saxonica* of 1624 has a totally different view. It distinguishes the "universal presence of God" *(praesentia Dei universalis),* which, as it states, is identical with "preservation and governing" *(conservatio et gubernatio)* or "providence" *(providentia);* the "gracious presence among Christians" *(praesentia gratiosa apud Christianos),* which consists in the whole work of salvation *(Heilswerk)* among men; and the "glorious presence among those who are saved" *(praesentia gloriosa apud beatos).* But in no case – so the *Decisio Saxonica* declares – can one speak of a "bare presence" *(nuda adessentia).* God's presence, it says, is always "operative" *(operosa).* And this view – it is Luther's view – asserted itself.[13] One can judge what this means by considering

[12] *Ex. Ordin.* I, 220. Similarly *Institut.* III, 247.

[13] Cf., e. g., Calov, *Syst.* II, 612: "The omnipresence of God is a relative attribute by the power of which God is present for all creatures not only with the nearness of His being but also with His power to produce intended results and His working" *(Omnipraesentia Dei est attributum respectivum, vi cuius Deus non tantum substantiae propinquitate, sed etiam efficacia ac operatione adest creaturis omnibus).*

how much easier it would have been for the dogmaticians if, when defining God's relationship to what is evil or when stating what human freedom is, they had distinguished here between "bare" *(nuda)* and "operative presence" *(operosa adessentia)*. Conversely, however, here one also sees the continuing power of Luther's knowledge. At the same time is becomes clear here that so far as the philosophy of life is concerned, early Lutheranism concerns itself at least potentially with God's presence.

Meanwhile, however, the problems of what is evil and of human freedom made it necessary to differentiate the operative presence of God. This the dogmaticians did in the doctrine of divine providence. Now it has become clear to what extent this doctrine, on principle, views God's sovereignty over the world differently from the way this sovereignty must be viewed in accordance with the strict doctrine of predestination. The dogmaticians put providence and the operative presence of God together. Providence results from the realization of God's living nearness. The doctrine of predestination moves God far away. In relation to the creatures divine providence is "preservation" *(conservatio)* and "governing" *(gubernatio)*. In the discussions of "preservation" *(conservatio)* the dynamic element of the philosophy of life again becomes evident: it is "creation" *(creatio)* or "continuous production" *(productio continuata)*. Nature is never a machine that runs idle – a machine that was put in operation in one way or another. Nature exists only because God – understood in Luther's sense – is in nature. But God is in nature as the Creator, as "One who is full of activity everywhere" *(semper ubique actuosus)*. And here there is no exception among the creatures. Even the devil, even the wicked, would crumble into nothingness at once if the Creator were to withdraw His activity in them (WA 18, 753, 14 ff.). Nevertheless, a difference must prevail here. The devil, the wicked, and every human being who sins must have relative independence. We have already met with this thought. Both Luther and Melanchthon recognize man's freedom "in minor matters" *(in inferioribus)* (cf. *The Primal Experience* and *Justification and Philosophy of Life*). The dogmaticians attempt to make allowance for this idea by differentiating "God's governing" *(gubernatio Dei)* as "permitting" *(permissio)*, "hindering" *(impeditio)*, "directing" *(directio)*, and "determining" *(determinatio)*. It is clear that here one becomes lost again in the narrowing down that is characteristic of scholasticism – the narrowing down that mortally endangers the basic conception of the Lutheran philosophy of life.

It is self-evident that Luther, too, had become aware of the problem posed by the necessity to differentiate when discussing the activity of

God. But he was aware of this in a manner that was elemental. Consequently, his awareness was deeper. In nothing that he says about God's activity in the world does he ever lose sight of the wrath and the love of God. The activity of what is evil in the world does not go hand in hand with the activity of God. The only way Luther can ever describe the relationship of these two activities to each other is by saying that they are at war. Nowhere is this clearer than it is in his writing against Erasmus, which is said to be "purely deterministic." Christians know, Luther says here, that "in the world two kingdoms are engaged in the most violent conflict" *(duo esse regna in mundo pugnantissima).* Satan rules in the one; Christ rules in the other (WA 18, 782, 20). Or the "world" appears as God's opponent. The world and its god cannot bear the Word of the true God. But God cannot be silent. "Since those two gods are at war, what besides uproar could now arise in the whole world?" *(Quid iam illis duobus diis bellantibus nisi tumultus fieret in toto mundo?)* To put an end to this struggle would be tantamount to doing away with the Word of God. If this struggle were not going on, one would have to doubt the reality of the Word (626, 22 ff.). Here man cannot be a spectator, "because if God is in us, Satan is not present, and nothing but good is present" *(quia si Deus in nobis est, Satan abest et non nisi bonum adest)*—and vice versa (670, 6). But neither are God and the devil spectators when man makes decisions, as would have to be the case according to Erasmus' doctrine of freedom. Not even for a moment is man free to decide in favor of the one or the other. He is always in the power of the one or the other of the "combatants who are engaged in the most violent warfare with each other" *(agitatores mutuo bellacissimi)* (750, 5 ff.). But this is not a matter of a struggle between good and evil in a flatly moral sense. On the contrary, it is a matter of belief and unbelief. The struggle of the "world" is "rage against the Gospel" *(furor adversus Euangelion)* (710, 19). The devil spurs and urges "enslaved man to will and to do with all his power that which is contrary to grace" *(homo servus, ut totis viribus contrarium gratiae et velit et faciat)* (750, 3).

In this way Luther's doctrine of God's activity in the world now arrives at its point of contact with the impact of the Gospel *(evangelischer Ansatz).* This activity can neither be traced back to mere predestination, nor can it be described as a neutral "activity in the creatures" *(operatio in creaturis).* It is always condescension in the sense in which Hermann Bezzel uses this term (cf. *The Doctrine of the Two Natures*). We have already established the fact that justifying faith is also faith in destiny; now it holds true that faith in destiny as justifying faith is faith in the activity of God's love in the world. This leads to two results. In the first place, the aforementioned unfulfillability of what is ethical is done away with in this faith in destiny. For justifying faith brings freedom. In the second place, here the statement that "the finite is capable of containing the infinite" *(Finitum capax infiniti)* takes on its full meaning. Faith knows "that heaven and earth [are] full of the fire of divine love, full of life and righteousness, full of glory and praise, so that, in contrast, hell with its fire, with death and sin, would be nothing but a thing that is pictured" (WA 20, 229, 19). Why would the finite earth not be "capable of containing" *(capax)* the infinite "fire of divine love"? If it were not capable of this, there could not be a single human being with faith. Finally, however, here it also becomes clear that the Lutheran faith in providence is not to be understood in a sense as purely fatalistic as it was often described. In itself submission to God's will, even "joyous submission," is not yet "Lutheran Christianity," as Emanuel Hirsch thinks he can discover in the writings of Fichte.[14] "We must struggle," says Luther, "and we have no rest. Nevertheless, Christ remains the Victor and the Lord. If our life is nothing else than a struggle, He has recognized us as angels." *(Streiten müssen wir und haben keine Ruhe. Tamen Christus victor manet et Dominus. Si nostra vita nihil aliud quam pugna, suscepit nos zu Engeln.)* (WA 49, 583, 2.) Struggling is not submission. Faith is never a resting. It must always undergo the hardest struggle of all – the struggle against fear of God, yes, even against the wrathful God Himself.

In this way a lively, indeed a tempestuous movement makes itself felt in Luther's philosophy of life. Just as there is no resting existence *(Sein)* of God either in the world or outside it, no "bare presence" *(nuda adessentia)* among the creatures, so there is also no "existence" *(Sein)* of man in the world, indeed no "existence" *(Sein)* of the world itself either. If Luther's purely dynamic view of the presence of God in the creatures corresponds to the removal of the magical philosophy of life by means of the modern philosophy of life, his conception of world affairs as a struggle is resumed in the philosophy of Jacob Böhme and in the natural philosophy of Schelling and Goethe.[15]

[14] E. Hirsch, *Die idealistische Philosophie und das Christentum,* 1926, pp. 221 f. — Cf. also W. Lütgert, *Die Religion des deutschen Idealismus und ihr Ende* III. 1925, p. 286.

[15] Cf. Heinr. Bornkamm, *Luther und Böhme,* 1925. — On Schelling: Heinr. Knittermeyer, *Schelling und die Romantische Schule,* 1929. — On Goethe: Tobias Pöhlmann, *Goethes Naturauffassung in neutestamentlicher Beleuchtung,* 1927. Primarily, of course, the limit according to the "Christian" view of nature is pointed out here. — We confine ourselves to a brief statement about Goethe. Our source is a little essay, *Die Natur,* which dates from the 1780's. As late as 1828 Goethe

To make Goethe a saint of Lutheranism would be just as absurd a venture as it would be to make him a "Christian." Perhaps it would not be quite so absurd to make him a saint as it would be to make him a "Christian." His conception of nature is so rich and is characterized by such clear-cut distinctions – likewise nourished in so many ways by the actual study of nature – that one sees that great gulfs separate him from Luther. Nevertheless, he erred in thinking that Spinoza was his ancestor. His connection with Spinoza is obvious. Like Spinoza, he denies the transcendence of God as this is understood by the church. Like Spinoza, he is filled with reverence of the universe. And here there is no bridge from Goethe to Luther. But where in Goethe do we find Spinoza's dualism, the theory that the world is explicable in terms of mind and matter *(Denken und Ausdehnung)?* Is there an inner relationship to Goethe's view of nature when mind and matter are designated as "attributes" of God? Spinoza's nature is dead. She knows no polarity. She knows no growth – not even development. Spinoza is enamored of fatalism. He knows only that "the infinite is capable of containing the finite" *(Infinitum finiti capax).* Goethe, too, knows this. Like Luther, however, he also knows the opposite – if it is permitted to grant validity for a moment to his equation of God with nature. "All men are in her," he says of nature, "and she is in all men." But his view agrees fully with Luther's statement that this is not a resting "existence" *(Sein).* Nature "changes eternally and does not stand still for a moment. She has no conception of what it means to remain, and she has put her curse on the thought of standing still. . . ." "She shoots forth her creatures out of nothing and does not tell them whence they come or where they are going. They are only to run. She knows the course." This can sound fatalistic. Yet man has a curiously dialectical relationship to nature. "We live in her midst and are strangers to her. She speaks unceasingly to us and does not betray her secret to us. . . ." "He who follows her trustfully she takes to her heart as a child. Out of everything she gives she makes a benefit, for first she makes it indispensable. She delays in order that one may desire her; she hurries in order that one may not grow tired of her. . . ." "One obeys her laws even when one resists them; one works with her even when one wants to work against her. . . ." "Her crown is love. Only through love does one come near her. She puts gulfs between all living things, and she wants to devour everything in order to draw everything together. By means of a few sips from the

acknowledged this essay as a "comparative" which was followed by the "superlative." Thus in a letter to Chancellor von Müller. Both writings are found in the fortieth volume of the Cotta edition.

cup of love she compensates for a life full of trouble. . . ." "She has put me here; she will also lead me out. I entrust myself to her. Let her have power over me. She will not hate what she has made."

For him who knows what the impact of the Gospel *(evangelischer Ansatz)* is, everything that forms the basis of Luther's philosophy of life is missing here. Christ is missing here. The transcendence of God is missing. At the very beginning the cry of hopelessness is missing – the cry that accompanies Luther's primal experience *(Urerlebnis)*. Obviously the span that the aging Goethe constructs between spirit and nature cannot compensate for all this. But here a sensation of the immanence of God is speaking – a sensation of the kind that could spring from Luther's philosophy of life. This sensation has the same relationship to Schleiermacher's sensation of dependence that Luther has to Calvin. Here there is a simultaneous within and without, a constant revelation and at the same time a secret, a constant cleavage that leads to the struggle of all against all yet in the end wants to create the possibility of love. "Life," it is said of nature, "is her most beautiful invention, and death is her knack of having much life." This does not come from Spinoza. Nor does it come from Giordano Bruno. "One sees," Goethe writes about this essay to Chancellor von Müller forty years later, "one sees the tendency toward a new kind of pantheism in the fact that an inscrutable, absolute, humorous, self-contradictory being is thought of as the basis of world phenomena." Goethe certainly regards this "being" as impersonal. But even a theologian like Richard Rothe found that the most elementary concept of God is that "of the absolute, taking this word as a noun of the neuter gender." Here as well as there this is not Luther's God! But the "self-contradiction" leads to the recollection of the span between the wrath and the love of God that connects Jacob Böhme with Luther. "Inscrutable," "absolute" – this is more than "nature." It is a final recollection of the "hidden God" *(Deus absconditus)*. And it is more than the brilliant fantasy of the poet. "She shoots forth her creatures out of nothing and does not tell them whence they come or where they are going." And in spite of this uncertainty there is the call through love to love. "That heaven and earth are full of divine love," said Luther. He, too, said this in spite of the "objective uncertainty," to speak with Kierkegaard.

Here Goethe's philosophy of life and Luther's are related. Here Goethe, without knowing it, is being propelled by a great movement that cannot be derived only from the Renaissance, from humanism, and from antiquity. He is plucking fruits from a tree that grew in the soil of the Lutheran belief in God.

32. Close Connection with the Earth[1]

Where Luther enunciates the immanence of God most sharply, he at the same time warns against the erroneous belief that one has God when one has the things in which He "is" (WA 19, 492, 6 and 19–21). When giving this warning, Luther is thinking of the obvious danger of idolatry. But he has more than this in mind. He knows that one can actually encounter God in those things. But if one does not yet believe in Him, they are weapons in His hand. They are parts of the entire sphere in which we are compelled to live and together with which we are destined for death (cf. *The Primal Experience*). Not even by justification are we by any means removed from this natural entanglement in our environment. Although God's justifying verdict is heard by the transcendental I, it applies to the empirical I. Thus we continue to be the same human beings with all our physical contents, character traits, recollections, and capabilities. The sharpening of our life "to a mathematical point" *(ad punctum mathematicum)* means "accusation" *(accu-*

[1] Joh. Bugenhagen, *Annotationes in Epistolas Pauli ad Galatas, Ephesios, Philippenses, Colossenses, Thessalonicenses, I. et II. Tim., Tit., Philem., Hebraeos, Nup. rec.*, 1525. — Georg Weinreich, superintendent and professor at Leipzig, *Leichpredigt für Prof. und Dr. med. Simon Scheibe,* Leipzig, 1597. — Bruno Hartmann, *Die Meyen Blumen des Bacchi unnd der Veneris Kinder in allen Landen. Zum Schrecken, Buss und Besserung und trewhertziger Warnung Gepredigt . . . ,* Grünberg in Hesse, 1612. — Georg Kilius, pastor in Baldestedt, *Encoenia oder Kirmess-Predigten,* Leipzig, 1612. — Melchior Othonius, pastor in Burgpfarrenbach, *Homo Stella, das ist Vergleichung dess Menschen mit den Sternen. . . . Sermon über den Abschied des Kaufmanns Thomas Imminger aus Regensburg . . . ,* Nürnberg, 1613. — M. Joh. Kauffmann, *David Sponsus, das ist eine Ehrn und Hochzeitspredigt, wie sich David, nach Absterben Nabals, mit der vernünfftigen Abigail anderweit verehelicht habe,* Nürnberg, 1613. — Daniel Wülfer, preacher at the St. Lorenz Church in Nürnberg, *Elisae Hohn, Lohn, Cron, Das ist die gantze Historia des h. Propheten Elisa . . . in 58 Predigten . . . ,* Nürnberg, 1663. — Heinrich Müller, *Geistliche Erquickstunden,* 1644, quoted according to a reprint, Hof, 1738. — Hans Jac. Christoph v. Grimmelshausen, *Der abendteuerliche Simplizissimus,* ed. by Adelb. Keller, *Bibl. d. Lit. Ver.* in Stuttgart, vols. 33 and 34, 1854. — Joh. Conr. Dürr, professor in Altdorf, *Comp. Theol. Moralis,* Altdorf, 1675. — Joh. Christoph Becmann, *Lineae Doctrinae Moralis,* Leipzig and Frankfurt, 1686. — Erich Klingner, *Luther und der deutsche Volksaberglaube,* Palaestra, Vol. 56, 1912, and *Archiv. f. Ref.-Gesch.* X, 288 ff., 1912—13. — A. Römer, *Luther und die Trinksitten, Vierteljahrsschr. "Die Alkoholfrage,"* 1917, pp. 100 ff. — Chr. Stubbe, *Luther und der Trunk, Internat. Monatsschr. z. Bek. d. Alkoholismus,* 1917, nos. 9 ff. — Kurt Dietr. Schmidt, *Die Alkoholfrage in Orthodoxie, Pietismus und Rationalismus (Die Alkoholfrage in der Religion,* No. 2), 1927. — Ad. Allwohn, *Luther und der Alkohol,* ibid., No. 3, 1929. — Hartmann Grisar, S. J., *Luther II,* 244 ff., 1911. — H. Böhmer, *Luther im Lichte der neueren Forschung,* 5th ed., 1919. — Christof Schubart, *Luther und die Jagd, Mitteilungen der Luther-Gesellschaft,* 1920, pp. 35 ff. — N. Söderblom, *Humor och melankoli och andra Lutherstudier,* 1919. — H. Steinlein, *Luthers und Melanchthons Stellung zum Schauspiel, Die Theatergemeinde,* Munich, Oct. 1928. — M. Rade, *Zum Teufelsglauben Luthers, Marburger Theol. Studien,* 1931, 2d part.

satio), not, as in German mysticism, a diminution of consciousness. Consequently, the things with which we are connected are not changed by penitence and justification. They attract the attention of the believer exactly as they attract the attention of the godless person. Of course, a change has occurred to the extent that they can no longer frighten us. God deals with me in a manner that is different from the treatment I must fear as long as I seek Him only in the world. Death, which the world prepares for me, is the beginning of life.

This hope of "eternal life" is the common possession of all Christians. For all Christians this leads to a shifting in their assessment of the world. But does the world become worthless? When compared with the eternal "worth," it surely does. To achieve this worth the Christian will "count everything as loss" (Phil. 3:8). According to the Pauline-Lutheran doctrine of justification, however, this cannot be the final word. "All creatures are good." Since they are God's creatures, how could they not be good? And the believer need not conclude a posteriori what the primal cause is before he gains this certainty. He knows that God is the Creator. But this knowledge does not become faith until, as is always the case when there is faith, the reference "for me" *(pro me)* is added. I believe that God has created and still preserves me as well as all creatures. Here the emphasis is both on the "me" and on the "as well as." God has not created me as one who is isolated; He has created me as a creature in the sum total of all. Here faith in my Creator has to become a hymn of praise to the preservation of my environment and of the world in general. Luther cannot separate either God or himself from the natural environment. It has been sufficiently emphasized that for him Gospel and justification are something different from nature and world, but also that this difference cannot be characterized by means of the concept of invisibility. Nor does Luther's faith want to be an intensified "spirituality" *(Geistlichkeit).* In the claim to have this intensified "spirituality" he sees a recollection of the temptation "You will be like God" *(Eritis sicut Deus)* and at all events the beginning of the end of faith. From Erasmus, Luther demands "that He be God for you here as well as in the future and in all things, on all occasions, at all times, and in all your works" *(ut tibi sit Deus tam hic quam in futuro et in omnibus rebus, casibus, temporalibus et operibus)* (WA 18, 726, 12). If God is gracious to me, He is gracious in any case, whenever I have to do with Him, therefore also in nature. In the very first edition of his *Loci* Melanchthon points out that the concept of promise in the Old Testament is also applied to temporal goods and that for this reason the Christian, too, may refer it to his whole attention.[2] It is God's gracious Word that constitutes the promise — not the object to which the promise refers. That He promises me anything at all — this is the revelation of His love, and since the promise is proclaimed to me and thus also applies to me, it is a way of stating that He forgives me my sins. This does not by any means do away with the uniqueness of the revelation of Christ. But in one respect Christ belongs completely in the world of creatures and dare not be detached from the world that surrounds Him. His uniqueness as a creature, however, cannot be fully understood until clarity has been established as to when nature was temporalized in history.

Early Lutheranism resounds with the hymn of praise Luther intoned in his Small Catechism to the creatures of God. Sermons, hymns, and prayers are full of this praise, and the main mistake made by the dogmaticians — aside from their wooden way of speaking about the subject — consists in the false position they have assigned to the doctrine of creation. This prevents them from being able to pull all the stops of the joy of faith, because at the beginning of their works, where they speak about creation, they do not yet give the reader any knowledge whatever of what faith is. But when faith realizes that the creatures are ruled over by God, a complete attitude *(Gesamthaltung)* over against the natural world results. This attitude dominates man even when he does not think of God in an individual case. The same thing happens in the ethos. The feeling that man and nature belong together has lost its terrors. The dead Christ, it is stated in a funeral sermon which alludes to Ecclus. 40:11, has been "buried in the earth, which is the mother of us all" (Othonius, p. 17). "I had measured the heavens," Kepler wanted inscribed on his own tombstone, "now I am measuring the shadows of the earth" *(Mensus eram coelos, nunc terrae metior umbras).* "Time always shows that it is often my stepmother; soon it will be my dear little mother; it comforts me and makes me happy" *(Die Zeit sich heltt zu aller frist, dass sie offt mein Stiefmutter ist, Bald ist sie mein*

[2] Plitt-Kolde, p. 143: "There are in Scripture in addition to this promise of eternal blessing also promises of temporal things, such as the promise that was made to Noah, just as in the Law there are very many promises concerning the earth, concerning wealth, etc., which are not only figures of the spiritual promises but in themselves are evidences of the grace and mercy of God, so that they comfort and buoy up our consciences that they may glorify God" *(Sunt in scripturis praeter hanc promissionem aeternae benedictionis etiam promissiones rerum temporalium, qualis est ea, quae facta est Nohae, quales pleraeque sunt in lege de terra, de opulentia etc., quae non modo figurae sunt spiritualium promissionum, sed per sese sunt testimonia gratiae et misericordiae dei, ita ut consolentur et erigant conscientias nostras, ut deum glorificent).* Cf. op. cit., p. 180.

liebs Mütterlein, Tröstet und macht mich frölich sein) (Johann Kauffmann). Time, which is our transitoriness, as well as the grave and the earth have not only lost their terrors for him who believes; we are laid to rest in the earth, because we belong to the earth as children belong to their mother. We *want* to belong to the earth, because we believe in Him who made us related to the earth. To be sure, death retains its terror even for Christians. It *should* retain its terror. When we see others dying, God puts "one mirror of death after the other before our eyes – mirrors by means of which He wants to remind us of our mortality" (Weinreich). "Paying the debt of nature" is a constantly recurring way of expressing the fact that we must die (e. g., Grimmelshausen II, 707). Because death has a reverse side that is eschatological, it can be overcome only by faith. But because it is nature, too, we experience in it the relationship with "the mother of us all." [3]

Lutheranism's close connection with the earth is no religion of nature. Here there is no deification of nature. What is said here about nature always pertains first of all to us ourselves. But neither can there be any hostility toward nature here. Nor can there be even an estrangement from nature. With nature we share death. With us nature shares life. It is nature's state of being alive that attracts Luther's admiring attention again and again. It is not the existence of the world that he regards as the real miracle of creation. He does not want anyone to compare the creation of the world out of nothing to the work of a blacksmith, who shapes dead material; he wants it compared to the birth of man, to the growth of the trees out of the earth (Erlangen edition, *ex. lat.* 18, 282). When he wants to illustrate the splendor and the wonderful quality of life in God's creation, he nearly always points to the life of the animals, to the field, and to the garden. He marvels at the tiny organs of the insects. Wonderingly he asks how God is able to let so many trees grow to satisfy man's need for wood. This friendship for nature has a homespun quality. Here one notes the Wittenberg countryside. Nor can Luther get away from the greatness of the impression made by nature. He and his friends saw the aforementioned comet of 1538 "with the greatest admiration" *(summa cum admiratione)*. But he does not grasp the magnificence of the Alps, even though he once crossed them. He speaks slightingly of Switzerland, because in that country there are

[3] In the sermon he delivered at the funeral of his sovereign, Duke George of Silesia, the court preacher Laur. Starcke does not hesitate to compare the grief for him who had fallen asleep with the grief of animals: "If oxen bellow because of a dead ox, why, then, should a human being not do so? Reason teaches him, and inborn love impels him, to mourn." (*Leichenpredigt,* Liegnitz, 1586, quoted according to a reprint in 1595.)

"only mountains and valleys" *(Table Talk* 3, 3621). Here, however, the feeling at the bottom of all this is important. Between him and the life and activity of nature he sees no basic boundary line. He regards the begetting and the birth of man as wonderful. Yet he considers the life of nature equally wonderful. To him children are precious gifts. If they are at his table when apples, nuts, and peaches are served, he shares their heartfelt joy. Then he tells how sweet the pomegranates and the oranges tasted in Paradise. He enjoys the happiness of married life. He is glad to read that the patriarch had fun with his wife (WA 43, 449, 40). "Woman is a delightful companion in life" *(Vitae iucunda socia mulier) (Table Talk* 1, 12).

Luther's belief in demons is part of this awareness of nature. These poltergeists, satyrs, and all the rest of the devil's vermin affect our senses with noises and all kinds of strange phenomena. The devil himself makes use of all the means provided by the world of nature. He prefers to work at night. He frightens people in pits, in dismal forests, indeed even in the study. As God's monkey he apes God. He even begets human beings. Of course, these human beings soon betray their origin and quickly perish – all this in order to harm people, to mislead them, and to deprive them of faith. One cannot say that Luther was superstitious in an undiscriminating manner. Many people are afraid to spill salt. Luther makes fun of this fear. He calls it a "great superstition" *(magnam superstitionem) (Table Talk* 5, 6373). When asked whether the unfortunate creatures he speaks of have a soul, he replies: "I do not know; I have not asked God about this" *(Table Talk* 1, 323). In his explanation of the First Commandment and the Second Commandment he attacked many popular customs of his time that were founded on superstition.[4] He also attacks the notion that the souls of departed persons attract attention in the poltergeists (WA 10 III, 196, 18 ff.). What he writes about devils and demons is completely unspeculative. He has no interest whatever in the devil's metaphysics. Even concerning the angels he says that Scripture does not describe their creation, since no opportunity for speculation is to be given *(Table Talk* 1, 319). But the devil is the terrible enemy who seeks to balk God's purposes everywhere. *That* the devil is this terrible enemy and *that* he tries this everywhere is shown by the struggling that takes place throughout the cosmos. Luther wants to use the word "armies" in Gen. 2:1, because all creatures were and are summoned against him. "For

[4] WA 1, 252; WA 6, 224, 15 ff. — There are many writings against sorcery. Cf., e. g., Jodocus Hocker, preacher at Osnabrück, *Eine getrewe, wolmeynende Christliche warnung wider die Gottlosen Teuffelbeschwerer oder Banner,* Frankfurt am Main, 1564.

all creatures are armies of God, and they all serve as soldiers in accordance with their situation. The trees bring forth fruits and leaves, the earth brings forth grasses and grains, etc.; if Satan were able, he would prevent all this. Therefore all creatures are soldiers." *(Sunt enim omnes creaturae exercitus Dei atque militant quaeque pro sua conditione. Arbores proferunt fructus et folia, terra herbas et frumenta etc.; quae si posset Satan, impediret omnia. Ideo omnes creaturae sunt milites.)* When Luther adds here that the Elbe, too, is a "soldier of God" *(miles Dei),* and that no one can stop its course, the immediacy of his awareness of the cosmic struggle for God's creation becomes clear *(Table Talk* 1, 664).

After all, the struggle between good and evil belongs in the fields of ethics and eschatology. Here it is the feeling that man has kinship with nature in general that matters. Obviously the expression of this feeling is subject to change. But the implied rejection of a spiritualization of man is essential for Lutheranism. At all events, such a spiritualization would have to be unbearable if it were derived from faith or even equated with faith. As long as early Lutheranism remained true to Luther's belief, it was consciously engaged in a struggle against every neo-Platonic disregard for the material world as well as against every confusion of the ethos with a deadening of emotional life. "For God wants nature preserved, not destroyed" *(Deus enim vult servatam naturam, non extinctam),* said Luther. The Holy Spirit does not corrupt and destroy nature; He heals the destruction and the corruption of nature in man. Therefore the natural affections for parents, brothers, and sisters remain. "They are not abolished through grace; they are aroused" *(Non tolluntur per gratiam sed excitantur).* It is reported that Christ, too, grew angry, suffered pain, mourned, and became indignant. One can sin with all these emotions. But that which is natural in them cannot be sinful. Like "love and conjugal desire" *(amor et appetitus conjugalis),* they have been put into man's heart (WA 44, 493, 6 ff.). For this reason God abhors the apathy of the Stoics and does not love the academicians, who suppress all their natural emotions (533, 13 ff.). Bugenhagen asks why a creature of God, which, according to 1 Tim. 4:4, is good per se, must be sanctified and by what means it must be sanctified. He points to woman, who is certainly a good creature of God but can also be misused. The creature is sanctified, he says, through the Word, which we may believe and which states that everything is ours if we ask God for it and receive it from Him (*Annot.*, p. 206 f.).

Here there was no place for the puritanical cheerlessness of social life. One can have respect for the somber portraits of the Geneva saints.

But in spite of one's best intentions it would be impossible to regard those Geneva saints as men who were made free and happy by the Gospel. In this connection one thinks of Philip II of Spain, another man who could not laugh. He laughed only once in his life – when he got the news of St. Bartholomew's Eve. Into what a grimace laughter is distorted in the definition given by the Reformed Professor Johann Christoph Becmann at Frankfurt an der Oder! He says: "Elation of spirits because of sudden joy is laughter, and sudden giving way to laughter because of something disgraceful in another person is commendation" *(Elatio spirituum ob gaudium subitaneum est risus, risusque passio subita sui ex indecoro alieno facta commendatio).* This is no longer a laughing occasioned by merriment – unless one regards the enjoyment of someone's discomfiture as the purest kind of laughter. It is a sure sign of the invasion of Lutheranism by a strange spirit when pietism begins to subject laughter to censorship. "It is better to weep with Jesus," says Heinrich Müller, "than to laugh with the world. One will not find Christ when one laughs. Where do you read that He laughed? But He is very kindly disposed to tears." Luther had not been afraid to say about God Himself that when He sees the happiness of married people, "He laughs and is happy on this account" (WA 34 I, 62, 20). If, as the Bible does, we can speak of God only anthropomorphically, no one who can laugh without troubling his conscience will be able to find anything offensive in this. And how plainly one hears the laughter of the table companions in much of Luther's *Table Talk!* Just as Luther thinks that loneliness and melancholy belong together, so he thinks that sociability and good cheer belong together. He condemns laughter that arises from bitterness and wickedness (WA 43, 453, 8 ff.). But with regard to Rom. 12:15 he says: "Now if someone is happy, we should not have the sour look the hypocrites have. They want to be something special, and in their unseemly earnestness they pretend that they alone are wise and holy. All those who are happy and do not have the sour look they have they call fools and sinners. No, the joy of happy people should please us if it is not against God." (WA 17 II, 54, 22.)

It will still be necessary to show how Luther's happiness is founded on basic optimism. This happiness must be achieved every day, and, like life as a whole, it constantly bears the stamp of a conquering "nevertheless." It is superfluous to say that Luther is also acquainted with the dangers inherent in natural pleasures, that he knows how close the causes of such pleasures can be to sin. Alongside the joyful acceptance of the world there is in all early Lutheranism the warning against the devils of pleasure, of amusements, of dancing, of drinking, of lying, of life at court, and of excesses in the matter of dress. But there was no trace of later pietism's basic mistrust of all natural happiness and sociability. Thus Pastor Georg Kilius of Baldestedt (1612) finds that it is "also right, proper, and praiseworthy – and God can surely permit this – either for a person himself to take a drink in accordance with propriety when he is alone or to arrange a fine, good, and proper party *(Collation)* and social gathering, just as it is one of the greatest joys on earth, next to wife and child, to sit at table in good confidence with honorable people. Now when one invites someone without harming him or other people, either because of friendship or for the sake of business or gratitude, or for recreation and pleasure; or if otherwise good friends get together – everyone at his own expense – in the confidence that no one will be slandered, gossiped about, or be brought to judgment, but that good things will be said about them, that they will speak confidentially to one another of their personal affairs, seek advice and comfort, eat and drink in accordance with propriety, so that they remain sober, do not forget God, do not neglect anything, and do no harm to body and soul, to property and conscience – such banquets *(Convivia)* the Son of God approves of, and He Himself attends them gladly. . . ." Then there is a reference to the wedding feast at Cana.

The dangers incident to drinking, dancing, and amusements were well known. One realized that the natural pleasure the sexes take in each other is a contributing factor in connection with dancing. But since this pleasure is also one of the emotions brought about by the Creator, this in itself was not a reason for branding dancing as immoral. "Since dancing is also customary in the world, among the young people who have matrimony in view, it is not to be condemned if it is done decently, without shameful conduct, words, or gestures, merely for pleasure" (WA 24, 419, 10). In dancing Bugenhagen found a tribute to matrimony: "If it is done in honor of matrimony, which the Lord wants to be honored because it is of His making, let us dance when it is done in honor of matrimony. In that case, just as I have said about pleasure, it can take place; but one cannot permit people to be attracted by it to lust." *(Si fit in honorem matrimonii, quod dominus vult honorari, quia eius factura, Item saltemur, quando fit in honorem matrimonii, ut dixi de letitia, fieri potest, sed quod personae hoc trahantur ad libidinem, non pati potest.)* [5] After pietistic criticism had set in, dancing was still to be

[5] Buchwald, *Ungedruckte Predigten Bugenhagens,* p. 305. Cf. Melanchthon, *CR* 20, 578: "Dances have been instituted and permitted in order that courteousness may be learned in crowds and friendship may be brought about between young men and girls; for in this way manners are shown. Moreover, they provide oppor-

permitted, at least as "recreation" (Dannhauer-Mayer, p. 439). This was already a rationalistic-utilitarian way of thinking. The immediacy of natural pleasure was gone. At least in the textbooks. Other types of amusement had a similar fate. For Luther the noblest "amusements" were music and fencing. Music, he said, drives cares away; fencing serves as physical exercise (*Table Talk* 3, 3470). Dürr still recommends sports for the cultivation of agility and bodily health, likewise to harden men for the defense of the fatherland. Again Dannhauer regards only the recreational purpose as valid. Taking walks befits a physician more than it befits a theologian.[6] No one but the aged may with a good conscience apply himself to leisure. For God wants man to work. And A. H. Francke expresses the opinion: "If the world, as is its custom, pleads that one's spirit must be amused, such a [Christian] has a totally different disposition and finds no greater joy and amusement – indeed no true joy and amusement of his spirit – than when he thinks of God or of godly things." Here, of course, natural things are not included among the godly things. For this statement has to do with the frequently discussed question whether it is permitted to love creatures.[7] It is well known that this model educator forbade the children in his institutions to play, prescribed eight hours of instruction every day, even on Sundays, and, on top of this, compelled the children to say "Thank you" for the many whippings they got. All this in order that the gracious Savior might be their sole pleasure. At all events, this taught them to hope for a better hereafter. Luther had thought that "little children are the finest playthings" (*spielfögel)*; in the playing of children he found a recollection of Paradise, and his table companions saw that he himself "had the best fun with his little son Martin" (*optimum jocum habuit cum filiolo suo Martino)* (*Table Talk* 4, 4364).

Toward drinking Luther took the same "natural" position that he took toward eating. Both are necessary for life. One should be doubly grateful to the Creator if, over and above this, both taste as good as nuts taste to children and a good drink tastes to the aged. Children should drink milk; the aged should drink wine (*Table Talk* 2, 1706). Wine is

tunity for living respectably; and when affection has been invited, girls may then go about more respectably and with greater confidence." (*Choreae sunt institutae et concessae, ut civilitas discatur in frequentia et contrahatur amicitia inter adolescentes et puellas; sic enim spectantur mores. Item praebent occasionem honeste vivendi et invitato animo puellae postea honestius et certius ambire possint.)*

[6] To be sure, from time immemorial "taking walks" was always a suspect occupation. Cf. Luther, WA 1, 252, 27; in addition, the *General-Artikel für d. Albertin. Sachsen* of 1557. See what is said about the duties of pastors under *The Later Doctrine of the Office and the Nature of This Office.*

[7] Walch, *Religionsstreitigkeiten der ev.-luth. Kirche* II, 396.

blessed and is recommended in Scripture; beer is merely a "human tradition" *(traditio humana)* (*Table Talk* 1, 254). But wine causes gout; beer causes dropsy *(Table Talk* 3, 3693). For this reason one should be temperate, like Adam in Paradise, when he still had good judgment. Fasting is a fine outward training. The devil reaches out his hand for wine, just as he does for all creatures. The demon dwelling in alcohol is the devil of excessive drinking *(Saufteufel).* In his exposition of Psalm 101, this classic criticism of the "swinish" *(sewisch)* life of the princes (1534), Luther finds that the devil of excessive drinking is the national devil of Germany. "Our German devil will be a good wineskin and must be called Guzzle *(Sauff)*. . . . Preachers have tried to check this with God's Word; persons in authority, with prohibition; some of the nobility themselves, with mutual pledges. Every day great and dreadful damage, disgrace, and all the misfortunes that happen to body and soul before our eyes have tried to check it and still do. It is reasonable to suppose that all this should deter us. But Guzzle remains an almighty idol among us Germans and acts like the sea and dropsy." (WA 51, 257, 6 ff.) No contemporary preached as emphatically against the devil of alcohol as Luther did. Heinrich Böhmer conclusively exploded the legend that Luther himself was a drunkard, after Hartmann Grisar, S. J., had already spoken about this matter with reservations. It is possible that if there had been promise of success, Luther himself would have abstained completely out of consideration for the "weak," as Louis Harms later gave up smoking his pipe. In the case of his nephew, Luther regarded wine as poison which the latter should avoid entirely, since he was unable to control himself after enjoying it *(Table Talk* 4, 5050). On principle, Luther could not have taken a vow that would have been binding for the duration of his life. Aside from this, however, he could never have identified wine as such with the devil, just as he could not have done this in the case of woman, whom the devil can also use for the purpose of temptation and seduction. To him this would have been ingratitude to God.

The loss of clear thinking and good manners was regarded as the main evil in connection with the enjoyment of wine and beer. "They rave," says Magister Bruno Hartmann of the children of Bacchus and Venus, "and rage like senseless brutes. They rant and slobber, shout and bark, yell and spit, curse and swear, so that the hair of pious people stands on end and these people are scared to death." But in spite of this the same Hartmann does not yet consider the promotion of "good spirits" by means of wine a sin in itself. On the contrary, because wine makes one happy, one should enjoy it with gratitude. This heightened joy is what is meant by the "Christian bit of tipsiness" *(christliches Räuschlein)* for the sanctioning of which the early theologians were so severely blamed. For they always speak of this as being the opposite of the devil of excessive drinking *(Saufteufel)*. Thus Grimmelshausen, one of their contemporaries, describes the ideal realm of the sylphs as follows: "There one finds no drunkards or topers; but when one honors another person with a drink, they are both satisfied with a Christian bit of tipsiness" (II, 762). It is self-evident that the wholesome effect on the body was not forgotten.[8] Although Valentin Ernst Löscher no longer had any sense of fun and humor, he still drank his Wittenberg beer and wine, "no matter how it was." In the controversy in which he was engaged he justified the love for creatures. Accordingly, he also indulged in the pleasure of collecting coins and books.[9] To be sure, on the Tenth Sunday after Trinity in the year 1748 he also delivered a powerful sermon against the Saxon court and government – a sermon in which he called for penitence and which approaches Luther in prophetic power.[10] It was not until the advent of pietism that the joy wine can produce, as well as its demonic possibilities, was condemned. There was a desire to prove that the success which "Reformed orthodoxy" had striven in vain to achieve did not come about until pietism demanded temperance.[11] One scarcely does pietism itself a service by judging it on the basis of its successes. August, the elector of Saxony who became a Catholic, had been a pupil of Spener! And it is well known what kind of life he led after this. The successes achieved by pietistic antialcoholism extended only to the narrowest pietistic circles. He who idealizes these successes must also acknowledge the reasons on which they were based. But if these reasons are in opposition to the impact of the Gospel *(evangelischer Ansatz)*, those successes were bought at a price evangelical Christendom cannot pay without surrendering. The alcohol problem is not a concern of the kingdom of Christ; it is a cultural problem. Therefore it is to be solved with cultural considerations, which can be done differently today from the way it could be done in Luther's time. Here again the only thing essential

[8] Cf., e. g., Bugenhagen's gratitude to the elector for a shipment of Torgau beer, which had restored the health of several persons — among them a baker who was dangerously ill — and his praise of the "Torgau bock beer" *(gedubbelt Torgauisch Bier)* in Vogt, *Bugenhagens Briefwechsel*, 1888, pp. 303 ff.

[9] Blanckmeister, *Der Prophet von Kursachsen, Val. Ernst Löscher*, 1920.

[10] Blanckmeister, *Säschsische KG*, 1899, p. 329.

[11] K. D. Schmidt, pp. 15 f. Schmidt's otherwise excellent presentation did not do justice to orthodoxy, since he had not taken Hans Leube's book on the reformatory ideas of orthodoxy seriously enough.

is that all creation remain God's creation and that reflections concerning expediency do not kill man's feeling of belonging in a direct manner to God's creation.

One side of the vital consciousness of being a creature is turned toward the world. It is as changeable as the world itself. Therefore Lutheranism, by affirming this in all its immediacy, took part in all the various styles in which the vital consciousness of modern times has expressed itself. One can observe this in its so-called professional representatives. Theology, too, has its history of style. Even the format of its books show this. The quarto format of the time of the Reformation – the format decorated with the lettering characteristic of the Renaissance – is followed by the gigantic baroque folio volume of the francophile duodecimo, finally by the practical handiness advocated by the Enlightenment. This extends to the method of presentation. What Luther and Brenz write is as stable as the oak chest of their age. Melanchthon's *Loci* is like the old Leipzig town hall with its long rows of coordinated gables and the Biblical inscription that still greets every Leipzig Fair. In Chemnitz' *Examen concilii Tridentini* and in Gerhard's *Loci* the counterreformational style of their opponets drives its waves over to us. Nicolai casts his eye on the soaring angels of the altars of his time. On the cover of his *Systema*, with its 10,000 quotations, Calov puts a maze of stuccowork. The writing of Semler, Löffler, Teller, and Gabler is as transparent as the square and unimaginative glass windows of the churches in which the rationalists delivered their lectures. One is inclined to say that their writing harmonizes with their names. Family life in the parsonage and the outward deportment of the pastor are subject to the same changes of style. The traditional shaved face of Luther's time is followed by the full beard of the clerics, the turned-up mustache, and the wig. Then there is a repetition until the mustache of the age that preceded ours comes into vogue. The only thing that remained the same in the parsonage was the large number of children – a genuine expression of the close connection with the earth. "The more children, the more happiness," Luther had said.

It is self-evident that in the general cultural life there are other and more tangible evidences of the succession of styles. But that the language of theology as well as the pastor and his family – where one can assume with the greatest certainty that religious motives are effective – have a part in this may surely be regarded as proof that here no other principle counted than that of being natural in natural things. Just as demonic possibilities were recognized in drinking, so they were recognized in "fashion" *(Mode)*. The devil of excesses in dress appears alongside the devil of drinking.[12] But it is not the innovations per se that stir up criticism; it is the threat of demoralization and of an increase in foreign influence that does so. These two dangers produce a retarding element in the attitude toward fashion. Accordingly, there are, of course, sermons on the devil of excesses in dress and sermons on luxury, even governmental regulations with regard to clothing; but these sermons and these regulations serve to ward off those dangers, and it is by no means their purpose to establish standard apparel for the citizens of the kingdom of God. Luther regarded it as an honor to marriage when a bride decked herself out in special finery. And when Veit Ludwig von Seckendorff, in his *Christian State (Christenstaat)*, complained in particular about the fancy clothing worn at weddings, the reasons that induced him to do so were primarily economic. He thought that clothes were "invented because of extreme need and because of modesty." He admitted, however, "that God Himself gave the permission and the means to make a work of honor out of a miserable covering for one's shame and that one should also thank God for decent clothing, finery, and the like" (II, 2, 13). Nor are there ascetic-spiritualizing reasons for the struggle against an increase in foreign influence. This struggle serves to preserve national individuality and is an indirect way of giving expression to the close connection with the earth.

Art was always the most direct and the final expression of the consciousness of living in the world. Hans Preuss has described the style of expression the modern denominations have created in pictorial art.[13] But even his basic thought — that a definite kind of piety is at the bottom of all genuine art — has a denominational qualification. The Lutheran and the Catholic can agree with him. The consistent Calvinist must reject this thought. And not only for ethical-ascetic reasons. The Calvinist will not recognize as "Christian" a piety that expresses itself in the artistic representation of the physical world. His belief in God ushers him out of the world in every respect. The more positively he recognizes the otherworldliness of God, the purer he is. His relationship to the natural world is limited to a minimum of contact. But this minimum is also subject exclusively to representation through the divine Law, to the essence of which God's otherworldly viewpoints belong. The whole pattern of life resulting from obedience to this Law aims exclusively at the hereafter. Here there is no more room for a "purposeless" repre-

[12] *Von zerluderten, zucht und ehrerwegen pluderichten Hosenteufel, vermanung und warnung. Getruckt zu Frankfurt a. M.*, 1563.

[13] Hans Preuss, *Die deutsche Frömmigkeit im Spiegel der bildenden Kunst*, 1926. Furthermore, *Luthers Frömmigkeit*, 1917; *Luther und der gotische Mensch*, 1919; *Dürer, Michelangelo, Rembrandt*, 2d ed., 1921; *Bach, Mozart, Wagner*, 2d ed., 1922.

sentation in art of what is beautiful than there is for amusement. Preuss's strong emphasis on the immanence of God is not accidental. He also makes a distinction between art that is pious and art that is not pious. There is a kind of painting that is completely absorbed in the creature and forgets the deep dimension of faith — even when it depicts Biblical subjects. But the world also affords a pleasure that is both pleasure afforded by God and pleasure in God. This, of course, also requires an inner freedom — a freedom that cannot thrive in the soil of the Calvinistic dogma of predestination and the legal ethic that is a part of this dogma.

The question remains whether it is right to restrict the denominations more or less to a particular artistic style that is appropriate for them. This is what Preuss does. He believes that he can do so because he also gives very strong emphasis to the interlacement of the denominations with the nations. That this holds true for Lutheranism will be shown when sociology is discussed (Vol. 2). But the question is whether Lutheranism is to be understood morphologically as a product arising from the impact of the Gospel *(evangelischer Ansatz)* and the special nature of particular peoples or whether, on the contrary, a main characteristic of Lutheranism does not consist per se in becoming a people, in connection with which the coalescence with a particular nationality was not essential but was merely "accidental," that is, historically necessary. Preuss holds to the former opinion. But even if one cannot concur in his view, all the relationships included in what he says make it necessary for Lutheranism to find expression in pictorial art. Even in ecclesiastical art, which is Preuss's primary concern, the will to take definite form becomes apparent — the will that does not for a moment deny its close connection with the earth.

But that is what matters here. If the world is not only in opposition to God but is also His creature, then one may not only know that He is near, but one may also feel His nearness. And not only in the teleology of the development of the world but also in what is creatural per se. The eye of faith will see the beauty of the world as the conquering of demonic darknesses. Its ear will hear inexpressible things in music — things that are of divine origin. "With all the greater joy and courage should Christians, as is proper, lift up their voices in the congregation as well as at home, because they know that God has such love for spiritual music in the church as well as in the home, forgets Himself, as it were, because of it, and guarantees *(haftet)* that He will remain in such a congregation with grace and blessing as though He Himself were united with it." That God forgets Himself because of this, as it were — this is a bold statement of Wülfer (p. 88), the pastor of the Church of St. Lorenz in Nürnberg. Here the expression of music is felt as an expression of God's self-surrender to the creatural world. This faith can be founded only on faith in Christ. But where it is, it gives birth to the psyche that portrays itself in art – not in order to be alone but in order to expend itself. In this soil Johann Sebastian Bach could thrive – Bach, who certainly "draws from mystical depths" but at the same time created a work of pure objectivity. Even the most subjective elements in his cantata for Pentecost become the proclamation of Someone entirely different. Here at last questions of style are silent. Here one stands on the borderline between the here and the hereafter.

The poet seems to have the easiest task when it is a matter of giving artistic expression to belief in God as part of the consciousness of being in the world. He has words at his disposal. Apparently he need only *speak* of God in order to show his piety. If he does this, he can certainly take part directly in the proclamation of the Gospel. Even the proclamation in the church seeks a cultic form, the structure of which always presupposes artistic feeling and ability (cf. *Worship*). The parables of Christ are poetry too. In order to justify the academic plays of his time, Dannhauer even declares that the whole Apocalypse is a comedy in which the Holy Spirit lets the Babylonian harlot tread the boards with all the attributes of a harlot (p. 442). And by doing so he certainly does not want to make light of the last book of the Bible. Not only Goethe but also Luther's opponents have recognized the poetic ability found in Luther's translation of the Bible. But this direct relationship of the poet to the proclamation of the Gospel is not the only thing that lets us take pleasure in what he creates. He who considers a poem or a play heathenish merely because it does not contain the name of God judges like one who calls Paul Gerhardt a sun worshiper because the word "God" does not occur in the first stanza of his morning hymn "The Golden Sun Full of Joy and Bliss" *(Die güldne Sonne voll Freud und Wonne)*. The earthy farces of Hans Sachs, the fate-laden tragedies of Shakespeare or Hebbel, the novels of Gustav Frenssen – apart from *Hilligenlei*, a work written for the purpose of showing his qualifications – can produce for the viewer or the reader exactly the same genuine joy that the epics of Milton, Klopstock, and Sandor Petöfi can produce. In this way they can also relate him to God. By drawing us into what he presents, the poet lets us see ourselves as if we were others. When we do so, however, we always remain ourselves. Thus the poet elevates us in our consciousness of being in the world exactly as do wordless chamber music or the pastels of Latour; and when we have reached the final stage of elevation, he makes us ready to ask the Creator for redemption – which the poet, of course, is unable to give us.

Chapter Six

TIME

33. Cross and Vale of Tears [1]

The Lutheran's close connection with the earth is his consciousness of being a creature. This is a definite characteristic of the psyche "of one who has been reborn." There is also a close connection with the earth that is not consciousness of being a creature, and there is consciousness of being a creature that is intolerable. Even Nietzsche and Richard Dehmel agreed that there are earthborn and earthbound emotions. But they do not know themselves as creatures of God. The latter knew himself only as world; the former, only as a human being. Both felt the demonic element in themselves. The one wanted to escape this by becoming nature pure and simple. The other wanted to surmount it and rise to divinity. The former stumbled in his flight and was overtaken. Nietzsche was successful in his affirmation of the demon. But the demon devoured him. And there is also an unbearable consciousness of being a creature. Hölderlin had it, even in his pantheistic period. But he did not find his way about among the great number of gods. He got lost among them and perished. Heinrich von Kleist also had it in the conflict between destiny and deed. He sought the redeeming You. He did not find it; he perished.

[1] Johann Hülsemann, *Freudiger und behertzter Abscheid des . . . Johannis Hoppii, der Philos. u. Artzney berühmten Doctoris u. Professoris . . .*, Leipzig, 1654. — Michael Julius, superintendent in Gotha, *Hiskias Pestilenti ulcere decumbens . . .*, Erfurt, 1599. — Cf. the writings mentioned in note 1 under *Close Connection with the Earth.*

G. W. Leibniz, *Philosophische Werke: Die Theodizee*, translated by A. Buchenau *(Philos. Bibl. Bd. 71)*, 1925. — C. Lülmann, *Leibniz' Anschauung vom Christentum, Zeitschr. f. Philos. u. philos. Kritik* III, 60 ff., 1898. — Ernst Cassirer, *Leibniz' System in s. wiss. Grundlag.*, 1902. — O. Lempp, *Das Problem d. Theodizee in d. Philos. u. Literatur des 18. Jahr. bis auf Kant u. Schiller*, 1910. — W. Lütgert, *Die Erschütterung des Optimismus d. d. Erdbeben von Lissabon, BFchrTh.* V. 3, 1901. — Wilhelm Hausenstein, *Vom Geist des Barock*, 1920. — W. Dilthey, *Gesammelte Schriften* III, 1927.

The believer's close connection with the earth unites him and all creatures into a single home community. It manifests itself in sensitiveness to the beauty of the world. It lets one rejoice with those who are happy. It manifests itself to no lesser degree in the humble realization that our bodies belong to "mother earth," from which they have their origin and to which they return. Cheerfulness cannot be based on it, and it cannot overcome the sadness caused by the necessity to die. Perhaps its manifestations cannot be distinguished from the attitude of a person who does not have faith. Even Schiller sang a hymn of high praise to joy. When Theodor Storm died, Liliencron wrote: "Surely no one took the smell of the earth out of forest and field as you did." And in the literature of the world there is scarcely a manlier readiness to return to the earth than the last lines of his poem "Kolin," where he writes: "Yet one day you and I will be buried in the sand unto everlasting rest. Who knows where?" In all this there lives a bit of Lutheranism. But it is heather that has been pulled out. It lasts a long time. But it withers in the end. Schiller was followed by Schopenhauer; Storm, by Steiner; Liliencron, by the public-spirited society for the prevention of the death of soldiers – by pacifism.

The consciousness of being a creature can be felt logically and without pain in the soil that results from the impact of the Gospel *(evangelischer Ansatz)*. Faith lives because of the "hereafter" of God's forgiveness of sins (cf. *Justification and Philosophy of Life*). In this way, of course, everything the "world" can offer is made relative. But what is promised to me is thereby also promised to a creature. Forgiveness of sins is God's acknowledgment that He is the Creator. Consequently, faith knows of no irreconcilable antagonism between God and the world. When the relationship in which God stands to the creatures as their Creator has dawned on faith, this relationship beams toward it from everything that is beautiful and alive in the creatural world. To faith "heaven and earth" are "full of the fire of divine love, full of life and righteousness" (cf. *God and the World*). But the "world" is not a homogeneous quantity. Again and again we have realized that there are secret or open divisions and tensions, that the demonic element is engaged in a struggle against God and His work. In early Lutheranism this realization is so vivid that the joyful consciousness of being a creature – the joyful consciousness that is based on justification – can often seem to collapse at last in crippling pessimism. Even those who could have had better knowledge made use of Luther's designation of the world as a "vale of tears" in order to ascribe to Lutheranism an altogether quietistic-pessimistic conception of life.

Above all, a widespread mood of doom is clearly in evidence. Amid the joyful dawning of the Reformation one senses it in the sermons of Bugenhagen and later in the Latin sermons *(Postilla)* (*CR* 24, 18, 29 f.) of Melanchthon or in the sermons Andreä preached against the Turks. Lukas Osiander opposed the calendar reform because, as he thought, the Last Day was near. And again and again one encounters the statement that the evening of the world has come. Tycho Brahe found that the new star that appeared on November 11, 1572, "had been shown to the world that was approaching its evening" *(advesperascanti mundo exhibitum)*. And when the announcement was made at the Reformation Jubilee in 1717 that the Saxon electoral prince had gone over to the Roman Church, the pastor at Leubnitz wrote to Löscher: "Evening is approaching; now, Christ, it shall remain ours" *(Advenit vesper, noster nunc Christe maneto)*.[2] Of course, the thought that the end of the world is imminent is common to all Christians. Perhaps one can even say that it is common to all men. That the world as a whole is dying is also an immanent assumption of the impact of the Gospel *(evangelischer Ansatz)*. But the mood of doom of the sixteenth and the seventeenth centuries is not really based on the sharpening of the consciousness of being in the world "to a mathematical point" *(ad punctum mathematicum)*, as it is in Luther's primal experience *(Urerlebnis)*. On the contrary, it is brought about by inner-worldly details: the menacing comet, the danger from the Turks, or, as Melanchthon puts it, the "catastrophes" *(ruinae)* of the German Empire. In the literature of the Thirty Years' War the growing demoralization and the great dying out of culture in Germany affect thoughtful spirits in the same way.

If this whole mood of doom counterbalances in a very serious way the joy that is part of the consciousness of being a creature, one must nevertheless ask whether and how the mood of doom and the consciousness of being a creature can be reconciled with each other, if at all. The thought that the end of the world is near appears as a resumption or even as a continuation of the apocalyptic mood of the latter part of the Middle Ages. For the time being we shall postpone discussion of this thought (cf. *End of the World*), since it can be understood only within the framework of eschatology as a whole. Here the attitude toward the inner-worldly causes has primary importance. First of all, it shows that Lutheran connection with the earth wants to be assessed as genuine consciousness of being in the world, not as an illusion.[3] It is just as correct

[2] Brahe, preface to *De nova stella;* Blanckmeister, *Löscher*, p. 72.

[3] Cf. the comments of Hans Preuss on Luther's common sense, *Luthers Frömmigkeit,* 1917, pp. 6 ff.

to call pestilence, war, and calamity by fire and water misfortunes as it is to speak of the happiness of wedlock or the beauty of music. If the man of faith relates them to God's activity, one is, of course, immediately confronted first of all with the divergence in the philosophies of life that are in conflict with each other. The magical man senses in them the aforementioned touching of a string whose vibrational range will also sometime or somehow take hold of him himself. To Melanchthon the "fearful positions of the stars" *(horrendi positus siderum)* but also the unconfirmed reports about the approach of the Turks and the immediate danger of pestilence that disturbs the operation of the university are "signs" *(signa)* that mean something, and nothing good at that; they are "portents" *(prodigia)* that mean something, and something terrible at that. In the same way Tycho Brahe views every new star as a "portent" *(ostentum),* and in countless sermons calling for penitence the comet or the Turk appears as a warning *(Menetekel)* the consequences of which one does not know in detail, of course, but concerning which one only knows that they will be a misfortune. It is easy for an atmosphere that is fundamentally fatalistic to thrive in this soil — an atmosphere that can resemble basic pessimism.

But great sadness often laments and sobs even where one does not need the detour by way of the magical echo between earth and heaven in order to be terrified by dangers and calamities. One's whole natural life, says Brenz, is in reality merely an exhaling of life and a thought of death.[4] We begin to breathe the moment we are born. Thus we begin to exhale life. When man, says Hülsemann in a funeral sermon, has reached the goal of his desires after many exertions and privations, and God gives him a position of honor in public life and says to him: "Here you have to work; bestir yourself here — at the very time he does this and everyone benefits by what he does, then God gives him such a blow that he falls down like a cabbage stalk or a sunflower, is taken away, and is cut off in a trice; there then lies everything on which great diligence and toil have been spent for twenty or thirty years."[5] Yet this is not only the thought of death in Luther's primal experience *(Urerlebnis)* — the thought that arises when one's whole life and God stand face to face — but it is an inner-worldly pessimism. It is natural for this thought to be intensified during the baroque period, of which the skulls and the painted pallor of death are as much a part as are the fanfares of roused vitality.[6] The medieval "art of dying" *(ars moriendi)* awakens again. A Lutheran

[4] Brenz, *Homil. in Joan.*, p. 737.

[5] Hülsemann, *Leichenpredigt für Joh. Hopp, Exordium.*

[6] Cf. Wilhelm Hausenstein, *Vom Geist des Barock,* 1920, pp. 40 f.

literature of death comes into being — a literature devoted to a downright cultivation of the thought of death. "How many sheep, how many calves, how many fish do you have buried in you? You are a grave for the dead, and you do not think of the grave." (Heinrich Müller, p. 30.)

It has already been shown that this absorption in the thought of death no longer has a necessary theological connection with Luther's "anxiety" (cf. *Fear*). Obviously he, too, is acquainted with all inner-worldly anxieties, including the physical dread of death, and feels all human pains. Like Dürer and Jacob Böhme, he knows what melancholy is. But this is something that must positively be overcome. It is true that in *A Sermon on Preparing for Death (Ein Sermon von der Bereitung zum Sterben)* (1519) he still demands that one familiarize oneself with death while one is living; but when one is about to die, one should think of life (WA 2, 687, 12 ff.). Here the fear of death is already a consequence of the "timidity of nature" *(Blödigkeit der Natur)* that should be overcome. Luther remained convinced that man's sadness is "natural"; that is, it is connected with sin's corruption of nature (*Table Talk* 2, 1279). Consequently, Luther saw in sadness a downright "tool" *(Instrument)* of the devil (*Table Talk* 3, 2840; 4, 5155). All sadness comes from the devil (*Table Talk* 1, 832), Because the devil is its originator, one need not be surprised to learn that it causes sickness not only of the spirit (*Table Talk* 3, 2889) but also of the body (*Table Talk* 5, 6024). Over against this diabolical origin of melancholy Luther does exactly the opposite of what the artists of death *(Sterbekünstler)* of the baroque period recommend. He knows that sadness thrives best in solitude. The feeling of being forsaken arises in solitude, and thus it becomes a trial *(Anfechtung)* (WA 17 II, 189, 19). Therefore one should flee solitude and seek sociability, in order that we may become happy (*Table Talk* 1, 122). The devil cannot bear to see people happy, and for this reason he cannot abide music (*Table Talk* 1, 194). But God wants us to be happy. For this reason He created the sun and everything else (*Table Talk* 1, 124). Therefore one should joyfully use the creatures, even eating and drinking, and especially music, as remedies for melancholy (*Table Talk* 3, 2951 b; Enders 8, 277, 16). Therefore one must also take pleasure in the jolly talkativeness of Magistrate Christoph Gross, who cheers up those who are afflicted with melancholia (*Table Talk* 3, 2935 b).[7]

Now it is doubtless sufficiently clear that Luther is a sworn enemy of pessimism and that he does not want the aforementioned moods of earthbound happiness to be cultivated merely out of a feeling of com-

[7] WA 37, 480, 19: "Our Lord God . . . did not make the head that I should hang it in this way; that is the way He created the beasts . . ."

plaisance toward the old Adam. According to the Calvinistic conception — at least to the extent that it is later expressed in Puritanism and in Methodism — optimism is innate in man. That it must be driven out of him and that a serious, dark conception of life must be substituted — this is the goal of ethical training. Luther declares: "Sadness is innate in us" (*Table Talk* 2, 1279). If anyone were to say that he is generalizing his personal disposition here, he would counter this objection by pointing to the transsubjective reasons: the three "terrible" images of sin, death, and the "unavoidable picture of hell and eternal damnation" (WA 17 II, 686, 32 ff.). And to him who would pretend to know nothing about this by virtue of his natural disposition he would say: "You are fixing your thoughts only on the surface of life." Then he would try to give this person the perspective of death. For Luther, too, says that man must pass through the dark side of life in order to arrive at the affirmation of life. Later, of course, he would scarcely have repeated what he had said in his first lecture on the Psalms, when he had actually asked his hearers to seek distress *(Querite angustiam)* (WA 3, 63, 25). He knows that "despair" *(desperatio)* can be "salutary" *(salutaris).* But the believer will not court despair on this account. On the contrary, Luther knows that *reasons* for despair cannot fail to appear. We must go through — but actually through! The night is terrible when God leaves us alone (WA 24, 576, 33). But "still it will come about that you are left alone" (WA 28, 219, 3). Yes, "trouble and anxiety . . . preserve us well in Christianity" (WA 31 I, 95, 14). Trouble and anxiety are the trials of our faith, and the worst of these trials occur when we experience no trials at all (WA 6, 223, 28). By means of all trouble, all suffering, and all trials God wants to urge us to call upon His holy name (223, 14 ff.). If we do this, He places before us the image of His Son, who is here for us and reveals to us God's order: "The order of the matter is that death and sin exist in nature before life and righteousness" *(Ordo rei est, quod mors et peccatum est in natura ante vitam et justitiam)* (WA 39 I, 347, 1). "God shows His mastery *(kunst)* by making something out of nothing, piety out of sin, life and holiness out of death" (WA 24, 576, 19). For this reason Christ is the real Conqueror of melancholy, since He overcomes death. He commands us: "Rejoice, be happy, be confident; let not your heart be troubled" *(Laetamini, gaudete, confidite, non turbetur cor vestrum)* (*Table Talk* 1, 835). In faith in the living Christ we become certain that just as Satan is the spirit of sadness, so God is the Spirit of joy (*Table Talk* 2, 2342a). "Where Christ is, there joy is" *(Ubi Christus, ibi gaudium)* (WA 20, 365, 13). Therefore "let everyone become a falcon, which can disappear on high in such trouble. Only let him first be certain, and let him not doubt, that God does not send him such trouble in order to destroy him . . . but that He wants to drive him to prayer, to calling, and to battle." (WA 31 I, 95, 3 ff.) Here indeed all quietistic pessimism is gone. Instead, there is a tempestuous power of faith, which faces not only the trials of conscience but also the oppressive experiences of life. It is precisely in suffering that the Christian can celebrate his greatest triumphs. There he has his "great joy" *(magnum gaudium).* The greater the assault from without, the more he can – laugh (WA 34 II, 12 ff.).

Thus suffering again puts the Christian on the borderline between the here and the hereafter. Suffering should hurt him, says Luther in the first of the sermons he delivered at Coburg in 1530; yet for him this suffering is sweet and easy.[8] He feels pain; but faith in the promised deliverance makes him happy, just as all faith in a promise does. "If I want to be a Christian, I must also wear the court uniform; dear Christ does not supply any other garb at His court. *It is necessary to suffer.*" (WA 32, 29, 31; Enders 1, 31, 21.) But by causing us to follow in the footsteps of the suffering Christ this suffering becomes "sheer holiness" *(eitel heiligtum)* for us ourselves. For me it will be a cross that leads to victory of life over death. In this sense Luther counts the "healing power *(Heiltum)* of the holy cross" – that is, misfortune, persecution, tribulation, and every evil – among the characteristic marks of the "holy Christian people" of the church (WA 50, 641, 35 ff.). And here again that which happens on earth becomes a battle for him. By means of the cross God wants to make us similar to Christ – Luther's recollection of the Franciscan ideal and of German mysticism. But the devil wants to make use of the cross in order to deprive us of faith in the Word of promise. "Thus the two heroes meet; each does as much as he can. The devil always brews one misfortune after the other; for he is a mighty, evil, and restless spirit. Therefore it is time that God be concerned about His honor. . . ." (WA 32, 37, 10.) Victorious faith in the Word of promise is God's victory. Therefore here, too – where Luther speaks about the necessity of suffering – he can conclude: "Just rout suffering and the cross from your heart and mind to the best of your ability. Otherwise the evil becomes worse if you think about it for a long time." (34, 19.) He turns with the greatest sharpness against the voluntary courting of suffering – which makes many fanatics of his time medieval men through and through, not "modern" men.

Suffering as the Christian's cross – from now on this remains a gen-

[8] Cf. the beautiful jubilee publication by Herm. Bechmann, *Der Coburger Luther,* 1930.

eral theme of the Lutheran conception of life. A rationalization of this suffering is already under way in the writings of Melanchthon. He enumerates ten different causes of suffering known by the Christian in contradistinction to the pagan philosophers, and he mentions five consolations afforded by the divine Word which enables one to recognize in them the divine teleology. But Luther's idea of the cross has not yet disappeared entirely in Melanchthon's writings. Endurance and patience are a "sacrifice" *(sacrificium)* which we bring to God as true service (*CR* 21, 950). Even in the Mecklenburg *Kirchenordnung* one section, which calls to mind Luther's "marks of the church" *(notae ecclesiae)*, has the heading "Why the Church Has Been Put Under the Cross" (Sehling, *KO* V, 177). And in the subsequent literature all the New Testament answers to the question about the cause and the purpose of suffering are revived: purification, chastisement, proof of God's love, steeling for the struggle with evil, hope of the hereafter.[9] Suffering is called "the dear cross" which no Christian escapes and which is no longer an affliction for him. "Thus the dear cross – poverty, sickness, and the like – still remains even among those who have already overcome God through true faith" (Balduin, p. 16). And Othonius gives a genuinely Lutheran interpretation of the "vale of tears" when he says "that here in this vale of tears we also wander about and travel in this miserable life on the temporal road between heaven and hell, in order that we may travel to heaven if we take hold of Christ by means of a true living faith."[10]

Here for the first time the cheerfulness of the Lutheran consciousness of being a creature becomes comprehensible. Belief in God provides it with its basic depth. In the face of suffering, however, this belief in God has its capacity to bear and its redeeming power only as belief in Christ. Just as a purely naturalistic consciousness of life – a consciousness that did not have its basis in belief in God – followed close on the heels of the Lutheran consciousness of being a creature, just as a kermis Lutheranism – a Lutheranism that wanted to reap joy where only death

[9] Cf., e. g., Brenz, *Homil. in Joan.* XV, 759. — Selnecker, *Ex. ordin.* IV. 410 ff. — Wülfer (see note 1 under *Close Connection with the Earth*), p. 390. — M. Julius, pp. 27 ff., where with instructive harmlessness he places side by side as causes of pestilence: the poisoning of the air; the influence of the stars; decay and "manure puddles"; visiting dying persons and the contagion connected with this ("and there is probably something to this"); and finally the divine will to punish. — Kilius (see note 1 under *Close Connection with the Earth*), p. 48 (in a sermon delivered at the dedication of a church).

[10] Cf. Luther in *Lectures on Hebrews*, 192, 4: "For thus it happens that the believer hangs between heaven and earth, and 'sleeps,' as the psalm says, in midair, that is, is suspended in the air and crucified in Christ" *(Sic enim fit ut fidelis inter coelum et terram pendeat et inter medios aeres, ut psalmus ait, "dormiat," hoc est in Christo in aere suspensus crucifigatur).*

had been sown — followed close on the heels of earthbound cheerfulness, and just as pietism's artificial attitude toward dying followed close on the heels of Luther's idea of death, so the immanent optimism of the Enlightenment followed close on the heels of the optimism of the cross.

When all branches of learning had been emancipated from the supervision of the church, the natural sciences began the independent construction of the new world picture (cf. *Relativity of the World Picture*). Now it was no longer the ultimate purpose of theology to synthetize all knowledge under the heading "Christian." In the writings of Luther theology gave thought to the meaning of its name. It was concerned with the world and man only in their functional relationship to God. This did not mean that theologians like Melanchthon and Löscher had no command of the secular knowledge of their time. Conversely, the aforementioned independent construction of the new world picture produces the type of naturalist who "lives solely in his learning," seeks his "satisfaction" there, and is engaged in building a philosophy of life and a conception of life that conform to this attitude. It is true that the naturalist cannot escape the theological problem, particularly when, as a rule, he has a relationship to the church, as the scholar of the eighteenth century still did; but it is precisely theology that confronts him with its ever-increasing emphasis on "natural revelation" when he constructs a purely immanent philosophy of life. What made Gottfried Wilhelm von Leibniz great was the fact that he, the commanding spirit of all the learning of his age, did not withdraw from the theological question. Dilthey, of course, deplores this as a compromise, as a concession to Leibniz' position at court.[11]

But the way Leibniz does this and the answers he seeks to the theological question show him in his complete connection with what Dilthey designates as a modern philosophy of life. With Descartes and Bruno he shares the idea of the one, all-controlling teleology of the universe. With Kepler and Newton he shares the realization of the universality of natural laws. He shares Galileo's and Newton's conviction concerning the dynamic of world affairs, and he shares Bruno's conviction concerning their vitality. It is just as wrong to call the mere fact that he gives an ethical interpretation of teleology a concession to Christianity as it is to make this statement about the preponderance of the aesthetic element that makes him related to Shaftesbury.

Now, however, it is significant for the turn of events that Leibniz

[11] Dilthey, *Die neue weltliche Kultur, Gesammelte Schriften* III, 67: "Thus this mighty spirit was fated to seek a compromise between his modern ideas and the concepts of the traditional Christian philosophy of life." — One could say the same thing about Fichte and Hegel, yes, even about Goethe!

treats the theological question as "theodicy." To him it is in God that the active and the ultimate causes of world affairs are identical — a genuinely Aristotelian system that connects him with Melanchthon and Thomas.[12] When one speaks of "prestabilized harmony," the adjective points to the origin, and the noun points to God's teleology. And what Leibniz says about the various kinds of necessity could just as well have been stated by Thomas and for the most part is stated by him. To be sure, Leibniz quotes Luther's *On the Bondage of the Will (De servo arbitrio)* in substantiation of this. Thus he becomes the first to explain Luther's writing in a manner that mistakes the periphery for the center. Traces of this exegesis have remained up to the present time.[13] Strictly speaking, however, Leibniz remains within the framework of a cosmology that is founded on and supported by his aesthetic consciousness of being in the world. He does not come to the truly theological question until he gives consideration to the actual disturbances of the harmony of the world, that is, to that which is apparently or really unteleological. And his answer can appear to be a simple continuation of Lutheran optimism.

Leibniz, too, states that his belief in God accounts for his optimism. God *must* be might, wisdom, and goodness — this is shown by the world as it is. Here one is brought up short. Was Luther wrong when, on the basis of his primal experience *(Urerlebnis)*, he inferred from the world something entirely different, namely, that God cannot be known or, at all events, that only the "angry" God can be known? Did Luther merely take a gloomier view, or was his view more profound? Leibniz bases his teleological proof of the existence of God on the perfection of the world, and it is his purpose to prove that the world is the most perfect world one could imagine. But this is purely a dogma. Schopenhauer and Eduard von Hartmann "proved" the opposite. But the fact that Leibniz had this optimistic belief actually did place him into the development of Lutheranism. Prepietistic Lutheranism also has a full realization of the goodness and the beauty of the world. Conversely, Leibniz, too, is conscious of the disturbances which prepietistic Lutheranism seeks to overcome with the thoughts of "trial" or the "cross." Occasionally Luther, too, balances the good with the evil. When he does so, he, like Leibniz, concludes: "We have more cause for joy than for sorrow" (*Table Talk* 2, 1279). And when he accounts for this by referring to God, who said: "I live; you, too, shall live" *(Vivo ego et vos vivetis)* — Leibniz, too, could have said yes to this. For Luther and for early Lutheranism this

12 On Leibniz and Aristotle cf. Peter Petersen, *Geschichte der Aristotelischen Philosophie im protestantischen Deutschland,* Leipzig, 1921, pp. 340 ff.

13 Cf., e. g., *Theodizee,* pp. 43, 65, 67 f., 79, 94, 314 (!), 428.

optimistic faith is founded exclusively on belief in Christ. At the end of his writing against Erasmus, Luther, too, asks about the compatibility of empirical evil with divine justice. The disharmony of "virtue and happiness" – to speak with Kant – can, he declares, only lead to the conclusion that either there is no God or that God is unjust (WA 18, 784, 35 ff.). When finally he points to eternal life, in which the correct proportion between reward and punishment is established, one is reminded of Kant's "moral" proof of the existence of God, which, incidentally, can already be found in the writings of Melanchthon (*CR* 21, 939). But for Luther this is not a matter of a postulate. No, it is a matter of faith in the strict sense. He introduces the reference to eternal life by reminding us of the "Gospel and the knowledge of grace" *(Evangelium et cognitionem gratiae)* (WA 18, 785, 14 ff.). But from this it follows that Luther's aforementioned optimistic comparison of the causes of joy and the causes of sorrow only seems to be thought of as empirical. When one looks at the matter in a purely immanent way, the causes of sorrow can by no means be interpreted as their opposite. Only faith changes them into their opposite, because it is precisely in the added pain that faith is conscious of the proof of divine love.

To be sure, by means of his optimistic belief in God Leibniz, too, seeks to view the evil in the world as something that is good in the higher sense. He differentiates evil that is metaphysical, evil that is physical, and evil that is moral. Metaphysical evil consists in creatureliness, finiteness, and limitation; physical evil, in pains, grief, and hardships; moral evil, in wickedness. God, he says, could certainly have created a world without these imperfections. But then the world would also have forefeited some of its perfection. For an accurate examination of the world shows that the good that is present outweighs those imperfections by far. We just do not notice that the normal possession of health and the possibility of doing our duty are also something good. We are not aware of this until we lack one of these good things. This observation is especially true of the moral evil. The sum total of wickedness in the world is much smaller than the sum total of goodness. But evils are absolutely necessary in order to achieve harmony. It is only by contrasting perfection with imperfection that perfection becomes visible. Of course, some evils are to be regarded as punishment, but only because they are a means for improvement and thus help to achieve the harmonious final goal. Wickedness has no real value as something that exists. It could have this value only if it had its basis in the "region of eternal truths." But it consists in "deprivation," that is, in the fact that this region has not become operative here. God put wickedness into His world plan because it was only at this price that He could create free beings, that is, beings who are morally responsible. Like all evil, it contributes to harmony by urging one to do good. History proves that good for others often resulted from an evil deed of individuals. Wickedness performs the function that dissonances perform in music. It does not obstruct the impression of the perfect harmony God wanted to attain in the world; it makes this impression possible. Now Christ appears in connection with all this. It is only through sin that we have gained Jesus Christ, the Redeemer! [14]

This is theodicy — vindicating God because of the evil in the world. Its relationship with the optimism of Lutheranism so far as the philosophy of life is concerned is clear.[15] Although here Leibniz is always at pains to paralyze the contrast between Lutheranism and Calvinism, still one can also see in his polemics against the Reformed doctrine of predestination a relationship even with the Lutheran belief in God. Here, however, the basic position is completely changed. "God should not be judged and measured in His works; but, on the other hand, He does not do anything that is unjust" *(Deus in suis operibus sol nit geurteilt und gemessen werden, sed econtra non facit iniquum)* (WA 16, 148, 1). This is Luther's verdict concerning every kind of theodicy. Like Paul, he says that man must justify himself before God.[16] Here the opposite is now true. Man stands fast. His rational explanation of the world must be unalterable. It is not for nothing that Leibniz prefaces theodicy with the "Discussion of the Agreement of Faith with Reason." This almost has the effect of a threat against God. Our reason comes from Him. Therefore He must justify Himself before our reason. Luther also knows that reason comes from God. But for him sin is not an object of the rational explanation of the world; it is an inevitable element in itself. "If there is a God, whence evil." *(Si Deus est, unde malum?)* — this is the basic question of Leibniz' theodicy. This very way of putting the question rules out the personal responsibility of the one who asks it. Luther's conscience rebels against this. To him it is a profanation of God's majesty to ask as if the questioner were merely a spectator and not the accused. Because

[14] Leibniz quotes the ancient Easter hymn: "O sin of Adam, certainly necessary, which was destroyed through Christ's death! O blessed guilt, which deserved to have a Redeemer like this and One so great!" *(O certe necessarium Adae peccatum Quod Christi morte deletum est! O felix culpa, quae talem ac tantum Meruit habere redemptorem!)* (P. 102.)

[15] The Lutheran doctrine of Holy Communion also influenced him. It led him to his definition of the relationship of substance and mass. Cf. Guhrauer, *G. W. Frhr. v. Leibniz,* 1846, I, 77; II, 48.

[16] Cf. above all the comments in *Lectures on Romans* II, 52 ff., on the "justification of God."

reason asks in this way, it is guilty of this profanation and is therefore bound up with sin. But Leibniz considers reason not only the witness but also the judge of what God does. It is only on this account that he can arrive at the thought of a quantitative comparison between the sum total of the good and the sum total of the evil in the world. In doing so he keeps completely within the bounds of the empirical world. If he actually took his universe as a whole and sharpened it "to a mathematical point" *(ad punctum mathematicum)* when opposing it to God, sin would not be an isolated evil in the world but would be the actual expression of the relationship of the creature to its Creator, therefore the point of the whole – the point that is directed against God. Then God is not in need of vindication; man is.

He who has read Luther's explanation of Psalm 90 or his book against Erasmus will not doubt for a moment that Luther was not more pessimistic than Leibniz without a reason. On the contrary, he will realize that Luther actually had a deeper understanding than Leibniz had. Luther thought out the idea of wickedness, while Leibniz toned it down by subordinating it to the concept of evil. Leibniz lived on the optimism of the Lutheran belief in God without being willing to pay the necessary price for it. That he was able to do so was confirmed above all by what can be observed in sociology, namely, that the ideas and the motives engendered by the Reformation have a wider field of activity than the evangelical belief in God from which they resulted. In their totality they lead to the picture of historical Lutheranism which, when looked at from a purely historical point of view, has a greater sphere than the number of people who shared Luther's evangelical faith. But this very fact makes it justifiable and also necessary to regard Lutheranism as a supraindividual phenomenon in the history of thought – a phenomenon that included many individuals, even though it had consciously or unconsciously divorced itself from the impact of the Gospel *(evangelischer Ansatz)*. The optimism of the philosophy of life in question dominates the entire eighteenth century. To be sure, the earthquake that occurred in Lisbon in 1755 gives it a serious jolt; but it wins its complete victory in German idealism. Here it is established anew primarily through Hegel, and even after the collapse of the school of Hegel it continues to be operative in the subsequent epoch of evolution in the fields of natural science and history. In the end the relationship with Luther's optimism was no more than a totally external one. But the opinion spread – not without the fault of theology and the church – that the relationship between the immanent optimism of progress and the evangelical faith was not only external but basic. For this reason the terrible disappointment of the great war could be interpreted as a refutation of this faith in the "love and justice of God." And the realization of the actually ensuing breakdown of an immanent-optimistic belief in God could be one of the reasons for the return to the "real" Luther.

The idealistic interpretation of Lutheran optimism makes it clear that consciousness of being a creature becomes consciousness of time and to what extent this is true. Lutheran optimism is the beginning of the temporalizing of the spatial world.

34. History [1]

In the consciousness of being closely connected with the earth man experiences his direct relationship to his environment. And he affirms this relationship. But when he experiences painful contact with his environment as a "cross," this immediacy is destroyed. Man's feeling is split. "It is necessary to suffer," says Luther. But at the same time he continues: "Just drive suffering and the cross from your heart and mind to the best of your ability" (cf. *Cross and Vale of Tears*). This is at once an affirmation and a denial. This splitting has its transcendental possibility in faith. In its psychical actuality, however, it transforms the state of suffering into a receding event. As soon as "suffering" is recognized as a "cross" and is joyfully affirmed, it is always "in the past" for the believer. To be sure, it was not lost. It leaves experience behind. But in Hegel's sense it is "negated."

This, however, is only a special case. A similar splitting is experienced in general in the close connection with the earth even when this connection expresses itself in cheerful consciousness of being a creature. Then, of course, man puts himself completely into nature; but he knows that at the same time he is something different from the blossoms in the garden and the stars in the sky. As a type and as a personal individual he is a human being. He gathers experience. In experience all direct contacts with his environment become events in the past. But comparison with others teaches man that once upon a time he himself, together with his experiences, was "in the past." Perhaps, however, the genus homo lives on — the genus homo in which the

[1] R. Rocholl, *Die Philosophie der Geschichte*, Vol. I, Göttingen, 1878. — Ernst Schäfer, *Luther als Kirchenhistoriker*, Gütersloh, 1897. — W. Köhler, *Luther u. die Kirchengeschichte*, Erlangen, 1900. — E. Menke-Glückert, *Die Geschichtsschreibung der Reformation und Gegenreformation*, Osterwieck in the upper Harz, 1912. — Moritz Ritter, *Die Entwicklung der Geschichtswissenschaft an den führenden Werken betrachtet*, Munich, 1919. — Karl Völker, *Die Kirchengeschichtsschreibung der Aufklärung*, 1921. — Herbert Vossberg, *Luthers Kritik aller Religion*, Leipzig, 1922. — Emil Clemens Scherer, *Geschichte und Kirchengeschichte an den deutschen Universitäten*, Freiburg, 1927.

experiences of all individuals are preserved beyond the end of my life. Where this is felt, historical thinking begins. This always presupposes a splitting of the consciousness of being in the world. It transforms a state into an event that is condemned to the past at the very moment it is recognized as an event. But by constantly remaining the present for himself the human being who thinks historically divorces himself from the environment which always becomes an event, that is, the past. Here, too, the splitting takes the place of the homogeneity and the immediacy of the consciousness of being in the world. The state of direct relationship to the world becomes a moment. The spatial relationship itself becomes a momentary event. It perishes in the consciousness of time.

In itself this temporalizing of the consciousness of being in the world has nothing to do with faith. From Thales to Heraclitus, from Spinoza to Hegel, it is the way of philosophy as an interpretation of the world. Luther, too, reached this point without faith. For only on this assumption can one understand that initial demand "that we transfer ourselves outside time" *(ut transferamus nos extra tempus)* (cf. *The Primal Experience*). What he says about sharpening the consciousness of life "to a mathematical point" *(ad punctum mathematicum)* is the recognition of life as a "moment." But when in this "moment" man hears God's verdict of forgiveness, then he is confronted by a timeless You which, removed from condemnation to the past, is rather an eternal present. It is precisely at the very end of the consciousness of time that a new splitting takes place here for the man of faith: I am fading, but God's verdict declares that I am imperishable. And only this splitting corresponds entirely to the aforementioned splitting that takes place in the face of suffering. When the believer refers suffering to God, he thinks of God not only as the cause – every cause belongs to the past – but he hears in it the promise of life for him who is to die. Therefore suffering felt as a cross always contains a reference to the futurity of God, thus to victory over the past.

In this elementary sense the revealed consciousness of time cannot be separated at all from the Christian belief in God. It is even a characteristic of the Old Testament belief in God. One finds it in the writings of Paul and Augustine as well as in the writings of Thomas Aquinas and Luther. But it would not be correct simply to equate Luther's consciousness of time with the consciousness of transitoriness. The impact of the Gospel *(evangelischer Ansatz)* teaches that although God condemns the sinner to death, He nevertheless pardons him unto life. The affirmation of man through God permeates the condemnation of the entire content of his life as "sin"; but as pardon it is actually the affirmation, the recognition of His own creature. The same affirmation in the denial was encountered in the conception of the relationship between God and the world. Nor can it be otherwise in God's relationship to time. Although the moment in which I hear God's verdict is the abolition of time, yet because this happens to my moment, it is at the same time a recognition of this moment. But this is true of the world moment in general. It is wholly history, wholly time. Therefore God confronts this moment as Someone entirely different. But not only this. Just as He is active in the affairs of the world as One who is "always full of activity everywhere" *(semper ubique actuosus)*, so He also has a positive relationship to history. Christ is the temporalizing of God.

To be sure, this temporalizing of God is more than His general "operative presence" in the creatures. As the incarnation it is related first of all to this "operative presence" as man is related to the creatures that are not human. For man it establishes his special place in the universe. Dilthey declared that the view "according to which man is the goal of creation and that everything else is a means for him" was "a terrible teaching" (*Ges. Schr.* III, 63). He considered Leibniz the liberator "of all previous theology, which, in Judaizing selfishness, had made man the center of the universe" (26). Strange praise for the "founder of German idealism," at the peak of which Hegel surely stands! If the objective spirit needs the subjective spirit in order to arrive at knowledge of itself and thus to become the absolute spirit – and if the subjective spirit is the spirit of man and thus the absolute spirit came to itself in the knowledge of Hegel – the chair of philosophy at the University of Berlin, which both Hegel and Dilthey occupied, is the "center of the universe." In laying claim to this Dilthey scarcely thought differently from Hegel. He differed from him only insofar as he did not express it. But at all events Hegel stood on Christian ground insofar as he gave preference, after all, to Christ as the center of history. "All history takes its course up to that time and from then on," we read in his history of philosophy. Although God is the center of the universe for the Christian philosophy of life, in His incarnation He also gives the immanent course of history a focal point, and at the same moment man – at any rate the Man Christ – has become the "center of the universe."

Of course, one needs faith in order to know and recognize this. But faith is not related to mere consciousness of the world as subjective knowledge is related to objective knowledge. The very opposite is true. All knowledge of the world is *my* knowledge. But in the Word concerning Christ, which announces forgiveness to me, I hear that I am known, and known by One who I myself am not. That this knowledge of God, of which mankind is the object, is a knowledge out of love and in love – this is an essential element of the revelation of Christ. But since evangelical faith cannot separate the relationship "Christ for me" from the relationship "Christ for all," God's incarnation becomes for it the pivotal point of its whole conception of history. What happens to me in Christ happens to all men so far as God is concerned. If He affirms me in my moment, He affirms the moment of all men. He affirms the moment of history. Here He affirms as He always does: under judgment because of sin. But history is not sin, just as nature is not sin and "original sin" is not "the substance of man." God's affirmation of history is just as critical as His attitude toward individuals is.

Even in Christ God's relationship to the world is critical. Even in Christ God condemns sin. Not Christ's sin, to be sure, but the sin "of the whole world." Thus Christ establishes the unity of historical mankind. But the sinless Christ is at the same time the other Adam, therefore a new dawning of history. In this way God's critical attitude toward history, which has its formal basis in his otherworldliness *(Jenseitigkeit)*, becomes an inner-historical matter. Whether there are phenomena in history that must be equated with the "kingdom of Christ" can be left undecided at this point (cf. *The Kingdom of Christ*). But faith cannot doubt that this Kingdom is active in history, since faith itself lives by this activity. For this a later theology coined the concept of the history of salvation *(Heilsgeschichte)*. As early as 1521 Melanchthon used the expression "divine history" *(historia divina)* in his *Loci*.[2] It is clear that so far as its content is concerned, this expression is not foreign to Luther either. To Luther the whole life of the historical Christ is the history of salvation (cf. *Propter Christum* and *The States and Offices of Christ*). He also took all Old Testament history as he found it in the Old Testament, and for this reason he also saw in it a direct activity of God in history. But the idea of the later Reformed federal theology concerning a gradually ensuing realization of salvation in history was foreign to Luther. This idea has its forerunners in Montanism and in the "eternal" *(aeternum)* Gospel of Joachim von Floris, which diluted the absolutely central significance of Christ into a relative significance. Their "third kingdom" celebrated its resurrection

[2] Plitt-Kolde, p. 170: "Now those who have this faith truly give assent to every word of God, to the threats and the promises of divine history" *(Jam omni verbo dei, minis et promissionibus historiae divinae vere assentiuntur, qui sic fidunt)*. It is possible, of course, that written history is meant here. Thus "divine history" could be used as a synonym for Holy Scripture. The same expression is certainly employed in this way by the authors of the *Magdeburg Centuries*.

in the writings of Lessing, Fichte, and Ibsen. The ideas pertaining to a history of salvation did not become part of Lutheran theology until they were set forth by Johann Christian Konrad von Hofmann, of Erlangen, the only Lutheran theologian who was also recognized by the Reformed Church.[3] Luther had a doctrinal interest in only one point of the range of ideas pertaining to the history of salvation: in the actual historical revelation of God in Christ.[4] This certainly does not preclude tracing the history of salvation throughout the Old Testament, provided that when doing so one has the same frank attitude toward the sources that Luther had. But for evangelical faith this can have no other significance than the Old Testament as a whole had for Luther. It is the prophecies contained in the Old Testament that bind him as well as the early Melanchthon to this part of Holy Scripture. This alone is likewise the basis of the interest in those who bore and proclaimed the prophecies. And here the thought of the divine authorization and inspiration of these prophecies also has its logical place (cf. *Canon, Inspiration, Means of Grace, and Apologetics*).

It would be a mistake to think that the aloofness of Luther and early Lutheranism vis-à-vis the idea of the gradual progress of the history of salvation was due to a lack of a sense of history. The very opposite is the case. This aloofness gives expression to the determination to let history be history. Karl Holl has shown in an impressive manner how this endeavor also dominates Luther's exposition of Scripture more and more.[5] And so far as the presentation of history is concerned, one need only compare Sebastian Franck's *Chronica* (1531) with Melanchthon's *Chronicon Carionis*.[6] There everything is history

[3] Gottlob Schrenk's proof of Hofmann's dependence on the Reformed Pastor Krafft in Erlangen (*Gottesreich und Bund*, Gütersloh, 1923, pp. 330 ff.) is worthy of high praise. Yet it was not necessary for Krafft to acquaint Hofmann with the idea of a gradual realization of salvation. This idea is common property of German idealism.

[4] I refer here to Vossberg, who (op. cit., p. 89) summarizes as follows: "On the one hand, therefore, Luther allots to the Israelitic-Jewish history of religion the theocentric type; on the other hand, he allots to it the egocentric type in its two main expressions — worship of creatures and piety that consists in works. Here it is clear how closely Luther could link the past to the immediate present. In the prophetic religion he saw the evangelical piety of faith; here he recognized his own religion. Under the covering of the idolatrous and legalistic religion of Israel he saw monkish as well as enthusiastic piety. *The eras and the individual differences escape him, and he saw successive events on one level.*"

[5] *Luthers Bedeutung für den Fortschritt der Auslegekunst, Ges. Aufsätze* I, 5th and 6th ed., p. 544.

[6] On Franck cf. Arnold Reimann, *Sebastian Franck als Geschichtsphilosoph (Camenius-Schriften zur Geistesgeschichte, No. 1)*, Berlin, 1921. — The *Chronicon Carionis* in the version of 1558 is found in *CR* 12, 711 ff. Melanchthon's substantial share in it was proved by E. Menke-Glückert, op. cit., pp. 26 ff. and 143 ff.

of religion; here everything is profane history. Certainly Melanchthon also acknowledges God as the Originator and the Leader of history. From Him come the states, the sciences, and the arts. He checks tyrants and sees to it that among the monarchies of the world there is relief from tyranny. But this activity of God is viewed within the framework of what God does in the world in general. Melanchthon actually writes world history which, with a genuine consciousness of time, also relativizes every happening at the moment at which it becomes an event. It is Melanchthon the humanist who constantly advances to the sources and lets the sources speak in the words of their authors, who seeks to satisfy from the sources the burning need of a genuine knowledge of history. The sources must relate how it "actually was" — but that it really *was*. He praises the writings of Moses because they are older sources for the history of the nations than the sources of the Greeks are (*CR* 9, 80). Luther sets a similar value on Moses, but he believes that Moses was dependent on older written sources (*Table Talk* 1, 291) — a noteworthy contribution to his doctrine of inspiration! Even in the foreword to the *Loci* Melanchthon promises to adhere to the "historical succession" (*historica series*) of the Biblical accounts because he does not want to invent new things, as Hesiod and the heretics did (21, 254; 605 f.). If one can see in this the program of a "theology in conformity with the history of salvation" (*heilsgeschichtliche Theologie*), he surely did not carry it out. For him the "historical matters" (*historica*) cease with the account of the Resurrection. Then Christ's discourses bring the "articles of faith" (*articuli fidei*), above all the "exposition of the Law and the Gospel" (*explicatio Legis et Evangelii*); and Paul wrote the necessary "discussions" (*disputationes*) of these matters (606). Fortunately, in the crucial passages of the final editions of the *Loci* Melanchthon adhered more to Paul the debater than he did to the historical sequence of the Biblical books. He did this exclusively in the edition of 1521. If the invasion of dogmatics by a humanistic overestimation of historical treatment is of dubious value, it became all the more important for the historical thinking of subsequent Lutheranism.

In the writings of Lorenzo Valla (1405–57) the humanistic struggle for the historical sources already includes a clear attack on the official historical picture of the Roman Church as this picture had been classically presented by Tolomeo of Lucca. For Tolomeo this picture serves to build the canonistic substructure of the empirical church. Claims to legal title are based on history. In this respect the relationship of the Reformation to historical criticism is not accidental either. It enters the humanistic struggle. It did not begin this struggle. But the *Magdeburg*

Centuries brought the struggle to an end. Therefore the criticism of church history by the Reformation is by no means "unconditioned." The untenability of the direct divine institution of the Roman Church had become certain to Luther on the basis of history. This untenability follows from the impact of the Gospel *(evangelischer Ansatz)*, which has a completely different basis, and from the new conception which the impact of the Gospel *(evangelischer Ansatz)* presents of the nature of the church. This knowledge, which springs from faith, needed no historical props. Nor could it be shaken by historical knowledge. All the historical proof adduced by the canonists and the historians on the other side could have validity only for those who regarded as binding the three characteristics of Catholicism mentioned by Vincent of Lérins and who shared Vincent's conviction that historical legal titles can be the basis of divine canonical law. When Luther and his associates took up the historical battle, they could hope for nothing else for their cause than to shake the position of the opposition; they could not hope to substantiate their own cause. Even before the Disputation at Leipzig, Luther came to the historical realization that it had taken a long time to develop the primacy of the pope, that for centuries it was not recognized at all, that later it was recognized only with limitations, and that by treating it as an article of faith one branded as heretics not only Cyprian, Athanasius, and all the Eastern theologians but also the apostles, to whom it was unknown.[7] In this way it had been proved that not one of the three characteristics mentioned by Vincent of Lérins could be enlisted as proof of the divine primacy of the pope. But this historical evidence also became deadly for the dogmatical presupposition of the opposition.

Nevertheless, evangelical faith also had a positive relationship to this historical knowledge. By denying — for God's sake — the papal legal institution's claim to absolutism it affirmed — again for God's sake — the relativity of history. Therefore proof of the fallibility of the councils had to follow. Therefore the rejection of the binding force of tradition for faith. Among inner-historical products only Scripture should retain its divine right — not, however, because of its historical reliability but as the Gospel concerning Christ, that is, as promise for our moment. Finally, therefore, the Formula of Concord's relativistic assessment of its own confessions as testimonies of "those who were living at that time." The historical relativism of the modern world goes back to early Lutheranism as well as to the Renaissance. In connection with the latter it leads to the break with Christianity by dissolving the Roman Catholic

[7] Letters to Dungersheim, Enders 1, 366 f.; to Spalatin, 2, 4 ff.

authority. In connection with the former the very opposite is true. Here it has its support in the evangelical belief in God. The results of early Lutheranism's historical way of thinking are similar to the results that come about in the domain of sociology. They cannot convince anyone of the truth and the necessity of the impact of the Gospel *(evangelischer Ansatz).* But they give proof of the mighty impulses the impact of the Gospel *(evangelischer Ansatz)* has passed on to the new world. The transcendent basis of the belief in God in the Gospel freed the church historian on principle from apologetic reservations. But it was also the prerequisite to a purely immanent treatment of profane history. This basic emancipation of historical thinking opened the door to the independent representation of history at the Lutheran universities. Melanchthon himself delivered lectures on history. The charter of the University of Marburg provides for the university's own professorship of history, the first full-time professorship of this kind at a German university. Hermann von dem Busche, Luther's admirable humanistic comrade in arms, becomes the first to occupy this chair. Through him it immediately becomes the most highly esteemed chair in the faculty of liberal arts. While the humanistic science of history still clings for the most part to the classical historians of ancient times and of early Germany, Goldenhauer, who succeeded Von dem Busche, begins to lecture on provincial and contemporary subjects.[8] Landgrave Philip himself had a pronounced sense of history. Greifswald got a professorship of history of its own in 1544; Tübingen, in 1557. In Königsberg the chair of history is combined with the chair of rhetoric; in Jena, with the chair of ethics.[9]

The great program of reform that Luther drew up for the universities in his *To the Christian Nobility of the German Nation Concerning the*

[8] H. Hermelink, *Die Philipps-Univ. Marburg,* 1927, pp. 61 f. and 144 f.

[9] Scherer, op. cit., pp. 34 ff. Scherer, of course, cannot refrain — obviously with reference to Friedrich Paulsen, *the* Protestant authority in these matters — from repeating the old assertion that "at first the spirit of Lutheranism was unfavorably disposed toward learning" and that "together with the breakdown of the humanistic movement the ecclesiastical and social upheavals that began with the spreading of Lutheranism brought about a general disorganization of the educational system" (p. 29). But when, in spite of this, he praises what Melanchthon did for the introduction of the study of history at the universities — which is greatly to Scherer's credit in connection with this assessment of Lutheranism — he surely could have concluded that only one of two things can be correct: either that humanism broke down as a result of the Reformation — then what Melanchthon accomplished must be charged to humanism, not to Lutheranism — or that Melanchthon achieved this as a humanist — then humanism cannot have broken down as a result of Lutheranism.

Actually the demand that history be represented at the universities stems — from Luther, who made this demand as early as the year 1520. It is found in *To the Christian Nobility of the German Nation (An den christlichen Adel deutscher Nation)* (WA 6, 458, 34).

Reform of Christendom (An den christlichen Adel deutscher Nation von des christlichen Standes Besserung) opens up a large number of historical perspectives. Here consciousness of the history of his own people comes to life. Here the extra-political and the inner-political, the ecclesiastical-political and the cultural-political demand grows out of historical knowledge. Centuries went by before this knowledge of the connections the present also has with the past in inferences drawn from similar cases became fruitful for historical research in the entire multiplicity of historical factors. But in Johannes Sleidan, who wrote a history of the League of Smalcald, a vivid feeling for historical events is already combined with the new critical approach. Of course, this feeling is facilitated for him by the fact that he writes contemporary history. But it is surely a different matter if the older chronicler describes only external events or the historian Sleidan tries to understand events on the basis of the play of historical forces. Moritz Ritter finds fault with Sleidan for centering his attention on a single fact as he does on a single official document. Not without justification. Sleidan describes events. In addition, he describes them as deeds of individual persons. But behind these there are at least two great collective forces: the old and the new doctrine. To be sure, he is unable to tell how these two final causes of the contemporary movement lead to an inner motivation of the individual acts. The persons and the groups are rigid quantities. But between them the aims play hither and thither, and Sleidan, who thinks in terms of functions, is not able to put this into words. As far as is possible, he lets the documents speak. True, he still clings to the single document. He still combines externally, not intuitively. But what progress is to be seen in the very fact that here the sources themselves are brought to the reader! This is the last step on the way from saga to the science of history in the modern sense, from myth to the critical writing of history. Machiavelli still works with reports. In Sleidan the critical approach, which is not satisfied until it has firsthand sources, is victorious.

Sleidan's little presentation of world history still clings — as Melanchthon does — to the pattern of the four world monarchies. It would probably have been asking too much if one had expected him to have an understanding of the dissolution of the old German Empire — the dissolution that had been hastened by the schism. But in his *Commentaries on the Status of Religion and the State Under Emperor Charles V (Commentarii de statu religionis et rei publicae Carolo V. Caesare)* [10] an

[10] Menke-Glückert, p. 74: "The very title, with its separation of religious and political matters, shows Sleidan's dependence on Melanchthon's views with regard to history."

understanding of the innermost dynamic of German history — the dynamic that springs from the polarity of the religious and the political motives — is actually expressed for the first time on the basis of the sources. In this sense a straight line leads from Sleidan through Bogislav Philipp Chemnitz, the Swedish historiographer who was a grandson of Martin Chemnitz, and Samuel Pufendorf to Leopold von Ranke, who himself had a high regard for Sleidan's little history of the world — even though especially the latest stage includes the influx of an immeasurable wealth of new discoveries, viewpoints, questionings, and also a capability of psychological empathy, over against which Sleidan's quotations of documents impress one as being immature. Even Ranke's works are still dominated to a large extent by the feeling for the aforementioned polar dynamic. This is also expressed in his feeling for irreligiousness. Of course, Ranke — entirely apart from the one time he combined historical divination with reproductive ability — is unthinkable without German idealism. But even the idealistic conception of history as such belongs into a train of development from which early Lutheranism cannot be excluded.

It has already been pointed out in another connection that this retrospective glance at the church history of the past had a background that was different from the intention to refute the historical claims of the opposition (cf. *Catholicity*). The elementary thought concerning the birth of the church from the Gospel led to the question of the historical origin of the church. But it also led to the idea of catholicity. This had to be distinguished from the conviction that there have been believers at all times. On the contrary, it means that the Word of the Gospel has never been silent. Thus it gives expression to the consciousness of the historical continuity of the church. But for this very reason it directs one's attention to history itself. How fruitful this train of thought could be for historical research is shown by Joachim Camerarius' history of the Bohemian Brethren, which, to be sure, was not printed until a generation after the author's death.[11] But what Camerarius did contained the seed of the work that is the basis of all modern church history: the *Magdeburg Centuries*.[12] In his biography of Luther, Johann Cochläus had still jibed that the Lutherans had searched all the libraries in vain, but that in all the centuries they had not been able to find a single teacher of the church — Rupert alone excepted — who had sanctioned

[11] *Historica narratio de Fratrum Orthodoxorum ecclesiis in Bohemia, Moravia et Polonia,* 1605.

[12] *Ecclesiastica Historia integram ecclesiae ideam . . . complectens . . . congesta per aliquot studiosos et pios viros in urbe Magdeburgica,* Basle, 1559—74.

Luther's dogmas.[13] A few years later Matthias Flacius gave the first answer in his *Catalog of the Witnesses to the Truth (Catalogus testium veritatis)* (1556). Soon after this he gave the second answer in the *Magdeburg Centuries.* This lightning struck. Lutheranism no innovation? In inner agreement, on the contrary, with Christian history? The Spanish court insists on a refutation. For this purpose it proposes the University of Alcalá. The Jesuits are insistent. The Roman curia is insistent. Under the chairmanship of Giovanni de Morone the committee of German bishops *(die deutsche Kongregation)* makes itself the seat of the opposition.[14] Rome had been hit at the core. For Lutheranism had rediscovered itself in history. Among the fourteen "advantages" *(utilitates)* the foreword to the *Magdeburg Centuries* places the thought of continuity at the head. In doing so it adheres strictly to the dogmatic relationship of catholicity to the church as this relationship had previously been developed.[15] Church history shows "perpetual agreement in the teaching of each article of faith in all ages" *(perpetuum consensum in doctrina singulorum articulorum fidei omnibus aetatibus).* The reader will realize "that this very form of the teaching which we now have in our churches because of the great kindness of God is that very ancient one, not a new one; genuine, not adulterous; true, not fabricated" *(quod haec ipsa doctrinae forma, quam nunc in Ecclesiis nostris ex ingenti Dei beneficio habemus, sit illa ipsa vetus, non nova; germana, non adulterina; vera, non commentitia).* The main defects of the work – the external division according to centuries and the stereotyped treatment of the in-

[13] Cochlaeus, *Commentaria de actis et scriptis Mart. Lutheri Saxonis, St. Victor. prope Mogunt.,* 1549, p. 132.

[14] *Nuntiaturberichte aus Deutschland, III. Abt. 3. Bd.,* ed. by K. Schellhass, Berlin, 1896, pp. 216 f. and 258 f.

[15] It could, of course, appear to be a break with the Lutheran idea of the church when first of all it is mentioned in general as the primary purpose "to see before our eyes the idea of the church of our Lord Jesus Christ depicted as in a painting. . . . It is an article of faith to believe in the holy catholic church." *(Ideam Ecclesiae Domini nostri J. Chr. ob oculos videre quasi in tabula depictam. . . . Est fidei articulus, credere Ecclesiam sanctam Catholicam.)* One could object that it is impossible to depict that which is believed. But this would have validity only if the character of the church so far as faith is concerned consisted in its "invisibility" — which, however, is in contradiction to the Lutheran conception of the church. On the contrary, here that which causes the church to show its activity in the world and in this very way to give evidence of its faith is added as the center of the entire presentation: "Therefore church history of this kind teaches that by the marvelous mercy and power of God the church in which God is operative is gathered in all ages through the ministry of the Divine Word and exists by reason of this ministry" *(Docet igitur historia eius modi Ecclesiastica, quod omnibus aetatibus mirabili Dei clementia et potentia ministerio verbi divini colligatur et consistat Ecclesia, in qua Deus est efficax).*

dividual epochs from the same functional points of view – have been criticized often enough. But the second of these defects is amply counterbalanced by the fact that in this way for the first time a presentation of the history of culture, of the history of government, and of the history of dogma came into being on the basis of the sources. To be sure, one misses the psychological empathy of the modern historian, just as one misses this in the case of Sleidan. Here Gottfried Arnold was the first to make a definitive change in the field of church history.[16] But no later achievement can diminish the service which the authors of the *Centuries* rendered to the history of dogma. Here the methodical strictness with which they presented the "objective" teaching throughout the centuries was by no means out of place. Here Arnold, the pietist for whom "the human soul" "is decisive" throughout the history of the church, must give way.[17] It is self-evident that the *Centuries* also had to point out "the origins and the increments of errors and the corrupting influences" *(origines et ingrementa errorum et corruptelarum)* in history. Here one sees their confessional ties. But the history of dogma that is completely free from this has not yet been written. Furthermore, one would have to ask whether a historian who is unwilling on principle to make a distinction between truth and error is capable at all of feeling his way into the doctrinal controversies of the past. That the verdict of the *Centuries* concerning the dogmatic development after the fifth century is predominantly pessimistic will easily be understood from their own position amid the doctrinal controversies of this century. They stood against three fronts. It is all the more remarkable that they did not let this keep them from holding firmly to the thesis of continuity. And is Adolf Harnack's history of the dogma of the ancient church or the presentation of the development of doctrine given by Friedrich Loofs less pessimistic? Scarcely anywhere in the *Centuries* is there such spite as is self-evident in the writings of many historians of dogma when they come to speak about the Lutheran Formula of Concord. And how few students of church history there undoubtedly are who realize that in their use of the sources – not only in investigating but also in combining them – they still follow the same path today that was opened up by the authors of the *Centuries!* Adolf Harnack's *History of Missions and the Spreading of Christianity in the First Three Centuries (Geschichte der Mission und Ausbreitung des Christentums in den ersten drei Jahr-*

[16] Proof in Erich Seeberg, *Gottfried Arnold, Die Wissenschaft und die Mystik seiner Zeit,* Meerane in Saxony, 1923.

[17] Thus Erich Seeberg, op. cit., p. 67.

hunderten) reads like a new edition of the corresponding sections of the *Centuries.*[18]

The father and organizer of the gigantic work called the *Magdeburg Centuries* is the same Matthias Flacius Illyricus who up to the present time appears in all descriptions of the century of the Reformation as a distinctive example of dogmatic pugnacity, yes, of the "dogmatic one-sidedness" of the entire age. But this age was not one-sided; it was two-sided. For Flacius the dogmatician history has become a passion. He is never satisfied with secondhand descriptions. He does not rest until he discovers the primary sources.[19] In Frankfurt he has a permanent representative who is to procure writings of the Waldensians from the merchants of Lyons. For a half year Marcus Wagner makes excerpts at the library of the imperial councilor Kaspar von Neidbruck in Vienna. When he announces the discovery of a Greek manuscript of Gregory of Nazianzus and another of Alcuin, a messenger on horseback is to bring these manuscripts to Magdeburg at once. All the libraries to which access is in any way possible – in Prussia, in Austria, in Bavaria, in Copenhagen, in Scotland – are ransacked. But this is not done in a haphazard manner; it is done according to a fixed program. It goes without saying that this search included all documents pertaining to heresy trials. But who before Flacius had thought of searching for all the rituals that were in use before Gregory the Great? Feverish work is done in Magdeburg itself. Seven students make excerpts under the direction of Flacius, Johann Wigand, Matth. Judex, and Basilius Faber. Decisions with regard to all the more important questions are reached in the plenary meeting of the leaders. Finally the dedicatory letter of the first volume makes mention of the amanuensis who made a fair copy of the result.

The very circle of the co-workers who searched and assembled shows that this is not a private hobby of Flacius. The passion for history spreads. Money is needed to carry on this mighty work. The editors sacrifice their own means. Although a plea for support does not have the desired success, nevertheless the King of Denmark promises 200 gulden a year, which, to be sure, were never paid. But the city of Lindau as well as noblemen and citizens of Augsburg and Nürnberg contribute. Ottheinrich, the count palatine, as well as Andreas Fugger in Augsburg

[18] Cf., e. g., the sections "on the place and the propagation of the church" *(de loco et propagatione ecclesiae)* in the individual *Centuries* and the source material brought together here for the first time with the corresponding sections in Harnack!

[19] On what follows cf. W. Preger, *M. Flacius Illyricus und seine Zeit,* 1859, II, 413 ff. — W. Schulte, *Beiträge zur Entstehungsgeschichte der Magdeburger Zenturien,* 1877. — Schaumkell, *Beitrag zur Entstehungsgeschichte der M. Z.,* 1898.

offer the treasures of their libraries. Here the historical-minded new era draws one of its first breaths.[20] The battle which the Wittenbergians of that time and the theologians of Leipzig fight against the work before it appears surely has other reasons than personal irritability over against Flacius. The Wittenbergians point to Melanchthon's *Chronicon* in order to emphasize the uselessness of the *Centuries.* If the authors are unwilling to abandon the project, they should at least not call it a *History (Historia);* they should call it *Commentaries (Commentarii),* as Sleidan had titled his work.[21] Here, too, Philippism contends against Gnesio-Lutheranism. Philippism believes that historical thinking should be schooled in the ancient teachers. It is true that the school of Melanchthon, like Flacius, attaches great importance to the *Catalog of the Witnesses to the Truth (Catalogus testium veritatis).* In his *Methods of the Subjects of Doctrine (Methodi locorum doctrinae)* (1569) Simon Pauli has a long "Series of Doctors in the Church from the Creation of the World" *(Series doctorum in ecclesia a mundo condito),* in which the names not only of Luther and Melanchthon but also those of Alcuin and Albertus Magnus are set off in the printing. By and large, however, the historical picture is just as stable as the Ptolemaic world picture. At best, one can write commentaries on it. But here Gnesio-Lutheranism follows in the footsteps of Luther by contending for the completely independent knowledge of history exactly as it accepted as definitive Luther's destruction of Ptolemy's celestial spheres when it espoused Luther's doctrine of Holy Communion.[22]

Here, in the seventeenth century, the letdown ensues. It is similar

[20] A sermon delivered in the following century by Johann Saubert, of Nürnberg, may serve as an example of the modern assessment of the library. In this sermon God Himself is described as the Librarian: *Liber Providentiae Divinae specialis. Das ist Denkzeddel Gottes, darinn die recht Gottesfürchtige auffgezeichnet finden* (on Mal. 3:16), Nürnberg, 1643. Here we read: "The profitable use of the text. In the first place, for teaching. They give us (1) a teaching concerning God's library." According to Ps. 139:16 and Apoc. 5:1, God has in His possession, in the first place, the book of general election; in the second place, according to Dan. 7:10, the books of judgment; thirdly, "the book of God's special election," in which instances of the forgiveness of sins, the hearing of prayers, and other comfortings are recorded — "They are surely written in God's memorandum" (Mal. 3:16) — thus a sort of card index; fourthly, the real "book of life."

[21] Cf., e. g., the defense of the Magdeburgians *De ecclesiastica historia, quae Magdeburgi contexitur. Narratio contra Menium et Scholasticorum Wittebergensium epistolas,* with the appended reply of the Wittenbergians (*Cum responsione scholasticorum Wittebergensium ad eandem,* Wittenberg, 1558), in which Flacius is suspected in a downright perfidious manner of spending on himself the money that had been collected, and in which the collaborators are stirred up against him.

[22] That even in his exegesis Flacius was a genuine disciple of Luther is shown by Holl, op. cit., pp. 578 ff.

to what took place in the struggle for the Copernican world picture. The passion for history cools off. Even Johann Gerhard and Quenstedt, with their wealth of patristic evidence, reap the fruits of the research carried on in the century of the Reformation. It is true that Georg Calixt thought historically; but his knowledge was meager, even though he had been privileged to inspire Hermann Conring to devote himself to history (*Rechtsgeschichte,* Vol. II). Not until the appearance of Ernst Salomo Cyprian, who was superintendent in Gotha, and Valentin Ernst Löscher does the passion — and at the same time the two-sidedness that characterized Flacius — awaken again. The two Walchs follow — father and son — the one even more industrious than the other. Johann Matthias Schröckh follows in Wittenberg. At the command of Emperor Joseph II his church history in forty-five volumes is introduced even at the general seminaries of Austria.[23] This, of course is greater praise for Schröckh than it is for the emperor, who acted here from the same rationalistic motives that prompted him to issue the command to bury the dead in sacks in order to save wood. Weighty inner changes in the conception of church history take place. Johann Lorenz von Mosheim left the division between truth and error to two great parties in the history of the church. In the writings of Ludwig Timotheus Spittler the last remnant of transcendence has disappeared. But the passion for history remained.

But by becoming a passion, history also took possession of man. It forms him and draws him into its incessant movement. It begins to dominate his consciousness of the world. Man feels that he carries history within himself just as history carries him within itself. He himself, the man, is history — no longer as an individual, it is true, but as a type, and not as a constant type but as a type that has come about and is in the making. Since he devotes himself to history, history lifts him beyond himself and promises him endless progress. But the fact that man and history become one presupposes a prestabilized identity. It is an act of the spirit that perceives. The world as history is the evolution of the spirit which, in the end, finds itself again as presupposition and origin of the world. In the writings of Fichte and Hegel history is thought out to the end. Fichte does this in one way; Hegel does it in another way. Their philosophy of identity has been materialized by Karl Marx and Lenin. But in spite of all even their philosophy of life is, historically speaking, exactly like that of Charles Darwin. There is no longer an existence of the spatial world. Einstein's theory of relativity proceeds from the fact that time is differentiated in itself. It ends in the doctrine

[23] According to Franz Zach, *Modernes oder kathol. Kulturideal,* 3d ed., 1925, p. 262. — On the historical arrangement of the entire theology — the arrangement that began with Buddeus and Chr. Matth. Pfaff — cf. Stolzenburg, op. cit., pp. 53 ff.

of the "bending of space" *(Krümmung des Raumes).* Today physics and astronomy end in the second thermodynamic axiom, that is, in the realiziation that the loss of warmth causes energy to die. They have capitulated to the fact that time cannot be turned back.

What the German Reformation contributed to the evolution of the modern consciousness of time consists primarily in the dissolution of the stability of Rome. This was not only an ecclesiastical act. It was an event bound up with the higher degree of civilization man had attained. Just as the earth was the firm basis of the entire astronomical system, so Rome was the spatial center of the life of mankind. Eternal Rome was and remained what it had been since the days of the apostles. Leo X was pope in exactly the same sense in which Peter had been pope. Through the Reformation, Rome was snatched into the stream of history. Whether one considers the history of the papacy a depravation, as Luther and Flacius do, or progress, as modern historians of the Roman Church do, makes no difference to historical thinking as such. For Luther the "Babylonian captivity of the church" was not bound locally to Avignon; it was a chapter in the history of the church. The story of how the science of history acquired its own chairs at German universities has been told. As a historian Flacius breached antiquity. German idealism completed the work that was begun at that time. Like Luther, it felt every splitting of man that is experienced when the world becomes temporalized. It sought to overcome this splitting by means of the philosophy of identity. The question is whether this is the solution. It is the same question that cropped up when Luther and Leibniz were compared (cf. *Cross and Vale of Tears).* It cannot be answered here in any other way than it was answered there. We, too, affirm the flight of time, together with all "progress in the history of thought" *(geistesgeschichtlicher Fortschritt).* We do this because we, together with Luther, have learned "that we should transfer ourselves outside time and look at our life with the eyes of God" *(ut transferamus nos extra tempus et oculis Dei inspiciamus nostram vitam).* And this affirmation of the temporalizing of the world made and continues to make the eschatology of Lutheranism possible.

35. The Kingdom of Christ [1]

The authors of the *Magdeburg Centuries* declare in their foreword that it was their intention to present "the outward appearance of the

[1] E. Hirsch, *Die Reich-Gottes-Begriffe des neueren europäischen Denkens,* Göttingen, 1921. — *Die Reden von L. Ihmels, Phil. Bachmann, der Bischöfe von Tammerfors (Gummerus) und Hadersleben (V. Ammundsen) auf der Stockholmer Weltkirchenkonferenz. Amtl. deutscher Bericht von A. Deissmann,* Berlin, 1926, pp. 132 ff., 512 ff., 518, 618 ff.

kingdom of Christ" *(regni Christi faciem).* A dangerous undertaking for a church historian! For since he, like every historian, must deal with worldly facts and occurrences, the danger of equating the kingdom of Christ with any simple or compound factor of history seems well-nigh unavoidable. Of course, the statement becomes understandable immediately when one remembers that the Apology, for example, makes no distinction between the kingdom of Christ and the church (IV, 16, 52; cf. Luther, Enders 4, 9, 3). When Melanchthon devotes a special chapter in his *Loci* to the kingdom of Christ in addition to the chapter he devotes to the church (*CR* 21, 920 ff.), here, as everywhere, it is his Biblicism that leads him to do this. He dare not ignore the numerous passages in the New Testament that deal with the kingdom of God, the kingdom of Christ, and the kingdom of heaven. But what he then states thetically about this never goes beyond his dogma of the church so far as the content is concerned: Christ at the right hand of God is our Intercessor, grants forgiveness of sins to the believers, gives them the Holy Spirit, sanctifies them, and will resurrect them unto eternal life. For this purpose the office of the ministry was instituted. The Spirit becomes active through the preaching of the Gospel. Until the Last Day the church — suddenly this word crops up as a synonym — must suffer persecution. The wicked are always intermingled with the church. In the Apology, Melanchthon seems to be thinking of a certain difference in emphasis. "The church is the kingdom of Christ in contradistinction to the kingdom of the devil" *(Ecclesia est regnum Christi distinctum contra regnum diaboli)* — the church is to be designated as the kingdom of Christ when its nature is to be illustrated by its opposite. And the way the authors of the *Centuries* carry out their program shows that they, too, are aware of this difference in emphasis. Ideally speaking, the church which they present as a historical factor is, of course, the kingdom of Christ, approximately in the Melanchthonian sense. The history of dogma is the history of the preaching of the Gospel. The persecutions of the Christians appear as an expression for the "church under the cross" *(ecclesia sub cruce).* At the same time, however, the "church" is also the scene of the struggle between error and truth, between tyranny and the spirit of Christ. Corruption falls to its lot. The moment this happens, it is, to be sure, still the church in one sense or another for the authors of the *Centuries;* but it is no longer the kingdom of Christ. The Antichrist creeps in and seats himself on Christ's chair. Nevertheless, the struggle of the believers continues to be a struggle for the "church," from which Satan must again be expelled. But this struggle is by no means concerned only with the pure doctrine. It is concerned to an equal degree with worship and with the ethos. For this reason one cannot say that to the authors of the *Centuries* or to Melanchthon the kingdom of Christ is identical with the "invisible church." On the contrary, here the kingdom of Christ is the church in its ideal state. The kingdom of Christ cannot be falsified, but the church surely can be – without on this account losing its essential relationship to the kingdom of Christ.

That the New Testament idea of a kingdom was brought into a firm relationship to the church is easy to understand. Both concepts give expression to a supraindividual solidarity. But according to everything that was taught about the church, the two could not stand in a rival relationship to each other. If, however, attention was paid to the usage of the New Testament – obviously, as in Melanchthon's case, this was always the reason for the use of the idea of a kingdom – one was confronted with the "kingdom of God" primarily in the preaching of Jesus. And now it is significant how obviously Christ's proclamation of the kingdom is related to the impact of the Gospel *(evangelischer Ansatz)*. "When Christ taught penitence and the remission of sins," says Martin Chemnitz, "the evangelists say that He preached the kingdom of God" *(Quando Christus docuit poenitentiam et remissionem peccatorum, dicunt Evangelistae: praedicavit regnum Dei)* (*Loci* II, 247b). Lutheranism's basic conception of the kingdom of God could not be expressed more felicitously. At the same time the bridge built from Paul to the synoptists is clearly visible here.[2] In Luther this thought is always in the foreground. It actually identifies the kingdom of God with the Gospel. Concerning Jesus' proclamation of the kingdom Luther says: "And He gives this and that coloring to what is nothing else than the remission of sins" *(Et sic et sic colorat, quod aliud non sit quam remissio peccatorum)*.[3] Therefore this kingdom is called the kingdom of the blind and the poor (WA 36, 383, 31). It is a "kingdom of consolation" *(regnum consolationis)* (385, 21). "Christ's kingdom is a hospice, and if one enters it, all sins are forgiven" *(Christi regnum est hospitale, in quod si venerit, dimissa sunt peccata omnia)* (WA 15, 729, 2). The sick in this hospice

[2] In Scripture Nik. Hemming finds a fivefold meaning of the idea of the kingdom: (1) the preaching of penitence, (2) synonymous with the Gospel, (3) the fruits of the preaching of the Gospel, (4) future salvation, (5) the visible church (*Postil*, sermon for the Fifth Sunday after Trinity). — In addition, cf. Heerbrand, *Comp.*, 1585, pp. 328 ff. — Schilter and Harbard, *Capita*, pp. 689 ff.

[3] WA 15, 724, 3. Cf. WA 1, 694, 17; WA 12, 675, 4; WA 17 II, 268, 29; WA 37, 90, 15; WA 49, 138, 32. — Nik. Hercko's (superintendent at Arnstadt) Catechism of 1554: "What is the kingdom of God? It is the holy Gospel, God's grace, the forgiveness of sins, redemption and everlasting life through Christ, here and there forever." (Reu, *Quellen II*, 2, p. 254.)

are those lost sheep which the Good Shepherd seeks and knows how to find (WA 20, 368 ff.).

It is clear how here the idea of a kingdom is traced back strictly and logically to the impact of the Gospel *(evangelischer Ansatz).* Here one finds the reason for the emphasis with which the kingdom is described to us in the Catechisms as a kingdom that comes to us, as a gift. Because we always find it when we receive it, the kingdom is something that has already been "given." Luther says in reply to Erasmus: "The kingdom is not being prepared; it has been prepared. In fact, the sons of the kingdom are being prepared; they are not preparing the kingdom" *(Regnum non paratur, sed paratum est; filii vero regni parantur, non parant regnum)* (WA 18, 694, 26). Yet this cannot exhaust the idea of the kingdom. Only with reference to the "King" *(rex)* can it be designated as a "kingdom" *(regnum).* In conformity with New Testament usage, Luther obviously calls it the kingdom of God as often as he calls it the kingdom of Christ. But the first designation is ambiguous. God established a kingdom when He founded the world. This is His dominion over "temporal life." Man was connected with this kingdom in such a way that he himself should rule over the creatures under him. This is a matter of government. It concerns the jurists (WA 49, 137, 13 ff.). "After that one there is another government. This is twofold: the government of the Law, which Moses established, and the second one, which God establishes here" [namely, in John 20:19-23] *(Post illud est aliud regiment. Das ist zweierley: Legis, quod Moses gestiftet hat, Alterum, quod Dominus hic stiftet.)* Therefore this last kingdom of God is the kingdom of Christ. Here God rules through Christ in a way that is different from the way He rules in the first two kingdoms. This third kingdom was made necessary by sin, death, and the devil. "There belongs the kingdom of Christ, who has been appointed King for this purpose, that He may be Lord over death and life, and His kingdom should be concerned to deal with sin and death" *(Da gehort Christi reich zu, qui ad hoc positus Rex, ut sit Dominus super mortem, vitam, et suum regnum sol damit zu thun haben, ut zu handeln habe cum peccato et morte)* (WA 49, 138, 7).

Therefore the kingdom of God with which faith alone is concerned is the kingdom of Christ. "Christ is King and Lord in the kingdom of God" (WA 11, 249, 27). This is the "kingly authority of Jesus." In fact, we can call it this in Luther's sense too. Christ is "King over the people of God" *(rex super populum Dei)* (WA 36, 50, 20). The elect, says Bugenhagen, "are called the kingdom of Christ, the kingdom of God, the kingdom of heaven, in which God Himself reigns" *(dicuntur regnum Christi, regnum Dei, regnum coelorum, in quibus Deus ipse regnat)*

(*Annotationes,* p. 98). Subjects belong to the kingdom just as the King does. Bugenhagen calls them the elect. They *are* the kingdom of Christ. "Christians," says Luther, "should be certain that they are the kingdom of God" (WA 17 II, 185, 8). Therefore the kingdom is not only an idea, as one could conclude from the fact that it is equated with the forgiveness of sins. Just as it has an actual King, so it also has actual members. But who are these? The elect! The "Christians" *(Christenmenschen)!* But in the Lutheran sense this means nothing else than sinners. Christ is "the King of sinners" *(Rex peccatorum)* (WA 36, 385, 4). A strange paradox! In the struggle against sin God establishes a kingdom made up only of sinners! "It is strange that Christ does not want sins, and in spite of this there is no one in this kingdom who is not a sinner; no one is righteous" *(Mirum est, quod Christus non vult peccata, et tamen nullus est in hoc regno nisi peccator, probus nemo)* (WA 15, 726, 12). But now the "kingly authority" is commensurate with this assembling of the members of the kingdom. Christ administers justice as every king does. But He can do what no one else is able to do. His justice is perfect. "The kingdom of Christ has justice, the scepter, what is right to the highest degree" *(Christi regnum habet justitiam, sceptrum, quod rectissimum)* (WA 40 II, 527, 13). "There we shall reach the mathematical point by taking hold of justice" *(Illic attingemus punctum mathematicum arripiendo justitiam)* (l. 9). Christ's work is the justification of the sinner. He lets His scepter rule "because we believe Christ; by believing in Him we allow ourselves to be judged by Him" *(quia nos credimus Christum; credentes in eo, patimur ab eo judicari)* (l. 2). Therefore here that "mathematical point" *(punctum mathematicum)* is reached which we encountered for the first time in Luther's primal experience *(Urerlebnis)* and then in the doctrine of justification. Even membership in the kingdom of Christ is attached to a mathematical point, namely, to exactly the same point at which the sinner becomes justified. The sinner is justified under the otherworldly verdict of God. But this applies to the empirical man. Conversely, the empirical human beings are the kingdom of Christ. But they are members of this kingdom only at a mathematical point, because it is only as believers that they are members of the kingdom. Christ's kingdom "exists in the spirit and in faith" (WA 19, 137, 1). "Those who belong to the kingdom of God are all true believers in Christ and under Christ" (WA 11, 249, 26).

For this reason the kingdom of Christ can never become a secular kingdom. Luther emphasizes this as indefatigably as Melanchthon does. The kingdom of Christ is and forever remains a "spiritual kingdom" *(regnum spirituale)* (WA 41, 231, 14; 542, 17). "The kingdom of Christ is not a worldly kingdom!" *(Regnum Christi non mundanum!)* This is shouted to three opponents. On this the Augsburg Confession bases its polemics against the secular jurisdiction of the bishops (Art. 28). Melanchthon shouts it to the Anabaptists (*CR* 21, 920). In Mömpelgard, Andreä shouts it to the disciples of Calvin (*Acta,* p. 97). But here, too, the contrast secular-spiritual is something different from the contrast visible-invisible. Perhaps the latter contrast would be formally tenable, but it is coupled to such an extent with the traditional Platonic-Neoplatonic philosophy of life that it cannot be employed here any more than it can be employed with reference to the "church." For it could give the impression that in the kingdom of Christ it is a question of spiritualizing some existent but rival factor of history or a conception advocated elsewhere. To be sure, the rival conceptions of the Roman Church as well as of the Baptists are actually more forcefully oriented at "visible" points. And in the eschatological sharpening of the idea of a kingdom Melanchthon had criticized the "great, carnal, Jewish" conceptions of chiliasm both in the Augsburg Confession (Art. 17) and on many other occasions. But here, too, the difference is not "intellectual." According to Luther's canon, which has already been quoted, it is "spiritual" (WA 23, 189, 8). What was said about the church applies equally to the "kingdom of Christ." This kingdom is not invisible in the Platonic sense; it is "hidden" *(absconditum)* in the evangelical sense.[4] For here, too, "everything God does is contradictory." If this is already to be seen in the paradoxical assembling of the members of this kingdom — only sinners — it is no less true of the nature of Christ's regal authority. "This is contradictory, to be Lord in this way over the people of God and nevertheless to be a beggar and the most despised man on earth" (WA 36, 50, 9). "Yes, tell me, what shall we do with a King who establishes His kingdom in such a way that He is the first to let Himself be tortured, and tortured as shamefully as a thief and a murderer, which really ruins the thing completely?" (WA 41, 231, 10.) "Thus it shall happen to Him on the way, that His kingdom continues through death and through the passing from this life to the Father" (232, 7). He also *rules* accordingly. Over all those who let themselves be found by Him and listen to His Word "Christ makes the sign of the cross and says: 'Your sins are remitted

[4] *Lectures on Hebrews* 110, 20: ". . . the people of Christ . . . although it seems to be an exile, not a kingdom; and to be dying, not to live; and not in glory but in ignominy" *(. . . populus Christi . . . cum non videatur esse regnum sed exilium, nec vivere sed mori, nec in gloria sed ignominia).* — WA 25, 326, 30: "Christ in glory, but in such a way that He is a stumbling block for all; no one will believe that He is Christ or King" *(Christus in gloria sed ita, ut omnibus sit scandalo, nemo credet eum esse Christum aut regem).*

unto you'" (WA 37, 91, 13). And for Him, of course, this "making the sign of the cross" has a different meaning from the meaning it has in the symbolical act of the priest who pronounces absolution. It is rather the symbol of "the kingdom of Christ in the cross" *(regnum Christi in cruce)*, as Luther calls it (31 II, 428, 8); it is "the kingdom of Christ covered with the cross" *(regnum Christi cruce tectum)*, as Melanchthon calls it (Apology IV, 18). Because this kingdom never *is* but always comes into being and is active, it needs the opposition in the victory over which it reveals its glory. Because Christ lets those who are His *overcome* suffering, they must first sink down in suffering. If He wants to make saints out of sinners, He can receive only sinners. If He wants to give them life, He must first let them die. What Luther says about death is true of all these powers: "When it is necessary for me to die, I cling to the King Jesus Christ, who shall perform the office of making the blind see, of comforting distressed hearts" (WA 36, 386, 3). Christ "wants to be the King who helps those who are dead, sinners, and prisoners under the Law. 'This is My kingdom,' He says." (384, 29.)

It is undoubtedly clear *how very far the Lutheran understanding of the "regal authority of Christ" is at this point from all more or less theocratic conceptions and aspirations* that surrounded it on the right and on the left. But it surely was a serious error when modern interpreters concluded from this that Lutheranism is decidedly quietistic. This would also be in open contradiction to the previously developed consciousness of being in the world – the consciousness that has a pronounced militant character. But the thoughts concerning the kingdom of Christ itself are really anything but quietistic. In fear of death Luther sees a disavowal of the kingdom. "He who flees from death has disavowed the kingdom of God, because He is Lord of the result of death, not of flight from death" *(Qui mortem fugit, regnum Dei abnegavit, quia dominus est exitus mortis, non fugae mortis)* (WA 4, 712, 26). At all times in the history of the world, however, contempt for death – which, according to what has just been said, is a characteristic of the children of the kingdom – was one of the most powerful forces of triumph. Here Luther is as far away from stoical fatalism as he is from courage that clutches at hopes of miracles (WA 33, 324, 25 ff.). Luther's *Whether One May Flee from Death (Ob man vor dem Sterben fliehen möge)* (1527) was written in the face of the plague. "But if anyone," we read there, "is affected with dread at the sight of those who are sick, he should take courage; and he should strengthen and comfort himself in such a way that he has no doubt that it is the devil who stirs up such aversion, fear, and dread in the heart. . . . Begone, devil, with your terrifying. And because it annoys you, I will spite you by going all the sooner to my sick neighbor in order to help him." (WA 23, 355, 24 ff.) Here one sees the militant motif in Luther's contempt for death. The close connection this contempt has with "moral" impulses is equally evident.

But both are necessarily connected with the idea of the kingdom of Christ. This is the kingdom of the forgiveness of sins, because it "is ruled by the substantial and simple Word of the Gospel" *(solido simplicique Evangelii verbo regitur)* (WA 7, 743, 7; *Lectures on Hebrews* 111, 16). For this reason Luther also calls it the "kingdom of good consciences" *(regnum bonarum conscientiarum)* (759, 27). But as this kingdom of good consciences it, like the good conscience of an individual, is constantly engaged in combat with everything that opposes it. Among the powers of terror it is primarily sin that has eaten its way into the inner nature of man and for this reason must be overpowered every hour. In connection with the idea of the kingdom Luther also warns against taking the forgiveness of sins to mean carnal freedom (WA 15, 730, 2). "The kingdom of Christ does not rest; it sweeps" *(Regnum Christi non feyret, es treybet das fegen)* (729, 18). He who wants to live in this kingdom must sweep out sin, because the struggle against sin is also the purpose of the forgiveness of sins. The battle Christ fought against sin on the cross is our battle too. The fact that in the struggle against sin Luther is so powerfully aware of the feeling of kindred with Christ that the believer has – even though in the case of the former the struggle is entirely different in nature from what it is in the case of the latter – shows once more to how great a degree sin, as Luther views it, is an "objective" power that can never be overcome by good deeds, never only by means of the "positive" ethos. When Luther was especially close to German mysticism, he could describe the evolution *(das Werden)* of the kingdom of God as an evolution *(ein Werden)* of virtue in man.[5] Here

[5] *Exposition of the Holy Lord's Prayer,* 1518 (WA 9, 136, 12): "The kingdom of God does not come until there is peace, humility, decency, chastity, love, and other fine virtues. It exists in beautiful tranquility, without anger, without hatred, without favoritism, without deception, without cunning. It is altogether kind, friendly, truthful, without guile, gentle, benevolent, obliging. It begins here in this time, but in yonder life it is finished. . . . Pay careful heed to yourself, whether you are more inclined to do what is good or more inclined to do what is evil. If you find in yourself that you have a desire to do what is good and to be heartily friendly and obliging; if you recognize that you are wholly insignificant and that you are less worthy than all creatures; if you are willing to help the poor — then the kingdom of God has begun in you. Thus man becomes more and more virtuous until we die. In yonder life this will be finished." — Cf. the *Frankforter* (*Eyn deutsch Theologia,* edited by Luther for the second time in the same year), ed. by Uhl, p. 17: "And if then man does not pay regard to, seek, or desire anything else than the eternal good alone and does not look out for himself or what is his but seeks only the glory of God in all things, there will be the joy, bliss, peace, tranquility, and comfort of the eternal good, and all this belongs to man. Then man is in the kingdom of heaven." — Cf. also *Lectures on Hebrews* 116, 20 ff.

one misses the clear basic thoughts of the impact of the Gospel *(evangelischer Ansatz)*. To be sure, those who want to deduce from this very fact that there is a close relationship between Luther and German idealism are scarcely right either. For this "kingdom of God" that is said to begin in man is surely something different from Kant's and Fichte's kingdom of ethical purposes. Precisely where Luther is related to the *Frankforter* one finds the ethical purposes – if they exist at all – entirely on the periphery. The idea of solidarity plays no role whatever. The "ethical ideal" is the molding of the individual soul for eternity. But even later Luther retained the idea of the activity of the kingdom in the believer. It is connected with the belief in God's operative presence in him – the belief that was discussed in conjunction with the doctrine of the "mystical union" *(unio mystica)*. "For in God's kingdom God alone should speak, rule, act, bring about, and work" *(Denn ym reich Gots sol Gott alleyne reden, regirn, thun, schaffen und wircken)*. He says the same thing in his collection of Lenten sermons of 1525 (WA 17 II, 185, 11).[6] And in his *On Secular Authority, to What Extent One Owes It Obedience (Von weltlicher Oberkeit, wie weit man ihr Gehorsam schuldig sei)* (1523) Luther describes the members of Christ's kingdom as those who "have the Holy Spirit. He teaches them and brings it about that they do wrong to no one, love everybody, gladly and joyfully suffer wrong, even death, from everyone." (WA 11, 250, 2.) The kingdom of Christ is nothing else than "the forgiveness of sins between God and men and also among men" *(remissio peccatorum zwischen got et homines et inter homines quoque)* (1524; WA 15, 724, 3).

Therefore it is incorrect to say that Luther thought of the kingdom of Christ as being quietistic in an ethical sense. The impression that he really did so can arise as long as he is dependent on the mystics. The clearer his doctrine of justification becomes, the more activistic his ethos becomes. For to the same degree he is freed from reflecting on himself. But now as before, to be sure, the believer's battle is directed against sin *in himself!* True, it is possible for a Christian to make an impression on this or that person in his environment with his personal friendliness and his capability of loving, which belong to the fruits of faith; but that this influence of man on man forms the effective basis of the great social orders or could actually "arrange" *(ordnen)* these orders was out of the question for him because "Christians live far apart from

[6] In the *Festpostille* (1527) it is then stated unambiguously: "Of the kingdom of God . . . that it is nothing else than the Word, which preaches forgiveness of sins, and this is the holy Gospel. For in this kingdom there is sheer grace and goodness, sheer forgiveness and remission of sin, sheer love and friendliness." (WA 17 II, 268, 26 ff.)

one another" (WA 11, 257, 37). "A Christian is indeed a rare bird" *(Es ist gar ein selczamer vogel umb einen Christen)* (WA 10 III, 397, 8). In this sense Luther always remained a pessimist. And so far the age of church history that would justify another view has not yet come. But it is both actually and basically impossible for the kingdom of God to be able to supply the pattern for the social orders among men. This is impossible because no one is a Christian in the sense that the battle against sin has already been fought out in him. That the Christian, too, is in need of outward discipline on God's part — this is not only the rule; it is the inevitable result of the fact that we are human beings. And even faith does not free us from being human beings. For Luther, of course, the cross — that is, the discipline — to which God subjects the Christian is simply the characteristic of Christians. For this reason, however, one must, *on principle,* take man's sin into consideration in connection with every social order. *The social orders treat it as potential and actual sin; the kingdom of Christ treats it as sin that is forgiven. This is the difference.* Therefore they will remain separated until the end of the world as *kingdoms of two kinds.* That the Christian does not thereby surrender the civil world to godlessness; that, on the contrary, there is and should be a *personal union* between both kingdoms; that the motif of love, which is conceived of in a specifically evangelical way, also contributes toward an inner change in civil life; and that it is particularly the Lutheran Christian who has unfolded exceedingly important activity in history — all this will be dealt with when sociology is discussed.

Luther's conception of the kingdom of Christ asserted itself in early Lutheranism. It can be found as early as 1524 in the sermon which Johann Eberlin von Günzburg delivered on the twofold kingdom — even though here it is oriented toward the contrast with the kingdom of the devil.[7] "Now this is called the kingdom of God because He rules in it through faith, and because through His death He has gained this spirit for us. There, through Christ, we now expect from God all that is good. We believe that we have a kind Father, who has taken us into His grace and has forgiven our sins through Christ. . . . And for this reason sin, death, the devil, and hell are gone; everything has been conquered." Then there is a reference to the Word of God, which grants the spirit that fights incessantly against sin in one's own flesh. The Apology, too, emphasizes not only the connection of the kingdom with the Gospel, with the spirit, and with faith but also its healing power in the hearts — the healing power that subdues the devil and manifests the power of

[7] L. Enders, *Flugschriften aus der Reformationszeit,* No. 18, Halle, 1902, pp. 89 ff. — Cf. Max Radlkofer, *Johann Eberlin v. G.,* 1887, pp. 130 f.

Christ in our weakness (III, 68). This now makes it possible to answer the question whether the Apology defined the relationship of the kingdom of Christ to the church in Luther's sense. The answer must be yes. Provided that the kingdom of Christ gains and keeps its members through the Gospel, fills them with the spirit of Christ, lets them overcome sin, death, and hell, it is nothing else than the church. Conversely, provided that Christ rules in the church through the cross, through His own cross as well as through the cross He imposes on the members of the kingdom – that is, provided that the church proclaims the Gospel – the church is the kingdom of Christ. But it loses this character the moment it mistakes Christ for Moses. Every interpretation of the kingdom of Christ as an ethical institution would, in Luther's sense, have to be opposed in the strongest manner possible. "The kingdom of Christ does not consist in works, in efforts, because no rule, no law, not the Mosaic Law either, can lead us to that knowledge [which has previously been defined as *justitia* in the evangelical sense]; but we arrive there through the Gospel" *(Regnum Christi non consistit in operibus, studiis, quia nulla regula, nulla lex neque Mosaica potest nos ad illam cognicionem perducere, sed evangelio eo pervenimus)* (WA 31 II, 439, 10; cf. WA 20, 368, 29). It was entirely in Luther's sense when Caspar Huberinus, who is otherwise very close to Bucer but differs completely from him here, gives the simple definition: "The kingdom of Christ is the Gospel; for through the Gospel the fatherly favor, grace, and mercy of God toward us are announced, and in the Gospel itself Christ, the Son of God, is presented as our Savior with all His merits, with His death, suffering, and resurrection" *(Regnum Christi est Euangelium: per Euangelium enim paternus favor, gratia et misericordia Dei erga nos annunciatur nobisque in ipso filius Dei Christus servator noster cum cunctis suis meritis, morte, passione et resurrectione offertur).*[8] This gave to the Wittenberg Reformation the tempestuous, sweeping power that made it possible here for a church which wanted to be the kingdom of Christ in the strict sense instead of the sociological misrepresentation of the church to fight its way through. But it *was* this church only because, and only as long as, it wanted and had nothing more than the Gospel. "Where the Holy Gospel," we read in the *Kirchenordnung* of Duke Henry of Saxony (1539), "comes into a city or village and drives out Satan and the pope, we should heartily rejoice that we again have these things pure: the Gospel, Baptism, the Sacrament, absolution, etc. For where these things are to be found, there Paradise has begun again, there is the kingdom

[8] C. Huberinus, *Homiliae Cathechisticae* . . . , Frankfurt, 1554, p. 112. Cf. pp. 108 ff.

of heaven, as Christ Himself says." (Sehling, *Kirchenordnungen,* I, 1, p. 265.)

The clear-cut separation of the kingdom of Christ from all sociological structures that are merely secular was the sense of Luther's doctrine of the two spheres (Vol. II, *Schöpfungsordnung*). The *Oeconomia* of Justus Menius shows how near the return to the Augustinian conception was. On the other hand, the concrete ecclesiastical-political situation could mislead one into mixing matters of state with matters of the church, as this was done very frequently by Philip of Hesse and afterwards, on principle, to a lesser degree in the Thirty Years' War. To the extent that this took place, the inner identity of the kingdom of Christ with the church was always lost. In general, however, the determination to keep away from the use of force in the service of the church was one of the inalienable characteristics of Lutheranism, simply because Lutheranism did not want the identity of the kingdom of Christ with the church to be lost. "Therefore," says Bugenhagen even before the outbreak of the Peasants' War, "he did not want any battering of heads in the name of Christ. Our fanatics want to defend the Word of God with the sword, but it is powerful enough; it can protect itself. . . . Some of our people have the Bible in one hand and the sword in the other. This does not make the devil sorry." *(Noluit ergo, das man sich Christi nomine solde umb die köpffe schlagen. Nostri schwermerii volunt dei verbum gladio defendere, sed satis potens est, potest seipsum tueri. . . . Quidam ex nostris in una manu habent biblia, in altera gladium, do ist dem teuffel nicht leyd.)*[9] Here the use of weapons, which, as service to the state, is a matter of divine right in Bugenhagen's sense too, becomes the expression for the power of the devil, because it wants to be of service to the kingdom of Christ. It cannot be denied that the use of power which Bucer as well as Calvin demanded for the kingdom of God because they understood it to be something different from what Luther understood it to be brought a mighty increase of power to the states that accepted the idea of the kingdom. And one can understand why Oliver Cromwell's idea of a kingdom — this kingdom of Christ in the boots of a cuirassier — always made a deep impression on those who wrote political history. Every Christian wants to see the kingdom of Christ depicted. The Hungarian Anabaptists made an impression on Simplicissimus because he thought he saw this wish fulfilled there. Among them he found "the kind of delightful harmony that seemed to be attuned to nothing else than to increase the human race and the kingdom of God in all respectability." Just as today many worshipers of certain ideas concerning the kingdom

[9] *Sermons,* p. 112 (Feb. 21, 1525). Cf. *Annotationes,* p. 177, on 2 Thess. 2:8.

of God record every unbuilt battleship as a victory of the kingdom of Christ, so Simplicissimus admired the chamber pots under the beds of these pious people.[10] The moment this conception of the kingdom of Christ has conquered the whole world, not only Lutheranism but also the Gospel is dead. Luther once reproached Rome for being the seat of the Antichrist. Today it would be equally proper to direct this reproach to another address. Someone else steals into a church from which the Gospel silently makes off. There is no exception to this rule in the history of the church (WA 18, 743, 32).

But in the idea of the kingdom of Christ there is something else — something that our linguistic instinct does not necessarily connect with the church. In it there is the element that has to do specifically with the philosophy of life. It has already been shown that justification places Luther face to face with the hereafter. If the justifying Gospel is not only the news about Christ but also Christ's own deed, through which He rules His own, here man, who hears this news in faith, is no longer alone on the boundary between the here and the hereafter. The hereafter gets a personal content. And this content takes hold of man's psyche. This was the sense of the "mystical union" *(unio mystica).* Through the idea of the kingdom, however, the believer is called out of the wholly personal dialog into an immeasurable solidarity. "The glorious company of the apostles," exults the *Te Deum,* "the goodly fellowship of the prophets, and the noble army of the martyrs praise Thee, Lord. The holy church throughout the world doth acknowledge Thee." So far does the church's idea of catholicity reach. But the *Te Deum* includes a far greater circle. "Thee, Father, the world eternally honors far and wide. To Thee cherubim and seraphim continually do cry. . . . Thy divine power and glory extend throughout heaven and earth. . . . Thou, Christ, the King of glory, Thou art the Father's everlasting Son." Here the kingdom expands into the cosmic. To be sure, it is an elementary tenet of the Christian philosophy of life that God is Lord over heaven and earth; but that He is Lord as the Father of Christ and that He rules the world through Christ — it is only in the idea of the kingdom that these two facts find expression.

At the same time, however, this threatens to tear the previous outlook of the Gospel, of the church, completely away from Christ and His kingdom. It was the knowledge of the world, in which nature and morality were combined for Luther, that enabled him to be aware of the wrath of God at the outset. The Gospel was in sharp contrast with this. And that which is unworldly and antiworldly was a necessary element

[10] Grimmelshausen II, 782.

of the righteousness that avails before God, the proclamation of which guarantees the right and the reality of the church. To be sure, in the revelation of Christ a new relationship of God to the world was also disclosed: "Heaven and earth full of the fire of divine love." Yet the strained state of affairs remained – the struggle of the demonic element against God, the deep dissension that even Goethe was aware of in nature too. Faith cannot doubt that none of these demonic powers – sin, death, and the devil – are a match for God in the long run. But as faith in Christ it also knows how God overcomes these powers in order to win everything for Himself. This does not take place by means of the simple use of power; it takes place in the sign of the cross, by means of His incarnation, by means of sacrifice and death (WA 25, 327, 8 and 11). But the goal of *this* way is victory, conquest, and glory. It is the *resurrection* that discloses the meaning of the cross. Therefore the resurrection is a necessary element of the Gospel. As news about the cross, the Gospel is the antithesis of the whole world; as news of the resurrection, it is the promise of a new world. For man, as a creature of God, cannot be separated from his close connection with the earth. If God wants to have him, He takes him into the community of the creaturely world as a creature. The part of man that resists this is not the close connection with the earth per se; it is sin, that is, man's entanglement with the "world" in the ethical sense, with the world as the area in which wickedness attacks and in which wickedness rules.

And this hope not to be the only one who has overcome death when Christ is ultimately victorious, and to come together then not only with several other "Christians who live far away from one another," but to celebrate the day of resurrection with the sum total of all Christians – this is the cosmic content of the idea of the kingdom of Christ. Only in this way can one understand the constantly recurring statement that this kingdom shall encompass "heaven and earth." At the conclusion of his exposition of Psalm 82 (1530) Luther spoke about the kingdom of Christ in a manner that could lead to a theocratic misconception. Since secular government, he argues, breaks down again and again in the face of the important tasks God has assigned to it, God had to establish another kingdom – a kingdom that is a match for secular government. This is the kingdom of Christ. But "Christ practices aright the three divine virtues mentioned above. He advances God's word and those who preach it; He makes and keeps law for the poor; He protects and rescues the miserable. The service of God in Christendom is justice, peace, righteousness, life, salvation. Of this kingdom of Christ the Gospels and the epistles of the apostles preach and testify so fully that there is no need to speak further of them here." (WA 31 I, 218, 24.) Yet that the kingdom of Christ is by no means to be understood here either as an improved form of political rule is clear from the fact that Luther adds that here one finds "a different righteousness, wisdom, and power." This proves that here, too, Luther does not believe that he is unfaithful to his other conception of the kingdom of Christ. Yet in the aforementioned enumeration of Christ's virtues as a Ruler there is a seemingly foreign element: He punishes the godless and the tyrants. This cannot be limited to the rule over sin and death, which Luther also ascribes to God. For it is precisely from those who are oppressed by the godless and the tyrants that this rule is to bring liberation. Accordingly, they – the godless, as the bearers of sin – are to be punished, and punished by Christ, who "is the supreme Ruler in all the world." If one does not want to take this as a complete break with Luther's belief in Christ as this belief is enunciated elsewhere, this idea can be understood only eschatologically. And Luther gives one a right to do so when he says: "For with this life worldly righteousness comes to an end. But the righteousness of Christ and of those who are His in His kingdom remains forever."

But this very reference to the judgment in the consummation of the kingdom of Christ designates a point at which it is no longer possible to equate the kingdom with the church. Here, too, the early dogmaticians wanted to uphold this equation by accepting the medieval concept of the "church triumphant" *(ecclesia triumphans)*. But since this concept was bound up with all kinds of theocratic hopes and claims, it would have been better if they had not done so. At all events, the "church triumphant" *(ecclesia triumphans)* no longer needs the functions that make up the essence of the "church." Their doctrine which ascribes to Christ both the "kingdom of power" *(regnum potentiae)* and the "kingdom of grace" *(regnum gratiae)* is a different matter. The danger connected with this teaching will be discussed when the field of sociology is taken up. It consists in the possibility of a new interpretation – an interpretation according to which these kingdoms will be regarded as empirical. In the context of the kingdom of Christ the separation of both concepts can appear to be precarious, but it cannot obscure the intrinsic element of truth. As Lord of His kingdom Christ has power over heaven and earth (WA 51, 22, 4). Otherwise it would be necessary to conclude that the powers of death are invincible. And this would lead us to despair. Again, however, this power must be understood to be dynamic in the strict sense. It does not reveal itself in the stability of a representative building; it does so in the incessant subduing of opposition. Faith knows that Christ subdues this opposition, but our eye sees nothing of this.

From what has been said one sees what significance the kingdom has so far as a philosophy of life is concerned. In the first place, it means that the man of faith should not become submerged in the isolation he experiences when he comes face to face with Christ. On the contrary, he is standing in the new solidarity of the kingdom of Christ. It is true that the *use* this kingdom makes of its power is different from that which takes place in secular kingdoms, but the *sphere* of its power encompasses heaven and earth. In the second place, however, this kingdom is engaged in constant combat; for at the same time the world is filled with the powers of death. But the only verdict faith can arrive at is that this struggle of the kingdom of Christ, which can never suffer defeat, *progresses victoriously*. As a mighty forward movement *(processus)* it adapts itself to the consciousness of time. More than this, it gives a deeper meaning to this consciousness. The victory of the kingdom *needs* time. If God wanted it to be different, He Himself would not have become time in Christ. Just as time is an abstraction of our human life and for this reason can only be *experienced* by us, so conversely, the idea of the kingdom establishes the sense of a supraindividual content of time. Just as for the individual there is only time that has been experienced, so for the kingdom there is only time that is dynamic: as the course of progressive struggling and conquering. To be sure, this interlacement of the kingdom with time does not imply that it is secularized. Neither does the incarnation of God, who instituted the kingdom. "For the kingdom of Christ also exists and is operative here below on earth among people" (WA 51, 11, 22). But since it always wins its victories only by leading through death to life, it simultaneously shuts off time. For death is the end of time that has been experienced. There is no longer any progress for one who is dead. By taking death for granted the kingdom of Christ sets a goal for life, and in doing so it sets a goal for time. But by overcoming death and all its helpers at the same time it is, in the third place, the resurrection. If we think back to Luther's statement that the Christians *are* the kingdom, it follows that as the resurrection the kingdom of Christ is also the resurrection of its members. But not only death but also sin and the devil – both are inseparably connected with death – are overpowered. Therefore every victory over sin is at the same time a beginning of the resurrection. In the idea of the kingdom of Christ time and eternity are combined, and this has never been expressed more simply and with greater faith than Luther stated it in the Large Catechism in connection with the Second Petition of the Lord's Prayer. This idea gives to Lutheranism's militant consciousness of being in the world its deepest meaning and at the same time the necessary conclusion. The kingdom is the beginning of the end. At the same time, however, it is the beginning of eternal life.

36. End of the World [1]

The kingdom of Christ is the solidarity of those who are justified. Just as justification places the individual before the hereafter, so the idea of the kingdom places the world as a whole before the hereafter. The world is time – time as flight. Our entire consciousness of being in the world has dissolved in time. "But what crossing over is," says Luther, "experience teaches us. For we cross over every day." *(Transire autem quid sit, docet nos experientia. Quotidie enim transimus.)* (WA 47, 624, 31.) It has been shown how early Lutheranism is filled with a deep feeling of being closely connected with the earth – but also with the consciousness of the aging of the world. "The world approaching its evening" *(Mundus advesperascens)* (cf. *Cross and Vale of Tears*). "*Heaven and earth are gradually changing and growing old,*" says Luther, "and the strength of the rest of the creatures is not as great as it was at the beginning of creation" *(Coelum et terra paulatim mutantur et veterascunt, neque tantae sunt vires reliquarum creaturarum, quantae initio creationis fuerunt).* This is the practical anticipation of the second thermodynamic axiom of modern physics. "Just as farmers bear witness that nature is gradually growing old" *(Sicut testantur rustici naturam paulatim sensecere)* (WA 44, 628, 13 ff.). One cannot underestimate this natural awareness of what is happening in the world. It has been shown that no pessimistic conception of life on the part of Lutheranism resulted from this. But optimism was based on something different from mere natural feeling. For this reason, however, it was also not necessary to resist the thought of the flight of time. In the frankness with which this thought was affirmed there is a genuine sense of reality. But it is a sense of reality with an eschatological background. Just as death comes to the individual, so it comes to the world in general – inevitably. Both are God's work; both are God's judgment. No one knows the when of the end of the world. Luther was opposed to all Biblicistic computations of the destruction of the world. In the most concrete statements about this – in the eschatological discourses of Jesus – he found that Matthew and Mark interweave two different things. Much has already been ful-

[1] Paul Althaus the Younger, *Die letzten Dinge*, 3d ed., 1926, and *Der Friedhof unserer Väter*, 3d ed., 1928. — E. Sommerlath, *Unsere Zukunftshoffnung*, *AELKZ*, 1927, No. 50. — Additional literature in *RGG* II, 2d ed., pp. 353, 361 f., 463.

filled, e. g., the destruction of Jerusalem (WA 15, 748, 5 ff.). The last things began long ago. We Christians are "the last piece of the world. We are the last to belong in heaven." *(das letzte Stück de mundo. Nos ultimi, qui ghen himel gehorn.)* (WA 41, 388, 41.). One should say with John and Paul that the last hour of the world has come. "Let us always be prepared" *(Semper parati simus)* (WA 47, 626, 34). This readiness at any moment is the application of the thought of the end of the world in a manner that befits a Christian. All computations are a delaying or indeed a denial of readiness. Nikolaus Selnecker turns with fury and contempt against the "expectants" *(Exspektanten)* of his time who cannot come to a decision to say yes or no in the confessional controversies, who want to wait and see how matters turn out. The Word of Christ, says Selnecker, demands decision, a waiting for an outcome that is not uncertain but is certain.[2]

But just as the death of the individual acquired a new meaning through the Gospel — or acquired no meaning at all until the Gospel was proclaimed — so the Gospel gave a new meaning to the end of the world. Although that which our natural feeling teaches is correct in both instances, the Gospel shows that the end is at the same time the beginning. It leads to the border of the here, but it speaks to us and to the world from a hereafter. Not until then does the end of the world become a direct deed of God. It is not a death of the world from the weakness of old age. It is the Last Day. It is the Last Judgment. That this, according to what Paul says, is to happen in an instant — "this is something inscrutable; it is not believable" *(das ist ein heimlich Ding, ist nicht credibile)* (WA 49, 734, 1). On the contrary, the end of the world is a part of faith. In the preaching of the seventeenth century the children of the world still appear as those "who do not believe in the judgment of the world." To be sure, this judgment is a part of faith only because at the same time it is a new beginning. For faith this beginning is already the present. We have the Spirit as a pledge, "the redemption according to the soul" *(redemptio secundum animam)*; but we are waiting until our bodies take part in this liberation (WA 49, 510, 1 ff.). Through this, however, we are united with all creatures. Here, therefore, it is not only a matter of an especially favored treatment of my individual corporeality. Once more Luther's whole connection with the earth finds downright passionate expression in the sermons he delivered in 1544 and 1545 on Rom. 8:18 ff., and perhaps it is ex-

[2] Selnecker, *Christliche Psalmen* (see note under *The Office of the Ministry*), preface.

pressed even more powerfully in his sermons on 1 Cor. 15:35 ff.[3] In his sermons on Rom. 8:18 ff. he, together with Paul, describes the "groaning of creation," which, by human fault, is subject to vanity and would like to be free in order to serve those who are free. He describes how creation finally rebels in its torment. "There the sun and all creatures say: 'Slay; it is time'" *(Ibi dicit Sol et omnes creaturae; schlag tod, es ist zeit).* It also anticipates the instantaneous character of the end. "So powerful is the thunderclap that it smashes oak trees to pieces in an instant" *(so mechtig ist der Donnerschlag, ut Eichen in momento zuscheitert).* In the sermons on 1 Cor. 15 Luther's comparisons with nature are well-nigh inexhaustible. Why does the farmer throw grain into the earth? "Why do you not eat it or give it to the pigs?" *(Cur non edis vel das porcis?)* "Why should it rot here?" "Gardener, madam, you are a gravedigger; you are burying the grain." But just wait! "Come Pentecost, there will be something else to see." Thus the creatures become preachers. Garden and field promise a resurrection just as the Word does. All creatures "cry out: 'Believe, believe; do not doubt!'" *(schreien: Crede, crede, ne dubita!)* They show that God has put death before life. They have a presentiment of freedom – provided that man has become free!

To be sure, they cannot give certainty of eternal life. Everything perishable is but an image. That the end is at the same time the new beginning is known only to faith, which here, as always, is faith in Christ. With faith, however, the resurrection is given directly, not by means of a conclusion a posteriori. Again, as at all decisive points of Luther's theology, the "great emphasis" *(magna Emphasis)* of the "for me" *(Pro me)* crops up. We believe in the resurrection because Christ rose. For I believe in the risen Christ only if He rose *for me.* If He rose only for Himself, His resurrection does not concern me (WA 49, 723, 16). For "Easter does not concern us, nor the Last Day" *(gehet uns der Ostertag nicht an, nec extremus dies)* (763, 8). Here the relationship of the Gospel to resurrection becomes clear. So does its relationship to the end of the world. An actual limit is set for the world by the opposite of the world. This, of course, is not only the opposite of the world; it is also a conquest. But what does Christ's resurrection mean "for me"? Here Luther points, for one thing, to the Pauline parallel to Baptism. Then, however, the idea of the kingdom brings the procurement. "We are His members. . . . the head cannot be without members. . . . the

[3] WA 49, 503 ff. The basic thoughts are identical with those in the sermons delivered in 1535 on Rom. 8 (WA 41, 301 and 311 ff.). Unfortunately, the transcripts are missing. Furthermore, WA 49, 395 ff., 723 ff., 727 ff., 761 ff.

whole resurrection must take place, it belongs to one body" (396, 1 ff.). We shall follow Him (728, 2). Since the beginning of the world our life and Christ's life are "embodied in each other" *(ineinander geleibet)*. Therefore "everything is mixed together, His own and our resurrection" *(ist alles ineinander gebrewet, ipsius et nostra resurrectio)*. That *all* are resurrected – this is the power and the might of the resurrection of Christ (762, 2 ff.).

One of the most absurd and most malicious slanders to which early Lutheranism has been subjected again and again up to the present time is the charge that it recognizes only an eschatology of the individual. A look at the sermons and prayers of the seventeenth century convinces one that the opposite is true. So do the hymns of Bartholomäus Ringwald, Philip Nicolai, and Johann Matthäus Meyfart – hymns to be found in every hymnbook. The fact that Luther speaks of the relationship of the hope of resurrection to the "mystical body of Christ" *(corpus mysticum Christi)* should convince one that the aforementioned charge is unfounded. Nor is the relationship Luther speaks of abandoned in Nicolai's *Freudenspiegel des ewigen Lebens* (cf. *Unio Mystica)*, which, in many respects, begins to resort to pronounced individualization. Since the *Loci* of 1535, Melanchthon always treats the doctrine of the last things in direct connection with the doctrine of the kingdom of Christ *(CR* 21, 523 f.; 924 f.). In the writings of Johann Gerhard and the dogmaticians succeeding him the doctrine of the last things comes immediately after the doctrine of the church; for the doctrine of the three states, with the long discussions it interjects, belongs here. A basic change does not occur until the analytical method that is so highly praised today is employed. In compliance with this method, the ideas of salvation, together with the doctrine of God as the "highest good" *(summum bonum)*, are placed at the beginning. As a result, dogmatics concludes very prosaically with the "domestic state" *(status domesticus)*, as is the case in Baier's work. This development, however, takes place in a manner exactly parallel to the pietistic Jesus eschatology, which is not Lutheran in origin and flows into the rationalistic hymn to "personal immortality." It is understandable, of course, that the final destiny of the individual is uppermost at the open grave. But even in the funeral sermons of a Balduin, a Weinreich, and a Hülsemann the view is raised often enough into the cosmic, toward the judgment of the world, toward the great idea of "being gathered to one's fathers." The death of the individual is not "the soul's rest in God"; it is "the return home to the fatherland" and entrance into the communion of saints. Everything Melanchthon says about dogmatics is directed toward this basic thought.

In countless places, even in the Apology, he says that God's work of salvation consists in gathering a church for Himself. The way proceeds from isolation to the gathering. At present this gathering is concealed. But it comes into view on the Last Day. A reference to this is to be found in the testimony of the forty days after Easter: "Christ wanted this resurrection, His own and that of others, and these intimate meetings and conversations of the forty days among the apostles and the rest of the circle associated with them to be clear and evident testimony of the resurrection and eternal life" *(Voluit Christus hanc suam et aliorum resuscitationem et hos familiares congressus et colloquia dierum quadraginta apud Apostolos et reliquum coetum ipsis conjunctum illustre et evidens testimonium esse de resurrectione et vita aeterna)* (*CR* 21, 925). The conclusion of Christ's work is this, "that there will be a gathering of the peoples, namely, the church" *(futuram esse congregationem populorum, scilicet Ecclesiam)*.[4]

The consummation of the church and of the kingdom of Christ; the hope of resurrection by virtue of the connection with Christ, who is the Head of His body; the end of the world – all this is universal eschatology. Early Lutheranism, however, unanimously and logically rejected every form of chiliasm – open and disguised, courageous and cowardly.[5] Chiliasm would like to assure the halo for itself without paying the necessary theological price for it. The conception of a "thousand-year kingdom" within the framework of the present cosmos – even if the cosmos is freed from its demonic tormentors – was totally incompatible with the Lutheran way of expressing the idea of the kingdom of Christ. Although the individual can say with Paul that he is buried with Christ into death through Baptism and accordingly can experience the beginning of the kingdom as the present, the cosmos as a whole cannot say or do this. If it is also true of the cosmos that the new life presupposes death, then *the end of the world* – the end on a radical scale – comes before the resurrection. But even every diluted form of chiliasm is impossible here. A diluted form is to be found where in an increasing improvement of world affairs – especially of the position of man, his regulations, arrangements, views, and ambitions – one sees an approach to the perfection that is promised to the kingdom of Christ. It has been shown that this presupposes a conception of the kingdom that is at variance with the Gospel. Here the question is whether the consummation of the kingdom is the end of an immanent *development*. That

[4] Thus Martin Makenrot in a discussion in 1553, *CR* 10, 828.

[5] *Augustana,* Art. 17. Cf. Apology VIII, 59. — Luther, WA 47, 561, 12 ff. Melanchthon, *CR,* 21, 519, 920.

the kingdom is in a state of progress is clear from its activity in time (cf. *The Kingdom of Christ*). But it wins its victories in those who become righteous – become righteous *in the sight of God,* not in the sight of men. Perhaps even human observers find that according to their inner-worldly standards the believer is better and more perfect than the nonbeliever. Nietzsche denied this. Lenin likewise. But even when the believer is measured according to the Decalog or the demands of the Sermon on the Mount, the fulfillment of these demands is neither the condition for entrance into the kingdom of Christ nor a mark of membership in this kingdom. For man belongs to this kingdom always only as a sinner, even though he belongs as a sinner to whom sin has been forgiven. Perhaps the ethical progress we think we observe in the world has an indirect connection with the work of the kingdom. We can never establish this. The only thing that is certain is this, that where ethical progress is equated with the kingdom of Christ, the Antichrist has his hand in the game. Therefore if the kingdom makes progress, this progress can be deduced only from the fact that the *proclamation* of the kingdom makes progress. For it is only in this way that we know anything at all about it. Although this will be an ever-new incentive for the church to proclaim the Gospel in the world ever more extensively and ever more pressingly by means of preaching and missions, it is again impossible to establish empirically how many hear this call in faith. That "the Word shall not return void" is purely an article of faith. For this reason, however, the progress of the kingdom of Christ can only be believed; it cannot be gauged from an immanent development.[6]

[6] If from this teaching and from the corresponding total attitude of Lutheranism one has concluded that Lutheranism has been inactive, has not fostered missions, and has no future (Paul Althaus the Younger, *ZsTh,* 1929, p. 364; *RGG* II, 350), this very judgment shows the unevangelical endeavor to confuse believing with observing. But the verdict is also historically incorrect. There are altogether different reasons for the "futurelessness *(Zukunftslosigkeit)* of the German Lutheran Church." The fact that the critic adds the word "German" here is no accident. He would scarcely have had the courage to make the same statement about the Lutheran churches of Scandinavia. And there is more than one reason for this. If there is a difference between the Lutheran Church in Germany and the Lutheran Church in Scandinavia with respect to their "future," the reason is not to be found in the eschatology, which is identical in all churches of the Augsburg Confession; it is to be found elsewhere. At another place (*Communio sanctorum,* 1929, p. 82) the same critic says: "The Lutheran Church saw in the other church its opponent or the object of evangelization; it took little joy in, and gave little honor to, what others contributed." A downright grotesque distortion of the state of affairs! Where in all the world did the Lutheran Church "evangelize" among other churches? If it actually had done this, the charge of "inactivity" — as this charge is meant by the critic — would be unjustifiable. Conversely, however, the Lutheran Church itself has always been merely "the object of evangelization" — from the days of Calvin and Laski down to the present time. And the picture that makes the impres-

For Luther the fact that the kingdom of Christ and its progress are *concealed* is essential. "Thus," he says where he speaks of the hope of the future, "our eyes are closed to the worldly, visible things; and their hope is directed toward the eternal, invisible things. Grace does all this through the cross into which the godly life that is intolerable to the world brings us." (WA 10 I, 43, 19.) The "first advent" *(erste tzukunft)*, which began with Christ's first coming, is "still hidden." It was, and today it still is, an "appearance" only for faith (44, 1 ff.). Thus the kingdom of Christ is in the sign of the cross, which includes the fact that it is unrecognizable empirically. Therefore one could sooner suppose that the facts of the empirical world contradict faith not only in its activity but also in its progress. This conception is based on the pessimistic conception of history which, since the days of early Christianity, thought it had to observe a strengthening of the powers of evil in the world and expected a final unsurpassable development, finally even a personal incarnation of that which is demonic, during the last time before the end of the world. Since this directs one's attention to the empirical "signs" of the empirical world, one cannot regard this conception of history as a direct statement of faith. Faith is concerned with

sion of "futurelessness" on the critic has developed from the results of this evangelization. Measured by the standards of the critic, these results probably speak for the superiority of the other side. But he who asks by what means these results were achieved will not have the audacity to record this superiority as closer proximity to the kingdom of Christ. To characterize it would require volumes. That the three electoral families to which the most important parts of the German Lutheran Church entrusted themselves went over to other churches one after the other and then — with the exception of the family that became Catholic — either suppressed the Lutheran Church with means that are not found in the Gospel or, to the extent that they were able, prevented it from unfolding its own individuality — this led to the result at which they had arrived when the German State Church came to an end.

So far as "missionlessness" *(Missionslosigkeit)* is concerned, that which is necessary has already been said about this matter (cf. *Missions*). One can speak of "inactivity" *(Tatlosigkeit)* on the part of Lutheranism only if one either again applies the standards of an unevangelical conception of the kingdom of Christ — then the North American Puritans are obviously the unachieved ideal in the matter of energy. Concerning the relationships between the joy with which they worked *(Werkfreudigkeit)* in the service of the kingdom of God and their greed for profit, concerning the brutality with which they reduced the person who served to the level of a thing, how they taught the Indians to scalp — concerning all this one hears nothing among the pacemakers of the western "kingdom of God." In one of his collected essays Heinrich Böhmer has adduced material to illustrate this. Or else the "inactivity" is meant to be ethical unfruitfulness. Then one can only ask whether the research of a Flacius or a Bogislav Phil. Chemnitz, Johann Michael Moscherosch's criticism of morals, the linguistic achievements of Lutheran pastors in the small nations of the East; whether the campaigns of Charles XII, the reforms of Freiherr vom Stein, and the policy of Bismarck were not "deeds" — and leave the verdict to the reader.

this only to the extent that it is nevertheless convinced of the ultimate victory of the kingdom of Christ and also visualizes the overwhelming magnitude of this victory by considering the very intensity of the final resistance. Luther, Melanchthon, and early Lutheranism as a whole shared the aforementioned view and expectation. The theology of the Enlightenment broke with it. In the nineteenth century the view came to life again in connection with Lutheran eschatology.[7] If here, too, one separates calculation and preparedness, no Christian can act as though the Antichrist were not standing at the door. If he takes the imminent nearness seriously, he will, of course, redouble his forces in the struggle against evil. Against the gathering might of the demons he will appeal to all the ethical motives in his environment, and as "jurist, sheriff, or hangman" – to use Luther's words – as physician, laborer, teacher, or members of parliament he will fight to the knife. This belongs in the field of ethics. But if the words "With might of ours can naught be done" do not ring through his soul, he confuses the history of civilization with eschatology. Faith in the Christ who is to come presupposes – if it actually *is* faith – the knowledge and the confession that its counterpart cannot be overcome by means of our ethos.

We shall act as though it *could* be overcome. But we know that this is not the case. "Carnal peace is not to be hoped for in this life" *(Pax carnalis in hac vita non speranda),* said Bugenhagen *(Annotationes,* p. 46). In this matter we have become more optimistic. Peace among nations, among classes, and among races is possible. Luther thought that a "battle" like the one that took place when Jerusalem was destroyed would not occur again (WA 15, 749, 1). But if this peace were to become a peace between good and evil, the Antichrist would have won the ultimate victory. The struggle between good and evil dare not cease. For peace between good and evil would always be the end of what is good and therefore the victory of what is evil. For the Christian, however, this struggle is ultimately the struggle of the Gospel. Because "there can be no unity in *doctrine,*" for this reason "before the Last Day comes," there will be "such uproar, division, dissension, and slaying in the world that one will fear that Christ and the Gospel will be entirely lost" (WA 47, 555, 24). Consequently, the "Last Day" will have the character of an actual revelation of Christ. Surely "this will be

[7] Cf., e. g., R. Rocholl, *Phil. d. Geschichte* II, 497 — in spite of his conception of history, which, on the whole, is optimistic: "Its manifestation is a demand of history. For its theme is man. Thus man must be revealed in both directions — in his relationship to God and in his enmity against God, in his love and in his hatred. Moreover, only the life of the person makes both revelations possible." Finally, Sommerlath, op. cit.

a war against all the ungodly and devils" *(das wird ein Krieg sein contra omnes impios et Teuffel)*. And the result will be: "everything dead, all creatures too" *(alles tod, et omnes creaturae)* (WA 49, 741, 5). But if this is to be God's ultimate victory, *this* death and *this* end of the world must look different from the way they would look if the devil had been victorious. The only thing the devil wants to do is to kill. And they do look different. For Christ comes with "ineffable majesty" (WA 45, 325, 4). Again He is standing on the borderline between the here and the hereafter. Up to this time the justification of the sinner was the hereafter for faith. Now, however, the hereafter is the justification of the sinner. He hears what he has believed: that it is only the verdict of the Judge that justifies. And he sees what he has believed.

The history of the world is not the judgment of the world; the end of the world is. In the history of the world the wicked are mingled with the good. They are not separated until the end has come. And they are separated as only Christ can separate. "The kingdom of Christ is victory over death" *(Regnum Christi victoria mortis)* (WA 49, 767, 6). Death no longer has a spear. For its spear, sword, sting, "with which it strikes, slays, stabs man, is sin" (772, 6). But sin has been forgiven. Thus death is disarmed. Eternal life dawns. "Christ wants to be our Consolation." "This is the end of the song" (723, 18). But the judgment is a real judgment and a real separation. If this were a historical procedure, there would probably also be a development from unbelief to faith. But there is always either the one or the other. And the borderline between time and eternity is crossed "in an instant" *(in momento)* (732, 4). If it is crossed with an evil conscience, the judgment of the Last Day would have decided for hell. For the hell about which the story of the rich man in the Gospel speaks is "the evil conscience" (WA 10 III, 192, 15). To be sure, here, after the Last Judgment, Luther expects another "hell," concerning which the Augsburg Confession states that in it the godless are condemned to everlasting punishment (Art. 17). But if this is an everlasting dying, here, too, the sting of death is sin, the unforgiven sin of the evil conscience – just as, conversely, he who has received mercy rejoices: "Where is the evil little dog now, the evil conscience, the poison of sin, which wanted to drive me to despair?" *(Wo ist nu das bose hundlin, mala conscientia, sunde gifft, quae me volebat adigere in desperationem?)* (WA 49, 776, 3.) Is there no end of the torment? A restoration? Being eternally dead instead of eternally dying? He who puts this question thinks of eternity as prolonged time.

But time has an end. "For here one must put time out of one's mind and know that in that world there is neither time nor hour, but that everything is an eternal moment" (WA 10 III, 194, 10; cf. WA 10 I, 1, p. 44, 2 ff.; WA 17 II, 253, 19). *That world* – it is as if in this thought the whole enormous tension were slackened and released – the tension into which the Lutheran, from the time of the primal experience *(Urerlebnis)* all the way through justification and the experience of the church, has been placed in his ethos as well as in his philosophy of life. The terrible conflict between should and must, with which this tension begins, the paradox of "at once a sinner and not" *(Semel peccator et non)* of justification, the strain of the will to stand in two spheres and to maintain itself in both, the abyss between the here and the hereafter, the raging battle in the world of the creatures, the sting of temptation and offense, the resigned maintaining of faith under the cross – all this trembles and surges contrapuntally through the hope of "that world." This is certainly the much-maligned "hereafter mood" *(Jenseitsstimmung)* of early Lutheranism! They went through this world as "candidates for eternity" *(candidati aeternitatis).*[8] Those who have a different view go through this world as "candidates for death" *(candidati mortis),* which no one will deny. The hope for "that world" implies that there is a debasement of the present world. Yet not only this. It would be *only* a debasement if the end of the world were to be the beginning of "pure spirituality." But the theme of "that world" is resurrection. Certainly then everything is "completely different" *(totaliter aliter).* The preaching of the church does not grow tired of emphasizing this. "In eternal life," says Melchior Othonius,[9] "there is joy without grief, life without death . . . over against the subtle swiftness of the children of God in eternal life the light facility of Asahel is great weakness. Over against the very great beauty of the blessed the finest attractiveness of Absalom" is "great hideousness and filth. The great wisdom of Solomon" is "great foolishness and stupidity." But just as there is a final identity of the man of time and eternity, so there is of every creature of God. For He created none in order to annihilate them in the end. Thus in the creation of the world the eye of hope sees the image of, the reference to, and the preparation for, the eternal world of God. "Ah, I think, it is so beautiful here, and Thou bestowest such kindness on us on this poor earth! What will really happen after this world?" Thus Paul Gerhardt sings as he strolls through the fields in the summer. This "hereafter mood" not only debases the world; it glorifies the world. "That which is beautiful," says Goethe, as Johann

[8] Thus Hülsemann in his funeral sermon for the physician Hopp. See note 1 under *Cross and Vale of Tears.*

[9] See note 4 under *Reconciliation and Predestination in the Confessions in Conjunction.* — Cf. Joh. Saubert, *Die neue Creatur, wie sie von dem Apostel Paulo angedeutet wirdt, Gal. 6,* Nürnberg, 1625.

Peter Eckermann relates, "is a primal phenomenon. Although it itself never appears, its reflection becomes visible in a thousand manifestations of the creative spirit." For the Christian "that world" is identical with the primal phenomenon. Luther judged that "this life is nothing but the anticipation or rather the beginning of the future life" *(haec vita nihil nisi praecursus aut initium potius futurae vitae)* (WA 18, 785, 19), that the present world is but a framework for the new building – a framework that is torn down when the building is completed *(Table Talk* 2, 2741). "That world" appears as the answer to the great question which the present world puts to us. In the aforementioned passage from his writing against Erasmus, Luther expects from it the solution of the problem of theodicy – not, to be sure, as Leibniz' "justification of God" – and Melanchthon expects the answer to the great why *(Cur)* of our destiny *(CR* 9, 1098). As a genuine humanist Melanchthon views heaven as an academy which differs from the one at Wittenberg because it is so pleasantly quiet and in which he intends to converse with the apostles, the prophets, and the church fathers about the pure doctrine *(CR* 7, 319). For Samuel Lange, the Leipzig botanist, Leonhard Beer delivers a funeral sermon on the heavenly garden (1664).

But they are all unanimous in saying that eternal life is resurrection: a new body, a new heaven, a new earth. A new body, totally different from the present one (WA 49, 733, 4) but a new body nevertheless, because God will be praised by all creatures (727, 7; 729, 4). The resurrection is accompanied by the "renewing of all creation" *(renovatio universae creaturae) (CR* 21, 525; WA 47, 613, 33) – "like the green seed in the spring" (WA 49, 770, 2). Now the creatures are wearing only their "work clothes; afterwards they will put on an Easter coat and Pentecost clothing" (WA 44, 628, 16). All to the praise of Him who is the Master of all beauty. All praise sung by faith at the present time is but a beginning of the eternal hymn (WA 5, 254, 20 ff.). But in all the cosmomorphic picturesqueness of this hope the thought of that which is deepest and last is not missing. The same Othonius who hopes to excel Asahel, Absalom, and Solomon in heaven finds the ultimate reason for this in the fact that man's "will shall be directed wholly in and according to God's will." The gathering of the church, which, according to Melanchthon, is the end of God's ways, has been completed. The "communion of saints" *(communio sanctorum)* in which Luther believed is united with its Lord.

Works by Early Dogmaticians

Baier, Johann Wilhelm, *Compendium Theologiae positivae, Ed. 5., Jenae, 1704* (the first edition appeared in 1686)

Brochmand, Caspar Erasmus *(Hafniensis), Universae Theologiae Systema, Ed. 6., Ulmae, 1664* (the first edition appeared in 1633)

Buddeus, Johann Franz, *Institutiones Theologiae dogmaticae, Francof. et Lips., 1741* (the first edition appeared in 1723)

Calixt, Georg, *De praecipuis christianae religionis capitibus disputationes, Helmestadii, 1648*

Calov, Abraham, *Systema locorum theologicorum, 12 Tomi, Witteb., 1655—77*

Chemnitz, Martin, *Examen Concilii Tridentini, 4 partes, Francof., 1606* (the first edition appeared in 1565—73)

Chemnitz, Martin, *Loci theologici, ed. Polyk. Leyser, 3 Tomi, Francof., 1591*

Cundisius, see Hutter

Gerhard, Johann, *Loci theologici, ed. Ed. Preuss, 9 Tomi, Berol., 1863.* In order to make it possible to use the earlier edition by Johann Friedrich Cotta (20 volumes, 1762—1789), which is more widely known, the quotations are indicated according to this edition. Since Preuss always gives the volume and the page of the Cotta edition in the margin, one can find the quotations in both editions without any difficulty. The first edition appeared in 1610—22.

Hafenreffer, Matthias, *Loci theologici, Ed. 3., Tub., 1603* (the first edition appeared in 1600)

Harbard, see Schilter

Heerbrand, Jakob, *Compendium theologiae, Tub., 1575,* and the same work, *Lips., 1585.* Since the *Compendium* was issued by Heerbrand himself in two widely differing presentations — each one differing repeatedly — it was necessary to quote one of the two editions at a time. They are kept separate by the Formula of Concord.

Hesshusius, Tielmann, *Examen theologicum continens praecipuos locos doctrinae christianae,* 1587

Himmel, Joh., *Syntagma disputationum theologicarum methodicum, Erf., 1630*

Hollaz, David, *Examen theologicum acroamaticum, Stargardae Pomeranorum, 1707*

Hutter, Leonhard, *Compendium locorum theologicorum, Witteb., 1696* (the first edition appeared in 1610). Among the various revisions and amplifications there are also quotations especially from *L. Hutteri Compendium theologicum notis illustratum a Gothofredo Cundisio, Ed. 3., Jenae, 1660*

Hutter, Leonhard, *Libri Christianae concordiae explicatio, Witteb., 1608*

König, Joh. Friedr., *Theologia positiva acroamatica, Rost., 1665,* and *Ed. 8., Lips., 1691*

Kromayer, Hieronymus, *Theologia positivo-polemica, Francof. a. M., 1683*

Matthias, Christian, *Systema theologicum minus, Hamburgi, 1654*

v. Mosheim, Johann Lorenz, *Elementa theologiae dogmaticae, ed. a Chr. Ern. de Windheim, Norinb., 1758*

Nicolai, Philipp, *Opera omnia, ed. G. Dedekenn, Hamb., 1617,* and *Alle Teutschen Schriften,* edited by G. Dedekenn, 3 parts, Hamburg, 1617.

Pauli, Simon, *Methodi praecipuorum locorum doctrinae ecclesiae, Magdeburgi, 1569*

Quendstedt, Johannes Andreas, *Theologia didactico-polemica sive Systema theologicum, 4 partes, Witteb., 1691*

Rhegius, Urban, *Loci theologici, ed. Joh. Freder, Francof., 1545*

Scherzer, Joh. Adam, *Systema Theologiae, Lips., et Francof., 1698*

Schilter, Zacharias, and Harbard, Burchard, *Capita purae et incorruptae doctrinae Christianae primaria, Lips., 1598*

Seiler, G. F., *Ausführliche Vorstellung der Christlichen Religion,* Giessen, 1781

Selnecker, Nikolaus, *Institutio Christianae religionis, 3 partes* (the place of publication is not given), *1579*

Selnecker, Nikolaus, *Examen Ordinandorum, 4 partes, Lips., 1593*

Semler, Johann Salomo, *Institutio ad doctrinam Christianam liberaliter discendam, Halae, 1774*

Töllner, Joh. Gottlieb, *System der dogmatischen Theologie, 4 Bücher,* Nürnberg, 1775

Wegscheider, Julius August Ludwig, *Institutiones Theologiae Christianae dogmaticae, Ed. 6., Halae, 1829*

Weller, Hieronymus, *Opera omnia, ed. Samuel Bened. Carpzov, Lips., 1702*

The titles of the monographs dealing with dogmatics are given in full where these works are mentioned in the text. The systematic presentations of ethics will be named in the second volume.

Index

Abyssinia 291, 399 f.
absoluteness 82 f., 87
absolution as act of judge 356
acceptance of old creeds 200—210, 289, 362; *see also* symbols
accusatio sui; see self-accusation
Aelian 419
Aepin, Johann 249
Africa 392 f.
agitation for unity 282
agreement in doctrine 275, 278
Alardus, Franziskus 251
Alber, Matthäus 313
Albertus Magnus 489
Albrecht, Duke of Prussia 286, 421, 423, 426
Alcalá 486
Alcuin 488 f.
Aleander 23
Alen 285
Aliaco (Cardinal d'Ailly) 302, 305
alien righteousness 109 f., 141, 150, 155
alien work of God 212
Allwohn, Ad. 321 f., 448
Alsfeld 236
Altdorf (Elsass) 180
Altdorf b. Nürnberg 302
Althamer, Andreas 66
Althaus, Paul, the Elder 166 f., 291, 321, 331
Althaus, Paul, the Younger x, xiii, xix, 87, 194, 255, 301, 507, 512
Ambrosian Hymn 205, 211
Amerbach 281
Amerbach, Bonifacius 281
Amerbacher, Georg 66, 115
America 8, 393, 400, 513
American Lutheranism 8
Ammundsen, V. 491
Anabaptists 297
angry God 51, 107, 119, 124, 132, 213, 472
Ansbach 24, 91 f., 94, 110, 115, 152, 183, 185, 203, 264 ff., 273, 277, 293, 326, 330
Amsdorf 134
Andreä, Jacob 129, 222 f., 232, 237 f., 250, 287, 291, 315, 330, 337, 362, 416, 465, 496
Andreä, Joh. Val. 352, 366
Anselm 110, 224 f.
anthropomorphism 212 f.
Antichrist 492, 503, 512, 514
antinomians 85, 88, 374
anxiety 6, 21, 69 f.; *see also* fear
in Luther 44, 467
Apocrypha 193
apologetic theology 191—200, 407, 416
on natural knowledge 56 ff.
on trustworthiness of Scripture 200
Apostles' Creed 92
as basis and content of faith 205
and continuity of church 286
as prayer 212
states and offices of Christ in 237 f., 248, 252
appropriating grace of Holy Spirit 141, 153
aptitudo passiva 29
Aquila, Caspar 125
Arabia 392, 399, 439
Archimedes 418
architecture 338 f.
Argoli, Andrea 427
Aristarchus of Samos 418
Aristotle 20, 39, 408, 427, 432, 439, 472
Arius, Arians 205 f., 222 f., 227
Armenia 291, 386, 392
Arminians 41, 386
Arndt, Johann 45 f., 154, 160, 166, 337
Arnold, Gottfried 487
Arnstadt 493
art 460
art of Christian dying 46, 48
articles of faith 264, 269 f., 272, 481
ascension 250
Asia 392, 395, 401
Asia Minor 387
Asmus *(Wandsbecker Bote)* 48
astrology 417, 433 ff.
Athanasian Creed 205 ff.
Athanasius 482
Augsburg 99, 209, 271, 273 f., 282 f., 284 f., 378, 488
Augsburg Confession (*see also* confessions)
and constitutional law 9
dogma of church in 267 f.
justification in 96 f.
office of ministry in 339 f.

and old creeds 209
and presupposition of God 17 f.
Augsburg Interim 99
August, Duke of Saxony 296, 322, 334
August, Elector of Saxony 395, 458
Augustine 41 f., 73, 80, 127, 160, 170, 174, 216 ff., 257 f., 284, 287, 408, 410, 438, 477
Aulén, G. 211
Aurifaber 174, 298, 424
Austria 335, 377, 427, 488, 490
authority of Holy Scripture 182 ff., 185, 188 ff.
in *Ansbach Counsel* 183
and Biblicism of Bucer 186
in *Copenhagen Articles* 183
in early history 182
in Melanchthon 184 f.
in *Schwabach* and *Marburg Articles* 185 f.
autonomy 25, 31, 35, 76, 113, 437
Avignon 281, 491

Bach, J. S. 338, 460, 462
Bachmann, Philip ix, 211, 491
Bagow 370
Bahamas 393
Baier, Johann Wilhelm 33, 56, 69, 104, 126 f., 144 ff., 192, 195, 230, 240, 300, 307, 510
Baldestedt 448, 455
Balduin, Frederick 198, 219, 352, 470, 510
Balkans 394
Bamberg 421
Baptism; *see* Sacrament of Baptism
Baptists 297
Baragua 393
Barby 226
Barth, Karl xxiii, 301
Bartholinus, Peter 430
Basle 256, 281
Baumgarten-Crusius 100
Baumgartner, Hier. 202, 271 f.
Bavaria 488
Bayreuth 265, 293
beautiful 464, 516 f.
Bechmann, Hermann 469
Becker, Fritz 337
Beckmann, Franz 418
Becmann, Johann Christoph 448, 454
Beer, Leonhard 517
Beham, Johann 265
Bellarmine, Robert 3 f., 32, 100, 109, 400
Bengel, Johann Albrecht 4, 48, 129, 318, 391
Berlin 302, 478
Bernard 166 ff., 170 f., 257
Bernegger 427, 434
Beyer, Hartmann 282
Beza, Theodor 137, 158, 223, 235, 246, 308
Bezzel, Hermann 228, 236, 444
Bible; *see* Holy Scripture
Biblicism 185 f., 199 f., 276, 416, 430
birth of Christ; *see* incarnation
bishops 346, 349 f., 384
Bismarck 513
Blanke, Fritz 59
Blankmeister 384, 458, 465
Blarer 335
Blaufelden 66
Blecher, C. 127
Bodenbach 146
Boethius, Heinrich 93
Bogenritter, G. W. 352
Bohemia 290, 298, 312, 346, 349 f., 372, 485
Bohlin, Torsten 59, 211
Böhme, Jacob ix, 47, 434, 445, 447, 467
Bohmer, Heinrich 17, 448, 457
Bohmer, Just. Henning 367
Borbis 376
Bornkamm, Heinrich 445
Bradwardina 409 f.
Brahe, Tycho 234, 427 f., 431, 434, 439, 441, 465 f.
Brandenburg (Kur-) 302, 305, 328, 395
Brandenburg-Ansbach 270, 377; *see also* Ansbach
Braun, Friedrich 129, 434
Braun, Wilhelm 28
Brazil 393
Bremen 312
Brenz, Johann 83, 100, 104, 129 ff., 131 ff., 134, 138 f., 156 ff., 159 f., 164 ff., 186, 222 f., 228, 232 f., 239 f., 241 ff., 247 f., 250, 258 f., 275, 278, 282, 300 f., 304, 306, 308, 312 ff., 317 ff., 333, 352, 379, 459, 466, 470
Breslau 364
Brieger 77
Briggs, Charles Augustus vii
Brilioth, Y. 301
Brochmand, Caspar Erasmus 93, 126, 156, 288, 343
Brubach, P. 282
Brück 270 f.
Brunner, E. 59
Bruno, Giordano 432, 447, 471
Brunswick 210, 222, 273, 298, 354, 374
Bryant, William Cullen xviii
Bucer, Martin 95 f., 186 ff., 281, 307, 501 f.
Buchenau, A. 463
Buchwald 295, 298, 456
Bückmann, R. 385
Buddeus, Johann Franz 32 f., 69, 156, 230, 439, 490
Buddha 408
Bugenhagen 92, 98, 150, 249, 273, 295, 298, 327, 329 f., 333 f., 336, 354, 448, 453, 455, 458, 465, 494 f., 502, 514
Bullinger 311
Bultmann, R. 59
Burckhardt 377

Burckhardt-Biedermann, Th. 281
Burgdorf, Martin 17
Burgfarrnbach 129, 448

Calixt, Georg 164, 195, 201, 209 f., 276, 286 f., 490
Calov, Abraham 56, 65, 143, 146, 156, 193 f., 195, 219, 251, 287, 354, 372, 383, 407, 430, 442, 459
Calvin 10, 103, 137, 194, 219, 249, 300, 306 f., 311 f., 315, 363, 384, 407, 447, 496, 502, 512
Calvinism, Calvinists 40, 83, 126, 135, 143, 158, 195, 219, 223, 235, 244 f., 251, 280 ff., 311, 319, 356, 407, 415 f., 460, 468, 474
Camerarius, Joachim 421 f., 485
Campanius, Johann 398
canon 191—200
care of souls
  in church regulations 364
  in Luther 363
  in Melanchthon 365
carnal peace 514
Cantiuncula 281
Carlstadt 185, 300
Carpzov, Benedikt, II 365, 367, 375
Carpzov, David Benedikt 356
Carpzov, Johann Benedikt, I 352, 355 f.
Caspari, W. 340
Cassierer, Ernst 463
Catharinus, Ambrosius 259, 262, 264, 267
Catholicism 6
catholicity 274—291, 355, 362, 377, 485
  Baptism and 290
  and Calvinism 280 ff.
  as claim 208, 285
  corrective of, in Scriptural principle 287 f.
  and external separations 280
  importance of confessions for 278
  in Luther 278 f.
  as mark of church 275
  in Melanchthon 275, 278
  origin and continuity of 285 f.
  and Roman Church 282
  and Sacrament of Altar 301
causality 410 f.
Celle 302
ceremonial requirements 91, 324 f.
certainty 68, 82 f., 87 ff., 102, 122, 130 f., 133, 135 f., 290, 509
Chamier, Daniel 3
Charles V, Emperor 23, 484
Charles XII, King of Sweden 452
Chemnitz, Martin 3, 32, 45, 54 f., 56, 73, 103, 109, 153, 159 f., 162, 193, 222 f., 228, 230, 232, 236, 238, 241 ff., 248, 286, 288 f., 300 f., 303 ff., 307 f., 327, 332, 355, 459, 485, 493
Chemnitz, Bogislav Philipp 485, 513
Cherbury, Herbert v. 56
Chiaramonti, Scipione 427
Chile 393
chiliasm 496, 511
China 392, 398
Christ (*see also* states and offices of Christ; Christ and His work)
  as basis of certainty 87
  birth of 224 f., 238 f., 245 ff.
  as Book of Life 221
  church as abode of 155, 166, 258
  critical significance of 85 f.
  under curse and without sin 112
  divine majesty of 242 ff.
  faith bound to 83 ff.
  finding of, in Bible 189 f.
  God and man in 223
  and historical work of reconciliation 127 f.
  indwelling of; *see* indwelling
  justice of, as King 495
  kingdom of; *see* kingdom of Christ
  on Last Day 515
  as Liberator 120 f.
  as Logos 226, 238
  as Mediator 104, 120, 122, 128
  merit of 116 f.
  as mirror of Father's heart 66
  obedience of 116 f., 239
  omnipresence of 231, 235, 313 f.
  remaining in 154 ff.
  as revealed God 108
  putting on of 169
  righteousness of 116, 127
  as Sacrifice of atonement 115
  in Synoptic Gospels and in Paul 225
  two kinds of union with 158, 164
  two natures of; *see* doctrine of two natures
  and unity of Person 227
  as "wrapped up" in flesh 111 f.
Christ Crucified 67, 72, 85, 108, 122, 139 f.
Christ and His work
  in Luther 86, 108, 111 ff., 119 ff., 171 ff., 212, 222 ff., 234 ff., 248 ff., 493 ff., 505
  in Melanchthon 108, 116 f.
Christian
  and influence on social order 499 f.
  and Law 181
  love between Christ and 171
Christian, Wilhelm, Duke of Brandenburg 288

Christocentric character of Luther's theology 66 f., 72, 92, 223
Christoph, Duke of Württemberg 251, 313, 333, 395
Chrysostomus, Olaus 276
church 255—274 (*see also* kingdom of Christ)
 as body of elect 258, 277
 and canon 191 f.
 catholicity of 274—291; *see also* catholicity
 as Christ's abode 155, 258
 and Christ's promise to be present 267
 continuity of 286 f., 485 f.
 under cross 470
 divine right of, as whole 371
 and doctrine 201
 and ecclesiastical authorities 255, 277
 false teachers in 268, 271
 founding of, from above 287, 289
 gathering of 511
 Gospel as "substance" of 259
 as invisible 258, 261 f.
 and justification 259
 as kingdom of Christ 492, 501
 legally constituted form of 256
 as local congregation 265, 341, 369 ff.
 in Luther 256 ff., 286
 in Luther in 1521 260
 Luther not destroyer of 255 ff.
 marks of 260 ff., 268, 275, 292
 in Melanchthon 268 ff., 287, 290, 324
 in motion 390 f.
 and presence of Holy Spirit 220
 and resurrection 511
 spirituality of 258 f., 260 ff., 277
 and state 181, 379, 383, 502
 testimony of, and canon 193
 and Word 259, 263, 265, 285
church discipline 360 f.
church government 285, 367—385, 396 f.
 and capability of inner action 368
 and consistories 375, 380 f.
 as department of state 383
 divine right of church as whole 371
 and doctrinal responsibility of estates 377
 and episcopal office 384
 not hierarchy 373
 institution of pastoral office as beginning of 368
 in Luther 373 ff.
 in Melanchthon 379 ff.
 and Melanchthon's theocratic blunder 380 f.
 as pastoral function and as special governing function 374
 by princes 374 f.
 and visitations 373 f.
church history 10, 285 f., 482 ff., 486 f., 492
church organization
 in Luther 368 ff.
 in Melanchthon 379 f.
church triumphant 505
church year 338 f.
Chyträus, David 33, 57
Cicero 52
Class, Valentin 399
Claudius, Matthias 48
Clavius, Christoph 427
clergy and laity 341, 345
close connection with earth 121, 448—462
 and art 460
 and correct feeling about nature 450
 and dancing 455 f.
 death and 451
 and devils and demons 452
 and drinking 456 f.
 and emotions 463
 and happiness 454 ff.
 and history of style 459
 and laughter 454
 and music 456, 462
 and poetry 462
 and praise of Creator and creatures 450
 and qualitative view of world 449
 and recreation 455 f.
 and sociability 454 ff.
 split consciousness of 476
Coburg 273, 424, 469
Cochläus, Johann 485 f.
combat 147 f., 149
 kingdom of Christ as 498
comfort
 in afflictions 97
 in certainty of election 130, 133
 for distressed consciences 101 f.
 in doctrine of two natures 236, 248
communication of attributes 231 ff.
communion 257 f., 316
communion of saints 257, 259, 262
 death as entrance into 510
 as united with Lord 517
 and unity 277
commutative imputation 163, 170 f.
complaint of Tholuck on absence of alarmed consciences 49 f.
concrete aspects of life 141
concupiscence 29
Confessio montana and dogma of church 266
confessional constant 5, 8, 11 f.
confessional unity 280
confessions 7 f., 9 ff., 17 f., 217
 and acceptance of old creeds 200—210, 289

not cause of divisions 289
Christ and His work in 115 f.
and "doctrine of Gospel" 190
dogmatic theology in 206
dynamic of 4 ff., 8, 11
ethos of 4, 13
justification in 90—106
and Scriptural principle 182 f.
significance of, for unity and catholicity 278
soteriological knowledge of Gospel in 181
as testimony 210
twofold orientation of 201, 203
wrath of God in 41
Congo 392
congregation 265, 341, 349, 369 ff.
Conring 490
conscience 35 ff., 39 f.
and complaint of Tholuck 49 f.
fears of 45, 50, 102
Law and 35 f.
consciousness 25
of being creature 39
concrete aspects of 141 f.
and justification 82
in original opposition to God 18
and renewal 151
renunciation of contents of 80, 167, 411
consistories 375, 380 f.
constant 5, 8, 11 f.
Constantinople 290 f.
Consul, Stefan 394
contingency 130, 439
continuity
of church 286 f., 485 f.
of worship 331
contradictions, existential 28 ff., 32 f., 35, 38, 44, 107
contrition 100, 102, 145 f., 150, 152
self-accusation in 147
conversion 100
in Luther 145 f.
in Melanchthon 148 f.
repentance equated with 146
in Selnecker 148
in Simon Pauli 148
three reasons for, in Melanchthon 148 f.
cooperation of God 149 f., 163
cooperating grace 150
Copenhagen 51, 90, 92, 115, 183, 202, 266, 271, 317, 319, 326 f., 342, 359, 488
Copenhagen Articles (*see also* Copenhagen)
and dogma of church 266 f.
on excommunication 359
on justification 92
on worship 326
Copernicus 418 ff., 426 ff., 431 ff.
Cortez 385
cosmic expansion and kingdom of Christ 503
councils 7, 184, 264, 482
Counter Reformation 6
Courland 328, 333, 370
creation 451, 459
faith and 450
groaning of 509
renewing of 517
creatures 449 f., 453, 459
and aging of world 507, 509
as channels for God's goodness 214
in German mysticism 79
in Luther 27, 440, 443, 451, 514
praise of God for 450
as preachers of resurrection 509
primal relationship to 27 f.
creeds of ancient church; *see* symbols
critical significance of Christ 85 f.
Cromwell, Oliver 502
cross (*see also* cross and vale of tears)
and concealed progress of Kingdom 513
conquering of 469 f., 476
making sign of 497
suffering as, and mark of Christian 469 f.
theology of 72 f.
cross and vale of tears 44, 46, 406, 463—476, 491, 507
and fight against melancholy 467
no illusions 466
and imminent optimism 475
in Leibniz 471
and mood of doom 465
as other kinds of close connections with earth 463
not pessimism 466
theodicy and 474
Cruciger, Caspar 64, 170, 174 f., 422
Crüger, Peter 427
Crypto-Calvinism 10, 308
Cuba 393
Culmbach 66, 279, 322 f.
Cundisius 126
Curcelläus 386
curse 111 ff.
Cyprian 482
Cyprian, Ernst Salomo 490
Cyril 158, 319
Dalmatinus, George 283, 287 f., 328
Dalton 282
Damasus 283
dancing 455 f.
Dannhauer 396, 438, 456, 462
Danzig 195, 427
Darien 393
Darwin 490
Dau 8
De servo arbitrio 21 ff., 121 f., 126, 133, 213, 472
De Wette 83
death 18 f., 21, 28
and art of dying 46, 48
and earth 451
and end of world 515
as entrance into

communion of saints 510
and feeling of God's wrath 40 f.
flight from 497
and life 61 f.
sin as sting of 515
thoughts of, and transitoriness 46 ff., 466 f.
Decisio Saxonica 244, 246, 405, 442
decision 89, 137, 181
Dedekenn, G. 143, 160
defection from faith 88 f.
Dehmel, Richard 463
Deissmann 491
Delitzsch, Franz 255
Democritus 419
demons 435 f., 452
Denifle 10
Denmark 276, 280, 282, 398, 402, 428, 430, 488
Denzinger 23, 109, 255, 272
dependence and responsibility 29 f.
Descartes 471
descent into hell 249
despair 22, 30, 36 f., 44, 122, 468
devil at work in 47
and inability to bear 49
as *salutaris desperatio* 22, 118
Dessau 214
destiny 26 ff. (*see also* fate)
God's power over 118, 121, 137, 438 f.
and guilt 29 f., 35, 43 f.
love of 28
in Melanchthon 44
and original sin 33
responsibility and 44
determinism 24 f., 31, 130, 138, 409 ff., 438
Deus absconditus; see hidden God
Deutschmann, J. 57
devil 47, 125, 469, 497
in Luther 452, 456 f., 467, 515
dialectic
as change of conspectus 62 f.
in Luther 59 ff.
as procedure 60 f., 71
Dieckhoff, A. W. 127, 179, 255
Dietrich, Veit 337, 397, 421
Dilherr, Johann Michael 432, 435
Dilthey, Wilhelm 407, 463, 471, 478
discipline; *see* church discipline
disposition 86, 94, 96
distance from God 30, 43, 164
Dithmarschen 334, 427
divine plan 60
divine majesty 69, 121 f., 203, 206
of Christ 242 ff.
receiving of, by believers 157, 160, 164 f.
and wrath of God 39, 44 f.
divine service 322 f. (*see also* worship)
emotion in 338
knowledge of God as 323
prayer as 323 f.
doctrina Evangelii; see doctrine of Gospel
doctrine (*see also* dogma)
agreement in 271, 273, 275, 278 f., 514
and church 201
doctrine of church; *see* dogma of church
doctrine of God 86, 121, 211—222, 362
and philosophy of life 406
doctrine of Gospel 190, 201, 269 f., 274, 369 f.
doctrine of two natures 86, 112, 216, 222—236, 428, 444
and beginning in birth of Christ 224
comfort in 236
and concern to preserve unity of Christ's Person 226 f.
and confessions of Lower Saxony 236
and God's suffering 227 f.
Luther's approach to 223
mercy and 229 f.
in Synoptic Gospels and in Paul 225
dogma 7, 179—253
and faith 201 f.
history of 187, 487
and Scripture 185
dogma of church 255—274, 287, 367
in Augsburg Confession and Apology 267 f.
in *Copenhagen* and *Schwabach Articles* 266 f.
formulation of, and *Ansbach Counsel* 264
in Hungarian *Confessio montana* 266
impact of Gospel in 257
and importance of doctrinal unity 271, 273, 278 f., 514
and "invisible" church as *abscondita* 261 f.
and Luther, non-destroyer of church 255 ff.
and Melanchthon's stand 270
and Ritschl 269 f.
and spiritualizing of church 258 f., 260 ff., 277
dogmatics 4, 221, 406 f.
analytical method in 510
in confessions 206
dominant force 5, 7, 11
Donatists 267
Dörffel, Samuel 431
Dorsch, J. G. 286
doubt 53
concerning election 125
about God's wrath 40
as primal sin 49, 88 f.
sin as 49, 88 f.
Drabitzius, Laurentius 352

dread 20 f., 43 ff., 47 f., 58, 117, 467
and devil 497
Dresden 46, 338, 370, 384
Drews, Paul 167, 216, 227, 231, 238, 247, 340, 367, 385, 399
drink 456 f.
Dryden, John xviii
Dungersheim 482
Dunte, Ludwig 365
Dürer 460, 467
Dürr, Joh. Conr. 448, 456
dynamic
of confessions 4 ff., 8, 11
of Lutheranism 179

earth; *see* close connection with earth; world
East Frisia 314
East India 402
Eastern Church 290 f.
Ebbinghaus, Jul. 59
Eber, Paul 300
Eberlin, Johann, v. Günzburg 500
Ebner, Erasmus 421
Eck 258
Eckermann, Peter 517
Eckhart, Meister 79
edict of 380, 284
Edict of Worms 23, 25, 377
Egypt 386, 392
Einbeck 222
Einstein 424, 490
Eisenach 277
elect 124
as church 258, 277
as kingdom of Christ 494 f.
election 125, 130, 133, 221; *see also* predestination
Emden 223, 311
emotion 100
and earth 463
in divine service 338
vs. fear 44, 47 f., 169
and Holy Spirit 218, 453
and natural pleasure 455
Empedocles 419
Emser 262, 264
end of world 252, 465, 507—517
and concealed progress 512 f.
computations of 507
faith and 508
Gospel and new meaning of 508 f.
as judgment of world 515
mundus advesperascens 465, 507, 509
pax carnalis non speranda 514
"that world" 516
and universal eschatology 510 f.
Enders, L. 500
Engelder, Theodore xix
England 17, 200, 280, 407
Enlightenment 6, 28, 33, 41 f., 49, 56, 75 f., 99 f., 105, 197, 211, 433
enmity against God 22, 27, 38, 51
contrition as 146
and Gospel 64 f.
sin as, in Luther 30 f.
sin as, in Melanchthon 32
episcopal jurisdiction 355, 384
epochs 4 f., 12
Erasmus 21 ff., 29, 31, 60, 66, 83, 86 f., 118, 122, 131, 134, 138 f., 147, 182, 222, 257, 411, 439, 444, 449, 473, 475, 494
Erlangen 198, 480
Esau 22, 118
Erlauthal 312
Ernst the Pious of Gotha 291, 366, 399
eschatology (*see also* end of world)
and kingdom of Christ 504, 510
in Luther 507, 513 f., 516
in Melanchthon 510 f., 516
universal character of 510 f.
Esslingen 222, 330, 362
eternal life 161, 164, 473, 508 f., 516
as resurrection 517
ethical behavior 438
joy as motive of 69 f.
justification and 142
ethical person 18
ethical purposes and kingdom of Christ 499, 501
Ethiopia 291, 386, 392
ethos 4, 13
faith and 142, 150 ff.
Eusebius 288
Evjen 8
exclusive terms 103
excommunication 359, 382
existential contradictions 28 ff., 32 f., 35, 38, 44, 107

Faber, Basilius 488
Faber, Friedrich 24
Fabricius, Johann 431
Fabricius, Johann Albrecht 393
Faero Islands 391
faith
as acceptance of doctrines 267, 269
as acceptance as true 92 f.
as active ferment in man of sin 148
and activity in man in Flacius, Gallus, Chemnitz 152 f.
Apostles' Creed as basis and content of 205
as bound to Christ 83 f.
and change in psychic make-up 144
as contrary to appearance 71 f., 93, 98, 123, 139
and creation 450
as creator 211, 215
and cross 469, 476
definition of 68, 84, 93, 101
as dependent on Christ 83 ff.
dogma and 201 f.
and end of world 508
and ethos 142, 150 ff.

as fashioned by love 99
foundation of 122
as fulfillment of First Commandment 100
Gospel as basis of 122
of infants 298
and inner man 168
not intensified spirituality 449, 453
I-relationship of 68, 75, 412
and knowledge of Christ 101
and knowledge of God 211
in Luther 60 ff., 68 ff., 79, 123, 211 ff.
as mathematical point 81, 102, 106, 153
as mediation of antitheses 62 f., 71, 107, 114
vs. natural knowledge of God 57
mere passive of 151
"precious company" of 93
and office of preaching 95
paradoxical character of 103
possibility of defection from 89
preaching about 206
and progress of kingdom of Christ 512
as psychological act 152
not *qualitas* 78 f.
vs. reason 63
as reason for justification 99 f.
relationship of penitence to 50, 64
without repentance 50
resurrection and 509
and righteousness of God 93, 95, 97
and salvation of I 215
in things not seen 123
thinking vs. 63 f.
transcendental birth of, and psyche 147 f.
as trust and obedience 100
as venture 70 f.
and Word of God 105
faith and psyche 94, 140 to 153, 155
and *ordo salutis* of later dogmaticians 142
and twofold subjectivity 140
faith-righteousness 105
false teachers 188, 268
Farel 361
fashions 459 f.
fatalism 23 ff., 28
fate 23, 26, 130, 438
love of 28
fear 6, 26 ff., 43—49, 69 f., 467
and beginning of rationalization 44 f.
correct position on, in Jacob Böhme 47
cultivation of 45
vs. emotion 44, 47 f., 169
as founded on fact 119
in Kierkegaard 48
in Luther 44, 467
in Melanchthon 45
psychologizing of, in literature on dying 45 ff., 106
in Schopenhauer 49
in sermonic literature 47 f.
fears of conscience 45, 50, 102
feeling, knowledge of God as 161; *see also* emotion
Fenger, J. Ferd. 385, 398
Ferm 8
Feuerbach, Ludwig 58, 102, 437
Fichte 445, 471, 480, 490, 499
fides creatrix in Luther 211, 215
Figueiredo, Manuel de 427
finitum capax infiniti 230, 441, 445
Finland 391
Flacius (Illyricus), Matthias 29, 33, 41, 53 f., 104, 133 f., 144, 152, 194, 222, 226, 279, 286, 486, 488 ff., 491, 513
Florida 393
Floris, Joachim v. 479
force 502
foreknowledge 137 f.
"forensic" 103 ff., 149
forgiveness of sins 66, 83, 95, 97, 104 f., 107
Christ as subject of promise of 108
as content of righteousness of God 96 f.
and imputation of righteousness 106, 114 f., 117, 412
as kingdom of God 493, 499
and life and salvation 319
in Lord's Supper 318 f.
and reconciliation 127
and regeneration 143
as rule of pastor 345
in viaticum 319
forms of expression 5, 7, 12
Formula of Concord 9
on justification 101 f.
on predestination 133 f.
on symbols 207 f., 209
unio mystica in 160
on wrath of God 41
Förstemann 278
Foscarini 427
France 304, 316, 318, 386
France, Anatole xvii
Francke, A. H. 385, 456
Francke, E. 385
Franconia 270 f., 377
Frank, Fr. H. R. xiii, 28, 42, 90, 126, 238, 249
Frank, Sebastian 480
Frankforter, Der 79, 498
Frankfurt a. d. O. 427, 454
Frankfurt am Main 280, 303, 349, 428, 488
v. Frauenstädt 49
Freder, Johann 217, 266
Frederick IV, King of Denmark 398
Frederick William I, King of Prussia 335
free will 21, 23 ff., 31 f., 85, 122
denial of 25
freedom 34, 48, 121, 128, 410
in Luther 121, 151

in Melanchthon 24, 439
Freiberger, Seb. 352
Freiburg 281
Frenssen, Gustav 462
Freylinghausen, J. A. 42
Frick, Heinrich 321, 385, 396, 399
Fricke, Otto 223, 250
Friedensburg, Walter 425
Friedrich, Count of Württemberg and Mömpelgard 223
Frisch, Chr. 428
Fritschel, Gottfr. 398
Fröhlich, Ambrosius 394
Fugger, Andreas 488
fulfillment
concept of 74, 117
of Law 36, 74, 224

Gabler 459
Gädicke, Peter 352
Galileo 427, 471
Galley, A. 146
Gallus, Nik. 152
gathering 316
of church 511
Gebhardt, Friedrich 321
Geiselmann, Josef Rupert vii
Geneva 366, 453 f.
Gennrich, Paul Wilhelm 223
George, Duke of Silesia 451
George, Margrave of Brandenburg-Ansbach 270, 272
Georgia, Transcaucasia 395
Georgiewitz 291
Gerhard, Johann 3 f., 32 f., 41, 45 f., 49, 55 f., 104, 109 f., 128, 146, 163 f., 193 f., 198, 209, 219, 239, 252, 266, 286, 288 f., 296, 307, 337, 353, 355 f., 374, 393, 399 ff., 407 f., 438, 459, 490, 510
Gerhardt, Paul 46, 70, 337, 462, 516
Gerlach, Stephan 104, 157 f., 158, 160, 223, 233 f., 236, 250
German Empire 9, 284
German idealism 478, 485, 490 f., 499
German mysticism 26, 79 ff., 140, 166 ff., 170, 411, 449, 469, 498
Germany 282 ff., 334, 376 ff., 386 f., 407, 465, 483, 512 ff.
Gerson 166
Gess 238
Gessner, Salomon 251
Giessen 243 ff., 385
gloom 18, 23, 44, 465 f.
glory of Christ 103, 140, 206
glory of God 103, 140, 262
God 86, 121, 211—222 (*see also* Christ; predestination)
activity of, in history 481
alien work of 212
as angry God 124, 132, 213
arbitrariness of 37 f., 86
cooperation of 149, 163
definitions of 56, 221
distance from 30, 43, 164
empirical evidences of goodwill of 53
freedom of 213, 216, 440
immanence of, in creatures 440 f.
incomprehensibility of 122
indwelling of 161, 165
as Judge 105
judgment and grace of 107
knowledge of 44 f., 161, 211, 213 ff., 323
as Lawgiver and Creator 37 ff., 53
love of, for creature 214
in Luther 20 ff., 39, 107 f., 211 ff., 437 f., 440
majesty of 69, 121 f., 157, 160, 164 f., 203, 206, 242 ff.
in Melanchthon 217 f.
natural proofs of existence of 51 f., 55
in opposition to God 108, 110, 115
participation of, in suffering of Christ 227 f.
as personal "You" 215
power of, over destiny 118, 121, 137, 438 f.
presupposition of, in Augsburg Confession 17 f.
as pure love 172, 175, 216
secret counsel of 131 f., 138
separation from 119 f.
and world; *see* God and world
wrath of; *see* wrath of God
as Zealot 39
God and world 27, 57, 214, 234, 431—447, 464
and Aristotelian concept 432
and astrology and medicine 434 f.
beginning of scientific prognosis in Melanchthon 435
and contact in impact of Gospel 444
and *Decisio Saxonica* 442
and *finitum infiniti capax* 441, 445
and God's immanence in creatures 440 f.
and God's power over destiny, but not fatalism 438 f.
and Goethe 446
in Luther 27, 437 f., 441, 444, 448, 451 f., 464, 514
and Luther and Kant 437, 473
and magical philosophy of life 433
and two kingdoms at war for Luther 444
God's call 20, 26, 43, 106, 143, 211, 215, 324
Goethe 18, 26 f., 47, 408, 437, 445 ff., 462, 471, 504, 516
"good human beings" 55
good works; *see* works

goodwill of God
  empirical evidences of 53
  and reason 214 f.
  trust in 214
Görlitz 47
Gogarten, Friedrich 21, 49, 59, 77
Goldenhauer 483
Goslar 222
Gospel 59—176
  authority of 183
  as basis of faith 122
  not court of decision 181
  as dynamic of Lutheranism 179
  enmity against God and 64 f.
  hearing of 63 f., 68, 412
  as historical account of Christ 65, 189
  kingdom of God as 493, 501 f.
  in Luther 65, 72 f., 180, 340, 493
  as mark of church 260
  in Melanchthon 179
  and missions 385 ff.
  and new meaning of end of world 508
  as promise 179 f.; *see also* promise
  as revelation 62 f., 65
  right doctrine of 272 f.
  as "substance" of church 259
  transsubjectivity of 102
  and twofold divine judgment 62, 70
  and Wittenberg Reformation 501
  and wrath of God 64 f.
Gotha 335, 463, 490
Gotthard, Georg 276
Göttingen 222
Gottschick, J. 166 f., 173, 292, 321
Graff, Paul 292, 300, 334 f.
Graul 402
Graz 427
great and noble 18
Greece 290, 386
Greenland 391, 400
Gregory XIII 427
Gregory the Great 488
Gregory of Nazianzus 488
Gregory of Rimini 409
Greifswald 425, 483
Grenzel 336
Griebler, Bernhard 131
Grimmelshausen 448, 451, 458, 503
Grisar, Hartmann 448, 457
Grockland 391
Gross, Christoph 467
Gross, Franz 231
Grössel, W. 385, 399
Grossgebauer, Theophil 149, 365
Grotius, Hugo 402
Grubenhagen 222
Grützmacher, R. H. 73, 179, 195
Grynäus, Simon 417
Guatemala 393
Guhrauer 474
guilt 22, 25 f., 29 f., 35, 37, 40, 43 f., 46, 74 f., 118
Gummerus 491
Günther, Ludwig 429 f.
Gussmann 66, 95 f., 104, 186, 190, 266, 273, 278 f., 282, 322
Gustavus Adolfus, King of Sweden 397 f.
Gustavus Vasa, King of Sweden 397

Haas 8
Hadeln 334, 362, 370
Hadersleben 491
Hafenreffer, Matthias 24, 55 ff., 104, 142, 179, 192 f., 197 ff., 229, 242, 266, 307, 355, 428 ff.
Haggenbusch, Anton 303
Haiti 393
Halberstadt 222
Hallesbye, Ole 59
Hamburg 92, 98, 150, 222, 236, 249, 282, 329 f., 354, 359
Hameln 222
Hänichen, M. Daniel 129
Hannover 222
happiness 454 ff.
Harbard, Burch. 126 f., 493
Hardeland, O. 77, 385
Hardenberg, Albert 305 f.
hardening of heart 22, 31, 124, 138
Harless, Ad. xiii, 339
v. Harling, O. 396
Harms, Claus 304
Harms, Louis 402, 457
Harnack, Adolf 487 f.
Harnack, Theodor 17, 35, 42, 116, 173, 249
Hartmann, Bruno 448, 457
Hartmann, Johann Ludwig 352
Hartmann, Julius 313, 366, 427
v. Hartmann, Eduard 472
Hassler, Joh. Leo 129
hatred of God 31 ff.
Hausenstein, Wilhelm 463, 466
Hausmann, Nik. 377
hearing 63 f., 68, 345, 412
heathen 388 f.
heaven, spatial conception of 251, 415
Hebbel 462
Heerbrand, Jakob 33, 55 f., 135, 189, 276, 283, 287, 307, 291, 394, 431, 434, 493
Hefelbower 8
Hegel 13, 200, 390, 407, 471, 475 ff., 478, 490
Heidegger, Johann Heinrich 313
Heidelberg 67, 310
Heiler, Friedrich viii, 5, 274
Heiling, Peter 402
Heim, Karl 59
hell 37, 249, 515
Helmstedt 210
Hemming, Nik. 127, 276, 493
Henke, E. L. Th. 201, 210
Henneberg 273, 328, 334, 370
Henry, Duke of Saxony 501
Heppe, Heinrich 10, 194
Heraclitus 477
Herbart 437
Herberger, Valerius 48
Herborn 352

Herbst, Wilhelm 191, 194
Hercko, Nik. 493
Herder 437
hereafter
joy of 516
in Luther 412 f.
Hering, H. 166, 173, 336
Hermann, Rudolf 59
Hermann v. d. Busche 483
Hermelink, H. 77, 425, 483
Herrlinger 342
Herrnhuter 6
Hesiod 481
Hess, Johann 364
Hesshusius, Tilemann 54, 250, 301
Hessia 273, 396
hidden God 22, 35, 43, 49, 71, 83, 108, 118, 121, 124 f., 132, 139, 211, 235, 410 f., 412, 447
adoration of 131 f.
hierarchy and church government 373
Hilbert, Gerhard 321, 379
Hildesheim 222
Himmel, Johann 146
Hipler, Franz 418
Hirsch, Emanuel 77, 81, 89, 101, 211, 421, 445, 491
history 5 f., 8, 11, 189, 286, 476—491; *see also* church history
activity of God in 481
and Christian belief in God 477
Dilthey and Hegel on 478
of dogma 187, 487
and German idealism 490 f.
and humanistic historical criticism 481 f.
and inspiration 481
in Luther 483 f.
and *Magdeburg Centuries* 486
in Melanchthon 479, 483, 491
in Old Testament 479
passion for 488
pessimistic conception of 513
Philippism vs. Gnesio-Lutheranism 489
as profane history 481
and Ranke 485
and relation to impact of Gospel 483
in seventeenth century 490 f.
and Sleidan 484
and split with consciousness of connection with earth 476
Hochstetter 127
Hocker, Jodocus 452
Hof 266
Höfling, J. W. Fr. 291, 300
Hofmann, Johann Christian Konrad v. 238, 480
Hofmann, Melchior 333
Hölderlin 463
Holl, Karl 35, 77, 89, 90, 173 f., 255, 367, 385, 387, 480, 489
Hollaz, David 32 f., 56, 105, 116, 141, 145, 149 f., 195, 240
Holmquist, Hjalmar 334
Holstein 251
Holy Scripture 179—191
in *Ansbach Counsel* 183
and apologetic theology 200
authority, sufficiency, perspicuity of 182 ff., 188, 190
and Biblicism of Bucer 186
Christocentric character of 190, 225
not codex 187
in confessions 181
in *Copenhagen Articles* 183
efficacy of 194 ff.
expounding of 184
and historical investigation 193 f.
and history of dogma 187
Law and Gospel in 189
in Melanchthon 184 f.
as norm for church doctrine 187 f., 191
and old creeds 208
vs. oral Word 340
and reason 184
in *Schwabach* and *Marburg Articles* 185
testimonies for, in Melanchthon 197 f.
and written and oral proclamation 188
Holy Spirit
appropriating grace of 141, 153
and emotion 218, 453
indwelling of 160, 169 f., 499
internal testimony of 192, 199
personality of 220
presence of, in church 220
and reborn man 153 f.
and Word 185, 195
Homer xviii
Hopp, Johannes 463, 466, 516
Hospinian, Rudolf 3
Huber, Samuel 126 f.
Huberinus, Caspar 501
Hübner, Friedrich ix f., xiii
Hülsemann, Johann 164, 209 f., 219, 286, 300, 314, 353 f., 372, 463, 466, 510, 516
Hungary 51, 104, 266, 279 f., 289, 305, 327, 335, 342, 370, 376, 502
Hunnius, Aegid. 127, 192, 198, 219 f., 223, 241, 250, 277, 290 f., 300 ff., 314
Hunnius, Nicolaus 223, 251, 352
Huschke, E. 339
Huss 258, 277
Huswedel 236
Hutter, Leonhard 3, 55 f., 146, 210, 219, 276, 290, 300, 302, 305, 318, 343, 353 f., 372, 430
hypotheses 9 f.

Ibsen 480
Iceland 391, 400
idealism 18, 76, 151; *see also* German idealism

Ignatius 319
Ihmels, L. xiii, 59, 90, 179, 200, 230, 255, 277, 280, 301, 321, 491
illuminatio 142
imitation of Christ 165 f., 169
immanence 25, 102
Imminger, Thomas 129, 448
immortality 510
immortality of soul 52
impact of Gospel 11 f., 15, 179, 181, 184, 194, 201, 203
  and doctrinal qualification of pastor 351 f.
  and doctrine of church 257
  and doctrine of God's activity 444
  and doctrine of Trinity 221
  and God and world 44
  and history 482 f.
  and justification and philosophy of life 408 f.
  and kingdom of Christ 494
  and missions 385
  and office of keys 356 f.
  and Sacrament of Altar 315 f.
  and worship 322
imperfection 152
imputatio commutativa 114, 163, 167
imputation 83, 86, 93, 95, 97, 102, 105 f., 108 ff., 114 f., 117, 120, 127, 412
incarnation 112, 224 f., 238 f., 245 ff.
incarnate God 72, 233 f., 321
India 387, 392
indwelling 156 ff., 161, 165
  of Christ in Luther 167 ff.
  of Holy Spirit 160, 169 f., 499
  and inwardness of man 168
  of Trinity 160, 165
  Word and 156
infant baptism 292, 296 f.
  in Luther 297
  in Melanchthon 298 f.
information 65, 67, 106
inherent righteousness 149
inspiration 56, 191—200
  and history 481
  and interpretation 196 f.
  and Old Testament 480
  and revelation 198 f.
intercession and reconciliation 129
internal testimony of Holy Spirit 192, 199
interpretation 196 f.
Italy 386
Iwand, Hans Joachim 77

Jacob, Günther 35
Jakobskötter, Ludwig 338 f.
Japan 392
Jena 483
Jerome 169
Jews 395
Joestel, Gregorius 216
Johann Ernst, Duke of Saxony 397
Johann Georg, Elector of Brandenburg 222 f., 395
Johann Georg I, Elector of Saxony 223, 421, 423
Johann Sigismund, Elector of Brandenburg 302, 305, 395
John Frederick, Duke of Saxony 377
Jonas, Justus 40, 279, 282
Jordan, Christof 192
Jörgensen, A. Th. 90, 266
Joseph II, Emperor 490
joy 162, 169, 450, 465, 468
  of hereafter 516
  as motive of ethical behavior 69 f.
joyful disposition 152
Judas 118, 146
Judex, Matth. 488
judgment 27 f., 63 f., 81, 85
  end of world as 507
  and grace 107
judicial; *see* forensic
Julius, Duke of Brunswick 286
Julius, Michael 463, 470
juridical terminology 74 f., 97; *see also* forensic
justification
  absoluteness and certainty of 82 f., 87 ff.
  and Christ's indwelling 167 ff.
  in confessions; *see* justification in confessions
  and consciousness 82
  crisis of doctrine of 110
  declaratory character of 105
  doctrine of, and spirituality of church 258 f.
  faith as reason for 99 f.
  giving proof of 96
  as key to Scriptural principle 190
  in Luther 69, 73—90, 411; *see also* Christ
  marks of 103
  as mathematical point 495
  in Melanchthon 97 ff.
  and moral activity 142
  and philosophy of life; *see* justification and philosophy of life
  and pre-Reformation theology 75 f.
  and psyche 78
  and reconciliation 128
  and regeneration 143
  and renewal 149
  and righteousness of Christ 127
  and sanctification 144
  transsubjectivity of 103
  and *unio mystica* 164, 166
justification in confessions 90—106
  in *Ansbach Counsel* 91 f.
  in Augustana and Apology 96 f.
  central position of 90
  in *Copenhagen Articles* 92
  and criticism of Bucer 95
  and Enlightenment 100
  in Formula of Concord 101 f.

as forensic doctrine 103 ff.
in Georg Major 99
in Osiander 101
in *Schwabach Articles* 94
and Socinians 100
and synergism 100
justification and philosophy of life 153, 405—414, 438, 443, 464
and agnostic determinism 410 f.
beginning of discussions on 405
and perspective in impact of Gospel 408 f.
present and hereafter in Luther 412 f.
validity and personality of God 413 f.
justice 40, 82
of Christ as King 495
Justinian, Emperor 274, 283, 285
justitia dei; see righteousness of God
justus ex fide vivit 77

kingdom of Christ 479, 491 to 507, 512
and chiliasm 496, 511
church and 492, 501
and cosmic expansion 503
in Eberlin v. Günzburg 500 f.
elect as 494 f.
endangered by ecclesiastico-political situation 502
not ethical institution 499, 501
eschatological significance of 504
forward movement of 506, 512 f.
and immanent development 511 f.
not "invisible" but *absconditum* 496
not kingdom of ethical purposes 499
as kingdom of consciences 498 f.
as kingdom made up of sinners 495
in Luther 493 ff.
in Melanchthon 492, 496
and philosophy of life 503, 506
and psyche 503
regal authority of Christ not empirical theocracy 497
and use of force 502
viewed as constant combat 498
kingdom of God
forgiveness of sins as 493, 499
as Gospel 493, 501 f.
Kadner, S. 43
Kaftan, Julius 42, 59, 77
Kähler, Martin 42
Kähler, S. A. 425
Kahnis 218, 255
Kant 34 f., 52, 59, 83, 100, 408, 411, 437 f., 463, 473, 499
Kasimir, Margrave 91
Kaspar v. Neidbruck 488
Kattenbusch, F. 59, 201, 255
Kauffmann, Johann 448, 451
Kefel, Samuel 236, 314
Keller, Adelbert 448
Kepler 57, 426 ff., 429 ff., 432, 434, 450, 471
Kierkegaard 48, 242, 447
Kilius, Georg 448, 455, 470
Kinder, Ernst ix
Kirkewall 391
Kleist, Heinrich v. 463
κλῆρος 354
Kliefoth, Th. F. D. 225, 335, 339
Klingner, Erich 448
Klopstock 47, 462
Knittermeyer, Heinrich 445
Knittlingen 399
Knolle, Theod. 321, 330
Knorn, Chr. Fr. 28
knowledge of Christ 84 f., 108
faith and 101
and predestination 124
knowledge of God 35, 44 f., 50, 211, 213 f.
as divine service 323
and faith 211
as feeling 161
personal character of 215
rationalization of, in dogmaticians 54 ff.
knowledge of Law 52
knowledge of sin 30, 66, 74
Koepp, W. 154, 158, 160, 164
Köhler, Karl 339
Köhler, Walther 200, 301, 476
Kohlmeyer, E. 255, 263
Kolde 24, 66, 94, 97, 115, 202, 267, 271, 278
König, Joh. Friedr. 56, 126, 129, 141, 145, 150 f., 156, 162, 240, 251, 307
Klettenberg, Fräulein v. 47
Königsberg 222, 483
Köstlin, H. A. 340
Köstlin, Julius 116, 173
Krafft 480
Kroker, E. 434
Kromayer, Hieronymus 33, 291
Kropatscheck, Friedrich 182
Krüger, J. Fr. 321
Kügelgen, C. W. v. 100
Kunze, Johann 90, 194
Kuzmany, K. 335, 370

Labrador 393
laity 341
Lamparter, Ed. 396
Lang, Heinrich 77
Lange, Samuel 517
Langenfass, Friedr. 385
Lapland 391, 397 f., 400
Lasko, Johanna 282, 300, 512
Last Day 508, 514 f.
Latomus 152, 223
Latour 462
Laubach 303
Lauerer, H. 230
laughter 454
Lausanne 7
Lauterbach, A. 332, 424

Lavater 417
Law
  not for believer 181
  concept of 74 f.
  and conscience in Luther 35 f.
  element of order in 37
  fulfillment of 36, 74
  giving of 36, 74
  implanted in heart 36
  knowledge of 52
  love of 38
  as objective power 117
  Pauline doctrine of 30, 33
  preaching of 357, 374, 383
  and primal experience 35 ff.
  revelation of God in 35 f., 65
  sin as deviation from 31, 33
  task of, as accuser 40
  unconditional validity of 18, 74
  and worldly domain 181
  and wrath of God; *see* Law and wrath of God
Law and Gospel 56
  in Bible 189
  in call 143
  self-testimony of 197
  unconditional validity of 18, 74
Law and wrath of God 35 to 43
Law-revelation 35 f.
Leibniz 385, 398, 401, 437, 439, 463, 471 ff., 478, 491, 517
  Luther and 472, 474
Leipzig 155, 210, 222, 232, 256, 258, 290, 309, 313, 370, 421, 425, 459, 482, 489, 517
Leisnig 364, 379
Lempp, O. 463
Lenin 490, 512
Leo X 491
Lessing 199, 480
Leube, Hans 282, 352, 458
Leubnitz 465
Lewin, R. 396
Leyser, Polycarp 311, 352, 354
libertinism 23 ff., 90, 130
Lietzmann, Hans 79, 273, 298, 354, 374
life
  and death 61 f.
  forgiveness of sins and 319
  in God's creation 451
  as mathematical point 19 f., 26, 477
  totality of 20, 25 f.
  as union with Christ 158, 164
Liljenbladt 398
Liliencron 464
Lilienthal 200
Lilje, Hanns xi
Lindau 488
Linz 428
Lisbon 427, 463, 475
literature of transitoriness 46, 467
Lith, v. d., Joh. Wilh. 299
Livonia 280, 333, 400
Loewenich, Walther v. 59
Löffler, Jos. Fr. Chr. 75, 354, 459
Logos 112, 224, 226, 238, 241
Löhe, Wilhelm 255, 276, 335, 339, 390, 402
Lohmeyer, L. 418
Lommatzsch, Siegfried 35, 59
Löner, Caspar 266
loneliness 37, 257, 321, 339
Loofs, Fr. 77, 97, 167, 250, 487
Lord's Supper; *see* Sacrament of Altar
Löscher, Valentin Ernst 46, 384, 458, 465, 471, 490
Louvain 427
love 93 f.
  between Christ and believer 171
  God as 172, 175, 216
  of God for creature 214
  and mystical union 158, 161, 171
  reciprocal relationship of 173 ff.
  and unity of church 257
love of destiny 28
love of Law 38
Lower Saxony 45, 176, 222, 232, 236, 240 f., 243, 250, 300, 305, 307, 313
Loy 127
Lübeck 57, 222, 402
Lucian 227
Ludwig the Bavarian 255
Ludwig, Duke of Württemberg 399, 401
Lufft, Hans 422
Lülmann, C. 463
Lüneburg 222
Lütgert, W. 445, 463
Luther
  on anxiety 44, 467
  on Baptism 291 ff.
  on bishops 346, 349 f., 384
  on care of souls 363
  on catholicity 278 f.
  on Christ and His work 86, 108, 111 ff., 119 ff., 171 ff., 212, 222 ff., 234 ff., 248 ff., 493 ff., 505
  on church 256 ff., 286
  on church and congregation 369 ff.
  on church government 373 ff.
  on church organization 368 ff.
  on confessional unity 280
  on creation 451
  on creatures 27, 440, 443, 451, 514
  and *De servo arbitrio* 21 ff., 121 ff.
  on demons 452
  dependence of Lutheranism on 11
  on devil 452, 456 f., 467
  on dialectic 59 ff.
  on drink 456 f.
  on Eastern Church 291
  on eschatology 507, 513 f., 516
  on faith 60 ff., 68 ff., 79, 123, 211 ff.

on faith and ethos 142, 150 ff.
on freedom 121, 151
on God 20 ff., 39, 107 f., 211 ff., 437 f., 440
on God and world 27, 437 f., 441, 444, 448, 451 f., 514
and Goethe 446
on Gospel 65, 72 f., 180, 340, 493
on happiness 454 ff.
on history 483 f.
on indwelling of Christ 167 ff.
on infant baptism 297
on Jews 395
on justification 69, 73 to 90; *see also* Christ
on kingdom of Christ 493 ff.
on Law and conscience 35
and Leibniz 472, 474, 491
on Lord's Supper 301 ff.
on mission 385 ff.
and mysticism 79 ff., 140, 167 ff.
on office of ministry 340 ff., 361 ff., 368 ff.
on optimism 454
on ordination 346
on pessimism 466 f.
on philosophy of life and world picture 410 ff., 417, 437 ff., 448
on power of keys 356
on prayer 324, 330
on predestination 121 ff.
on Psalm 90 18, 19
on repentance 145 ff.
on revelation 66, 71; *see also* Christ
on sacraments 292
on salvation egoism 68, 214 f.
on Scripture principle 180 f., 184 f., 188 ff. 195
on separations 284
on sin 30; *see also* justification, Law, conscience
on suffering 468 f.
on symbols of ancient church 204 ff.
on Trinity 216
on universal priesthood 340
on visitations 351, 358, 372
on vocation 347 f.
on worship 324 ff.
Lutheranism 9 ff., 13
dependence of, on Luther 11
Gospel as dynamic of 179
and missions in 19th century 402
Lütkemann, Joachim 48
Lyon 488

Machiavelli 484
Mädler, J. H. v. 418 ff., 427
Maestlin, Michael 426 ff., 431, 434
Magdeburg 300, 303, 305, 330, 332, 353, 479, 481 f., 485 ff., 488 f., 491 ff.
magical philosophy of life 417, 433
magna emphasis 68, 82, 214, 509
majesty of God; *see* divine majesty
Major, Georg 99, 102f., 152
Makenrot, Marlin 511
Malmö 266
man
"from birth" 29
creature-consciousness of 39
as different person through faith 144
faith and activity in 152 f.
gloomy picture of 18 f.
as God's creature 30
and history 490
inwardness of 168
in new setting 144, 147
responsibility of 21, 24 ff., 32
twofold subjectivity of 140 f.
Manichaeus, Manichaeans 23, 223
Mansfeld 222, 238, 279 f., 285, 300, 301 f., 304, 314 f., 318, 328, 332
Marbach, Erasmus 135
Marburg 10, 185, 202, 234, 266, 302, 304, 312, 315, 425
Marcus of Venice 392
marks of church 260 ff., 268, 275, 292, 349
Marsilius of Padua 342
Marx, Karl 58, 490
Mass 91, 310, 324 f.
mathematical point
faith as 81 f., 102, 106, 153
justice of Christ as 495
justification as 495
life as 19 f., 26, 81, 477
and rational view of world 412
righteousness of God and 81 f., 94
transcendental I as 140 f.
Matthes, Kurt 367
Matthias, Christian 33, 193
Maurer, Wilhelm viii f., xiii
Mayer, F. E. vii
Mayer, Friedrich 396, 438, 456
Mead, Sidney E. vii
means of grace 191—200
Mecklenburg 222, 353, 360, 370, 470
mediation of antitheses 62 f., 71, 107, 114, 243
medicine 434 f.
Mehl, O. 336
Meier, Heinrich 290 f.
Meiser, Hans ix
Mejer, Otto, 367, 383
melancholy 48, 454, 467
Melanchthon
on astrology 417, 434
on care of souls 365
on catholicity 275, 278
on Christ and His work 108, 116 f.
on church 268 ff., 287, 290, 324; *see also* kingdom of Christ
on church discipline 360 f.
on church government 379 ff.

on church organization 379 f.
on confessional unity 280
on contingency 130, 439
on Copernicus; *see* Copernicus
on destiny 44; *see also* fate
on Eastern Church 291
on episcopal jurisdiction 355
on eschatology 510 f., 516
on faith and ethos 142
on fate, fatalism 130, 438
on freedom 24, 439
on God 217 f.; *see also* presdestination *and* Christ
on Gospel 179
on history 479, 491
on infant baptism 298 f.
on justification 97 ff.
on kingdom of Christ, 492, 496
on mission 386, 397
on mood of doom 465 f.
on natural sciences 421 f., 424, 434 ff.
on natural theology 51 ff., 417
on office of ministry 342
on ordination 351
on philosophy of life 405, 417 ff., 439 ff.
on power of keys 360 f.
on predestination 129 f.
on qualification as to doctrine 351
on reconciliation 126 ff.
on Scripture principle 197
on sin 32
on suffering 470
on symbols of ancient church 203, 207
theology of 9 f.
on *unio mystica* 154, 156
on wrath of God 40
Memmingen 129, 434
Mencel, Hieron. 222
Mendoza, Johannes 392
Menius, Justus 103, 489, 502
Menke-Glückert, E. 476, 480, 484
Mentzer, Balthasar 196, 220, 223, 246, 276, 300, 353 f., 370
mercy 65, 72 f., 93, 110, 123, 137
call for, as part of repentance 146
and two natures of Christ 229 f.
and wrath of God 212 f.
mere passive 78, 96, 151
merit 40, 76, 96, 104
of Christ 116 f.
and *sola fide* 320
Merkel, Franz Rud. 385
Merseburg 328
Merz, Georg 17, 77
Metz 281
Mexico 385, 393
Meyer, Johann 201, 292
Meyfarth, Johann Matthäus 510
Michael the Ethiopian 291
Michelangelo 460
Milton 462
Minges 76
ministry; *see* office of ministry
Mirbt, E. 109, 385, 421, 427
missions 385—402
attempts at, among Turks 394
in Bengel 390 f.
as church in motion 390 f.
among Jews 395
and Löhe 390 f.
in Luther 385 ff.
among Laplanders 397
in Melanchthon 386, 397
in nineteenth century 402
obligation of, in Luther 386 ff.
and religio-geographical knowledge in Nicolai 391 f.
no resting from Christianizing of world 386 ff.
and state church 399
Missionsgedanke (idea of missions) 385 f.
Missouri 127
Mithobius, Burkard 419 f.
modalism 227
Moe, Olaf 8, 276
Möhler, Johann Adam vii
Moller, Justus 146
Moller, Martin 46 f., 251
Mömpelgard 223, 235, 246, 300, 312, 315, 331, 405, 496
Montaigne, J. 281
Montius, Joh. Baptista 392
mood of doom 465 f.
moral sense 25, 52
moralism 52, 75 f.
Mörlin, Joachim 99, 300, 352 f., 354
Morocco 393
Morone, Giovanni de 486
Morphe 5, 7, 14
morphology of confessions 3 ff., 10 ff.
mortification 299
Moscherosch, Johann Michael 513
Moscow 391
Moses, commandments of 36
Mosheim, Johann Lorenz v. 230, 490
Mauritania 387, 393
Mozambique 392
Mozart 460
Müller, A. V. 17, 166
Müller, Adolf 418, 420 f., 427, 430
Müller, Hans Michel 35, 77
Müller, Heinrich 46, 448, 454, 467
Müller, Karl 186, 367
v. Müller, Chancellor 446 f.
multivolipresence 232
Münster in W. 376
Murner 261 f.
Musäus, Johann 28, 56, 127, 386
Musäus, Simon 53 f., 133
Musculus, Andreas 222, 235, 251, 269, 300
music 330, 338 f., 456, 462, 467
Mylius, Georg 302, 352
mysterium 162, 170 f., 260

mystical union; *see unio mystica*
mysticism 18, 26, 80, 85, 140, 167, 174, 411, 449, 469, 498
  in Luther 79 ff., 140, 167ff.

natural knowledge 50 ff., 54, 56 f., 211
  apologetic theology on 56 ff.
  repentance as break with 50 f.
natural sciences 417, 421 f., 424, 434 ff.
natural theology 41, 44, 49—58, 417
  Flacius' correct view of 53 f.
  in Melanchthon 51 ff., 417
nature (*see also* earth)
  friendship for 450 ff.
  and Goethe 446
  as growing old 507
  not machine 443
  as reflecting God's love 445, 464
  revelation of God in 215
Naumburg 330
Netherlands 282
Nettesheim, Agrippa v. 433
Neuenburg 180
Neve, J. L. 255
"nevertheless" 123, 198, 454
Newton 471
Nicaragua 393
Nicene Creed 185, 202, 206, 209, 377
  and Melanchthon 207, 218
Nicolai, Philipp 143, 160 ff., 164 ff., 175, 251, 258, 300, 307, 311, 319, 391 ff., 395, 401, 459, 510
Nidaros 391
Niedbruck, Kaspar v. 488
Niemeyer 186
Nienberg 336
nihil sine Christo 65 ff., 190, 222
Nihusius 209
Nietzsche 18, 26, 58, 463, 512
nineteenth-century theology 12 f.
  kenoticists of 238
  and Lutheran missions 402
  and proportional interpretation of wrath of God 42
Nördlingen 352
Normann, Georg 334
Norway 391
Noth, Gottfried 223
Nürnberg 265, 271, 273, 280, 282, 299, 361, 377, 421 ff., 432, 448, 462, 488 f.

obedience 28, 100, 148
Oberpfalz 416
Occam 83, 182, 415
Oecolampadius 234, 281, 300 f., 315, 319
Oetinger 48
offer 65
Offermann 8
office of ministry 339—351, 367 f. (*see also* later doctrine of ministry and nature of office)
  in Augsburg Confession 339 f.
  as divine institution 342 f.
  and governing function 374
  in Luther 340 ff., 361 ff., 368 ff.
  in Melanchthon 342
  and obligation with respect to doctrine 351
  and ordination 346, 451
  practical aspect of 341 f.
  and priesthood of all believers 256, 340
  and principle of independence 348 f.
  and qualification of called person 350 f.
  and vocation 348
later doctrine of office of ministry and nature of office 352—367, 368, 381
  absolution as act of judge 356
  care of souls in Luther 363
  care of souls in church regulations 364
  and division of spiritual authority 355
  excommunication in church regulations 359
  main function: preaching of Word 361
  office of shepherd and moral supervision 365
  and power of binding 357, 360 f.
  and private confession 365
  theological basis in later dogmaticians and in church regulations 353 f.
old creeds; *see* symbols
Old Testament 75
  authority of 184
  Gospel in 185, 189, 480
  history in 479 f.
  and inspiration 480
Oldersum, Joh. v. 314
omnipotence 121 f., 170, 439
omnipresence of body of Christ 231, 235, 313 f.
On Monastic Vows 10
opposition to God 18, 30 ff., 43, 51, 53 f.
optimism 48, 454, 472 f., 475, 507
order
  concept of, in worship 329, 332, 341
  and Law 37
order of salvation 102, 128 f., 142, 153
ordination 346 f., 351
organization; *see* church organization
ὄργανον ληπτικόν 106
Origanus 427
Origen 220
original sin 29 ff., 44, 51
  destiny and 33
  in Flacius 53 f.
  and primal experience 29 f.

Orkney Islands 391
Osiander, Andreas 85, 101 ff., 110, 116, 421 f.
Osiander, Lukas 291, 465
Osnabrück 452
Ostorodt, Chr. 100, 226
Otho, Lucas Valentin 426
Othonius, Melchior 129, 448, 450, 470, 516 f.
Ottheinrich 488
Oettingen, Al. v. 291
Otto, Rud. 179
Otto, Valentin 426

Padua 342, 427
Palatinate 7, 416
Palestine 392
Palladius, Joh. 276
Palladius, Peter 197
Pandocheus, Joh. 126
papacy
  church in midst of 277
  long development of 482
  as sect 282
Pappus, Johann 236, 251, 287, 298, 314
Paracelsus 434
paradoxical character
  of act of justification 98
  of faith 103
  of God's deeds 60
Pareus, David 310 f.
Paris 402
"passive fitness" 29 f.
past and responsibility 29
Patripassianism 227 f.
Pattensen on Leine 93
Pauli, Simon 56, 148, 489
Paulsen, Friedrich 483
peace 514
peace of conscience 51, 130 f.
  and new obedience 148
peasants' revolt 180
Pehrson, Per 276
Peisker, Martin 21
Pelagianism 54, 409 f.
penitence 145 f. (*see also* repentance)
  and Baptism 299
  in medieval church 39
  permanent necessity of 102f.
  relationship of, to faith 50, 64
Persia 392
perspicuity of Scripture 184 f., 188 ff.
Peru 393
pessimism 19, 23, 44, 46, 466 f., 507
Peter the Alexandrian 283
Petersen, Peter 472
Petöfi, Sandor 462
Petri, Benedictus 398
Petri, Friedrich 223, 235, 300, 315
Petri, L. A. 402
Petzel, Christopher 311, 314
Peurbach, Georg v. 425
Pfaff, Chr. Matth. 32, 490
Pfeffinger 103
Pfeiffer, August 57
Pharaoh 22, 31, 118
Pharisee and tax collector 59, 62, 64
Philipp, Landgrave of Hessia 273, 483, 502
Philipp II of Spain 454
Philippi 42
Philippists 237, 251
philosophy of life 6, 12, 130
  justification and 405 to 414
  kingdom of Christ and 503, 506
  in Melanchthon 405, 417 ff., 439 ff.
  and world picture in Luther 410 ff., 417, 437 ff., 448
Photius 283
pietism 6, 458, 510
  and natural happiness 454 f.
  and objective reconciliation 109
  and "regeneration" 143
  and thoughts of death 46
piety 101
Pindor, Josef 385, 394
Pinguente 394
Pisa 427
plan of salvation 134
Plato 52f., 219, 221, 261, 321, 408
Plauen in Vogtland 431
Pleninger 32
Plitt, G. 24, 169, 299, 385, 450, 479
Poach 174
poetry 462
Pöhlmann, Tobias 445
polemicists 3 f.
Pontoppidan, Erik 266, 326
Popi, Alexander xviii
Poland 198, 280
Pomerania 328, 330, 334, 339
Pomesanien 328, 359
Portia, Count Bartholomäus v. 286
Portugal 392
Potsdam 6
power of keys 356 f., 360 f.
Prague 428
praise of God
  in Ambrosian Hymn 211
  and His creatures 450
  in worship 338
prayer
  Apostles' Creed as 212
  as divine service 323 f.
  in Luther 324, 330
preaching 189, 260, 346
  about Christ 222 f.
  church doctrine as stable element in 201, 206
  faith and 95
  about faith 206
  as main function of pastor 361
  as main part of divine service 324
  as public matter 341 f.
  right accent in 201
preceding grace 103
predestination 83, 121, 439
  as annihilating blow to free will 122
  in Brenz 131, 138
  and election to life 133, 221
  in Formula of Concord 133 f.
  in Luther 121 ff.
  in Melanchthon 128 f., 138
  and reason 47, 133
  for sake of faith 123
  subsidiary significance of doctrine of 122 ff.
  thought of, and faith 122 f., 124

predisposition 29
Preger, W. 488
preliminary questions on Gospel and faith 59 to 73, 75
pre-Reformation theology and justification 75 f.
Pressel, Th. 131, 298
Preuss, Hans 20, 182, 321, 460 f., 465
"priest" 354
priesthood of all believers 256, 340 ff., 353
primal dread 30, 44 f., 47, 58
primal experience 17—28, 35, 43 f., 443, 448, 477
  and agnostic determinism 410 f.
  and divine and human judging 62
  and Law 35 ff.
  as means 71
  and original sin 29 f.
  and Schopenhauer 49
primal relationship to creatures 27 f.
principal sin 29, 40, 119
private confession 335, 365
pro me 68, 75, 82, 114, 121, 150, 172, 204
  in Lord's Supper 317
  and resurrection of Christ 509
Procksch, O. 75
proclaimed God 72, 122, 138 f.
proclaimed Gospel 65, 67
  progress of 512
  written and oral 188
progress
  as concealed under cross 513
  faith and 512
  and kingdom of Christ 506, 512 f., 387
promise 65 f., 97, 104 f., 108, 124, 179 f., 204, 267, 294, 449 f., 504
propter Christum 106 to 117, 479
  and *aliena justitia* 109
  and Christ as *deus revelatus* 108
  and Christ's love for mankind 113
  and concept of substitution 114 f.
  and crisis of doctrine of justification 110
  and danger of illusion 107
  and *imputatio commutativa* 114
  and incarnation 112
  justitia dei and forgiveness of sins 107
  and synonomous terms in confessions 116
propter Christum and *per fidem* 86 f., 97 f., 101, 108, 111, 117, 127
Protestantism 10
Providence 443
Prowe, Leop. 418, 420 f., 423, 425 f.
Prussia 286, 331 f., 373, 425, 427, 488
psyche
  affected by union with Christ 169
  in Baptism 299
  depth of 168
  faith and 94, 140—153, 155
  justification and 78
  kingdom of Christ and 503
  and transcendental birth of faith 147 f.
psychic I 140 f.
psychologizing of concept of fear 47, 106
Ptolemy 418 f., 426, 430, 436, 489
Pufendorf, Samuel 485
pure doctrine 267, 273

qualification as to doctrine 350 f., 362
Quenstedt 56, 69, 109, 129, 141, 145, 149 f., 156, 219, 244, 307, 352, 361, 407, 490
quietism 165 f., 497, 499
Quito 393

Rade, M. 166, 448
Radlkofer, Max 500
Rakau 100, 198, 219
Ranke, Leopold v. 485
Rathmann 195
ratio 408 (*see also* reason)
  as natural relationship 20, 22, 25, 59
rationalistic concept of sin 34
rationalization of fear 44 f.
rationalization of knowledge of God in dogmaticians 54 ff.
readiness 508
real presence 157, 159, 231 ff., 303 ff., 311 ff.
reason
  vs. faith 63
  and God's goodness 214 f.
  and God's wrath 32, 39 f., 45
  in Kant 35
  and morality 52
  and omnipotence of God 121 f.
  and predestination 47, 133
  revolt of, against God 53 f.
  and Scripture 184
reborn man 150 f.
  in Baptism 299
  and Holy Spirit 153 f.
Rechtenbach, Ludwig 331
reciprocal relationship of love 161, 173 ff.
reconciliation 120
  Christ's historical work of 127 f.
  double meaning of 127
  intercession and 129
  justification and 128
  in Melanchthon 126 ff.
  objective doctrine of 109
  and redemption 120
  satisfaction and 127
  in sermon literature 129
reconciliation and predestination in confessions in conjunction 126 to 140
  and double meaning of reconciliation in confessions 127
  and individualizing of concept in sermon literature 129

predestination in Melanchthon, Brenz, Formula of Concord 133 f.
and synthesis of Melanchthon and Brenz 138
reconciliation and predestination in Luther in disjunction 107, 117 to 126
and *De servo arbitrio* 121
and faith and doubt 125
and God as master of destiny 121
and redemption 120
and *salutaris desperatio* 118
and subsidiary significance of doctrine of predestination 122 ff.
recreation 455 f.
redemption
according to soul 508
acts of 248 f.
reconciliation and 120
reform
not founding of new church 210
and missions 385
questions pertaining to 91
and social conditions 180
Reformed Church
and liturgical sense 335 f.
and Sacrament of Altar 303, 309 f.
regeneration 102, 146
in Formula of Concord 144
as gradual and growing 145
justification and 143
in Nicolai 143
and pietism 143
Regensburg 129, 428, 448
Rehlinger, Conrad 282
Reiffenstein, W. 40
Reimann, Arnold 480
Reimers, Nikolaus 427
Reinhard 34
Reinhold, Erasmus 422, 425 f., 427, 434
relationship to God 28, 30 f., 33, 39, 47 f., 53, 213
revision of 64, 106
relativity of world picture 57, 235, 251, 414 to 431, 471
and emancipation of theology from world picture 423
in Erasmus Reinhold 425
and evangelical pastors as astronomers 431
and intolerance in later Biblicism 430
in Joachim Rhaeticus 420 f.
in Johann Kepler and Matthias Hafenreffer 428
and magical world picture in Melanchthon the humanist 417
and Melanchthon's attitude toward Copernicus 418
no spatial conceptions of heaven 415
and stand taken by Lutheran universities in 17th century 426
Rembrandt 460
renewal 99, 149, 151, 153
cooperation of reborn with God in 149 f.
imperfection of 152
and sanctification 149
renovatio and *sanctificatio* in Scherzer, Grossgebauer, Quenstedt, Hollaz 149
renunciation 80, 167, 411
repentance 25, 50 (*see also* penitence)
and break with "natural knowledge" 50 f.
call for mercy as part of 146
as equated with conversion 146
in Luther 145 ff.
new obedience as third factor in 148
repristination 5, 13
resistance 31, 100, 136
responsibility 21, 24 ff., 32
and decision 137
dependence and 29 f.
and destiny 44
and personal relationship to God 212
resurrection
of Christ and members 509 f.
and creatures 509
eternal life as 517
and faith 509
glory of 248
and promise of new world 504
and testimony of 40 days 511
as theme of "that world" 516
retrogression 12
Reu 8, 33, 93, 251, 276, 394, 493
Reuss Younger Line 335
Reuter, Alfred 367
Reutlingen 104, 273
revealed God 72 f., 108, 118
revelation 22, 211, 234
of God in Law 35 f., 65
of God in nature 215
Gospel as 62 f., 65
and inspiration 198 f.
in Luther 66, 71
purely objective concept of 71, 108
and science 57
and supranaturalism 198 ff.
theology of 125, 134
and Word of God 194
Rhäticus, Joachim 418, 420 ff., 423, 425, 434
Rhegius, Urban 66, 217, 224, 266, 276, 290, 394
Rhein 336
Rhelin, Joh. 352
Rhiestedt 319
Rhodius, Ambrosius 427
Richard, J. W. 127
Richard of St. Victor 218
Richter, Aem. Ludw. 367, 379
Richter, Julius 385, 399
Richter, Martin 385
Rieker, Karl 367, 383

Rietschel, G. 340
Riga 328, 333
right *(jus)* 110
righteousness of Christ 116
  and justification 127
righteousness of God 76 f., 102, 107 (*see also* imputation)
  as alien righteousness 109 f., 141, 150, 155
  as bound to Christ 83
  as constructed from faith and divine imputation 83, 97
  vs. empirical justice 82
  and faith 93, 95
  and faith-righteousness 105
  forgiveness of sins as content of 96 f.
  as gift 77 f.
  as knowledge of Christ 108
  and legal element in term 75, 97
  and mathematical point 81 f., 94
  as righteousness that avails before God 110, 141
  as righteousness that holds true of empirical I 150 f.
  and self-judgment 80 ff.
  transsubjective validity of 97 f.
Rimini, Gregor v. 409
Ringwald, Bartholomäus 510
Ritschl, Albrecht 9, 42, 90, 101, 104, 158, 164, 173, 255, 267, 269 f., 272, 324
Ritschl, O. 90, 104, 194, 210
Ritter, Moritz 476, 484
Rocholl, Rudolph ix, xiii, 301, 336, 417, 476, 514
Roeskilde 197
Rohne 8
Rohnert, W. 194
Roman Catholic Church
  Baptism in 276
  and catholicity 282
  and Sacrament of Altar 309 f.
Romano, Adriano 427
Rome 283, 290, 418, 427, 486, 491
Römer, A. 448
Rörer 160, 175, 252, 337
Roskilde 197
Rostock 46, 222, 425
Roth 174
Rothe, Richard 447
Rückert, H. 73
Rudelbach 335, 402
Rudolf II, Emperor 428
rule of faith *(regula fidei)* 115
Runge, David 236
Rupert 485
Rupprecht, Joh. 228, 236
Rurer 190
Russia 391 f.

Saalfeld 425
Sachs, Hans 462
Sacrament of Altar 6, 158, 231 ff., 252, 281, 300 to 321, 414 f.
  and accusations against Luther 302
  as based on institution 303
  and communion 316 f.
  and consciousness of catholicity 301
  not foreign substance 320
  forgiveness of sins in 318 f.
  and impact of Gospel 315 f.
  in Luther 301 ff.
  modus in 305 f.
  omnipraesentia non inclusiva 313 f.
  and oral eating 307 ff.
  and *pro me* 317
  in relation to Roman and Reformed Church 309 f.
  in remembrance 317
  and unworthiness 308 f., 358
  and viaticum 319
Sacrament of Baptism 291 to 300
  assuring significance of 295 f.
  in Catholic Church 276
  and catholicity 290
  ecumenical significance of 291 f.
  external character of 292
  infant baptism 292, 296 f., 298 f.
  as initiation 296
  institution as basis of 293
  in Luther 291 ff.
  as necessary to salvation 292
  and penitence 299
  promise in 294
  psyche in 299
sacraments in Luther 292
saints 20, 257, 263
salvation 68
  doctrine of, and doctrine of Trinity 220
  and forgiveness of sins 319
  as God's work alone 121
  history of 479 f.
  relationship of faith to 121 f.
salvation egoism *(Heilsegoismus)* 68 f., 93, 97, 214 f.
  in Luther 68, 214 f.
Sam, Conrad 96, 99, 187
Samland 328, 359
Samos 418
sanctification 102, 149
  justification and 144
  renewal and 149
  striving for 143
  as synonym for justification 144
Santo Domingo 393
Sartorius, E. 218, 238
Sasse, Hermann xxiii, 255, 340
satisfaction 75, 115 ff.
  and reconciliation 127
Saubert, Johann 156, 489, 516
Savaria, Hadrian 400
Saxony 50, 92, 129, 176, 209, 222, 244, 251, 270 ff., 296, 322, 364,

370, 377, 395, 397, 405, 458, 465, 501
Scandinavia 334, 394, 397, 512
Schäfer, Ernst 476
Schall, J. 291
Scharf, Johann 286
Schaudig, Paul 336
Schaumkell 488
Scheel, Otto 17, 77, 166, 194, 292
Scheibe, Simon 448
Scheibel 402
Schellhass, K. 486
Schelling 437, 445
Schempp, Paul 194
Scherer, Emil Clemens 476, 483
Scherer, M. G. G. 8, 340
Scherzer, Joh. Adam 56, 149
Schickard, Wilhelm 427
Schiller 34 f., 463 f.
Schilter, Sacharias 126 f., 493
Schinder, Carl C. xiii
Schleiermacher 13, 34, 59, 200, 324, 447
Schlüsselburg, Conrad 90, 9, 126, 352
Schmid, Heinrich 201, 282, 301
Schmidt, Friedrich Wilhelm 211
Schmidt, Hans Wilhelm 59
Schmidt, Kurt Dietrich 448, 458
Schmidt, Sebastian 21, 219, 301
Schmidt, Wilhelm Ferd. 90, 97, 101
Schneckenburger, M. 4, 126
Schnepf 335
Schöberlein, Ludwig Fr. 218, 238, 240
Scholl, Johann 196, 223, 276
Schoner, Johann 417, 421
Schopenhauer 49, 464, 472
Schopper, Jacob, the Younger 302
Schorer, Christoph 129, 434
Schornbaum, K. 91, 270
Schott, Erdmann 28
Schrenk, Gottlob 480
Schroekh, Johann Matthias 490
Schubart, Christof 448
Schubert, H. v. 17, 91, 94, 186, 255, 270 f.
Schulte, W. 488
Schütz, Johann 319
Schwabach 94 ff., 99, 115, 185, 227 f., 266 ff., 340
Schwarzburg 334
Schwenckfeld, Schwenckfeldians 222, 238
science and divine revelation 57
Scotland 312, 488
Scotus, Duns 76
Scriptural principle 92, 182 ff., 226, 416
  and catholicity 287 f.
  justification as key to 190
  in Luther 180 f., 184 f., 188 ff., 195
  in Melanchthon 197
Scriver, Christian 48, 337, 401, 434
Seckendorf, v. 377, 398 f., 401, 460
Seebach, Count 384
Seeberg, Erich 17, 166, 487
Seeberg, Reinh. 76, 194, 200, 211, 218, 255
Sehling, Emil 92, 292, 296, 322, 327 ff., 330 ff., 339, 353 f., 359 f., 362, 364, 370, 383, 470, 502
Seiler, Georg Fr. 198 ff.
self-accusation 25, 82, 85, 90, 94, 101 f., 140, 145, 147, 167 f.
self-determination 26
Selnecker, Nikolaus 33, 56, 111, 148, 158, 160, 163, 192, 200, 219, 228, 233, 240 f., 248, 250, 286, 300 f., 305, 319, 331, 339, 380, 432, 439, 442, 470, 508
Semler, Johann Salomo 34, 459
Sening, Johann 276
separation 277, 280, 284, 289
Sermon on Mount 512
settlement according to reason 39
seventeenth century, theology of 12 f.
Shaftesbury 471
Shakespeare 462
"shalt" 21 f., 35, 37, 43
shepherd, office of 365 f.
Shetland Islands 391
Siegfried, Theod. 35
sight *(conspectus)* 62 ff.
Sigwart, Joh. Georg 32, 352 f., 364, 372
Silein 335, 370
Silesia 427
Sillem, C. H. W. 282
sin 27, 28—35, 40, 75, 119 (*see also* conscience, justification, Law)
  battle against 147 f., 149, 498
  as deviation from Law 31, 33
  in dogmaticians of Enlightenment 33
  doubt as 49, 88 f.
  as enmity against God 18, 30 ff.
  as failure to make use of freedom 33 f.
  hostility to 147
  in Kant 34
  as lawlessness 32 f.
  in Luther 30
  in Melanchthon 32
  and original sin 30 ff.
  in Schiller 34 f.
  and social order 500
  as sting of death 515
  as unbelief 35 f., 148
sinner 38, 59, 64, 103
  in kingdom of Christ 512
  and righteous 59, 61 f.
Slavonia 385, 394
Sleidan, Johannes 484 f., 487, 489
Slowakia 335
Smalcald 216, 275
sociability 454 ff.
social order
  influence of Christian on 499 f.

and reform 180
sin and 500
Socinians 3, 41, 100, 105, 199, 219, 226, 353, 386
sociology 13 f.
Soederblom, N. 7, 276, 448
Sohm, Rud. 367
sola fide 320
sola gratia 121
Sommerlath, E. 301, 507, 514
South America 393
Spain 386, 393, 486
Spalatin 482
Spangenberg 330
Spener 365, 458
Spengler, Lazarus 282, 298
Speratus, Paul 305
Speyer 285, 377
Spindler, Georg 416
Spinoza 26 ff., 408, 446 f., 477
spirituality
of church 258 f., 260 ff., 277
faith as 449, 453
Spittler, L. T. 490
Sprottau 46
Spurgeon 187
Stadener 276
Stange, Carl 17, 90, 97, 211, 292
Starcke, E. 77
Starcke, Laur. 451
state 181, 379, 383, 502
state church and missions 399
states and offices of Christ 86, 236—253, 415, 479
and acts of redemption 248 f.
in Apostles' Creed 237 f., 248
and ascension 250
and *Decisio Saxonica* 244
and descent into hell 249
and *Extra Calvinisticum* 244 f.
and Giessen Christology 244 f.
and Hafenreffer's picture of incognito 242 f.
and kenoticists of 19th century 238
and North Germans 241, 248
and old Würtembergians 239 f.
and Schöberlein's statement 238
and sitting at right hand 252 f.
and Tübingen camp 244
Staupitz 17, 146, 166
Steiermark 428
Stein, Freiherr v. 513
Steiner 464
Steinlein, H. 367, 396, 448
Stellhorn 127
Stendal 370
Stettin 24
Stintzing, R. 256
Stockholm 7, 491
Stolzenburg, A. F. 32, 156, 490
Storm, Theodor 464
Strassburg 94, 180, 236, 287, 427
Strasser, E. 321, 385
Striegel, V. 133
Stubbe, Chr. 448
Stunica, Didacus a 427
Stuttgart 282, 428
style 6, 338 f., 459
Suabia 180, 185 f., 202, 227 f., 266 ff., 271, 300 f., 316, 340, 429
submersion in own thinking 18
substitution, concept of 114 f.
suffering 46, 181, 406, 468 f., 470
suffering of God in Brenz, Chemnitz, Selnecker 228 f.
sufficiency of Scripture 185 f., 188 ff.
superstition 452
supranaturalism 99, 198 f.
Sweden 280, 334, 391, 397 f., 430, 485
Switzerland 156, 182, 250 f., 271, 273, 278, 280, 309, 312, 451
Sybel, Heinrich v. 418
symbolics 4, 7
symbols 7
acceptance of; *see* acceptance of old creeds
Calixt on 209
Formula of Concord on 207 f., 209
in Luther 204 ff.
in Melanchthon 203, 207
synergism 100, 103, 148 f.
system of Christology 229 ff.
Tammerfors 491
Tarnov, Paul 352
Tauler 79 f., 166
Te Deum 503
teaching profession 362
Teller 459
terminology 6
of Bible 186 f.
in doctrine of justification 73 ff.
tension 26
of God as Lawgiver and as Creator 38 f.
testimony
of church 192 f.
of confessions 210
of creeds 207 f.
Thales 477
Theodosius I, Emperor 285
"that world" 516
theocracy
of Melanchthon 380 f.
and regal authority of Christ 497
theodicy 472, 474, 517
theologia crucis 72 f.
Thieme, Karl 77
Thimme, W. 194
thinking 48, 64
vs. faith 63 f.
submersion in 18
technique of, in mysticism 80, 85, 140, 167, 411
wrath of God as product of 119
Tholuck, August 49, 58
Thomas Aquinas 76, 182, 408, 472, 477
Thomasius, Gottfried xiii, 116, 238
time
end of 515 f.
world as 507

Töllner, Johann Gottlieb 33 f., 41 f.
Tolomeo of Lucca 481
Torgau 249 f., 278, 323, 355, 458
totality 29, 35, 38
in Baptism 298 f.
of God's righteousness 82
of life 20, 25 f.
of man's corruption 53
Trankebar 391, 398
Traub, G. 83
Trebitz, K. 255
Trescho, Sebastian Friedrich 46
Troeltsch, Ernst 4, 7, 49, 73 f., 76, 407, 418
Truber 394
Tübingen 157, 223, 244 f., 283, 291, 395, 425 ff., 483
Turkey 331, 386, 389, 392, 394, 399, 439, 465
Turks, mission work among 394
transcendental birth of faith and psyche 147 f.
transcendental I 69, 79, 89, 140
and agnostic determinism 411 f.
involution of 80 ff.
as mathematical point 140 f.
and reflection on origin of Bible accounts 196
and righteousness of God 150 f.
transitoriness 46, 48, 466 f.
transubstantiation 305 f.
transsubjectivity 102 f.
Trinity
common doctrine of 203
doctrine of, as source 183, 185
and impact of Gospel 221
indwelling of 160, 165
in Luther 216
in Melanchthon 217 ff.
and Nicene Creed 207
Scriptural proof of 219 f.
speculative approach to doctrine of 218 f.
trust 83, 94, 100, 152
Christ as basis of 108
in God's goodwill 214
two kingdoms 444
two natures of Christ; *see* doctrine of two natures
twofold divine judgment 62, 70
twofold righteousness 150
twofold subjectivity 140 f.

Uhl 498
Ulm 95 f.
unbelief
as greatest sin 29, 40, 119
sin as 35 f., 148
Ungnad v. Sonegg 394
unio mystica 101, 154 to 176, 258, 318 f., 499, 503, 510
Biblical grounds for 156
in followers of Melanchthon 157 f.
in Formula of Concord 160
as I-you relationship 170
and justification in Brenz 164
in later dogmaticians 163
in Luther 154, 156, 166
in Melanchthon 154
as relationship of love 158, 161, 171
relationship of, to mysticism 174
in Würtembergians 157
United States; *see* America
unity
agitation for 282
in confession 279 f.
and confessions 278
in doctrine 271, 273, 275, 278 f., 514
love and 257
of spirit, faith, hope, love 277
supraterritorial 279
Urach 395
Urerlebnis; see primal experience
Vadstena 398
vale of tears; *see* cross and vale of tears
validity 23, 36, 82
of Law and Gospel 18, 74
question of, and personality of God 413 f.
of righteousness of God 97 f., 110, 141
Valla, Lorenzo 481
Venezuela 393
Venice 392
Vergil xviii
Vetter, P. 340
viaticum 319
Vienna 291, 394, 488
Vietor, Johann 236, 247
Vilmar, A. 339
Vincent of Lérin 187, 209, 287 f., 482
Virck, Hans 180
virtue 52, 79, 100 f., 104
visitations 351, 358, 372 ff.
Vives, Ludovico 160
vivification 102
in Luther 151
Vlahovic 394
vocation 142, 347 f.
Vogelsang, Erich 223
Vogt 458
Völker, Karl 476
Vollert, W. 90
Vollrath, W. 17
Voltaire 386
voluntarism 32
Voss, Johann Heinrich xviii
Vossberg, Herbert 386, 476, 480
Vurpillot, E. 225

Wächter, O. 4, 48, 129, 318, 391
Wagner, Marcus 488
Wagner, Richard 460
Walch, J. G. 127, 456, 490
Walter, Joh. v. 17, 278
Walther, Ferd. 127, 340
Walther, Wilhelm 77, 90, 173, 179, 255, 396
Warko, A. 90
Warneck, Gustav 385, 393, 397 ff.
Wegscheider 34, 42, 100 f., 199 f.

Weiganmeyer, Joh. Georg 352
Weigle 8
Weinmann, Erh. 104
Weinreich, Georg 448, 451, 510
Weltanschauung 6, 12; *see also* philosophy of life
Welz, Just. v. 402
Wendell 8
Wendland, Johann 164
Wentz 8
Werdermann 352
Werner, Pastor in Barby 226
Westphal, Joachim 249, 282, 300, 311
Westminster 315, 327
Wigand, Johann 301, 303, 488
Wilster 251
Windsheim 336
Winkelmann, Johann 146, 196, 223 f., 276
Winter, Karl 194, 255
with eyes of God 19, 26 f., 81, 141, 491
Wintzingerode 331
Wittenberg 208, 216, 222, 232, 243, 249, 251, 256, 270 f., 276 f., 280 f., 291, 300, 309, 313, 326, 331, 340 f., 352, 370, 391, 420 ff., 425 ff., 451, 489 f., 501, 517
Wolf, Ernst 17, 146, 166
Wolf, Johann 321
Wolf, Rudolf 418, 426
Wolmar 333
Word 84, 218
  dissemination of 340
  faith and 105
  and Holy Spirit 185, 195
  and indwelling 156
  as life and substance of church 259, 263, 265, 285
  as means of grace 195
  revelation and 194
works 24, 99, 149 f.
  faith and 142
  trust in 74
world (*see also* end of world; God and world)
  aging of 465, 507, 509
  as approaching its evening 465, 507
  Christianizing of 386 ff.
  Law in 181
  qualitative view of 448
  rational view of, as mathematical point 412
  relativity of picture of; see relativity of world picture
  as time 507
Worms 376 f.
worship 321—339, 462
  in *Ansbach Counsel* and *Copenhagen Articles* 326
  in Bugenhagen and church regulations 329
  and ceremonial requirements in Luther 324 f.
  concept of order in 332, 341
  conservative attitude in 327
  contemplative element in 336 f.
  desire of supraterritorial uniformity in 333 f.
  discipline in 328
  and dissolution of liturgical sense 335 f.
  divine service in Culmbachians and in Luther 322
  historical continuity of 331
  beyond impact of Gospel 322
  in Luther 324 ff.
  praise of God in 338
  restriction of forms in 332
  song and prayer in 330
  and style, architecture, church year 338 f.
wrath of God 17—58
  and alien work 212
  in confessions 41
  and divine majesty 39, 44 f.
  in dogmaticians of Enlightenment 41 f.
  in dogmaticians of 19th century 42
  in exact proportion to sin 41 f., 45
  and Gospel 64 f.
  and human feeling 41
  and human law 42f.
  as illusion 107
  inexplicability of 40
  in Johann Gerhard 41
  Law and 35—43
  in Luther 39
  in Melanchthon 40
  and mercy 212 f.
  as product of thinking 119
  and *propter Christum* 111
  and reason 32, 39, 45
  revelation of, in Law 37
  thought of, eliminated from mind 64
Wrede, Ad. 23
Wülfer, Daniel 448, 461, 470
Wunsiedel 192
Württemberg 104, 176, 223, 235, 245 f., 251, 282, 291, 313, 331, 335, 366, 377, 394 f., 399, 427 ff.
Wyclif 23, 258, 268, 409

Xenophon 52

young Luther 9 f., 17
Yucatan 393

Zach, Franz 9, 490
Zahn xiii
Zasius, Ulrich 256, 287
Zentgraf, Joh. Joach. 21
Zephyrius, Ernst 302
Zepper, Wilhelm 352
Zezschwitz, G. v. 367
Zinzendorff 69, 173, 335
Zoch, Laurentius 381
Zöckler, Otto 57 f., 429
Zöllner 255
Zürich 311
Zwickau 377
Zwingli 10, 130, 180, 235, 237, 250, 252, 280 f., 297, 300, 302, 306, 312 f., 314, 386

INDEX TO SCRIPTURE PASSAGES

Genesis
- — 57, 406
- 2:1 — 452

Leviticus
- 16 — 27

Psalms
- 9 — 261
- 32 — 348
- 45 — 82, 419
- 51:6 — 31
- 51:12 — 160
- 65 — 214
- 68:23 — 343
- 78:69 — 419
- 82 — 504
- 90 — 18, 23, 26, 81,475
- 101 — 457
- 117 — 386
- 139:16 — 489

Ecclesiastes
- 1:4 — 419

Isaiah
- 5:9 — 236
- 53:6 — 116
- 53:11 — 84

Daniel
- 7:10 — 489

Haggai
- 2 — 386

Malachi
- 3:16 — 489

Matthew
- — 507
- 8:27 — 242
- 9 — 353
- 11:27 — 242
- 16 — 263 f., 183
- 16:17 — 356
- 17:2 — 242
- 18 — 265, 359
- 18:14 — 297
- 18:18 — 340, 356
- 18:20 — 242
- 19:14 — 297
- 20:28 — 116
- 22:1 ff. — 171
- 24:35 — 242
- 28 — 267
- 28:19 — 185, 353

Mark
- — 507
- 1:15 — 221, 225
- 16:15 — 353, 386
- 16:16 — 295

Luke
- 10 — 353
- 10:20 — 242

John
- — 225, 242
- 1:1 f. — 185
- 1:29 — 116
- 3:16 — 221
- 6 — 307, 318
- 6—8 — 174
- 6:37 — 221
- 6:40 — 221
- 6:56 — 156
- 10 — 362
- 14 — 220
- 14:23 — 155 f.
- 15 — 158, 174
- 15:1 ff. — 155
- 17 — 156, 162
- 17:6 — 125
- 17:22 f. — 154
- 20:19-23 — 494
- 20:21 — 343, 353
- 20:22 — 344
- 20:23 — 345, 356

Acts
- — 349 f.
- 1:9 — 251
- 10:43 — 279 f.

Romans
- 1:17 — 76 f.
- 1:18 — 77
- 3:24 f. — 116
- 3:28 — 204
- 4:3 ff. — 93
- 4:5 — 97
- 4:24 — 116
- 5:10 — 116
- 5:19 — 239
- 6:4 — 295
- 8 — 133, 509
- 8:7 — 32
- 8:9-11 — 95 f.
- 8:18 ff. — 508 f.
- 10:17 — 221
- 12:1 — 323
- 12:15 — 454
- 13 — 382
- 14:10 — 104

1 Corinthians
- — 320
- 2:1 — 198
- 5 — 360
- 6 — 162, 165
- 6:15 ff. — 155
- 6:17 — 156, 158
- 6:19 — 156
- 10:12 — 89
- 10:16 — 159, 316
- 11:29 — 308
- 12 — 162
- 12:28 — 372
- 14 — 346
- 14:16 — 346
- 14:32 — 354
- 14:40 — 332
- 15 — 509
- 15:28 — 156
- 15:35 ff. — 509

2 Corinthians
- 5:18 — 116
- 13:3 ff. — 157
- 13:13 — 159

Galatians
- — 34
- 2:19 — 156
- 2:20 — 155, 157, 167, 169
- 3:27 — 169, 292
- 6 — 516

Ephesians
- 1 — 264, 266
- 1:7 — 116
- 1:21 — 231
- 1:22 ff. — 329
- 2:20 ff. — 329
- 3:17 — 157, 159
- 4 — 162, 236
- 4:5 f. — 260
- 4:11 — 372
- 4:12 — 329
- 5 — 170
- 5:19 — 330
- 5:23 — 155
- 5:32 — 155

Philippians
2 — 239, 247
2:5 ff. — 236, 238
2:7 ff. — 247
3:8 — 449

Colossians
— 225
1:14 — 116
1:23 — 386
2:7 — 329

2 Thessalonians
2:8 — 502

1 Timothy
4:4 — 453

2 Timothy
3:16 — 198

Titus
— 346
3:5 — 295

Hebrews
— 193, 225, 253
4:14 — 313
11:1 — 71, 93
11:3 — 55

James
— 193, 293

1 Peter
— 116, 253
3:18 ff. — 249
4:11 — 343

2 Peter
— 193
1:4 — 156 f., 175

1 John
2:2 — 116
3:4 — 32 f.
4:10 — 116

2 John
— 193

3 John
— 193

Jude
— 193

Revelation
— 193, 462
2:6 — 311
5:1 — 489

Ecclesiasticus
40:11 — 450